D0758967

Brink's Modern
Internal Auditing

Update Service

BECOME A SUBSCRIBER!
Did you purchase this product from a bookstore?

If you did, it's important for you to become a subscriber. John Wiley & Sons, Inc. may publish, on a periodic basis, supplements and new editions to reflect the latest changes in the subject matter that you *need to know* in order to stay competitive in this ever-changing industry. By contacting the Wiley office nearest you, you'll receive any current update at no additional charge. In addition, you'll receive future updates and revised or related volumes on a 30-day examination review.

If you purchased this product directly from John Wiley & Sons, Inc., we have already recorded your subscription for this update service.

To become a subscriber, please call **1-877-762-2974** or send your name, company name (if applicable), address, and the title of the product to:

mailing address: **Supplement Department**
John Wiley & Sons, Inc.
One Wiley Drive
Somerset, NJ 08875

e-mail: **subscriber@wiley.com**
fax: **1-732-302-2300**
online: **www.wiley.com**

For customers outside the United States, please contact the Wiley office nearest you:

Professional & Reference Division
John Wiley & Sons Canada, Ltd.
22 Worcester Road
Etobicoke, Ontario M9W 1L1
CANADA
Phone: 416-236-4433
Phone: 1-800-567-4797
Fax: 416-236-4447
Email: canada@wiley.com

John Wiley & Sons, Ltd.
The Atrium
Southern Gate, Chichester
West Sussex PO 19 8SQ
ENGLAND
Phone: 44-1243-779777
Fax: 44-1243-775878
Email: customer@wiley.co.uk

John Wiley & Sons Australia, Ltd.
33 Park Road
P.O. Box 1226
Milton, Queensland 4064
AUSTRALIA
Phone: 61-7-3859-9755
Fax: 61-7-3859-9715
Email: brisbane@johnwiley.com.au

John Wiley & Sons (Asia) Pte., Ltd.
2 Clementi Loop #02-01
SINGAPORE 129809
Phone: 65-64632400
Fax: 65-64634604/5/6
Customer Service: 65-64604280
Email: enquiry@wiley.com.sg

Brink's Modern Internal Auditing

Sixth Edition

Robert R. Moeller

WILEY

John Wiley & Sons, Inc.

This book is printed on acid-free paper. ∞

Copyright © 2005 by John Wiley & Sons, Inc. All rights reserved.

Published by John Wiley & Sons, Inc., Hoboken, New Jersey.

Published simultaneously in Canada.

No part of this publication may be reproduced, stored in a retrieval system, or transmitted in any form or by any means, electronic, mechanical, photocopying, recording, scanning, or otherwise, except as permitted under Section 107 or 108 of the 1976 United States Copyright Act, without either the prior written permission of the Publisher, or authorization through payment of the appropriate per-copy fee to the Copyright Clearance Center, Inc., 222 Rosewood Drive, Danvers, MA 01923, 978-750-8400, fax 978-646-8600, or on the web at www.copyright.com. Requests to the Publisher for permission should be addressed to the Permissions Department, John Wiley & Sons, Inc., 111 River Street, Hoboken, NJ 07030, 201-748-6011, fax 201-748-6008.

Limit of Liability/Disclaimer of Warranty: While the publisher and author have used their best efforts in preparing this book, they make no representations or warranties with respect to the accuracy or completeness of the contents of this book and specifically disclaim any implied warranties of merchantability or fitness for a particular purpose. No warranty may be created or extended by sales representatives or written sales materials. The advice and strategies contained herein may not be suitable for your situation. You should consult with a professional where appropriate. Neither the publisher nor author shall be liable for any loss of profit or any other commercial damages, including but not limited to special, incidental, consequential, or other damages.

For general information on our other products and services, or technical support, please contact our Customer Care Department within the United States at 800-762-2974, outside the United States at 317-572-3993 or fax 317-572-4002.

Wiley also publishes its books in a variety of electronic formats. Some content that appears in print may not be available in electronic books.

For more information about Wiley products, visit our Web site at *www.wiley.com*.

Library of Congress Cataloging-in-Publication Data:
Moeller, Robert R.
    Brink's modern internal auditing / Robert Moeller.-- 6th ed.
        p. cm.
    Includes bibliographical references and index.
    ISBN 0-471-67788-4 (cloth)
    1. Auditing, Internal. I. Title: Modern internal auditing. II. Title.
    HF5668.25.B74 2005
    657'.458--dc22

                                                    2004016916

Printed in the United States of America
10 9 8 7 6 5 4 3 2 1

To my best friend and wife,

Lois Moeller

About the Author

Robert R. Moeller has over 25 years experience in internal auditing, ranging from launching new internal audit functions in several companies providing internal audit consulting and serving as audit director for a *Fortune* 50 corporation.

Moeller has an MBA in finance from the University of Chicago and an undergraduate degree in engineering; he has accumulated a wide range of professional certifications including the CPA, CISA, PMP, and CISSP. He was appointed the national director of information systems auditing for the major public accounting firm of Grant Thornton. There he developed firmwide audit procedures and directly managed information systems audits, and assumed responsibility for their Chicago office information systems consulting practice.

In 1989, Moeller was recruited to build and organize the first corporate information systems audit function for Sears Roebuck, an organization that then consisted of AllState Insurance, Dean Witter, and Discover Card, as well as the Sears retail operations. He went on to become their audit director, initiating numerous new practices. He has been active professionally in both the Institute of Internal Auditors and the AICPA. He was president of the IIA's Chicago chapter, served on its International Advanced Technology Committee, and was chair of the AICPA's Computer Audit Subcommittee.

In 1996, Moeller launched his own corporation, Compliance and Control Systems Associates, Inc., and presented seminars on internal controls and corporate governance throughout the United States. He was then talking about Sarbanes-Oxley issues well before the Act. He has helped launch a new consulting practice for EMC Corporations, has worked as a consultant and project manager, specializing in the telecommunications industry, and managed a cellular telephone financial system project on a worldwide basis. More recently, he has led in a series of Sarbanes-Oxley Section 404 projects in manufacturing, finance, and other industries. He continues to stay well-connected with the overall profession of internal auditing.

Robert Moeller lives with his wife, Lois, in the Chicago area. They enjoy sailing on Lake Michigan in the summer, skiing in Colorado and Utah, and participating in Chicago's theatre, opera, and music scene.

Contents

Because of the rapidly changing nature of information in this field, this product may be updated with annual supplements or with future editions. **Please call 1-877-762-2974 or email us at** *subscriber@wiley.com* **to receive any current update at no additional charge.** We will send on approval any future supplements or new editions when they become available. If you purchased this product directly from John Wiley & Sons, Inc., we have already recorded your subscription for this update service.

CONTENTS

Preface

In 1941, the clouds of war—initiated by such dictators as Hitler, Mussolini, and Stalin—were surrounding much of the world. At the same time, Victor Z. Brink completed his New York University PhD thesis. While the "maximum leader" dictators were predicting one kind of violent revolution, Brink's PhD thesis outlined a much more benign revolution, a revolution in the way that internal auditors should perform their work. Prior to the 1940s, internal auditors were essentially in-house assistants to their company's public accounting firms, often performing little more than clerical financial auditing support duties for those external auditors. Brink's thesis argued that a much better role for internal auditors should be servants to management, not external auditor assistants.

Brink then went off to service in World War II, but not before the wheels were put in place to publish his thesis as a book for business leaders. Its title was *Modern Internal Auditing*. With the United States gearing up for total war and looking to better utilize every scarce resource, the first edition of *Modern Internal Auditing* (published by John Wiley & Sons in 1942) caused many managers to consider how they might better organize their internal audit functions. Brink's book strongly proposed that internal auditors could and should be much more significant members of an organization's management team. The *modern* internal auditor that Brink envisioned served management by going beyond routine accounting verification procedures and taking a broader approach of *supplying service to management* as part of his or her internal audit activities.

Brink returned from the war and became director of internal audit for the Ford Motor Company. He also worked with others, such as Brad Cadmus and Larry Sawyer, to build and better define this new profession called internal auditing. A final result of the work of Brink and others was the establishment of the Institute of Internal Auditors (IIA), now a major professional accounting organization, responsible for setting standards and providing guidance to the profession of internal auditing. Often, authors of significant and groundbreaking business books "go to sleep" after their first or second editions. However, Brink kept active in the profession, revising his original 1942 edition three times over the years, either by himself or in collaboration with others in later editions.

Although Brink introduced new concepts and technologies in the subsequent editions, he never lost his basic philosophy that internal auditing should provide a basic and essential *service to management* in the modern organization. Robert Moeller took general responsibility for the fifth edition of *Modern Internal Auditing* released in 1999, and had an opportunity to meet with Vic Brink and discuss internal auditing concepts from the very early days leading to the development of that edition. Vic Brink was an impressive, interesting man, with an ongoing concern for the practice of internal auditing. This sixth edition preserves Brink's important concept of internal audit's responsibility to management but also introduces many of the changes and concepts that continue to make internal auditing exciting and important.

Each new edition of *Modern Internal Auditing* has focused on changes that were then affecting the profession of internal auditing. The fifth edition, for example, emphasized the growth of computers and information systems as a change that has very much impacted internal auditors over the last 50 to 60 years. At the time of the first edition of *Modern Internal Auditing*, the digital computer essentially did not exist and companies were just beginning to use 80- or 90-column punched-card tabulating equipment for some of their elementary statistical recordkeeping applications. There was no need to mention these machines in the first edition of this book because they were just not that important to businesses. Mainframe computers, behemoths that weighed tons and occupied major areas of floor space, were introduced in larger companies starting in the 1960s, but internal auditors initially were not concerned with them. This was the era in which audits were performed *around* the computer; that is, if a total had been generated by the computer and printed on some report, it was assumed to be correct because "the computer figured it out." Auditors were primarily concerned that the input controls were adequate. Internal auditors had little to do with these computer systems besides perhaps checking to see if the door to the computer room was locked or that candy and soft drinks were not being consumed in the computer room. The fifth edition tried to give some broad internal audit guidance in many information systems–related areas.

This sixth edition is released in the midst of a new era of concerns and responsibilities for internal auditors. The concerns regarding corporate governance, associated with the collapse of Enron Corporation, MCI, Adelphia, and others as well as the collapse of the then prominent public accounting firm, Arthur Andersen, led to the passage of the Sarbanes-Oxley Act (SOA) by the U.S. Congress in 2002. This legislation has a worldwide impact on organizations and both internal and external auditors. In many respects, SOA has given internal audit functions a level of "new respect" in the eyes of their corporate audit committees, management, the external auditors, and a much broader public.

This book has an overall objective to give the reader an overview of the many issues facing internal auditors today as well as areas of good internal audit practices. An example is the SOA Section 404 review, an internal controls document and testing process that has become a major concern for organization management today. Chapter 6, "Evaluating Internal Controls: Section 404 Assessments," provides internal audit guidance for these important SOA review requirements. In addition, an overall theme of the periodic editions has been to introduce and emphasize newer areas that should be of interest to internal auditors. The early editions of this book under Victor Brink described the operational approach to internal auditing, a major and important change from the compliance- and financial-related approaches of most internal auditors at that time. Similarly, the previous fifth edition by this author discussed such new areas of internal audit interest as the COSO (Committee of Sponsoring Organizations) internal controls framework, the importance of ethics and codes of conduct, and auditing systems under development. These were not common topics of interest for internal auditors at that time, but were areas that were believed to be of interest for the modern internal auditor. Perhaps ahead of our time, the topics on COSO internal controls as well as ethics and codes of conduct are important elements of today's SOA-driven world.

This edition continues to follow this theme of introducing newer areas of internal control or management concern that should at least be of interest to today's modern internal auditor. An example of this approach is Chapter 22, "Infrastructure Service- and Support-Delivery Controls, on the information technology infrastructure library (ITIL) standards for information systems service-delivery and service-support standards. This may become an important set of standard practices for many organizations in the future. However, in covering a broad set of topics, space does not allow for detailed discussions of areas discussed in separate chapters such as business continuity planning or audit sampling.

This edition should provide today's internal auditor with an introduction to many practices important to internal auditing. To the internal audit manager or chief audit executive (CAE), the chapters that follow are designed to give an overview of all aspects of modern internal auditing. To the staff internal auditor, the chapters are designed to give some information that should be of importance to the internal audit professional, such the previously referenced ITIL model or the Chapter 5, "Understanding and Assessing Risks: Enterprise Risk Management," discussion of the soon to be released (at the time of publication) of the COSO Enterprise Risk Management (ERM) framework.

These chapters should also be important to members of the audit committee of the board of directors as well as senior managers in the organization who deal with internal auditors on a regular basis. The chapters should provide an overview of what internal audit does, its operating practices, and the standards that create to day's profession of modern internal auditing.

PART ONE

Foundations of Internal Auditing

CHAPTER ONE

Foundations of Internal Auditing

1.1 WHAT IS INTERNAL AUDITING?

An effective way to begin this book about modern internal auditing is to refer to the professional standards of the Institute of Internal Auditors (IIA). This internal auditor professional organization defines the practice of internal auditing as follows: *Internal auditing is an independent appraisal function established within an organization to examine and evaluate its activities as a service to the organization.*

This statement becomes more meaningful when one focuses on its key terms. *Auditing* suggests a variety of ideas. It can be viewed very narrowly, such as the checking of arithmetical accuracy or physical existence of accounting or other business records, or more broadly, as a thoughtful review and appraisal at the highest organizational level. In this book, we use the term *auditing* to include this total range of levels of service, from detailed checking of accounting balances to higher-level operational appraisals.

The term *internal* defines work carried on within the organization by its own employees. Internal auditing work is distinguished from such audit-related work carried on by outside public accountants or other parties (such as government regulators) who are not directly a part of an organization.

The remainder of the IIA's definition of internal auditing covers a number of important terms that apply to the profession:

- *Independent* means auditing that is free of restrictions that could significantly limit the scope and effectiveness of the review or the later reporting of resultant findings and conclusions.

- *Appraisal* confirms the need for an evaluation that is the thrust of internal auditors as they develop their conclusions.

- *Established* confirms that internal audit is a formal, definitive function in the modern organization.

- *Examine and evaluate* describe the active roles of internal auditors, first for fact-finding inquiries and then for judgmental evaluations.

- *Its activities* confirm the broad jurisdictional scope of internal audit work that applies to all of the activities of the modern organization.

- *Service* reveals that help and assistance to management and other members of the organization are the end products of all internal auditing work.

- *To the organization* confirms that internal audit's total service scope pertains to the entire organization, including all personnel, the board of directors and its audit committee, stockholders, and other interested stakeholders.

Internal auditing can also be recognized as an organizational control that functions by measuring and evaluating the effectiveness of other controls. When an organization establishes its planning and then proceeds to implement its plans in terms of operations, it must do something to monitor the operations to ensure the achievement of its established objectives. These further efforts can be thought of as *controls*. While the internal audit function is itself one of the types of controls used, there is a wide range of other controls. The special role of internal audit is to help measure and evaluate those other controls. Thus, internal auditors must understand both their own role as a control function and the nature and scope of other types of controls in the organization.

Internal auditors who do their job effectively become experts in what makes for the best possible design and implementation of all types of controls. This expertise includes understanding the interrelationships of various controls and their best possible integration in the total system of internal control. It is thus through the control door that internal auditors come to examine and evaluate all organizational activities to provide maximum service to the organization. Internal auditors cannot be expected to equal—let alone exceed—the technical and operational expertise pertaining to the many activities of the organization. However, internal auditors can help the responsible individuals achieve more effective results by appraising existing controls and providing a basis for helping to improve those controls.

1.2 INTERNAL AUDITING HISTORY AND BACKGROUND

It is normal for any activity—including a control activity such as internal auditing—to come into being as a result of emerging needs. The business organization of 1942, when modern internal auditing was just getting started, was very different from our twenty-first century organization of today. For example, aside from some electromechanical devices and activities in research laboratories, computer systems did not exist. Organizations had no need for computer programmers until these machines started to become useful for various record keeping and other computational functions. Similarly, organizations had very rudimentary telephone connections where switchboard operators routed all incoming calls to a limited number of desktop telephones. Today, we are all connected through a vast, automated worldwide web of telecommunications and the Internet. The increasing complexity of modern business and other organizations has created the need for a similar specialist in various business controls: the internal auditor. We can better understand the nature of internal auditing today if we know something about the changing conditions in the past and the different needs these changes created. What is the simplest or most primitive form of internal auditing and how did it come into existence? How has internal auditing responded to changing needs?

At its most primitive level, a self-assessment or internal auditing function can exist when any single person sits back and surveys something that he or she has done. At that point, the individual asks him- or herself how well a particular task has been accomplished and, perhaps, how it might be done better if it were to be done again. If a second person is involved in this activity, the assessment function would be expanded to include an evaluation of the second person's participation in the endeavor. In a small business, the owner or manager will be doing this review to some extent for all enterprise employees. In all of these situations, the assessment or internal audit function is being carried out directly as a part of a basic management role. However, as the operations of an organization become more voluminous and complex, it is no longer practicable for the owner or top manager to have enough contact with every aspect of operations to satisfactorily review their effectiveness. These operations review responsibilities need to be delegated.

Although this hypothetical senior manager could build a supervisory system to try to provide a personal overview of operations, that same manager will find it increasingly difficult to know whether all of the interests of the organization are being properly served as it grows larger and more complex. Are established procedures being complied with? Are assets being properly safeguarded? Are the various employees functioning efficiently? Are the current approaches still effective in the light of changing conditions?

The ultimate response to these questions is that the manager must obtain further help by assigning one or more individuals to be directly responsible for reviewing activities and reporting on the previously mentioned types of questions. It is here that the internal auditing activity comes into being in a formal and explicit sense. The first internal auditing assignments usually originated to satisfy very basic and sharply defined operational needs. The earliest special concern of management was whether the assets of the organization were being properly protected, whether company procedures and policies were being complied with, and whether financial records were being accurately maintained. There was also considerable emphasis on maintenance of the status quo. To a great extent, this internal auditing effort was initially viewed as a closely related extension of the work of external auditors.

The result of all of these factors was that these early internal auditors were viewed as playing a relatively narrow role in their organizations, with limited responsibility in the total managerial spectrum. An early internal auditor often was viewed as a financially oriented checker of records and more of a police officer than a coworker. In some organizations, internal auditors had major responsibilities for reconciling canceled payroll checks with bank statements or checking their mathematics in regular business documents. In retail organizations, internal auditors often were responsible for reconciling daily cash sales to recorded sales receipts.

Understanding the history of internal auditing is important because this old image still persists, to some extent, for today's modern internal auditors. This is so even though the character of the internal auditing function is now very different.

Over time, the operations of various organizations increased in volume and complexity, creating managerial problems and new pressures on senior management. In response to these pressures, management recognized the possibilities for better utilization of their internal auditors. Here were individuals already set up in an audit function, and there seemed to be every good reason for getting greater value from these individuals with relatively little increase in cost.

At the same time, internal auditors perceived these opportunities and initiated new types of services themselves. Thus, internal auditors gradually took on broader and more management-oriented responsibilities in their work efforts. Because internal auditing was initially largely accounting-oriented, this upward trend was felt first in the accounting and financial-control areas. Rather than just report the same accounting-related exceptions—such as some documentation lacking a supervisor's initials—internal auditors began to question the overall control processes they were reviewing. Subsequently, internal audit valuation work began to be extended to include many nonfinancial areas in the organization.

In 1942, the Institute of Internal Auditors (IIA) was launched. Its first membership chapter was started in New York City, with Chicago soon to follow. The IIA was formed by people who had been given the title internal auditor by their organizations and who wanted to both share experiences and gain knowledge with others in this new professional field. A profession was born that has undergone many changes over subsequent years and has resulted in the type of modern internal auditor discussed in this book.

New business initiatives, such as the COSO (Committee of Sponsoring Organizations) internal control framework discussed in Chapter 4, "Internal Controls Fundamentals: COSO Framework," or the Sarbanes-Oxley Act (SOA) discussed in Chapter 3, "Internal Audit in the Twenty-First Century: Sarbanes-Oxley and Beyond," and Chapter 6, "Evaluating Internal Controls: Section 404 Assessments," have caused a continuing increase in the need for the services of internal auditors. In addition, some newer environmental forces have created needs in such areas as protection from industrial hazards, support of quality-control programs, and different levels of business responsibility, including ethical standards. This need for ethical standards includes higher standards for corporate governance, greater involvement of boards of directors and their audit committees, a more active role for stockholders, and a changed role for the outside public accountant.

Ethics, whistleblower programs, and codes of conduct issues will be discussed in Chapter 9, "Whistleblower Programs and Codes of Conduct." As a result of these new business directions, the services of internal auditors have become more important to a wide range of interested parties in the organization. There are now more and better-qualified internal auditing personnel and a higher level of organizational status and importance attached to them. The IIA has grown from its first, 25-member charter chapter in 1942, to an international association with over 90,000 members and hundreds of local chapters worldwide. At the same time, the importance of internal audit has been recognized by many professionals through their Standards for the Professional Practice of Internal Auditing, as will be discussed in Chapter 12, "Internal Audit Professional Standards." The internal audit profession has reached a major level of maturity and is well positioned for continuing dynamic growth.

Internal auditing today involves a broad spectrum of types of operational and financial activity and levels of coverage. In organizations today, internal auditing has moved beyond being a staff activity roughly tied to the controller's organization, although internal audit's role is constantly being redefined. SOA has been a major driver of change for internal auditors. While they once only had a nominal reporting relationship to the audit committee of the board, SOA has strengthened and formalized that reporting relationship. However, in some other organizations, internal audit continues to function at just a routine compliance level. In other situations, internal audit still suffers from being integrated too closely with regular accounting activities and limits virtually all of its audit work to strictly financial areas. These are all exceptions that do not reflect the potential capabilities of the modern internal audit organization. They may also reflect the lack of progressive attitudes in the overall organization.

Today, modern internal auditors have expanded their activities to all operational areas of the organization and have established themselves as valued and respected parts of the senior management effort. With renewed emphasis from SOA, the modern internal auditor today is formally and actively serving the board of director's audit committee. While internal audit organizations once had an almost nonexistent, dotted line reporting relationship to their audit committee—with little direct communication—the chief audit executive (CAE) today has direct and active level of communication with that same audit committee. This overall situation reflects major progress in the scope of internal audit's coverage and level of service to all areas of the organization. The internal auditing profession itself, through its own self development and dedication, has contributed to this progress and has set the stage for a continuing upward trend. Internal audit's service responsibilities to the audit committee will be discussed in Chapter 8, "Internal Audit and the Board Audit Committee."

1.3 RELATIONSHIPS OF OPERATIONAL, FINANCIAL, AND INFORMATION SYSTEMS AUDITING

During the 1960s, there was a strong tendency for many to use the term of *operational auditing* in place of the traditional *internal auditing*. The rationale was that *internal auditing* was a term tied too closely with basic financial auditing, including the external auditor's review of both financial control activities and financial statements. Internal auditors called themselves operational auditors because of their desire to focus more of their efforts on the other operational activities in the organization that could potentially point to areas for increased profit and overall management service. In its most extreme form, the so-called operational auditing function would disassociate itself entirely from the so-called financial areas. They would claim, for example, to have no expertise on the financial controls surrounding an accounts receivable operation. Rather, they might look at process controls and ignore the issue of whether the cash received was properly recorded and tied to financial accounts, including the general ledger. Management often became confused and dismayed when their internal auditors all but ignored these important accounting or financial-related issues. This separation of responsibility created issues of both substance and self-interest for the *operational audit*–oriented internal auditors.

Traditionally, internal auditors had been concerned with both accounting and financial processes, and some expertise in these areas had generally been considered to be essential. Coverage of accounting and financial controls and processes also provided an opportunity for expanding the range of internal audit services into the broader operational areas. Since accounting and financial records directly or indirectly reflect all operational activities, financially oriented internal audit reviews often open doors to the other activities. This combination of operational and financial internal audit practices as well as information systems auditing will be considered throughout this book. In terms of strategy, an internal audit abandonment of accounting and financial areas can create a vacuum that would invite the emergence of other audit-type functions. Chapter 26, "Internal Audit Quality Assurance and ASQ Quality Audits" for example, will discuss how many traditional internal auditors in the past ignored the International Organization for Standardization (ISO) "quality" movement in its early days, leading to an almost separate profession of quality auditors.

An internal audit function today needs to have an adequate coverage of key accounting and financial areas, and the responsibilities of whomever does that will inevitably spill over into an overview of broader operational areas. The failure to cover key financial areas was one of the arguments external audit firms made to senior management when they offered to provide internal audit outsourcing services. For some years leading up to the enactment of SOA, it almost appeared that the public accounting firms were taking over internal auditing through their outsourcing arrangements. Now, an organization's external auditors are prohibited from also performing internal audits for the same organization. These new SOA-mandated rules will be discussed in Chapter 3.

In the wake of SOA and the internal control assessment requirements of the Act's Section 404 requirements (discussed in Chapter 6) internal audits' roles and responsibilities are changing again as we move through the first decade of the twenty-first century. Internal auditors today are a much more important element in an organization's overall internal control framework than they were not that many years in the past. To be effective here, an internal auditor must gain a strong understanding of internal controls, and any internal audit involvement with SOA Section 404 reviews require some understanding of generally accepted accounting principles (GAAP) and their related financial controls. Therefore, internal auditors today need to understand financial and operational as well as information systems controls. An objective of this book is to cover all three of these areas, but to cover them in a manner whereby they are not considered separate internal audit practices, but represent skills and knowledge that should be used by all internal auditors.

CHAPTER TWO

Management Needs: Internal Audit's Operational Approach

2.1 INTERNAL AUDIT'S MANAGEMENT FOCUS

Starting with the first edition in 1942, this book has continually emphasized that *service to management* should be the major mission of internal audit. In the earlier days, this internal audit mission objective was fairly narrow and emphasized more the needs of middle to senior management, such as a financial controller interested in the controls covering accounting processes. Over time, this internal audit mission has been broadened to cover the board of directors, stockholders, all levels of employees, government, and society. The controlling mission of internal audit today is service to the overall organization, including those responsible for its governance. However, that mission still must have a strong internal management focus. While the recipients of internal auditing services have special needs, management effectiveness is often the most major concern. If an organizational unit is not well managed, everyone associated with it suffers. At the same time, management's tasks are becoming more complex because of a rapidly changing worldwide environment with regard to changing technology, markets, regulatory factors, and societal values. These factors make it important for internal audit to take a broad approach to the concept of service and assistance to the organization at every level and in every way. In order to properly assist management, an internal auditor must continuously strive to understand management needs, in terms of both general concepts and the unique characteristics of a particular organization. Auditors need to understand some general concepts of management theory and processes, how managers set their objectives, and how they identify and solve problems to achieve those objectives. All internal auditors must learn to think like organization management in order to form partnership relationships and communication links.

Another important reason to understand management theory and practice is that internal auditors themselves are managers. Their roles include supervising audit projects and directing overall internal audit tasks. Internal auditors must be able to develop objectives and strategies to achieve those objectives, working through people and with other resources, just like other managers. Auditors cannot be qualified counselors to management if they cannot effectively manage their own operations. Internal auditors should provide a model that can be observed and followed by others in the organization. In this way, internal auditors will also be viewed as likely candidates for other management-level positions in their organizations.

This chapter considers some of the more general concepts of management and also discusses communication techniques that will help an auditor gain a better understanding of management needs. This chapter should be read in conjunction with other audit management chapters such as Chapter 4, "Internal Controls Fundamentals: COSO Framework," and Chapter 14, "Directing and Performing Internal Audits," among others. Effective internal auditing involves understanding management needs and working with management to serve those needs. That understanding is an essential ingredient for establishing internal audit credibility such that management will respect and listen to internal audit's counsel. Working together, managers and internal auditors can achieve increased effectiveness and promote overall organizational welfare.

2.2 OPERATIONAL AUDITING CONCEPTS

A basic theme and message in this chapter and throughout this book is that an internal auditor is primarily an operational auditor, no matter whether reviewing a cash management process, information systems service delivery, or Sarbanes-Oxley Act (SOA) Section 404 internal controls. The expression "operational auditor" can cause some confusion with noninternal auditors who often tend to think that all auditors, whether internal or external, do about the same tasks. That is certainly not true. Internal auditors, with their strong operational approach, have a unique and important role in service organization management at all levels.

The objective of operational auditing is, as defined in the IIA's "Statement of Responsibilities" standards[1] "to assist members of the organization in the effective discharge of their responsibilities." To accomplish this, internal auditors must place themselves in the position of both general and departmental management to see things from both perspectives and to provide constructive service and recommendations to the overall organization. This starts with an internal auditor gaining a clear understanding of management's objectives in some areas as well as a good knowledge of the operations that will be reviewed. This places an internal auditor in a much different role than the public accountant external auditor who primarily focuses on the organization's published financial statements and the supporting financial auditing standards. An internal auditor may become involved in some of these financial accounting issues, but will primarily focus on organizational processes and operations. Many of these operational areas will be discussed in greater detail in other chapters of this book.

Internal auditors should regularly take an operational approach in their audits and appraisals of management performance. For example, today they often will be helping to complete the SOA internal controls assessment requirements, called Section 404 and discussed in Chapter 6, "Evaluating Internal Controls: Section 404 Assessments." By doing this work, they will improve the overall internal controls environment and will help to satisfy a corporate legal requirement. However, line or operational management may not see much additional value in these reports unless internal audit serves management through appraisals of operations and suggestions for improvement when appropriate. Managers of business operations will be more interested in such areas as:

- Suggestions to improve operations at all levels to help managers achieve their objectives

- The manner in which the results of operations, including audit recalculations of performance, are reported back to senior management levels

- The impact of overall organizational policies, instructions, and allocations on the operation being reviewed

In many larger organizations where many employees have little direct contact with senior management, internal auditors may be one of the few groups with regular, face-to-face links with senior corporate management beyond periodic financial performance reports or other high-level meetings. Managers at all levels look to internal auditors to appraise their operations and to make constructive suggestions. While it may sometimes be necessary, management is not looking to an internal auditor to make a series of minor, nit-picking recommendations. Internal audit has the high-level objective of serving management's needs through constructive operational auditing recommendations.

2.3 UNDERSTANDING AND WORKING WITH MANAGERS AND MANAGEMENT

While the words *management* or *manager* suggests a variety of different concepts; most people are aware that management requires skills distinct from those needed for more repetitive work. An excellent accountant may not be able to supervise a group of other accountants or a product development engineer may be unable to successfully manage a small engineering project development group. In its simplest form, management presents an image of someone getting a job done and doing it in an effective manner. The concept of management often suggests an individual or a group of individuals who are dealing with large and complicated problems. A common thread of any management activity is a systematic approach to accomplish some defined organizational or group objective.

There are a wide range of concepts used, in terms of nature and scope, to develop formal definitions of management. Some view management as a science, while others feel that good management is almost an art. A compact and useful definition for the internal auditor is: *Management is the process of achieving the effective utilization of resources.* This definition recognizes that management is an active process, that it deals with human and other resources, and that its end objective is the effective utilization of those resources. This process is the most basic aspect of what management is all about. Managers attempt to get the best possible results in the best possible manner. In business, this normally means maximum profitability, based on long-term standards and giving fair consideration to the rights of all parties.

Management requires both decision-making skills and the ability to get things done through others. The manager must decide on the objectives to be accomplished and select the resources needed to accomplish these objectives. This management process is broken down into detailed areas where necessary decisions are made. The basic functions of management have really not changed much throughout our industrial age. While technologies and business practices change, good management concepts generally have remained unchanged. Early editions of this book used a definition by Gulick and Urwick, who described the functions of management in 1937[2] as *planning, organizing, staffing, directing, coordinating, reporting, and budgeting.* With some modifications, these management functions are still valid today. The effective internal auditor should keep these concepts in mind when managing all aspects of the internal audit function as well as when evaluating management controls as part of internal audit projects. A more detailed description of these management concepts includes:

- *Planning.* A manager must decide what needs to be done and must set short- and long-term goals to achieve those objectives. In order to do this, the manager must make his or her best effort to understand the economic, social, and political environment in which the organization will be operating and the resources available to make the plans work. As one example, plans entirely feasible during a period of strong economic growth may be utterly impractical in a time of recession. Planning also includes the management function of *budgeting,* since a budget is a plan to spend money to accomplish certain objectives. Planning is the foundation for all the other functions and is a necessary component in all levels of an organization.

- *Organizing.* This involves breaking down any work effort into basic elements and then bringing them back together to accomplish total work requirements. Management objectives and the work necessary to attain them dictate the skills needed. In organizing, the manager must decide on the positions to be filled and on the related duties and responsibilities. That is, what positions or functions will be responsible for performing the planned work? Because the work done by individual members of the organization will be interrelated, some means of coordinating these efforts must be provided. *Coordinating* is an essential component of organizing rather than a management function in itself.

- *Staffing.* In organizing, the manager establishes position descriptions and decides which skills are required for each. Staffing is the function of attempting to find the right persons for required jobs. An established organization, of course, should already have both a structure and appropriate people to fill the authorized positions. Nevertheless, both building an organization and staffing it are likely to be continuing management tasks since changes in plans and objectives often require changes in the organization and may occasionally necessitate a complete reorganization. Staffing is not a one-time effort. People are continually leaving for multiple reasons, while changes or growth in the organization create new or different positions. Although many of these activities are part of the human resources function, all managers must be deeply involved with them.

- *Directing.* This is the important process of giving the correct guidance to people in the organization as needed. Since it is difficult to predict the problems and opportunities that will arise in day-to-day work activities, position descriptions must be couched in rather general terms with the manager providing ongoing direction. The manager must make sure that all team members are aware of the results expected in each situation, must help to improve skills, and must provide guidance on how and when to perform certain tasks.

- *Controlling.* Current work accomplishments are affected by changing conditions and varying human capabilities. Controlling is a function where the manager must determine how well tasks have been accomplished, identify deviations from plans, and make changes to bring work teams in line with overall goals. Although sometimes considered a separate function, *reporting* is an element of controlling. Reports are made so that the manager, as well as others, may see what is happening in order to change course if necessary. Controlling is also the area in where internal audit has special expertise.

These functions focus on the administrative aspects of management, and internal audit focuses many of its review activities in these areas. However, a manager must also be a leader in moving the organization in new directions. As Peter Drucker wrote in his classic description of management, "Managing a business cannot be bureaucratic, an administrative, or even a policy-making job. . . . [It] must be a creative rather than adaptive task."[3] In other words, the real manager is always an innovator.

Innovating should be considered an additional key function of the manager. A second function is representing the organization to outside groups. There are other additional functions that could be mentioned, but they are essentially subfunctions. For example, communicating is often considered a major part of a manager's job. Unless the manager can communicate with staff, important ideas and concepts may be missed. However, achieving good communication is really part of the *directing* function in which the manager attempts to ensure the overall success of the organization through communication with subordinates.

Internal auditors should always have a good understanding of the management process. They are working with all levels of managers on their internal audit assignments and must manage their own processes and activities.

2.4 ATTRIBUTES OF MANAGEMENT

While many organizations in the past were often isolated, with their markets local or restrained by limitations in communications and transportation, the typical organization today operates in a more complicated and often global environment. However, those organizations in the past "good old days" were affected by many similar attributes even though things traveled at a much slower pace. For example, as early as the 1880s, the price of grain in Kansas was influenced by grain prices in the Ukraine and in Argentina. It took a few days for that price information to travel to the market in Kansas and much longer for grain to actually be transported to these other markets, but they each were influencing factors. Similar examples can be found going at least back to Roman times. Today, speed of communications and such factors as the Internet have just increased this environmental complexity.

Modern environmental factors include economic, competitive, technological, political, and social matters. They should be in the mind of an internal auditor when attempting to understand why management does or does not take some action. For example, economic factors, including dimensions of the state of world, national, and regional economies, can have a major influence on an organization. When thinking about an organization and its business processes, an internal auditor might raise a series of questions such as: Who uses these products and why? How strong is that demand in terms of other needs? Where are the users of the product? Are there other, competitive products or services? There are also factors relating to the supply of the product or service. Where do the materials come from that are needed to produce the aforementioned products, and what is their availability? What kinds of facilities are needed and what kind of production processes are involved? What are the requirements in terms of capital, specialized knowledge, and marketing? Finally, factors relating to demand and supply must be considered in terms of whether there are acceptable profit potentials.

Economic factors have an impact on all organizations, whether a private-sector industrial corporation, a not-for-profit service organization, or a governmental unit. For example, United Parcel Service (UPS) in the United States has largely taken over small parcel delivery from the U.S. Postal Service due to UPS's ability to provide better service at a lower cost structure. The U.S. Postal Service, once a virtual monopoly, could not effectively compete when faced with these economic factors. An internal auditor should always consider the role of economic, competitive, technical, and even political factors when performing internal audits in an organization. That understanding will be valuable for a better understanding of management needs.

This discussion of environmental factors has been from the standpoint of the entire organization. However, management entities also exist at lower levels, including subsidiaries, divisions, departments, and the like. The environmental factors previously discussed also include the authority and controls of the higher organizational levels, to which lower-level management entities are accountable. Also included are the resources available from upper-level management that augment and better define the environmental factors as well as constraints of various kinds that may be imposed by the senior-level management.

In addition to these environmental factors, an internal auditor also needs to understand other key attributes that help to define the overall process of management. Some of the more important of these include:

- *Dependence on People.*   People are the most important resources the effective manager must utilize. They are important in terms of their knowledge, skills, and experience, and have a unique importance that goes far beyond those considerations. An effective manager is directly dependent on people to implement plans through their definitive actions. Thus, an internal auditor must understand how people, or the human resources of an organization, can operate in an effective manner to provide a maximum contribution toward the achievement of managerial goals and objectives. As part of understanding an organization's human resources, management has a continuing challenge to find the best possible fit and integration of individuals within overall organizational goals. These human resources range from senior management to the support staff in an organization. Each has its own general interests, motivations, and needs; management needs to understand these factors to best utilize human resources.

- *Focus on Decision Making.*   Managerial action is based on various types of decisions with some at a very high level, such as a major new line of business, while others are at relatively lower levels. All have common elements in their decision-making process with respect to decision principles and methodology. The problem must be identified, alternatives explored using all information available, and a decision made on the action to be made. This decision-making process is similar for managers at all levels, and only differs due to the magnitude of the problem, the extent to which information is available, the available decision alternatives, and the potential risks associated with the decision outcomes. The factors of time, risk levels, and costs all affect this management process. The effective manager should survey these issues, identify the most significant issues, and then attempt to make the best decisions. Internal auditors should follow this decision-making process to help assemble the correct supporting data when making a recommendation. This will also help the internal auditor to better understand how management reacts to audit report findings and recommendations.

- *Effect of Risk Level.*   There are risks associated with every management decision. If a wrong decision is made, there may be the risk of increased costs associated with that wrong decision, including wasted resources, diminished future performance, or even legal liability for the organization or the responsible manager. To a considerable extent, risk can be reduced by better management information about operational and environmental factors. Of course, every decision would be risk-free if the manager had what is hypothetically called perfect information. There are costs associated with obtaining the various types and levels of information desired, and probability factors will affect the desired results. As a result, total certainty is impossible because of both practical and absolute limitations. This means that management decisions reflect the levels of risk deemed to be acceptable to the particular responsible manager. Managers and their overall organization have varying appetites for risk, and each manager must make evaluations within the parameters of decision authority and risk preferences. The effective internal auditor should have a good understanding of this risk assessment process. Chapter 5, "Understanding and Assessing Risks: Enterprise Risk Management," discusses the entire process of evaluating risk in the context of the COSO Enterprise Risk Management (ERM) framework. In order to understand management's needs, an internal auditor also needs to understand management's willingness to accept or avoid risks.

- *Management Is Judged by Results.* Virtually everything a manager does is judged by how those actions further the achievement of established organization goals and objectives. Managers should be primarily interested in results as opposed to letting an intermediate process be an end in itself. This attribute of judging overall management effectiveness has been a rationale for some hostile management takeovers. Corporate raiders have taken over many otherwise successful companies with the argument that they could achieve better short-term financial results by selling off under-performing assets and undertaking other restructuring actions. Although an organization might have been considered otherwise successful, these raiders promised better results and often took over the organization and then reported improved short-term results. There are always decision variables that cannot be fully predicted or adequately evaluated. As a result, the merits of some managerial decisions may be controversial, and managerial excellence is measured by the quality of its results. Internal auditors should be aware of these issues when attempting to understand management's needs. If management wishes to achieve the best results for the overall organization, the auditor should attempt to support and corroborate those decisions.

- *Time Span for Appraising Results.* Judging management by its results raises questions as to the time frame in which those results are to be evaluated. A manager often can achieve short-term results such as improved profitability even though those decisions will undermine longer-run profits. For example, quality can be temporarily sacrificed with resulting short-term profits, but this action can be so damaging to customer satisfaction that future products are no longer purchased. Good managers should think in terms of the longer term and resist the often-tempting shortcuts that endanger longer-term potentials. When management understands this, the correct decision should be clear. However, the evaluation may be complicated by how long of a time span should be allowed for decisions made today and how willing stockholders are willing to wait for longer-run rewards. A further complicating factor is the difficulty of measuring long-term effects. Managers often innocently make bad estimates in these areas or are victims of wishful thinking. In other cases, lower-level managers ignore long-term consequences because they will not be directly involved when final outcomes become evident. There are many published accounts of this practice, where a manager achieves short-term results at a unit and because of those results either is promoted or leaves to join a different organization. The successors must deal with the long-term results of these short-term decisions. Auditors can often play an important role in this short-term versus long-term results decision process. An internal auditor frequently identifies operational issues that may have long-term negative implications even though the short-term results are not nearly as obvious.

A central truth of management is that conditions are always changing. A valued employee leaves the organization, a new invention makes existing practices obsolete, consumer preferences shift, or something else unforeseen develops. As a result, many dimensions of the management process must be reappraised or redirected. An organization's capacity to foresee such possibilities and to adapt to them is a measure of its ability to survive and prosper. This adaptive approach often takes a rather unstructured management style. At the same time, however, there are needs for standardization and regularity, including effective internal control processes.

2.5 MANAGEMENT AND THE INTERNAL AUDITOR

The successful internal auditor needs to have a general understanding of the management concepts discussed in this chapter. While some of this understanding can come from college training, most will come from exposure to experienced managers on audit assignments within the organization, or from other professional contacts. Finally, it can come from an ongoing program of auditor self-education. There are numerous trendy books on management published continually. Many of these receive a lot of attention for a year or two and then are quickly forgotten, but there are also some classic books on management that will allow an internal auditor to gain a better understanding of management fundamentals. The previous reference to a book by Peter Drucker is a good example—he has written a stream of excellent management books over the years. An internal auditor also might want to talk with a professor of management at a local graduate school of business for other recommendations. An extended reading program will greatly enhance an internal auditor's knowledge and skills in the important practice of management.

In the typical business organization, success is measured by the ability to grow and be profitable. In our free enterprise system, a business organization that is not profitable over a period of time is either not providing needed products or services or is not being effectively managed. Although this profit measure does not exist in government or in some not-for-profit organizations, there are comparable yardsticks available there, including the achievements of various types of service levels rendered or the quantity or quality of services delivered. This measure of profitability is similar for individual units with any organization. On those levels, success is measured by individual contributions overall organization profitability through meeting budget expectation, delivering successful new products, or any of a stream of other measures.

An individual internal auditor as well as the entire internal audit department should think of its success in terms of some measure of success. Many of these success factors will be discussed in other chapters of this book. For example, Chapter 13, "Internal Audit Organization and Planning," talks about planning and organizing the entire internal audit department, while Chapter 21, "Reviewing and Assessing Application Controls," discusses reviewing and assessing information systems applications controls. Success in either of these areas or success for the overall internal audit function is measured by the effective completion of internal audit tasks. In each of these areas, internal audit is satisfying management's needs. However, the most important way an internal auditor can understand the needs of management is to develop ongoing channels of communication with management. This process is often both quite easy and difficult for the internal auditor. It is easy because internal audit often has communication links with the highest levels of management. Internal audit, as discussed in Chapter 8, "Internal Audit and the Board Audit Committee," reports to the audit committee of the board of directors, and has an ability to communicate face to face with senior members of management. Because of this high level of communication, internal auditors can contact almost any level of management within the organization to establish a meeting and to discuss matters of audit interest.

Internal audit must take specific steps to establish communication links with all levels of management in order to better understand their needs. Many of the operational audit projects described in other chapters of this book require this understanding of management's needs. For example, internal audit cannot perform an effective audit of the information systems service support functions, as discussed in Chapter 20, "Software Engineering, the Capability Maturity Model, and Project Management," unless they are aware of management concerns and approaches in this area. Internal audit must establish communication channels through its planning process, through participation in various advisory meetings and boards, and through frank discussions with management over the results of audits.

The basic internal audit role of service to management starts with understanding management's problems and needs. It then goes on to involve a partnership role between the manager and internal audit at all operational levels—a partnership role that extends to helping management to achieve its goals and objectives to the maximum extent possible. Such an effective partnership role can be achieved in many ways. The following are essential ingredients of a sound program to achieve these desired results:

- Internal audit must provide basic audit protective services but, at the same time, help management achieve desired improvements. Moreover, protective contributions often provide an important foundation for making constructive contributions.

- Internal audit should be continuously alert to use its independence from actual operational responsibilities to identify, evaluate, and support issues of significant management interest.

- The capacity to interface in a persuasive manner with managers at all levels should be exercised whenever practical. This requires having a combination of a strong operational understanding and appropriate personal contacts and conduct.

- Auditors must avoid the inherent temptation to use their potential power with management and other auditees. Such actions generate auditee resistance that later will block ongoing constructive relationships.

- Internal audit's focus on internal controls should be used as the credential for the analysis and review of many operational areas. Since the technical expertise of the auditee is typically superior, the auditor's focus on control provides a more acceptable justification of the audit assistance offered.

- There must be respect given at all times for the responsibility that managers have for operational results. Audit recommendations must stand on their own merits, as judged by those who have operational responsibility.

- There should be a blending of the objectives of any audit at its operational levels with the necessity for upward disclosure within the framework of total organizational welfare. This focus should help to neutralize any lower-level audit conflicts due to the more senior management exposure of internal audit.

Service to the organization through assistance to management at all levels is a major goal for internal auditors. This justifies the efforts of internal audit to see its job through the eyes of management and to render all possible assistance for maximum management goal achievement. The problems of management are complex and continually changing in light of both internal and external environmental factors. This means that management increasingly needs the assistance of internal auditors and, in many cases, will welcome it when the ability and credibility of the internal audit function is established. It is a continuing challenge to internal auditors to render assistance to management through effective and significant audit recommendations.

ENDNOTES

[1] See Chapter 12, "Internal Audit Professional Standards," for an overview of IIA professional standards.
[2] Lester Gulick & Lyndall Urwick, "Notes on the Theory of Organization," *Papers on the Science of Administration*, New York: Institute of Public Administration, 1937.
[3] Peter Drucker, *The Practice of Management*, New York: Harper & Row, 1954, p. 47.

CHAPTER THREE

Internal Audit
in the Twenty-First Century:
Sarbanes-Oxley and Beyond

3.1   BACKGROUND: CHANGES IN FINANCIAL
AUDITING STANDARDS

Some internal auditors often avoided financial auditing issues in past years. They took pride in their skills as operational auditors and reserved financial auditing tasks to their external audit firm. Those external auditors reviewed financial controls and records leading up to the issuance of annual financial statements along with their auditor's reports on the fairness of those financial statements. Given their operational audit and internal controls skills, many internal auditors supported their external auditors over the years. This arrangement began to change somewhat during the 1990s. The major public accounting firms up through about the year 2002—then called "the Big 5"—began to take responsibility for organizational internal audit functions through what was called outsourcing. Through an arrangement with the audit committee, many internal auditors at that time found themselves to be employees of their external audit firms continuing to perform internal audits but under the management of their external auditors.

These outsourcing arrangements offered advantages to some internal auditors. Reporting to a large external audit firm, many outsourced internal auditors found greater opportunities for access to continuing education or the possibility to make promotional career transfers to other organizations. Outsourcing somewhat changed the tone of many of these internal audit functions. The public accounting firms managing an internal audit group tended to focus the attention of their internal audit resources more on audits in support of financial controls rather than operational issues. Although not every internal audit function was outsourced, this trend continued through the late 1990s in many major corporations.

As the 1990s ended, businesses were faced with predictions of computer systems and other process-related disasters as part of the Y2K millennium change to the year 2000. Although the millennium arrived with no major problems, the following year, 2001, brought with it some real disasters for U.S. accountants, auditors, and business in general. The long-running stock market boom, fueled by "dot-com" Internet businesses, was shutting down with many companies failing and with growing ranks of unemployed professionals. Those same boom years spawned some businesses following new or very different models or approaches. One that received considerable attention and investor interest at that same time was Enron, an energy trading company. Starting as a gas pipeline company, Enron developed a business model based on buying and selling excess capacity first over their and competitor's pipelines and then moving on to excess capacity trading in many other areas. For example, an electrical utility might have a power plant generating several millions of excess kilowatt hours of power during a period. Enron would arrange to buy the rights to that power and then sell it to a different power company who needed to get out of a capacity crunch. Enron would earn a commission on the transaction.

Enron's trading concept was applied in many other markets such as telephone message capacity, oil tankers, water purification, and in many other areas. Enron quickly became a very large corporation and really got the attention of investors. Its business approach was aggressive, but it appeared to be profitable. Then, in late 2001, it was discovered that Enron was not telling investors the true story about its financial condition. Enron was found to be using off-balance sheet accounting to hide some major debt balances. It had been transferring significant financial transactions to the books of unaffiliated partnership organizations that did not have to be consolidated in Enron's financial statements. Even worse, the off-balance sheet entities were paper-shuffling transactions orchestrated by Enron's chief financial officer (CFO) who made massive personal profits from these bogus transactions. Such personal transactions had been prohibited by Enron's Code of Conduct, but the CFO requested the board to formally exempt him from related code violations. Blessed by the external auditors, the board then approved these dicey off-balance sheet transactions. Once publicly discovered, Enron was forced to roll these side transactions back in to Enron's consolidated financial statements and forcing a restatement of earnings. Certain key lines of credit and other banking transactions were based on its pledge to maintain certain financial health ratios. The restated earnings put Enron in violation of these agreements. What once had looked like a strong, healthy corporation, Enron was soon forced to declare bankruptcy.

Because Enron was a prominent company, there were many "how could this have happened?" questions raised in the press and by government authorities. Another troubling question was, "where were the auditors?" Commentators felt that someone would have seen this catastrophe coming if they had only looked harder. The press at the time was filled with articles about Enron's fraudulent accounting, the poor governance practices of Enron's board, and the failure of its external auditors. The firm Arthur Andersen had served as Enron's external auditors and had also assumed responsibility for its internal audit function through outsourcing. With rumors that the SEC would soon be on the way to investigate the evolving mess, Andersen directed its offices responsible for the Enron audit to "clean up" all records from that audit. The result was a massive paper shredding exercise, giving the appearance of pure evidence destruction. The federal government moved quickly to indict Andersen for obstruction of justice because of this document shredding, and in June 2002, Andersen was convicted by a Texas jury of a felony, fined $500,000 and sentenced to five years' probation. With the conviction, Andersen lost all public and professional trust and soon ceased to exist.

At about the same time, the telecommunications firm WorldCom disclosed that it had inflated its reported profits by at least $9 billion during the previous three years, forcing WorldCom to declare bankruptcy. Another telecommunications company, Global Crossing, also failed during this same time period when its shaky accounting became public. The cable television company Adelphia failed when it was revealed that its top management, the founding family, was using company funds as a personal piggy bank, and the CEO of the major conglomerate Tyco was both indicted and fired because of major questionable financial transactions and personal greed. Only a few examples are mentioned here; in late 2001 and through the following year, 2002, many large corporations were accused of fraud, poor corporate governance policies, or very sloppy accounting procedures. Exhibit 3.1 highlights some of these financial failures. The press, the SEC, and members of Congress all declared that auditing and corporate governance practices needed to be fixed.

These financial failures helped to introduce some major changes to what had been well-established financial auditing standards and practices. They caused government regulators as well as the investment community to question and then reform the financial auditing standards setting process and a wide range of public accounting firm practices. Many organizations' CEOs and CFOs were characterized as being more interested in personal gain than in serving shareholders, audit committees were often characterized as not being sufficiently involved in organizational transactions, and external auditors and their professional organization, the American Institute of Certified Public Accountants (AICPA) received major criticism. Outsourced internal auditors caught this criticism as well; they were viewed as being tied too closely to their external audit firm owners. Many other previously accepted practices, such as the self-regulation of public accounting firms, were seriously questioned. By self-regulation, we refer to the AICPA's peer review process, where public accounting firm A would be given the responsibility

EXHIBIT 3.1

Early Twenty-first Century U.S. Financial Scandals

The following represent some, but not all, of the accounting scandals that took place in the United States in the period around early 2004. This list represents allegations reported in the financial press and situations where earnings restatements were necessary.

Company	What Happened
Adelphia Communications	Organizational funds used by founding family officers as a personal "piggy bank."
Enron Corporation	Massive accounting fraud discovered through improper off-balance sheet accounting.
Fine Host Corporation	CFO resigned because of financial fraud.
HealthSouth	Earnings fraudulently misstated over many years to satisfy analyst expectations.
Homestore.Com	Bogus sales reported to boost reported results.
ImClone Systems	CEO and founder engaged in massive insider trading based on advance knowledge of regulatory ruling.
Parmalat	At least $14 billion in fictitious cash reported for this Italian dairy products corporation.
Tyco	Accounting fraud coupled with the CEO using corporate funds for personal gain.
WorldCom	$3.8 billion in overstated earnings.
Xerox	Masked billions of losses through "creative accounting."

to review standards and practices for firm B. Knowing that firm B might be assigned to come back and review A a few years into the future, few firms ever found that much critical to say about their peers.

These financial scandals caused many changes with the passage in 2002 of the Sarbanes-Oxley Act (SOA) as the most significant event. SOA establishes regulatory rules for public accounting firms, financial auditing standards, and corporate governance. Through SOA, the public accounting profession has been transformed, the AICPA's Auditing Standards Board (ASB) has lost its authority for setting auditing standards, and the rules have changed for corporate senior executives, boards of directors, and their audit committees. A new entity, the Public Corporation Accounting Overview Board (PCAOB) has been established, as part of SOA and under the SEC to set public accounting auditing standards and to oversee individual public accounting firms. Although not directly covered in the legislation, SOA also has very much affected internal auditors as well.

This chapter discusses this very significant public accounting standards setting and corporate governance legislation, the Sarbanes-Oxley Act (SOA), with an emphasis on its aspects that are most important to internal auditors. SOA and the PCAOB represent the most major change to public accounting, financial reporting, and corporate governance rules since the SEC was launched in the 1930s. SOA represents the most important set of new rules for auditing and internal auditing today. The effective internal auditor should have a good understanding of these new rules and how they apply to today's practice of internal auditing.

3.2 "WHERE WERE THE AUDITORS?" STANDARDS FAILURE

The corporate accounting scandals and bankruptcies that surfaced in the early days of this twenty-first century, including Enron, WorldCom, and others, all happened in the same general time frame. Although these scandals did not raise questions about the quality and integrity of internal auditors, CPA certified external auditors were faced with multiple questions along the theme of "where were the auditors"? These external auditors were responsible for auditing the books and certifying that the financial statements were fairly stated. It is easy to suggest that the once highly regarded but now gone Arthur Andersen represented what had gone wrong with the major public accounting firms. Andersen had promised to improve its processes as part of a settlement with the SEC regarding botched audit procedures at Waste Management several years earlier. Andersen, however, evidently shrugged off that settlement the way a driver shrugs off the ticket for being caught in a speed trap. When they were implicated with Enron, regulators at the SEC soon honed in on Andersen's procedures. Enron's internal audit function had been outsourced to Andersen with the two audit groups essentially speaking in one voice, Andersen seemed to be more interested in providing consulting services to Enron than auditing its financial statements, and many Andersen auditors were quickly rewarded with senior management positions at Enron after brief periods on the financial internal audit staff.

Although Andersen was the center of attention for Enron, other external audit practices soon faced questioning. Based on off-the-books accounts, corporate executive greed, and other matters, it soon became apparent that some audited financial statements were not all fairly stated, per the traditional CPA/auditing terminology. Many situations were soon highlighted where the external auditors had missed some massive errors and frauds in their reviews of organization financial statements. Too often, the major public accounting firms were accused as selling their auditing services as a "loss leader" with the objective of using that audit work to gain assignments in more lucrative areas such as consulting or tax advisory. To many observers, the whole concept of "independent outside auditors" was seriously questioned. How could a team of outside auditors be independent, the critics asked, if key members of the financial staff had just recently been serving as auditors and then had accepted positions on the "other side." There were too many close ties, making independent, objective decisions difficult.

With a very few exceptions, there also was little evidence of internal auditors raising issues at these accounting-scandal-implicated corporations. Many of the internal audit departments at these corporations accused of accounting fraud had been "outsourced" to their responsible external audit firms. Prior to Enron's fall, there were published reports describing the "great partnership" that existed between the Arthur Andersen managed internal audit function at Enron and the Andersen external auditors. They shared offices, shared resources, and spoke essentially in one voice. This was really in contrast to the somewhat uneasy alliances that independent internal audit functions sometimes had had with their external auditors in the past. Although these internal audit outsourcing arrangements had been in place for many corporations over some years, the Enron situation raised many questions about the independence and objectivity of these outsourced internal auditors.

Internal and external auditors have historically been separate and independent resources. External auditors were responsible for assessing the fairness of an organization's internal control systems and the resultant published financial reports, while internal auditors served management in a wide variety of other areas as was discussed in Chapter 1, "Foundations of Internal Auditing." In the early 1990s, this separation began to change, with external audit firms taking overall responsibility for some internal audit functions. This trend started when larger organizations began to "outsource" some of their noncore functions. For example, rather than having their own janitorial function, with company employees acting in those roles, an organization's janitorial function might be "outsourced" to a company that specialized in providing janitorial services for many organizations. The previous in-house janitors would be transferred to the janitorial services company and, in theory, everyone would benefit. The organization that initiated the outsourcing would experience lower costs by giving a noncore function, janitorial services, to someone who better understood it. The outsourced janitor, in this example, also might have both better career possibilities and better supervision.

Internal audit outsourcing got started in the late 1980s. External audit firms went to their client firm's management and offered to "outsource" or take over their existing internal audit function. The idea appeared to make sense to senior management and audit committees on many levels. Senior management often did not really understand the distinctions between the two audit functions and were sometimes more comfortable with their external auditors. There were many reasons for this, and senior management and audit committee members were often enticed by the promised lower costs of internal audit outsourcing. In addition, many financial managers had got their start in public accounting, often in positions with the same external audit firm.

Although the Institute of Internal Auditors (IIA) initially fought against the concept, internal audit outsourcing continued to grow through the 1990s. The fifth edition of this book talked about this trend with a mixed message. It acknowledged that this was a then-growing trend that could benefit some individual internal auditors but also had many risks. Although a few independent consulting firms also made efforts to get into this market, internal auditor outsourcing continued to be the realm of the major public accounting firms.

This outsourcing or contracting out of some or all internal audit services had been a growing trend throughout the 1990s. An IIA sponsored survey[1] found that in 1996 in the United States and Canada some 25% of the organizations surveyed had contracted out some if not all of their internal audit functions, with public accounting firms doing the bulk of this work. The reasons given in the IIA survey for decisions to contract out internal audit services included cost savings, adding specialized audit skills, and to "clean house of incompetent people or at least those with a perceived lack of value." That last comment received 10% of the survey responses and certainly should have been disturbing to some internal audit professionals. This trend to outsource internal audit services continued through the 1990s, with the major public accounting firms becoming increasingly involved in internal auditing. There was not much concern expressed about auditor independence and objectivity, except perhaps from internal audit managers who had been forced out because of outsourcing. Enron and the other accounting-scandal-related firms put these objectivity questions and concerns back on the table.

Beyond outsourced internal auditors, an even stronger criticism of the major public accounting firms at that time was aimed at their strong and lucrative practice of providing consulting services for the organizations they audited. The consulting arm of a firm might be engaged to install a financial system at a client corporation, and then auditors from that same firm would assess the internal controls for that just implemented system. This arrangement pointed to objectivity issues and conflicts of interest, and Enron provided many examples here. This had been an ongoing concern by the SEC and other public accounting critics. In 2000, the SEC had proposed rules that would limit the amount of consulting work that a public accounting firm could perform for the companies they also audited. That SEC proposal was halted through a massive lobbying effort by the AICPA. With revenues from auditing always under pressure, the major public accounting firms did not want to give up their lucrative consulting practices.

As the professional organization for public accounting, the AICPA was responsible for establishing financial auditing standards as well as reviewing and initiating appropriate external auditor disciplinary measures through a peer review process. With the failure of Enron and Arthur Andersen, the AICPA found itself the target of considerable criticism. In addition to their fight to allow auditing and consulting at the same client, they had been accused, in the late 1990s, of deferring to wishes of the then Big 5 accounting firms when the AICPA had backed off from proposed standards that would have made auditors more responsible for detecting financial fraud.[2] Questions were also raised about the quality review and disciplinary processes, both largely based on a peer review process. Peer reviews created an environment where almost everyone passed the test. Prior to Enron, the now much-maligned Arthur Andersen had gone through peer review and passed with flying colors. The business world had changed after Enron and WorldCom, but the public accounting profession and the AICPA initially did not.

The end result was that the SEC now defines public accounting rules, which were included in the Sarbanes-Oxley Act (SOA), passed in 2002. A major component of SOA is the Public Company Accounting Oversight Board (PCAOB), an independent entity to govern and regulate the public accounting industry and to establish financial auditing standards. SOA has totally changed the rules for financial auditing, corporate governance, the role of external audit firms, among other matters. SOA has a major impact on all internal auditors, whether working in the United States or elsewhere for essentially any form of organization. The sections following discuss major aspects SOA and the PCAOB, with an emphasis on their impact on internal auditing.

3.3   SARBANES-OXLEY OVERVIEW: KEY INTERNAL AUDIT CONCERNS

The official name for this U.S. federal legislative act to regulate the accounting and auditing practices of publicly traded companies is the "Public Accounting Reform and Investor Protection Act." It became law in August 2002 with some detailed rules and regulations still being released, some over two years later as this book went to press. The law's title being a bit long, business professionals generally refer to it as the Sarbanes-Oxley Act from the names of its congressional principal sponsors, and it is referred to as SOA throughout this book. Others refer to the law with the name SOX.

SOA has introduced a totally changed process of issuing external auditing standards, reviewing external auditor performance, and giving new governance responsibilities to senior executives and board members. Among other matters, the SEC has taken over the process for establishing auditing standards from the AICPA through the Public Company Accounting Oversight Board (PCAOB). This board also monitors external auditor professional ethics and performance. As happens with all comprehensive federal laws, an extensive set of specific regulations and administrative rules is being developed from the broad guidelines in the SOA text, and the SEC has been given that responsibility.

The provisions of the SOA also have a major impact on internal auditors, particularly in U.S. publicly traded organizations. Internal audit now must act somewhat differently in their dealings with audit committees, senior—and in particular financial—management, and external auditors. Because of the breadth of U.S. business throughout the world, SOA has an impact on virtually all internal auditors. The effective modern internal auditor should develop a general understanding of SOA's provisions as well as its specific provisions affecting internal audit.

U.S. federal laws are organized and issued as separate sections of legislation called Titles with numbered sections and subsections under each. Much of the actual SOA text only mandates rules to be issued to the responsible agency, the SEC for SOA. These upcoming specific SOA rules to be developed by the SEC may or may not be significant to most internal auditors. For example, Section 602 (d) of Title I states that the SEC "shall establish" minimum professional conduct standards or rules for SEC practicing attorneys. While perhaps good to know, an internal auditor will typically not be that concerned about these specific rules yet to be promulgated. Others may be of more interest to internal auditors. Section 407 of Title I again says that the SEC will set rules requiring the disclosure that at least one audit committee member must be a "financial expert." While this definition of a "financial expert" is subject to ongoing interpretation, this is important information for a chief audit executive (CAE) who will be dealing with both members of the audit committee and senior management. That "financial expert" will or should have some understanding of an effective internal controls review process as well as audit committee and internal audit interactions. Since this "financial expert" may very well be new to the organization's audit committee, this may be a key liaison contact for internal audit.

Exhibit 3.2 summarizes the major Titles of SOA and includes those more significant to internal auditors. The sections following provide descriptions of those key portions of SOA that are important to internal auditors. SOA is the most important financial legislation passed in the United States since the early 1930s, and it has caused changes for internal auditors, external auditors, and corporate governance in all corporations. While SOA is directed at corporations with SEC-registered securities, its concepts if not its actual rules will almost certainly encompass a wider swath of worldwide organizations over time.

EXHIBIT 3.2

Sarbanes-Oxley Act Key Provisions Summary

The following are the major sections of SOA of interest to internal auditors. A more detailed description of each is included in the text of this chapter.

Section	Subject	Rule or Requirement
101	Establishment of PCAOB	Overall rule for the establishment of PCAOB, including membership requirements.
104	Accounting Firm Inspections	Schedule for registered firm inspections.
108	Auditing Standards	The PCAOB will accept current standards, but will issue new ones.
201	Out of Scope Practices	Outlines prohibited practices such as those related to internal audit outsourcing, bookkeeping, and financial systems design.
203	Audit Partner Rotations	The audit partner and the reviewing partner must rotate off an assignment every five years.
301	Audit Committee Independence	All audit committee members must be independent directors.
302	Corp. Responsibility for Financial Reports	The CEO and CFO must certify the periodic financial reports.
305	Officer and Director Bars	If funds are received as part of fraudulent/illegal accounting, the officer or director is required to personally reimburse funds received.
404	Internal Control Reports	Management is responsible for an annual assessment of internal controls.
407	Financial Expert	One audit committee director must be a designated financial expert.
409	Real Time Disclosure	Financial reports must be distributed in a rapid and current manner.
1105	Officer or Director Prohibitions	The SEC may prohibit an officer or director from serving in another public company if guilty of a violation.

(a) SOA Title I: Public Company Accounting Oversight Board

The AICPA formerly had responsibility for public accounting firms through its administration of the Certified Public Accountant test and the restriction of AICPA membership to CPAs. State boards of accountancy actually licensed CPAs, but the AICPA had overall responsibility for the profession. Auditing standards for new issues or concerns were set by the AICPA's Auditing Standards Board (ASB) through a process that involved member task forces to develop proposed standards changes, extensive individual member and firm reviews of draft standards, and the eventual issuance of those new or revised financial audit standards. Auditing standards were based on generally accepted auditing standards (GAAS), with a series of specific numbered auditing standards called Statements of Auditing Standards (SAS). Much of GAAS was just good financial auditing practices such as the understanding that certain transaction must be backed by appropriate documentation. The SAS's covered more specific areas requiring better definition. SAS No. 79, for example, defined internal control standards, or SAS No. 99 was titled "Consideration of Fraud in a Financial Statement Audit." Internal control standards will be discussed in Chapter 4, "Internal Controls Fundamentals: COSO Framework" and the SAS No. 99 fraud standard is discussed in Chapter 11, "Fraud Detection and Prevention." The AICPA's code of professional conduct stated that CPAs were required to follow and comply with those auditing standards when applicable.

The AICPA's GAAS and numbered SAS standards had been accepted by the SEC prior to SOA and set the foundation for what constituted the reviews and tests necessary for a certified audited financial statement. Much has now changed since SOA! While previously there was not much noise about whether the process of establishing auditing standards was "broken," SOA now has taken this audit-standard-setting process out of the hands of the AICPA and its ASB.

The PCAOB is a totally new nonfederal, nonprofit corporation with the responsibility to oversee all audits of corporations subject to the SEC. It does not replace the AICPA but assumes responsibility for many functions that were formally managed by AICPA members for themselves. The AICPA will continue to administer the CPA examination, with its certificates awarded on a state-by-state basis. The PCAOB is defined in Title I of SOA legislation along with nine separate other sections. PCAOB is an entity for overseeing external but not internal auditors. However, because of the changes in the audit process and corporate governance, PCAOB rules will have an impact on the manner in which internal auditors coordinate their work with external auditors as well as the overall process of corporate governance. If for no other reason, the new SOA rules say that an internal audit function can no longer be run as an outsourced unit of a corporation's external auditors.

(i) PCAOB Administration and Public Accounting Firm Registration. The PCAOB consists of five members appointed by the SEC with three of them *required* to be non-CPAs. The legislation is insistent that the PCAOB is not to be dominated by CPA and public accounting firm interests. A board member can be considered as one of the two CPA representatives even if that member was a former practicing CPA. In addition, the PCAOB chairperson must not have been a practicing CPA for at least five years. These are strong rules with an objective of keeping the board from being dominated by CPAs and public accounting firms. It can almost be expected that PCAOB will be dominated by lawyers and "public interest activists" going forward. When this legislation was being drafted, the AICPA mounted a major lobbying effort to keep the PCAOB under CPA control. Ongoing accounting scandals, however, made their case weak, and today the AICPA has lost their authority and responsibility for self-regulation for the auditors of SEC-registered organizations.

The current PCAOB chair, William McDonough, is the former chief accountant in the SEC's Division of Enforcement and co-chairman of the SEC's Financial Fraud Task Force. In those roles, the new PCAOB chair coordinated, monitored, and advised SEC staff conducting accounting and financial reporting investigations and initiated enforcement and disciplinary proceedings. Although a practicing CPA in past years, the first chair has a background as a lawyer and government regulator. This will probably be the background of typical PCAOB members going forward.

The PCAOB is responsible for overseeing and regulating all public accounting firms that practice before the SEC. This really means any corporation that has stock registered to trade on any U.S. exchange or has registered debt issuances. Private or small corporations are currently not included nor are not-for-profits and governmental entities. PCAOB's responsibilities include:

- *Registration of the Public Accounting Firms That Perform Audits of Corporations.* This registration is much more detailed than just filling out an application form, paying a fee, and beginning business. The registering firm must disclose the fees collected from the corporations they have audited, provide data on their audit and quality standards, provide detailed information regarding the CPAs who will be performing their audits, and disclose any pending criminal, civil, or administrative actions. A firm can be denied the right to register due to any PCAOB questions regarding their background.

- *Establish Auditing Standards.* These standards include auditing, quality control, ethics, independence, and other key audit areas. Although many of these initial standards will be essentially the same as the previous ASB standards, a new process for the overall setting of auditing standards has been established here. As there are continuing demands for more continuous auditing and health and safety sustainability reporting, we can probably expect a whole different dimension of these standards in the future.

- *Conduct Inspections of Registered Public Accounting Firms.* The PCAOB has responsibility for quality-related reviews of registered firms. In the past, this was the AICPA peer review process, where firms often found little to say in criticism of their peers. This is an area that will evolve as PCAOB gets itself better established, but public accounting firms can almost certainly expect to receive more detailed, stringent reviews.

- *Conduct Investigations and Disciplinary Procedures.* These procedures apply to an entire registered firm or just to individuals within those firms. Wrongdoing discovered in formal investigations can result in sanctions that would prohibit a firm or an individual auditor from performing audits under PCAOB—a kiss of death.

- *Perform Other Standards and Quality Functions as the Board Determines.* The PCAOB may get into other areas to protect investors and the public interest. As the need for auditing services evolves, these standards will certainly change and evolve.

- *Enforce SOA Compliance.* Although there is still much to be determined, PCAOB will be responsible for enforcing compliance to SEC rules beyond the SOA overall legislation. This may result in a variety of administrative law actions or other procedures as appropriate.

There is a required annual registration process for public accounting firms practicing before the board. This registration application data will become of public record, and a public accounting firm's litigation matters and other traditionally somewhat confidential data will become a matter of public record.

The PCAOB registration process and the available published data may be of particular value for an organization that is not using one of the Big 4 accounting firms (formerly the Big 5, now sometimes called the Final 4). There are several medium-sized and smaller but very highly credible public accounting firms that can provide excellent, high-quality services. However, if an organization is using one of these smaller public accounting firms, it would be very prudent to check these PCAOB registration records.

(ii) Auditing, Quality Control, and Independent Standards. SOA's Title I, Section 103 gives PCAOB the authority to establish auditing and related attestation standards, quality-control standards, and ethics standards for registered public accounting firms to use for their financial audits. The PCAOB has been given the authority to take over the standards setting process that was built over many years by the AICPA's Auditing Standards Board. Using impartial language, the SOA text recognizes that these new PCAOB auditing standards may be based on "proposals from one or more professional groups of accountants or advisory groups." While this is an area still under development and subject to future change, the current set of auditing standards, known as Statements of Auditing Standards (SASs), remain in effect. For example, the internal control review audit standard, SAS No. 78, was based on the COSO (Committee on Sponsoring Organizations) internal control model has become one of the new PCAOB standards. We can expect new standards in other areas soon. Beyond SAS's covering auditing, there have been other AICPA standards as well. These were the SSAEs and SSARs. The Statements on Standards for Attestation Engagements (SSAE) cover situations where the CPA does not perform actual audit tests but examines or even observes some area or circumstance and then *attests* to what was observed or found. The Statements on Standards for Accounting and Review (SSAR) are standards for the bookkeeping-type tasks that a CPA may perform. These are not formal audit procedures and are not included as part of PCAOB responsibilities.

The IIA's *Standards for the Professional Practice of Internal Auditing*, discussed in Chapter 12, "Internal Audit Professional Standards," fall in this latter category as well. They cover the work of internal auditors that may be used to support an external auditor's formal work in some area, such as internal controls. IIA Standards are designed to support all internal auditor review work but are not for an external auditor's audit and attest work. When an internal auditor was working in support of the external audit counterparts on some review task, the work should have been done following external audit guidelines. Even with a new set of PCAOB standards, the reliance on traditional audit standards will continue. There will only be a conflict if some future PCAOB standard is widely divergent from some element of the IIA standards. In that situation, the IIA standards will have to be revised.

SOA mandates that the PCAOB develop standards with the following minimum requirements:

- *Audit Workpaper Retention.*   Standards require that audit workpapers and other materials to support the auditor's report must be maintained for a period of not less than seven years. This requirement is certainly a response to the infamous Andersen document shredding, and every internal audit department should consider maintaining their internal audit documentation with at least the same retention period. While an operational audit workpaper and audit reports may not have the same retention needs as the financial audit materials, members of the audit committee and corporate management will expect that same level of retention from internal audit. In these days of electronic media, it is not enough to file workpapers as hard-copy documents that are difficult to retrieve. Internal audit functions need to have documentation standards to define the necessary requirements for the set of workpapers necessary to support an audit. Too often, internal auditors have filed as a workpaper "permanent file" such trivia as the menu from that neat restaurant they visited on an extended audit to some remote location. Internal audit workpapers will be discussed in Chapter 15, "Workpapers: Documenting Internal Audit Activities."

- *Concurring Partner Approval.*   Standards require a concurring or second-party approval for each audit report issued. This can be done by another member of the same public accounting firm or an independent reviewer. The major public accounting firms have all had independent review processes for their issued reports and workpapers, but these were sometimes done more for after-the-fact quality-control review rather than audit decisions. Under the new SOA rules, a second external audit partner must "sign on the dotted line" and personally and professionally commit to the findings and conclusions in any audit. With other SOA audit report requirements outlined below, both signing partners must agree to all of the potential alternative issues outlined there.

  There is message for internal auditors in this standard. Many internal audit departments are too small to allow for a second, concurring auditor to be assigned to audit engagements, and even if there is a larger internal audit department, this concept of a concurring auditor has generally not been used. In addition, the new IIA standards outlined in Chapter 12 do not call for such a concept. The IIA standards only state that the CAE is responsible for communicating the results of the audit to responsible parties. However, with an increasing emphasis on SOA rules, an effective internal audit function should perhaps consider installing ground rules for when a second audit report approval is appropriate.

  The concurring opinion here refers to the external auditor's formal opinion, in the conclusion of an audit, stating the client's financial reports are "fairly stated" in accordance with GAAP. Because of different interpretations of various GAAP rules in some audit situations, SOA has mandated those second, concurring opinions. The opinions expressed in internal audit reports typically do not require that same level of gravity. For example, an audit report on the auditor's observation of a physical inventory would not need a concurring opinion if the report covered primarily compliance observation findings, such as the failure to distribute documented counting instructions. However if, in the internal auditor's opinion, the inventory taking was so lacking in internal controls that the final results might be suspect, a second concurring or review auditor opinion might be helpful.

SOA does not cover standards for internal audit report opinions and certainly not internal audit concurring opinions. However, it may be appropriate for an internal audit department to include a reviewing auditor or concurring auditor opinion on some reports. Exhibit 3.3 outlines guidelines for including a concurring internal auditor on the final report.

- *Scope of Internal Control Testing.* SOA standards require the external auditor to describe the scope of the testing processes as well as the findings from that testing. The result of this will be more detailed descriptions of testing procedures in reports and report addendums as well as probably more extensive testing procedures. In the past, external auditors have sometimes used increasingly strained theories to justify their use of the most minimal of test sizes. External auditors were frequently faced with very large test populations and then tested only a very small number of

EXHIBIT 3.3

Guidelines for a Concurring Second Internal Auditor Opinion

ACTION STEPS

1. Does the chief audit executive (CAE) or a designate sign off on all audit reports issued?

2. Does the senior auditor who performed the work and/or a responsible audit manager also sign the audit report?

3. Prior to the CAE's sign-off, is there a process in place for the CAE's review of the detailed report findings and necessary supporting materials?

4. When audit report findings are highly technical—such as for information systems or complex accounting issues—are all issues fully understood by persons signing the report?

5. When consultants or other outside parties have been used to develop the audit conclusions, is this identified in the report and is their sign-off secured for documentation purposes?

6. Are processes in place to ensure that all persons signing an internal audit report personally have acknowledged that they are personally and professionally responsible for the report content?

7. If an internal auditor refuses to sign off on an audit report, are there procedures in place to document that refusal and secure a second opinion if necessary?

8. For a smaller, limited-resources audit department, have arrangements been made to obtain a concurring signature from some other party, either a knowledgeable person in the organization or an outside consultant?

items. If no problems were found, they expressed an opinion for the entire population based on the results of this very limited sample. Although tests designed and administered by internal auditors have typically had a larger sample size, both will need to pay greater attention to the scope and reasonableness of their testing procedures. Chapter 7, "Internal Controls Frameworks Worldwide: CobiT and Others," discusses evaluating and testing internal controls as part of SOA, while Chapter 16, "Gathering Evidence Through Audit Sampling," describes how an internal auditor can effectively use audit sampling as a testing process.

- *Evaluation of Internal Control Structure and Procedures.* PCAOB standards will include guidance for the review and evaluation of internal controls. Because it has become a recognized worldwide standard, the final PCAOB standards follow the COSO model of internal control, as discussed in Chapter 4. SOA further specifies, however, that the external auditor's evaluation contain a description of material weaknesses in such internal controls as well as any material noncompliance found on the basis of the auditor's testing. This requirement points to the need for more detailed and comprehensive internal controls reporting.

    Internal control reviews are areas where internal auditors can very much assist the organization and senior management through their focused reviews. For external auditors, the bar has really been raised. In past years, external auditors did much of the internal control evaluation work themselves, sometimes reviewing the internal controls over a process that their consultants had previously installed. Needless to say, not many material control weaknesses were often found. Under SOA, the external auditors are only required to assess the effectiveness of internal controls based on their reviews of documentation performed by others within the organization being reviewed. Normally, a management team or outside consultants will be charged with documenting internal controls and testing their effectiveness. The external auditors are to assess this internal control documentation and perform other tests they may feel necessary to satisfy their audit requirements.

    This entire process of evaluating SOA internal controls, often called Section 404 reviews, is discussed in much greater detail in Chapter 6, "Evaluating Internal Controls: Section 404 Assessments." Internal audit's role in this process has very much changed and has been expanded. Internal audit can take a passive role in assisting management in performing their own internal control reviews, can take a more active internal role where needed, or can assist the external auditors in performing their internal control assessments. Although their role will vary depending on a variety of factors, the modern internal auditor today will have a much more significant role in helping organizations to achieve SOA internal controls compliance.

    An interesting SOA internal control review requirement is that for companies with many locations in the United States and/or internationally, all significant locations are supposed to be *evaluated annually* and not just on a rotation basis for the purpose of determining the effectiveness of the internal control system. Whether this work is performed by external or internal auditors, this really expands the scope of the overall audit. Planning for internal control reviews at large, multilocation organizations will require detailed planning and coordination between internal and external audit under the overall supervision of the audit committee.

- *Audit Quality Control Standards.*   The PCAOB also is mandated to release audit quality-control standards for the issuance of audited financial reports. These quality standards have not yet been released at press time. In the past, the AICPA's quality standards were fairly high level and limited to their peer review processes for large firms. In October 2002, the AICPA became registered under ISO 9000 standards. The growing importance of these ISO quality standards will be discussed in Chapter 24, "HIPAA and Growing Concerns Regarding Privacy." ISO is a worldwide standards process, and internal auditors should gain a general understanding of the ISO process and how it fits into their organization.

- *IIA Professional Standards.*   Discussed in Chapter 12, they require that internal audit departments have a quality-improvement and -assessment program. In the past, internal auditors had a single-sentence fairly general professional standard for internal audit quality assurance. Current IIA standards now have several distinct standards for quality-assurance and -improvement programs. This is much stronger guidance than in the past, and they should help an internal audit department better comply with this new era of ISO 9000 and SOA quality standards.

  While the PCAOB will eventually issue its own specific quality standards, the SOA legislation states that every registered public accounting firm is required to have standards related to:

  ○ Monitoring of professional ethics and independence

  ○ Procedures for resolving accounting and auditing issues within firm

  ○ Supervision of audit work

  ○ Hiring, professional development, and advancement of personnel

  ○ Standards for acceptance and continuation of engagements

  ○ Internal quality inspections

  ○ Other quality standards to be proscribed by the PCAOB

  These are fairly general quality standards, and we can expect that over time the AICPA or some other body will release a fairly specific set of them that can be applied to all registered public accounting firms if not to all firms. In a similar sense, we can expect that the IIA, the American Society for Quality (ASQ), or some other body will establish a set of quality standards that will be applicable to all internal audit departments. ASQ quality audits are a whole new dimension for internal auditors and are discussed in Chapter 24.

- *Internal Audit Implications of the PCAOB Standards.*   An internal auditor might ask what does all of this PCAOB standards stuff have to do with me? Some internal auditors will claim that as an internal auditor, there are the IIA *Standards for the Professional Practice of Internal Auditing*, and there is little need to become concerned here. However, while it cannot be predicted with absolute certainty, these newer PCAOB financial auditing standards will have an impact on internal auditors as well as their external audit counterparts. The new SOA rules for corporate governance very much increase the role and responsibility of the audit committee for many firms, and the internal audit function will become even more closely aligned with them. Chapter 8, "Internal Audit and the Board Audit Committee," discusses how internal audit can work with and support their board of directors audit committee.

Government rulemaking bodies often move slowly, and the effective internal audit function should closely monitor these evolving PCAOB standards and modify internal audit department processes to follow what will eventually be external and internal audit best practice standards. The latest current or proposed draft rules can best be found on the PCAOB Web site (www.pcaobus.org). Interestingly, a private provider of SOA-related information grabbed the pcaob.org registration, leaving the official oversight board to have to contend with pcaobus.org name.

PCAOB financial auditing standards will cause significant changes in the manner in which internal audits are planned, performed, and reported. An organization's external auditors will be working under the SOA rules, and the audit committee will expect their external and internal auditors to operate inconsistent in a manner. Whether it is quality standards, effective internal control testing, or many other areas, the effective internal audit department should modify its procedures to comply with these evolving PCAOB standards.

(iii) Inspections, Investigations, and PCAOB Disciplinary Procedures. The PCAOB is empowered to conduct a continuing program of registered accounting firm inspections to assess their compliance with SOA rules, SEC rules, and professional standards. Interestingly, here and throughout the legislation are references to public accounting professional standards but no specific reference to the AICPA. While groups such as the Canadian Institute of Chartered Accountants (CICA) play that role for companies headquartered in Canada, the AICPA had set the auditing standards framework for all. The text of the SOA statute either ignores the AICPA or only mentions them in general terms. Still, the AICPA is a powerful professional organization and will continue to play a role in providing guidance to public accountants. The AICPA also is beginning to take a more active role in areas that are not covered in SOA. Their peer review standards and processes, in the past, were limited to the major public accounting firms with many SEC-registered clients. With PCAOB taking over this larger firm quality review process, the AICPA announced in early 2003 that they would be administering and scheduling peer reviews for the many smaller firms that have no SEC-registered clients.

As part of the 2002 SOA legislation, the PCAOB quality inspections or reviews were initially scheduled to be performed annually at the larger registered public accounting firms and once every three years if a registered firm conducted less than 100 financial statement audits. This was a fairly aggressive schedule, and the board was given the authority to adjust this schedule. The years 2003 and 2004 got the PCAOB off to a slow start in initiating these reviews. Only one of the Big 4 firms was reviewed in 2003 due to a variety of review process startup problems. That first review had been planned for up to 15,000 hours covering about 70 different offices. Despite this slow start, the full review process should soon be underway.

These PCAOB inspections focus on the public accounting firm's performance in the audits selected for review and on the issuance of associated audit reports. The reviews are empowered to identify any act or an omission to act that is violation of the rules established by the SOA, PCAOB, SEC, AICPA–type professional standards, and that firm's own quality control policies. A long list of things to review! These reviews are often lengthy and intense exercises as compared to the AICPA-administered peer reviews of the old days. Although not designated as reviews of an internal audit function, these peer reviews could very much affect an internal audit department as well. Because internal auditors coordinate their work with their external audit counterparts, some internal audit work could also be subject to inspection as part of a PCAOB review. While it was the external auditor's responsibility to review and monitor performance, problems could result in some nasty accusations.

These inspections cover selected audits and reviews completed during the prior period and include selected offices and individual auditors. The reviews are performed to evaluate the quality-control system of the firm reviewed as well as documentation and communication standards. Work performed by internal audit for the public accounting firm could be included here. The inspections are documented in a formal inspection report that is to be reported to the SEC and state boards of accountancy. When appropriate, the PCAOB will initiate disciplinary procedures.

The PCAOB reviews of the public accounting firm audits performed probably can include internal audit's activities in supporting the external auditors as well. Following the COSO internal control framework, as discussed in Chapter 4, internal audit is a key component of an organization's control foundation. Internal audit's plans, workpapers, and completed audit reports should always be ready and available for the possibility of such a PCAOB review.

SOA's Title I, Section 105 covers public accounting firm investigations and disciplinary procedures in some detail. The PCAOB is authorized to compel testimony, to require the production of audit work, and to conduct disciplinary proceedings. The latter many range from temporary suspension of an individual or firm, to substantial fines, or even to barring from the profession. The enforcement process follows the same general rules as for any federal administrative legal actions, whether a violation of a SEC securities rule or a pollution complaint under the Environmental Protection Agency.

Section 106 consists of one brief paragraph on foreign public accounting firms that has resulted in much controversy. It says that if any foreign public accounting firm prepares an audit report for an SEC-registered corporation, that foreign public accounting firm is subject to the rules of the SOA, the PCAOB, and related SEC rules. In addition, the board can require those foreign firms to register under SOA rules, with their audit workpapers and the like subject to inspection.

Our multinational world is filled with many non-U.S. public accounting firms. These foreign public accounting firms are governed by their own national public accounting standards, some of which are modeled on AICPA standards and others—so they claim—are stronger than U.S. standards. Other firms follow the evolving set of international accounting standards discussed in Chapter 27, "Control Self-Assessments." No matter what standards they had followed, SOA initially said that they would be subject to these SOA rules if one of their clients has its securities listed on a SEC regulated stock exchange, such the New York Stock Exchange or NASDAQ. This has resulted in some firms no longer wanting to be listed on a U.S. stock exchange. The argument is that the reach of U.S. law is too long or broad. PCAOB has slightly modified some rules or extended registration periods at present, and we may see further changes going forward.

(iv) Accounting Standards. SOA's Title I concludes with one section that affirms that the SEC has authority over the PCAOB, including final approval of rules, the ability to modify PCAOB actions, and the removal of board members. PCAOB is an independent entity responsible for regulating the public accounting industry, but the SEC is really the final authority. The concluding section here recognizes the U.S. accounting-standards-setting body, FASB, by saying that the SEC may recognize "generally accepted" accounting standards set by a private entity the meets certain criteria. The act then goes on to outline the general criteria that the FASB has used for setting accounting standards.

There is and always has been a major difference between accounting and auditing standards. The former define some very precise accounting rules, such as saying that a certain type of asset can be written off or depreciated over no more that X years. These are the principles called GAAP. Auditing standards are much more conceptual, highlighting areas that an external auditor should consider when evaluating controls in some area. These financial auditing standards became increasingly loosely interpreted as we went into the 1990s with management frequently under pressure to continually report short-term earnings growth, and with external auditors who sometimes refused to say "No." The result was the financial scandals of Enron and others as well as Andersen's audit document destruction upon news that the SEC was coming. SOA and the PCAOB now oversee public accounting companies. Internal auditors should always be aware of that relationship.

(b) SOA Title II: Auditor Independence

While SOA Title I set up the new PCAOB, Title II contains a set of rules that very much changes the external auditor and the public accounting industry. Over the years, the traditional rules of auditor independence were increasingly relaxed. Perhaps the most major issue here has been the external audit firm's promotion of consulting services. Consulting was viewed as a more profitable business than strict financial auditing, and the major external audit firms gave the impression that they were selling their auditing services as promotional "loss leaders" in order to sell more consulting services.

SOA Title II contains a series of rules that very much prohibit many recent external audit firm activities. With the exception of a prohibition on external firms outsourcing the internal audit functions of their clients, there is not too much in SOA Title II that directly affects internal audits. However, the effective internal auditor should have an understanding of these new rules for discussions with management and for an ongoing understanding of internal audit's relationship with their external auditors. This section briefly summarizes the SOA Title II new rules.

(i)   Limitations on External Auditor Services.   Section 201 of SOA has made it illegal for a registered public accounting firm to contemporaneously perform both audit and nonaudit services at a client. The prohibitions include internal auditing, many areas of consulting, and senior officer financial planning. For the internal audit professional, the most significant element here is that it is now illegal for a public accounting firm to provide internal audit outsourcing services if it is also doing the audit work. This means that the major public accounting firms are now essentially out of the internal audit outsourcing business for their financial audit clients. They can provide these services to organizations that are not their audit clients, but such an arrangement often introduces a major complexity in the financial audit process. Other firms, including independent spin-offs from public accounting firms, can still provide internal audit outsourcing, but the era when an internal audit professional became a contactor or employee of his or her public accounting firm is essentially over.

In addition to providing outsourced internal audit services, SOA prohibits public accounting firms from providing other services, including:

- *Financial information systems design and implementations.*   Public accounting firms have been installing financial systems—often of their own design—at clients for many years. This is no longer allowed. Internal auditors will need to have a greater understanding of installed financial systems and will no longer be pressured to sometimes look the other way because their external auditors were responsible for an installed financial system.

- *Bookkeeping and financial statement services.*   Public accounting firms previously offered accounting services to their clients in addition to doing the financial audits. Even for major corporations, it was not unusual for the team responsible for the overall financial statement audit also to do much of the work necessary in building the final consolidated financial statements. This is no longer allowed; in-house accounting groups now have the responsibility to analyze, document, and build their financial statements prior to the financial statement audit.

- *Management and human resource functions.*   Prior to SOA, external audit firms took on many responsibilities in these areas. They often identified senior-level professionals from their own firms and helped to move them to client management positions. The result was an environment where virtually all of the accounting managers in an organization often were alumni of their external auditors. This was sometimes frustrating for internal auditors who were not from that same public accounting firm. Avenues from promotion above certain levels seemed limited because of "old-boy" network connections with the external audit firm.

- *Other prohibited services.* Although these do not have that much impact on internal audit, SOA also specifically prohibits external audit firms from offering actuarial services, investment advisor, and audit-related legal services.

Tax services are not included here. Although a prohibition was included in the initial drafts of SOA, there were massive protests from the public accounting firms. Tax services were allowed, but in early 2003 the CEO of the telecommunications company Sprint was forced to resign because of his personal involvement in a dodgy tax avoidance scheme that had been suggested by the firm's external auditors.[3] The tax scheme was based on stock options and the price of the stock, raising questions in the press about the external auditor's role and interests. There may be more to come on this matter in the future.

The overall theme here is that external auditors are authorized to audit the financial statements of their client organizations and that is about all. SOA allows that beyond the above-prohibited activities, external auditors can engage in other nonaudit services only if those services are approved in advance by the audit committee. With the increased scrutiny of audit committees under SOA, many will be wary of approving anything that appears to be at all out of the ordinary.

These SOA external audit service prohibitions will have major impacts on internal audit professionals for many organizations. Because external audit firms are *just the auditors*, internal auditor professionals should find increased levels of respect and responsibility for their role in assessing internal controls, making internal consulting recommendations, and promoting good corporate governance practices. Internal audit's relationships with audit committees will be strengthened, as they will seek increasing help for services that were sometimes assumed by their external audit firms. New groups of professional service firms will be organized to help with installing financial systems, providing bookkeeping services, or managing internal audit functions outsourced under the new SOA rules.

Organizational management will find it necessary to use more scrutiny in their selection of outside service providers. With the changed environment under SOA, many new service providers have appeared. Some are spin-offs from the traditional public accounting firms, while others are new entities. Exhibit 3.4 is a checklist of things to consider when contracting for some of the types of services formerly supplied by external audit firms. Working with nonexternal-audit consultants will be discussed in more detail in a later section.

(ii) Audit Committee Preapproval of Services. Section 202 of SOA's Title II specifies that the audit committee must approve all audit and nonaudit services *in advance*. While audit committees have or should have been doing this all along, that approval was often little more than a formality prior to SOA. Audit committees in "the old days" often received little more than a brief written and/or verbal

EXHIBIT 3.4

Contracted Audit-Related Services Checklist

ACTION STEPS

1. If a registered external audit firm proposes providing additional, nonaudit services, determine that the audit committee and other parties are aware of SOA prohibitions.

2. Working with corporate legal services, ascertain that any firm providing contracted services is properly registered and licensed.

3. Through review and examination, determine that the firm providing contracting services has no direct connection with the current external auditor.

4. Also through review and examination, attempt to determine that the firm providing contracting services has no direct relationship with organization officers, board members, or their families.

5. If the services are to be supplied by the registered external audit firm and if these are for major projects, determine that the nature of these services has been presented to the audit committee and their approval received in advance.

6. For the smaller, less than 5% of the audit fee, nonaudit projects, establish a log to record the nature of the services and accumulated costs.

7. If nonaudit extra work proposed by the registered audit firm appears to violate specific SOA prohibitions, such as those for financial systems consulting, consult the responsible audit committee representative about the matter and resolve it.

8. Work with audit committee members responsible for approving additional work to establish appropriate project and accumulated cost documentation.

9. Develop processes to ensure that all audit-committee-approved additional service work is disclosed in the proxy.

10. Ascertain that all additional, nonaudit work is performed following good project management procedures, including a formal statement of work and documented completion procedures.

11. In cases where the outside provider work is performed by the external audit firm but could have been supplied by other consulting resources, provide data regarding potential decision options to the audit committee representative.

report from their external auditors that was approved in the same perfunctory manner that business meeting minutes are often approved. SOA changes all of this. Audit committee members can now expose themselves to criminal liabilities or stockholder litigation for allowing some prohibited action to take place.

Of course, there are many minor matters regarding external auditor activities that should not have to go through this formal audit committee in advance approval process. Using legal terminology, SOA sets *de minimus*[4] exception rules for these audit committee permission requirements. Per the SOA, preapproval is not required for some nonauditing services if:

- The aggregate dollar value of the service does not exceed 5% of the total external audit fees paid by the organization during the fiscal year when the services were provided.

- The services were not recognized as nonaudit service by the organization at the time the overall audit engagement was initiated.

- These services are brought to the attention of the audit committee and approved by them prior to the completion of the audit.

These exceptions give the external audit firm and the audit committee some flexibility. However, the nature and accumulated dollar value of these additional nonaudit services must be carefully monitored throughout the course of a fiscal year to maintain a level of compliance. The CAE should become involved in this process to help ascertain that all provided extra services continue to be in compliance with the SOA rules. In addition, when an audit committee approves any nonaudit services, these must be disclosed to investors through the annual proxy statement.

SOA allows that the audit committee may delegate this nonaudit services preapproval authority to one or more of the outside directors on the audit committee. This would reduce the strain of handling lengthy audit committee business matters, but will put even more responsibility on a few audit committee members over and above the many new legal responsibilities mandated by SOA. Chapter 8 discusses potential roles for internal audit to better serve their audit committees in much greater detail.

(iii)   External Audit Partner Rotation.   Another section of SOA Title II makes it unlawful for a public accounting firm's lead partner to head an audit engagement for over five years. This is a matter that the major public accounting firms had self-corrected well before SOA. Lead partners from the major firms had been rotated on a regular basis, although there may have been exceptions with smaller firms and smaller engagements. While lead partner rotation had been common, SOA makes the failure of a firm to not rotate a criminal act.

SOA does not really address the common practice in audit partner rotation where a given person will play the lead on an audit and then continue to serve in an advisory role after his or her term. That advisory role partner can often maintain the same level of responsibility as the designated lead partner. If the CAE sees this situation as a potential violation of SOA rules, the matter should be discussed with the chair of the audit committee for possible action.

Full audit partner rotation may bring a challenge to the internal audit function. Internal audit may have been working comfortably with the designated audit partner and the associated team. Internal audit practices for working with a new audit team or responsible audit partner are discussed later in this chapter.

(iv)   External Auditor Reports to Audit Committees.   External auditors have always communicated regularly with their audit committees in the course of the audit engagement as well as for other matters of concern. In the aftermath of Enron and other corporate scandals, however, the level of communication was often found to have been limited. Prior to SOA, a member of management might negotiate a "pass" from the public accounting partner on a suggested accounting treatment change, but the matter often was only reported to the audit committee in the most general of terms if at all.

SOA has changed this. External auditors now are required to report on a timely basis all accounting policies and practices to be used, alternative treatments of financial information discussed with management, alternative financial accounting treatments, and the approach preferred by the external auditor. The whole idea here is that external auditors must report to the audit committee any alternative accounting treatments, the approach preferred by the external auditors, and management's approach. This really says that if there are disputed accounting treatments, the audit committee should be well aware of the actions taken.

This requirement really points to the need for good audit committee documentation. While board members not serving on the audit committee may not be accustomed to this SOA level of required documentation, the CAE can assist here by suggesting the types of documentation approaches that internal audit uses on a regular basis. Chapter 8 discusses audit committee responsibilities under SOA and areas where internal audit can be of help.

(v) Conflicts of Interest and Mandatory Rotations of External Audit Firms. As discussed previously, it had been common for members of the external audit firm team to get offers to move to their audit client firms as a CFO or other senior financial positions. SOA Title II, Section 206 now prohibits external auditors from providing any audit services to a firm where the CEO, CFO, or chief accounting officer participated as a member of that external audit firm on the same audit within the last year. This really says that an audit partner cannot leave an audit engagement to begin working as a senior executive of that same firm that was just audited. There were some really outrageous examples of this switching of roles as part of the Enron scandal. As discussed at the beginning of this chapter, Enron was the perhaps most notorious of corporate wrongdoers, and many of the questionable actions that Enron took became a playbook for SOA regulations.

The SOA prohibition is limited to public accounting partners, and external audit staff members and managers can still move from the public accounting firm team to various positions in the auditee's organization. In addition, the CAE is not included in this prohibition. There continues to be value for some persons beginning their careers in public accounting and then moving to junior or mid-level management positions at organizations where they were assigned as auditors.

Initial drafts of SOA proposed, in addition to required partner rotation, mandatory audit firm rotation. It was initially proposed that an organization was required to change its external auditors periodically. That was met with massive objections from the major public accounting firms and from many corporations. Today, many organizations retain their external audit firms for decades. Both sides feel that such long relationships foster a better understanding of the organization being audited. In addition, when an organization changed auditors under the auditing standards in the past, it often raised investor questions. The feeling of many audit partners as well as corporate executives was that continuous audit services to one organization built up a level of trust to promote more efficient and better audits. While organizations do not change auditors that regularly, the fall of Andersen saw its past clients searching for a new external auditor.

In the final versions of SOA, mandatory auditor rotation was put on hold. The General Accounting Office (GOA) was mandated to perform a one-year review and study the potential effects of mandatory auditor rotation. The GOA study was released in December 2003 with recommendations for mandatory rotation. The result of this study was a series of howls from public accounting critics, no rotation at present, and perhaps some changes in the future.

(c) SOA Title III: Corporate Responsibility

While SOA Title II set up new rules for external auditor independence, Title III, prescribes audit committee performance standards and a large set of new rules, and some major regulatory changes for audit committees that were not all that regulated until recently. This is an area where internal auditors should have a greater level of interest as well as a role. New York Stock Exchange–listed companies as well as banks have been required to have audit committees composed of independent directors, and NASDAQ has passed similar rules in late 2003. However, beyond that, there were few governance rules covering corporate audit committees. SOA has changed all of that!

SOA Title III established a wide range of new rules for audit committees. The audit committee that in the past did little more than approve internal and external audit annual plans now has some significant responsibilities. In some respects, the SOA legislation raised the role of the audit committee to a very high status in the organization. Internal audit should recognize this role and provide support whenever appropriate.

(i)   Public Company Audit Committee Governance Rules.   Under SOA, *all* listed companies in the United States are required to have an audit committee composed of only independent directors. The firm's external audit firm is to report directly to the audit committee, who is responsible for their compensation, oversight of the audit work, and the resolution of any disagreements between external audit and management. While major corporations in the United States have had audit committees for some years, these rules have tightened and have very much changed. Many other companies with smaller boards of directors, often dominated by insiders, have had to make some major adjustments. Internal audit department have had a reporting relationship to their audit committees for some years as well. However, that was often a weak link in the past. The CAE often had a nominal direct line reporting relationship to the audit committee with a very strong dotted line to the CFO. Internal audit reported to and met with the audit committee on a quarterly basis, concurrent with board meetings, but with limited interim communications. That reporting link must now be much stronger and active.

Each member of the board's audit committee must be a totally independent director. To be considered independent, an audit committee member must not accept any consulting or other advisory fees from the organization and cannot be affiliated with any subsidiary or related unit of the organization. In the past, some corporations have lavished "consulting fees" on their outside directors as a means of compensation or reward. Since they now cannot pay these consulting fees to audit committee directors, the total extent of these often-lavish corporate director rewards will almost certainly decline.

SOA and SEC regulations regarding audit committee members now require that at least one member of the audit committee be a "financial expert." Per current SEC regulations, a "financial expert" is a person who, through education and experience:

- Understands GAAP and financial statements
- Is experienced in preparing or auditing financial statements of comparable companies and applying these principles in connection with accounting for estimates, accruals, and reserves
- Is experienced with the structure and nature of internal controls
- Has had experience with audit committee functions or operations

These are rather stiff rules for audit committee member qualifications since many independent board member candidates, who might otherwise be natural candidates to serve on an audit committee, would have difficulty qualifying as such a "financial expert." These qualification rules will almost certainly be somewhat relaxed over time.

Audit committees are to establish procedures to receive, retain, and treat complaints and to handle whistleblower information regarding questionable accounting and auditing matters. This really says an audit committee must become effectively almost an ongoing separate entity rather that a subset of the board that flies to some location and meets quarterly. While SOA allows the audit committee to hire independent counsel and other advisors, an organization's internal audit function can be a good resource to help establish these procedures. Internal audit is a truly independent resource within an organization and can be a major resource in helping the audit committee become SOA compliant.

An ethics department is another often quasi-independent function that exists in many larger corporations that can help an audit committee launch a whistleblower function. These corporate ethics functions are built around corporate codes of conduct and often have a hotline-type function to allow employees to point out a reported theft or to complain about some form or harassment. Both the U.S. Sentencing Commission's Organizational Sentencing Guidelines, introduced in Chapter 9, "Whistleblower Programs and Codes of Conduct," and the COSO internal control standards, covered in Chapter 4, talk about the need for strong ethics standards in an organization. Internal audit can be a natural resource to help launch and facilitate effective ethics and whistleblower functions for the audit committee.

The whistleblower function described in SOA covers reported information regarding questionable accounting and auditing matters. SOA is trying to address an issue reported during the Enron debacle where an accounting department employee tried to get the attention of the external auditors or an Enron financial officer to recognize some improper accounting transactions. The employee's concerns were rebuffed. An ethics whistleblower or hotline function can often provide help in this type of situation. Today, ethics functions are often tied to the human resources department or are otherwise not viewed as independent of senior management. Internal audit can act as a conduit for SOA accounting and auditing whistleblower reports.

(ii) Corporate Responsibility for Financial Reports. Prior to SOA, organizations filed their financial statements with the SEC and published the results for investors, but the responsible corporate officers who authorized those reports were not personally responsible. The bar has now been raised! The CEO, the principal financial officer, or other persons performing similar functions must certify for each annual and quarterly report filed that:

- The signing officer has reviewed the report.
- Based on that signing officer's knowledge, the financial statements do not contain any materially untrue or misleading information.
- Again based on the signing officer's knowledge, the financial statements fairly represent the financial conditions and results of operations of the organization.
- The signing officers are responsible for:
    1. Establishing and maintaining internal controls.
    2. Have designed these internal controls to ensure that material information about the organization and its subsidiaries is made known to the signing officers during the period when the reports are prepared.
    3. Have evaluated the organization's internal controls within 90 days prior to the release of the report.
    4. Have presented in these financial reports the signing officer's evaluation of the effective of these internal controls as of that report date.
- Signing officers have disclosed to the auditors, audit committee, and other directors:
    1. All significant deficiencies in the design and operation of internal controls that could affect the reliability of the reported financial data and have, further, disclosed these material control weaknesses to organization's auditors.
    2. Any fraud, whether or not material, that involves management or other employees who have a significant role in the organization's internal controls.
- Have indicated in the report whether there were internal controls or other changes that could significantly affect those controls, including corrective actions, subsequent to the date of the internal controls evaluation.

Given that SOA imposes criminal penalties of fines or jail time on individual violators of the act, these signer requirements place a heavy burden on responsible corporate officers. Corporate officers must take all reasonable steps to make certain that they are in compliance. There is a provision here that these requirements still apply even if the organization has moved its headquarters to outside of the United States. In 2000 and 2001, there were numerous U.S. corporations that moved corporate registration to offshore locations, such as Bermuda, primarily for income tax purposes.

This personal sign-off requirement has raised major concerns from corporation CEOs and CFOs. This requirement will cause a major amount of additional work for the accounting and finance staffs preparing these reports as well as signing officers. An organization needs to set up detailed paper-trail procedures so that the signing officers are comfortable that effective processes have been used and the calculations to build the reports are all well documented. The organization may want to consider using an extended sign-off process where staff members submitting the financial reports sign-off on what they are submitting. Internal audit should be able to act as an internal consultant and help senior officers establish effective processes here. The audit workpaper model, with extensive cross-references, might be a good approach. Exhibit 3.5 provides an example Officer Disclosure Sign-Off type of statement that officers would be requested to sign. This exhibit is not an official PCAOB form, but is based on an SEC document, showing the types of things as officer will be asked to certify. We have highlighted a couple of important phrases here in *bold italics*. Under SOA, the CEO or CFO is asked to personally assert to these representations and could be held criminally liable if incorrect. While the officer is at risk, the support staff— including internal audit—should take every precaution possible to make certain the package presented to the senior officer is correct.

Exhibit 3.5

Sample Officer Disclosure Signoff

CERTIFICATE OF AN OFFICER REGARDING SARBANES-OXLEY COMPLIANCE

Certification: Understanding that we intend to rely upon these statements, the undersigned hereby certifies, represents, and warrants to each of them and to the Company as follows:

1. I have read those portions of the accompanying draft of the covered filing that relate directly to the scope of my responsibilities as an employee and officer of the Company (the "certified information").

2. Based on my knowledge, the certified information, as of the end of the period covered by such filing, did ***not contain an untrue statement of a material fact*** or omit to state a material fact necessary to make the statements therein, in light of the circumstances under which they were made, not misleading.

3. Based on my knowledge, to the extent of the scope of the certified information, the certified information fairly presents, in all material respects, the financial condition, results of operations and cash flows of the Company as of the close of and for the period presented in the covered filing.

4. I am not aware of any deficiencies in the effectiveness of the Company's disclosure controls and procedures that could adversely affect the Company's ability to record, process, summarize, and report information required to be disclosed in the covered filing.

5. I ***am not aware of any significant deficiencies or material weaknesses*** in the design or operation of the Company's internal controls that could adversely affect the Company's ability to record, process, summarize, and report financial data.

6. I ***am not aware of any fraud, whether or not material,*** that involves the Company's management or other employees who have a significant role in the Company's internal controls.

Signature: _____.
Dated this _____ day of _____, 200_.
Print Name:
Title:

In an interesting twist of the legal language used, this section makes reference to the organization "auditors" rather than the term "registered public accounting firm" as used in Title II. While there have been no legal rulings to date and while this author cannot hold himself out as a legal expert on such matters, this Title III of the Act would appear to refer to auditors in its broadest sense and certainly include both internal and external auditors. A CAE should recognize this and take appropriate steps to work with corporate officers to expand and improve internal controls and the like. An internal audit function must place a strong emphasis on performing reviews surrounding significant internal control areas. This can be done through a detailed risk assessment of the internal control environments, discussions of these assessments with corporate officers, and then a detailed audit plan documenting how these internal control systems will be reviewed.

Internal auditors should take particular care, given SOA rules, on the nature and description of any findings encountered during the course of their audits, on follow-up reporting regarding the status of corrective actions taken, and on the distributions of these audit reports. Many internal audits may identify significant weaknesses in areas of the organization that are not material to overall operations. A breakdown in the invoicing process at one regional sales office may be significant to the performance of that sales region for the corporation, but will not be a materially significant internal control weakness if the problem is local and does not reflect a wider, pervasive problem, or if the problem was corrected after being discovered by internal audit. The CAE should establish good communications links with key financial officers in the organization such that they are aware of audits performed, key findings, and corrective actions taken. Internal audit should also provide some guidance as to whether reported audit findings are material to the organization's overall system of internal control. Similar communication links should be established with members of the audit committee.

(A) MATERIALITY

The question of how much or what is "material" has been an open question among public accounting professionals for years. Prior to SOA, the public accounting firms used guidelines along the lines that only if an error or internal control failure altered reported earnings per share by some fraction of a cent, the matter would be considered material for purposes of financial reporting. All other errors were considered nonmaterial. This would mean that the auditors for a large corporation could discover an error in a transaction of a very large value—perhaps several million dollars or more—but they would not investigate the reasons for that error or would make some further adjustment because they considered it "nonmaterial" for an organization with accounts valued hundreds of millions. This decision to define a transaction as material was really an auditor's judgment call. Of course, the error that was considered to be nonmaterial to the external auditors might often be considered much more material or significant to the internal auditors.

The SEC has indicated that *their* existing legal standards for materiality will now apply. That is, information is now generally considered to be material if:

- There is a substantial likelihood that a reasonable investor would consider it important in making an investment decision, and

- There is a substantial likelihood that that the information would be viewed by the reasonable investor as having significantly altered the total mix of available information

The SEC has taken a further position that quantitatively small accounting errors may still be considered material under certain circumstances and that simple percentage thresholds for determining are not appropriate.

This really says that all involved parties in the financial audit process need to develop a consistent understanding on what is a material error. An internal control error causing an accounting error that is reported in an internal audit report but ignored by the external auditors could cause trouble for the corporation's officers signing the final financial reports if they are unaware of or ignore the reported error. Given the era in which SOA was enacted, all parties would probably benefit from lowering standards for materiality such that more potential errors are viewed as material.

Internal audit needs to work closely with their external auditors as well as with the audit committee to ensure that both audit teams have a consistent definition of materiality when reporting errors or omissions. Both audit teams should try to coordinate findings here. There is no need for a situation where external audit has ignored some internal controls that a recently issued internal audit report identifies as "serious." Such a discrepancy places the senior officers signing off on the report in a potentially difficult situation.

(B) PENALTIES FOR REPORTING FAILURES

SOA Section 906, located toward the end of the long, multiparagraph SOA legislation, schedules a series of criminal penalties for any corporate officer who signs or certifies a financial statement while knowing that that the report is not in compliance with all of the requirements of SOA. Maximum penalties are defined as fines of not more than $5 million and/or 20 years' imprisonment. A stiff penalty for an accounting executive found to be in violation! Such fines will be imposed only if a wrongdoer is charged, tried, and convicted. The actual penalty would be based on the Organizational Sentencing Guidelines as will be discussed in Chapter 9. Those guidelines say that if an organization has an effective compliance program that is in place and working, the penalties will be reduced per a documented set of factors. However, compliance programs must be authorized and championed by senior management. Thus, the senior manager who is found to be guilty of violating SOA financial statement rules is really at risk.

It is difficult to predict how this penalty process will play out over time. If good corporate governance practices become widespread and if we have fewer Enron-type situations occurring regularly, those penalty statutes will remain on the books with not much enforcement action. Some sort of nasty failure could really turn things the other way with some corporate executives prosecuted because "they should have known." Strong internal control monitoring and reporting systems are needed. Internal audit can really help!

(iii) Improper Influence over the Conduct of Audits. SOA further states that its is unlawful for any officer, director, or related subordinate person to take any action, in contravention of a SEC rule, to "fraudulently, influence, coerce, manipulate, or mislead" any external CPA auditor engaged in the audit, for the purpose of rendering the financial statements materially misleading. These are strong words in an environment where there had often been a high level of discussion and compromise between the auditors and senior management when a significant problem was found during the course of an audit.

In the past, there often were many "friendly" discussions between management and the external auditors regarding a financial interpretation dispute or proposed adjustment. The result was often some level of compromise. This is not unlike an internal audit team in the field that circulates a draft audit report with local management before departing. After much discussion and sometimes follow-up work, that draft internal audit report might have been changed before its final issue. The same things often happened in reports covering annual quarterly or final results. SOA now has some very strong rules to prohibit such practices. The rules evolved during the Congressional hearings leading up to the passage of SOA where testimony included tales of strong CEO's essentially demanding that external auditors "accept" certain questionable accounting entries or lose the audit business. There can still be these friendly disputes and debates, but if an SEC ruling is explicit in some area and if the external auditors propose a financial statement adjustment because of that SEC rule, management *must* accept it without an additional fight.

There can be a fine line between management disagreeing with external auditors over some estimate or interpretation and management trying to improperly influence its auditors. External audit may have done some limited testing in some area and then proposed an adjustment based on the results of that test. This type of scenario could result in management disagreeing with that adjustment and claiming the results of the test were "not representative." While the external auditors, particularly under SOA, have the last word in such a dispute, internal audit can often play a facilitating role here. Internal audit resources, for example, can be used to expand the population of some audit sampling test or to perform other extending observations or testing regarding the disputed area. Doing this, internal audit is not helping to improperly influence the conduct of an audit but helping to resolve the matter.

(iv) Forfeitures, Bars, and Penalties.   Title III concludes with a series of other detailed rules and penalties covering corporate governance. Their purpose is to tighten exiting rules that were in place before SOA or to add new rules for what often seemed to be outrageous or at least very improper behavior prior to SOA. These new rules outlined below will not impact the audit committee, internal, or external auditors directly, as they are directed at other areas in what was believed to be corporate governance excess.

(A) FORFEITURE OF IMPROPER BONUSES

Section 304 requires that if an organization is required to restate its earnings due to some material violation of securities laws, the CEO and CFO must *reimburse* the company for any bonuses or incentives received on the basis of the original, incorrect statements issued during the past 12 months. The same applies for any profits received from the sale of organization securities during that same period. During the SOA Congressional hearings, multiple instances were cited where a company had issued an aggressive, but unsupportable earnings statement, its key officers had benefited from bonuses or the sale of stock from that good news, and then the company soon had to restate its earnings due to some material noncompliance matter. There would not have been those CEO and CFO bonuses under the revised, correct interpretations. SOA places a personal penalty on senior corporate officers who had benefited from materially noncompliant financial statements.

(B) BARS TO OFFICER OR DIRECTOR SERVICE

Section 305 is another example of how SOA has tightened up the rules. Prior to SOA, federal courts were empowered to bar any person from serving as a corporate officer or director if that person's conduct demonstrated "substantial unfitness to serve as an officer or director." SOA changed the standard here by eliminating the word "substantial" saying that the courts can bar someone from serving as a director or officer for *any* conduct violation.

(C) PENSION FUND BLACKOUT PERIODS

A standard rule for 401K and similar retirement plans is that a fund administrator can establish a blackout period over a limited time period that prohibits plan participants from making investment adjustments to their personal plans. A plan participant with a substantial amount of his or her retirement funds in company stock could, because of bad company news, transfer funds from that company stock to a cash based money market fund or some other investment option. These blackout periods are usually instituted for purely legitimate reasons such as a change in plan administrators. An Enron-related complaint during the SOA hearings was that there was a blackout in place during those final weeks before the bankruptcy, preventing employees from making changes to their plan. However, those same blackout rules did not apply to corporate officers who had their own separate plan and who, in some cases, got out of Enron before things totally collapsed. SOA rules now state that the same blackout periods must apply to everyone in the organization, from staff to corporate officers.

(D) ATTORNEY PROFESSIONAL RESPONSIBILITY

Section 307 covers revised rules for attorney professional conduct and has become very controversial. An attorney is required to report evidence of a material violation of securities law or a similar company violation to the chief legal counsel or the CEO. If those parties do not respond, the attorney is required to report the evidence "up the ladder" to the audit committee of the board of directors. SOA's initial rules also allowed that if an attorney discovered such a securities law violation, the attorney should withdraw from the engagement reporting the violation particulars, what lawyers call a "noisy withdrawal" approach.

The controversy here is the SOA is effectively dictating an attorney to violate the rules of attorney-client privilege. Under traditional rules, if a subsidiary executive met with an attorney to discuss some matter that constituted a potential violation of SOA, the attorney and the subsidiary manager client would work out the issues. Now, that attorney is supposed to blow the whistle on this discussion and bring the matter potentially all the way to the audit committee.

After several postponements, the final rules still have not been settled here as this book went to press.

(E) FAIR FUNDS FOR INVESTORS

The final section of Title III states that if an individual or group is fined for a violation through administrative or legal action, the funds collected from the fine will go to a "disgorgement" fund for distribution to the investors who suffered because of the fraud or improper accounting actions. The same rule applies to funds collected through a settlement in advance of court proceedings. Properties and other assets seized will be sold and also go into that disgorgement fund. The whole idea here is that investors who lost because of individual corporate wrongdoing may benefit from a financial settlement from such a fund.

(d) SOA Title IV: Enhanced Financial Disclosures

This Title of the SOA is designed to correct some financial reporting disclosure problems, to tighten up conflict of interest rules for corporate officers and directors, to mandate a management assessment of internal controls, to require senior officer codes of conduct and other matters. There is a lot of material here, and internal auditors might give particular attention to the internal controls review rules outlined below.

(i) Disclosures in Periodic Reports. Many of the unexpected bankruptcies and sudden earnings failures of companies around the time of the Enron failure were attributed to extremely aggressive, if not questionable, financial reporting. With the approval of their external auditors, companies pushed this to the limits and often used such tactics as using optimistic pro forma earnings to report their results or moved their corporate headquarters offshore to minimize taxes. While these tactics were in accordance with GAAP and existing laws, public outcry caused SOA to tighten up some rules and make other actions difficult to perform or illegal.

SOA mandated that the SEC develop rules that pro forma published financial statements must not contain any material untrue statements or omit any fact that makes the reports misleading. Further, the pro forma results must reconcile to the financial conditions and results of operations under GAAP. Pro forma financial reports present an "as if" picture of a firm's financial status by leaving out nonrecurring earnings expenses such as restructuring charges or merger-related costs. However, there is no standard definition and no consistent format in the financial world for reporting pro forma earnings. Depending on the assumptions used, it was possible for an operating loss to become a profit under pro forma earnings reporting. For example, for its 2001 fiscal year, Cisco Systems Inc., a San Jose, CA–based maker of computer networking systems, reported net income of $3.09 billion on a pro forma basis but simultaneously reported a net loss of $1.01 billion on a GAAP basis. Cisco's pro forma profit specifically excluded acquisition charges, payroll tax on the exercise of stock options, restructuring costs and other special charges, an excess inventory charge, and net gains on minority investments.

Cisco certainly was not alone here as many companies had reported pro forma earnings showing ever-increasing growth, while their true, GAAP results were not so favorable. The problem with these two sets of numbers is that investors and the press frequently ignored the GAAP numbers focusing on the more favorable pro forma results.

Perhaps the major issue that brought Enron down was a large number of off-balance-sheet transactions that, if consolidated with regular financial reports, would show major financial problems. They eventually were identified and consolidated with Enron's other financial results, moving Enron toward bankruptcy. SOA now requires that quarterly and annual financial reports must disclose all such off-balance-sheet transactions that may have a material effect on the current or future financial reports. These transactions may include contingent obligations, financial relationships with unconsolidated entities, or other items that could have material effects on operations. While many of the SOA financial disclosure rules are really the responsibility of external auditors, this is an area where internal auditors might be of help. It is often the internal auditor, on a visit to a distant unit of the company, which encounters these types of off-balance-sheet arrangements in discussions with field personnel. If something significant, the internal auditor should communicate the details to the audit committee or the external audit engagement partner.

There may be more to come regarding the rules for off-balance-sheet transactions. The SEC is directed to complete a study on off-balance-sheet disclosures within 18 months after the mid-2002 passage and to submit a report to Congress and the president six months later. This would push any potential new rules out further into the future.

(ii)   Expanded Conflict of Interest Provisions and Disclosures. The hearings that led to the passage of SOA often pictured corporate officers and directors as a rather greedy lot. Large relocation allowances or corporate executive personal loans were granted and subsequently forgiven by corporate boards. It is difficult to see these arrangements as anything other than a potential conflict of interest situation. A CEO, for example, that convinces the board to grant the CFO a large personal "loan" with vague repayment terms and the right to either demand payment or forgive, certainly creates a conflict of interest situation. Although a series of exceptions are allowed, SOA makes it unlawful for any corporation to directly or indirectly extend credit, in the form of a personal loan, to any executive officer or director.

With the initial lack of guidance from the SEC, the executive officer loan prohibition has caused some problems for corporations. While there is no question about the propriety now of the board giving an executive a massive cash advance on loan, the officer who takes his or her spouse out for dinner at a business meeting and charges that dinner on the company credit card might also be considered as being granted a corporate "loan" in terms of the executive's company credit card charge.

Although there has been some SEC clarifying guidance, organizations should look at a wide variety of practices to see which are allowed under the loan prohibition rule. Many otherwise normal business transactions could be treated as executive "loans" under these rules. The CEO should discuss company policies in this area and potentially imitate a detailed review of company loan procedures.

Another section of Title IV requires that all disclosures under SOA, as discussed previously, must be filed electronically and posted "near real time" on the SEC's Internet site. This would make the filing of such information much more current. Internal audit should potentially consider evaluating the control systems in place to handle such SEC online reporting. This is an area where reporting was often hard-copy based in the past, and there could be a risk of improperly transmitted or security leaks without proper internal control procedures.

(iii) Management's Assessment of Internal Controls. SOA requires that each annual report filing must contain an internal controls report that states management's responsibility for establishing and maintaining an adequate system of internal controls as well as management's assessment, as of that fiscal year ending date, on the effectiveness of the installed internal control procedures. The external auditors are to attest to and report on the internal control assessments made by management. This is a major step in corporate governance that should be of particular interest to internal auditors with their ongoing internal control related review work.

Chapter 4 discusses how earlier internal control standards have evolved into the COSO standard internal control framework. That process was not without controversy. Among the various studies and commissions studying internal control procedures, the SEC proposed in 1979 mandatory management reports on the system of internal controls. That proposal raised a storm of protest because both public corporations and external auditors claimed it was an onerous task and there was no clear definition for internal controls. The SEC then dropped that proposal. The COSO internal control framework was subsequently released and incorporated in AICPA auditing standards. Time has passed, and the SEC is now defining the rules for internal control following the COSO framework. Chapter 4 contains a summary of the COSO framework and its importance for internal auditors. SOA internal control requirements are covered in Section 404, and Chapter 7 discusses these SOA evaluations of internal controls.

(iv) Financial Officer Codes of Ethics. SOA requires that corporations must adopt a code of ethics for their senior officers, including the CEO and principle financial officers, and disclose compliance with this code to the SEC as part of the annual financial reporting. SOA has now made this a requirement for senior officers, and today's modern internal auditor needs to understand how organizations should establish such ethics functions and build a corporate culture to support them.

Employee codes of ethics or conduct have been in place in some organizations for many years. They evolved to more formal ethics functions in larger corporations in the early 1990s, but were often established with the main body of employees in mind rather than the officers. These codes defined a set of rules or policies that were designed to apply to all employees. They covered such matters as policies on the protection of company records or on gifts and other benefit issues. Chapter 9 contains a more detailed discussion on codes of conduct as well as launching a whistleblower function and ethics program under SOA rules.

SOA brings organization codes of conduct to new levels. Since the mid-1990s, this area has become very important for many organizations. With a growing public concern about the needs for strong ethical practices, many organizations have appointed an ethics officer to launch such an initiative with a code of conduct as a first step. However, while that code of conduct received senior officer endorsement, it was often directed at the overall population of employees, not the senior officers.

SOA does not address the content of these organization-wide codes of ethics, but focuses on the need for the same standards for senior officers as for general employees in the organization. SOA specifically requires that an organization's code of ethics or conduct for senior officers must reasonably promote:

- Honest and ethical conduct, including the ethical handling of actual or apparent conflicts of interest between personal and professional relationships

- Full, fair, accurate, timely, and understandable disclosure in the organization's financial reports

- Compliance with applicable governmental rules and regulations

Many larger organizations today have established ethics type functions, but smaller ones frequently have not. Internal audit can play an important role in helping their organization achieve compliance with SOA ethical rules for officers. If an ethics function is not in place, internal audit and the CAE can help to launch such a function for all members of the organization, board members, officers, and employees

If an organization has a code of conduct, the CAE can play a key role in ensuring that this code applies to all members of the organization and that it will be consistent with SOA rules. With the approval of the audit committee, the CAE should launch a project to ensure that the existing code of conduct procedures are consistent with the SOA rules and that these ethical rules are communicated to all members of the organization, including the officers. The key issue here is making sure that the existing code of conduct covers the above SOA rules, that it has been communicated to senior management, and that these officers have formally agreed to comply with it. While others in the organization can make certain that the existing code of conduct is consistent with SOA, the CAE is a key person to communicate that information to the audit committee.

An organization faces a greater challenge here if they have no formal ethics function, no code of conduct, or a code that has not been effectively communicated throughout the organization. Here again, the CAE can serve as a prime communicator/facilitator between the audit committee and the overall organization and can play a key role in establishing SOA code of conduct compliance for the officer group and throughout the organization. While SOA compliance processes can be established just for the senior officers enumerated in SOA, this is the ideal time to launch an ethics function throughout the organization that applies to both senior management and to all employees.

A strong ethics function should be promoted throughout the organization and not just as an SOA legal requirement. A good set of ethical standards can get an organization through a crisis situation and help it to move in the right directions. A motivation for SOA and its strong provisions in these areas was the perception that certain corporate officers were operating on the basis of personal greed with no consideration for strong ethical values.

The ethical requirements of SOA can help any organization to better set themselves up for ongoing ethical business conduct practices. With an overall understanding of how to establish such ethics programs, internal audit can work with both management and the audit committee to establish a program that will be SOA complaint and will enhance overall organization ethical standards. See Chapter 9 for more detailed guidance on ethics and whistleblower programs.

(v)   Other Required Disclosures.   Title IV of SOA concludes with three other sections that will not directly affect internal audit but have an ongoing impact on organizational governance. SOA legislation authorizes the SEC to develop the detailed rules necessary to implement it. While SOA rules have been largely established, they may continue to change over time. Internal auditors and all members of management should always consult counsel or other advisors for detailed current interpretations of SOA rules when implementing compliance programs.

(A) SECTION 407 ON AUDIT COMMITTEE FINANCIAL EXPERT DISCLOSURES

As discussed previously, at least one member of every corporate audit committee must be identified as a "financial expert." Starting with SOA's initial passage, this requirement has resulted in extensive concerns and discussions. Some internal auditors with CPA credentials who have worked on financial audits and who have trouble managing their personal household budgets may wonder about the requirements of a "financial expert." Some current audit committee members have expressed the same concerns.

Many board and audit committee members today do not come from an audit or accounting background but from such areas as finance or overall corporate management. They had relied on their financial "experts" to supply the necessary support. With SOA, the board must designate one of its audit committee members as the "financial expert." This requirement resulted in new board of director searches for persons who can claim such qualifications. It will probably also result in one or another audit committee member being designated that financial expert, whether or not the candidate's background meets SOA requirements to the letter of the law. The downside for that person is the designated "financial expert" may become very liable if there is a corporate SOA rules violation problem. Others may argue as a defense in an enforcement or litigation action that they did what they did because they relied on their audit committee "financial expert."

The CAE or other members of the internal audit staff will often be greater "financial experts" than the designated audit committee member. Internal audit should consider taking a role of advising the audit committee "expert" on the ongoing financial issues affecting the organization. This could be limited to as little as sending press clippings to that audit committee member on current financial issues in the specific company or industry or could be expanded to more detailed consultations. This would be a further expansion of internal audit's service to management.

(B) SECTION 408 ON SEC ENHANCED DISCLOSURE REVIEWS

All listed U.S. corporations are required to file Form 10K annual and other financial reports with the SEC. While the issuing companies filing those reports would anticipate a SEC review in some detail, the hearings leading to SOA revealed that these reviews were not always that comprehensive. Prior to SOA the detailed corporate disclosures reported as SEC report footnotes often did not receive sufficient detailed attention. Just as an individual hopes that his or her federal income tax return will not be subject to a detailed audit all that often, corporations and their external auditors have had the same hopes. Some of the massive corporate accounting and financial problems leading up to the passage of SOA might have been detected had there been a more diligent SEC review.

SOA mandates the SEC to perform an "enhanced review" of the disclosures included in *all* company filings on a regular and systematic basis and no less often than once every three years. As part of that disclosure review, the SEC is mandated to do a detailed review of the reports' supporting financial audit materials. The SEC can decide to either perform an enhanced review of disclosures as soon as possible or to wait to schedule the review through the three-year window. This enhanced review could be triggered by any one of the following situations:

- If the corporation has issued a material restatement of its financial results.
- If there has been a significant volatility in its stock prices compared to others'.
- If the corporation has a large market capitalization.
- If this is an emerging company with significant disparities in its stock price to earnings ratio.
- Corporation operations significantly affect material sectors of the national economy.
- Any other factors the SEC may consider relevant.

This really says that the SEC may more regularly schedule such an extended disclosures review for large "Fortune 500"–sized companies, leaders in some sectors of the economy, or where stock prices are out of average ranges. Of course, with the "other factors" consideration, virtually any corporation could move to the head of the list for such an extended review.

The SOA text and the SEC rules published to date do not provide much detail on the nature of these planned enhanced reviews. Financial statement disclosures that are part of published financial reports and are included in the section called "Management's Discussion & Analysis (MD&A)" in the SEC's 10K report. They cover a wide range of issues, including transactions with unaffiliated subsidiaries or derivative trading activities. Unusual or hard to classify transactions are disclosed and discussed here. Exhibit 3.6 lists a few, but certainly not all, of the types of financial statement disclosures that would be subject to an SEC enhanced review.

Financial disclosures are documented as footnotes on published financial reports. To many, they are stated in terms of complex financial gibberish that few understand. A recent article in *BusinessWeek* magazine summarizes the problem:

> However, no amount of reform will matter if people don't bother to read the information companies give them. And the sad fact is few investors and shockingly few professional analysts ever bother combing through financial documents.[5]

The CAE as well as many others in the organization can argue that a proposed disclosure is unreadable, but the lawyers preparing these may argue otherwise. Good corporate governance practices would argue that these documents need to be better understood by investors, but legal and accounting specialists will insist on the precise but convoluted language found in many of these documents.

The SEC plans to require simplified language and to perform these "enhanced reviews" of the financial statement disclosures for the corporations selected. They have allowed that this disclosure review may lead to a full audit of the financial statements for the period reviewed, almost putting the SEC in a financial audit role. If they find inconsistencies between the disclosures and reported financial statements, the result could be financial statement restatements. Detailed rules have not been released at the time of publication, but Section 408 enhanced reviews could have some interesting implications.

EXHIBIT 3.6

SEC-Mandated Financial Statement Disclosure Examples

Financial-reporting disclosures are mandated by the SEC and appear on an organization's 10K annual and 10Q quarterly reports in the Management's Discussion & Analysis sections. Matters are discussed in the form of detailed legal-sounding text and often are not easily understandable by investors. Examples of the types of matters discussed include:

- *Restatements of Previously Issued Financial Statements.* If necessary, this is a discussion of why an organization had to restate its earnings. It is often described in fairly lengthy text discussions along the lines of:

  "an oversight in collecting data for the calculation for certain postretirement benefit liabilities at the fiscal years . . ."

- *Changes in Accounting Principle.* Again, this will be a detailed description but can be difficult to understand and interpret. This again stated along the lines of:

  "the Company implemented a change in accounting principle to reflect more appropriately investment returns and actuarial assumptions . . ."

- *Critical Accounting Policies.* This may be a general discussion covering such matters as policies for revenue recognition, certain government contracts, or environmental costs.

- *Liquidity and Capital Resources.* This would be a series of broad and very general statements asserting to the company's health.

With the large number of SEC registered companies, the not-unlimited number of SEC staff members to do such reviews, and the probable time requirements for any such enhanced review, the SEC will probably have a challenge in completing its goal of once every three years enhanced reviews of financial statement disclosures for major corporations. The many smaller SEC-registered corporations with no unusual accounting statement disclosures and low total capitalization values may very well miss the SOA every-three-years legislated review window.

(C) SECTION 409 ON REAL-TIME FINANCIAL STATEMENT DISCLOSURES

The last section under Title IV mandates that reporting corporations must disclose to the public "on a rapid and current basis" any additional information containing material financial statement issues. Formal SEC rules have not yet been established here, but corporations are allowed to include trend and quantitative approaches as well as graphics for those disclosures. This is a change from traditional SEC report formats that allowed only text with the exception of corporate logos. The concept is to get key data to investors as soon as possible, not through traditional slow paper-based reports.

Internal audit, in playing a strong SOA facilitating role, can help to ensure that the organization has such a real-time financial disclosure facility. The Internet might be an ideal facility for transmitting such data to an investor's Web site. The application needs to be reviewed for controls and security. Only company-authorized data should be reported to investors, and the site should have appropriate security controls. Internal audit should consider offering to perform a controls-related review for any application that is scheduled for this disclosures reporting. Continuous auditing processes and a powerful tool to help with this process, the XBRL (Extensible Business Reporting Language) reporting standard are discussed in Chapter 24. The results of the audit should be well documented, and there should be a follow-up process to ensure that there have been corrective actions to repair any control problems encountered during that audit.

(e) SOA Title V: Analyst Conflicts of Interest

This Title of SOA and other subsequent sections do not directly cover financial reporting, corporate governance, audit committees, and external and internal audit issues. They are designed to correct some of the other perceived abuses that were encountered during the SOA Congressional hearings. The internal audit professional should only be interested in them from a general-knowledge basis, as they generally do not directly affect internal audit.

Title V is designed to rectify some securities analyst abuses. Investors have relied on the recommendations of securities analysts for years. These analysts were often tied to large brokerage houses and investment banks but were analyzing and recommending securities to outside investors. When they looked at securities where their employer had an interest, there were supposed to be strong separations of responsibility between the people recommending a stock for investment and those selling it to investors. In the frenzy of the late 1990s investment bubble, these traditional analyst controls and ethical practices broke down. In the aftermath of the market downturns, analysts sometime recommended stocks seemingly only because their investment bank employer was managing the IPO. Also, investigators found such things as analysts publicly recommending a stock to investors as "great growth opportunity," while simultaneously telling their investment banking peers that the stock was a very poor investment or worse.

Abuses of this manner existed in many circumstances. While investment analysts once relied on their own strong self-governing professional standards, the SOA hearings revealed that many of these standards were ignored by strong and prominent securities analysts. Title V attempts to correct these securities analyst abuses. Rules of conduct have been established with legal punishments for violations. SOA, as well as other legal actions and resultant securities industry settlement agreements,[6] have very much reformed and regulated the practices of securities analysts. The result should be better-informed investors.

(f) SOA Titles VI and VII: Commission Authority, Studies, and Reports

These two SOA legislative titles cover a series of issues ranging from the funding authorization SEC appropriations to plans for future studies. These sections include new rules to tighten up on what had been viewed as regulatory loopholes in the past. Among these, the SEC can now ban persons from promoting or trading "penny stocks"[7] because of past SEC misconduct or can bar someone from practicing before the SEC because of improper professional conduct. The latter rule give the SEC the authority to effectively ban a public accounting firm from acting as an external auditor for corporations.

The professional misconduct ban could represent a major penalty to any public accounting firm or individual CPA that was found, through SEC hearings, to have violated professional or ethical public accounting standards. Although SOA outlines a process of hearings before any action is taken, individual CPA's or entire firms can be banned temporarily or permanently. This takes the monitoring and policing process away from the AICPA's key peer review process of the past, giving the regulatory authority to the SEC. While an individual negligent CPA can still work in non-SEC practice areas such as small business accounting or, for that matter, in internal audit, even a temporary ban can be a death knell for a public accounting firm. All concerned must be aware of and follow SEC rules and procedures, particularly these newer SOA rules.

Title VII authorizes the SEC to engage in a series of studies and reports with specified due dates for the delivery of those reports to appropriate congressional committees or federal agencies. There are an untold number of such legislatively authorized reports that are filed with Congress or government agencies, and some just disappear in some bureaucratic swamp. SOA authorizes five of these studies and reports:

1. **Consolidation of Public Accounting Firms.** This study is charged with looking at the factors that have led to consolidations among public accounting firms, the problems, if any, that business organizations face because of those consolidations, and whether and to what extent state and federal agencies impede competition among public accounting firms.

2. **Credit Rating Agencies.** The role of these agencies and their importance to investors will be studied.

3. **Securities Professionals Violations and Violators.** The study will look at violations and disciplinary practices over a four-year period, ending in 2001, for investment bankers and advisors, public accountants and their firms, attorneys, and others practicing before the SEC.

4. **Analysis of SEC Enforcement Actions.** Violations of security law reporting requirements will be studied over a five-year period.

5. **Study of Investment Banks.** This study will focus on whether investment banks and their advisors have assisted corporations in manipulating reported earnings. There is a specific emphasis here on Enron and Global Crossing.

The ongoing impact, if any, of these studies is yet to be determined. The analysis of enforcement actions is designed to help the SEC formulate the detailed rules that are still being released at present. This author is enough of a cynic to question the worth of a study that looks at why we have gone from the traditional Big 8 or 5 major public accounting firms to what we have at present.

(g) SOA Titles VIII, IX, and X: Fraud Accountability and White-Collar Crime

The next three titled sections of SOA seem to be very much of a reaction to the failure of Enron and the subsequent demise of Arthur Andersen. At that time, even though Andersen seemed very culpable to outside observers for its massive efforts to shred company accounting records, Andersen initially argued that they were just following their established procedures and had done no wrong. The courts eventually found what became a criminal conspiracy and Arthur Andersen is essentially no more. Now, Title VIII of SOA has established specific rules and penalties for the destruction of corporate audit records.

The statute is much broader then just the Andersen matter and applies to all auditors and accountants, *including internal auditors*. The words here are particularly strong regarding the destruction, alteration, or falsification of records involved in federal investigations or bankruptcies: "Whoever knowingly alters, destroys, mutilates, conceals, covers up, falsifies or makes false entry in any record, document, or tangible object with the intent to impede, obstruct, or influence the investigation . . . shall be fined . . . [or] imprisoned not more than 20 years, or both." Taken directly from the statute, some strong words! This really says that any organization should have a strong records retention policy. While records can be destroyed in the course of normal business cycles, any hint of a federal investigation or the filing of bankruptcy papers for some affiliated unit should trigger activation of that records retention policy.

A separate portion of this section establishes rules for corporate audit records. Although we tend to think of SOA in terms of primarily rules for external auditors, it very much applies to internal auditors as well. Workpapers and supporting review papers must be maintained for a period of five years from the end of the fiscal year of the audit. SOA clearly states that these rules apply to "any accountant who conducts an audit" of a SEC-registered corporation. While internal auditors have sometimes argued in the past that they only do operational audits that do not apply to the formal financial audit process, the prudent internal audit group should closely align their workpaper record retention rules to comply with this SOA five-year mandate.

Several of the sections of the legislation are designed to tighten up things and to correct what were viewed by others as excesses. One of the reported excesses leading up to SOA was reported instances where corporate officers got large loans from their board of directors based on stock manipulation and performance that was later found to be improper. Boards of directors regularly forgave those loans after some period of time. Now, SOA states that these debts cannot be forgiven or discharged if they were incurred in violation of securities fraud laws. The executive—now probably the ex-executive—who received the forgiven loan is now obligated to repay the corporation. Another section here extends the statute of limitations for securities law violations. Now, legal action may be brought no later than two years after discovery or five years after the actual violation. Since securities fraud can take some time to discover, this change gives prosecutors a bit more time.

The Organizational Sentencing Guidelines are a published list of corporate penalties for violations of certain federal laws. If an organization is found to be guilty, the punishment or sentencing could be reduced if there had been an ethics program in place that should normally reduce the possibility of such a violation. While the basic concepts of the Sentencing Guidelines are still in place, SOA modifies them to include the destruction or alteration of documents as offences. Chapter 9 talks about the Sentencing Guidelines in greater detail.

Section 806 of SOA adds whistleblower protection for employees of publicly traded organizations that observe and detect some fraudulent action and then independently report it to the SEC or to some other outside parties. By employee, SOA means officers, contractors, or agents as well. Any person who observes that illegal act can "blow the whistle" and report the action with legal protection from retaliation. The SOA whistleblower language does not include the provisions found in other federal contract whistleblower provisions where the person reporting something may be rewarded with some percentage of the savings reported.

Securities law violations and whistleblowing raises an issue for internal auditors. More than almost anyone in the organization, internal audit has access to virtually all organization records. Following the code of ethics, as defined by the Institute of Internal Auditors, any violations discovered here should be handled not by a report to the SEC but through a report to proper levels of senior management. If an internal auditor discovers a security law violation by a senior financial officer, the matter would normally be first reported to the CEO. However, if the CEO is involved in the action, internal audit should report the matter to the audit committee for resolution. While an employee at a different level in the organization may not feel comfortable reporting something to an audit committee member, the CAE certainly has that established level of communication. Where an IIA standard appears to be in conflict with a law, such as SOA, the law takes precedence.

Title VIII concludes with a very brief section 807 defining the criminal penalties for shareholders of publicly traded companies. Summarized here, it simply states that whoever executes or attempts to execute a scheme to defraud any persons in connection with a corporation's securities or fraudulently receives money or property from that sale shall be fined or imprisoned not more than 25 years or both. A strong potential penalty for securities fraud! The regulations, rules, and penalties outlined in SOA have made following the rule extremely important.

Title IX then contains a series of white-collar crime penalty enhancements, going through existing criminal law penalties and raising maximum punishments. For example, the maximum imprisonment for mail fraud has now grown from 5 years to 20 and the maximum fine for ERISA retirement violations has gone from $100,000 to $500,000. These increased penalties, coupled with the provisions of the Organizational Sentencing Guidelines create an environment when an increasing number of persons found guilty of white-collar crimes may have to spend time in prison.

Finally, section 906 of SOA Title IX introduces a strong new requirement on corporate CEOs and CFOs. Both must sign a supplemental statement with their annual financial report that certifies that the information contained in the report "fairly represents, in all material respects, the financial condition and results of operations." These effectively personal certifications are coupled with penalties of fines up to $5 million and 10 years for anyone who certifies such a statement while knowing they are false. Since these are personal penalties, the prudent CEO and CFO must take *extreme care* to make certain that all issues are resolved and that the annual financial statements are correct and fully representative of operations. Title X then is a "Sense of the Senate" comment that corporate income tax returns should be signed by the CEO. Again, responsibility is placed on the individual officer, not the anonymous corporate entity.

(h) SOA Title XI: Corporate Fraud Accountability

While prior sections focused on the individual responsibilities of the CEO, CFO, and others, the last SOA title also defines overall corporate responsibility for fraudulent financial reporting. Various sections focus on other existing statutes, such as the Organizational Sentencing Guidelines, and both reaffirm the rules for corporations and increase penalties. The SEC also is given authority to impose a temporary freeze on the transfer of corporate funds to officers and others in a corporation that is subject to an SEC investigation. This was done to correct some reported abuses where some corporations were being investigated for financial fraud while they simultaneously dispensed huge cash payments to individual officers. A corporation in trouble should retain some funds until the matter is resolved.

Section 1105 also gives the SEC the authority to prohibit persons from serving as corporate officers and directors. This applies to persons who have violated certain of the SOA rules outlined earlier. While this will not be an automatic ban, the SEC has the authority to impose this ban where it feels appropriate. The idea is to prevent the corporate wrongdoer who has been found culpable of securities law violations at one corporation to then leave that corporation to go on and serve at another.

3.4 IMPACT OF THE SARBANES-OXLEY ACT ON THE MODERN INTERNAL AUDITOR

The previous sections here are a very general overview of the Sarbanes-Oxley Act, or SOA. While this discussion did not cover all sections or details, the intent is to give internal audit professionals an overall understanding of key sections that will have an impact on the annual audit of an organization and its audit committee. Whether a large, "Fortune 100"–sized corporation, a smaller company not even traded on NASDAQ, or a private company with a bond issue registered through the SEC, all will come under SOA and its public accounting regulatory body, the PCAOB. Internal auditors will first see these changes in their dealings with their external auditors. Relationships have changed, and the internal audit professional will no longer see consultants from the public accounting firm installing a new accounting system or perhaps have a fear that the internal audit department will be "outsourced."

Exhibit 3.7 contains a checklist to help internal audit to implement some of these new SOA rules. These rules are consistent with the IIA standards discussed in Chapter 12. The end result will be an SOA-compliant organization and a better, more effective internal audit department. New rules and responsibilities have been established for audit committees, and the chief audit executive with a good general knowledge of SOA's provisions can become a valuable advisor to both that audit committee and corporate management. While both will be exposed to many other sources of information, such as specialized consultants, and internal auditor should be able to provide very valuable insights.

EXHIBIT 3.7

SOA Rules Implementation Checklist

ACTION STEPS
1. The audit committee needs to have procedure in place for recording and following up on accounting and auditing complaints or concerns. Internal audit should be able to provide support here.
2. A hotline procedure needs to be implemented to allow anonymous, confidential complaints or tips from employees. There should be adequate follow-up procedures in place to investigate and take appropriate action based on those calls.
3. Internal audit's CAE should take steps to establish an ongoing communications link with the designated independent audit committee "financial expert." The designated "financial expert" should be kept informed of ongoing audit and control issues.
4. The CAE should establish a good communications link with the partner in charge of the external audit. If there are questions whether the registered external audit firm is following is following SOA rules for such things as partner rotation, the CAE should discuss this first with the audit partner and bring it to the attention of the audit committee if necessary.
5. Documentation should be in place to ensure that published financial reports reflect all material correcting adjustments and off-balance-sheet transactions. A member of internal audit should assist in this review.
6. Using normal internal audit procedures to review audit evidence, the CAE should offer support for the organization's CEO if requested.

EXHIBIT 3.7 *(CONTINUED)*

SOA Rules Implementation Checklist

7. Using internal audit confirmation letter type procedures, the CAE should offer help in establishing a confirmation procedure for the existence of executive loans.

8. Internal audit should work the treasurer to ensure the procedures are in place to disclose all insider stock transactions within the SOA required two-day limit.

9. Internal audit should initiate manual reviews covering the effectiveness of internal controls supporting financial procedures. The findings and recommendations from those reviews should be reported to senior management.

10. Working with the organization's existing code of conduct and SOA requirements, care should be taken to issue a code of conduct for all senior officers.

11. Records should be established to confirm that the executive level code of conduct has been acknowledged and signed.

12. Internal audit should work with the organization's ethics function or others responsible for the code of conduct to launch a code of conduct for all organization employees.

ENDNOTES

[1] Jamie Kusel, Ralph Schull, and Thomas H. Oxner, "What Audit Directors Disclose about Outsourcing," Institute of Internal Auditors, Altamonte Springs, FL, 1996.

[2] "CPAs: Bloodied and Bowed" *BusinessWeek*, January 20, 2003.

[3] "Sprint Case Shows New Risk to CEOs When Things Go Bad," *Wall Street Journal*, February 11, 2003.

[4] An abbreviation of a longer Latin phrase "de minimis non curat lex" which literally means the law is not concerned with trivial matters. The phrase is generally used as a way of categorizing that, which is not worth litigating over.

[5] "What Good Are Disclosures That Go Unread?", *Business Week*, March 26, 2002.

[6] U.S. Securities & Exchange Commission, "SEC, NY Attorney General, NASD, NASAA, NYSE and State Regulators Announce Historic Agreement to Reform Investment Practices," December 20, 2002, www.sec.gov/news/press/2002-179.htm.

[7] *Penny stocks* is a term that refers to very low priced stocks—usually less than $1.00 per share. Normally very speculative investments, penny stocks attract naïve investors wishing to make big profits and unscrupulous brokers.

PART TWO

Importance of Internal Controls

CHAPTER FOUR

Internal Controls Fundamentals: COSO Framework

4.1 IMPORTANCE OF EFFECTIVE INTERNAL CONTROLS

Internal control is the most important and fundamental concept that an internal auditor must understand. An internal auditor reviews both operational and financial areas of the organization with an objective of evaluating their internal controls. Virtually all internal audit procedures focus on some form of this evaluation of internal controls. While internal auditors generally have a good understanding of what is meant by internal controls, others may respond to a "can you define good internal controls?" question with answers along the lines of one or more characterizations:

- Good internal controls means everything is well documented—which is a correct answer.

- Good internal controls mean strong security processes—correct again.
- Good internal controls mean the debits equal the credits—also true.

Although many professionals use the term, they often have to step back and think about it when asked for a definition. Yet, internal controls are a positive set of general procedures necessary for all well-managed and well-functioning business systems. A common textbook application of internal control is:

> Internal control comprises the plan of organization and all of the coordinate methods adopted within a business to safeguard its assets, check the accuracy and reliability of its accounting data, promote operational efficiency, and encourage adherence to prescribed managerial policies. This definition recognizes that a system of internal control extends beyond those matters which relate directly to the functions of the accounting and financial departments.

That long and rather academic-sounding definition says that a system or process has good internal controls if it (1) accomplishes its stated mission, (2) produces accurate and reliable data, (3) complies with applicable laws and organization policies, (4) provides for economical and efficient uses of resources, and (5) provides for appropriate safeguarding of assets. All members of the organization are responsible for the internal controls in their area of operation and for making those internal controls function.

Lawrence (Larry) Sawyer, a contemporary of Vic Brink and a founder, with Brink, of the profession of internal auditing, has called control evaluations the auditor's "open sesame."[1] That is, an internal auditor's skills in assessing the internal controls in operation for various specialized areas of an organization will open doors to an internal auditor throughout the organization. The examination and appraisal of internal controls are normally components, either directly or indirectly, of every type of internal auditing assignment. An internal auditor's special competence in the control-evaluation area justifies reviews covering a wide range of operational activities, even though the auditor may not possess specialized knowledge about the operational details surrounding those activities.

The chapter discusses the fundamentals of internal controls both from some very basic definitions of control systems and with some background on how we have arrived at what is called the COSO internal controls framework. An understanding of that internal control framework is essential for achieving the Section 404 internal control requirements of the Sarbanes-Oxley Act (SOA) as will be discussed in greater detail in Chapter 6, "Evaluating Internal Controls: Section 404 Assessments." Another COSO-related framework is its Enterprise Risk Module (ERM). ERM is sometimes mistakenly described as an updated version of COSO and will be discussed in Chapter 5, "Understanding and Assessing Risks: Enterprise Risk Management."

4.2 FUNDAMENTALS OF INTERNAL CONTROLS

To effectively review internal controls, an internal auditor needs to have a good basic understanding of the nature of controls, *a definition of a control system,* as well as the overall concept of the types and nature of an organization's operating internal control processes. The first of these two concepts, the idea of a control system, is perhaps the easier. This concept goes back to the basic principles of mechanical and paperwork procedures that exist throughout one's everyday life. Control systems are necessary for all areas of activity, both inside and outside today's organization, and the concepts and principles used are the same no matter where the control system is encountered. The automobile can provide a good analogy of a control system. When the accelerator is pressed, the automobile goes faster. When the brake is pressed, the automobile slows or stops. When the steering wheel is turned, the vehicle turns. The driver *controls* the automobile. If the driver does not use the accelerator, brake, or steering wheel properly, the automobile will operate *out of control.*

An organization is similar to an automobile. There are a variety of systems at work, such as the manufacturing and sales processes, information systems, and accounting operations. If management does not operate or direct these systems or process components properly, the organization may operate out of control. The effective control of an organization, of course, is much more complicated, but a significant failure of one or another component can cause the entire organization to operate out of control. An internal auditor should first develop an understanding of these control systems and then assess them to determine if the components of the system are properly connected and if management is properly operating the controls that allow it to manage the system. This type of system or process is often referred to as the organization's system of *internal controls.*

Internal auditors are often called on to describe control systems to their management and to convince them of the importance of controls even when management may have other priorities. An internal auditor must be a spokesperson for the importance of internal controls, but to be effective, must have a good understanding of basic internal control objectives and components. The purpose of any control system is to attain or maintain a desired state or condition. The system of internal control should be able to satisfy various objectives established by management for that control area. A basic control system has four elements:

1. **Detector or Sensor Element.** There must be some type of measuring device that detects what is happening in the particular element of the system being controlled (e.g., a thermostat in the home that connects to the furnace). An internal auditor often is the sensor who observes some problem as part of a normal audit review.

2. **Selector or Standard Element.** The detector that reports on current conditions must have some type of a standard to compare what is actually happening to what should be happening. The thermostat is set to a desired temperature and linked to a thermometer measuring the actual temperature. Fluctuations above or below the user-supplied temperature setting cause the furnace to take action. Internal audit will make recommendations based on standards and best practices as discussed in Chapter 14, "Directing and Performing Internal Audits."

3. **Controller Element.** This element alters the behavior of the area under control based on a comparison between the detector and standard results.

The thermostat turns off the furnace when the heat reaches some certain predetermined level and restarts the furnace again when the level drops.

4. **Communications Network Element.**   The control system communications network is simply a vehicle for transmitting messages between the control sensor and the entity being controlled. A home heating thermostat has a connection between the sensor on the furnace—usually away from the living area—and the measuring unit in the home living space.

These four elements can be called a control system because they are separate but interrelated components of an overall control process. Exhibit 4.1 illustrates such a conceptual control system. There are many other examples of these types of control systems in everyday life. The same elements repeat themselves in more complex systems.

Many business processes do not have this level of automatic control system in place because their formal detector and even selector controls are limited. Nevertheless, even manual systems have some control elements, and an internal auditor should look for these elements when reviewing internal controls. Of course, internal auditors themselves often serve as a type of control system detection element by helping to make sure that the control system is working effectively.

(a) Detective, Protective, and Corrective Control Techniques

Following the system described in Exhibit 4.1, control techniques can be further categorized as *preventive, detective, corrective,* or a combination of the three. The

EXHIBIT 4.1

Elements of a Control System

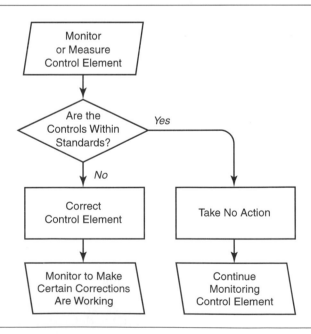

sum of these three basic control techniques should provide management with reasonable assurance that a particular process is operating properly:

- *Preventive controls* are built into a system to prevent an error or undetected event from happening. A very elementary type of preventive control is an organization structure that establishes a separation of duties over certain functions. Another is a locked door to prevent unauthorized access to critical equipment.

- *Detective controls* are designed to alert management of errors or problems as they occur, or shortly after. A cash count and reconciliation of cash register sales at the end of the day is an example of such a detective control. An alarm that sounds when the locked door is forced open is another.

- *Corrective controls* are used in conjunction with detective controls to recover from the consequences of the undesired events. An insurance policy to pay for losses is one type of corrective control. A guard to apprehend the intruder who forced open the locked door and sounded the alarm is another corrective control technique.

Preventive, detective, and corrective control techniques are important elements in an overall system of control. While it is often more cost-effective to install preventive controls in a system, detective controls are also needed, and detective controls are usually of little value unless some form of corrective action or control is also in place. Internal audit acts as a type of detective control to determine, among other matters, that the preventive controls are working properly. Because internal auditors are not "police officers," however, management must implement the corrective actions to respond to any reported control findings. Since these controls should always be tied directly or indirectly to control objectives that may vary widely in nature and scope, the manner in which control is exercised can also vary. Preventive, detective, and corrective controls can be considered to operate on three different levels:

1. **Steering Controls.** This level of control identifies events that will prompt interim action to aid in the achievement of larger objectives. These interim events can be very precise or broad. The common characteristic of steering controls is that they are usually preventive and call attention to the need to take managerial action on a timely basis. Various types of gauges in a manufacturing process indicate conditions that require particular processing actions. A drop in dealer orders may highlight the problem of declining market acceptance and the related need to adjust production schedules. In other cases, a broad index of economic trends can alert management to changing conditions that should spark protective or other opportunity-oriented actions.

2. **Yes-No Controls.** These controls are designed to function more automatically, to be protective, and to assure the accomplishment of desired results. In their simplest form, a yes-no control could be a quality-control gauge on a mechanized assembly line that checks product parts for exact specifications. Parts that are out of tolerance are routed to a rework area.

This control could also be a required approval signature on a business form to help ensure that an authorized individual has reviewed the document. The common element here is a pre-established control device or arrangement that, under normal conditions, will more or less automatically assure desired protective or improved actions.

3. **Post-Action Controls.**   A third control somewhat overlaps with the other two discussed, but is distinctive because managerial action comes later and takes the form of after-the-fact corrective action. The action may be taken to repair a product that has been damaged or to dismiss or reassign an employee. That after-the-fact action happens immediately or may require extended analysis. The analyses done by internal auditors are typically directed to recommending the most effective type of after-the-fact action, even though that action may be very much future-oriented. This recommendation can be directed to correcting established preventive, detective, or corrective types of control.

An internal auditor should try to develop an understanding of these very basic control systems concepts. These concepts are useful whenever an auditor is asked to evaluate, document, and understand an internal control system or process. This type of internal control systems thinking will allow an auditor to break down and analyze any process, whether a large complex process or a simple almost manual procedures into its internal control components. The next step is to map these internal controls concepts against a recognized and accepted framework. This leads to what is called the COSO framework. The following sections will define and discuss the COSO internal control framework in greater detail.

4.3   INTERNAL CONTROLS STANDARDS: BACKGROUND DEVELOPMENTS

The preceding section described internal control systems, a very important concept for the modern internal auditor. A problem with these definitions is that there was no consistent agreement among many interested persons of what was meant by "good internal controls." This section briefly describes some of the past definitions used for internal control and presents a definition of internal control that was first introduced in the United States in 1992 and has been accepted by virtually all professional auditing and accounting organizations. This definition is also the foundation for Sarbanes-Oxley Act (SOA) definition of internal controls and should provide internal auditors with a general understanding of the objectives and components of a system of internal control. These internal control concepts are very important for the modern internal auditor and will be used in other chapters in this book.

(a)   Early Definitions of Internal Control Systems

As discussed, the concept of internal control has been used by auditors since the very early days of auditing to define the process of how management mechanisms work. In the very first edition of this book, Vic Brink talked about the importance of understanding and evaluating internal control systems and provided a definition of internal control that helped to launch the internal audit profession. Other interested parties, including external auditors, developed their own similar but not totally consistent definitions of internal control.

The early definitions of internal control, developed by the American Institute of Certified Public Accountants (AICPA) and used by the Securities and Exchange Commission (SEC) in the United States to develop regulations covering the Securities Exchange Act of 1934, provide a good starting point. Although there have been changes over the years, the AICPA's first codified standards were called the Statement on Auditing Standards (SAS No. 1).[2] This standard covered the practice of financial statement auditing in the United States for many years and also was similar to definitions used by the Canadian Institute of Charter Accountants (CICA). SAS No. 1 used the following definition for internal control:

> Internal control comprises the plan of organization and all of the coordinate methods and measures adopted with a business to safeguard its assets, check the accuracy and reliability of its accounting data, promote operational efficiency, and encourage adherence to prescribed managerial policies.

The original AICPA SAS No. 1 was further modified to add administrative controls and accounting controls to the basic internal control definition:

> Administrative control includes, but is not limited to, the plan of organization and the procedures and records that are concerned with the decision processes leading to management's authorization of transactions. Such authorization is a management function directly associated with the responsibility for achieving the objectives of the organization and is the starting point for establishing accounting control of transactions.

> Accounting control comprises the plan of organization and the procedures and records that are concerned with the safeguarding of assets and the reliability of financial records and consequently are designed to provide reasonable assurance that:

> a. Transactions are executed in accordance with management's general or specific authorization.

> b. Transactions are recorded as necessary (1) to permit preparation of financial statements in conformity with generally accepted accounting principles or any other criteria applicable to such statement and (2) to maintain accountability for assets.

> c. Access to assets is permitted only in accordance with management's authorization.

> d. The recorded accountability for assets is compared with the existing assets at reasonable intervals and appropriate action is taken with respect to any differences.

The overlapping relationships of these two types of internal control were then further clarified in these pre-1988 AICPA standards:

> The foregoing definitions are not necessarily mutually exclusive because some of the procedures and records comprehended in accounting control may also be involved in administrative control. For example, sales and cost records classified by products may be used for accounting control purposes and also in making management decisions concerning unit prices or other aspects of operations. Such multiple uses of procedures or records, however, are not critical for the purposes of this section because it is concerned primarily with clarifying the outer boundary of accounting control. Examples of records used solely for administrative control are those pertaining to customers contacted by salesmen and to defective work by production employees maintained only for evaluation personnel per performance.

Our point here is that the definition of internal control, as then defined by the AICPA, was subject to changes and reinterpretations over the years. However, these earlier AICPA standards stress that the system of internal control extends beyond just matters relating directly to the accounting and financial statements. Over this period through the 1970s, there were many internal control guidelines published by the SEC and AICPA as well as voluminous interpretations and guidelines developed by major CPA firms.

Internal auditors were not that affected by these changing definitions. Internal auditors have always extended their work beyond internal accounting controls to the effectiveness of the total system of internal control. Internal auditors have historically believed that internal accounting control is part of a larger control system, with the lines of demarcation as to where internal accounting control fits in the total system never exactly clear.

(b) Foreign Corrupt Practices Act of 1977

Just as the scandals of Enron and others in the early years of this century brought us the Sarbanes-Oxley Act (SOA), the United States experienced a similar situation some 25 years earlier. The period of 1974 through 1977 was a time of extreme social and political turmoil in the United States. The 1972 presidential election was surrounded by allegations of a series of illegal and questionable acts that eventually led to the president's resignation. The events were first precipitated by a burglary of the Democratic Party headquarters, then located in a building complex known as Watergate. The resulting scandal and related investigations became known as the Watergate affair. Investigators found, among other matters, that various bribes and other questionable practices had occurred that were not covered by legislation.

In 1976, the SEC submitted to the U.S. Senate Committee on Banking, Housing, and Urban Affairs a report on its Watergate-related investigations into various questionable or potentially illegal corporate payments and practices. (The phrase "potentially illegal" is used because many legal statutes in place at the time were somewhat vague regarding these activities.) The Senate report recommended federal legislation to prohibit such bribes and other questionable payments, and the Foreign Corrupt Practices Act (FCPA) was enacted in December 1977. The act contained provisions requiring the maintenance of accurate books and records and the implementation of systems of internal accounting control, and prohibitions against bribery. Internal controls soon came back on to the radar screen of internal and external auditors. The FCPA provisions apply to virtually all U.S. companies with SEC-registered securities. Using terminology taken directly from the act, SEC-regulated organizations must:

- Make and keep books, records, and accounts, which, in reasonable detail, accurately and fairly reflect the transactions and dispositions of the assets of the issuers.

- Devise and maintain a system of internal accounting controls sufficient to provide reasonable assurances that:

  o Transactions are executed in accordance with management's general or specific authorization.

  o Transactions are recorded as necessary both to permit the preparation
     of financial statements in conformity with generally accepted account-
     ing principles or any other criteria applicable to such statements, and
     also to maintain accountability for assets.

- Access to assets is permitted only in accordance with management's general or specific authorization.
- The recorded accountability for assets is compared with the existing
  assets at reasonable intervals, and appropriate action is taken with respect
  to any differences.

The special significance of FCPA requirements was that, for the first time,
management was made responsible for maintaining an adequate system of
internal accounting control. The act required organizations to "make and keep
books, records, and accounts, which in reasonable detail, accurately and fairly
reflect the transactions and dispositions of the assets of the issuer." Similar to
today's SOA, the FCPA record keeping requirements applied to public corporations registered with the SEC.

In addition, the FCPA required that organizations keep records that accurately reflect their transactions "in reasonable detail." While there is no exact definition here, the intent of the rule was that records should reflect transactions in
conformity with accepted methods of recording economic events, preventing off-
the-books "slush funds" and payments of bribes. The fraud provisions of the
FCPA on loss prevention and fraud investigation are discussed in Chapter 11,
"Fraud Detection and Prevention." The FCPA also required that companies with
registered securities maintain a system of internal accounting controls, sufficient
to provide reasonable assurances that transactions are authorized and recorded to
permit preparation of financial statements in conformity with generally accepted
accounting principles. FCPA also states that accountability is to be maintained for
assets, access to assets is permitted only as authorized, and recorded assets are to
be physically inventoried periodically, with any significant differences analyzed.

The main reason for the FCPA, the bribery provisions, are applicable to both
SEC-registered corporations and all other U.S. domestic concerns. The act prohibits bribes to foreign officials to influence or assist an organization in obtaining
business, with the offer or gift intended to induce the recipient to misuse an official position, such as to direct business to the payer or a client. Excluded from the
definition of foreign official are government employees whose functions are clerical or ministerial in nature. Thus, so-called grease payments to minor officials to
get their help in expediting some process are permissible. Passed over 25 years
ago, the FCPA was a strong set of corporate governance rules, and because of the
FCPA, many companies' boards of directors and their audit committees began to
take a more active part in directing reviews of internal controls.

(c) FCPA Aftermath: What Happened?

When enacted, the FCPA resulted in a flurry of activity among major U.S. corporations. Many organizations then initiated major efforts to assess and document
their systems of internal control. Organizations that had never formally documented procedures, despite a long chain of internal audit reports pointing out

that weakness, now embarked on major documentation efforts. This responsibility for FCPA documentation was often given to internal audit departments who used their best efforts to comply with the internal control provisions of the act. The reader should recall that this was in the late 1970s and very early 1980s when most automated systems were mainframe batch-oriented devices, and graphics tools were often little more than plastic flowchart templates and #2 pencils.

Considerable efforts were expended in these efforts, and many consultants and seminar presenters became wealthier in the process. One of the major public accounting firms at that time ran a series of advertisements in major business publications showing a small flowchart template with a message that this firm could use this plastic flowchart template to help client organizations solve their FCPA problems. Of course, much more was needed than a flowchart template. Even though systems and processes change relatively often, many large organizations developed extensive sets of paper-based systems documentation with no provisions, once they had been completed, to update them. As a result of the FCPA, many organizations also strengthened their internal audit departments significantly.

Many writers anticipated a wave of additional regulations or legal initiatives following the enactment of the FCPA. However, this did not occur. Legal actions were essentially nonexistent, no one came to inspect the files of assembled documentation, and today the FCPA has dropped off of the list of current "hot" management topics. The FCPA is still very much in force, but is more recognized as an anticorruption, antibribery law. An FCPA-related search on the Web today will yield few if any references to the act's internal control provisions. The law was amended in the early 1990s but only to strengthen and improve its anticorruption provisions.

When enacted in 1977, the FCPA emphasized the importance of effective internal controls for many U.S. corporations. Although there was no consistent definition at the time, the law heightened the importance of internal controls in the corporation. Its antibribery provisions continue to be important. It was an important first step for helping organizations to establish effective internal controls. Although it dates back to an era of minimal automation and many manual processes, it provided a good precursor to today's SOA requirements. Perhaps, if there had been more attempts at achieving FCPA internal controls compliance, we would never have had SOA.

4.4 EFFORTS LEADING TO THE TREADWAY COMMISSION

With all of the various published approaches for documenting internal controls, it soon became obvious to many parties involved in this process, including auditors as well as business and financial managers, that we did not have a clear and consistent understanding of what was meant by the term "internal control." As discussed, external auditors thought in terms of "internal accounting control," while internal auditors had their own broader definitions. Concurrent with these internal control definitions–friendly debates, the financial press and others in the United States began to call for external auditors to express an opinion on an organization's internal controls as part of their audits of financial statements.

Back in the late 1970s, external auditors only reported that an organization's financial statements were "fairly presented." There was no mention of the adequacy of internal control procedures supporting those audited financial statements. The FCPA had put a requirement on the reporting organizations to document their internal controls but did not ask external auditors to attest to whether an organization under audit was in compliance with any internal control reporting requirements. The SEC, which regulates publicly held companies in the United States, began a study on whether external audit reports were adequate. As a result, a series of studies and reports were completed over about a 10-year period to define better both the meaning of internal control and the external auditor's responsibility for reporting on the adequacy of those controls.

(a) AICPA and CICA Commissions on Auditor Responsibilities

The AICPA had formed the high-level Commission on Auditor's Responsibilities in 1974 to study the external auditor's responsibility for reporting on internal controls. This group, better known then as the Cohen Commission, released its report in 1978, recommending that corporate management be required to present a statement on the condition of their company's internal controls along with the financial statements. These Cohen Commission initiatives were taking place concurrently with the development and initial publication of the FCPA. At about the same time, the CICA's Commission on Auditor Expectations released a report in 1978 with similar conclusions.

In the United States, the Cohen Commission's report initially ran into a torrent of criticism. In particular, the report's recommendations were not precise on what was meant by "reporting on internal controls," and external auditors strongly expressed concerns about their roles in this process. Many external auditors were concerned about potential liabilities if their reports on internal control gave inconsistent signals due to a lack of understanding over what were internal control standards. Although auditors were accustomed to attesting to the fairness of financial statements, the Cohen Commission report suggested that they should express an audit opinion on the fairness of the management control assertions in the proposed financial statement internal control letter. The issue was again raised that management did not have a consistent definition of internal control. Different organizations might use the same terms regarding the quality of their internal controls, with each meaning something a little different. If an organization reported that its controls were "adequate" and if its auditors "blessed" their assertions in that controls report, the external auditor could later be criticized or even suffer potential litigation if some significant control problem appeared later.

The Financial Executives Institute (FEI) then got involved in this internal controls reporting controversy. Just as the IIA is the professional organization for internal auditors and the AICPA or CICA represent the public accountants in the United States and Canada, respectively, the FEI represents senior financial officers in organizations. The FEI released a letter to its members in the late 1970s endorsing the Cohen Commission's recommendations on internal control reports. They suggested that publicly held organizations should report on the status of their internal accounting controls. As a result, publicly held corporations began to discuss the adequacy of their internal controls as part of the management letters typically included as part of annual reports. These internal control letters were not required and those issued did not follow any standard format. They were an entirely voluntary initiative and often were included in the CEO's management letter summarizing operations. They typically included comments stating that management, through its internal auditors, periodically assessed the quality of its internal controls. The same letters sometimes included "negative assurance" comments indicating that nothing was found to indicate that there might be an internal control problem in operations.

This term *negative assurance* will return again in this discussion of internal controls. Because an external auditor cannot detect all problems and because of the risk of potential litigation, their reports often have been stated in terms of a negative assurance. That is, rather than saying that they "found no problems" in an area under review, an external auditor would state that they did not find anything that would lead them to believe that there was a problem. This is a subtle but important difference.

(b) SEC 1979 Internal Control Reporting Proposal

Using both the Cohen Commission and FEI's recommendations, the SEC subsequently issued proposed rules calling for *mandatory* management reports on an entity's internal accounting control system. The SEC stated that information on the effectiveness of an entity's internal control system was necessary to allow investors to evaluate better both management's performance and the integrity of published financial reports. This SEC proposal raised a storm of controversy. First, many CEOs and CFOs felt that this was an onerous requirement on top of the then newly released FCPA regulations.

Questions were once again raised from many directions regarding the definition of internal accounting control, and while organizations might agree to voluntary reporting, they did not want to subject themselves to the civil and legal penalties associated with a violation of SEC regulations. The SEC soon dropped this 1979 internal control reporting proposal, but promised to re-release the regulations at a later date. The SEC proposal was important, however, in that it emphasized the need for a separate management report on internal accounting controls as part of the annual report to shareholders and the required SEC filings. This tentative regulation caused larger public companies to begin to issue voluntary internal control comments or letters in their annual reports.

(c) Minahan Committee and Financial Executives Research Foundation

In parallel with the SEC's proposed rules on internal control reporting, the AICPA formed another committee, the Special Advisory Committee on Internal Control, also called the Minahan Committee. Their 1979 report pointed out the lack of management guidance on internal control procedures and acknowledged that most of the published guidance on internal controls was found in the accounting and auditing literature. This guidance would not necessarily come to the attention of or to be completely relevant to a business manager in other areas of an organization, such as operations, who had a need to understand internal control concepts.

At about the same time, the FEI Research Foundation (FERF) commissioned two studies in this area. The first researched published literature and considered definitions used for the characteristics, conditions, practices, and procedures that define internal control systems. This report,[3] published in 1980, pointed out the vast differences in the definitions of various professional standards-setting groups in what constitutes an effective system of internal control. FERF also released a related research study in 1980[4] that attempted to define the broad, conceptual criteria for evaluating internal control.

These two efforts pointed out the need to find a better and more consistent meaning of internal controls. A regulatory group such as the SEC could not realistically draft requirements for reporting for internal control unless both the organizations developing those reports and the investors who read them all had a consistent understanding of the concept.

(d) Earlier AICPA Standards: SAS No. 55

Prior to SOA, the AICPA was responsible for external audit standards through Statements on Auditing Standards (SASs) that were released from time to time and were codified in an overall set of professional standards. As discussed previously regarding SAS No. 1, these standards were once almost engraved in stone, with little change for many years. They formed the basis of the external auditor's review and evaluation of financial statements. During this same period of the 1970s and 1980s, the public accounting profession, in general, and the AICPA were criticized that their standards did not provide adequate guidance to either external auditors or the users of these reports. This problem was called the "expectations gap," in that public accounting standards did not meet the expectations of investors.

To answer this need, the AICPA released a series of new SASs on internal control audit standards during the period of 1980 to 1985. These included, SAS No. 30, *Reporting on Internal Accounting Control,* which provided guidance for the terminology to be used in internal accounting control reports. The SAS did not provide much help, however, on defining the underlying concepts of internal control. Much of these standards were viewed by critics of the public accounting profession as too little too late. For example, SAS No. 48, *The Effects of Computer Processing on the Examination of Financial Statements,* was issued in 1984 and provided guidance on the need to review both the computer system applications controls and such general controls as physical security. Although there had been massive technological changes in the way computer systems were constructed, at the time SAS No. 48 was issued external auditors were still using guidance from the early 1970s.

The AICPA subsequently released a whole new series of auditing standards that better defined many problem areas facing external auditors. One of these, SAS No. 55, defined internal control from the perspective of the external auditor and defined internal control in terms of three elements:

- The control environment

- The accounting system

- The control procedures

SAS No. 55 presented a somewhat different approach to understanding internal control than had been used by the AICPA in the past, as well as by other standard-setting groups, such as the IIA.

An organization generally has other internal control structure policies and procedures that are not relevant to a financial statement audit and therefore are not considered by the external auditors. Examples include policies and procedures concerning the effectiveness, economy, and efficiency of certain management decision-making processes, such as setting of an appropriate price for products or deciding whether to make expenditures for certain research and development activities. Although these processes are certainly important to the organization, they do not ordinarily relate to the external auditor's financial statement audit.

SAS No. 55 defined internal control in much broader scope than had been traditionally taken by external auditors. However, this was still a narrower view than the scope traditionally taken by internal auditors. This AICPA definition, however, provided a basis for the COSO report definition of internal control and SAS No. 78, both discussed later in this chapter. The interests of internal auditors extend beyond internal accounting control to the effectiveness of the total system of internal control, and that internal accounting control is part of a larger system. SAS No. 55 became effective in 1990 and represented a major stride toward providing external auditors with an appropriate definition of internal control.

(e) Treadway Committee Report

The late 1970s and early 1980s were a period of many major organizations' failure in the United States due to factors such as high inflation, the resultant high interest rates, and high energy costs due to extensive government regulation. Organizations sometimes reported adequate earnings in their financial reports, and their external auditors attested that these same financial reports were fairly stated, only to have the organization suffer a financial collapse shortly after the release of such favorable audited reports. Some of these failures were caused by fraudulent financial reporting, although many others were caused by high inflation or other factors causing organizational instability. Several members of Congress proposed legislation to "correct" these potential business and audit failures. Bills were drafted and congressional hearings held, but no legislation was passed.

In response to these concerns, the National Commission on Fraudulent Financial Reporting was formed. Five professional organizations sponsored the Commission: the IIA, the AICPA, and the FEI, all discussed previously, as well as the American Accounting Association (AAA) and the Institute of Management Accountants (IMA). The AAA is the academic professional accountants' organization. The IMA is the professional organization for managerial or cost accountants. This organization, formerly called the National Association of Accountants, sponsors the Certificate in Management Accounting (CMA).

The National Commission on Fraudulent Reporting, called the Treadway Commission after its chairperson, had as its major objectives the identification of the causal factors that allowed fraudulent financial reporting and the making of recommendations to reduce their incidence. The Treadway Commission's final report was issued in 1987[5] and included recommendations to management, boards of directors, the public accounting profession, and others. The Treadway

Commission report again called for management reports on the effectiveness of their internal control systems and emphasized key elements in what it felt should be an effective system of internal control, including a strong control environment, codes of conduct, a competent and involved audit committee, and a strong internal audit function. The Treadway Commission report again pointed out the lack of a consistent definition of internal control, suggesting further work was needed. The same Committee of Sponsoring Organizations (COSO), which managed the Treadway report, subsequently contracted with outside specialists and embarked on a new project to define internal control. Although it defined no standards, the Treadway report was important because it raised the level of concern and attention regarding reporting on internal control.

Other internal control–related activities took place about the time the Treadway Commission's report was released. As discussed earlier, the AICPA initially released its SAS No. 55 auditing standard on internal control, and the SEC responded to the Treadway recommendations by proposing additional management reporting on internal control.

The internal control–reporting efforts discussed here are presented as if they were a series of sequential events. In reality, many of the internal control–related efforts took place in almost a parallel fashion. This massive effort over nearly a 20-year period redefined internal control, a basic concept for all auditors, and increased the responsibility of many other participants in an organization's internal control structure. The result has been the COSO internal control framework, discussed in the sections following and elsewhere in this book. The COSO framework for internal control is an important concept for the modern internal, auditor.

4.5 COSO INTERNAL CONTROL FRAMEWORK

As mentioned, the acronym COSO stands for the five professional auditing and accounting organizations that developed this internal control report; its official title is *Integrated Control–Integrated Framework*. Throughout this book, it is referred to as the COSO report, its commonly accepted name. The sponsoring organizations contracted with a public accounting firm and used a large number of volunteers to research and develop the report, and then released a draft in 1990 for public exposure and comment. More than 40,000 copies of the COSO draft version were sent to corporate officers, internal and external auditors, legislators, academics, and other interested parties. Formal comments regarding this draft were requested and the internal control review procedures portion of the study, discussed later, was field tested by five public accounting firms.

The final COSO report was released in September 1992.[6] The report proposes a common framework for the definition of internal control, as well as procedures to evaluate those controls. In a very short number of years, the COSO framework has become the recognized framework or standard for understanding and establishing effective internal controls in virtually all business organizations. This section will provide a fairly detailed description of the COSO framework while Chapter 6 will discuss how to use COSO to evaluate internal controls. That latter evaluation description will be based on SOA Section 404 evaluations, an important and significant area for internal auditors.

(a) COSO Framework Model

Virtually every public corporation has a complex control procedures structure. Following the description of a classic organization chart, there are levels of senior and middle management in its multiple operating units or within different activities. In addition, control procedures may be somewhat different at each of these levels and components. For example, one operating unit may operate in a regulated business environment where control processes are very structured, while another unit may be an entrepreneurial start-up operation with a less formal structure. Different levels of management in these organizations will have different control concern perspectives. The question "How do you describe your system of internal controls?" might receive different answers from persons in different levels or components in each of these organizational units.

COSO provides an excellent description of this multidimensional concept of internal controls. It defines internal control as follows:

> Internal control is a *process,* affected by an entity's board of directors, management, and other personnel, designed to provide reasonable assurance regarding the achievement of objectives in the following categories:

- ○ Effectiveness and efficiency of operations
- ○ Reliability of financial reporting
- ○ Compliance with applicable laws and regulations

This is the COSO definition of internal control. The definition should be very familiar to internal auditors. It follows the same theme that Vic Brink used as a definition of internal auditing in his first 1943 edition of *Modern Internal Auditing* and all subsequent editions. He defined internal auditing as:

> Internal auditing is an independent appraisal function established within an organization to examine and evaluate its activities as a service to the organization.

While COSO focuses on financial reporting controls, Brink used the broader definition of service to management to define what the new profession of internal auditing was then. That definition is still important today.

Using this very general definition of internal control, COSO uses a three-dimensional model to describe an internal control system in an organization. Exhibit 4.2 defines the COSO model of internal control as a pyramid with five layered or interconnected components composing the overall internal control system. These are shown with a component called the control environment serving as the foundation for the entire structure. Four of these internal components are described as horizontal layers, with another component of internal control, called communication and information, acting as an interface channel for the other four layers. These components are described in greater detail in the following sections. Exhibit 4.3 shows this same COSO model from a slightly different perspective. Here, the three major component of internal control—effectiveness and efficiency of operations, reliability of financial reporting, and compliance with applicable laws and regulations—give three dimensions to this model. Just as the pyramid structure of Exhibit 4.2 showed the internal control structure as the environment for all internal control processes, this view adds equal weight to each of these three components.

EXHIBIT 4.2

COSO Component of Internal Control

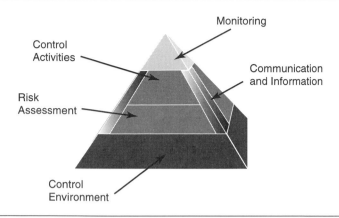

Auditors and mangers should consider and understand their internal controls in this multilevel and three-dimensioned manner. While this is true for all internal audit work, the concept is particularly valuable when assessing and evaluating internal controls using the COSO framework. The paragraphs following describe this COSO framework in greater detail.

(i) COSO Internal Control Elements: The Control Environment. The foundation of any internal control structure for any organization is what COSO calls the *internal control environment*. COSO emphasizes that this entity internal control environment foundation has a pervasive influence on how business activities are structured and risks are assessed in any organization. The control environment serves

EXHIBIT 4.3

COSO Internal Control Model

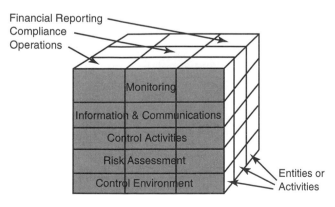

Relationship between Control Components,
Objectives, and Organization Entities

as a foundation for all other components of internal control and has an influence on each of the three objectives and all activities. The control environment reflects the overall attitude, awareness, and actions of the board of directors, management, and others concerning the importance of internal control in the organization.

Organization history and culture often play a major role in forming this control environment. Where an organization historically has had a strong management emphasis on producing error-free products, senior management continues to emphasize the importance of high-quality products, and this message has been communicated to all levels, this becomes a major control environment factor for the organization. However, if senior management has had a reputation of "looking the other way" at policy violations, this message will be similarly communicated to other levels in the organization. A positive *tone at the top* by senior management will establish the control environment for the organization.

The following sections outline some of the major elements of the COSO control environment component of internal control. Internal auditors should always try to understand this overall control environment when performing reviews of various organization activities or units. In some instances, they may want to perform specific reviews of some or all of these control environment factors covering the overall organization. In small organizations, the control environment factors will be more informal. However, internal audit should still look for the appropriate control environment factors in any entity and consider them as essential components of internal control. Following SOA guidance, if the control environment appears to have major deficiencies, internal audit should discuss these concerns with the audit committee.

(A) INTEGRITY AND ETHICAL VALUES

The collective integrity and ethical values of an organization are essential elements of its control environment. These factors are often defined by the tone-at-the-top message communicated by senior management. If the organization has developed a strong code of conduct that emphasizes integrity and ethical values, and if all stakeholders appear to follow that code, internal audit will have assurances that the organization has a good set of values.

As discussed in Chapter 3, "Internal Audit in the Twenty-First Century: Sarbanes-Oxley and Beyond," and further in Chapter 9, "Whistle-blower Programs and Codes of Conduct," a code of ethics or conduct is an important component of organizational governance. Although an organization may have a strong code of conduct, its principles can often be violated through ignorance rather than by deliberate employee malfeasance. In many instances, employees may not know that they are doing something wrong or may erroneously believe that their actions are in the organization's best interests. This ignorance is often caused by poor moral guidance by senior management rather than by any employee intent to deceive. An organization's policies and values must be communicated to all levels of the organization. While there can always be "bad apples" in any organization, a strong moral message will encourage everyone to act correctly. When performing a review in a given area, the internal auditor should always ask questions to determine if appropriate messages or signals have been transmitted throughout the organization.

Internal auditors should have a good understanding of the organization's code of conduct and how it is applied throughout the organization. If the code is out of date, if it does not appear to address important ethical issues facing an organization, or if management does not appear to be communicating the code to all stakeholders on a recurring basis, internal audit should remind management of the significance of this deficiency, both in the course of audits in other areas and as a special message to management. If the organization does not have a formal ethics office function, internal audit may often be asked to suggest changes and to help in the dissemination of the organization's code of conduct.

While the code of conduct describes the rules for ethical behavior in an organization and while senior members of management should transmit a proper ethical message throughout their organization, other incentives and temptations can erode this overall control environment. Individuals in the organization may engage in dishonest, illegal, or unethical acts if their organization gives them strong incentives or temptations to do so. For example, an organization may establish very high, unrealistic performance targets for sales or production quotas. If there are strong rewards for the achievement of these performance goals—or worse, strong threats for any missed targets—employees may be encouraged to engage in fraudulent or questionable practices to achieve those goals. The kinds of temptations that encourage stakeholders to engage in improper accounting or similar acts include:

- Nonexistent or ineffective controls, such as poor segregation of duties in sensitive areas that offer temptations to steal or to conceal poor performance

- High decentralization that leaves top management unaware of actions taken at lower organization levels and thereby reduces the chances of getting caught

- A weak internal audit function that has neither the ability nor the authority to detect and report improper behavior

- Penalties for improper behavior that are insignificant or unpublicized and thus lose their value as deterrents

There is a strong message here both for internal auditors performing their various reviews and for the internal audit organization in total. First, the internal auditor should always consider these control environment factors when performing reviews. A good internal auditor should always be skeptical and perform appropriate levels of tests when reviewing various areas of operations. When things look "too good," the auditor might want to look a bit harder. This is not just to find something in the course of a review but to assess whether deficiencies in the control environment may lead to possible fraudulent activities. Procedures for fraud investigations are discussed in Chapter 11.

A strong internal audit function should be a major component of the COSO control environment. If internal audit finds that management is placing constraints on the internal audit function, internal audit should remind management of the importance of internal audit as part of the organization's overall internal control structure and should go to the board of director's audit committee, if necessary, to achieve corrective action.

(B) COMMITMENT TO COMPETENCE

An organization's control environment can be seriously eroded if a significant number of positions are filled with persons lacking required job skills. Internal auditors will encounter the situation from time to time when a person has been assigned to a particular job but does not seem to have the appropriate skills, training, or intelligence to perform that job. Because all human beings have different levels of skills and abilities, adequate supervision and training should be available to help the person until proper skills are acquired.

An organization needs to specify the required competence levels for its various job tasks and to translate those requirements into necessary levels of knowledge and skill. By placing the proper people in appropriate jobs and giving adequate training when required, an organization is making an overall *commitment to competence*, an important element in the organization's overall control environment. Internal auditors often find it valuable when reviewing a functional area to assess whether adequate position descriptions have been created for the various functions under review, whether procedures are in operation to place appropriate people in those positions, and whether training and supervision are adequate.

While an important portion of the control environment, an assessment of staff competence can be a difficult internal audit review area. How does an auditor determine that the staff is "competent" with regards to its assigned work duties? If an internal auditor visits a remote subsidiary operation and finds that no one in the accounting department there seems to have any knowledge of how to record and report financial transactions, and also that no training program exists to help these "accountants," the auditor easily can raise control environment issues for this operating unit. However, the auditor should exercise extreme caution before attempting to check on the background and training of some individual manager at the headquarters facility. A personality conflict or difference of opinion is no reason to question someone's competence.

(C) BOARD OF DIRECTORS AND AUDIT COMMITTEE

The control environment is very much influenced by the actions of an organization's board of directors and its audit committee. In the years prior to SOA, boards and their audit committees often were dominated by senior organization management, with only limited, minority representation from outside directors. This created situations where the boards were not totally independent of management. Company officers sat on the board and were, in effect, managing themselves, often with less concern for the outside investors. As discussed in Chapter 3, SOA has changed all of that. Boards now have a more important corporate governance role, and audit committees are required to be truly independent

An active and independent board is an essential component of an organization's control environment. These independent board members should ask appropriate questions of top management and should give all aspects of the organization their detailed scrutiny. By setting high-level policies and by reviewing overall organization conduct, the board and its audit committee have the ultimate responsibility for setting this "tone at the top." Even if not required by SOA, this same principle applies to the board of directors of a private organization or boards of trustees for not-for-profit and other public bodies.

(D) MANAGEMENT'S PHILOSOPHY AND OPERATING STYLE

The philosophy and operating style of top management has a considerable influence over an organization's control environment. Some top-level managers frequently take significant organizational risks in their new business or product ventures, while others are very cautious or conservative. Some managers seem to operate by the "seat of the pants," while others insist that everything must be properly approved and documented. Still others take very aggressive approaches in their interpretations of tax- and financial-reporting rules, while others go by the book. These comments do not necessarily mean that one approach is always good and the other bad. A small, entrepreneurial organization may be forced to take certain business risks to remain competitive, while one in a highly regulated industry would be risk averse. Called an organization's appetite for risk, this concept is discussed in Chapter 5.

These management philosophy and operational style considerations are all part of the control environment for an organization. Internal auditors and others responsible for assessing internal controls should understand these factors and take them into consideration when evaluating the effectiveness of internal controls. While no one set of styles and philosophies is always the best for all organizations, these factors are important when considering the other components of internal control in an organization.

(E) ORGANIZATIONAL STRUCTURE

The organizational structure component provides a framework for planning, executing, controlling, and monitoring activities for achieving overall objectives. This is an aspect of the control environment that relates to the way various functions are managed and organized, following the classic organization chart. Some organizations are highly centralized, while others are decentralized by product, geography or other factors. Still others are organized in a matrix manner with no single direct lines of reporting. Organizational structure is a very important aspect of the organization's control environment. No one structure provides a preferred environment for internal controls.

There are many ways in which the various components of an organization can be assembled. Organizational control is a part of a larger control process. The term *organization* is often used interchangeably with the term *organizing* and means about the same thing to many people. *Organization* sometimes refers to hierarchical relationships between people but is also used broadly to include all of the problems of management. This book and other sources generally use the term organization to refer to the organizational entity, such as a corporation, a not-for-profit association, or any organized group. This section considers the organization as the set of *organizational arrangements* developed as a result of the organizing process.

An organization can be described as the way individual work efforts are both assigned and subsequently integrated for the achievement of overall goals. While in a sense this concept could be applied to the manner in which a single individual organizes individual efforts, it is more applicable when a number of people are involved in a group effort. For a large modern corporation, a strong plan of organization control is an important component of the system of internal control. Individuals and subgroups must have an understanding of the total goals and objectives of the group or entity of which they are a part. Without such an understanding, there can be significant control weaknesses.

Every organization or entity—whether a business, government, philanthropic, or other type of unit—needs an effective plan of organization. The internal auditor needs to have a good understanding of this organizational structure and the resultant reporting relationships, whether a functional, decentralized or matrix organizational structure. Often, a weakness in organizational controls can have a pervasive effect throughout the total control environment. Despite clear lines of authority, organizations sometimes have built-in inefficiencies that become greater as the size of the organization expands. These inefficiencies can often cause control procedures to break down, and the auditor should be aware of them when evaluating the organizational control environment in the functional organization.

(F) ASSIGNMENT OF AUTHORITY AND RESPONSIBILITY

This area of the control environment, as defined by COSO, is similar to the organizational structure area previously discussed. An organization's structure defines the assignment and integration of the total work effort. The assignment of authority is essentially the way responsibilities are defined in terms of job descriptions and structured in terms of organization charts. Although job assignments can never fully escape some overlapping or joint responsibilities, the more precisely these responsibilities can be stated, the better. The decision of how responsibilities will be assigned is often concerned with avoiding confusion and conflict among individual and group work efforts.

Many organizations of all types and sizes today have streamlined operations and pushed their decision-making authority downward and closer to the front-line personnel. The idea is that these front-line employees should have the knowledge and power to make important decisions in their own area of operations rather than be required to pass the request for a decision up through organization channels. The critical challenge that goes with this delegation or empowerment is that although it can delegate some authority in order to achieve organizational objectives, senior management is ultimately responsible for any decisions made by those subordinates. An organization can place itself at risk if too many decisions involving higher-level objectives are assigned at inappropriately lower levels without adequate management review. In addition, each person in the organization must have a good understanding of the organization's overall objectives as well as how his or her individual actions interrelate to achieve those objectives. The framework section of the actual COSO report describes this very important area of the control environment as follows:

> The control environment is greatly influenced by the extent to which individuals recognize they will be held accountable. This holds true all the way to the chief executive, who has ultimate responsibility for all activities within an entity, including internal control system.

(G) HUMAN RESOURCES POLICIES AND PRACTICES

Human resources practices cover such areas as hiring, orientation, training, evaluating, counseling, promoting, compensating, and taking appropriate remedial action. While the human resources function should have adequate published policies in these areas, their actual practices send strong messages to employees regarding their expected levels of ethical behavior and competence. The higher-level employee who openly abuses a human resources policy, such as a plant smoking ban, quickly sends a message to other levels in the organization. The message grows even louder when a lower-level employee is disciplined for the same unauthorized cigarette, while everyone looks the other way at the higher-level violator.

Areas where these human resources policies and practices are particularly important include:

- *Recruitment and Hiring.* The organization should take steps to hire the best, most-qualified candidates. Potential employees' backgrounds should be checked to verify their education and prior work experience. Interviews should be well organized and in depth. They should also transmit a message to the prospective candidate about the organization's values, culture, and operating style.

- *New Employee Orientation.* A clear signal should be given to new employees regarding the organization's value system and the consequences of not complying with those values. This is when new employees are introduced to the code of conduct and asked to formally acknowledgment acceptance of that code. Without these messages, new employees may join the organization lacking an appropriate understanding of its values.

- *Evaluation, Promotion, and Compensation.* There should be a fair performance-evaluation program in place that is not subject to an excessive amount of managerial discretion. Because issues such as evaluation and compensation can violate employee confidentiality, the overall system should be established in a manner that appears to be fair to all members of the organization. Bonus incentive programs are often useful tools to motivate and reinforce outstanding performance by all employees.

- *Disciplinary Actions.* Consistent and well-understood policies for disciplinary actions should be in place. All employees should know that if they violate certain rules, they will be subject to a progression of disciplinary actions leading up to dismissal. The organization should take care to ensure that no double standard exists for disciplinary actions—or, if any such double standard does exist, that higher-level employees are subject to even more severe disciplinary actions.

Effective human resource policies and procedures are a critical component in the overall control environment. Messages from the top of strong organizational structures will accomplish little if the organization does not have strong human resources policies and procedures in place. Internal audit should always consider this element of the control environment when performing reviews of other elements of the internal control framework.

(H) COSO CONTROL ENVIRONMENT IN PERSPECTIVE

Exhibit 4.2 showed the components of internal control as a pyramid, with the control environment as the lowest, or foundation, component. This concept of the control environment acting as the foundation is very appropriate. Just as a strong foundation is necessary for a multistory building, the control environment provides the foundation for the other components of internal control. An organization that is building a strong internal control structure should give special attention to placing solid foundation bricks in this control environment foundation.

Internal auditors should always be aware of the control environment components in place when performing reviews of their organizations. In many instances, internal audit may find internal control exceptions in other areas of their review that are attributable to the lack of a strong control environment foundation. For example, they may find that employees in a given unit are violating some travel expense rule that is defined in a company policy statement. The excuse by local management may be that the rule doesn't apply to them or that everyone is doing what the auditors found. Depending on the nature of the issue, this may be a situation where internal audit should talk with appropriate persons in senior management and point out the control environment problem here.

(ii) COSO Internal Control Elements: Risk Assessment. With reference back to the Exhibit 4.2 COSO pyramid, the next level or layer above the Control Foundation is Risk Assessment. An organization's ability to achieve its objectives can be at risk due to a variety of internal and external factors. As part of its overall control structure, an organization should have a process in place to evaluate the potential risks that may have an impact on the attainment of its various objectives. While this type of risk-assessment process does not need to be a formal quantitative risk-assessment process as discussed in Chapter 5 there should be a minimum understanding of the risk assessment process for an entity. An organization that has an informal objective of "no changes" in its marketing plans may want to assess the risk of not achieving that objective due to the entry of new competitors that may place pressures on the objective of doing the same as in the prior year. Risk assessment should be a forward-looking process. That is, many organizations have found that the best time and place to assess their various levels of risks is during annual or periodic planning process. This risk-assessment process should be performed at all levels and for virtually all activities within the organization. COSO describes Risk Assessment as a three-step process:

1. Estimate the significance of the risk.

2. Assess the likelihood or frequency of the risk occurring.

3. Consider how the risk should be managed and assess what actions must be taken.

The COSO risk assessment process puts the responsibility on management to go through the steps to assess whether a risk is significant and then, if so, to take appropriate actions. This process should be familiar to internal auditors. For example, Chapter 18, "Business Continuity Planning and Disaster Recovery," discusses computer security risk assessment issues as part of business continuity planning. This is the process whereby an auditor might assess both whether a computerized application is critical to the organization and whether it has an adequate disaster recovery backup plan. Internal audit can assist members of management who are not familiar with this type of a risk assessment process.

COSO emphasizes that risk analysis is not a theoretical process, but often can be critical to an entity's overall success. As part of its overall assessment of internal control, management should take steps to assess the risks that may affect the overall organization as well as the risks over various organization activities or entities. A variety of risks, caused by either internal or external sources, may affect the overall organization.

(A) ORGANIZATIONAL RISKS FROM EXTERNAL FACTORS

Technological developments can affect the nature and timing of research and development, or lead to changes in procurement processes. Other external factor risks include changing customer needs or expectations that can affect product development, production, pricing, warranties, or competition that can alter marketing or service activities. New legislation or regulations can force changes in operating policies or strategies, and catastrophes, such as the World Trade Center 9/11 terrorist attack, can lead to changes in operations and highlight the need for contingency planning.

(B) ORGANIZATIONAL RISKS FROM INTERNAL FACTORS

A disruption in the organization's information systems processing facility can adversely affect the entity's overall operations. Also, the quality of personnel hired and methods of training and motivation can influence the level of control consciousness within the entity, and the extent of employee accessibility to assets, can contribute to misappropriation of resources. Although now remedied by SOA, the COSO report also cited the risk of an unassertive or ineffective board or audit committee that can provide opportunities for indiscretions.

(C) SPECIFIC ACTIVITY-LEVEL RISKS

In addition to organization-wide risks, consideration should also be given to the risks at each significant business unit and key activity, such as marketing or information systems. These activity-level concerns contribute to the organization-wide risks and should be identified on an ongoing basis, built into various planning processes throughout the organization. Internal auditors should be aware of the risk assessment processes in place for various activities and should assess their effectiveness when performing reviews over these activities. Where no such risk assessment process exists, internal audit should highlight this need as an audit report finding and recommendation.

All too often, management may have a process in place that gives the appearance of risk assessment but lacks any substance. For example, a new product authorization approval form will have a box for the requester to describe the level of risks associated with the proposed product. Local management may consistently describe them as "low," with no further analysis. This assessment may not even be questioned until there is some type of massive failure. When performing reviews in these areas, internal auditors should ask to see the analysis or to discuss the reasoning behind the "low" risk assessment. If nothing exists, the auditor will have an issue to report to senior management.

The risk assessment element of COSO is an area where there has been recently much misunderstanding and confusion. COSO recently released a new framework called the Enterprise Risk Model (ERM) as a way for an overall enterprise to understand and evaluate "big picture" ERM risks. As this book goes to press, ERM has just been finalized after its draft release; it will be discussed in some detail in Chapter 5. Because both frameworks were released by the same COSO organization and because the framework models look similar, some have mistaken ERM for a replacement for COSO. This is not the case. The COSO framework described here covers internal controls for an individual entity within an enterprise with risk assessment being one factor. The new ERM framework covers the entire entity and beyond. These are really two separate issues and one is not a replacement for the other. Assessing risk and the new ERM framework will be discussed in Chapter 5.

(iii) COSO Internal Control Elements: Control Activities. The next layer in the COSO internal control model is called control activities. These are the policies and procedures that help ensure that actions identified to address risks are carried out. This internal control component includes a wide range of activities and procedures, from establishing organization standards with appropriate segregation of duties to reviewing and approving key operations reports properly. Control activities should exist at all levels within the organization, and in many cases, they may overlap one another.

The concept of control activities should be familiar to the internal auditor who develops a procedure to sample a set of invoice records from an A/P system to test whether invoices were properly coded and discounts properly calculated. The control activity here is to determine if the invoices were correctly handled. The audit procedure may be to use sampling techniques to select a representative set of these invoice records, and then to check each of the selected items for compliance with selected control criteria. Just as an internal auditor performs such control activities, other levels of management should have similar control activities in place to ascertain that their control objectives in various areas are being achieved.

(A) TYPES OF CONTROL ACTIVITIES

Many different definitions of controls are used, including manual, computer system, or management controls, or preventive, corrective, and detective. While no one set of control definitions is correct for all management situations or for all organizations, COSO suggests a series of control activities that might be implemented by an organization. While certainly not an all-inclusive list, the following list represents the range and variety of control activities in the modern organization:

- *Top-Level Reviews.*   Management at various levels should review the results of their performance, contrasting those results with budgets, competitive statistics, and other benchmark measurements. Management actions to follow up on the results of these top-level reviews and to take corrective action represent a control activity.

- *Direct Functional or Activity Management.*   Managers at various levels should review the operational reports from their control systems and take corrective action as appropriate. Many management systems have been built to produce a series of exception reports covering various activities.

For example, a computer security system will have a mechanism to report unauthorized access attempts. The control activity here is the management process of following up on these reported events and taking appropriate corrective action.

- *Information Processing.* Information systems contain many controls where systems check for compliance in a variety of areas and then report any exceptions. Those reported exception items should receive corrective action by systems automated procedures, by operational personnel or by management. Other control activities here include controls over the development of new systems or over access to data and program files.

- *Physical Controls.* An organization should have appropriate control over its physical assets, including fixtures, inventories, and negotiable securities. An active program of periodic physical inventories represents a major control activity.

- *Performance Indicators.* Management should relate sets of data, both operational and financial, to one another and take appropriate analytical, investigative, or corrective action. This process represents an important organization control activity that can also satisfy financial- and operational-reporting requirements.

- *Segregation of Duties.* Duties should be divided or segregated among different people to reduce the risk of error or inappropriate actions. This is a basic internal control procedure.

These items, included in the COSO report, represent only a small number of the many control activities performed as part of the normal course of business. These and other activities keep an organization on track toward achieving its many objectives. Control activities usually involve both a policy establishing what should be done and procedures to affect those policies. While these control activities may sometimes only be communicated orally by appropriate levels of management, COSO points out that no matter how a policy is communicated, it should be implemented "thoughtfully, conscientiously, and consistently." This is a strong message for internal auditors reviewing control activities. Even though an organization may have a published policy covering a given area, an internal auditor should review the established control procedure that supports the policy. Procedures are of little use unless there is a sharp focus on the condition to which the policy is directed. All too often, an organization may establish an exception report as part of an automated system that receives little more than a cursory review by the report's recipients. However, depending on the types of conditions reported, those exceptions should receive appropriate follow-up action, which may vary depending on the size of the organization and the activity reported in the exception report.

(B) INTEGRATION OF CONTROL ACTIVITIES WITH RISK ASSESSMENT

Control activities should be closely related to the identified risks discussed previously as part of the COSO risk assessment component. Internal control is a process, and appropriate control activities should be installed to address identified risks. Control activities should not be installed just because they seem to be the "right thing to do" if management has identified no significant risks in the area where the control activity would be installed. All too often, management may still have control activities or procedures in place that perhaps once served some control-risk concern, although the concerns have largely gone away. A control activity or procedure should not be discarded because there have not been control violation incidents in recent years, but management needs periodically to reevaluate the relative risks. All control activities should contribute to the overall control structure.

The previous comments refer to what might be called "dumb" control activities that once had a purpose but currently accomplish little. For example, business data processing computer operations centers, up through the 1970s, had input-output clerks who manually checked file-record count reports from various programs in automated systems. Computer operating system facilities effectively automated those control procedures long ago, but some organizations continued to employ these procedures long after they were needed. If there had been a record count exception, the operating system would have flagged the problem and initiated corrective action long before any reports were delivered. This is a "dumb" control because it now accomplishes little or nothing in today's control environment. While some controls will cease to have importance, other basic controls, such as a strong separation of duties between incompatible functions, should always remain in effect.

(C) CONTROLS OVER INFORMATION SYSTEMS

COSO emphasizes that control procedures are needed for all significant information systems—financial, operational, and compliance related. With information systems controls a key activity in the overall control environment, COSO breaks down information systems controls into general and application controls. General controls apply to much of the information systems function to help ensure adequate control procedures over all applications. A physical security lock on the door to the computer center is such a control that as a general control for all applications running at that data center.

Application controls refer to specific information systems applications. A control in a weekly payroll application program that flags as a potential error any employee from being paid for over 80 hours in a given week is an example of an application reasonableness control. People may work extra hours, but it is doubtful many will record over 80 hours in a week. COSO highlights a series of information systems control areas for evaluating the overall adequacy of internal controls. General controls include all centralized data center or computer systems controls, including job scheduling, storage management, and disaster recovery planning. These controls typically are the responsibility of data operations specialists in centralized computer or server centers. However, with newer, more modern systems connected to one another through telecommunications links, these controls can be distributed across a network of server-based systems.

COSO concludes with a discussion on the need to consider the impact of evolving technologies whose impact should always be considered when evaluating information systems control activities. Due to the rapid introduction of new technologies in many businesses, what is new today will be considered mature tomorrow and will soon be replaced by something else. COSO has not introduced anything new with regard to information systems controls, but has highlighted this subject's importance in the overall internal control environment. Again, the effective internal auditor needs to have a strong understanding of information systems controls such as will be discussed in Part Five of this book, Chapters 18 to 23.

(iv) COSO Internal Control Elements: Communications and Information. The Exhibit 3.2 pyramid model of COSO internal controls framework describes most components as layers, one on top of another starting with the control environment as the first layer or foundation. The information and communication component, however, is not a horizontal layer but spans all of the other components. In the original draft of COSO, information and communication were treated as two separate components, to make the framework less complex, they were combined in the final draft. Information and communication are related, but are really very distinct internal control components. Both are important portions of the internal control framework. Appropriate information, supported by automated systems, must be communicated up and down the organization in a manner and time frame that allow people to carry out their responsibilities. In addition to formal and informal communication systems, organizations must have effective procedures in place to communicate with internal and external parties. As part of any evaluation of internal controls, there is a need to have a good understanding of the information and communication flows or processes in the organization.

(A) RELATIONSHIP OF INFORMATION AND INTERNAL CONTROL

Various types of information are needed at all levels of the organization in order to achieve operational, financial reporting, and compliance objectives. The organization needs proper information to prepare the financial reports that are communicated to outside investors. It also needs both internal cost information and external market preference information to make correct marketing decisions. This information must flow both from the top levels of the organization on down to lower levels. COSO takes a broad approach to the concept of an information system; it recognizes the importance of automated systems, but makes the point that information systems can be manual, automated, or conceptual. Any of these information systems can be either formal or informal. Regular conversations with customers or suppliers can be highly important sources of information and are an informal type of an information system. The effective organization should have information systems in place to listen to customer requests or complaints and to forward that customer-initiated information to appropriate personnel.

The COSO framework also emphasizes the importance of keeping information and supporting systems consistent with overall organizational needs. Information systems adapt to support changes on many levels. Internal auditors often encounter cases where an information system was implemented years before to support different needs. Although its application controls may be good, the information system may not support the current needs of the organization.

COSO takes a broad view of information systems, both automated and manual, and points to the need to understand both manual systems processes and automated systems technologies.

Strategic and Integrated Systems. Accounting and financial processes were the first automated systems in organizations, starting with the unit record or "IBM card" accounting machines in the 1950s and then moving to the earliest computer systems. Most organizations have upgraded their automated systems over time, but their basic mix of supporting automated applications may not have changed significantly. An organization will have its general ledger, payroll, inventory, accounts receivable, accounts payable, and related financial-based processes as core information systems, without too much else. COSO suggests that the effective organization should go a step further and implement both strategic and integrated information systems.

By a strategic system, the COSO report suggests that management should consider the planning, design, and implementation of its information systems as part of its overall organizational strategy. These strategic systems then support the organization's business and help it to carry out its overall business missions. There have been many examples of companies that developed strategic information systems to support their business strategies—systems that moved them even further forward. Examples here range from American Airlines, which developed its SABRE automated reservation system back in the 1960s, greatly enhancing its ability to sell tickets and make more effective use of its resources to Amazon.com, Inc. with its fairly recent one-click order fulfillment system for customer Internet book orders. Not every organization has the resources or needs to develop systems of the nature or scale of SABRE or Amazon; however, even smaller systems should be designed and developed to support the organization's strategies. These strategic systems will allow organizations to understand and to respond better to changes in their marketplaces and control environments.

COSO also emphasizes the importance of integrating automated information systems with other operations. Examples would be a fully automated manufacturing system that controls both production machines and equipment inventories or a highly automated distribution system that controls inventory and schedules shipments. These comments about strategic information systems are a step forward or into the future when contrasted with the information systems–related comments from earlier internal control standards. COSO makes the point, however, that it is a mistake to assume that just because a system is new, it will provide better control. Older systems have presumably been tried and tested through use, while the new system can have unknown or untested control weaknesses. The internal auditor can play a significant role in assessing whether controls are adequate in new automated systems by reviewing these new systems while under development.

Quality of Information. COSO has a brief report section on the importance of the quality of information. Poor-quality information systems, filled with errors and omissions, affect management's ability to make appropriate decisions. Reports should contain enough data and information to support effective control activities. Ensuring the quality of information includes ascertaining whether:

- The content of reported information is appropriate.
- The information is timely and available when required.
- The information is current or at least the latest available.
- The data and information are correct.
- The information is accessible to appropriate parties.

These points all circle back to today's SOA requirements. While the COSO framework holds up these quality of information points as objectives, SOA now effectively makes them requirements. As discussed in our SOA overview in Chapter 3, the CFO is effectively attesting to these points as they pertain to an organization's financial statements.

Internal auditors should always be aware of the quality of the information produced by all manual and automated systems. This concern goes beyond the traditional role of auditors, who have historically looked only at systems controls and given little attention to quality-related issues. Internal audit quality assurance practices will be discussed in Chapter 26, "Internal Audit Quality-Assurance and ASQ Quality Audits."

(B) COMMUNICATIONS ASPECT OF INTERNAL CONTROL

Communications is defined as an internal control element separate from information in this component of COSO's internal control framework. Communication channels provide the details to individuals to carry out their financial-reporting, operational, and compliance responsibilities. COSO emphasizes that communication must take place in a broader sense in dealing with various individuals and groups and their expectations. The existence of appropriate channels of communication is an important element in the overall framework of internal control. An organization needs to establish these communication channels throughout its various organization levels and activities, and between the organization and various interested outsiders. Although communication channels can have many dimensions, COSO highlights the separate components of internal and external communications. Internal auditors have always focused on formal channels of communication such as needs procedure manuals or published systems documentation. Internal audit reports frequently cite entities for a lack of documentation in their reviews. While that documentation is a very important element of communication, COSO takes an expanded view when considering internal control.

Communications: Internal Components. According to COSO, perhaps the most important component of communication is that all personnel should periodically receive messages from senior management reminding them that their internal control responsibilities must be taken seriously. The clarity of this message is important to ensure that the overall organization follows effective internal control principles. This message is part of the tone at the top, discussed earlier as part of the control environment, and it should be communicated throughout the organization.

In addition to these overall messages, all organizational stakeholders need to understand how their specific duties and actions fit into the total internal control system. If this understanding is not present, various parties in the organization will ignore errors and make decisions thinking no one cares. This is really the concept of an organization mission statement, as discussed in Chapter 9.

All stakeholders need to know limits and boundaries and when their activities may become unethical, illegal, or otherwise improper. People also need to know how to respond to errors or other unexpected events in the course of performing their duties. They typically require communication in terms of messages from management, procedure documentation, and adequate training. Internal auditors often encounter these issues in the course of their reviews. While auditors may have historically presented some audit report finding about a lack of documentation and treating it as a fairly minor point, both COSO and SOA emphasize that this lack of documentation may mean a lack of appropriate internal control communication channels.

Communication must flow in two directions, and COSO emphasizes that stakeholders must have a mechanism to report matters upward throughout the organization. This upward communication has two components: communication through normal channels and special, confidential reporting channels. Normal reporting refers to the process in which members of the organizations are expected to report status information, errors, or problems up through their supervisors. This communication should be freely encouraged, and the organization should avoid "shooting the messenger" when bad news is reported. Otherwise, it will be understood throughout the organization that employees should report only good news, and managers may not become aware of significant problems. Because personnel may sometimes be reluctant to report matters to their immediate supervisors, the whistleblower programs discussed in Chapter 9 are essential. This section of COSO concludes with a discussion of the importance of communication channels between top management and the board of directors. Per the COSO framework now in place for over 20 years, management should take care to inform the board of major developments, risks, and occurrences. The board, in turn, must independently review operations and communicate their concerns and decisions to management. These were recommendations as part of the COSO framework that did not receive sufficient attention until they became the law through SOA.

External Communication. Organizations need to establish appropriate communication channels with interested outside parties including customers, suppliers, shareholders, bankers, regulators, and others. This communication should go beyond the public relations–type of function that large organizations often establish to talk about themselves. Similar to internal communication channels, external information must flow in two directions. The information provided to outside parties should be relevant to their needs so they can better understand an organization and the challenges it faces. The organization that sends out highly optimistic reports to outsiders when many inside the organization realize there are problems is also giving an inappropriate message to its own employees. This is what was occurring in the events leading up to SOA when some organizations were reporting fraudulent results.

External communications also can be a very important way to identify potential control problems. Customer complaints, involving such matters as service, billings, or product quality, often can point out significant operating and control problems. There should be independent mechanisms established to receive these messages and to appropriately act on them. This form of communication should be investigated and corrective action taken when necessary.

Management should also establish appropriate communication channels with outside parties such as financial analysts or even regulators. Open and frank two-way communications may alert the organization to potential communication problems or allow it to discuss and solve any problems in advance of adverse publicity.

Means and Methods of Communication. There is no one correct means of communicating internal control information within the organization. The modern organization can communicate its messages through many vehicles, including bulletin board announcements, procedure manuals, Webcasts, videotaped presentations, or speeches by members of management. Often, however, the action taken by the communicator either before or after the message will give a stronger signal to the recipients of that communication. COSO summarizes this internal control element as follows:

> An entity with a long and rich history of operating with integrity, and whose culture is well understood by people through the organization, will likely find little difficulty in communicating its message. An entity without such a tradition will likely need to put more into the way the messages are communicated.

(v) COSO Internal Control Elements: Monitoring. The capstone of the pyramid internal control framework model, as shown in Exhibit 4.2, is the monitoring component. While internal control systems will work effectively with proper support from management, control procedures, and both information and communication linkages, a process must be in place to monitor these activities. Monitoring activities has long been the role of internal auditors, who perform reviews to assess compliance with established procedures; however, COSO now takes a broader view of monitoring while still reserving a significant portion of that activity to internal audit.

COSO recognizes that control procedures and other systems change over time. What appeared to be effective when it was first installed may not be that effective in the future due to changing external conditions, new personnel, new systems and procedures, and other factors. A process should be in place to assess the effectiveness of established internal control components and to take corrective action when appropriate. While this certainly points to the role of internal audit, this internal control component cannot be relegated to the auditors while management remains somewhat oblivious to potential control problems. An organization needs to establish a variety of monitoring activities to measure the effectiveness of its internal controls.

Monitoring can be accomplished through a series of separate evaluations as well as through ongoing activities. The latter—ongoing activities—refer to processes that monitor performance and make corrective action when required.

(A) ONGOING MONITOR ACTIVITIES

Many routine business functions can be characterized as monitoring activities. Although auditors and others do not always think of these in that sense, COSO gives the following examples of the ongoing monitoring component of internal control:

- *Operating Management Normal Functions.* Normal management reviews over operations and financial reports constitute an important ongoing monitoring activity. However, special attention should be given to reported exceptions and potential internal control deviations. Internal control is enhanced if reports are reviewed on a regular basis and corrective action initiated for any reported exceptions.

- *Communications from External Parties.* This element of monitoring is closely related to the component of communication from external parties discussed earlier. External communication measuring monitors, such as a customer complaint telephone number, are important; however, the organization needs to monitor closely these calls and then initiate corrective action when appropriate.

- *Organization Structure and Supervisory Activities.* While more senior management should review summary reports and take corrective action, the first level of supervision and the related organizational structure often plays an even more significant role in monitoring. Direct supervision of clerical activities, for example, should routinely review and correct lower-level errors and ensure improved clerical employee performance. This review is also an area in which the importance of an adequate separation of duties is emphasized by COSO. Dividing duties between employees allows them to serve as a monitoring check on one another.

- *Physical Inventories and Asset Reconciliation.* Periodic physical inventories, whether of store room stock or negotiable securities, are an important monitoring activity. An annual inventory in a retail store, for example, may indicate a significant merchandise loss. A possible reason for this loss could be theft, pointing to the need for better security controls.

These are examples from a longer list in the COSO report. They illustrate procedures that are often in place in organizations but are not thought of as ongoing monitoring activities. Any activity that reviews organizational activities on a regular basis and then suggests potential corrective actions can be thought of as a monitoring activity.

(B) SEPARATE INTERNAL CONTROL EVALUATION

While COSO points out the importance of ongoing monitoring activities to support the internal control framework, COSO also suggests that "it may be useful to take a fresh look from time to time" at the effectiveness of internal controls through separate evaluations. The frequency and nature of these separate special reviews will greatly depend on the nature of the organization and the significance of the risks it must control. While management may want to periodically initiate an evaluation of its entire internal control system, most reviews should be initiated to assess a specific area of control. These reviews may often be initiated when there has been an acquisition, a significant change in business, or some other significant activity.

COSO also emphasizes that these evaluations can be performed by direct line management through self-assessment types of reviews. Internal audit is not required to perform the review unless requested by senior management; the scheduling of these will be dependent on audit's risk assessment process and the resources available to schedule and perform reviews. Considerable time may pass before internal audit may have scheduled a normal review in a given area of operation. However, responsible management in that area should consider scheduling and performing its own self-assessments on a more regular basis. Chapter 27, "Control Self-Assessments," discusses how internal audit can aid the organization through formal control self-assessment processes. The internally generated review can point out potential control problems and cause operating management to implement corrective action. Because these self-assessment reviews will typically not be as comprehensive as normal audit assessments, internal audit can be requested to perform a more comprehensive review over the same general area if potentially significant problems are encountered through such a limited review.

Internal Control Evaluation Process. COSO talks about the evaluation process for reviewing a system of internal controls. The controls evaluator should first develop an understanding of the system design, identify its controls, test those controls, and then develop conclusions on the basis of the test results. This is really the internal audit process. COSO also mentions another approach for evaluation called *benchmarking,* an approach that is occasionally performed by internal auditors. Benchmarking is the process of comparing an organization's processes, control procedures, and other activities with those of peer organizations. Comparisons may be made with specific similar organizations or against published statistics from similar industry groups. This approach is convenient for some types of measurement but filled with dangers for others. For example, it is fairly easy to benchmark the organization's size, staffing levels, and average compensations of a sales function against comparable organizations in the same general industry; however, the evaluator may encounter difficulties in trying to compare other factors due to the many small differences that make all organizations unique. The control self-assessment process described in Chapter 27 is an alternative approach that may achieve some of the benefits of benchmarking without going through an extended analysis.

Evaluation Action Plans. COSO discusses the importance of control documentation, particularly when statements about controls are made to outside parties. However, COSO recognizes that not all control procedures lend themselves to formal documentation. Many are informal and undocumented although regularly performed and highly effective. COSO makes the point that these undocumented controls can be tested and evaluated in the same manner as documented ones. While an appropriate level of documentation makes any evaluation of internal control more efficient and facilitates employees' understanding of how the process works, that documentation is not always essential.

These COSO comments about undocumented system documentation seem to run almost contrary to SOA provisions discussed earlier in Chapter 3. The external auditors reviewing an organization's internal financial controls systems will almost certainly request to see some level of systems documentation as part of their assertion review work. If an existing process is informal and undocumented but effective, the review team will need to prepare some level of its own documentation to explain how the process works and the nature of its internal controls.

(C) REPORTING INTERNAL CONTROL DEFICIENCIES

Whether internal control deficiencies are identified through processes in the internal control system itself, through monitoring activities, or through other external events, these internal control deficiencies should be reported to appropriate levels of management in the organization. The key question for the internal audit evaluator is to determine what should be reported given the large body of details that may be encountered, and to whom the reports should be directed. COSO states that "all internal control deficiencies that can affect the entity's attaining its objectives should be reported to those who can take necessary action." While this statement initially makes sense, the experienced internal auditor will realize that this directive is difficult to implement.

The modern organization, no matter how well organized, can be guilty of a variety of internal control errors or omissions. COSO suggests that all of these should be identified and reported, and that even the most minor of errors should be investigated to understand if they were caused by any overall control deficiencies. The report uses the example of an employee's taking a few dollars from the petty cash fund. While the amount may not be significant, COSO urges that the matter be investigated rather than ignored, since "such apparent condoning personal use of the entity's money might send an unintended message to employees." External auditors regularly apply the concept of materiality when performing their reviews. That is, they may decide that some errors and irregularities are so small that they are not material to the overall conclusion that the external auditor will reach. While the operational efficiency of administrative control is of prime importance, materiality should also be considered when evaluating internal controls in general. SOA does not really discuss materiality issues, but it certainly will be a major factor in an external auditor's Section 404 assessments or any enforcement actions.

COSO concludes by discussing to whom to report internal control deficiencies in the organization. In one paragraph, COSO provides guidance that is useful for evaluations:

> Findings on internal control deficiencies usually should be reported not only to the individual responsible for the function or activity involved, who is in the position to take corrective action, but also to at least one level of management above the directly responsible person. This process enables that individual to provide needed support or oversight for taking corrective action, and to communicate with others in the organization whose activities may be affected. Where findings cut across organizational boundaries, the reporting should cross over as well and be directed to a sufficiently high level to ensure appropriate action.

SOA has tightened up this COSO reporting guidance with its requirement for a formal Disclosure Committee, as briefly discussed in Chapter 6. Matters that appear to be of a material nature become an almost immediate CFO and audit committee reporting issue. The organization should also develop reporting procedures such that all internal financial control deficiencies, whether encountered through a SOA Section 404 review or through internal audit reviews of ongoing operations, are reported to appropriate levels of the organization. Management reporting and monitoring is a highly important aspect of internal control.

4.6 UNDERSTANDING, USING, AND DOCUMENTING COSO INTERNAL CONTROLS

The previous sections have provided an overview of the COSO internal control framework, a very important tool for today's modern internal auditor. There is much good guidance information in the previously referenced full COSO report and interested internal auditor can easily obtain access and download copies through the coso.org Web site. We have tried to highlight many of the important points in the COSO framework, but a detailed study will give much more valuable background information.

The next important step for an internal auditor is to use COSO concepts to understand and document internal controls. We will cover this in some detail for reviews of internal controls for several example systems or process areas in Chapter 6. Under what is called Section 404, SOA requires that organizations must understand, document, test, and evaluate the internal controls of major processes and systems. COSO is the suggested tool for this process, and the chapter will describe this COSO-based internal control review process.

We started this chapter with quotes about the importance of internal controls from the internal audit pioneers, Vic Brink and Larry Sawyer, with the latter's very important comment that internal controls are an internal auditor's "open sesame." An understanding of internal control processes will allow an internal auditor to look at and analyze a series of diverse business process steps and then visualize them in terms of an internal controls system.

Those "open sesame" comments were made when internal auditors and others did not have consistent approaches and definitions to understanding internal controls. Our earlier comments in this chapter pointed out some of these problems as well as the long road that external auditors and others have traveled to develop a consistent approach to understanding and evaluating internal controls. While the role of the likes of the Minahan Committee, discussed in this chapter, is primarily of interest to the researcher at this point in time, our explanation of what it took to get to COSO points out the importance of this important internal control framework approach or standard for auditors, management, and others.

ENDNOTES

[1] Lawrence B. Sawyer, *The Practice of Modern Internal Auditing,* Altamonte Springs, FL: The Institute of Internal Auditors, 1988.
[2] American Institute of Certified Public Accountants, "Statement on Auditing Standards No. 1," New York: AICPA, last updated in 2002.

[3] Kenneth A. Merchant, *Fraudulent and Questionable Financial Reporting: A Corporate Perspective*, Morristown, NJ: Financial Executives Research Foundation, 1980.

[4] R. K. Mautz and J. Winjum, *Criteria for Management Control Systems*, Morristown, NJ: Financial Executives Research Foundation, 1981.

[5] Report of the National Commission on Fraudulent Financial Reporting, National Commission on Fraudulent Financial Reporting, 1987.

[6] Committee of Sponsoring Organizations of the Treadway Committee, Jersey City, NJ: AICPA, 1992.

CHAPTER FIVE

Understanding and Assessing Risks: Enterprise Risk Management

5.1 AUDITING AND UNDERSTANDING RISKS

Risk management has always been a component of internal audit planning and assessment processes. The idea was for internal auditors to have a formal process to help understand risks and to focus efforts in higher-risk areas. In the past, auditors often just used good audit judgment—common sense—to focus audit attention on riskier areas. It did not take too much audit analysis to decide that there were greater risks in controls surrounding treasury funds supporting the disbursement of stockholder dividends than internal controls for office petty cash. While certain of these risk-based decisions were easy, others were not as obvious. Internal auditors today should have a consistent approach for understanding and assessing the audit risks, both the risks associated with individual audit entities as well as overall risks facing their organization.

This chapter provides an approach to help internal auditors better understand the various risks that will have an impact on their audit activities, a process to select riskier areas for audit assessments, and procedures for internal auditor risk management. We will introduce the new Committee of Sponsoring Organizations (COSO) Enterprise Risk Management (ERM) framework that has just been released as this book goes to press but soon will almost certainly become an important standard for internal auditors and internal controls specialists. The chapter then introduces a methodology for assessing organization process risks, scoring and ranking those risks, and then for assessing and controlling those risks. Risk management is an important tool for the internal auditor. Today's modern internal auditor should focus on understanding relative risks when planning and developing internal audit activities.

5.2 UNDERSTANDING RISKS: COSO ENTERPRISE RISK MANAGEMENT INTEGRATED FRAMEWORK

Understanding risks is a very important part of the audit planning and delivery process. The effective auditor needs to focus the always limited audit resources on higher-risk areas, while deferring other lower-risk situations until more time or resources are available. The COSO internal control framework introduced in Chapter 4, "Internal Controls Fundamentals: COSO Framework," includes a risk assessment component. In order to understand and build effective internal controls, an internal auditor needs to understand the risk components of that overall COSO internal controls environment. However, while COSO tends to focus on risks within a process, the new Enterprise Risk Management (ERM) framework provides a tool to assess risks throughout the entire organization or enterprise.

In past years, many managers and internal auditors have not had a formal, consistent approach for analyzing and identifying higher-risk areas in their organizations. Some used elaborate approaches for identifying higher-risk processes, while others used little more than a "gut feel" or "seat of the pants" common-sense approaches. There has been a need for a formal risk analysis approach to provide an effective and consistent approach for evaluating and understanding the riskier areas in the organization. A consistent definition and approach to risk assessment and evaluation has been needed! This lack of a consistent definition of risk assessments is similar to the internal controls related conclusions of the Treadway Committee in its investigation of fraudulent financial reporting in 1978 as discussed in Chapter 4. Looking at the multiple reasons for fraudulent financial reporting, Treadway looked at internal controls and found that there was no consistent definition. The result then was the COSO internal controls framework, released in 1982 and now the all but totally recognized internal control framework standard. The COSO internal framework was discussed in Chapter 4.

Although there has not been a Treadway-type committee to raise these risk assessment issues, the COSO organization and others recognized the similar lack of a consistent definition for risk assessment and risk management. As a result, the same professional sponsoring organizations of COSO contracted with one of the major public accounting firms, PricewaterhouseCoopers (PwC) and launched a study to better understand and define risk management. The result was the Enterprise Risk Management (ERM) framework, first published in draft form in late 2003 and released in September, 2004 almost concurrent with the publication of this book. ERM provides a consistent and comprehensive framework or approach for understanding and evaluating risks for the overall organization, at an enterprise level.

This section provides an overview of the ERM framework, in its current draft format. While there may be some new interpretations in the just released final version of ERM, our description should be fairly similar to the final published ERM version. The following sections discuss how internal auditors can use this ERM framework to better understand, evaluate, and manage the risks they will encounter in their organizations and in their internal audit work. This ERM framework applies to all aspects of the organization and goes far beyond the individual process risk assessment described in Chapter 4 as an element of COSO.

Similarly to the COSO report, the ERM framework document starts at a very high level by defining Enterprise Risk Management as follows:

> Enterprise risk management is a process, effected by an entity's board of directors, management and other personnel, applied in strategy setting and across the enterprise, designed to identify potential events that may affect the entity, and manage risks to be within the risk appetite, to provide reasonable assurance regarding the achievement of entity objectives.

This ERM definition is a bit more complex than COSO's definition of internal control, as discussed in Chapter 4. The ERM framework introduces some newer concepts and terminology that will be used for considering risk management as well as some new concepts that have been used by specialized risk managers in the past, but are less familiar to many internal auditors. These newer ERM concepts should soon become part of the modern internal auditor's vocabulary:

- *ERM is a process.* As emphasized throughout this book, internal auditors should think in terms of *processes*, not applications or systems. Business processes represent an effective way to think of business activities with their defined beginning and ending points. Processes drive internal operations, streamline partner interactions, and set business rules for best practices. Well-defined processes form the basis for effective procedures and technology implementations. In the past, some have thought of the steps to pay a vendor bill just in terms of a traditional accounts payable system. However, thinking of this activity in terms of the vendor payable *process* often begins with the receipt and approval of vendor invoices, goes to an automated accounts payable system, and ends with the closeout and issuance of checks. Just as the vendor payable process is much more than just the accounts payable system, ERM should be thought of not as one system or procedure but as an overall organization-wide process.

  ERM is not one event or circumstance, but a series of actions that cover a wide range of entity activities. Because of the focus on risk, these actions should be pervasive and inherent in the way an organization is managed. Costs and cost containment should be a part of this ERM process thinking. Adding new processes, with an objective to improve risk management, can have important implications in the highly competitive marketplace that many organizations face. Adding new procedures separate from existing ones adds costs, and an organization should strive to build ERM processes into the fabric of existing operations.

- *ERM is affected by people.*   The people in any organization—the board of directors, management, employees, and related stakeholders—all significantly affect ERM processes by what they do and say. People's actions at all levels establish an organization's effective mission, strategy, and objectives. Although directors primarily provide oversight, they bring direction and approve strategy, certain transactions, and policies. While all employees and stakeholders are responsible for implementing and operating an effective ERM process, strong support from the board and senior management are essential. A strong "tone at the top" series of messages will ensure the success of organizational ERM processes. Without that strong message, cynics in the organization may view ERM-related messages as just another type of "slogan of the month" and will tend to ignore them.

   An ERM process will never be effective if only delivered as just a series of empty-sounding slogans or as thick procedures manuals that sit on bookshelves but receive little further attention. Even worse are the very complex Visio charts and Excel spreadsheets that are sometimes prepared to define a process. All members of the organization need to understand the importance of risk management throughout the overall organization and in their specific functions with respect to those organizational risks. A risk management process will never be effective unless it is embraced by a wide group of people in the organization.

- *ERM should be applied in setting organization strategy.*   An organization often defines itself through a formal mission statement and also establishes strategic objectives, the high-level goals that align with and support this mission. There is also a need to establish strategies to achieve those objectives, giving consideration to risks relative to any alternative strategies. These objectives should cascade throughout the organization, to its business units, divisions, and processes.

- *ERM must be applied across the organization.*   This aspect of ERM is almost implicit in the other elements of the ERM definition. To be a consistent risk management program, ERM must be applied consistently throughout all levels of the organization. Actions that take place at a corporate office level—often call the "C-level"—must also be applied at other less-senior levels. This implementation approach must go both ways. C-level practices should be communicated down to the "shop floor," and those front-line practices should be understood by senior organizational levels. While there are certainly responsibility and prerequisite differences here, broad ERM initiatives and themes should be applied consistently. A key ERM component here is what the ERM framework describes as the enterprise's risk appetite, as discussed in the next points.

- *Risk appetite should be considered.*   A concept *very key* to any ERM, "risk appetite" is the amount of risk that an organization is willing to accept in its pursuit of value. Depending on their business products, operating policies, and scope of operations, all organizations have different levels of risk appetites. This concept of risk appetite will be discussed throughout this introduction to ERM. For example, one organization may choose to open a facility in an underdeveloped country that may be risky but provides high potential returns. A different organization may seek to operate in less-risky but lower-return areas. These two alternatives are dependent on each organization's appetite for risk. Doing business in underdeveloped but potentially higher-return areas characterize an enterprise with a higher appetite for risk.

This concept of risk appetite is an important part of the COSO ERM. Internal auditors have always talked about the way that different organizations accept or tolerate risks, but ERM has clarified and better defined this practice through its use of the expression "risk appetite." It really says that there is nothing wrong with operating in either a high-risk or low-risk environment as long as management and the board recognize such a strategy and build various controls and procedures to limit the impacts of those risks occurring. The risk appetite philosophy, as defined by senior management, should be communicated and followed consistently throughout the organization.

- *ERM will only provide "reasonable assurance."* The term "reasonable assurance" is an auditing expression going back to the CPA's standard audit report. Because an auditor can never "guarantee" all aspects of an area reviewed, the CPA auditors reported findings by stating their observations and findings with a reasonable assurance—not 100%, but being fairly certain that the auditor's recommendations are accurate. Here a well-designed and operated ERM can provide management and the board of directors with reasonable assurances regarding the achievement of related objectives. In order for ERM to be effective in each of the categories of its entity objectives, the board, management, and internal audit should gain reasonable assurance that:

  o They understand the extent to which the organization's strategic as well as operations objectives are being achieved.
  o The organization's reporting is reliable.
  o They are in compliance with applicable laws and regulations.

  Reasonable assurance includes the notion that uncertainty and risk relate to the future, which no one can predict with certainty. Limitations also result from the realities that human judgment in decision making can be faulty, decisions on risk responses and establishing controls need to consider the relative costs and benefits, breakdowns can occur because of human failures such as simple errors or mistakes, controls can be circumvented because of collusion of two or more people, and management has the ability to override ERM decisions. These limitations preclude the board of directors and all levels of management from having absolute assurance that objectives will be achieved. This really says that no matter how strong or effective the supporting control processes, the possibility that something might not work should always be considered. That is a key element of risk management.

- *An effective ERM must focus on the achievement of objectives.* ERM can be expected to provide this reasonable assurance of achieving objectives relating to such areas as compliance with laws and regulations or the reliability of the organization's reporting. These matters are within an organization's sphere of control and are based on normal business activities. In other situations, the achievement of some strategic and operations objectives may be beyond the organization's span of control. Here ERM can only provide reasonable assurance that management and the board, in their oversight role, are made aware of the extent to which the organization is achieving their objectives, given these external and uncontrollable factors.

This definition of ERM defines the framework in a very broad manner. The pages that follow will discuss the ERM framework in some detail. ERM provides an important approach for thinking about risks and risk management—important for internal auditors whether specializing in information systems related auditing or any other internal auditing activity or for just general business operations.

5.3 ENTERPRISE RISK MANAGEMENT FRAMEWORK

Similar to the COSO internal control discussed in Chapter 4, ERM is described as a three-dimensional model with eight ERM levels, with ERM Monitoring at the base or foundation level and going up through the ERM framework with the Internal Environment at the top of the model. The framework model is further sliced from the front to back into four components, risks at an overall entity level, by division within that entity, by business unit, and by subsidiary. The concept here is that enterprise-level risks should be considered in terms of the total organization or enterprise and level by level for business subsidiaries. ERM, and each of its components, should be considered in the context of the total organization and through individual subsidiaries at a profit center type of level.

The ERM is further sliced in a third dimension with separate consideration for compliance, reporting, operating, and strategic ERM issues. Exhibit 5.1 shows

EXHIBIT 5.1

COSO Enterprise Risk Management Framework

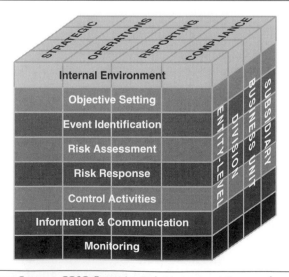

Source: PricewaterhouseCoopers, COSO Enterprise Risk Management Framework, copyright © American Institute of Public Accountants (AICPA), 2004

this ERM framework. The concept is that risks should be assessed and managed within any of these three dimensions with consideration given to other risk elements in the three-dimensional model. At first glance, this looks very similar to the COSO internal control model shown in Exhibit 4.3, but the ERM framework covers and describes enterprise-level risks rather than the internal control considerations of COSO. ERM is relevant to the entire organization as well as to individual business units, but this ERM framework allows focus on a specific risk element. One could focus on the top-right-back cell, representing the internal risk environment as it relates to compliance objectives of a particular subsidiary.

The sections that follow will discuss ERM on a layer-by-layer level with consideration given to the other two dimensions for each. As with the overall theme of this book, the discussions at each level focus on internal auditor–related internal control and security issues. Today's internal auditor should focus on risks at an enterprise level as part of effective audit, control, and security work.

(a) ERM Framework Internal Environment

While ERM is relevant to all organization entities, the manner in which management will apply this framework will vary widely from one enterprise to another. Factors determining these differences include the nature of the business, its size and complexity, the degree of regulation, tolerance for risk, and many other factors. The idea is that every organization operates in its own unique risk management framework, an environment its managers should understand as it evaluates and manages enterprise risks. The point is that every organization faces a different organization-level risk environment. There can be numerous examples of these differences. A biotech organization developing, testing, and marketing new drugs needs to establish a far different risk framework than an organization selling retail clothing. Organizational management should adopt an ERM internal environment framework for their organization that gives consideration to:

1. **Risk Management Philosophy.** An organization's risk management philosophy is reflected in both its communications and its everyday actions. While an organization will typically not openly advertise itself as taking on high- or low-risk projects, messages such as the importance of maintaining a high credit rating will communicate a low-risk philosophy to stakeholders. Similarly, new product releases that push the edge of technology point to a philosophy of accepting higher risks in product launches. There is nothing wrong with either approach. Employees, investors, and the public understand such risk philosophies and then expect them demonstrated in the organization's ongoing actions.

2. **Organization's Risk Appetite.** A concept that has been implicit in thinking about risks, ERM raises the term or concept of *risk appetite* as a major element of the ERM definition discussed earlier and an expression that should be used by managers and auditors in understanding organizational-level risks. Risk appetite is the amount of risk that an organization or its entity is willing to accept in pursuit of value. Organizations often consider their risk appetite in a quantitative sense, using a risk ranking approach.

Risk appetite should be considered as part of an organization's overall strategy-setting processes. Different strategies will expose an organization to different levels and types of risks. We can think of risk appetite in terms of two hypothetical technology organizations. One may be constantly launching new and innovative products, some of which are total winners while many rapidly fail. Such an organization has a high appetite for risk as compared to another that focuses on new products that are primarily minor improvements over older models—a low-risk approach. ERM applied in strategy setting helps management to select approaches consistent their risk appetite.

3. **Organization Risk Culture.** To quote the COSO ERM document, "Risk culture is the set of shared attitudes, values and practices that characterize how an entity considers risk in its day-to-day activities." This concept of risk culture usually flows from an organization's risk philosophy and risk appetite. If an organization, however, does not do an adequate job in defining its risk philosophy, its risk culture may form haphazardly with different risk cultures within different organization business units. The result may be some business units operating in a very conservative manner, while others are more aggressive. There is nothing wrong with either approach, but one or another should reflect the organization's risk culture. Where misalignment exists, management should perhaps take steps to reshape their risk culture by rethinking its risk philosophy, its risk appetite, and how it applies to the organization's ERM functions. This is not to say that all business units *must* have the same risk culture. Individual business units, functions, and departments may have slightly different risk cultures. Managers of some units are often prepared to take more risk.

4. **ERM and the Board of Directors.** As discussed in Chapters 3 and 4, the Sarbanes-Oxley Act (SOA) has increased the responsibilities and importance of an organization's board of directors and its audit committee. The board is also an important element in an organization's risk management processes through its review and scrutiny of organizational activities as well as its questions to management regarding strategy, plans, and performance. An active and involved board should question management's activities, present alternative views, and act in the face of obvious wrongdoing. An important external environment element in an organization's ERM philosophy, the board should have at least a majority of independent outside directors.

5. **Integrity and Ethical Values.** An organization's implementation of its strategy and objectives is based on its preferences, management values, and management styles. Management's integrity and commitment to ethical values influences values and styles. An important component of its ERM framework, management integrity is an essential prerequisite for ethical behavior in all aspect of organization activities. These management values must consider and balance the concerns of all stakeholders including employees, suppliers, customers, competitors, and the public. This ethical behavior and management integrity are important by-products of

organization culture. Stakeholders often participate in dishonest, illegal, or unethical acts because the organization gives them strong incentives or temptations to do so. For example, a strong emphasis on short-term results can offer stakeholders strong incentives and temptations for inappropriate actions. The whistleblower programs, mission statements, and codes of conduct, discussed in Chapter 9, "Whistleblower Programs and Codes of Conduct," and part of SOA, are important support mechanisms here. In order to manage its risks, an organization must first have strong integrity and ethical value support mechanisms.

6. **ERM Commitment to Competence.** As discussed in the COSO ERM standards, risk management competence reflects the knowledge and skills needed to perform assigned tasks. Management decides how well these tasks should be accomplished by balancing strategy and objectives against plans for the achievement and implementation of those objectives. Competent resources should be assigned to accomplish these objectives, but the trade-off between competence and cost should be considered. The ERM document makes the point that it is not necessary to hire an electrical engineer to change light bulbs. An appropriate level of competence requires basic employee skills and knowledge as well as the level training provided to accomplish the responsibilities of a job position. A lack of attention and budgets for training in the organization can reduce management's commitment to competence.

7. **Management's Philosophy and Operating Style.** As discussed at the beginning of this chapter, management styles have a major influence on how risks are accepted throughout the organization. An undisciplined senior management operating style may encourage an appetite for high-risk ventures and activities. Based on reported information, the management of Enron Corp—perhaps the prime rationale for SOA—had a senior management team with an aggressive risk-taking style. That philosophy bubbled down through the organization and contributed to its downfall. Other elements of management's philosophy and operating style include the preference for aggressive or conservative accounting principles, the contentiousness with which accounting estimates are developed, and attitudes toward information systems controls and effective processes. Internal auditors can frequently gain a front-line assessment of these attitudes in their operational reviews and management's responses to audit report findings.

8. **Organizational Structure.** The organizational structure provides a framework to plan, execute, and control organizational activities. Centralized or decentralized organization structures should be organized according to product line, geographic, or many other needs. However, whatever the organization structure, it should allow for effective risk management to help in the achievement of overall organizational objectives. Internal audit is specifically mentioned in the ERM integrated framework document with the comment: "For example, an internal audit function should be structured in a manner that achieves organizational objectivity and permits full and unrestricted access to top management and the audit committee of the board, and

the chief audit executive should report to a level within the organization that allows the internal audit activity to fulfill its responsibilities." SOA has taken care of this guidance, but the quote emphasizes the importance of internal audit as part of the ERM framework.

9. **Assignments of Authority and Responsibility.** This ERM internal environment element involves the degree to which individuals and teams are authorized and encouraged to use their own initiatives and solve problems. Chapter 13, "Internal Audit Organization and Planning," for example, discusses these organizational arrangements for internal audit functions ranging from organizations where most decisions are made by a central, corporate authority to ones where they are pushed out to remote field-based units. The trend today is toward much more pushing of this authority and responsibility down to lower levels in the organization and individuals. This delegation may mean surrendering central control of some business decisions to lower echelons, including the empowerment to sell products at discount prices, negotiate long-term contracts, or enter into joint venture alliances. Care must be given to delegating only to the extent required to achieve objectives. The concepts of risk identification and acceptance are important elements of this assignment of authority.

10. **Human Resources Polices and Procedures.** The skills and dedication of employees are what ensure the success of any organization. ERM emphasizes that practices pertaining hiring, orientation, training, evaluating, counseling, promoting, compensating, and taking remedial actions all send messages throughout the organization regarding the expected level of integrity, ethical behavior, and competence. Strong policies will encourage appropriate actions throughout the organization. At the other extreme, employees will tend to ignore rules with an "everybody does it" type of attitude. This type of thinking is discussed in Chapter 11, "Fraud Detection and Prevention," regarding the reasons why employees sometime commit fraud. The same is very true regarding attitudes for risk taking.

(b) Other ERM Framework Levels

The internal environment factors discussed in the previous section outline the key factors to consider in this basic or foundation level of the ERM framework. Internal environment factors represent one layer of and eight level framework models that include the following ERM levels:

1. Internal environment
2. Objective setting
3. Event identification
4. Risk assessment
5. Risk responses
6. Control activities
7. Information and communications
8. Monitoring

Space does not allow a discussion of the detailed elements in each of these areas. Some, such as monitoring, information, and communication, have the same titles as are found in the COSO framework. However, the details in these areas are more oriented to enterprise-level risk as opposed to internal controls. The reader can review the entire model from the COSO site on the net (www.coso.org). The basic point for an internal auditor to consider is that COSO ERM is a new, enterprise-wide framework that will almost certainly gain the attention of senior management in the future.

5.4 ERM AND COSO: WHAT'S THE DIFFERENCE?

In our world of acronyms and abbreviations, managers, auditors, and other professionals often do not understand the very distinct differences between COSO and ERM. That misunderstanding occurs because the COSO internal control framework was developed and issued by COSO in 1982. Now, many years later we have ERM, also issued by COSO. Making matters even more confusing, both the COSO and the ERM frameworks are based on three-dimensional models that look fairly similar. This has created some confusion and questions among many professionals, including:

- Is ERM an "improved" version of COSO?

- My organization has already prepared COSO documentation—will it have to be revised?

- COSO has five interrelated components, while ERM has eight, with several sharing the same names, such as controls activities or monitoring. What's different?

This confusion is still continuing as this book reaches publication and as ERM has just been released. The COSO Web site (www.coso.org) does not help matters. It simply lists ERM as an additional COSO publication with little explanation of the differences. One needs to dig a bit deeper to access the ERM Web site (www.erm.coso.org/Coso/coerm.nsf) to gain some specific information there. The ERM document, however, does not help matters. To find a description of the differences between COSO and ERM after release of the latter, the reader needs to go to an appendix at the end of the ERM report to understand that ERM is *not* a subset or revision of COSO. Again, things will change as ERM moves to a final document and preferably becomes more recognized, but at present there has been some confusion among many professionals.

Auditors should recognize that ERM is a risk assessment–based framework, while COSO is an internal controls framework. An organization will use ERM to understand and manage the risks that externally surround and affect an enterprise, while COSO will be used to understand and manage the internal controls that is necessary as part of an organization's internal operations. COSO has a risk management component for internal control–related risks, but ERM is more concerned with organization-wide external risks.

5.5   RISK RANKING AND RISK ASSESSMENTS

ERM provides a framework for internal auditors to better understand risks both in individual departments and throughout their enterprise or organization. An understanding of these potential risks will allow an internal auditor to devote more time to higher-risk areas and then develop audit procedures to review, test, and evaluate controls in higher-risk areas. This requires a multiple-step audit process. Given an auditor's basic understanding of the risk management process, risk-based auditing requires a four-step process:

1. Define the processes covering an organization's operations.
2. Rank and score processes on the basis on their relative risks.
3. Assess process risks with an emphasis on higher-risk areas.
4. Initiate actions to install controls over higher-risk processes.

The above four basic processes can be used to understand and assess relative risks in an organizational unit, whether a single department, the entire enterprise, or beyond. The concept here is similar whether an internal auditor is planning and deciding on which areas are candidates for an audit or a senior manger is focusing management attention on higher-risk areas. Understanding and focusing attention on these higher-risk areas is an important component of risk analysis. There is some level of risk associated with every business process or operation, but time and resource constraints require that we cannot look at all of them. This section discusses an approach for ranking and evaluating process risks in an organization. While the ERM framework allows risk assessments on an almost global scale, looking at the organization in total, at its competitors and more, internal auditors typically focus only on the risks within their organization or even the operating unit where internal audit has responsibility.

(a) Define Organization Processes

Internal auditors often think in terms of their *audit universe*, the number of auditable entities within the organization—the number of areas that can be subject to potential audit. This audit universe concept is discussed in the Chapter 13 discussion on organizing the internal audit function and on internal audit planning. The step here is to define all major processes within the entity, areas that may be subject to internal audit. Understanding the concept of a process is perhaps the important first step here. Processes are the systematic activities by which an organization conducts its affairs. For a vendor account payable operation, processes are more than just the individual payment transactions and the supporting automated application; the process is the steps from receiving and mailing the remittance received to delivery of payment. While a process will usually cover that entire accounts payable operation, it is sometimes valid to separate certain unique payable transactions as separate processes.

Defining that list of processes requires the participation of a wide group of people in the organization, internal audit, information systems, quality assurance, and both manager and staff in the area being evaluated. If an organization has not already gone through a process definition, a good first step is to get a senior management team to help sell this process identification exercise on a functional area by functional area basis. Exhibit 5.2 provides a framework for understanding organizational risks. The management team here should not focus on just an individual area, such as the accounting department, but across broad areas of operations.

(b) Rank and Score Processes Based on Relative Risk

An initial step is to develop some type of scoring or evaluation process to look at each of the identified processes and to rate them based on a consistent set of risk-related factors. There is no one correct scoring formula to use here; the various factors and scoring process depend on the types of processes being reviewed. Exhibit 5.3 is an example of such a scoring system used for selecting new systems under development to select for internal audit preimplementation reviews. The idea is to establish a set of factors to consider, assign each a relative criticality score, and then to calculate a weighted relative risk score for that process.

There is no one correct list or set or procedures. The idea is for internal audit to meet with management and discuss what areas or processes are jointly considered to be relatively riskier. It is sometimes best to derive a fairly lengthy list of factors to limit any bias in the process. If this is done as a single exercise, all processes under consideration should be scored. The same system should be used on an ongoing basis as new processes are launched and considered for risk-based analysis.

(c) Assess and Identify Higher-Risk Processes

The next step here is to apply factors and calculate the relative risk scores for all of the processes reviewed. This is an exercise that sometimes yields unexpected results. That is, internal audit and the team that established the risk factors and

EXHIBIT 5.2

Framework for Understanding Organizational Risk

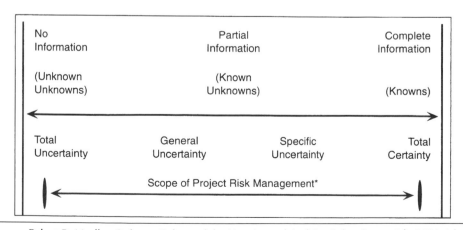

Source: Robert R. Moeller, *Sarbanes-Oxley and the New Internal Auditing Rules,* © copyright 2004, John Wiley & Sons. Used with permission.

EXHIBIT 5.3

RIsk Scoring Factors Example

An internal auditor should evaluate each application development project according to the following criticality scoring factors. Points should be assigned and then adjusted according to the weighting factors at the end of this chart. Each major criticality factor may receive a total score of up to 50 points. The sum of all the scores for all the factors for each application should not exceed 100 points. The highest scoring applications should be given priority as candidates for preimplementation review.

Criticality Factors	Normal Range	Assigned Score
I. Project Status		
A. *Nature of the application project:*		
New application developed in-house	8–10	_____
Purchased application package	5–8	_____
Major change affecting functionality	6–9	_____
Minor change	0–5	_____
B. *Past history of application change:*		
Significant changes over past two years	6–10	_____
Few changes in past two years	4–6	_____
Two years or more since last change	2–5	_____
New application (no changes)	0	_____
C. *Project development team:*		
Systems contractor, competitive bid	8–10	_____
Systems contractor, sole source	6–8	_____
In-house, remote location development	4–8	_____
In-house development group	2–4	_____
Packaged software with minor vendor changes	1–3	_____
D. *Project management team:*		
User group	8–10	_____
Information systems group	4–7	_____
Joint user and I/S management	1–4	_____
E. *Top management interest in project:*		
Project mandated by senior management	8–10	_____
Division or operating unit request	6–9	_____
Project initiated by middle management	5–7	_____
Individual user or department request	2–5	_____
"When time is available" request	0–3	_____
Project Status Score		=======

EXHIBIT 5.3 *(CONTINUED)*

RIsk Scoring Factors Example

Criticality Factors	Criticality Scores: Normal Range	Criticality Scores: Assigned Score
V. Impact of Application Failure		
A. *Impact of incorrect outputs:*		
Potential legal liability	10	______
Financial statement impact	9–10	______
Potential for incorrect decisions	4–8	______
Limited application decision support	1–4	______
B. *Impact of incorrect files or data:*		
Incorrect results passed to other systems	8–10	______
Corrupted data requiring reconstruction	6–9	______
Corrupted data requiring reprocessing	1–5	______
C. *Impact of failure on computer operations:*		
Scheduling problems with related systems	7–10	______
Schedule adjustment for reprocessing	4–6	______
End-user application (minimal impact)	1–5	______
D. *Impact of failure on project management systems:*		
Requirement to reschedule planned systems	7–10	______
Requirement to plan revised application	4–6	______
Requirement to plan application fixes	1–5	______
E. *Impact of application failure on personnel:*		
Need for extra management analysis time	8–10	______
Need for extra user clerical time	6–9	______
Need for systems or programmer efforts	2–6	______
Purchased software vendor support	1–4	______
Failure Impact Score		______

Summary and Weighting

Factor	*Score*		*Weighting Factor*		*Weighted Score*
Project Status	____	×	0.15	=	______
Audit and Control Significance	____	×	0.40	=	______
Technical Complexity	____	×	0.05	=	______
Interrelationship with Other Applications	____	×	0.10	=	______
Impact of Application Failure	____	×	0.30	=	______
Total Weighted Score			1.00		______

their relative scores may find some unexpected results. A process that has been considered relatively high risk may score lower than others. This may require some rethinking of the risk scoring process, but will typically mean that a process appears to have a higher or lower risk than was originally assumed.

(d) Initiate Actions and Install Controls for Higher-Risk Processes

The final step is to initiate plans to review and otherwise audit the identified higher risk areas. For internal audit this ties directly in to the internal audit planning procedures discussed in Chapter 13. Internal audit can use this same type of exercise to help organization management to assess and identify higher risk areas under ERM.

5.6 UNDERSTANDING RISKS FOR MORE EFFECTIVE AUDITING

Risk management, now and in the future, will be an important component of internal auditing. Internal auditors should develop skills to understand and then evaluate risks as part of their overall audit activities. While it is difficult to predict exact outcomes, the just released COSO ERM will almost certainly raise risk management to new and more significant levels of importance in the organization. That recognition will probably not come directly after the recent release of the ERM framework description but some time afterward and after management begins to recognize its importance. For example, the COSO internal control framework was "on the street" for some years before first the AICPA (American Institute of Certified Public Accountants) and now PCAOB (Public Corporation Auditing Oversight Board) has recognized its importance as an effective evaluation framework. The modern internal auditor should be prepared to better understand risks under ERM as years go by.

CHAPTER SIX

Evaluating Internal Controls: Section 404 Assessments

6.1 ASSESSMENTS OF INTERNAL CONTROLS AFTER THE SARBANES-OXLEY ACT

Reviews of internal controls have been a fundamental internal audit task since internal audit's earliest days. Although the language and suggested audit approaches have changed, internal controls reviews have been a topic going back decades. Chapter 4, "Internal Controls Fundamentals: COSO Framework," on the fundamentals of internal control discussed some of these changes leading up to today's COSO framework. Many internal audit groups began to experiment with the use of COSO as a tool to better evaluate internal controls soon after the framework was published. External auditors were faced with many of the same internal control issues, and they subsequently adopted the COSO framework internal control framework as part of a then AICPA auditing standard, Statement on Auditing Standards (SAS) No. 95.

External auditor internal controls reviews, however, came under major criticism during the hearings leading up to passage of the Sarbanes-Oxley Act (SOA). The concern was that external auditors would review and assess the internal controls surrounding a client's systems or processes and then would come back to perform their audit procedures based on the results of that internal controls review. That is, if the internal controls review found no significant problems surrounding some process, the external auditors could reduce their levels of testing through reliance on that same internal controls review. In order to not dig too deeply, auditors often gave a tentative pass on those internal control reviews in order to make the audit go a bit easier. The practice became even more of an issue because of independence concerns when consultants from that same external auditing firm built and installed an accounting system first, then members of the same firm reviewed its internal controls, followed by their auditing the process as well. This raised questions about the independence an objectivity of external audit-led internal controls reviews.

This whole issue was resolved and significantly changed as part of SOA Section 404. This very important section of the act essentially says that external auditors cannot review the internal controls of the same systems and processes that they are auditing. Another party—often from management—must perform the actual internal controls reviews, and the external auditors then subsequently review and attest to the results of those independent reviews of internal controls. Internal audit often also has a strong role in these Section 404 reviews, sometimes reviewing the internal controls themselves for external audit attestation and sometimes supporting their external auditor in completing this new internal controls review process. This chapter will discuss approaches to performing Section 404 reviews along with internal audit's potential role in this process.

6.2 SOA SECTION 404

After much speculation on how things would turn out, the Public Company Accounting Oversight Board's (PCAOB) final rules on audits of internal controls over financial reporting were issued in March 2004.[1] While these detailed rules are quite lengthy, SOA Section 404 requires an annual internal control report for registered corporations, as part of the SEC financial reporting, which shall:

1. State the responsibility of management for establishing and maintaining an adequate internal control structure and procedures for financial reporting

2. Contain an assessment, as of the end of the most recent fiscal year of the issuer, of the effectiveness of the internal control structure and procedures of the issuer for financial reporting

In addition, the public accounting firm that issued the supporting audit report is required to audit and report on the process that led to management's assessment of internal financial controls. An attestation made under this subsection shall be made in accordance with standards for attestation engagements issued or adopted by the board. Any such attestation shall not be the subject of a separate engagement.

Simply put, management is now required to report on the quality of *their* internal controls, and the public accounting firm responsible for the financial statement audit must attest to that internal accounting controls report. Management has always been responsible for preparing their periodic financial reports, and their external auditors previously only reviewed those financial numbers and certified that they were fairly stated after their audit. Now with SOA Section 404, management is responsible for documenting and testing their internal financial controls in order to prepare a report on their effectiveness. The external auditors will now review the supporting materials leading up to that internal financial controls report to assert that the report is an accurate description of that internal control environment.

To the nonauditor, this might appear to be an obscure or almost trivial requirement. Even some internal auditors that primarily specialize in operational audit reviews may wonder about the nuances in this process. However, audit reports on the status of internal controls have been an ongoing and simmering issue between the public accounting community, the SEC, and other interested parties going back to 1974. As discussed in Chapter 4, much of the debate, going through the 1980s, was that there was no recognized definition for what is meant by internal controls. The release of COSO in 1992 established a common framework for internal control that has become an accepted standard. Now, SOA has ended this debate. Management is now required to report on their internal controls with public accounting firms attesting to those internal controls reports.

(a) Launching the Section 404 Compliance Review: Identifying Key Processes

Every organization uses a series of processes to conduct its normal business activities. Some of these may be represented by automated systems, some are primarily manual procedures that are performed on a regular basis, while still others are a combination of automated and manual. The monthly financial report is an example of the latter. Automated accounting systems, including the general ledger system, support a large portion of this closing process. For most organizations, there is a major manual component here as well where manual accounting processes allow the organization to make adjustments to the results of its automated general ledger to close the books for the accounting period.

If they have not already done so, a very early step in a Section 404 review is for the organization to define and describe its major accounting processes. A preliminary first step here is to make certain that all parties have a clear understanding of what is meant by a process. This can cause confusion to some where a Web search for "process definition" will yield a long list of sites from software vendors and other firms that each have a different interpretation of a process. We would define a process as a particular course of action intended to achieve a result, such as the procedure of obtaining a driver's license. A process is a series of actions that have clearly defined starting points, consistent operational steps, and defined output points. A process results in a usable set of defined steps described with documents that allow it to be followed consistently over time periods and throughout the organization.

Internal audit can be a major help when an organization is defining key processes. For many organizations, internal audit has already defined their key processes through their annual internal audit planning process as discussed in Chapter 13, "Internal Audit Organization and Planning." For purposes of a Section 404 reviews, an organization should define its key processes. This process is much more than just documenting one or another automated application but includes all of the beginning and ending steps to allow an organization to perform some business function. For a payroll application, for example the compensation process will include all aspects of the systems and procedures necessary to compensate employees, ranging from the preparation of timesheets to the automated payroll calculation system to the steps necessary to distribute compensation checks, pay taxes and benefits, and much more. The concept here is to think about processes in a very big picture sense. As a first step, internal audit or whoever is responsible for the Section 404 review process should think of all basic business activities in an organization.

After discussions with management as well as with the external auditors, who should know the organization, this list will form a basis, or starting point, for future internal controls reviews. This process list will become a basis for understanding basic accounting flows and for launching a stream of internal controls reviews for the organization.

(b) Launching the Section 404 Compliance Review: Internal Audit's Role

There are few specific references to internal audit in the text of SOA, but the act specifically prohibits external audit firms from performing internal audit services for their audit clients. Although SOA does not specifically give this responsibility to internal audit, they have become an important resource in many organizations for the completion of SOA Section 404 internal controls assessments. Under SOA, another separate and independent function—often internal audit—will review and document the internal controls covering key processes, identify key control points, and then test those identified controls. External audit will review that work and attest to their adequacy. For many organizations, internal audit now has a much greater set of responsibilities and importance in this post-SOA world.

Internal audit's role in the Section 404 reviews in an organization can take several different forms as follows:

1. Internal audit can take the lead in actually performing the Section 404 reviews by identifying key processes, documenting their internal controls, and performing appropriate tests of those controls. Internal audit would be following a documentation format consistent with their external auditors but would be doing this work separately and independently. The external auditors would then be responsible for attesting to these reviews as performed by internal audit.

2. An in-house function or outside resources would be designated by the organization to perform the Section 404 reviews, and internal audit can act as a resource to support their external auditors in reviewing the results of the Section 404 work. This approach will reduce external audit resource costs provided there is some other resource available to actually perform effective Section 404 reviews.

3. Internal audit can work with and help the other corporate resources—either internal or external—that are responsible for the Section 404 reviews but not be directly involved with performing those reviews, either as independent internal auditors or as agents for their external audit firm. This approach

allows internal audit to devote more time and resources to other audit projects similar to those described in other chapters of this book. This also may be the only alternative for a very small internal audit function.

The chief audit executive (CAE), senior financial management and the audit committee should work with the external auditors to define responsibilities for the required Section 404 internal control reviews. In some cases all parties will decide that it is most efficient for management, other than internal audit, to take the second approach described earlier. External audit might make arrangements with internal audit to review and assess the adequacy of that internal controls review work. Internal audit would be working for external audit in reviewing and attesting to the results of those internal controls reviews but would not be performing the actual reviews. As mentioned, this type of arrangement will save on overall external audit costs by giving internal audit an important role in helping external audit in achieving the Section 404 review objectives. The negative side of this arrangement is that the management team or the consultants assigned often does not have the time, resources, or even training to perform these internal controls assessments. This arrangement only works effectively when an organization has another internal audit-like function such as a strong quality-assurance or risk assessment function. These are groups that understand how to review, document, and test internal control processes.

In alternative 1, internal audit performs the review work for corporate financial management for a subsequent but separate and independent assessment by the external auditors. The positive side of this arrangement is that internal audit is often the best and most qualified resource in the organization to perform these reviews. They understand internal controls, testing procedures, and good documentation techniques and often have the skill to effectively review supporting information systems applications. Although this arrangement will involve more external audit resources, this may be an effective way to complete the Section 404 review requirement. All parties must realize their roles and responsibilities here.

Section 404 reviews are an annual process, and an organization and its internal audit function can change that strategy in future years. There is no reason why the strategy selected should be the same every year going forward, except that changes always introduce increased costs and added time spent relearning approaches. All parties should develop an approach that appears most cost-effective to achieve these legally mandated detailed SOA requirements.

(c) Launching the Section 404 Compliance Review: Organizing the Project

Compliance with SOA Section 404 places a major challenge on SEC-registered organizations. While some may have previously taken a hard look at the COSO internal control framework, described in Chapter 4, and evaluated their internal controls using that framework, others may not have completed a COSO internal controls review in any level of detail. Organizations and internal audit functions that previously evaluated their own controls, in a COSO context, almost certainly have some work ahead, but at least should have an understanding of their internal controls environment. A second group may have relied on their external auditors who issued favorable financial reports, with only limited internal control work, as well as having relied on internal audit, who has been reviewing internal controls in various selected areas but never in totality. This second group faces a potentially major challenge in completing their assessment of internal controls. A third group are the often-smaller organizations that have given little attention to documenting their internal controls and frequently have a small, understaffed internal audit function as well. The latter are potentially facing a major challenge in establishing Section 404 compliance.

An effective internal audit function should play a very major role in helping an organization get ready for SOA and its Section 404 compliance. The external auditors that once did some internal financial controls assessment work as part of their annual audits are no longer directly responsible for these reviews. As discussed, those external auditors will review and attest to management's internal financial controls assessment report but cannot do the work themselves. As discussed in the prior sections, there are some very qualified and excellent consulting firms to help an organization to achieve SOA compliance, but the effective internal audit function should be in a key role to aid senior management here. Based on the IIA standards discussed in Chapter 12, "Internal Audit Professional Standards," internal audit should not be directly responsible for implementing the internal financial controls testing and documentation program that they will eventually be requested to review. They should not assume the role as project manager, but only play an active participant role on the implementation team. Internal audit's role in auditing new systems under implementation might prove a good example. Typically, internal auditors will serve on the team that is installing a new application and will recommend internal control improvements as the new application is being developed. However, they are not responsible for installing those changes or for the overall new system. Thus, they can return later and review the new system maintaining their independence.

An internal audit function should begin its Section 404 compliance review process by launching a formal, special project. While the actual project would vary based on the strength of the extent and sophistication of an organization's internal control processes, the project could be launched following these steps:

1. **Organize the Section 404 Compliance Project Approach.** Assign a project team to lead the effort. A senior executive such as the CFO should act as the project sponsor with a team of both internal and external (but not external audit!) resources to participate in the effort. Roles, responsibilities, and resource requirements should be estimated as well. Internal audit will often assume major responsibilities here.

2. **Develop a Project Plan.** The internal financial controls compliance project should be well in process prior to the organization's financial year end. While the existing plan can be updated in subsequent years, there will be a major challenge and "time crunch" for earlier years. The plan should focus on significant areas of organizational operations with coverage over all significant business units. Although there can be many variations here for developing such a plan, Exhibit 6.1 shows some of the major work steps—a work breakdown structure—that must be considered when planning a Section 404 compliance review project. Although the work steps described are at a fairly

EXHIBIT 6.1

Section 404 Compliance Review Work Breakdown Structure

1. Assemble review team. This may be led by internal audit or will consist of other review team members, with internal audit acting as a consultant (Note: this assumes that internal audit will not be supporting their external auditors for these reviews).

2. Agree on a consistent terminology for the review, including an understanding of financial assertions and risks.

3. Define project objectives.
   - Determine if the review will cover just financial areas or efficiency and effectiveness areas as well.
   - Determine the organizational units to be covered in review.
   - Review results from any previous Section 404 or internal audit reviews requiring follow-up.
   - Establish a project time line that allows time for the external audit review.
   - Review planned objectives with the CFO and audit committee.

4. Develop a detailed project plan covering processes to be reviewed.

5. Establish the review approach for each process/system included in the review.
   - Identify the types and nature of key process controls and the risks associated with failure of those controls.
   - Define the nature and types of possible errors and omissions.
   - Define nature, size, and composition of transactions to be reviewed.
   - Determine the volume, size, complexity, and homogeneity of individual transactions processed.
   - Establish guidelines for materiality and error significance.
   - Understand process transaction susceptibility to error or omissions.

6. Review approach and timing with external auditors.

7. Establish standards for review documentation and project progress reporting.

8. Complete preliminary reviews for each identified process or system, including new or updated supporting documentation.

9. Follow up and resolve any items requiring investigation.

10. Consolidate review work and prepare preliminary 404 report.

11. Review 404 report results with the CFO and release the report.

high level, the team should use these steps to develop a more detailed plan document to begin the internal financial controls review.

3. **Select Key Processes for Review.** Every organization uses or depends on a wide range of financial and operational processes. We have used the term *process* here as opposed to *system* because the latter is often used only to refer to automated processes. The payroll system, for example, is a set of automated routines that take time and attendance data and produce payroll checks or transfers into the employees' checking accounts. The payroll *process* is much larger, including the steps necessary to add a new employee, to process a pay increase, and to communicate with accounting and benefit systems. There can be numerous transaction flows in this overall process.

Internal audit and/or the Section 404 compliance team needs to review all organization processes and select the ones that are financially significant. This key process selection should focus on those where a failure could cause a major loss or expense to the organization, and this consideration should include all organizational entities, not just headquarter applications. The processes should then be ranked by the size of assets controlled, their materiality in terms of the overall financial resources of the organization, or other measures. Rather than just the size of assets managed, Exhibit 6.2 contains some planning considerations for a Section 404 review. In addition, Exhibit 6.3 contains some process review selection guidelines. The focus on these guidelines are more on information

<hr>

EXHIBIT 6.2

<hr>

Planning Considerations for a Section 404 Internal Controls Review

1. Determine status of review—Is this the first round of Section 404 reviews for the entity and a subsequent year follow-up?

2. If it is a new review, follow the work steps as outlined in Exhibit 6.1. Otherwise plan for a subsequent-period Section 404 review.

3. Review the detailed documentation covering prior 404 reviews, including process flowcharts, internal control gaps identified and remediated, as well as overall project-planning documentation for prior review.

4. Review any recently published PCAOB rules covering Section 404 reviews and related auditing changes, and adjust review procedures to reflect those changes.

5. Meet with the external audit firm responsible for the current Section 404 attestations and determine if there are any changes in documentation and testing philosophy from the prior review.

6. Review any organizational changes since the last review, including acquisitions or major reorganizations, and develop plans to modify the review coverage, if necessary.

7. Through meetings with senior and IT management, identify if new systems or processes have been installed over the last period and if those new changes have been reflected in updated documentation.

8. Review any internal control weaknesses identified in the last review and assess whether internal control corrections reported as installed appear to be working.

9. Assess the status of existing Section 404 documentation and determine the extent of new documentation preparation necessary.

10. Assuming that the prior Section 404 review was done by internal audit, determine that appropriate, knowledgeable, trained resources are available to perform the upcoming review.

11. Interview all parties involved in the prior Section 404 review exercise to assess any lessons learned and develop plans for corrective actions in the upcoming review.

12. Based on discussions with external auditors and senior management, determine the scope of materiality parameters for the upcoming review.

13. Determine that the software, if any, used to document prior review is still current, and make any changes necessary to have adequate tools in place to perform the upcoming review.

14. Prepare a detailed project plan for the upcoming Section 404 review, with considerations given to coordination of review activities at business entity units and external auditors.

15. Submit plan for approval by senior management.

systems–related considerations, but the exhibit provides some of the types of factors to consider. For example, in raising the question of whether the application software was purchased or built in-house, the organization might—and probably should—decide that purchased software often has a lower risk. Internal audit can assist in developing documented procedures to justify why one process was more worthy or significant for detailed review than another. Many internal audit groups already have a criticality selection process in place; such processes are discussed in Chapter 14, "Directing and Performing Internal Audits." The external auditors reviewing selection criteria may ask for such justifications and may add their own insights into the processes they feel should be view as review candidates.

4. **Document Selected Process Transaction Flows.** The next step, and an important one, is to prepare transaction flow documentation for the key

EXHIBIT 6.3

Process Review Selection Guidelines

The following questions can serve as a guide for selecting key processes to review as part of a SOA Section 404 review exercise. While there is no right or wrong answer to any of these, these should help allow the team selecting key processes to consider key factors

I. Process or System Status

A. Nature of the process or system to be reviewed:
-Is this a new system or process developed in-house?
-Is it a newly purchased application package?
-Have there been major changes over past period affecting functionality?
-Have past changes been described as only minor changes?
-Is there adequate current documentation supporting the process?

B. Past history of process or system changes:
-Have there been significant changes over past two years?
-Have changes been minor in the past two years?
-Have there been two years or more since the last change?
-Is this a new process or with no recent changes?
-Is there an adequate document change control process in place?

C. Process or system development team:
-Is the development or management of the process handled by an outside contractor?
-Is an in-house group responsible for process development and management?
-Is the process a purchased packaged solution with only minor local changes?

D. Top management interest in process of project:
-Is this an enterprise-level process mandated by senior management?
-Does the system or process responsibility reside at an operating unit level?
-Is this a process initiated by middle management?
-Is this an individual user or departmental responsibility?

II. Audit and Control Significance

A. Type of system or process:
-Does the process support financial statement balances?
-Does it support major organizational operations?
-Is it primarily for logistical or administrative support?
-Is this a less critical statistical or research application?

EXHIBIT 6.3 *(CONTINUED)*

Process Review Selection Guidelines

B. Past internal audit or SOA review involvement:
-Has there been a prior SOA review, including control improvement recommendations?
-Have prior reviews concluded with only limited recommendations?
-Have prior Section 404 test results found no significant internal control problems?
-If controls improvement recommendations have been made in prior reviews, do matters appear to have been corrected?
-Is this a process that was never formally reviewed?

C. System or process control procedures:
-Are there process-generated internal controls?
-Are there run-to-run controls with other systems or processes?
-Is the process primarily operating in a batch mode or with manual controls?

III. Impact of Process Failure

A. Impact of incorrect reported results. Would a process failure result in:
-Potential legal liability?
-Financial statement impact?
-Potential for incorrect management decisions?
-Limited decision support risks?

B. Impact of application failure on personnel. Would a process failure result in a:
-Need for extra management analysis time?
-Need for extra user clerical time?
-Need for a wide range of specialized resources?

processes selected. This can be an easy step for some organizations where there has been a COSO-type review with key flowchart documentation prepared previously. Then, the existing documentation should be reviewed to determine that it is still accurate, and it should be updated as required. Process documentation is much more of a challenge if the organization has never documented its processes or if what documentation it has is just represents old automated system transaction flows.

There are a variety of accepted documentation protocols supported by various automated tools. Exhibit 6.4 is an example of a simple flowchart describing a payroll timecard process for an organization. The goal for these flowcharts is to describe key organizational processes at a very high level. This shows the steps to initiate the process, actions such as recording a transaction at a very high level, and key decision points. The documentation should show key transaction flows and control points. The space below the chart would contain a detailed process description. Although a variety of flowchart styles can be used, this example chart has notations where transactions are initiated, where data is recorded, where the transaction is authorized, and where processing takes place. The numbers referenced here refer to process flowchart procedural steps.

A key need for any documentation is a supporting process to keep it updated. Three-ring notebooks full of process documentation sheets will be of little value in the future if they have never been updated. Organizations should establish procedures to ensure that all changes to previously documented systems are noted when required. Whoever led the project to document SOA processes should potentially be given the responsibility for maintaining this documentation. We have suggested that internal audit should take a major role here, but this ongoing maintenance task would probably not be an appropriate responsibility for internal audit.

5. **Identify, Document, and Test Key Internal Controls.** This can be a major effort! Using some form of criticality analysis, key organizational internal financial control processes should be identified, compliance tested, and the results documented. Documentation is very important here, because when the external auditors review these processes, they will need to examine this documentation in order to attest that controls are in place and operating. This is an area where internal audit should play a key role in advising the internal financial controls project team. These steps will be discussed in greater detail in the paragraphs that follow.

6. **Assess Selected Process Risks.** Once an organization has defined and documented its key processes, the next step is to assess risks to determine what might go wrong. Here, the team that first identified key process areas and then documented them should go through a detailed "what could go wrong?" type of analysis. The reviewers should ask questions about the potential risks surrounding the process. For example in an accounts payable process, could someone gain access to the system and then arrange to cut themselves an unauthorized check? Could system controls be sufficiently weak that multiple payments might be generated to the same authorized vendor? There could be numerous risks of this sort. A management team should go through each of the selected processes and highlight potential risks in such an open-ended set of questions and then focus on the expected supporting controls. Based on background, this is very much the type of analysis where internal audit can play a very valuable role. Exhibit 6.5 is an example of this type of risk assessment review for an accounts payable process and points to a review approach that should be developed for any key process. We have selected accounts payable (A/P) as an example process because it is fairly easy to understand in most circumstances. In many cases, existing internal audit programs can meet this need.

7. **Assess Control Effectiveness through Appropriate Test Procedures.** System controls are of little value if they are not working effectively. An internal auditor or other reviewer can sometimes determine that appropriate controls do not appear to be in place or are ineffective. In that case, the conclusions from the assessment should be documented, discussed with the process owners, and an action plan developed to take corrective actions to improve the controls. If the reviewer asks about the approval process necessary to generate an A/P check and is effectively told there is no process beyond initial approval of the invoice, the reviewer will determine that this an obvious internal control weakness that should be documented and discussed for planned corrective action.

EXHIBIT 6.4

Payroll Timecard Process

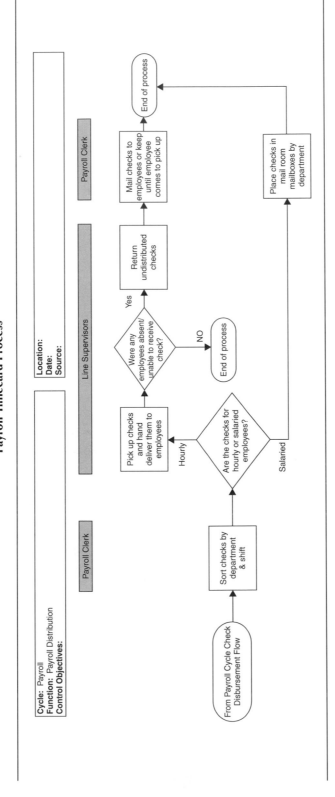

Cycle: Payroll
Function: Payroll Distribution
Control Objectives:

Location:
Date:
Source:

EXHIBIT 6.5

Sample Accounts Payable Review Procedures

1. Are accounts payable personnel independent from purchasing and receiving functions?

2. Are debit memos, adjustments, and other noncash debits to accounts payable approved and periodically reviewed by supervisory personnel?

3. Are there defined cut-off procedures at month end that are continually monitored by supervisory personnel?

4. Are month-end accruals and other credit accounts payable estimates and adjustments reviewed by management?

5. Are all accounts payable vouchers and debit memos prenumbered?

6. Are all vendor invoices date and time stamped in sequential order, and is the sequence periodically checked?

7. Are all unused forms controlled?

8. Are records maintained for all voided forms?

9. Are daily runs of total cash disbursed to accounts payable compared to the check run?

10. Is accounts payable subledger maintenance separate from maintenance of the general ledger?

11. Are accounts payable trial balances and general ledger control accounts periodically reconciled and reviewed by supervisory personnel?

12. Are reconciliations of monthly vendor account statements made against unmatched open purchase orders and receiving reports; and reviewed by a supervisor?

13. Is receipt of vendor account statements performed by someone other than the accounts payable bookkeeper?

In most instances, the initial assessment of internal controls will require testing. Audit testing has been a common process for both internal and external auditors in their reviews of controls. For financial audits, these audit tests were once extremely extensive with often-large attribute and variables sample transactions taken and sample results evaluated. Attribute sampling is used for evaluating internal controls and variables sampling is used for estimating financial balances. Evaluation of the results of these samples allowed an auditor to draw conclusions regarding whether financial results were fairly stated or internal controls appear to be working. A powerful tool, this statistically based audit sampling is less common today because of pressures for audit efficiency. Attributes can be a powerful tool to assess internal controls today and to state with some measure of statistical confidence that the internal controls tested are working or not. Audit sampling techniques for internal auditors will be discussed in Chapter 16, "Gathering Evidence through Audit Sampling."

Whether using a statistically based sample or not, the SOA process reviewer should virtually always use one or more sample transactions to test a process. If a complex but a largely paper-based process with many people-based approval steps, the SOA reviewer might borrow from classic internal audit techniques and try a "walkthrough" type of test. The idea is to take a single transaction—such as a vendor's invoice requiring

EVALUATING INTERNAL CONTROLS: SECTION 404 ASSESSMENTS

approval before the A/P check is generated—and individually walk that transaction through each of the processing steps prior to cutting the A/P check. Again, this is a test to assess internal controls over a process. If the results of the test are positive, the process reviewer could determine that the process appears to be working correctly, with adequate internal controls. This is an exercise that should be familiar to all internal auditors. The "test of one" transaction test should then be followed by a more extensive sample of transactions. For this single A/P walkthrough example, a detailed sample of perhaps 10 to 30 transactions might be selected to determine that the process is working effectively.

8. **Review Compliance Results with Key Stakeholders.** Senior financial and executive management will ultimately be responsible for the final Section 404 report. The project team should review their progress with senior management on a periodic basis, highlighting their review approaches and the short-term corrective actions initiated. Similarly, since they must formally attest to the results of this internal financial control review, the external auditors should be kept informed of progress and any outstanding issues in process of resolution.

9. **Complete Report on the Effectiveness of the Internal Control Structure.** This is the final step in Section 404 compliance. Since this is not a one-time exercise, all work should be documented for follow-up reviews. The documentation process here is similar to a financial audit process, where results are documented in workpapers for ongoing periods. This is the report, along with the external auditor's attestation work, that will be filed with the SEC as part of the organization's 10K annual report.

This Section 404 compliance project can be a major undertaking and certainly will require considerably more time and effort than is expressed in the limited number of work steps described in this chapter. As has been discussed, this is really a key area where internal audit should play a very significant but advisory role. The level of work required will depend on the level of internal control work that has previously been performed in the organization. Many if not most larger organizations have embraced some form of COSO internal control reporting, such as the CobiT internal control framework, and have strong internal audit functions in place that have performed internal audit reviews of those installed internal controls. Often through the leadership of internal audit, these organizations have reviewed, tested, and documented their internal controls following the COSO framework standard. Such organizations will have an easier task in achieving Section 404 compliance on a continuing basis. SOA requires that companies evaluate the effectiveness of their internal controls over their financial-reporting processes. In the past, internal audit may have focused on COSO internal control factors, emphasizing the effectiveness and efficiency of operations, leaving financial controls to the external auditors. Now, the internal control review team or other designated persons may have to change their emphasis.

The work involved here may require some time in reviewing past COSO audits and updating program guidance or making changes to broaden scope as required. If the COSO-related review had been just an internal audit project, financial management, and other members of management should be included and "brought up to speed." A major task here will be to document all internal controls, the tests performed, and the results of those tests.

At the present time in these early days of SOA, there are still organizations that have not fully embraced a COSO-type framework in their management of internal controls. There are many SEC-registered corporations today whose internal audit functions have performed some internal control reviews but have not otherwise embraced a COSO internal controls model throughout the organization. These are often organizations where the internal audit function is relatively small with activities focused on operational efficiency–related reviews or financial internal audit work in support of their external auditors. Almost certainly if internal audit has not been involved in such a COSO internal control review program, management in total has not as well.

Many organizations will have a challenge in maintaining compliance procedures for SOA Section 404. Internal audit functions here may have to go through a total reengineering process, training staff, revising audit approaches, and seeking outside control review help. A major task here may be for the CAE to meet with the audit committee and senior financial officers to explain how internal audit work will be tailored to meet SOA Section 404 requirements. As we have discussed, internal audit may not necessarily take responsibility for these reviews, even though internal audit is often the most qualified resource in the organization to perform them. Internal audit can independently perform the review with the external auditors attesting to their work subsequently. Based on the information gathered and reviews by management, the project team responsible for the Section 404 compliance effort should develop an audit action plan to begin this process. Time and resources will not allow them to cover all control areas during a given period so that their emphasis should be placed on significant business with potentially high risks for financial misstatements.

Smaller organizations with little or no internal audit resources face the greatest challenge under Section 404. While the typical internal audit professional today may ask "how can this be possible, doesn't everyone have an internal audit function?" that is not the situation for many. Indeed, while NYSE registered corporations are required to have an internal audit function and NASDAQ listed corporations have similar requirements, there are many other SEC-registered corporations that do not have an internal audit function or have a very low-level type of function. These are the many smaller corporations whose stock trades on what were called "pink sheets," small almost private companies. All, however, are subject to SOA requirements. In addition, there are numerous essentially private organizations that have some bond offering registered with the SEC, making them subject to SOA.

Section 404 represents a major challenge for these small corporations. They have the same SOA requirement to formally review and document their internal financial controls, to identify any weaknesses, and to take appropriate corrective actions. Such a review can be accomplished by the financial management team with help by an internal audit function, if it exists. Otherwise, the CFO and the financial teams can take on this responsibility, if there are sufficient time and other resources. The best solution here may be to contract for outside services.

6.3 INTERNAL CONTROL REVIEW PROCESS: IMPORTANCE OF FINANCIAL ASSERTIONS

Financial assertions is a term that will be familiar to many CPA-trained external auditors but may cause some other internal auditors to just shrug shoulders an think it is a theoretical concept of little concern to them. For example, a search of the IIA's Web site (www.theiia.org) provides little information. However, understanding the whole concept of financial assertions will allow internal auditors to better tailor the Section 404 internal controls and to better communicate with their external auditors, whether performing Section 404 reviews as part of management for external audit or as contractors to their external auditors.

The concept starts with a formal recognition that management is responsible for their organization's internal controls and the preparation of the financial statements. These financial statements are prepared under a series of what is called assertions covering the state of affairs at the balance date and the results of its operations for the period then ended. In broad terms, management is being asked to strongly proclaim or assert that the financial statements, the financial statement items and underlying account balances and supporting internal controls are free of material misstatements or errors. That is, that the financial statement items, and underlying account balances and classes of transactions are, in all material respects, complete, valid, and accurate.

This broad concept of financial statement assertions is broken down by level of aggregation and depicted in a tabular format. The idea is to tie each significant internal control to a management assertion. This assertion concept used by external auditors is a good way to identify these various risks as follows:

- *Existence.*   Assets, liabilities, and ownership rights should exist at the time of the review. Taking a physical inventory shortly before the financial statement date reduces the risk that those assets and other items will not exist at the time of the financial statement.

- *Occurrence.*   Recorded transactions must represent the events reported. The risk is that something like a recorded sale has really not taken place at the statement date.

- *Completeness.*   All events during the reporting period should have been recognized or considered during that period. The risk is that there may be unrecorded transactions during the period.

- *Rights and Obligations.*   The recorded assets and liabilities are bona fide at that point in time. The risk is that some other party may have an interest.

- *Valuations of Accounts.*   All transactions should be recorded at appropriate amounts and in correct accounts. The risk is possible misstatement.

- *Presentations and Disclosures.* Items in the financial statements are properly described and are fairly presented. Again, the risk is possible misstatement.

The idea here is that various internal controls will be identified, and each of these internal controls should be tied to a specific assertion. An internal control in manufacturing materials receiving department may include a provision that all goods received are properly recognized and recorded as inventory or work-in-process. The assertions this is associated with are Existence and Occurrence. Yes, management should properly recognize that the goods were received and properly recorded. When identifying internal controls for purposes of a Section 404 review, internal audit should connect each internal control with one or more of these assertions.

6.4 CONTROL OBJECTIVES AND RISKS UNDER SECTION 404

Although due dates have changed several times and may change again as this book goes to press, the current rule for Section 404 compliance is that all SEC-registered organizations with a financial year-ending date of July 1, 2004 or later are required to comply with SOA requirements. At the time of this book's publication, many organizations have just gone through their first round of Section 404 compliance assessments. The rules for non-U.S. corporations have been eased, and overall due dates may be extended further. However, Section 404 reviews represent a law that all SEC registered corporations will be required to live with going forward. Once that first Section 404 review has been completed, it is easy to just say something along the lines of, "Wow, we're done with that. Now let's get back to business as usual." However, it will not be that easy. Once an organization has gotten itself through its first Section 404 review, it should establish processes for a continuous monitoring, evaluation, and improvement process.

Going forward, the organization needs to monitor its key systems, determine if there were any changes in subsequent periods, and design internal control procedures to correct any control weaknesses or otherwise fill control gaps. This is an ongoing periodic exercise, and the team that first implemented the Section 404 compliance work will almost certainly have returned to normal job duties. This is the time to look at the Section 404 review work that was completed and make any necessary changes to improve the efficiency and value of these reviews. Given the time and resources expended in completing these reviews, an organization should use this material to improve its overall internal controls environment.

An organization's Section 404 documentation standards and materials needs to be reviewed and updated on a regular basis. Systems and processes change and acquisitions or corporate reorganizations modify the environment. In the paragraphs following, we suggest two approaches to help document internal controls to support SOA Section 404 and to document internal accounting controls in general.

(a) Developing an Internal Controls Matrix

A tabular matrix that supports the graphical diagram is an effective way to process document controls as well as to justify the steps needed to classify and assess the controls associated with a process. This type of matrix chart works best when tied with this type of process chart. However, an organization can describe its controls just using a verbal matrix chart without the supporting diagram. Exhibit 6.6 is an example of the type of control matrix that should be constructed for this type of a Section 404 review. It lists the controls within a process, the types of risks associated with each, the types of controls, the control

EXHIBIT 6.6

Control Matrix Example

	Control	Risk	Assertion	Control Type	Type	Critical Control
1.	Controller performs monthly income statement analysis comparing actual amounts to forecast and prior periods. All fluctuations or unanticipated balances are researched and documented.	Recurring entries are not posted or improperly posted.	Measurement/ Valuation	Manual	Detect	H
2.	Monthly reconciliations are performed for all balance sheet accounts. All fluctuations or unanticipated balances are researched and documented. Reconciliations are reviewed and approved by accounting, as evidenced by a manual signature.	Recurring entries are not posted or improperly posted.	Measurement/ Valuation	Manual	Detect	H
3.	Controller performs monthly income statement analysis comparing actual amounts to forecast and prior periods. All fluctuations or unanticipated balances are researched and documented.	Intercompany activity is not identified or recorded properly.	Measurement/ Valuation	Manual	Detect	H
4.	All invoices are reviewed and approved by the sales manager.	Invoices are not created properly or are not created for all customers.	Measurement/ Valuation	Manual	Prevent	H
5.	All invoices are reviewed and approved by the sales manager.	Invoices are generated for fictitious customers.	Measurement/ Valuation	Manual	Prevent	H
6.	Accounts receivable aging is reviewed by controller, independently of the invoice generation process.	Invoices are generated for fictitious customers.	Measurement/ Valuation	Manual	Prevent	L
7.	Monthly reconciliations are performed for all balance sheet accounts. All fluctuations or unanticipated balances are researched and documented.	Month-end entries are improperly posted or not posted at all.	Measurement/ Valuation	Manual	Detect	H
8.	Controller and accounting manager review entries for accounting and clerical accuracy.	Financial statements may contain clerical or other errors.	Existence/ Completeness	Manual	Detect	L

criticality, and the financial assertion that the control supports. Following an example from another accounting-related process, such a chart can be organized on a column-by-column basis as follows:

- *Summarized Control Points.* A brief paragraph describes each control point. In the first control in the exhibit, the controller performs a monthly income statement analysis. The description for each should be brief, with only enough information to describe the overall control.

- *Associated Risks.* A column lists the risks associated with each control. In this example, even though the controller reviews the income statement analysis, there is a risk that an item will not be posted correctly. There can be multiple risks associated with each control point, but the idea should be to identify only the more significant risks.

- *Related Assertions.* Financial and internal controls assertions were discussed previously. The ideal is to list one or more of the financial assertions that management can proclaim for each control to support the idea that it should be working. Under the Existence and Completeness assertions, management normally expects that all transactions in this example have been recorded for subsequent review.

- *Control Type.* For documentation and understanding purposes, the type of each control should be identified. In this example, they are all shown as manual, but other control types might include:

  - *Manual.* Controls are exercised manually by one or a group of individuals, such as the monthly reconciliations and account analysis performed by the accounting staff.

  - *Application.* These controls may consist of specific programs to process or edit a transaction, including edit checks, validations, and calculations, as well as nonprogrammed controls such as the manual balancing of computer-produced information.

  - *Preventive.* This type of control is usually applied to each transaction during the normal flow of processing to prevent errors from occurring.

  - *Detective.* This type of control is applied outside the normal flow of transactions processed or partially processed to detect and correct errors. Detective controls can be either manual or automated application controls.

  The definition of *control type* allows persons reviewing the control matrix to gain an overall understanding of the nature of each control point.

- *Control criticality.* Based on the nature of each control, the associated risks, and the type of control, each should be further classified by criticality as follows:

  - *High.* This is a significant control designed to prevent or detect the identified risk from going undetected. This control should be tested as part of regular Section 404 internal control testing as discussed below.

  - *Medium.* This control is not as significant and does not prevent the risk from going undetected. This control typically would not be tested in association with Section 404 testing.

A package of process flowcharts as well as internal control diagrams should be prepared for each key process. We have presented example formats, but some external auditors, who have overall responsibility for these Section 404 reviews may prefer slightly different approaches or formats. However, the formats presented should allow an organization to complete its Section 404 review materials in a credible manner and in a format that should allow external audit attestation.

(b) Testing Section 404 Internal Controls

As an essential component of the Section 404 review process, critical internal controls must be tested. If using the process-by-process control matrix charts as outlined earlier, the level of testing will depend on the criticality of a given control. This testing will follow the same procedures as the other aspects of these Section 404 reviews. That is, the team doing the actual internal controls documentation— and not external audit—would be responsible for appropriately testing the identified internal controls. This emphasizes the importance of internal audit doing the actual testing work or at least supervising the results of those tests. Internal auditors have skills in designing test plans and developing testing procedures, an area where many members of the organization may not have that level of experience. This is again another reason why internal audit may be the most appropriate group in the organization to design and perform an appropriate level of internal controls testing.

Internal controls testing, or what is also being called audit sampling, is discussed in Chapter 16. Whether for SOA Section 404 internal controls testing or for other internal audit tasks, testing is an important internal audit skill! The results of that testing are necessary to confirm that internal controls are working effectively as described. Of course, if the results of that testing indicates material control weaknesses, efforts should be initiated within the organization to improve control procedures as necessary or to design appropriate compensating controls.

6.5 DISCLOSURE COMMITTEE AND KEEPING SECTION 404 CURRENT

The SEC has recommended that SOA-affected organizations create a disclosure committee to consider the materiality of information discovered, to identify relevant disclosure issues, and to ensure that the material is disclosed to investors on a timely basis. In other words, someone should be responsible for reviewing all of the internal control review material presented, decide what is important or "material," and then decide when and if any matters are worthy of formal disclosure to investors. Such a disclosure committee will almost necessarily be a senior CEO- or CFO-level group. The sponsor for the SOA internal financial controls project review team should be at least a disclosure committee member with internal audit having a key representative as well.

A major task of this disclosure committee is to consider the materiality of any exception information encountered. This group is looking over the data that will be presented to the external auditors for their review and report. We can almost certainly expect that there will be a tendency, at least in the early years of

SOA, to err on the side of viewing too many matters as material. In the big picture of things in a large organization, there may be many internal control weaknesses that individually or collectively are not all that material. Since the disclosure committee will be going through some very important information, the CAE or another member of the audit team should suggest to management that internal audit could provide valuable information and insights to any newly formed disclosure committee.

An overall requirement of SOA Section 404 is that all documents and other work examined during a review must be maintained, following U.S. income tax guidelines, for a period of at least seven years. This says that all evidence that was part of a review, such as review workpapers, key reports reviewed, samples of data files, and other matters must be maintained in a manner that they can be retrieved at some future date for review and examination. While an organization may find material from the prior year useful to support a subsequent year review exercise, this old material will be required if the organization ever finds itself in some form of legal or regulatory crisis where it will need to prove it did or did not take some action. Every organization needs to develop some form of document retention process for keeping past copies of Section 404 review documentation and records in a manner that they can easily be retrieved if needed. Exhibit 6.7 contains some guidelines for keeping Section 404 documentation current and up to date. This can be a very complex process, the review work taking space and electronic files becoming unreadable due to changing formats or just age. Internal audit, with their experience in filing and maintaining past audit workpapers can be of major help in this process.

EXHIBIT 6.7

Keeping Section 404 Compliance Review Procedures Current

1. Develop a documentation standard for all Section 404 reviews, setting up minimum requirements for entering materials in documentation files. Documentation should include, at a minimum, a record of:

   - Planning and preparation records covering the SOA review scope and objectives
   - A list of all major organization processes as well as criteria for processes selected
   - The Section 404 review program; this is an approach that will be negotiated with the external auditors
   - Project plans for the planned review work including review activities, planned work steps, and overall budgets
   - The individual process review steps performed and evidence gathered
   - The 404 findings, conclusions, and recommendations for corrective action
   - Any report issued as a result of this work
   - Evidence of supervisory reviews

2. Launch procedures to document all significant accounts, processes, risks, and internal controls that conform to standards such as the COSO framework.

3. Launch procedures for the integrity of records with audit trails, document management, version control, and security measures that ensure the protection of data and documentation.

EXHIBIT 6.7   *(CONTINUED)*

Keeping Section 404 Compliance Review Procedures Current

4. For processes and systems included in past Section 404 reviews, establish ongoing procedures to:
   - Keep process documentation added, deleted, or updated on regular basis
   - Follow-up and resolve any issues highlighted from past Section 404 review including reasons for not including some processes that could be viewed as critical
   - Include results of interim internal reviews and testing for processes
5. Maintain the appropriate custody and retention of the documentation that supports Section 404 conclusions for a time sufficient to satisfy legal, professional, and organizational requirements.
6. Documentation should be organized, stored, and secured in a manner appropriate for the media on which it is retained and should continue to be retrievable for a time sufficient to multiple Section 404 review cycles and to meet legal requirements.

ENDNOTE

[1]PCAOB Release No. 2004-001, PCAOB, Washington, DC. March 9, 2004.

CHAPTER SEVEN

Internal Controls Frameworks Worldwide: CobiT and Others

7.1   BEYOND COSO: OTHER APPROACHES TO UNDERSTANDING INTERNAL CONTROLS

COSO (Committee of Sponsoring Organizations) has become the recognized framework for understanding and evaluating internal controls in the United States. However, COSO is not the *only* framework and perhaps not even the best or the easiest to use in some situations. The idea is to use a consistent approach that will satisfy the Sarbanes-Oxley Act (SOA) internal control requirements, known as Section 404 procedures and discussed in Chapter 6, "Evaluating Internal Controls: Section 404 Assessments." This chapter discusses an alternate internal control framework—with the ungainly name of CobiT. The CobiT framework is particularly effective when assessing internal controls in a strong information technology (IT) environment, such as an organization with highly automated processes or with IT-related products. CobiT often provides a useful tool for understanding and documenting an organization's internal controls under the requirements of SOA Section 404 when there is a high degree of automated systems.

    This CobiT framework is not a replacement for but a supplement to the COSO internal controls framework to help better understand and document controls, particularly in an IT environment. We will provide a high-level introduction to CobiT as well as to its use for Section 404 documentation. The chapter will also look at some international variations of COSO, the Turnbull framework for England and much of the European Community (EC) as well as the Control Framework developed by a committee of the Canadian Institute of Charter Accountants (CICA) and known as CoCo (Committee on Controls). COSO is becoming a worldwide framework for defining and understanding internal controls, but some of its international variations are equally appropriate and powerful. Just as an internal auditor working in an international environment thinks about financial accounts or values in terms of perhaps U.S. dollars or euros, an internal auditor in an international environment should be aware of COSO and its the non-U.S. variations.

7.2   COBIT MODEL: IT GOVERNANCE

The professional and business world is filled with acronyms or initials that have become words themselves. We use the word IBM today often not thinking that it stands for the corporation's original name, International Business Machines. COSO is quickly becoming such a word—we forget what COSO stands for and it just becomes descriptive term. (Chapter 4, "Internal Controls Fundamentals: COSO Framework," provided COSO explanations and background information.) While not at the same level of recognition, CobiT is an acronym becoming a word that stands for *Control Objectives for Information and related Technology*. Because of its emphasis on controls and technology, the first and last letters are usually capitalized. This is another important audit and control framework that can stand by itself or serve as a supplement to COSO and the IIA standards discussed in Chapter 12, "Internal Audit Professional Standards." Although its emphasis is more on information technology, all internal auditors should at least have an understanding of CobiT and its use as a tool for reviewing and understanding internal controls.

The CobiT standards and framework are issued and maintained by the Information Systems Audit and Control Association (ISACA) as well as its affiliated research arm, the IT Governance Institute. ISACA also is the professional organization that administers the CISA (Certified Information Systems Auditor) examination and program as well as the newer Certified Information Systems Manager (CISM) certification and examination. These and other professional certifications are discussed in Chapter 28, "Professional Certifications: CIA, CISA, and More." ISACA was originally known as the EDP Auditor's Association (EDPAA), a professional audit organization that was started in 1969 by a group of internal auditors that felt the IIA was not giving sufficient attention to the importance of computer systems and their technology controls as part of the audit process. We have almost forgotten that EDP stands for electronic data processing, an almost archaic term for information systems, and the professional organization became ISACA over time. ISACA continues to lead the IIA in providing guidance and standards for technology-related audit issues. As will be discussed in Chapter 12, the IIA has just now released a proficiency standard stating that all internal auditors should have a general understanding of information technology risks and controls.

This upstart EDPAA information systems audit professional organization originally began to develop information technology audit professional standards shortly after its formation. Just as the EDPAA evolved into ISACA, its initial standards became a very excellent set of control objectives that evolved into CobiT, now in its July 2000 third edition.[1] CobiT's stated mission is a good introduction to the sections that follow:

> The CobiT Mission: To research, develop, publicize and promote an authorative, up-to-date, international set of generally accepted information technology control objectives for day-to-day use by business managers and auditors.

CobiT has been enhanced with existing and emerging international technical, professional, regulatory and industry-specific standards. CobiT is designed to be both pragmatic and responsive to business needs, while being independent of the technical IT platforms adopted in an organization. To the first time reader, however, the CobiT materials may appear a bit formidable. The guidance material is scattered over multiple volumes with many charts, tables, and diagrams, published in a multivolume package with separate guidelines, and a quick-start guide. CobiT is an excellent internal audit tool for understanding and auditing IT systems in general, and we will try to provide an overview of CobiT in the sections that follow.

(a) CobiT Framework

Information is often the most valuable asset for virtually all organizations today, and management has a major responsibility to safeguard its supporting IT assets, including automated systems. A combination of management, users of IT, and auditors all need to understand these information-related processes and the controls that support them. This combination is concerned about the effectiveness and efficiency of their IT resources, the IT processes, and overall business requirements, as shown in Exhibit 7.1. The idea is that each of these three groups has somewhat differing concerns regarding the business requirements of their IT systems, the supporting IT resources as well as IT processes. Management is interested in the quality, cost, and appropriate delivery of its IT-related resources whose control components are the same three COSO internal control elements that were discussed in Chapter 4. The third leg of this framework is the IT processes that require appropriate levels of confidentiality, availability, and integrity controls. Internal controls over IT resources are very much based on the interdependencies of these three effectiveness and efficiency IT components.

In addition to three interconnected groups, CobiT looks at controls in three dimensions: IT Resources, IT Processes, and IT Information Criteria. These three dimensions fit on what is called the CobiT Cube (see Exhibit 7.2). Similar to the COSO framework cube discussed in Chapter 4, this model looks at IT controls from a three-dimensional perspective. However, its front facing dimension, with its pictorial description of processes has perhaps scared off some people from considering the use of CobiT in the past. The nontechnical person—and there are many—may look at the process diagrams on the face of the CobiT cube and

EXHIBIT 7.1

CobiT Framework's Principles

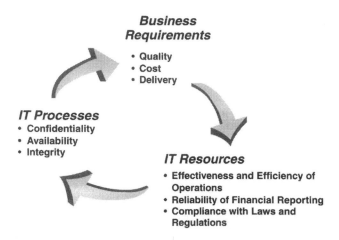

Source: *Control Objectives for Information and Related Technology* (COBIT®), 3rd Edition, © Copyright 1996, 1998, 2000, the IT Governance Institute® (ITGI), http://isaca.org and http://itgi.org, Rolling Meadows, IL 60008, USA. Reprinted by permission.

decide that this approach must be too technical. It is really not at all that technical, and we will describe and explain the CobiT and the framework in general in paragraphs that follow.

EXHIBIT 7.2

The CobiT Cube

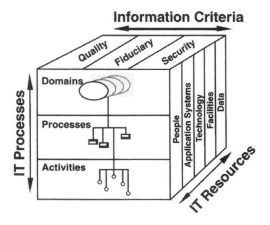

Source: *Control Objectives for Information and Related Technology* (COBIT®), 3rd Edition, © Copyright 1996, 1998, 2000, the IT Governance Institute® (ITGI), http://isaca.org and http://itgi.org, Rolling Meadows, IL 60008, USA. Reprinted by permission.

The IT Resources side, or dimension, of the CobiT cube represents all of an organization's IT assets, including its people, the application systems, installed technology, the facilities, and the value of data. This right-hand side of the CobiT cube represents all of the resources necessary for the control and administration of IT resources in an organization, and these resources, either individually or as groups, should be considered when evaluating controls in an IT environment. That is, in addition to the actual application systems, we must consider the technology used, the people responsible for those applications, and other IT supporting resources. We have started our CobiT description from the right-hand side of the CobiT cube, but control considerations always must be considered in terms of how they relate to other components on that on side of the CobiT cube as well as with others in this three-dimensional perspective.

The second and front-facing dimension to the CobiT framework is called IT Processes, and this consists of three segments: domains, processes, and activities. Domains are the natural groupings of IT processes and often match an organizational domain of responsibility. Within an IT organization, CobiT lists four specific domains:

1. **Planning and Organization.** This domain covers strategy and tactics to allow IT to best contribute to the business objectives of the organization. This is the strategic vision message for IT that should be communicated throughout the organization.

2. **Acquisition and Implementation.** IT solutions need to be identified, developed, or acquired, and both implemented and integrated with business processes. This domain covers changes in and maintenance of existing systems.

3. **Delivery and Support.** This area covers the actual delivery of required services, both application and infrastructure tools. The actual process of application data and application controls is covered within this domain.

4. **Monitoring.** This domain includes control processes, among them quality and compliance monitoring, as well as external and internal audit procedures.

Within the IT organization, the installed Systems Development Life Cycle (SDLC), procedures, discussed in Chapter 21, "Reviewing and Assessing Application Controls," could be viewed as part of the implementation domain, and quality assurance could be a part of the monitoring domain. The CobiT documentation materials describe each of these in greater detail. For planning and organization, it suggests the following specific processes:

- Define a strategic IT plan.
- Define the information architecture.
- Determine technological direction.
- Define the IT organization and relationships.
- Manage the IT investment.

- Communicate management aims and direction.
- Manage human resources.
- Ensure compliance with external requirements.
- Assess risks.
- Manage projects.
- Manage quality.

Individual processes are the next level down. They are a series of joined activities with natural control breaks. Finally, activities are the actions needed to achieve measurable results. Activities have a life cycle, whereas tasks are discreet. In terms of a life cycle, we can think of the SDLC process where the activity is designed, implemented, used over time, and then replaced with an improved process. We have used what we called the accounts payable (A/P) process in past discussions. CobiT would view A/P as an activity within the purchasing process and within the manufacturing domain. The tasks here would include such matters as producing the actual vendor check.

The third dimension to the CobiT model or cube is described as the Information Criteria, and this consists of three components: quality, fiduciary, and security. That is, all IT overall systems or processes should be evaluated with consideration given to these three criteria. These relate to the quality, cost, and delivery management concern factors described in Exhibit 7.1. The quality criteria covers quality-assurance issues and the overall quality of IT resources. Although mentioned throughout this book, internal audit quality-assurance processes are introduced and discussed in greater detail in Chapter 26, "Internal Audit Quality Assurance and ASQ Quality Audits." CobiT uses the term fiduciary to describe accounting and financial controls as one of its three Information Criteria dimensions. The third security component is covered in many other areas of this book, with an emphasis in Chapter 19, "General Controls in an E-Business and Networked Environment," including discussions on e-business and network controls.

The Exhibit 7.2 CobiT cube provides an interesting and effective way to look at IT controls. CobiT is really a powerful tool for understanding IT processes, business requirements, and control objectives. However, some of the CobiT published materials initially can become a confusing set of tables and charts that can be difficult to understand without some level of training. The following sections provide an interpretation for navigating CobiT and using it as a tool for better understanding and evaluating IT controls. CobiT can be an excellent audit tool for evaluating many types of IT controls with a particular emphasis on the SOA Section 404 discussed in Chapter 6.

(b) Navigating CobiT: Understanding the Framework

The CobiT cube has the three dimensions of IT Processes, IT Resources, and Information Criteria. IT processes are further defined as the domains of Planning & Organization, Acquisition & Implementation, Delivery & Support, and Monitoring. Each of these higher-level processes is still further defined as a series of detailed processes, with CobiT-assigned process numbers. The domain of Delivery & Support high-level process area, for example, consists of the suggested processes:

DS 1	Define and Manage Service Levels
DS 2	Manage Third-Party Services
DS 3	Manage Performance and Capacity
DS 4	Ensure Continuous Service
DS 5	Ensure Systems Security
DS 6	Identify and Allocate Cost
DS 7	Educate and Maintain Users
DS 8	Assist and Advise Customers
DS 9	Manage the Configuration
DS10	Manage Problems and Incidents
DS11	Manage Data
DS12	Manage Facilities
DS13	Manage Operations

These are suggested areas for the CobiT-suggested processes within this domain. A different organization in a different environment may want to define these differently. However, each of the 13 points in this example set of processes is matched against the other two dimensions of the CobiT cube: Information Criteria and IT Resources. This really says that when an internal auditor is reviewing control procedures covering the delivery and support of IT resources, the auditor should begin by considering the controls that are found within these 13 activities in this area. All may not always be appropriate or others may need to be added, but CobiT provides an excellent starting point.

Moving to the other side of the cube, CobiT separates IT Resources into the elements of people, applications, technology, facilities, and data. For each of the processes, the CobiT framework identifies whether that process is applicable to each of the IT Resources elements through a check in a matrix chart. For example, the previously mentioned process DS8, Assist and Advise Customers, is applicable to the IT Resource elements of people and applications but not the other three.

For the third dimension of the CobiT cube, the domain processes are matched against a set of Information Criteria factors:

- Effectiveness

- Efficiency

- Confidentiality

- Integrity

- Availability

- Compliance

- Reliability

Each of the individual processes is evaluated against each of these to identify whether they are primary or secondary control objective concerns.

Based on these three CobiT control cube dimensions, each IT process is evaluated through a four-step process:

I   The control of [*Process Name*]

II Which satisfy [*List of Business Requirements???*]

III Is enabled by [*List of Control Statements*]

IV Considering [*Control Practices for Process*]

This process makes greater sense when looking at an actual CobiT high-level control objective for Ensuring Compliance with External Requirements as part of the Planning & Organization objective. Exhibit 7.3 illustrates this process. Here,

EXHIBIT 7.3

High-Level Control Objective

Control over the IT process of

ensuring compliance with external requirements

that satisfies the business requirement

to meet legal, regulatory, and contractual obligations

is enabled by

identifying and analyzing external requirements for their IT impact and taking appropriate measures to comply with them

and takes into consideration

- laws, regulations, and contracts
- monitoring legal and regulatory developments
- regular monitoring for compliance
- safety and ergonomics
- privacy
- intellectual property

Source: Control Objectives for Information and Related Technology (COBIT®), 3rd Edition, © Copyright 1996, 1998, 2000, the IT Governance Institute® (ITGI), http://isaca.org and http://itgi.org, Rolling Meadows, IL 60008 USA. Reprinted by permission.

effectiveness and compliance are primary Information Criteria factors, while reliability is secondary. Other factors such as efficiency and availability are not of concern. Moving to the lower-right corner of the exhibit, the model shows that people, applications, and data are applicable IT Resource factors. The previously referenced CobiT guidance materials covers each of these CobiT domains and processes and can be found in several guidelines published by ISACA, including a summarized Framework booklet.[2]

Following the details in the CobiT guidance materials, there is excellent guidance for reviewing general controls for this and many other areas. The sections that follow describe CobiT as we move down to more detailed control objectives. The effective internal auditor is encouraged to explore the previously referenced ISACA published reference materials to gain more information on the CobiT approach to evaluating IT processes.

The Exhibit 7.2 CobiT Cube is very similar to the COSO model in Exhibit 4.3. As with the COSO approach, controls should be considered in a three-dimensional environment. While controls and procedures may be strong in one respect or dimension, they may need improvements in another. This becomes a very realistic way to evaluate IT controls and processes. CobiT uses this model as the basis to establish control objectives, audit, management, and implementation guidelines as discussed in the sections that follow.

(c) Control Objectives under CobiT

The term "control objectives" should be familiar to virtually all internal auditors. When reviewing any area of operations, an internal auditor needs to have some type of objective to determine or guide a review. When performing a financial audit, an auditor may establish a control objective that the transactions reviewed must be authorized and correctly classified, and that total balances should tie to the proper general ledger account. These would be considered the auditor's major control objectives. An internal auditor could also be concerned with other control objectives such as whether the documentation covering the financial system reviewed was current or whether the staff preparing the accounting transactions has received proper vendor training on the use of the financial system reviewed. These are all areas for an internal auditor to review, but priority in a financial review would be given to the more important control objectives such determining that the transactions reviewed were authorized.

Whether done formally or informally, establishing control objectives is an important part of the audit process. CobiT starts with the proposition that in order to provide the information an organization needs to achieve its objectives, IT resources need to be managed by a set of naturally grouped processes. The previously discussed published CobiT material defines a set of detailed processes as well as a control objective for each of these processes. We previously discussed the high level Planning & Organization process for Ensuring Compliance with External Requirements with a list of specific or detailed processes. Another example would be the Planning & Organization process to Define a Strategic IT Plan, a process an auditor would want to see in place for any IT function. A series of subprocesses are defined under this heading as well as a control objective for each. Exhibit 7.4 lists these subprocesses as well as examples of the detailed control objectives. Not every process and its related control objective will fit for every organization, but the CobiT material provides an excellent set of guidance material for establishing effective controls in an IT environment.

The next step is to consider each of these IT processes and to define the business requirements that those processes satisfy. For example, controls over the process of managing an organization's IT investments will satisfy a business requirement for controls over the disbursement of financial resources. This step is enabled by an operational budget established and approved by appropriate

EXHIBIT 7.4

CobiT Subobjectives Example: Define a Strategic IT Plan

1.1 IT Should Be Part of the Organization's Long- and Short-Range Plan

Supporting Control Objective: Senior management is responsible for developing and implementing long- and short-range plans that fulfill the organization's mission and goals. In this respect, senior management should ensure that IT issues as well as opportunities are adequately assessed and reflected in the organization's long- and short-range plans. IT long- and short-range plans should be developed to help ensure that the use of IT is aligned with the mission and business strategies of the organization

1.2 IT Long-Range Plan Process

Supporting Control Objective: IT management and business process owners are responsible for regularly developing IT long-range plans supporting the achievement of the organization's overall missions and goals. The planning approach should include mechanisms to solicit input from relevant internal and external stakeholders affected by the IT strategic plans. Accordingly, management should implement a long-range planning process, adopt a structured approach, and set up a standard plan structure.

1.3 IT Long-Range Planning—Approach and Structure

Supporting Control Objective: (Published as part of CobiT materials.)

1.4 IT Long-Range Plan Changes

Supporting Control Objective: (Published as part of CobiT materials.)

1.5 Short-Range Planning for the IT Function

Supporting Control Objective: (Published as part of CobiT materials.)

1.6 Communication of IT Plans

Supporting Control Objective: (Published as part of CobiT materials.)

1.7 Monitoring and Evaluating of IT Plans

Supporting Control Objective: (Published as part of CobiT materials.)

1.8 Assessment of Existing Systems

Supporting Control Objective: (Published as part of CobiT materials.)

Note: This is an example of CobiT's definition of processes and subprocesses. The CobiT guidance material includes a detailed Supporting Control Objective for each process.

■ 154 ■

levels in the organization with consideration given to funding alternatives, clear budget ownership, controls over the actual spending, and a cost justification and awareness of total cost of ownership, among other factors.

This process flow is shown in Exhibit 7.5. The published ISACA CobiT materials are filled with these factors to consider for each of the processes. In a first pass reading, the CobiT framework materials can be almost formidable with four identified domains each with 34 defined processes. Within each process, there are from 3 to 30 detailed IT control objectives defining controls that should be in place. Although complex, this forms a systematic and logical method for defining and communicating IT control objectives. It leads to the CobiT audit and management guidelines discussed in the next sections.

(d) CobiT Audit Guidelines

Effective reviews of IT controls and procedures have presented challenges to internal auditors ever since automated systems have become a major component of overall business processes. CobiT tries to improve this process. A major component of CobiT and its published materials is a set of generic and high-level audit guidelines to help with reviews of processes against IT control objectives. The CobiT audit process is built upon several generic guidelines that can be used for all processes as well as specific audit procedures oriented to each of the defined CobiT processes.

The CobiT generic guidelines are just that, *a guideline*, to identify tasks to be performed in assessing any process control objective. There are also process-specific guidelines with suggested audit steps to provide management assurance that a control is in place and working. While we suggest that the reader

EXHIBIT 7.5

Cobit IT Process to Control Practices Linkages

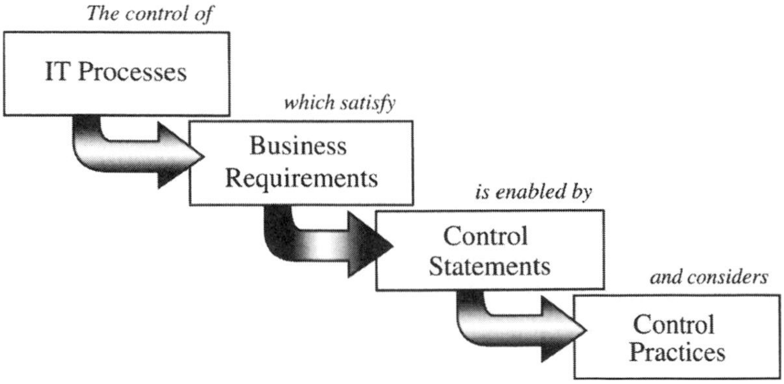

Source: Control Objectives for Information and Related Technology (COBIT®), 3rd Edition, © Copyright 1996, 1998, 2000, the IT Governance Institute® (ITGI), http://isaca.org and http://itgi.org, Rolling Meadows, IL 60008, USA. Reprinted by permission.

obtain the previously referenced CobiT materials for details and specific wording, the generic audit guidelines cover the following areas:

- *Obtaining an Understanding.* A description of the audit steps to be performed to document activities underlying the control objectives as well as to identify the control procedures in place.

- *Evaluating the Controls.* The guideline outlines audit steps to be performed in assessing the effectiveness of control measures in place or the degree to which the control objective is achieved. This is the step to basically decide what, whether, and how to test.

- *Assessing Compliance.* The audit steps to be performed to ensure that the control measures established are working as prescribed, consistently and continuously, and to reach a conclusion on the appropriateness of the control environment.

- *Substantiating the Risk.* This guideline outlines the audit steps to be performed to substantiate the risk of the control objective not being met by using analytical techniques and/or consulting alternative sources. The objective is to support the opinion and to "shock" management into action (CobiT's words!). Auditors have to be creative in finding and presenting this often sensitive and confidential information.

CobiT suggests that each of the four generic guidelines should be used for *every process* reviewed. Each guideline also contains guidance for obtaining direct or indirect evidence for selected items/periods, suggestions for limited reviews of the adequacy of the process deliverables, general guidance on the level of substantive testing, and additional work needed to provide assurance that the IT process is adequate.

The published CobiT materials also include specific audit procedures for each of the detailed processes. These are very generic documents with guidance along the lines of "Consider whether . . ." followed by lists of items specific to that process area. The general structure of these detailed processes follows these steps:

1. Items or areas to consider when evaluating controls.

2. Items to examine or test to assess compliance with control procedures.

3. Steps to perform to substantiate the risk of control objectives not being met.

4. The identification of such matters as IT failures to meet the organization's missions and goals, IT failures to meet cost and time guidelines, or missed business or IT opportunities

The result of all of this material is some excellent guidance material for assessing controls over IT processes. There is sufficient CobiT material to allow any internal auditor and a computer audit specialist in particular to review and assess controls for an IT organization. Although CobiT is heavily oriented toward

IT, these same procedures can be used as a basis for internal control reviews in many areas.

(e) Management and Implementation Guidelines

The overall CobiT materials also include sets described as Management and Implementation Guidelines. Unfortunately, the CobiT Management Guidelines do not fit as neatly with the other Framework and Audit Guideline materials. The CobiT Management and Implementation materials discuss an organization's maturity model along with the Software Engineering Institute's Capability Maturity Model (CMM)[3] discussed in Chapter 20, "Software Engineering, the Capability Maturity Model, and Project Management," and sections on critical success factors among other topics. This chapter will not be discussing this section of CobiT.

The Implementation Guidelines reaffirm who should benefit from CobiT and discuss steps to implement CobiT in the organization. It suggests multiple ways to implement CobiT ranging from a top-down approach through the CIO or audit committee to a mandate-regulated situation. The general recommendation is that internal audit—the chief audit executive (CAE)—should communicate the COBIT approach to appropriate senior operating and IT management. The CobiT framework, processes and control objectives should be communicated to teams such as the CIO's organization via education to help sell the overall CobiT approach.

7.3 USING COBIT FOR SOA SECTION 404 ASSESSMENTS

Chapter 6 discussed the SOA Section 404 internal controls assessment requirements and suggested a COSO-based internal audit approach for evaluating those controls. CobiT is another powerful tool, particularly in an environment with a heavy concentration in IT processes and resources, to help internal auditors perform these Section 404 as well as Section 302 reviews. Discussed in Chapter 3, "Internal Audit in the Twenty-First Century: Sarbanes-Oxley and Beyond," Section 302 is primarily concerned with the responsibilities of the CEO and CFO for financial reports and related disclosures. As part of this, SOA mandates that an organization's external auditors should perform limited quarterly reviews to determine whether there were any significant modifications to the internal control structure or changes in internal controls over financial reporting.

ISACA/IT Governance Institute documentation describes, in Exhibit 7.6, how the CobiT internal control framework can be mapped to the COSO model.[4] This shows that an internal auditor should use CobiT's prime objectives, from Planning & Organization to Monitoring & Evaluation, and use the controls objectives guidance for each of these to understand and evaluate internal controls through COSO's five components. The actual process, then, of performing the Section 404 compliance work is very similar to that outlined in Chapter 6 on Section 404 assessments. Whether using COSO in general or CobiT, the internal auditor reviewer moves through a series a processes from planning to performing risk assessments and on to identifying, documenting, and evaluating key internal controls.

EXHIBIT 7.6

Relationship between COSO Components and CobiT Objectives

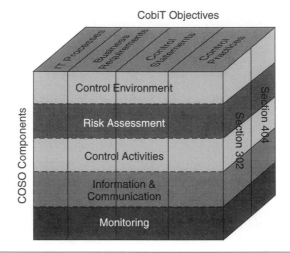

Because of CobiT's heritage in IT systems auditing, design, and processes, its documentation and guidance material relies very much on good systems design and software-engineering practices. For example, Chapter 20 describes the Capability Maturity Model (CMM) an approach for looking at IT organizations and processes in terms of relative maturity such as whether processes are ad hoc, defined and documented, or even better. Exhibit 7.7 shows this CMM controls reliability framework in terms of the relative design of operating effectiveness and the extent of this documentation.

With much more information about these reliability stages in Chapter 20, this controls reliability framework provides an internal auditor with a good way to assess internal controls over an individual process or over the entire organization. An internal controls assessment, for example, might find a Stage 0, nonexistent controls environment. This implies a complete lack of a recognizable control process and an inability to be in compliance with Section 404 requirements at any level. This is an extreme situation, and if an internal auditor is part of an organization that appears to have the attributes of a Stage 0 assessment, flags should have been raised or even "whistles blown" if controls are that weak. Ideally, internal audit should hope to find at least a Stage 2, and hopefully a Stage 3, environment. At Stage 3, controls and related policies and procedures should be in place and adequately documented at a level sufficient for management to be able to assert to the adequacy of these controls.

The published CobiT Section 404 review material, referenced previously, does an excellent job of matching IT and CobiT control objectives with the five COSO components. Based on the published CobiT guidance, Exhibit 7.8 shows how the major CobiT control objective areas match or link to the major COSO components of internal control. This link-up ties together even better by going a

EXHIBIT 7.7

Stages of Internal Control Reliability

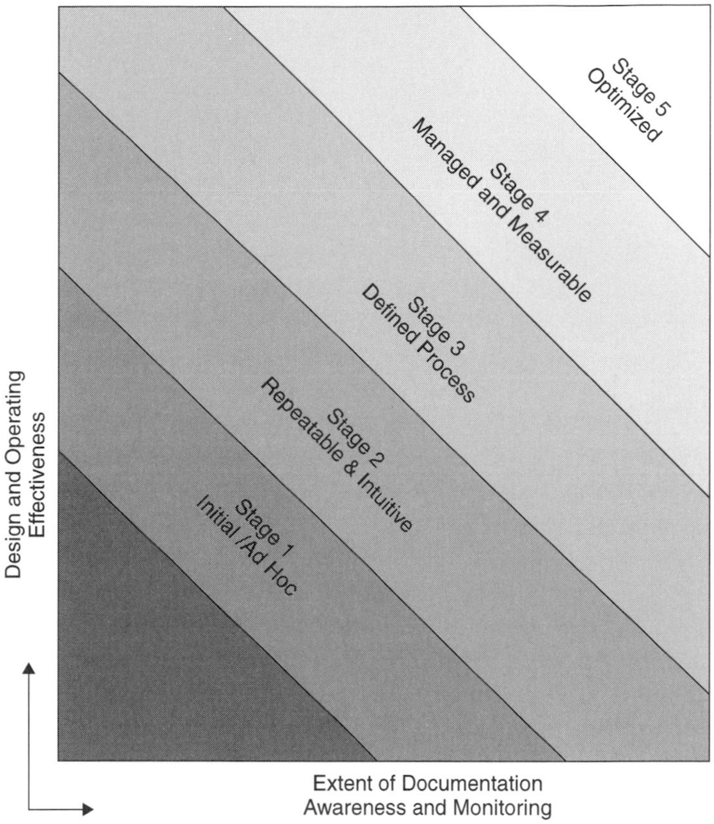

level lower. For example, CobiT objective of Managing Changes under the Acquire and Implement control objective affects the COSO components of Control Activities and Monitoring. The actual published CobiT detailed control objectives will tie to each of the COSO components. There is a close relationship between these CobiT and COSO control objectives and components.

The full set of CobiT control objectives will provide strong support for an internal auditor seeking to perform a SOA Section 404 internal controls assessment review. While the concepts can be used in any internal control area, the emphasis is on IT applications and processes. For many organizations, an understanding and assessment of those IT-associated internal controls is a key area to achieving SOA compliance. CobiT has been around for some years now, but for too long, many internal auditors viewed it as just specialized information systems audit tool and not a more general help for other internal audit work. Although its emphasis continues to be on IT, all internal auditors should explore the CobiT framework as an excellent tool for helping with SOA compliance requirements.

EXHIBIT 7.8

COSO and CobiT Relationships

	COSO Components				
COSO Control Objectives	Control Environment	Risk Assessment	Control Activities	Information & Communication	Monitoring
Plan and Organize					
Define a strategic IT plan		X		X	X
Define the information architecture			X	X	
Determine technological direction					
Define the IT organization and relationships	X			X	
Manage the IT investment					
Communicate management aims and direction	X			X	X
Manage human resources	X			X	
Ensure compliance with external relationships			X	X	X
Assess risks		X			
Manage projects					
Manage quality	X		X	X	X
Acquire and Implement					
Identify automated solutions					
Acquire and maintain application software			X		
Acquire and maintain technology infrastructure			X		
Develop and maintain procedures			X	X	
Install and accredit			X		
Manage changes			X		X
Deliver and Support					
Define and manage service levels	X		X		X
Manage third-party services	X	X	X		X
Manage performance and capacity	X		X		
Ensure continuous service	X		X		X
Ensure systems security	X		X	X	X
Identify and allocate costs					
Educate and train users	X			X	

EXHIBIT 7.8 *(CONTINUED)*

COSO and CobiT Relationships

Assist and advise customers				
Manage the configuration	X		X	X	
Manage problems and incidents			X	X	X
Manage data			X	X	
Manage facilities			X		
Manage operations			X	X	
Monitor and Evaluate					
Monitor the processes				X	X
Assess internal control adequacy					X
Obtain independent assurance	X				X
Provide for independent audit					

Source: Control Objectives for Information and Related Technology (COBIT®), 3rd Edition, © Copyright 1996, 1998, 2000, the IT Governance Institute® (ITGI), http://isaca.org and http://itgi.org, Rolling Meadows, IL 60008 USA. Reprinted by permission.

7.4   CANADA'S COCO FRAMEWORK

The Canadian Institute of Chartered Accountants (CICA) is the professional financial auditing and accounting organization in Canada. Similar to the AICPA's CPA certificate, the CICA awards Chartered Accountant certifications. After the release of the COSO framework and the AICPA's incorporation of it in U.S. audit standards, the CICA established a study group in 1995 to issue guidance on designing, assessing, and reporting on the control systems of organizations. The result is what is called the *Criteria of Control* (CoCo) framework.

According to CoCo, control comprises those elements of an organization—including its resources, systems, processes, culture, structure, and tasks—that, taken together, support people in the achievement of the organizations' objectives. Just as a U.S. native can often identify a Canadian resident through slightly different verbal expressions, there are some slightly different words in CoCo when compared to the U.S.-oriented COSO. While CoCo defines control objectives in terminology similar, but not identical to COSO, it emphasizes that the essence of control can be viewed as four connected high-level processes, as described in Exhibit 7.9:

- Monitoring and learning internal and external environments as well as monitoring assumptions

- Internal control purposes including understanding risks and policies, and establishing performance targets

- A commitment to ethical values, appropriate human resources policies, and an atmosphere of mutual trust

- A capability based on appropriate information processes, control activities, and information coordination

EXHIBIT 7.9

CoCo Framework

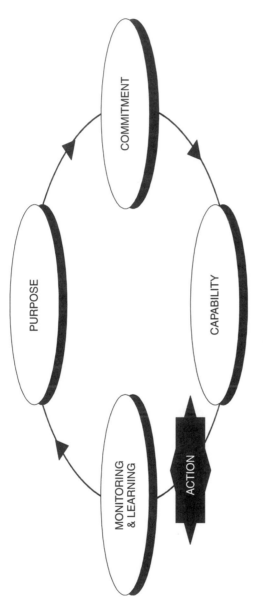

Purpose	Commitment	Capability	Monitoring and Learning
– Objectives (including mission, vision and strategy) – Risks – Policies – Planning – Performance targets and indicators	– Ethical values including integrity – Human resource policies – Authority, responsibility, and accountability – Mutual trust	– Knowledge, skills, and tools – Communication processes – Information coordination – Control activities	– Monitoring internal and external environments – Monitoring performance – Challenging assumptions – Reassessing information needs and information systems – Follow-up procedures – Assessing the effectiveness of control

Source: Robert R. Moeller, *Sarbanes-Oxley and the New Internal Auditing Rules,* © copyright 2004, John Wiley & Sons. Used with permission.

The CoCo framework has evolved since its inception from a prime focus on internal controls to more emphasis on risk management and corporate governance, and CICA has been shaping internal control concepts and developing a new terminology that will probably become codified in CICA future standards. The CoCo guidance states that it is management's overriding objective to ensure, as far as practical, the orderly and efficient conduct of the entity's business. Management discharges its internal control responsibilities through actions directed to:

- *Optimizing the Use of Resources.* Internal control assists management in optimizing the use of resources by ensuring, as far as practical, that reliable information is provided to management for the determination of business policies, and by monitoring the implementation of those policies and the degree of compliance with them.

- *Prevention or Detection of Error and Fraud.* A management internal controls objective is the prevention and detection of unintentional mistakes or errors and fraud—the intentional misrepresentation of financial information or misappropriation of assets. The guidance goes on to state that any controls here should be *cost-effective*. The cost of a possible control should be weighed against the relative likelihood of error and fraud occurring and the consequences if any were to occur, including their effect on the financial statements.

- *Safeguarding of Assets.* An organization's assets should be safeguarded partly through internal controls and partly through business policies. Internal control protects against loss arising from *unintentional* exposure to risk in processing transactions or handling related assets. The degree of *intentional* exposure to risk is determined by business policies.

- *Maintaining Reliable Control Systems.* These are the policies and procedures established and maintained by management either to collect, record, and process data and report the resulting information or to enhance the reliability of such data and information. Management requires reliable control systems to provide information necessary to operate the entity and produce such accounting and other records necessary for the preparation of financial statements.

The preceding paragraphs have briefly outlined the CoCo framework. CoCo provides a framework for control assessments, but really is not an assessment methodology along the line of the CobiT approaches discussed earlier in the chapter. CoCo targets all stakeholders and is intended to be "creatively interpreted and applied." Internal auditors use various assessment tools that range along a continuum. At one extreme, an audit approach can be based on searching for concrete evidence with no involvement of those responsible for the activities and processes under review. This approach would be most appropriate in the case of a forensic investigation into questionable or fraudulent activities as discussed in Chapter 11, "Fraud Detection and Prevention." At the opposite other extreme are self-assessment approaches that place responsibility for identifying issues and solutions with those who manage the activities and processes.

CoCo reviews are most effective when they incorporate a self-assessment approach. Only by soliciting perceptions of employees and management through such an approach can an internal auditor gain evidence about such control factors as shared ethical values and mutual trust. CoCo-based self-assessments are not appropriate for every circumstance. There are occasions in which audit objectives are specific and best addressed by a review of data and documents. However, CoCo provides a way to deal with issues that have their origins in overall management systems—which, we now recognize, are critical to the good functioning of overall control. In some respects, the CoCo self-assessment approach to evaluating internal controls has some similarities to the IIA's Control Self-Assessment approach discussed in Chapter 26.

While it is very consistent with the U.S. framework, CoCo represents a less structured model of internal control than the U.S.'s COSO. It certainly stands in stark contrast to the CobiT model. The CoCo control framework represents a different and less stringent way of thinking about internal control and provides a good way for management to think about how its organizations are performing. It is recommended that all internal auditors take a more detailed look at the CoCo model. A good starting point is www.cica.ca.

7.5   TURNBULL REPORT

Similar to Canada, the professional designation in the United Kingdom is chartered accountant, a certification that is obtained through gaining auditing experience and passing a comprehensive examination. The professional organization here is The Institute of Chartered Accountants in England and Wales as well as separate organizations for Ireland as well as for Scotland. There are separate chartered accountant designations and organizations for management accounting and public finance. Affiliated with the Chartered Accountants institutes, the Auditing Practices Board (APB) establishes and publishes statements of the principles called APBs, similar to what were the U.S. Statements of Auditing Standards (SAS) documents.

The United Kingdom was involved in some of the same concerns as the United States regarding improper financial reporting during the 1990s. Their focus was more on inappropriate statements made by directors but included failures of internal control as well. The result of a study in the United Kingdom was what is called the 1999 Turnbull report on internal control. The report is oriented toward directors of publicly traded companies and places a strong emphasis on objective setting, risk identification, and risk assessments when evaluating internal controls. The report calls on directors to regularly consider the following factors:

- The nature and extent of the risks facing the company
- The extent and categories of risk, which it regards as acceptable for the company to bear

- The likelihood of the risks concerned materializing

- The company's ability to reduce the incidence and impact on the business risks that do materialize

- The costs of operating particular controls relative to the benefit thereby obtained in managing the related risks

This set of considerations is very similar to the risk assessment approaches that were discussed in Chapter 5, "Understanding and Assessing Risks: Enterprise Risk Management." What is significant about the Turnbull approach to developing an effective system of internal controls is its emphasis on understanding business objectives and then analyzing risks as the first steps to designing effective internal controls. Turnbull then suggests a framework for evaluating the effectiveness of internal controls as shown in Exhibit 7.10. The idea is to understand the risks, to design controls based on those risks, and to perform tests to evaluate the controls.

Although there are some differences in the text, Turnbull provides the same three basic objectives of internal controls as was discussed for COSO and CoCo: effectiveness and efficiency of operations, reliability of internal and external financial reporting, and compliance with applicable laws and regulations. The really important concept of the Turnbull approach is the emphasis on risk assessment. Emphasis should be placed developing controls on high-impact and higher-likelihood risks. COSO provides the same general guidance, but the U.K. Turnbull approach perhaps does a better job in establishing a risk-based internal control environment. There is nothing to conflict with COSO, and an internal auditor might find value in reviewing the Turnbull report in greater detail.

7.6 INTERNAL CONTROL FRAMEWORKS WORLDWIDE

With a wide range of independent national accounting authorities and some differences in business practices worldwide, there are other variations of internal control frameworks or models. Most follow the COSO framework with its CoCo or Turnbull variations. For example, in Australia there is the Australian Conditions for Control (ACC). It is not the objective of this book to summarize internal control practices on a country-by-country basis.

The issue here is that COSO is soon to become the worldwide standard for reviews of internal controls. The explosive growth of investing and raising capital in the global markets has put an emphasis on the development of international accounting, auditing, and ethical standards. The result has been a set of international accounting and auditing standards that are designed to be applicable worldwide and become the dominant standards in countries that currently do not have strong national standards such as the United States, Canada, Britain, and many EC countries. The COSO model of internal control has become the effective worldwide standard for assessing internal controls, and all internal auditors should develop a strong understanding of COSO as explained in these chapters.

EXHIBIT 7.10

EXHIBIT 7.10

Turnbull Approach to Evaluating Internal Controls

Framework for forming an opinion on the effectiveness of
internal control

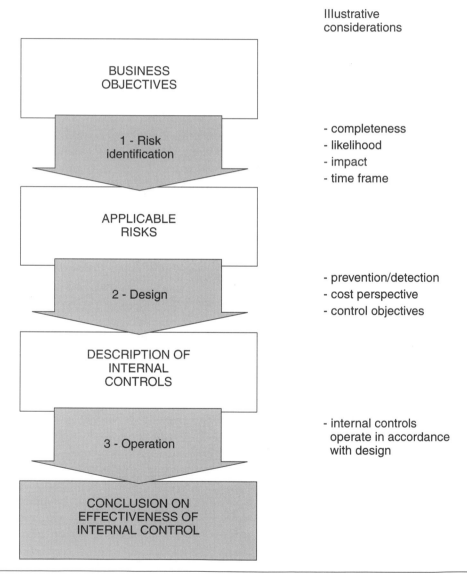

Illustrative
considerations

BUSINESS
OBJECTIVES

1 - Risk
identification

- completeness
- likelihood
- impact
- time frame

APPLICABLE
RISKS

2 - Design

- prevention/detection
- cost perspective
- control objectives

DESCRIPTION OF
INTERNAL
CONTROLS

3 - Operation

- internal controls
  operate in accordance
  with design

CONCLUSION ON
EFFECTIVENESS OF
INTERNAL CONTROL

Source: Robert R. Moeller, *Sarbanes-Oxley and the New Internal Auditing Rules,* © copyright 2004, John Wiley & Sons. Used with permission.

ENDNOTES

[1] *CobiT—Governance, Control and Audit for Information and Related Technology*, 3rd Edition, IT Governance Institute, Rolling Meadows, IL, 2000.

[2] *CobiT Framework*, 3rd Edition, IT Governance Institute, Rolling Meadows, IL, 2000.

[3] CMM is registered in the U.S. Patent and Trademark Office by Carnegie Mellon University.

[4] *IT Control Objectives for Sarbanes-Oxley*, IT Governance Institute, Rolling Meadows, IL 2003.

PART THREE

Internal Audit and Corporate Governance

CHAPTER EIGHT

Internal Audit and the Board Audit Committee

8.1 ROLE OF THE AUDIT COMMITTEE

A significant step in organizing an effective internal audit function is to obtain authorization and approval by the organization's audit committee of the board of directors. The audit committee provides this broad authorization for an internal audit function through a formal audit charter document. An audit committee also approves internal audit's overall plans for continuing activities through the current period and beyond. As one of the several operating committees established by the board, the audit committee has a rather unique role compared to other board committees. It consists of only outside directors—giving it independence from management—and should be composed of a specially qualified group of outside directors who understand, monitor, coordinate, and interpret the internal control and related financial activities for the entire board. As was discussed in Chapter 3, "Internal Audit in the Twenty-First Century: Sarbanes-Oxley and Beyond," one of those audit committee members must be designated as a "financial expert" per Sarbanes-Oxley Act (SOA) rules. In order to fulfill its responsibilities to the overall board of directors, to the stockholders, and to the public, an audit committee needs an internal audit function to become an independent set of "eyes and ears" inside of the organization, providing assessments of internal controls and other matters.

The comments in this chapter are based on a corporate structure organization such as a company with SEC registered stock. Other nonpublic organizations will benefit from this audit committee structure as well. For example, many not-for-profit private organizations are large enough to have a formal board of directors and an internal audit function. Although not mandated by SOA and SEC rules, these types of organizations will benefit from a board audit committee of only independent directors. An internal auditor in that form of organization would benefit both the internal audit function and the overall organization management by suggesting this type of audit committee approach.

While external auditors have a prime responsibility to an organization's board of directors for attesting to the accuracy and fairness of financial statements, internal audit has an even larger role in assessing internal controls over the reliability of financial reporting, the effectiveness and efficiency of operations, and the organization's compliance with applicable laws and regulations. Corporate boards of directors have had formal audit committees for some time, and internal audit has always had a long-term reporting relationship to their board of directors' audit committee. However, much has changed since the introduction of SOA in mid-2002. In past years, many audit committees met only quarterly for often brief sessions in conjunction with regular board meetings; those meetings were often limited to little more than approving the external auditor's annual plan, their quarterly and year-end reports, and reviewing internal audit activities on what appeared to be little more than a perfunctory basis. While NYSE rules, even prior to SOA, required that audit committees consist of only outside directors, many audit committee directors in the past often appeared to be "buddies" of the CEO with apparently little independent action. While internal audit's chief audit executive (CAE) has always had a direct reporting relationship to the audit committee, this often was little more than a theoretical relationship in which the CAE had limited contact with the audit committee beyond scheduled board meetings. SOA has now changed all of that!

A major issue that evolved from the collapse of Enron and related financial scandals at that time was the publicity and testimony that boards and their audit committees were not exercising a sufficient level of independent corporate governance. The Enron audit committee was frequently highlighted as an example of what was wrong. It was reported to have met some 30 minutes per calendar quarter prior to the fall of Enron. Given the size of the corporation at that time and the many directions it was pursuing, the Enron audit committee's attention appeared to be limited at best.

Even before the fall of Enron, the SEC was becoming interested in seeing audit committees acting as more independent, effective managers of a company's external and internal auditors. Also, what was called the Blue Ribbon Committee on Improving the Effectiveness of Corporate Audit Committees was formed in 1999 by the NYSE, SEC, AICPA, and others. It issued a series of recommendations on improving the independence, operations, and effectiveness of audit committees. The stock exchanges then adopted new independent director audit committee standards as listing requirements to be phased in over the next 18 months, and the then Auditing Standards Board of the AICPA raised standards for external auditors with respect to their audit committees. The subsequent financial failure of Enron and other companies showed that these earlier audit committee initiatives were not enough. The result was the legislative work that led to SOA.

This chapter discusses the expansion of the responsibilities of board of directors' audit committees since the passage of SOA and how an internal audit function can best serve its audit committee. Although an audit committee will typically have regular contacts primarily with the CAE, all internal auditors should have an understanding of this very important relationship. We will discuss heightened audit committee responsibilities and how internal audit can better work with an audit committee under SOA rules.

8.2 AUDIT COMMITTEE ORGANIZATION AND CHARTERS

An audit committee is an operating component of the board of directors with responsibility for internal controls and financial reporting oversight. Because of this oversight responsibility, audit committee members must be independent directors with no connection to organization management. There are no size restrictions, but a full board with 12 to 16 members will often have a 5- or 6-member audit committee. An audit committee may invite members of management or others to attend audit committee meetings and even to join in on the committee's deliberations. However, any such invited outside guests cannot be full voting members. An organization's board of directors is a formal entity given the responsibility for the overall governance of that audit committee for its investors or lenders. All members of the board can be held legally liable through their actions on any issue, and a board and its committees enact most of its formal business through resolutions, which become matters of organization record. The organization of the board's various committees, including the audit committee, is established through such a resolution. Exhibit 8.1 is a sample board resolution to establish an audit committee. This type of resolution is documented in the records of the board and not revised unless some circumstances require a change.

The Exhibit 8.1 resolution authorizing the audit committee is an example of the manner a board of directors sets rules for itself. Such resolutions are an example of corporate governance—setting the rules by which a corporation operates. Really not published in annual reports and the like, the existence of appropriate board resolutions only becomes an issue in matters of regulation and litigation when a board needs to rely on an authorizing resolution. Many corporate board audit committee authorizing resolutions were updated in 2002 to make them compliant with SOA.

While not a necessary requirement, many corporate internal audit functions regularly operate through a formal audit charter, a document approved by the board audit committee and senior management that outlines internal audit's role and responsibilities. Although the IIA provided some guidance for drafting an internal audit charter, these internal audit charters did not follow

EXHIBIT 8.1

Board Resolution Example: Authorizing the Audit Committee

ExampleCo Corp Board of Directors

Board Resolution No. XX, MM DD, 20YY

The Board of Directors authorizes an audit committee to consist of five directors who are not officers of ExampleCo. The Board will designate one member of Audit Committee as a Financial Expert, per the requirements of the Sarbanes-Oxley Act, and elect one member to serve as its chair for a term of three years. The ExampleCo Chief Executive Officer may attend Audit Committee meetings as a nonvoting member at the invitation of the Audit Committee.

The ExampleCo Audit Committee is responsible for:

- Determining that ExampleCo internal controls are effective and formally reporting on the status of those controls on an annual basis with quarterly updates.

- Recommending an external auditor to be selected on an annual basis through a vote by the shareholders.

- Taking action, where appropriate, on significant control weaknesses reported by internal audit, the external auditors, and others.

- Approving an annual plan and budget submitted by the external auditor.

- Approving annual audit plans to be submitted by the outside auditor as well as by internal audit.

- Approving the appointment and ongoing service of Internal Audit's Chief Audit Executive.

- Approving the annual internal audit plan and recommending areas for additional audit work as appropriate.

- Reviewing and distributing the audited financial statements submitted by the outside auditor.

- Establishing an ExampleCo whistleblower program that allows officers, employees, and other stakeholders to report financial accounting errors or improper actions and to investigate and resolve those whistleblower calls without any retribution to the original whistleblower.

- Circulating a Code of Ethics to senior officers and obtaining their assent on a quarterly basis.

- Initiating appropriate actions based upon any recommendations by the outside auditor or the Director of Internal Audit.

- Maintaining records on other consulting activities as mandated by the Sarbanes-Oxley Act.

An Audit Committee meeting will be held at least concurrently with each Board meeting and at other times as required.

The Audit Committee will meet privately with the outside auditor or the Chief Audit Executive to assess the internal control environment and to evaluate the independence of the audit function.

Approved: Corporate Secretary

---

any specific standards or format but formally stated, among other matters, that internal audit had full access to all records and facilities within the organization. Internal audit charters are discussed in Chapter 1, "Foundations of Internal Auditing," and cover an internal audit function but not the corporate board audit committee. The NYSE had suggested proposed board audit committee charters in December 1999 but with no requirement that an audit committee should have such a charter. SOA has now mandated that each audit committee must develop a formal audit charter to be published as part of the annual proxy statement.

The purpose of a board audit committee charter is to define the audit committee's responsibilities regarding:

- The identification, assessment, and management of financial risks and uncertainties
- The continuous improvement of financial systems
- The integrity of financial statements and financial disclosures
- Compliance with legal and regulatory requirements
- The qualifications, independence, and performance of independent outside auditors
- The capabilities, resources, and performance or the internal audit department
- The full and open communication with and among the independent accountants, management, internal auditors, counsel, employees, the audit committee, and the board

The audit committee is required to go before the overall board of directors and obtain authorization, through this charter document, for board audit committee activities just as the CAE, representing the corporate internal audit function, has regularly gone before the board audit committee. This audit committee charter is to be published annually as part of the organization's annual meeting proxy statement.

While some may look on this audit charter requirement as just some additional pages to add bulk to the proxy statement, it is a formal commitment by the board audit committee to ensure the integrity of financial statements and to supervise the internal and external audit functions. There is no single required format for this audit committee charter document, but the NYSE has published a model charter that has been adopted by many public corporations today. While formats vary from one corporation to another, audit committee charters generally include the following sections:

1. Purpose and Power of Audit Committee
2. Audit Committee Composition
3. Meetings Schedule
4. Audit Committee Procedures
5. Audit Committee Primary Activities
    a. Corporate Governance
    b. Public Reporting
    c. Independent Accountants

    d. Audits and Accounting

    e. Other Activities

6. Discretionary Activities

    a. Independent Accountants

    b. Internal Audits

    c. Accounting

    d. Controls and Systems

    e. Public Reporting

    f. Compliance Oversight Responsibilities

    g. Risk Assessments

    h. Financial Oversight Responsibilities

    i. Employee Benefit Plans Investment Fiduciary Responsibilities

7. Audit Committee Limitations

Although audit committee charters vary, many contain descriptions of these areas. Some appear to have been developed by corporate legal counsels with language to cover every possible contingency, while others are more clear and succinct. An excellent example of an easy-to-follow charter is Microsoft Corporation's 2003 audit committee charter, part of their Web site and shown in Exhibit 8.2. Although not included in our exhibit, the full text of that charter also outlines some 30 specific activities for the audit committee. For example, number 29 in that list states, "Meet with the General Auditor in executive sessions to discuss any matters that the Committee or the General Auditor believes should be discussed privately with the Audit Committee" and highlights the fact that this activity will occur two times per year.

Not every corporation is a Microsoft Corporation in terms of its size, sophistication, and resources, but all corporations with SEC registration must conform to SOA rules. Smaller entities will not have the resources or need to release a Microsoft-like Web-based audit committee charter. But, the smaller corporation must still have an independent director's audit committee, as mandated by SOA, as well as an audit committee charter. This is the type of board of directors' resolution document that would be part of corporate records.

Whether large or small, an organization still needs to have effective internal controls as well as an internal audit function. This is important today because a limited internal audit resource can no longer rely on its external auditors to perform required tasks that it had expected them to do in the past. The CAE for that small corporation should review materials published by the IIA, ISACA, or the AICPA and work with internal auditors from other small firms in the auditor's community to develop ideas and approaches. The local IIA chapter will typically have as members CAEs from other nearby similar-sized companies who should be willing to share thoughts and ideas.

EXHIBIT 8.2

Microsoft Corporation Audit Committee Charter

Role

The Audit Committee of the Board of Directors assists the Board of Directors in fulfilling its responsibility for oversight of the quality and integrity of the accounting, auditing, and reporting practices of the company and such other duties as directed by the Board. The Committee's role includes a particular focus on the qualitative aspects of financial reporting to shareholders, and on the company's processes to manage business and financial risk, and for compliance with significant applicable legal, ethical, and regulatory requirements. The Committee is directly responsible for the appointment, compensation, and oversight of the public accounting firm engaged to prepare or issue an audit report on the financial statements of the company.

Membership

The membership of the Committee shall consist of at least three directors who are generally knowledgeable in financial and auditing matters, including at least one member with accounting or related financial management expertise. Each member shall be free of any relationship that, in the opinion of the Board, would interfere with his or her individual exercise of independent judgment. Applicable laws and regulations shall be followed in evaluating a member's independence. The chairperson shall be appointed by the full Board.

Communications/Reporting

The public accounting firm shall report directly to the Committee. The Committee is expected to maintain free and open communication with the public accounting firm, the internal auditors, and the company's management. This communication shall include private executive sessions, at least annually, with each of these parties. The Committee chairperson shall report on Audit Committee activities to the full Board.

Education

The company is responsible for providing the Committee with educational resources related to accounting principles and procedures, current accounting topics pertinent to the company, and other material as may be requested by the Committee. The company shall assist the Committee in maintaining appropriate financial literacy.

Authority

In discharging its oversight role, the Committee is empowered to investigate any matter brought to its attention, with full power to retain outside counsel or other experts for this purpose.

Responsibilities

The Committee's specific responsibilities in carrying out its oversight role are delineated in the Audit Committee Responsibilities Checklist. The responsibilities checklist will be updated annually to reflect changes in regulatory requirements, authoritative guidance, and evolving oversight practices. As the compendium of Committee responsibilities, the most recently updated responsibilities checklist will be considered to be an addendum to this charter.

EXHIBIT 8.2 *(CONTINUED)*

Microsoft Corporation Audit Committee Charter

The Committee relies on the expertise and knowledge of management, the internal auditors, and the public accounting firm in carrying out its oversight responsibilities. Management of the company is responsible for determining the company's financial statements are complete, accurate, and in accordance with generally accepted accounting principles. The public accounting firm is responsible for auditing the company's financial statements. It is not the duty of the Committee to plan or conduct audits, to determine that the financial statements are complete and accurate and are in accordance with generally accepted accounting principles, to conduct investigations, or to assure compliance with laws and regulations or the company's internal policies, procedures, and controls.

Microsoft Corporation Audit Committee Responsibilities Checklist

A detailed list of responsibilities follows along with a schedule of the quarterly meeting when the activity will be covered.

8.3 AUDIT COMMITTEE'S FINANCIAL EXPERT AND INTERNAL AUDIT

A major audit committee criticism after the fall of Enron was that many board members serving on audit committees did not appear to understand financial and internal control issues. People were elected to board audit committees because of their business or professional backgrounds but often did not understand complex financial or internal control issues. SOA now requires that at least one of the audit committee's independent directors be what is called a "financial expert" with some fairly specific requirements for that role, as outlined in the Chapter 3 overview of SOA. This financial expert board member could very well be internal audit's best or closest audit committee ally and may very well be the starting point for the CAE to introduce or reintroduce internal audit to the board's audit committee. The typical audit committee member today and certainly that financial expert are certainly in a new and challenging position with legal mandates and lots of pressure.

SOA has caused many changes to corporate governance, the board of directors, and certainly the audit committee. In many situations, the CAE and internal audit may be a unique thread of corporate governance continuity, and internal audit can help its audit committee in this new era through a three-step approach:

1. Through a report and presentation, provide a detailed summary of current internal audit processes for risk assessments, planning and performing audits, and reporting results through audit reports.

2. Working with human resources and other resources, present plans to the audit committee to assist in launching the SOA-required ethics and

whistleblower program as discussed in Chapter 9, "Whistleblower Programs and Codes of Conduct."

3. Develop detailed plans for reviewing and assessing internal controls in the organization. A key component of SOA Section 404, internal control assessment requirements, as are discussed in Chapter 6, "Evaluating Internal Controls: Section 404 Assessments."

The first step is that internal audit should make a concentrated effort to explain its processes and procedures to the audit committee, the overall board, and to senior management with an emphasis on SOA's internal audit requirements. Once this board presentation is launched, it should become part of the annual internal audit planning process with ongoing changes being reported. However, even before launching any such presentation, internal audit should go through its own processes and perform what might be called a health check to assess current internal audit practices. This might point to areas where there is room for improvement. Exhibit 8.3 shows an internal audit health check

EXHIBIT 8.3

Internal Audit Health Check Assessment

Internal Audit (I/A) Processes

1. Does I/A have a formal set of standards and are those standards consistent with IIA Standards (as outlined in Chapter 12)?

2. Are new I/A members educated on the use of I/A standards and is overall compliance to standards monitored regularly?

3. Does I/A prepare an annual audit plan and is performance against the plan regularly monitored by the audit committee?

4. Are audit plans developed through a formal risk assessment process (see Chapter 5 on risk assessments)?

5. Are individual audits planned and supervised with sufficient attention given to adequate planning and staffing (discussed in Chapter 14)?

6. Is all I/A work documented through a formal set of workpapers and are those workpapers reviewed by appropriate levels of management (workpaper procedures are discussed in Chapter 15)?

7. Are audit findings reviewed, as appropriate, with management before release of final audit reports?

8. Are recipients of audit reports required to respond to recommendations with plans for corrective action and are those responses monitored (see Chapter 17)?

9. Are there special I/A procedures in place in the event or fraud or suspected fraud encountered during reviews (fraud detection is discussed in Chapter 11)?

10. Does I/A report the results of its activities regularly to the audit committee?

11. Are overall budgets developed for all I/A work and is performance monitored against those budgets?

12. Do all members of I/A receive adequate training on accounting, internal controls, and technology issues?

assessment internal survey that can be expanded or modified, depending on current conditions. The idea here is that internal audit should go through a rapid self-assessment, asking itself how it is doing at present and what it should do to improve, and then make improvements as required.

Once internal audit has gone through such a self-correction exercise, audit processes and ongoing activities should be presented to the audit committee as well the overall board and management. The idea is make certain that all parties are aware of internal audit's processes as well as ongoing issues. The session should be given to key members of management first, before the audit committee presentation to ensure that internal audit's message is well understood and consistent with other management initiatives. Depending on the organization and its past history, internal audit may receive too little or even too much credit for their role in the corporate governance process.

8.4 AUDIT COMMITTEE RESPONSIBILITIES FOR INTERNAL AUDIT

The corporate audit committee has a primary responsibility for the corporation's internal audit function. Prior to SOA, this had often been little more than a theoretical concept where internal audit reported to the audit committee "on paper" but effectively reported to the CFO or some other senior corporate officer. The modern internal audit function today should have a very active relationship with the organization's audit committee. These charters are often very specific regarding relationships with internal audit and typically require the audit committee to:

Review the resources, plans, activities, staffing, and organizational structure of internal audit. These areas will be discussed in Chapters 13, "Internal Audit Organization and Planning," and 14, "Directing and Performing Internal Audits."

1. Review the appointment, performance, and replacement of the CAE.

2. Review all audits and reports prepared by internal audit together with management's response. Audit reports and communications are discussed in Chapter 17, "Audit Reports and Internal Audit Communications."

3. Review with management, the CAE, and the independent accountants the adequacy of financial reporting and internal control systems. The scope and results of the internal audit, program, and the cooperation afforded or limitations, if any, imposed by management on the conduct of the internal audit program.

The above have been part of the relationship between internal audit and its audit committee over time, but the audit committee charter published in the proxy formalizes this arrangement. The CAE should work closely with the audit committee to ensure that the effective communication links are in place. The third point above on audit reports is an example. Some internal audit departments have developed the habit, over time, of supplying their audit committees with only summaries of internal audit report findings or just submitting what internal audit has decided are significant audit report findings. SOA put this in a new perspective. Internal audit should not just send the audit committee what it *thinks* they need to see. Rather, SOA mandates that internal audit should provide the audit committee with all audit reports and their management responses. Even when internal audit generates a large number of audit reports, as in the case of a retail organization with audits of many smaller store units that often have few significant findings, the audit committee should receive detailed information on *all audits* performed. Even though summary reports are provided, complete reports for all audits should be provided as well.

(a) Appointment of the Chief Audit Executive

While the CAE typically reports administratively to organization management, the audit committee is responsible for the hiring and dismissal of this internal audit executive. The board's compensation committee may also be involved when the CAE's designated as an officer of the organization. The objective here is not to deny organizational management the right to name the person who will administer the internal audit department, which serves the combined needs of organizational management and the audit committee. Rather, the significance of the audit committee's participation is to ensure the independence of the internal audit function when there is a need to speak out regarding issues identified in the review and appraisal of internal controls and other organizational activities.

The actual participation of the audit committee in the selection of the CAE can take a number of forms but typically involves a review of the proposed director's credentials followed by a formal interview. Organizational management—often primarily the CFO—consults with the chair of the audit committee regarding potential CAE candidates, allowing the audit committee time to review and comment on, and sometimes interview them, before any change is actually made. In many instances, the organization will be faced with the need to name a new CAE because the existing person has resigned or has been promoted. Management may suggest the promotion of someone from within the organization or the recruitment of an outsider, but the audit committee will have the final decision. Agreement on the adequacy of the candidate's qualifications to serve the needs of both management and the board of directors is an essential condition of an ongoing effective relationship between senior management and the audit committee.

The audit committee is usually not involved in day-to-day administrative matters regarding the CAE and the entire internal audit function and must take care to ensure the ongoing quality of the internal organization. For example, an incumbent CAE should continue to have opportunities for receiving a promotion or be given other responsibilities as a part of the organization's management development program. In other instances, senior management may express strong feelings that the CAE should be transferred or terminated because of some strong management concern. In the latter situation, the audit committee should review the suggested personnel action and provide the affected CAE with a fair hearing on the issues involved. The audit committee also may feel that the CAE is not doing an adequate job either in complying with the audit committee's requests or in directing the internal audit function, or both. In such a case, the chair of the audit committee would typically express those concerns to organizational management and start the process for a change in personnel. In an extreme case where there is disagreement regarding the CAE, the audit committee can always hire an outside consultant to perform the audit review work desired by the committee or can direct management, through board directives, to make a change.

The overall issue here is that the audit committee has the ability to hire or fire the CAE, but there must be an ongoing level of cooperation. The audit committee is not on-site on a daily basis to provide detailed internal audit supervision and must rely on management for some detailed support. The CAE or any member of internal audit cannot just ignore an appropriate management request by claiming that he or she only reports to the audit committee and is not responsible to organizational line management. Similarly, organizational management must make certain that internal audit is part of the organization and not some near outsider because of the audit committee relationship.

(b) Approval of Internal Audit Charter

As discussed in Chapter 1, an adequate internal audit charter serves as a basis or authorization for every effective internal audit program. An adequate charter is particularly important to define the roles and responsibilities of internal audit and its responsibility to serve the audit committee properly. It is here that the mission of internal audit must clearly provide for service to the audit committee as well as to senior management. An internal audit charter is a broad, but general document that defines the responsibilities of internal audit within the organization, describes the standards followed, and defines the relationship between the audit committee and internal audit. The latter point is particularly important because it sends a special message to senior management that the CAE can go to a higher authority—the audit committee—in the event of a significant controversy or internal controls issue.

The audit committee is responsible for approving this internal audit charter, just as the full board is responsible for approving the audit committee's charter. We are briefly discussing internal audit charters here because of this audit committee responsibility, but internal audit charters were discussed in greater detail in the Chapter 1 discussion on the foundations of internal auditing. Who is responsible for drafting this internal audit charter? In theory, perhaps, the audit committee might draft the document as a board committee activity. In reality, the CAE will usually take the lead in drafting this charter and/or suggesting appropriate updates to an existing charter to the chair of the audit committee.

While the internal audit charter authorizes the work that should be performed, the audit committee members may not be in a position to draft detailed audit charter requirements. The CAE typically works closely with the chair of the audit committee to draft this document for audit committee and overall board approval. In addition to the charter, the specific nature and scope of internal audit's service responsibilities to the audit committee should be formalized and outlined. These could include periodic written audit status reports, regularly scheduled meetings with the audit committee, and both the rights and obligations of internal audit's direct access to the audit committee. While this understanding typically does not require a formal audit committee resolution, both parties should have a clear understanding of the responsibilities of internal audit to present reports and to attend audit committee meetings. The acceptance of the internal audit charter and related provisions by all parties of interest means that internal audit is freed from barriers that might otherwise prevent it from making needed disclosures to the audit committee, even those of a very sensitive nature.

This charter statement of internal audit's relationship to the audit committee is especially important since internal audit's has a day-to-day working relationship with organizational management. While the audit committee selects the CAE, other members of the audit team are hired and paid by the organization, not the independent audit committee. Senior management often may forget that internal audit also has this special reporting relationship within the organization. This need for an adequate internal audit charter is sometimes discounted by organizational management on the grounds that there are *no restrictions* to internal audit's independence. Nevertheless, a strong internal audit charter, approved by the audit committee, is an important provision of corporate governance.

(c) Approval of Internal Audit Plans and Budgets

The audit committee should ideally have developed an overall understanding of the total audit needs of the organization. This high-level appraisal covers various special control and financial-reporting issues, allowing the audit committee to determine the portion of audit or risk assessment needs to be performed by either the internal or other providers. As part of this role, the audit committee is responsible for reviewing and approving all internal audit higher-level plans and budgets. This audit committee responsibility is consistent with its role as the ultimate coordinator of the total audit effort. While organizational management may have its own ideas about the total audit effort and how it should be carried out, and while the CAE has views as to what needs to be done, this is an audit committee responsibility. It is essential that the varying views of the key parties be jointly considered and appropriately reconciled, but the audit committee will have the final word here.

The review of all internal audit plans by the committee is essential if the policies and plans for the future are to be determined most effectively. The introduction of new audit responsibilities since SOA has changed roles that have been in place for years, and all interested parties should understand the nature of the total audit plan. Organizational management, internal auditors, and external audit alike then will know what to expect from the suppliers of audit services. The audit committee should assume a high-level coordination role. Although there are practical limitations as to how actively the audit committee can become involved in the detailed planning process, some involvement has a demonstrated high value. Typically, the chair of the audit committee is the most active person in this plan review, but even this person is subject to time limitations. Internal audit should prepare a comprehensive set of annual planning documents for the committee that give detailed plans for the upcoming year as well as longer-range plans for the future. Suggested formats for these plans are discussed in Chapter 5, "Understanding and Assessing Risks: Enterprise Risk

Management," and in Chapter 13. In addition, internal audit should prepare summarized reports of past audit activities and reassessments of its coverage to give the audit committee an understanding of significant areas covered in past reviews. Although internal audit should report its activities to the audit committee on a regular basis, this summary reporting of past activity gives an overview of past areas for audit emphasis as well as highlighting any potential gaps in audit coverage. Exhibit 8.4 is an example of a one-year audit plan for presentation to the audit committee. The CAE would present this type of report, listing particulars for each audit, to the committee, with supporting details to answer questions and discuss the details. The summary report on past activities is particularly important in that it shows the areas that had been scheduled in the prior year's plan and the accomplishments against that plan.

In many organizations, the annual audit plan is developed through both internal audit's risk analysis process and discussions with both senior management and the audit committee. Management and the committee may suggest areas for potential internal audit review. Internal audit should develop plans within the constraints of budget and resource limitations. If the audit committee has suggested a review of some specialized area but internal audit is unable to perform the planned audit due to some known constraints, the CAE should clearly communicate that deficiency to the audit committee.

(d) Review and Action on Significant Audit Findings

One of the audit committee's most important responsibility is to review and take action on reported significant audit findings that are reported to them by internal and external auditors, management, and others. While the audit committee has responsibility for all of these areas, the focus here is on the importance of internal audit reporting all significant findings to the audit committee on a regular and prompt basis. Part of this will occur through internal audit's distribution of all audit reports to the audit committee as part of the SOA requirements outlined in Chapter 3. While internal audit and others should certainly not filter audit findings and only tell the audit committee what they feel is "significant," the interests and efficiencies of all will be better served by internal audit regularly reporting significant audit findings as well as the status and disposition of those findings. Exhibit 8.5 is an example of such a significant findings report from a representative ExampleCo Corp.

Reacting to significant audit findings requires a combination of understanding, competence, and cooperation by all of the major parties of interest—internal audit, management, external auditors, and the audit committee itself. Total organizational welfare then becomes the standard by which to judge all internal audit services, as opposed to more provincial views that the interests of management and the audit committee may be to some extent conflicting. Within its own area of responsibility, internal audit should act aggressively in not just reporting these significant findings and stopping there, but should exercise ongoing monitoring actions to assess whether appropriate corrective action items are being taken.

EXHIBIT 8.4

One Year Audit Plan Summary for Audit Committee Review

ExampleCo Corporation 20XX Summarized Audit Plan

DIVISION	AUDIT	Risk Rank	Est. Start	Planned Finish	Total Hours	Total Costs	Comments
Electro	Inv. Planning Controls	8.4					Carry-over—From 20XX
Electro	Phys. Inv. Observation	9.5					
Electro	B-Plant Security	7.4					Physical & Logical Security
Electro	Materials Receiving	6.2					
Electro	Procurement Controls	6.8					Operational Assessment
Electro	New Marketing System	7.8					
Distribution	XML Order Controls	9.1					First Audit of Process
Distribution	Whse. Physical Security	5.3					Financial Controls
Distribution	Factory Labor Reporting	7.2					Operational Controls
Distribution	Product Incentive System	8.6					Audit Committee Request
Distribution	Prod. Warranty Returns	8.8					Operational Controls
Distribution	Business Continuity Planning	9.1					
Distribution	A/R Control Proceed	7.5					
Asia Pacific	G/L System Integrity	8.6					First Review of Unit
Asia Pacific	Labor Relations Stds.	8.2					First Review of Unit
Asia Pacific	Mfg. Control System	9.2					First Review of Unit
Corporate	Government Relations Dept.	5.3					
Corporate	Construction Contracts	7.3					
Total Internal Audit Projects							
Non-Audit	Training						
Non-Audit	Audit Administration						
Total Internal Audit for 20XX							

EXHIBIT 8.5

Internal Audit Significant Findings Report Example

ExampleCo Corporation

Audit Committee of the Board of Directors

Internal Audit Significant Audit Findings—May 31, 20XY

Status of Findings Reported in Prior Periods

- Jan XX—Disaster recovery plans have not been tested   — Open
- Jul XX—Physical security of abc plant poor   — Final rest
- Oct XX—Federal form S-1's not completed   — Corrected
- Nov XX—Poor project planning for Maxx Div   — In process
- Poor accounting controls over plant scrap   — Corrected

New Significant Audit Findings Added

- Mar XY—Poor controls over new WIP system   — Open
- Mar XY—Federal EEOC reports not filed   — Open

8.5 AUDIT COMMITTEE AND EXTERNAL AUDITORS

The audit committee has a major responsibility for hiring the principle external audit firm, approving its proposed budget and audit plan, and releasing the audited financial statements. While many aspects of this arrangement have remained unchanged over time, SOA has caused some significant changes here. As discussed in Chapter 6, the external auditors no longer can both perform and approve internal controls assessments. The Chapter 3 overview of SOA highlights that the consulting arms of the public accounting firms can no longer install financial applications that would be subject to external audit review. In addition, public accounting firms are prohibited from outsourcing the internal audit services for the organizations they audit. Audit committees need to be aware of and sensitive to these changes.

SOA requires that the audit committee approve all external audit services, including comfort letters, as well as any nonaudit services provided by the external auditors. At the time of this publication, external auditors are still allowed to provide tax services as well as certain de minimus service exceptions. External auditors are prohibited from providing the following nonaudit services contemporaneously with their financial statement audits:

- Bookkeeping and other services related to the accounting records or financial statements of the audit client
- Financial information systems design and implementation

- Appraisal or valuation services, fairness opinions, or contribution-in-kind reports

- Internal audit outsourcing services

- Management function or human resources support activities

- Broker or dealer, investment advisor, or investment banking services

- Legal services and other expert services unrelated to the audit

- Any other services that the PCAOB determines to be not permitted

Even though prohibited by external auditors, corporations will still need to contract for and acquire many of these types of services. These must be treated as special contracting arrangements, reported as part the annual financial reports. While it is in the best interests of the external audit firm to not get involved with such nonaudit services, internal audit should consider offering its services where appropriate and consistent with internal audit's charter.

8.6 WHISTLEBLOWER PROGRAMS AND CODES OF CONDUCT

As discussed in Chapter 3, SOA rules state that the audit committee must establish procedures for the receipt, retention, and treatment of complaints regarding accounting, internal accounting controls, or auditing matters, including procedures for the confidential, anonymous submission by employees of concerns regarding questionable accounting or auditing matters. This can be a documentation challenge, since much of this material must be held in a secure, confidential manner. The CAE will often be the only non-CEO and -CFO link between the audit committee and the corporation. Internal audit should offer its services to the audit committee—often to the designated financial expert—to establish documentation and communication procedures in the following areas:

- *Documentation Logging Whistleblower Calls.* SOA mandates that the audit committee establish a formal whistleblower program where employees can raise their concerns regarding improper audit and controls matters with no fear of retribution. A larger organization may already have an ethics function, as discussed in Chapter 9, where these matters can be handled in a secure manner. When a smaller organization does not have such a resource, internal audit should offer its facilities to log in such whistleblower communications, recording the date, time, and name of the caller for investigation and disposition. With a heritage of handling secure internal audit reports, internal audit is often the best resource in an organization to handle such matters. In all instances, SOA gives the audit committee the responsibility for launching and administering such a whistleblower program.

- *Disposition of Whistleblower Matters.* Even more important than logging in initial whistleblower calls, documentation must be maintained to record the nature of any follow-up investigations and related dispositions. Although the SOA whistleblower program does not have any cash reward component, complete documentation covering actions taken as well as any net savings should be maintained. Again, with its tradition of handling confidential matters, internal audit should offer to take responsibilities here in a secure confidential manner. This can be a very important activity because if an employee calls in a whistleblower matter, and it is later proven that this reported information got out and the whistleblower received some level of retaliation, the reporting employee can bring legal action against the corporation.

- *Codes of Ethics*. SOA gives the audit committee the responsibility to implement a code of ethics or conduct for a corporation's senior officers such as the CEO and CFO. The concept is to outline a set of "rules" for proper conduct and to have these senior officers to acknowledge that they have read, understand, and agree to abide by these rules. Chapter 9 will discuss these programs, and internal audit can play a leading role in helping the audit committee to implement such programs not just for a limited set of senior officers but for the entire organization.

8.7 OTHER AUDIT COMMITTEE ROLES

In this post-SOA world, the audit committee may frequently receive questions and queries regarding various accounting and auditing matters. Internal audit can offer to act as a secretary to the audit committee in documenting and handling these matters. Many of the points discussed in this chapter outline areas where internal audit can help the audit committee in handling some of its new SOA-related administrative chores. Even for a very large corporation, the audit committee many not involve more than perhaps six persons and will typically only be two in a smaller corporation. In addition, the typical independent director audit committee member is a busy person serving on multiple boards and with little direct administrative support. While the CEO or CFO's administrative support staff usually handles many administrative duties for board members, the new SOA rules require that the audit committee act independently. Internal audit is a natural resource to provide help.

Under SOA, the audit committee takes on a new and important role and internal audit is in perhaps one of the best positions to help facilitate that new role. The CAE has an opportunity for open access to the audit committee through presentations at periodic meetings and confidential one-on-one meetings. However, for many organizations in the past, that was often little more than a formality with limited true communication. As discussed throughout this book, SOA has changed these rules.

The audit committee and certainly its designated financial expert have been given a whole series of new responsibilities. Internal audit is in an excellent source to help audit committee members to fulfill their SOA new responsibilities through close communication as well as offering to take on certain audit committee documentation tasks. The broad acceleration of social expectations, the resulting impact on the areas of organizational responsibility, and the related growth of audit committees have generated new needs for the organization. As a result, there are new and expanding requirements for internal audit services that constitute both challenges and opportunities. SOA has changed much and the modern internal auditor should be aware of this expanded level of audit committee importance. Internal auditors should both respond to these SOA-mandated service needs and actively serve and work with their audit committees as part of an overall objective to provide maximum service to the organization.

CHAPTER NINE

Whistleblower Programs and Codes of Conduct

9.1 ORGANIZATIONAL ETHICS, COMPLIANCE, AND GOVERNANCE

Many of the more significant business failures over recent years, in the United States and elsewhere worldwide, were later shown by investigators, regulators, and journalists to be the result of unethical behavior on the part of business managers and CEOs. Historically, such failures are nothing new, and ethical lapses have occurred since the early days of business and trade—at least over the past 1,000 years. However, today's lapses often seem different, as access to information widely publicizes them and more people may be hurt due to the many people with stock market investments, retirement accounts, and other financial interests. The so-called robber barons of the 1880s had an attitude of "Let the public be damned!" This is not acceptable in today's society. The result has been an increased interest and attention in business ethics, including codes of conduct and whistleblower programs.

Internal auditors have been familiar with ethics programs and codes of conduct for some years. Internal audit's professional standards, as will be discussed in Chapter 12, "Internal Audit Professional Standards," have a code of conduct as a prominent component of IIA professional standards, and many internal auditors in recent years have become involved with reviewing and helping to enhance their organization's ethics programs. This area became even more important in recent years with the Sarbanes-Oxley Act (SOA) that mandated signed ethics or code of conduct statements from senior officers and called for audit-committee-directed whistleblower programs.

This chapter describes how to establish ethics and whistleblower functions that are consistent with SOA but also of value to all stakeholders in the organization: employees, officers, vendors, and contractors. Going beyond the SOA objectives to prevent fraudulent financial reporting, an effective ethics program is an important governance and compliance tool for the entire organization. Although whistleblower programs have been a component of U.S. defense-contracting labor laws for years, SOA now mandates the establishment of such programs in all registered public corporations. We will look at the guidelines here and the things internal audit can do to establish effective programs in the organization. We will also briefly look at the Organizational Sentencing Guideline, a U.S.-based "carrot-and-stick" approach to promote strong compliance programs. This chapter concludes with guidelines for performing operational and compliance audits over these functions.

9.2 LAUNCHING AN ORGANIZATIONAL ETHICS PROGRAM

As outlined in Chapter 3, "Internal Audit in the Twenty-First Century: Sarbanes-Oxley and Beyond," SOA mandates that corporate audit committees must have their CFO sign an ethics statement, but this is no guarantee that the CFO will always follow ethical business practices. The risks to the CFO of a major fine or even prison are stronger inducements. A strong set of CFO personal values and an ongoing commitment or desire to always "do the right thing" are even more important. While SOA's requirements are limited to senior financial officers in a corporation, an organization will generally find more value in launching and implementing such a program for the entire organization and its key stakeholders. While some ethics and code of conduct rules can be very specific to just the financial officers, organizations will find greater value in having one set of rules apply to all, and internal audit may want to consider advising management to move in that direction.

This section talks about how an organization can establish an effective ethics function, including a mission statement and a code of conduct. These are initiatives that are important today, but an organization cannot claim to have implemented an ethics program by just mailing a code of business conduct to everyone with instructions to read it. An effective ethics program requires a formal commitment by the organization and its employees and agents to "do the right thing."

Many organizations today already have elements of an ethics program in place, while others assume that they have good ethics practices because there have been no recent problems. All too often, those established "ethics programs" amount to little more than an employee code of conduct given to new hires on their first day on the job plus a few employee posters or brochures. That new employee is asked to read and sign the organization's code as part of completing such new hire materials as tax withholding forms, medical plan selections, and other employee options. All too often the code of conduct is signed, filed away, and forgotten. This does not constitute an effective ethics program for an organization.

The paragraphs that follow discuss some of the elements of an effective ethics program for an organization, from understanding the risk environment to launching an effective code of conduct. The effective organization should consider launching an organizational ethics program that applies to all stakeholders involved in the organization's operations. While the emphasis may be a bit different at various levels, all should be aware of the organization's values and overall mission. As a very natural party interested in good, ethical business practices, internal audit should be in a key position to help launch an organization-wide ethics function if one really does not exist or to help to improve on any current programs. This is clearly more than just SOA compliance!

(a) First Steps: Developing a Mission Statement

Every organization, no matter how big or small, needs a mission statement to describe its overall objectives and values. It should be a source of direction—a compass—let employees, customers, stockholders, and other stakeholders know what the organization stands for and what it does not. Once often little more than a nice but tired sounding slogan, an effective organization mission statement has become very important in our current era of strong organizational ethics and good corporate governance. Effective mission statements can be a great asset to an organization, allowing it to better achieve organizational goals and purposes.

Although it is years ago now, the Johnson & Johnson Tylenol crisis of the early 1990s provides a good example of the importance of strong corporate mission statement as a compass to provide direction. Johnson & Johnson, a major medical products provider, manufactured the popular over-the-counter pain reliever medication Tylenol®. In those days, such medications were sold in stores over the counter in screw-top bottles. Someone in the Chicago area opened a series of these Tylenol bottles, adulterated the contents with the poison cyanide, and replaced the bottles on the store shelves. Several people who purchased this tainted Tylenol subsequently died from cyanide poisoning. An investigation of these deaths quickly pointed to Johnson & Johnson and the poison-tainted Tylenol.

This whole matter put Johnson & Johnson under massive pressure. The corporation knew that it had extremely strong quality-control processes in place that would prevent such poison contamination from occurring within their own manufacturing facilities. They also knew that the contaminated products had appeared only in the Chicago area, while Tylenol was found on store shelves worldwide. A total product recall would be extremely expensive. However, Johnson and Johnson did not go through a long series of internal investigations and quickly did the right thing. They recalled all of their Tylenol products from store shelves worldwide and subsequently rereleased it in a newly designed sealed package. When asked why they were able to make such a very expensive recall decision so quickly with no evidence that they were at fault, the corporation stated that there was no need for a delayed decision. The Johnson & Johnson credo, their mission statement, dictated that decision. That Johnson and Johnson credo strongly states that the company's first responsibility is to supply high-quality products to their customers. At the time of the Tylenol crisis, everyone at Johnson & Johnson knew this, the credo had been posted widely in organization facilities, and there was no need for a decision. The whole unfortunate matter really highlighted the importance of a strong mission statement for an organization.

A strong corporate mission statement is an important element in any ethics and corporate governance initiative. Although most organizations will not face a crisis on the level of Johnson & Johnson with its tainted Tylenol in the 1990s, a stronger anchor of this sort might have helped some organizations to better avoid the accounting scandals in recent years that led to SOA.

Working with any ethics officer function and senior management, internal audit can help to evaluate any mission statement that may exist today or to rewrite or launch a new one if needed. The stakeholder ethics surveys discussed in the section following will highlight potential problems in any existing mission statement. If employees or other stakeholders are not really aware of any existing corporate mission statement or if they view it with little more than cynicism, there is a need to revisit and revise that document. A poorly crafted mission statement can often do more harm than good by creating cynical and unhappy organizational members who resist change. If the organization has no mission or values statement, there can be considerable value to assembling a team to develop a statement that reflects the organization's overall values and purposes. If an existing statement that was met with cynicism during the ethics survey, it is time to rework and revise that statement. However, any revised statement should be carefully crafted and delivered. If just rolled out with no preparation, it may be viewed with even more cynicism. A good mission statement also is a good starting point for the corporate "tone-at-the-top" message for today's corporation.

A good mission statement should make a positive statement about a corporation; it should hopefully inspire organizational members to harness their energy and passion and increase their commitment to achieving goals and objectives. The idea is to create a sense of purpose and direction that will be shared throughout the organization. Again going back some years ago, perhaps one of the best examples of a mission statement was expressed by U.S. president John F. Kennedy in the early 1960s:

> This nation should dedicate itself to achieving the goal, before this decade is out, of landing a man on the moon and returning him safely to Earth.

Those simple words describe a mission and vision much better than an extensive document of many pages. Sometimes called values statements or credos, examples of these statements can be found in the annual report of many organizations. Some are lengthy, while others seem to be little more than fluff. The best are closer to the above Johnson & Johnson credo or President Kennedy's moon landing statement in their style.

Once an organization has developed a new mission statement or has revised an existing one, it should be rolled out to all organization members with a good level of publicity. Using a tone-at-the-top approach, senior mangers should explain the reasons for the new mission statement and why it will be important for the organization. It should be posted on facility bulletin boards in the annual report, and in other places to encourage all stakeholders to understand and accept this mission statement. That mission statement should just not stand by itself. A series of other key steps are necessary, starting with surveys and other mechanisms to build an effective ethics and compliance function.

Sometimes, an internal auditor might argue that "I'm an internal auditor—I just review the controls that are in place. What do I have to do with launching an ethics function?" This is very true, and internal audit should always be involved with reviewing and commenting on the controls that others have established. However, the unique nature of ethics and compliance programs and their relationship to the overall organization point to an area where internal audit can take an even more active role in helping to implement these important organizational processes.

(b) Understanding the Risk Environment

Virtually every organization faces a mix of risks that might limit its business operations, growth, profitability, or other areas. In the aftermath of the dot-com bubble of the 1990s, many faced the risk of severe business downturns. In order to keep growing and showing ever-increasing growth as that dot-com era was beginning to slow down, too many organizations took the risk of bending the rules with regard to their financial performance. This was the path of Enron, WorldCom, and others, and also led to the U.S. Congress to pass SOA. Understanding an organization's risk environment is a first step to launching an effective ethics program.

While an effective ethics program can certainly not shield an organization from the risk of a major earthquake or some other cataclysmic event, it can help to shield it from a variety of other operational and business risks. Just as some accounting officers decided to "bend the rules" prior to SOA, these kinds of attitudes can present risks in many other areas. The office worker who copies company software programs for use on his or her home computer, the factory worker who skips product final inspection procedures to save time, or the vendor that ships fewer items than ordered because "they will never check" are all examples of bending rules and increasing risks to the organization. These kinds of practices often develop because of perceived senior management/staff disparities. The employee who regularly sees managers exceed expense account limits with no evident repercussions may soon try to bend the rules in other areas.

Internal audit can take a major lead here in surveying employee attitudes and practices. Ethics attitudes and risks can be assessed through either a targeted review of findings from past audits or special reviews based on employee and stakeholder ethics attitude surveys. Internal audit can accomplish this ethics survey work through coordination with the organization's ethics function, if such a group exists. The nature of such an ethics function will be discussed in the paragraphs that follow, and if the organization has a formal ethics function, internal audit should review the results of any other ethics surveys that may have been performed there, making plans to revise or update them as necessary. An ethics survey is a very good way to understand organizational attitudes and is an aid to support corporate governance processes.

(i) Ethics-Related Findings from Past Audits or Special Audits. Internal audit has completed a large number of compliance-related operational and financial audits over recent years, a reexamination of workpaper and audit report findings or even audit report responses may provide insights into overall ethical attitudes. Consistent workpaper findings covering "minor" infractions may point to overall trends in ethical attitudes. An example here would be an ongoing failure of employees to follow some relatively minor process or procedures such as securing a second approval signature on smaller-valued transactions, despite a policy calling for this second signature, or the failure to document new information systems, despite systems development documentation requirements. The responsible audit team may have decided the matter was "too minor" to include in summarized final audit reports, but such findings often point to potential ethical attitude problems. Even worse, sometimes these types of findings are reported in audit reports, only to be somewhat brushed off in the report responses.

Some of the ongoing "minor" findings mentioned may not point to ongoing ethical violations but to areas where rules just need to be changed. Some organizations, for example, have travel expense rules calling for every travel expense to be reported by a receipt, even if this includes highway tollbooth fares of 50 cents each. The driver can only get this postage-stamp-sized toll receipt by waiting in the cashier line rather than driving through a faster line that just accepts coins without receipts. Because managers and others may feel that rules requiring such minimal value receipts do not add value, expense reports lacking these receipts may be frequently submitted and approved with these less than $1.00 receipts missing. Such a matter may be noted but certainly not reported in audit reports. Does this situation represent an ethical violation for the organization? On one level, the answer may be yes, because a rule is a rule. However, an internal auditor reviewing past audit reports and workpapers for ethical problems might best work with the appropriate unit in the organization to get such unreasonable rules changed.

Internal audit might also consider launching a special audit to assess ethical attitudes. This would be a strong compliance review covering some key areas across the organization or a highly focused review in one department or group. This type of internal audit–initiated review will provide an overall assessment of ethical attitudes in the organization.

(ii) Employee and Stakeholder Ethics Attitude Surveys. Properly done, employee, officer, and stakeholder surveys can be an excellent way to assess ethical attitudes throughout the organization. The idea is to gather as much information as possible about ethical attitudes and practices from broad groups from the organization. These groups might include production-floor workers, if appropriate, office staff, senior managers, vendors, and other groups. While the ethics attitude survey would include some common questions, each group would also receive specific questions directed to their responsibilities. The senior officer group, for example, would receive the same set of organizational attitude questions given to all, but also might require additional specific SOA internal control–related questions.

Drafting a fact-gathering survey with a high hoped-for response level is never easy, and the use of specialized help should be considered. Rather than a series of questions requiring just Yes or No responses, the survey should consist of many "Have you ever . . ." types of questions, where persons completing the survey can provide as long or as short an answer as they wish. This open-ended response makes it more difficult to compile results, but interesting and valuable information may be retained. Exhibit 9.1 is an example of an ethics attitude survey that might be directed to supervisory, management, and other professional members of the organization.

EXHIBIT 9.1

Ethics Environment Survey Questions

1. Do you have access to current company policies and procedures?
2. If you have questions or need clarifications, do you have a mechanism to ask questions or seek advice?
3. When an established procedure does not appear applicable, given current conditions, is there a process for submitting it for review?
4. Do you feel that the rules and procedures apply just to other groups, such as regular employees if you are part-time or the headquarters operation if you are at a remote subsidiary?
5. Do you feel that your senior managers follow the same types and level of rules that you follow?
6. Has your supervisor ever told you to ignore some rule or procedure?
7. Do you feel that some of the published rules and procedures are trivial or out of date?
8. Are you familiar with the organization's mission statement?
9. What does the mission statement mean to you?
10. Are you familiar with code of business conduct?
11. Do you feel that this code of conduct is regularly updated to reflect current business activities and issues?
12. Do you feel that the code of conduct is applicable to other stakeholders such as officers, contractors, or vendors?
13. Do you feel that the rules are clear for violations of the code of conduct?
14. Have you ever reported an observed code of conduct violation? Were you satisfied with the results of that reporting?
15. Have you participated in any company-sponsored ethics training?
16. Do you understand how to report accounting, internal control or auditing concerns under the company's whistleblower program?
17. Do you feel that there is an effective mechanism to confidentially report violations of the code or other questionable acts?
18. Do you feel that there is an effective process in place to investigate reported compliance violations?
19. Have you observed any evidence that reported compliance violations are subject to disciplinary action?
20. Would you be reluctant to report a violation for fear of employer retaliatory actions?

A key requirement of this type of survey is that it must be as anonymous as possible. The surveys should be sent directly to employees' homes along with a cover letter from perhaps the CEO explaining the objectives and purpose of the survey. Prestamped return envelopes addressed to a special post office box should be included. The survey document would be designed with a primary objective of surveying ethical attitudes; however, if the organization has already established a whistleblower hotline function, as discussed later in this chapter, the survey could also allow people to report such matters. Summarizing survey results can be a major challenge with this type of survey, particularly if respondents have provided free-form responses. Internal audit or the ethics officer should be responsible for preparing such a report with the objective of reviewing the results with the audit committee and senior management. These types of report responses should not be distributed back to the employee/respondent group for confidentiality reasons. They should only receive a general thank you letter.

Either of these approaches will allow internal audit, a designated ethics office team, or others to gain a general understanding about the ethics environment in the organization. This is a first step to launching a formal ethics function or upgrading and enhancing an existing function. These surveys will provide general management with some insights into the overall ethics atmosphere in the organization. While not required under SOA, this information will bolster corporate governance practices by highlighting areas where improvements are needed.

(c) Summarizing Ethics Survey Results: Do We Have a Problem?

The results of an ethics attitude survey or assessments from past internal audits may provide some assurances that things are "pretty good" throughout the organization. More often, however, they can raise some troubling signs, ranging from small but ongoing compliance deviations to surveyed vendors claiming heavy-handed negotiation tactics or to employees stating that they have been asked to bend rules. The hard question with any such results is whether they represent troubling exceptions or the tip of a much larger ethics problem iceberg. At this point, internal audit and the organization's ethics officer should meet with senior management to develop some next steps.

Based on potential disturbing "red flags" from the surveys, it may be best to expand the mail survey process. Also, concerns that came out of those initial surveys may point to a need to expand the assessments to such groups as customers, agents, or vendors. If the survey results ended with inconclusive or mixed messages, another appropriate step would be to set up a series of focus group sessions, small groups of employees and stakeholders would be randomly selected and asked to meet together in an off-site location to discuss their perceptions of organizational ethical values. With a strong emphasis that any responses from such sessions are anonymous, a skilled facilitator could then lead the selected group through a discussion. These inputs and other data may form the basis for launching an organizational ethics program or enhancing any existing programs. As discussed in the following sections, an ethics program effort also requires a strong code of conduct as well as a whistleblower process to allow for the reporting of ethics violations.

While SOA talks about these ethics and whistleblower issues only in terms of senior financial officers and potential financial fraud, a strong, effective ethics program will benefit the entire organization in addition to providing SOA compliance. If the organization does not already have an established ethics program, internal audit can be a natural party to help establish this type of program.

9.3 CODES OF CONDUCT

While a mission statement is a keystone to hold together the overall structure of corporate governance, the code of conduct provides the supporting rules for organizational stakeholders. Although these codes have been in place at major corporations for many years, SOA now requires that corporations develop a code of ethics for their senior financial officers to promote the honest and ethical handling of any conflicts of interest and their compliance with applicable governmental rules and regulations. The issuance of this code of ethics is to be disclosed in the organization's periodic financial reports, and a financial officer's willful violation of that signed code could result in personal criminal penalties. While the SOA code is mandated, all organizations can benefit from a code that covers all stakeholders. While SOA uses the expression "code of ethics," we refer to it here by perhaps its more common name, the organizational code of conduct.

The effective organization today should develop and enforce a code of conduct that covers a set of appropriate ethical, business, and legal rules for all organizational stakeholders, whether they are the financial officers highlighted in SOA, all other employees, or the larger group organization stakeholders. While internal audit may not typically be the catalyst designated to draft or launch such a code of conduct, internal audit can be a key participant in both helping to launch and then determining that the organization has an effective code of conduct that promotes ethical business practices throughout the organization.

(a) The Contents: What Should the Code's Message Be?

A code of conduct should be a clear, unambiguous set of rules or guidance that outlines rules or what is expected of them as members of the organization, whether officers, employees, contractors, vendors, or any other stakeholders. The code should be based on both the values and legal issues surrounding an organization. That is, while all organizations can expect to have code of conduct prohibitions against sexual and racial discrimination, a defense contractor with many defense-contract-related rules issues might have a somewhat different code of conduct than a fast food restaurant operation. However, the code should apply to all members of the organization from the most senior level to a part-time clerical employee. A code of conduct rule prohibiting erroneous financial reporting is the same whether directed at the CFO for incorrect financial reporting or the part-timer for an incorrect or fraudulent weekly time card.

If the organization already has a code of conduct, the introduction of SOA might be an appropriate time to revisit that code. All too often, older codes were often originally drafted as rules for the lower-level employees with little attention paid to the more senior members of the organization. SOA and its overall corporate governance guidance was meant for those senior officers but should be delivered in such a manner that it will apply to all organizational stakeholders. Working with senior members of management and the audit committee, internal audit can examine any existing code of conduct to determine if those rules still fit in our present post-SOA era.

Whether preparing a revision to an existing code of conduct or developing of a new code, a joint team from a cross-section of management, including those in the legal and human resources areas, should be assembled to develop the code. The team should examine the business issues facing the organization and then draft a set of rules that are applicable to that organization, according to its business and related issues. The code's rules must be written in a clear manner so that the points can be easily understood by all. Exhibit 9.2 lists some examples of code of conduct topics. While this list does not apply to all organizations,

EXHIBIT 9.2

Example Code of Conduct Topics

The Following Are Topics Found in a Typical Organizational Code of Conduct:

I. INTRODUCTION
  A. Purpose of This Code of Conduct: A general statement about the background of this code of conduct.
  B. Our Commitment to Strong Ethical Standards: A restatement of the mission statement and printed letter from the CEO.
  C. Where to Seek Guidance: A description of the ethics hotline process.
  D. Reporting Noncompliance: Guidance for Whistleblowers—How to report.
  E. Your Responsibility to Acknowledge the Code: A description of the code acknowledgment process.

II. FAIR DEALING
  A. Our Selling Practice: Guidance for dealing with customers.
  B. Our Buying Practices: Guidance and policies for dealing with vendors.

III. CONDUCT IN THE WORKPLACE
  A. Equal Employment Opportunity Standards: A strong commitment statement.
  B. Workplace and Sexual Harassment: An equally strong commitment statement.
  C. Alcohol and Substance Abuse: A policy statement in this area.

IV. CONFLICTS OF INTEREST
  A. Outside Employment: Limitations on accepting employment from competitors,
  B. Personal Investments: Rules regarding using company data to make personal investment decisions.
  C. Gifts and Other Benefits: Rules regarding receiving bribes and improper gifts.
  D. Former Employees: Rules prohibiting giving favors to ex-employees In business.
  E. Family Members: Rules about giving business to family members, creating potential conflicts of interest.

V. COMPANY PROPERTY AND RECORDS
  A. Company Assets: A strong statement on the employees' responsibility to protect assets.
  B. Computer Systems Resources: An expansion of the company assets statement to reflect all aspects of computer systems resources.

EXHIBIT 9.2 *(CONTINUED)*

Example Code of Conduct Topics

> **C.** Use of the Company's Name: A rule that the company name should only be used for normal business dealings.
>
> **D.** Company Records: A rule regarding employee responsibility for records integrity.
>
> **E.** Confidential Information: Rules on the importance of keeping all company information confidential and not disclosing it to outsiders.
>
> **F.** Employee Privacy: A strong statement in the importance of keeping employees' personal information confidential from outsiders and even other employees.
>
> **G.** Company Benefits: Employees must not take company benefits to which they are not entitled.
>
> **VI. COMPLYING WITH THE LAW**
>
> **A.** Inside Information and Insider Trading: A strong rule prohibiting insider trading or otherwise benefiting from inside information.
>
> **B.** Political Contributions and Activities: A strong statement on political activity rules.
>
> **C.** Bribery and Kickbacks: A firm rule against using bribes or accepting kickbacks.
>
> **D.** Foreign Business Dealings: Rules regarding dealing with foreign agents in line with the Foreign Corrupt Practices Act.
>
> **E.** Workplace Safety: A statement on the company's policy of complying with OSHA rules.
>
> **F.** Product Safety: A statement on the company's commitment to product safety.
>
> **G.** Environmental Protection: A rule regarding the company's commitment to complying with applicable environmental laws.

these topics are appropriate for many modern organizations today. The key is that messages delivered in the code must be clear and unambiguous. This author was very involved in drafting a code of conduct for a large U.S. corporation several years ago. The following is an extract from that code of conduct on a section covering Company Assets, as an example:

> We all have a responsibility to care for all of the company's assets including inventory, cash, supplies, facilities, and the services of other employees and computer systems resources. If you see or suspect that another employee is stealing, engaging in fraudulent activities, or otherwise not properly protecting company assets, you may report these activities to your manager or to the ethics office.

These words are a good example to the tone and style of good code of conduct. It places the responsibility on the recipient of the code, tries to explain the issues in an unambiguous manner, and suggests expected responses and actions.

In addition to the code topics as well as the code rules, many organizations have found value in adding a set of questions and answers that accompany the points in the code. This allows the code's reader to better understand the issues as well as the types of questions that a perhaps more unsophisticated employee might ask regarding a code rule. The key to a clear set of code of conduct rules is that the team drafting a new or revised set of code of conduct points must make sure that the code materials are clear and understood by all. This can be a real editing challenge for the code of conduct team.

We have not included sample codes of conduct in this book because the codes of conduct for almost every organization are different in terms of style, format, and size. Some organizations publish rather elaborate documents, while others are very bare bones. Corporate codes of conduct, by their nature, are certainly not company trade secrets, and a call to a corporate information or public relations office will typically result in them sending sample copies of their code of conduct. A call to the corporate ethics department or the internal audit department usually will provide the same types of samples. Start with organizations in your industry that you respect to see how they have built their codes of conduct.

Global corporations face another issue when developing a code of conduct. Although a corporation may be headquartered in the United States, it may have significant operations worldwide where key managers, employees, and other stakeholders do not use English as their primary language. Although there will be the added costs of translation, consideration should be given to producing a version of the code of conduct in at least the major languages used in corporate operations. If there are many locations and just small numbers of various foreign language stakeholders, a summary of the main code of conduct in each of the local languages might be appropriate. However, those summary versions should certainly emphasize the same SOA financial fraud guidance that is contained in the primary code of conduct.

(b) Communications to Stakeholders and Assuring Compliance

An organization's code of conduct must be a *living document*. It has little value if it has been developed, delivered to all stakeholders with much hullabaloo, and then essentially filed and forgotten after that initial launch. If a new code of conduct or even a major revision of the existing code is produced, the organization should undertake a major effort to deliver a copy of that code of conduct to all employees and stakeholders. Given today's SOA emphasis, a good first step would be to formally present that new code of conduct to the organization's top mangers, and particularly to the financial officers. Codes of conduct in the past sometimes received only token acceptance from the senior officer group, with a feeling that it was really for the staff and not for them. The reported financial scandals leading up to SOA really highlighted this discrepancy. Both Enron and WorldCom had adequate corporate codes of conduct. However, corporate officers generally did not feel that the rules applied to them.

A disturbing example of the lack of high-level corporate officer code of conduct acceptance can be found in the ex-Enron CFO, Andrew Fastow. Because he knew that he would be violating the Enron corporate code of conduct with his off-balance-sheet schemes, Fastow went to the Enron audit committee and asked them to formally vote him an exemption from code of conduct rules! The audit committee did grant this exemption—one more step in the ultimate failure of Enron.

The senior management group should then formally acknowledge that they have read, understand, and will abide by the code of conduct. With the management team standing behind it, the organization should next roll out and deliver the code of conduct to all stakeholders in the organization. This can be done in multiple phases with delivery to local or more major facilities first followed by smaller units, foreign locations, and other stakeholders. Rather than just including a copy of the code with payroll documents, an organization should make a formal effort to present the code in a manner that will gain attention.

The new code can be communicated through a video by the CEO, training sessions, or by many other means to communicate the importance and meaning of that code of conduct. Special communication methods might be used for other groups such as vendors or contractors, but an organizational objective should be to get all stakeholders to formally acknowledge that they will abide by the organization's code of conduct. This can be accomplished by an Internet or telephone response system, where every organizational stakeholder is asked to respond to these three questions:

1. Have you received and read a copy of the code of conduct? Answer Yes or No.

2. Do you understand the contents of the code of conduct? Answer Yes if you understand this code of conduct or No if you have questions.

3. Do you agree to abide by the policies and guidelines in this code of conduct? Answer Yes if you agree to abide by the code and No if you do not.

The whole idea is to require every employee and stakeholder to acknowledge acceptance of the organization's code of conduct. Responses should be recorded on some form of computer database listing the employee's name and the date of his or her review and acceptance or rejection. Any questions from question 2 can be handled through the whistleblower program described later in this chapter. The idea is to have everyone—all of the stakeholders—buy into the code of conduct concept and agree to its terms. If someone refuses to accept the code because of questions, supervisors or others should discuss the matter with that person to achieve eventual resolution. The final issue here is that the organization should expect all employees to agree to accept and abide by the organization's code of conduct. Following that code of conduct is just another work rule, and consistent failure to abide by these rules should be grounds for termination.

The whole concept behind this code acknowledgment requirement is to avoid any "I didn't know that was the rule" excuses in the future when code violations are encountered. It is a good idea to go through code acceptance process on an annual basis or at least after any revision to the code document. The files documenting these code acknowledgments should be retained in a secure manner.

(c) Code Violations and Corrective Actions

The whole idea behind a code of conduct is that it lays out a set of rules for expected behavior in the organization. SOA requires that financial officers subscribe to a code containing rules prohibiting fraudulent financial reporting, among other matters. The financial officer who violates these rules is subject to strong penalties under SOA. However, the organization should release one code of conduct with guidance for all stakeholders—the SOA-impacted financial officers as well as all others, including employees at all levels, contractors, vendors, and others. In addition to publishing its code of conduct and obtaining stakeholder acceptance to the code, there is a need for a mechanism to report code violations and for investigating and handling those violations.

The objective here is that if the organization issues a strong code of conduct along with a message from the CEO about the importance of good ethical practices, all stakeholders are expected to follow those rules. However, we all know that people are people, and there will always be some who violate the rules or run on the edge. An organization needs to establish a mechanism to allow employees, or even outsiders, to report potential violations of the code in a secure and confidential manner. Much of that reporting can be handled through the whistleblower facility discussed later in this chapter. Other potential violations must be handled on a different level. Consider the female staff employee with a male supervisor who "hints" that sharing her sexual favors with him would be a good way to advance in the organization. A sexual harassment prohibition in the code of conduct will not necessarily stop the supervisor, and often the employee cannot easily walk into the office of a manager one level above the supervisor to report the situation. A process should be established for reporting all types of ethics violations.

In addition to the whistleblower or ethics hotline function described in section 9.4, the organization should establish other mechanisms for reporting potential code of conduct violations. Since some do not want to even call an ethics hotline, a well-publicized post office box address is sometimes very effective. Stakeholders could be encouraged to write to such a PO box, anonymously or not, to report ethics violations. Based on these responses, the ethics function, human resources, or some other appropriate function in the organization should investigate the matter and take action as necessary.

A code of conduct describes a series of rules for expected actions in the organization. When violations are found, the matter should be investigated and actions taken on a consistent basis, no matter what the rank of the organizational stakeholders. If the code of conduct prohibits making copies of corporate software—and it should—the penalties for a staff analyst in a remote sales office and a senior manger at corporate headquarters should be the same. Assuming that they both have read the prohibition in the code and acknowledged acceptance, penalties for violations should be consistent. Otherwise, there can be an atmosphere where the rules appear only to apply to some people.

Most code of conduct violations can be handled through the organization's normal human resources procedures, which probably include a process calling for verbal counseling or probation for a first offense and leading to termination if there are multiple reoccurrences. Some matters must be reported to outside authorities. A violation of SOA rules, such as a recently discovered undocumented off-balance-sheet arrangement, would be reported to the Security and Exchange Commission (SEC), and the theft of goods from a warehouse would be reported to a county prosecutor. When these matters are discovered and reported to outside authorities, the matter moves outside of the organization's hands. The overall goal here is that the organization must have some process in place to encourage all stakeholders to follow good ethical practices, as defined in the code of conduct, and to provide a consistent mechanism for reporting violations and taking disciplinary action when necessary.

(d) Keeping the Code Current

Many of the basic rules of good ethical behavior as well as basic organizational rules will not change from year to year. The sample rule about the protection of company assets, cited previously, stated that all stakeholders had a responsibility to care for their organization's assets, whether property, cash, computer resources, or other assets. That type of ethical rule will not change over time, while others may change due to business or other conditions. The author was involved with a retail organization, company A, which originally had a code rule prohibiting employees working for competitors. That was appropriate when a shopping mall salesperson worked for company A full-time. However, in a changing era of much part-time work, it was not appropriate to tell a half-time shopping mall salesperson that she could not work part-time for another retailer, company B, in the same shopping mall. The code of conduct rule here was changed to state that while on the job for company A, the employee's loyalty had to be only to A and not company B.

Organizations should review their published codes of conduct on a periodic basis and at least every two years to make certain that the guidance is still applicable and current. An organization today should review any current published code of conduct to determine if it reflects changes introduced by SOA. This might include a code statement regarding the need for accurate and timely financial reporting at all levels or the organization's commitment to avoiding any type of financial fraud. Changes to the code of conduct should not be treated lightly. Any revision to the code of conduct should go through the same announcement and rollout process described previously for code introductions. The revised code should be issued to all stakeholders along with an explanation of the changes and a requirement to reacknowledge acceptance as discussed previously.

As new employees and other stakeholders join the organization, they should be given the existing code of conduct with the same requirement that they read and affirm the document. Consideration might be given to creating an online video to explain and educate new employees regarding the code of conduct and the organization's commitment to it. Also, whether the code is revised or not, all stakeholders should be asked, on a periodic basis, to reaffirm that they have read and will continue to abide by the code.

Creating a new code of conduct revision and request for stakeholder reaffirmation can be an expensive task requiring dedicated organizational resources from the ethics, human resources, internal audit, and other functions. Along with the mission statement, an organization should keep its code of conduct and supporting principles in front of all stakeholders at all times. This can be accomplished through constant references to the code of conduct such as in bulletin board posters in all facilities, instructive questions and answers in publications, or as segments in employee training classes. Internal audit should play a key role in promoting the code and monitoring compliance through audit reviews and ongoing contacts through the organization.

9.4   WHISTLEBLOWER AND HOTLINE FUNCTIONS

As outlined in Chapter 3, SOA mandates that the audit committee establish procedures to "handle whistleblower information regarding questionable accounting or auditing matters." This whistleblower provision is an important part of SOA. Many of the questionable accounting practices that originally gave rise to the SOA came to light, at least in part, as a result of employees who "blew the whistle" and reported their concerns. Even before the scandals at Enron and others broke, whistleblower protections were included as part of many federal labor laws as a means to help regulators ferret out violations and wrongdoing. The whistleblower provisions of SOA are patterned after similar statutory schemes for protecting workers in the airline and nuclear power industries.

A whistleblower function is a facility where an employee or stakeholder who sees some form of wrongdoing can independently and anonymously report that action with no fear of retribution. The matter can be reported to the organization or to regulatory authorities. There can be no retribution against the employee; if there is, the employee can initiate legal action to recover damages. These whistleblower cases can inflict serious damage on an organization's reputation as well as on the careers of accused managers.

While whistleblower programs have been around for some years to support federal contracting laws, health and safety regulations, and other regulations, SOA moves these rules into the business offices of all U.S. publicly traded organizations. While the audit committee is required to establish these whistleblower procedures, other functions, such as the ethics, human resources, or internal audit department will need to actually set things up.

Organizations that have established ethics functions also have hotline or similar ethics question telephone lines. These ethics hotlines can provide a starting point for the SOA whistleblower function, but they typically need adjustments or fine-tuning. Too often, reported incidents are not investigated in a proper manner or confidentiality is not as strong as necessary. A slip-up here can cause major problems for an organization if the whistleblowing stakeholder feels that matters have not been resolved or that individual confidentiality has been compromised. Internal audit often can be a major aid in this process through reviews of the existing process, recommending appropriate controls, and providing guidance to the audit committee.

Whistleblower functions have been mandated by law for any organization involved in federal contracting and other federal regulations. Any employee or stakeholder who observes some type of improper activity can "blow the whistle" and report the incident. The matter is then investigated and corrected if the allegations prove true, and the original whistleblower may receive a proportionate reward from the savings that result. An employee whistleblower, for example, may observe that a contract calls for fasteners in a manufacturing part that must be of a certain gauge steel. The example assembly worker may discover that the organization is using a cheaper gauge of steel and can blow the whistle on the employer for this practice. These programs are often administered through a contract compliance office, human resources, or some procurement function.

The SOA-mandated whistleblower program throws another new challenge at the responsible audit committee member. The typical board of directors audit committee member *may* be aware of such an organizational function through past presentations, but almost certainly will not be aware of the processes necessary to establish an effective whistleblower program. Internal audit groups can often help the audit committee representative to establish an effective whistleblower program that will comply with SOA. This section discusses how to establish effective whistleblower programs and how internal audit can help to launch or refresh the function.

(a) Federal Whistleblower Rules

The U.S. Department of Labor (DoL) administers and enforces more than 180 federal laws covering many workplace activities for about 10 million employers and 125 million workers. Most labor and public safety laws and many environmental laws mandate whistleblower protections for employees who complain about violations of the law by their employers. SOA now adds federal whistleblower protection to all employees of SEC-registered organizations, and public companies will need to pay special attention to these new protections for corporate whistleblowers. SOA Section 806 establishes this whistleblower protection for stakeholders in publicly traded companies, allowing that no public company or any officer, employee, contractor, or agent of such company "may discharge, demote, suspend, threaten, harass, or in any other manner discriminate against an employee in the terms and conditions of employment because of any lawful act done by the employee." Those lawful acts occur when the employee provides information or otherwise assists in an investigation conducted by a federal regulatory or law enforcement agency, Congress, or company personnel regarding any conduct that the employee "reasonably believes" constitutes a violation of SEC rules and regulations or fraud statutes; or files, testifies, participates in, or otherwise assists in a proceeding—pending or about to be filed—relating to an alleged violation. In other words, the employee or stakeholder who perceives some financial wrongdoing and then reports the matter is legally protected during its investigation and resolution.

In many respects, whistleblower provisions are primarily designed to protect employees who think they have discovered some wrongdoing rather than as provisions to increase an organization's internal controls. Virtually any personnel action taken against a whistleblowing employee, including a demotion or suspension, can potentially be subject to legal action under this provision. Although there is not much whistleblower experience related to SOA at this time, if the experiences from other whistleblower statutes are applied to SOA, the SEC and DoL will broadly protect accounting and auditing whistleblowing employees. This says that an employee or stakeholder who registers a whistleblower complaint will be protected until the matter is resolved. SOA does seek to avoid frivolous complaints here by requiring that the whistleblower must have a "reasonable" belief that the practice reported constitutes a violation.

Under SOA, it is a crime for anyone "knowingly, with the intent to retaliate," to interfere with the employment or livelihood of any person—a whistleblower—who provides a law enforcement officer any truthful information relating to the possible commission of a SOA violation offense. Any whistleblowing employee who subsequently faces adverse employment action could potentially become a "protected informant" witness. Several legal sources have emphasized that this employee protection legislation is extraordinary and underscores the seriousness with which Congress views this subject.

SOA requires the audit committees to establish a process for the receipt and treatment of complaints received regarding accounting, internal accounting controls, or auditing matters, and for "the confidential, anonymous submission by employees" regarding questionable accounting or auditing matters. Stakeholders who believe that they have been unlawfully discharged or discriminated against, due to their whistleblowing action, may seek relief by filing a complaint, within 90 days after the date of the violation, with the DoL or by initiating federal district court action. The aggrieved will typically need to secure legal help to seek relief, but numerous law firms will be waiting to get involved. The process can be time-consuming and expensive for the accused corporation. The procedural rules here, including the burdens of proof for the employer and employee, will follow the Air 21 statute[1] for airline employees. For example, to prevail on a complaint before DoL, the employee must demonstrate that discriminatory reasons were a "contributing factor" in the unfavorable personnel action. Relief will be denied, however, if the employer demonstrates by "clear and convincing evidence" that it would have taken the same personnel action in the absence of protected activity.

An employee prevailing in such an action is entitled to full compensatory damages including reinstatement, back pay with interest, and compensation for the litigation costs and attorney fees. However, if DoL does not issue a final decision within 180 days of the whistleblower's complaint filing, the matter may be moved to the federal district court. Complicating matters further, the harmed whistleblower can take action on several fronts, seeking protection under federal and state laws as well as any collective bargaining agreement. Employers are exposed to potential "double jeopardy" for whistleblower actions with liability under both SOA provisions and state or federal laws on wrongful discharge and similar causes of action. In addition, the aggrieved whistleblower can seek punitive damages through separate court actions.

Based on administrative and judicial experiences in the nuclear energy and airline industries, whistleblower protection laws can become a potential minefield for corporations. If an employee makes any sort of accounting or auditing assertion regarding an improper or illegal act, that whistleblower is totally protected until the matter is investigated and resolved. There will be lots of trial lawyers in the wings eager to help the whistleblower and to file actions, particularly against major corporations with "deep pockets." In addition, a substantial body of DoL and court precedent exists in this area to support regulatory sanctions and personal remedies.

Based on over 20 years of experience with whistleblower protection laws, an impacted organization should attempt to strike a balance between the rights of employees to raise whistleblower concerns and the ability to manage the workforce. A positive work environment is needed in which employees feel free to raise concerns to management coupled with effective mechanisms to deal with any concerns raised. The strong ethics-related programs discussed in the first sections of this chapter—including mission statements and codes of conduct—will support this strategy.

(b) SOA Whistleblower Rules and Internal Audit

Under SOA, any employee or other stakeholder can become a whistleblower by reporting an illegal or improper activity covering accounting, internal control, and auditing. This should be an effective process when the potential whistleblower is a member of the corporate accounting staff who hears of plans for some fraudulent transactions or an employee at a remote unit that is not frequently visited by corporate staff, such as internal audit. Whistleblower rules are designed to encourage stakeholders to report these fraudulent or illegal acts and to very much protect the person who reported the matter. This raises a series of issues regarding internal auditors and internal audit reviews.

An objective of internal auditing is to review and discover the types of accounting, internal control, and auditing issues specified in SOA. Internal audit findings are reviewed with management and presented in a formal audit report where management can outline their plans for corrective action. However, what if the internal audit team discovers an accounting, internal control, or auditing matter that is not formally reported to management in the audit report? Can one of the audit team members independently report the matter under SOA whistleblower procedures? Can an internal auditor who encounters a SOA accounting and internal control matter that is not part of a scheduled audit take the whistleblower protection route to report the matter? What if the internal audit team member has not been performing well and fears termination. Can that shaky status auditor dig up some potential findings, perhaps from past workpapers, and report them outside of the audit department to obtain whistleblower protection and job security until the matter is resolved?

The internal audit team is clearly part of management, and internal auditors have a first responsibility to report any improper or illegal matters encountered during an audit to internal audit management for disposition. Internal audit team members should not attempt to work as independent whistleblowers as part of their internal audit work. Internal audit should develop a clear policy stating that any SOA accounting, internal control, or auditing matters encountered should during the course of a scheduled audit review be documented in the audit workpapers and communicated to internal audit management for resolution. Exhibit 9.3 outlines a potential internal auditor whistleblower policy. Both the internal audit team and the management of the functions audited should understand that the purpose of internal audit is not to let loose a team of potential whistleblowers on a department's books and records. Any illegal or improper items should be investigated and reported through the normal internal audit process.

EXHIBIT 9.3

Internal Audit Whistleblower Policy

To: Internal Auditors

Federal law, under the Sarbanes-Oxley Act, allows any employee of our company to "blow the whistle" and independently and confidentially report any improper or illegal matters involving accounting, internal control, or auditing issues. These matters can be reported to our 800-HELP facility for investigation and resolution. However, as a member of our internal audit team, your reporting responsibilities are different.

As a member of the internal audit team responsible for assessing our overall operations, you may regularly encounter major or minor improper or illegal matters involving accounting, internal control, or auditing Issues. It Is your responsibility to investigate, document, and report such matters as part of your normal internal audit work. The matters will be handled though our normal internal audit reporting processes. If you feel that your supervisor on an audit assignment is not giving sufficient attention to some matter, your first responsibility is to report and discuss the matter through internal audit channels, up through the audit committee.

You may encounter situations where It Is necessary to report incidents such as material wrongdoing in our Internal Audit department. In those instances, you have a right and indeed an obligation to report them through our 800-HELP facility.

John Doe, Chief Audit Executive

A situation could exist where an internal auditor does find some accounting or internal controls matter that gets somehow dropped from the audit process, perhaps in a senior auditor's workpaper review. The internal auditor has a first responsibility to get resolution on the matter through the internal audit department up through the chief audit executive (CAE) or the audit committee. If the internal auditor documents and reports the issue, but audit management elects to drop or ignore the matter, the internal auditor certainly then has the right and responsibility to report the matter through, hopefully, the organization's hotline functions or even through the SEC. Audit management and other processes should be in place to prevent such a frustrated internal auditor potential whistle-blower situation.

(c) Launching the Organizational Help or Hotline Function

Many organizations have already established help or hotline functions. Most include confidential telephone line facilities administered through the ethics department, the human resources department, or an independent provider. These are 800-number toll-free telephone operations, which often operate on a 24 hours, 7 days a week basis, and allow any employee or stakeholder to call anonymously and either ask a question, report a concern, or "blow the whistle" on some matter. The idea is to provide an independent facility where all stakeholders can ask questions or report possible wrongdoings at any level. These are not legally required functions, but facilities where employees or other stakeholders in a large organization can ask questions, report possible wrongdoings, and seek advice. The items reported may range from allegations of the theft of company property to human resource complaints to just asking questions about troubling issues. In most cases, the person who takes the telephone call will take all of the necessary information, asking questions when needed, and then pass the reported incident to an appropriate authority for investigation and resolution. The hotline operator will typically assign the reported incident a "case" number so that the caller can later check on resolution.

These employee hotlines were established in many larger organizations beginning in mid-1990. Often staffed with knowledgeable human resources veterans, the operators are often particularly skilled at addressing human-resource-related issues, such as treatment in the workplace. Where there have been any allegations of wrongdoing, the recorded case has been shifted to others for investigation, such as to the legal department. In some instances, these lines have turned into little more than corporate "snitch" lines where many minor gripes or infractions are reported, but they have been generally very successful.

While many established ethics hotlines were set up to be "friendly" in answering employee questions and giving some advice in addition to investigating reported incidents, using this same, already established facility for the SOA whistleblower program places some new controls and responsibilities on the function. While the more friendly help aspects of an ethics hotline can still apply, federal whistleblower rules require much more formalized processes, particularly in areas such as confidentiality, documentation requirements for all records, and efficient processing of any investigations. In addition, the employee calling in a SOA

EXHIBIT 9.4

Guidelines for Setting Up a Whistleblower Call Center

- Establish independent—preferably toll-free—telephone lines for the facility. The lines must not go through other company switchboards.
- Train all operators for the facility with the basic provisions of federal whistleblower rules. Also, establish scripts so that callers can be asked the same general questions.
- Advertise and promote the facility throughout the organization with an emphasis on the fact that callers will be able to check status of all items reported, all callers will be treated anonymously, and there will be no recrimination for caller actions.
- Implement a logging form to record all calls. Maintain the date and time of the call, the caller's name or identification, and the details reported.
- Establish a routing and disposition process so that who has the call information and the status of any investigation can be determined.
- Establish a secure database for all whistleblower data with appropriate password protection.
- Working with human resources, develop procedures to fully but anonymously protect any whistleblower from recrimination of any sort.
- Develop a process for closing out all whistleblower calls, documenting all actions, if there were any.

whistleblower allegation is legally protected from any future recrimination. In some respects, a bubble has to be encapsulated around the whistleblowing employee so that there can be no actions of any sort directed at that whistleblower by the employer until the allegation is resolved. While not SOA related, there have been situations, under other federal whistleblower laws, where an employee who called in the matter had her desk moved and successfully brought legal action for whistleblower discrimination. There is no reason to establish separate ethics help lines and SOA whistleblower lines. Callers would be confused about which to call in any event. However, with the SOA whistleblower requirement, control procedures need to be enhanced in any established ethics hotline facility. Exhibit 9.4 contains guidelines for setting up an ethics hotline program that will also serve as a SOA whistleblower facility.

The existence of an ethics hotline and whistleblower facility will be of little value unless it is communicated and "sold" to all members of the organization. A good way to initially launch these processes is through the employee code of conduct, discussed previously. Even if such a hotline has already been launched, the fact that the line can be used for any potential SOA whistleblowers needs to be communicated. The goal should be to investigate and promptly resolve all calls—and especially whistleblower calls—internally to avoid outside investigators and lawyers.

9.5 AUDITING THE ORGANIZATION'S ETHICS FUNCTIONS

The ethics and hotline function should not be exempt from the same types of operational or financial reviews that internal audit performs in all other segments of the organization. While different from such audit areas as asset management, marketing, or design engineering, which are periodically subject to operational or financial reviews based on potential audit risks, the ethics function should nevertheless be included in the same type of risk-analysis model used by internal audit for audit planning. Although the ethics code of conduct function may introduce minimal risks, the whistleblower function—particularly if administered internally—may present some major security and confidentiality risks. In addition, the CFO and other key officers are very much at risk if there are problems here.

The purpose of an internal audit review of the ethics and whistleblower function is to assess whether that ethics group is following good internal control procedures, making effective use of its resources, complying with good confidentiality procedures, and following its department charter authorizing the ethics function. While every ethics and whistleblower function may be a little different, internal audit should gain a detailed understanding of how the function operates and the procedures normally performed. As the organization's *ethics function,* internal audit should expect to find the ethics department procedures at least as good as internal audit regarding compliance with such areas as document confidentiality and compliance with organizational policies such as travel expenses. Other ethics functions' responsibilities may point to areas where internal audit can suggest improvements. For example, the ethics department's code of conduct normally should have an acknowledgment form or process whereby employees indicate that they have read and understand the code. An ethics function may not have established appropriate procedures here to ensure that all newly hired employees have gone through this code acknowledgment process. Internal audit can assess this process and recommend improvements where appropriate.

Exhibit 9.5 describes general audit procedures for a review of an organizational ethics and whistleblower function. Because of the close, ongoing relationship that should exist between the ethics function and internal audit, if an

EXHIBIT 9.5

Auditing the Ethics Function: Sample Audit Program

1. Ethics Function Administration.
   1.1 Develop an understanding and document the organization structure of the ethics function, including organization structure and reporting relationships.
   1.2 Review ethics function's charter and other key process documentation.
   1.3 Assess ethics function office security procedures for the adequacy of such matters as records, file, and workstation security.
   1.4 If outside contractors are used to provide ethics or hotline services, review and document contractual arrangements.
2. Code of Conduct Processes.
   2.1 Obtain copy of current Code of Conduct.
      2.1.1 Determine that code is current and regularly updated.
      2.1.2 Discuss code with a sample on organization staff to determine that they understand the code document.
      2.1.3 Discuss code with sample of managers to determine if there are concerns about the code's issues or content.
   2.2 Assess the adequacy of processes for obtaining code acknowledgments.
      2.2.1 Select a sample of employees and determine that they acknowledged acceptance of the code.

EXHIBIT 9.5 *(CONTINUED)*

Auditing the Ethics Function: Sample Audit Program

      2.2.2 Determine that all officers have accepted the code.

      2.2.3 Assess adequacy of procedures for any employees who fail/refuse code acknowledgment.

      2.2.4 Assess adequacy of code acknowledgment records.

    2.3 Assess adequacy of processes for updating code of conduct as required.

    2.4 Assess processes in place to distribute code to all organization stakeholders, including remote locations including foreign, vendors, and others.

3. Hot-Line/Whistleblower processes.

    3.1 Develop a general understanding of processes in place and determine they cover all areas including SOA matters.

    3.2 Assess adequacy of processes for logging calls received and documenting interactions.

    3.3 Review process for disposition of calls and select of sample of recent call to determine if processes appear adequate.

    3.4 Review overall security processes in place, including protection of key documents and individual whistleblower stakeholders.

    3.5 Meet with Human Resources to determine that adequate procedures are in place to protect/encapsulate any whistleblowers.

4. Audit committee responsibilities. Meet with audit committee representative to determine knowledge and understanding of the ethics and whistleblower programs in place.

operational review of ethics does come up as part of audit's risk analysis, the CAE should discuss the planned review with the ethics director in some detail to explain the reasons for and the objectives of the planned operational review. Privacy and confidentiality may become an issue in this type of review. A call to the hotline may have pointed to some form of potential employee malfeasance or an SOA whistleblower revelation, which ethics will want to keep highly confidential until the matter is resolved. Despite internal audit's ongoing exposure to other sensitive areas and issues in the organization, the director of the ethics function may be reluctant to have internal auditors review certain materials. The CAE should point out internal audit's ongoing exposure to other sensitive information and the requirements that it follow appropriate professional standards.

Assuming that these matters can be resolved appropriately, an operational review of an ethics function will give management additional assurances as to the integrity of controls in the ethics function, a component of operations where most managers have had little exposure or experience.

9.6   IMPROVING CORPORATE GOVERNANCE PRACTICES

A strong ethics program, based on a meaningful mission statement and a code of conduct, are key elements of any overall program of corporate governance in the organization. The accounting scandals that led to SOA were, in many respects, scandals at the top levels of the organization, whether caused by a scheming financial officer, a greedy CEO, or a don't-ask-any-questions public accounting firm. The executive teams at the accounting scandal companies set their own rules with little consideration given to the rest of the organization. The result has been SOA that is really focused on this same senior group. However, an overall strong ethics program will improve corporate governance practices for the entire organization rather than just the people in the executive office.

The following actions should be considered as part of launching an effective ethics and whistleblower strategy for the entire organization:

1. **Corporate Policy.** An organizational policy statement should be issued by senior management to emphasize that all stakeholders are encouraged, indeed have an obligation, to bring concerns about accounting and financial practices to the attention of management. The policy statement should also stress that management will not tolerate retaliation against employees who raise concerns. The policy can help foster an "open door" process for addressing issues, which, after all, is the most effective management approach.

2. **Employee Concerns Program.** A program must be established for the receipt and processing of concerns submitted by employees on a confidential or anonymous basis. An effective employee concerns program should include:

   ○ A central coordinator to process and investigate concerns

   ○ Controls to ensure an adequate investigation is consistently conducted, with proper documentation describing the resolution of the concerns

   ○ A feedback mechanism to advise the employee of the disposition and resolution of the reported matter

   ○ A process for periodically evaluating the effectiveness of the program

3. **Training of Supervisors.** Training should be conducted for all first-line supervisors and other managers on how to respond effectively to concerns raised by employees. Problems often escalate because of miscommunication between an employee and his or her supervisor. Cases of discrimination can turn on how a supervisor reacts to and handles a particular situation with an employee. Thus there is a strong need for effective training of supervisors and managers on the subtleties associated with potential whistleblower concerns.

4. **Guidance to Contractors.** Because public companies can potentially be "on the hook" for discriminatory acts by contractors, subcontractors, and other agents, special mechanisms should be put in place to guard against this, such as specific employee protection clauses in contracts.

5. **Employee Surveys.** Organizations should periodically conduct surveys of their workforce to assess the corporate "culture" and gauge whether employees feel free to raise concerns.

Major corporations and small ones alike are all now subject to SOA rules and requirements. The ethics and whistleblower processes discussed in this chapter are important for SOA compliance and for good corporate governance. Internal audit can play a key role in helping to launch as well as review these processes.

ENDNOTE

[1]The Wendell H. Ford Aviation Investment and Reform Act for the 21st Century (commonly known as Air 21) protects whistleblowers in the airline industry. A related act is the 1978 Energy Reorganization Act, which protects employees in the nuclear power industry from retaliation for their reporting of safety concerns.

CHAPTER TEN

Working with External Auditors

10.1 IMPORTANCE OF EXTERNAL AUDIT COORDINATION

Organizations receive their major auditing services from two different sources: internal audit and independent external auditors. Although each has very distinct responsibilities, there are many common objectives that can provide a basis for coordination between these two distinct audit functions. Since both audit functions work with the same organizational records and personnel, there is a possibility of unnecessary duplication of effort or avoidable excessive demands on organizational personnel without some level of coordination. These coordinated audit efforts should provide more effective audit overage for the organization served.

Internal audit should have an objective to coordinate work with their external auditors. This is not to state that they must work together on projects or that they must follow the same general audit approach for their various projects.

Rather, each should be generally aware of what the other is doing and plan work to avoid any obvious duplication of effort. While an internal auditor understands the differences between his or her goals and objectives and those of the external auditors, often many members of management do not. This matter is complicated further with internal audit's role as required by Sarbanes-Oxley Act (SOA) Section 404 requirements. Section 404 was discussed in Chapter 6, "Evaluating Internal Controls: Section 404 Assessments," and will be further referenced in this chapter. Those who are not acquainted with the audit process sometimes think that an auditor is an auditor is an auditor. That is, they may have the impression that all auditors are really about the same, even though the internal auditor plays a unique role in day-to-day audit processes. In addition quality auditors, as discussed in Chapter 26, "Internal Audit Quality Assurance and ASQ Quality Audits," have a somewhat different role than the Institute of Internal Auditors (IIA)–type professionals who are the major focus of this book.

This chapter discusses approaches for internal auditors to develop a better working relationship with external auditors, with consideration given to their role after SOA and its Section 404. While internal audit cannot dictate to external auditors the extent to which they should coordinate their work, both management and the board of directors audit committee generally will endorse this coordination. Internal audit cannot, of course, speak directly for the company's external auditors, but must endeavor to understand their special needs, requirements, and concerns in order to achieve effective coordinated audit efforts.

This chapter also discusses support for audit coordination as defined by the American Institute of Certified Public Accountants' (AICPA) Statement on Auditing Standards (SAS) No. 65, "The Auditor's Consideration of the Internal Audit Function in an Audit of Financial Statements,"[1] as well as the IIA's professional standards on coordination with internal auditors discussed in Chapter 12, "Internal Audit Professional Standards." These audit standards provide guidance to external and internal auditors in working together and coordinating their efforts. The two audit groups have some fundamentally different responsibilities, however, and internal audit management should be aware of them and communicate them to management in the event of questions. Internal audit should *never* be viewed as a subset of or junior partner to their external auditors!

10.2 PROFESSIONAL STANDARDS SUPPORTING AUDIT COORDINATION

The relationship of internal auditors to their external auditors has changed over the years and is still changing. To better understand the current environment for coordinating the internal and external auditing efforts, it is interesting to consider internal and external audit coordination since 1942, when the first edition of this book was published. At that time, internal auditing departments were often linked closely to the work of their external auditors. Historically, concerns about the then growing magnitude of independent audit responsibilities and the cost of this effort caused external auditors to recommend the creation of internal auditing departments to their clients. In these earlier situations, internal auditing tended to be viewed by all parties as a support function directly supportive of external audit's objectives. Additionally, these early internal auditing departments were often largely staffed by personnel drawn from public accounting practice. In addition, early internal audit work often consisted of work considered by external auditors to be necessary but time-consuming. For example, internal auditors working in support of their external auditors might reconcile certain checking accounts or perform test counts of inventories, both resource-consuming tasks but then considered necessary audit attestation steps. These tasks were often viewed by external audit as necessary but low-level work. With internal audit's help on these audit procedures, the net result was typically a close, coordinated effort between the internal and external auditors, but with internal audit playing a subordinate role.

In 1941, the Institute of Internal Auditors (IIA) was founded and the internal auditing profession moved toward the concept of modern operational auditing, as is discussed in this book, with its stronger emphasis on management service. This diversion from the earlier financial statement–oriented internal audit activities weakened the linkage to external auditors and, in turn, the closeness of their coordination. In some cases, the two audit groups operated totally autonomously, with only the most perfunctory contact and coordination. The changing atmosphere of the 1970s and 1980s, however, along with the enactment of the Foreign Corrupt Practices Act (FCPA) of 1977, the later COSO internal control framework, and today's SOA rules have again generated a much greater emphasis on the adequacy of an organization's system of internal accounting controls.

These initiatives and SOA Section 404 rules in particular were discussed in Chapter 6. Internal control developments have once more swung the pendulum back toward a closer but changing coordination effort between internal and external auditors in many organizations. Although internal and external auditors have different primary missions, there are important common interests, and close coordination between internal and external auditors should be strongly considered by internal audit and its chief audit executive (CAE). If an organization's internal audit management wants to promote coordination with the objective of overall efficiency and resource savings, and if the external auditors do not, the audit committee and senior management should be consulted for resolution. Conversely, if external audit wants to coordinate its efforts with internal audit and the latter does not want to cooperate, that internal audit function may be subject to serious questions from the audit committee and senior management.

(a) AICPA Support for Audit Coordination

External auditors in the United States were governed by the standards established by their professional organization, the American Institute of Certified Public Accountants (AICPA), which was responsible for, among other matters, defining educational and examination standards for external auditors, defining audit reporting requirements, and establishing auditing standards. These auditing standards were published in what are called Statements on Auditing Standards (SAS) documents. The AICPA's SAS standards are similar to the internal audit professional standards discussed in Chapter 12. However, since the investing public, owners, and government regulators relied on the work of and reports by external auditors, the AICPA's standards carried a much greater level of importance over past years. Rules and relationships here have changed since the enactment of SOA and the new regulator of external auditing, the Public Company Accounting Oversight Board (PCAOB). The PCAOB is currently adhering to established SAS standards but will be issuing new or revised auditing standards over time.

External auditing standards outline, among other matters, the extent of reliance that an external auditor can place on internal auditors in a financial statement review. The AICPA's major pronouncement in the area of internal audit coordination is its Statement on Auditing Standards No. 65, "The Auditors Consideration of the Internal Audit Function in an Audit of Financial Statements." This SAS was released in 1991 and supersedes their much earlier SAS No. 9, "The Effect of the Internal Audit Function on the Scope of the Independent Auditor's Examination." SAS standards provided the basis for what external auditors call generally accepted auditing standards (GAAS), the overall basis for their audit work.

The AICPA's SAS No. 65 defines audit coordination between internal and external auditors. This audit standard describes the role of both auditors, areas for joint audit participation, and external auditor responsibilities for financial statement audits. The first paragraphs of SAS No. 65 define the roles of external and internal auditors as follows:

> Paragraph 2. The [external] auditor's responsibility, when performing an audit in accordance with generally accepted auditing standards, is to express an opinion on the entity's financial statements. To fulfill this responsibility, the auditor maintains independence from the entity. The independent auditor cannot have a financial interest in the entity or have other relationships that might impair auditor objectivity as defined by the profession's independence rules. The auditor is also required to obtain sufficient competent evidential matter to provide a reasonable basis for the opinion.
>
> Paragraph 3. Internal auditors are responsible for providing entity management and its board of directors with analyses, evaluations, assurances, recommendations, and other information that assists in the effective discharge of their responsibilities. To fulfill this responsibility, internal auditors should maintain objectivity with respect to the activity being audited but they are not independent of the entity.

SAS No. 65 goes on to discuss procedures for external auditors to obtain an understanding of the internal audit function, to assess internal audit competence and objectivity, to coordinate work with internal auditors, and to evaluate the effectiveness of this work. It suggests ways in which this audit coordination can be accomplished, including:

- Holding periodic meetings
- Scheduling audit work
- Providing access to workpapers
- Exchanging audit reports and management letters
- Documenting responsibilities related to the audit
- Discussing possible accounting and auditing problems

SAS No. 65 strongly suggests, but does not mandate, that external auditors should consider the work of internal auditors when performing their financial statement attestation work. It states that external auditors can rely on certain work performed by internal auditors. Before making this reliance decision, however, they must gain an understanding of internal audit's activities, including its competency and objectivity. Based on a decision to rely, they can then coordinate their work with internal audit. However, auditing standards still correctly place the final responsibility for financial statement reviews on the external auditor—the independent public accountant.

Internal auditors should have an understanding of the key elements and requirements of SAS No. 65. This will enable internal audit to better understand external audit's decision process when deciding whether to use or not to use internal audit as part of its annual reviews. The SAS contains a flowchart, summarized in Exhibit 10.1, which directs external auditors to use the following steps in considering whether to use internal audit in their work.

1. **Obtain an understanding of the internal audit function.** An external auditor will want to gain an assurance that internal audit reports to proper levels in the organization; that audits are adequately planned, with measurements for plan performance; that internal audit has a quality-assurance process; and that audits are completed in accordance with IIA standards. In other words, an external auditor would want to determine if an internal audit organization was following many of the standards and practices outlined in chapters of this book.

2. **Assess the competence and objectivity of internal audit.** In addition to understanding the organizational structure of an internal audit function, an external auditor would want to assess the competency of individuals working in internal audit and the quality of their work product. This would include a consideration of the staff's educational levels, their professional experience as internal auditors, professional certifications, such as Certified Internal Auditor (CIA) or Certified Public Accountant (CPA), and programs for continuing professional education. (Professional certifications such as the CIA are discussed in Chapter 28, "Professional Certifications: CIA, CISA, and More.") This review step would also include an assessment of quality of workpapers and audit reports as well as the degree of supervision over internal audit activities.

3. **Consider the effect of internal audit on the external auditor's plan.** The external auditor should determine how internal audit might contribute to the overall audit objectives through testing and other procedures. This recognizes that the external auditor has a prime responsibility for forming the opinion on the fairness of the financial statements reviewed.

4. **Plan and coordinate work with internal audit.** Once the external auditor has determined that the internal audit function meets the external auditor's quality standards, audit work can be planned and coordinated.

5. **Evaluate and test the effectiveness of internal audit's work.** Per their standards, external auditors cannot just plan for internal audit to perform certain procedures and then rely on the results of that work with no further review. Just as internal audit management should review the work of auditors assigned to a project, external auditors are also required to evaluate the work of the internal auditors working with them on a project.

EXHIBIT 10.1

SAS No. 65 Internal Audit (I/A) Decision Flowchart

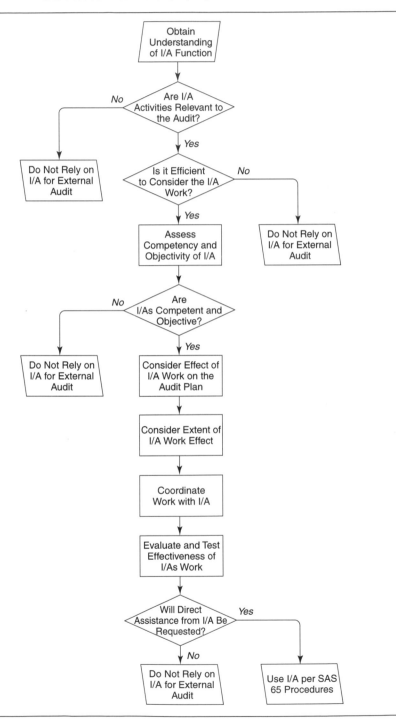

6. **Use internal audit to provide direct assistance to the external auditor.** SAS No. 65 allows external auditors to have internal auditors provide direct support on an audit assignment. This has been a common practice, as discussed in this chapter, but SAS No. 65 confirmed this practice.

SAS No. 65 defines the overall rules of the external auditor's use of internal audit resources to support the external auditor's very important attestation as to the fairness of the organization's financial statements. It does not say that the external auditors *must* use internal audit in their financial statement audits; however, it sets the basic rules that external auditors should use when evaluating an internal audit function and making a decision to use this very important resource. The internal audit function that follows the standards and guidance discussed in earlier chapters of this book should find no trouble in meeting an external auditor's requirements. If an internal audit function and its management want to support external audit in its annual financial statement reviews, internal audit management should discuss these SAS No. 65 measurement standards with their external auditors.

Internal audit should always remember that it has a unique and very important mission in its service to management. In many instances, internal audit management may not want to devote its resources to supporting the external auditors. However, internal audit should never place itself in a position where an organization's external auditors advise the audit committee and management that they cannot use internal audit due to SAS No. 65 problems. When internal audit does work for their external auditors on their financial statement audit, internal audit must always realize that the external auditor has the ultimate responsibility of attesting to the fairness of the organization's financial statements. Although SAS No. 65 provides guidance to external auditors for audit coordination efforts, it also clearly defines the unique role of the external auditor. Paragraph 21 states, in part:

> The responsibility to render an opinion on the financial statements rests solely with the [external] auditor. Even though the [external] auditor's work in obtaining an understanding of the internal control structure, assessing control risk, and performing substantive procedures may be affected by the work of the internal auditors, the [external] auditor should perform sufficient procedures to provide reasonable assurance that the financial statements do not contain material misstatements.

(b) Internal Audit Support for Audit Coordination

Audit coordination from the standpoint of internal auditors is covered by the IIA in its Standards for the Professional Practice of Internal Auditing, discussed in Chapter 12. The IIA standards recognize that "the scope of internal audit work encompasses both financial and operational objectives and activities," while the scope of the external auditor's work, determined by their professional standards, "is designed to obtain sufficient evidential matter to support an opinion on the fairness of the annual financial statement."

IIA Standards recognize that while oversight of the work of external auditors is the responsibility of the audit committee, internal audit's CAE should coordinate internal and external audit efforts, and that coordination should both ensure adequate audit coverage and minimize duplicated efforts. As discussed in Chapter 8, "Internal Audit and the Board Audit Committee," the responsibilities of the audit committee of the board of directors include the coordination of the total audit effort, both for internal audit and the independent public accountants engaged to carry out the annual external audit. The CAE is typically charged with the responsibility for managing this coordination. Performance Standard 2060 of the Internal Auditing Standards states:

> The chief audit executive should report periodically to the board and senior management on the internal audit activity's purpose, authority, responsibility, and performance relative to its plan. Reporting should also include significant risk exposures and control issues, corporate governance issues, and other matters needed or requested by the board and senior management.[2]

Just as external auditors have their own standards in SAS No. 65 outlining practices for coordination with internal auditors, the Standards for the Professional Practice of Internal Auditing, outlined in Chapter 12, outline the standards of practice and participation for internal auditors. The CAE should determine that the external audit team is aware of internal audit's standards and internal audit's compliance with those standards. This may require some educational efforts on the part of internal audit. Sometimes, external audit will be aware of internal audit standards in only a very general manner but will not understand the scope and comprehensiveness of those standards.

External auditors may have sometimes encountered internal audit functions that are not in compliance with IIA standards. They might then assume that all internal audit functions are the same and are deficient in their standards. When discussing any external-internal audit coordination, the CAE should describe and discuss internal audit's level of compliance with audit standards. Audit coordination can often be a very effective process that contributes to the overall control environment of the organization. Other times, there may be coordination problems when an external auditor chooses, for whatever reason, to operate in a manner that ignores or all but circumvents internal audit. The CAE may have to discuss coordination problems with the external audit engagement partner or even with the audit committee of the board.

10.3 INTERNAL AUDIT AND SOA SECTION 404 REVIEWS

SOA Section 404 reviews, as discussed in Chapter 6, introduce a different perspective to the concept of internal and external audit coordination. As explained in Chapter 6, *someone*, but not an organization's external auditors, is required to perform reviews of an organization's internal controls. The organization's external auditors are then required to review and attest to that independent review of internal controls, perform independent tests of the work as appropriate, and then perform an independent audit of the organization's financial statements. These new arrangements very much change the typical rules in the old pre-SOA days.

Prior to SOA, internal auditors often were very involved in external audit fiscal year-end reviews of organization's internal controls. In those old-rules days, the external audit firm sometimes did that review of internal controls required by auditing standards or delegated someone else—usually internal audit—to perform the review. The hearings that led to the passage of SOA frequently highlighted that those reviews were not always that independent. External auditors were alleged to have frequently looked the other way at internal control weaknesses, particularly when consultants for the same internal audit firm had built the system that contained the weak controls or when external auditors just ignored internal control weaknesses as part of their need to complete a financial statement audit.

As outlined in Chapter 6, SOA Section 404 has changed the rules for external audit firms, and internal audit has three separate options for reviewing internal controls as part of the SOA Section 404 internal controls assessment requirements:

1. **Internal audit can independently perform the Section 404 reviews for management.** With this approach, there will be no external audit coordination for internal audit. Following some general discussion with the internal auditors to understand their review objectives, internal audit would independently review, test, and document their significant internal controls. External audit would eventually review and attest to this work independently of internal audit and others in the organization.

2. **Internal audit can assist their external auditors in reviewing and attesting to the adequacy of the completed Section 404 internal controls assessments.** In this case, internal audit would be an independent contractor for their internal auditors. Some other independent entity—either management or other consultants would review, test, and document the adequacy of these significant internal controls. In this case, internal audit would step away from their normal service to management and act as contractors to their external audit firm.

3. **Internal audit can essentially do nothing regarding SOA Section 404 internal controls assessments.** In this mode, internal audit can go about its normal internal audit review procedures, per their published audit plans. There would essentially be no external audit coordination under this option.

Which one of these Section 404 review approaches is best in terms of external and internal audit coordination? Each can work, and each has its strengths and weaknesses. The best approach, perhaps, internal audit is to back away from close external audit coordination and to take the task of independently performing Section 404 review for management and for subsequent external audit attestation. Because of the time and resources required to perform these reviews, internal audit may have to back away from some other activities in its annual audit plan. However, this approach makes internal audit an entity very much independent of their external auditors in the completion of SOA Section 404 reviews and in internal audit's ongoing service to management.

10.4 EFFECTIVE INTERNAL AND EXTERNAL AUDIT COORDINATION

Effective coordination of internal and external audit activities starts with an understanding of their primary and secondary responsibilities. Internal audit's objective should be to develop coordinated efforts that are supportive of the needs of the two audit groups as well as the audit committee and organization management. Before internal audit can effectively coordinate its work with external audit, it must clearly have defined and understand its role in the organization. Starting with Chapter 1, "Foundations of Internal Auditing," this has been a theme throughout this book.

Chapter 1 described internal auditing as an independent appraisal function established to examine and evaluate activities, with the objective of assisting management in the effective discharge of its responsibilities. At the same time, internal audit should assist the organization in achieving a more productive use of its resources. Reporting to the board audit committee, internal audit operates independently but is still a member of the overall management team. It has a responsibility to review and assess the overall system of internal control in the organization, as outlined in Chapter 4, "Internal Controls Fundamentals: COSO Framework," and other chapters. Although internal audit is free to review any area of the organization, management will often suggest areas that require more internal audit attention. These areas of emphasis will often be defined in the internal audit's charter and mission statement, as was discussed as part of the foundations of internal auditing.

This is a broad, but still very unique responsibility within the structure of the organization. Internal audit reports to the audit committee and may also report functionally or administratively to a high level of senior management. Either of these can set some broad objectives governing internal audit activities. Although internal audit is charged with a broad set of objectives and responsibilities reporting to senior management and the audit committee, external auditors have an even broader responsibility because their reports also are directed to investors, bankers, and members of public interest groups. While internal audit is an independent entity within the organization, outsiders frequently do not always view internal audit as *totally* independent. Those outsiders—investors, lenders, and others—look to external audit to provide that independent assessment regarding the fairness of financial statements and other matters.

The modern organization operates in an environment in which it must interrelate in various ways with stockholders, customers, creditors, governmental agencies, and various other regulatory organizations. In these interrelationships, an organization must provide information and representations about its strength and ability to operate as an ongoing entity. These representations usually center on its financial statements, as expressed in periodic balance sheets, cash flow statements, and the results of operations or the income statement. While these financial statements are the responsibility of organizational management, they could contain errors or be prepared in a manner that misrepresents actual results. The financial statements need to be reviewed by someone outside the organization who can examine their supporting data and attest that the financial statements are fairly stated and in accordance with generally accepted accounting principles (GAAP). The primary mission of external auditors is to provide this independent opinion as to the fairness of the presentation of those statements.

In addition to their common responsibility for assessing the system of internal accounting controls, both internal and external audit functions have other common audit responsibilities. Some of these may result in conflicts. Internal audit, for example, should be interested in the organization's overall welfare, including that the external auditor provides service in a manner that renders good value for the fees charged and that minimizes interference with other ongoing organizational activities. Internal audit here should have the same basic interest as the external auditor as they would have with other vendors, with the special capability in this case of better understanding the manner in which this particular vendor product or service is provided.

While external auditors are interested in the overall welfare of their client organization, they cannot examine *every* system or account in that client organization, and must assess overall risks when performing their audit. This will include a SAS No. 65 assessment of the internal audit function. Management may look to the external auditor for counsel in evaluating the effectiveness of internal audit, including the range and quality of its services. External audit knows also that management will normally be expecting—if not insisting—that they give all possible consideration to the work of internal auditors while carrying out their financial statement audits.

While only external auditors can independently sign a financial statement audit report in a manner recognized by outsiders, internal audit often has the time and resources to perform some necessary audit activities in a manner that is often more cost-effective than external audit. For example, external auditors have a requirement to solicit independent confirmations of customer accounts receivable balances. The most effective way to perform this procedure is to make a selection from an automated accounts receivable file and to produce the confirmation requests using computer-assisted software. Assuming that the internal audit does not have full responsibility for SOA Section 404 reviews, they can often do a more cost-effective job of producing these confirmations to assist its external auditors. External audit might only set the selection criteria and supervise the results of the confirmation process. The result of this cooperative effort would be a cost-effective accounts receivable confirmation using the selected resources of both audit groups.

(a) Problems Limiting Audit Coordination

Because of its Section 404 role or for other reasons, the audit committee may decide to limit internal audit's participation in the external audit process. This may be precipitated by external auditors who are sometimes guilty of requesting that internal auditors perform extensive reviews of areas that would normally only receive minimal external audit attention. While this will increase external audit assurances, it may not be the most efficient use of internal audit resources. Management needs to be advised that limited internal audit resources cannot complete their own plans if they are constantly responding to external audit requests.

Although a decision may have been made to limit internal audit participation in external audit work, internal audit should continue to coordinate work through such things as sharing audit plans and audit reports. External auditors base much of their audit selection work on the concept of materiality. For example, they may ignore audit procedures on certain balance sheet accounts because they determine that any misstatements to those accounts are not material to the overall financial statement results. For many internal auditors, accustomed to more extensive audit testing, external auditor procedures are often based on very small sample sizes or limited inquiry and observation procedures will appear inadequate or even inappropriate. These issues can cause problems in auditor coordination. It is important that each group understand the scope and objectives of the other in order to promote more effective coordination.

There are many other problems that can have an impact on internal and external audit coordination. Most can be resolved, however, by close coordination between the CAE and the public accounting firm partner responsible for the audit engagement. Even if management has restricted any joint internal-external audit projects, internal audit has an obligation to review plans and activities with the external auditor in order to achieve a level of coordination.

(i) Right Attitude by Each Audit Group. Although internal audit will find an ample basis for generating an effective coordination effort, there is a further need of having a "right attitude" on the part of both internal and external audit. This goes beyond an understanding of the common interests just described and pertains to the sincerity and cordiality with which the two audit groups view each other. Audit professionals are human beings just like any other individuals, and can be subject to the same problems of pride, jealousy, distorted self-interest, inertia, lack of self-confidence, and other counterproductive forces. Too often, these problems unduly prevent an effective coordination effort. Both parties should be alert to the danger and encourage a more substantive approach to the problem. A healthy and friendly attitude is a necessary basis for cooperative efforts.

Some of these coordination problems are often due to the fee-based work of external auditors compared to the salaried compensation of internal audit. An internal auditor earning, for example, $80,000 per year cannot understand why an external audit staff member may be billing his or her time at $250 per hour. The internal auditor does a quick calculation and assumes that this external auditor must be receiving annual compensation in excess of $500,000. The internal auditor forgets that external auditors are not able to bill out 100% of their time, and that their audit firms have many other costs, which are built into an individual's billing rate. Both internal and external audit staff members are often compensated with comparable salaries. The difference is that internal auditors typically do not charge their time to other departments at an external audit type of billing rate.

(ii) Establishing an Understanding at Senior Management Levels. The effective coordination of internal and external audit efforts requires the understanding and support of senior management, typically the chief financial officer (CFO), the chief executive officer (CEO), and the chairperson of the audit committee. The CFO is usually the person who has the most direct interface with the external audit firm engagement partner. The CFO most often has line responsibility for the accounting and financial control activities that make up the system of internal accounting controls. These activities culminate in the financial statements that are reviewed by the external auditor. The CFO typically first works with external audit for an agreement on the nature and scope of the external auditor's review.

The extent to which the audit committee and the CFO stresses the importance of internal audit's input and the possibilities of audit coordination can become a major factor in deciding how much consideration is given to a coordinated effort by external audit. The CFO usually has responsibility for managing the overall costs of audit activities, including the fees charged by external audit, as presented in their annual proposal and reported in the proxy statement. As part of the negotiation over the scope of work to be performed and proposed fees, the audit committee and CFO can insist on certain levels of internal audit participation to help reduce external audit fees. This influence is, of course, all the more powerful when management plays a dominant role in the negotiation of the external auditor's fees.

SOA rules, as discussed in Chapter 3, "Internal Audit in the Twenty-First Century: Sarbanes-Oxley and Beyond," require the CEO and CFO to personally sign and to be responsible for financial reports and management reports attesting to the adequacy of the system of internal accounting control. Because of this, CEOs and CFOs have become deeply involved in the work of their external auditors, and, in turn, the coordination of the work between internal and external auditors. Needless to say, the deeper the involvement of the CEO and CFO in this coordination effort, the more serious is the approach to audit coordination.

The expanding role of the audit committee, in light of SOA, was discussed in Chapter 8. The audit committee, under the leadership of its auditing and accounting expert, takes direct responsibility for engaging and approving the terms of the engagement of the external auditors and takes an active role in coordinating internal and external audit efforts. This expanded audit committee role does not mean that the contributions of the other key parties are not extremely important. Effective coordination starts at the previously mentioned CAE, external audit engagement partner, and the CFO. However, the involvement of the audit committee under the leadership of a strong audit committee chairperson adds a very important force for achieving effective internal and external audit coordination arrangements.

In order to achieve effective coordination of internal and external audit activities, a proper understanding by all involved individuals is very important. Especially needed is an understanding of the responsibilities and interests of each audit group in order to coordinate the audit effort in a manner that will achieve all major objectives. It is especially important that there is a high-level of individual professional relationship between internal and external audit. This relationship includes the understanding that internal audit does not function primarily to assist external audit and that external audit resources should also be devoted to providing services to management for achieving operational objectives.

10.5 MOTIVATIONS FOR AND CONSTRAINTS OVER EFFECTIVE AUDIT COORDINATION

There are multiple factors that both encourage and limit effective coordination between internal and external auditors. Some of these factors tend to overlap, and they range from relatively low-level to those of high-level importance. Coordination at a lower level may, for example, be as basic as ensuring that representatives of the two audit groups do not arrive at a given location simultaneously, each with different objectives but seeking to examine some of the same records or interview the same employees. Coordination can also involve internal audit performing specified work directly under the supervision of members of the external auditing firm. In this instance, the motivation often is to reduce external audit staff time and thus reduce the cost of the external audit. However, the motivating factor can be one of higher-level cooperative assistance, including the coverage of defined portions of the audit work by internal audit with a later, relatively limited review of that work by the external auditors. Coordination could also include the exchange of findings and related information, together with joint discussions and agreement on further follow-up on the correction of identified deficiencies. Motivation at higher levels does not ignore the more elementary types of benefits, but it also focuses on the deeper common interests of achieving an effective system of internal controls.

Internal audit should have a special responsibility to encourage effective audit coordination because of its in-depth involvement with total organization operations. In many organizations, internal audit is in an especially advantageous position to know and understand various potential audit problems. Further, internal auditors often will have a good professional understanding of the work of external auditors, or will at least generally understand the external audit standards. Internal audit, therefore, can often take the initiative in proposing and helping to work out arrangements that will better satisfy external audit's needs.

Internal audit's responsibilities may also extend to exerting reasonable pressure on various members of management to ensure their support in working with the external auditors. This is often necessary because some members of management may not understand the differing roles of internal and external audit. Internal audit should attempt to explain to its line management the differences in audit scope and objectives. Internal audit often needs to negotiate various planned audit projects with external auditors. For example, if internal audit has performed a review in an area where external audit now plans to visit, internal audit should question why external audit cannot rely on the work of internal audit. Sometimes, internal audit may want to question a planned area of review if they have reasons to believe that external audit does not understand the audit risks in the area to be reviewed. External auditors often perform only a very limited risk assessment as part of their planning work and may decide to perform procedures that may not be all that necessary. Internal audit, because of its close knowledge of the organization, can suggest alternative audit approaches. This may even result in audit fee savings to the organization.

Internal audit must recognize, however, that external auditors are *independent*, and, thus, can perform their reviews in any area they feel necessary for performing their attest function. Internal audit can only recommend changes. However, if the external auditors are performing work that does not appear to be cost effective in the professional judgment of internal audit, this should be discussed initially with the external audit engagement partner. If the matter cannot be resolved, internal audit should bring these concerns to the audit committee and senior management.

When internal audit has serious reservations about some planned external audit procedure, an effective way to challenge that work is to request documentation covering their risk assessment of the area to be reviewed or the tests performed. External auditors should go through a set of risk assessments similar to those discussed in Chapter 5, "Understanding and Assessing Risks: Enterprise Risk Management," for internal auditors. Where there is a difference of opinion or where internal audit has performed a risk assessment over the same area but with different results, internal audit may want to go to the audit committee or senior management to raise these concerns. However, internal audit must always recognize that external audit is independent. If there is a serious dispute over audit procedures or other matters, the organization can always retain a new external auditor. This is a serious step, however, and should not be done casually. In addition, changing auditors sends bad signals to investors who may assume that problems exist. In addition, in today's post-SOA world, there are only a limited number of external audit firms, limiting options.

Potential constraints can stand in the way of effective audit coordination, ranging from very low-level, personnel-related conflicts to very significant management- or audit approach–related differences. Barriers to effective coordination concern anything that directly or indirectly weakens the overall audit effort. Many of these are based on the overall competency and charter of the internal audit function. As discussed previously, external auditors are required to assess the competency and objectivity of the internal audit function per SAS No. 65. Some of the SAS No. 65 factors that may be considered include:

- *Independence of the Internal Audit Function.* Chapter 1 discussed the necessity that internal audit should be an independent function within the organization. However, external auditors have somewhat different standards for their assessment of independence. For example, an internal auditor may be totally independent in action but may also be a cousin or some other relative to a key member of the organization's management. External audit might not view that auditor as independent. Similarly, the internal audit function may report to the organization's CFO or even a lower-level accounting director with only minimal connection to the audit committee. External auditors may not consider that internal audit function to be independent from the pressures of their direct management.

- *Adequacy of Internal Audit Standards.* SAS No. 65 requires that external auditors obtain an understanding of the internal audit function, including its standards. If internal audit follows the IIA's professional standards, as discussed in Chapter 12, or a related internal audit standards–setting group such as the General Accounting Office (GAO) standards for governmental auditors, there can be a basis for coordination. However, if such standards are not followed in spirit or action, external audit could decide to severely limit any internal audit coordination. In all fairness to external auditors, their professional reputations are always on the line, and the work of internal audit must meet adequate professional standards. A real constraint can exist, however, when internal auditors are not sufficiently objective to recognize the need to perform their own work using proper standards and practices.

Sometimes, internal audit may expect a level of external audit reliance on their work beyond that which is justified. For example, internal audit may have performed a review in a given area but not properly documented it through adequate workpapers. External audit may have to reperform some or all of these tests due to this inadequate internal audit documentation. They may feel that it is easier to just do all of the work themselves. Although the problem of achieving proper standards typically relates to internal audit, the problem can also exist in reverse. For various reasons, the work of external audit may not always meet the desired standards. For example, an external auditor may not have an adequate understanding of information systems controls. While this is a significant problem that must be communicated to senior management, internal audit may also decide to limit any coordination activities in this area. There may be other situations where internal audit may look upon such coordination with considerable skepticism. This is particularly the case when internal audit believes its competence and understanding of a specialized area is superior.

- *Possible External Auditor Organizational Deficiencies.* The condition can sometimes exist where partner-level persons responsible for the effective audit support coordination are aware of the situation, but where that message never reaches lower-level external audit personnel assigned to the engagement, such as in-charge auditors or managers based in different locations. The typical public accounting firm often has somewhat autonomous offices in various cities. If an audit engagement uses resources from multiple city offices, messages to coordinate the engagement with internal audit can sometimes be lost. Major problems can also exist in the form of overly rigid budgetary controls, where audit fee or schedule pressures do not allow sufficient time for properly planning internal audit participation. The external audit firm may set its own budgets and schedules without consulting with internal audit, which may not be aware of any plans for coordination until it has already made other plans for audit resources. These practical problems can become significant barriers to effective internal-external audit coordination.

- *Potential Legal Liability of External Auditor.* Another significant constraint to effective coordination is that external auditors are increasingly faced with legal responsibility for losses due to audit failures. Corporate failures after the fall of Enron and the enactment of SOA have exacerbated this situation. A frequent assertion made in legal proceedings against external audit is that injured parties relied on the auditor's "clean opinion," and the financial deficiencies that were disclosed later could have been identified if there had been a proper external audit effort. If internal audit standards or work quality is weak, the external audit team may be reluctant to place much reliance on the work of internal audit. Undue reliance by external audit on internal audit work could potentially be asserted or believed to be one of the bases for the failure to discover an audit deficiency.

As a result of these constraining factors, external auditors may sometimes be extremely cautious about entering into any significant audit coordination efforts.

If they do not see compliance with the internal audit standards, or see inadequate procedures, they may decide not to work with internal audit in any coordinated manner. However, they should always communicate these concerns to the organization's audit committee. If the concerns are valid, internal audit should consider improving its standards and procedures so that its work will be accepted by the external auditors in the future. The AICPA's SAS No. 65, as discussed previously, defines the factors external audit should consider when using the work of internal auditors. Since external audit is ultimately the party that will express an opinion on the fairness of the organization's financial statements, they must also make the final decision on using the work of internal auditors. Sometimes, external audit will fail to properly coordinate audit efforts despite the adequacy of internal audit standards and procedures. The CAE should determine the reasons for this failure. If the two parties cannot resolve the matter, both may want to bring their dispute to senior management or to the audit committee.

10.6 STEPS TO ACHIEVE EFFECTIVE AUDIT COORDINATION

Once decisions have been made to coordinate internal and external audit efforts, the specific components or types of coordination practices must be defined. These activities may vary with the size and complexity of the organization as well as with the size of the two audit groups. For some, certain coordination activities will take place in relatively simple forms between the two audit groups while each pursues its own mission. This will be particularly true if internal audit has been designated to perform the SOA Section 404 review for external audit's subsequent review and attestation. Both the IIA standards and SAS No. 65 outline various audit coordination activities that might be considered under the following seven broad categories:

1. Exchange of audit documentation
2. Face-to-face sharing of information
3. Use of common methodology
4. Collaborative work assistance
5. Cooperation and collaboration in auditor training
6. Supportive follow-up of audit findings
7. Joint audit project planning

(a) Exchange of Audit Documentation

This is a very basic type of coordination and includes workpapers and audit reports. The flow of those documents between the internal and external auditors includes:

- *Exchanges of Workpapers.* The sharing of internal audit workpapers with external audit is a common coordination effort. The logic is that external audit must examine those workpapers as part of its determination of the extent to which it can rely on the work of internal audit. In some cases, an internal auditor might be reluctant to expose workpapers that do not meet the desired standards of professional quality; however, that is a problem that needs basic correction on its own merits. Typically, no really good reason can exist for internal audit withholding working papers from external audit.

The reverse action—making external audit workpapers available to internal audit—is a slightly different problem. Some external auditors may feel in principle that such availability is not compatible with their independent status and broader responsibilities to the outside world. Also, external audit may in some cases not be too proud of the quality of some of its own workpapers. In still other instances, there may be timing problems due to the review procedures within the external audit firm. Generally, however, such availability should be extended by external audit, except in cases of a confidential nature. Even then, external audit should provide copies of selected extracts. Freer availability seems to be an increasingly accepted practice. Internal audit management should try to request access to selected external workpapers as part of the coordinated planning process.

- *Exchange of Reports.* The exchange of reports between the internal and external auditors seems to be a reasonable and typically general practice. The flow of reports from internal audit involves the same principles covered under workpapers. Internal audit reports should be distributed automatically to external audit. They constitute an important means of keeping external audit informed of internal audit findings and other activities. In some cases, certain internal audit reports may be of a confidential nature or not really within the concerns of external audit. However, this would be a very unusual situation.

In a typical external audit engagement, narrative-type reports in addition to the regular audit opinion letter are less common and vary with the terms of the individual audit engagement. Such narrative reports often cover special controls reviews or supplemental management advisory comments. These narrative reports are normally of interest to internal audit, although some external audit reports may be confidential. Otherwise, the reports should be available to internal audit as a standard distribution practice.

(b) Face-to-Face Sharing of Information

Internal and external auditors always should cooperate through a day-to-day exchange of needed information. Examples might include information about a new auditing standard, organizational changes, or the status of a new computer system that was under development. More extended requests might require extra efforts to provide responses, and at that point the factors of cost and effort required need careful consideration. The face-to-face sharing of information reaches a more comprehensive level when there is an ongoing sharing of overall audit-related information from one audit group to the other. Typically, internal audit is more likely to run into matters that would be of interest to external audit during internal audit's more detailed and broader coverage of operational activities. Typically also, external audit depends very much on such a flow of useful information, and this level of cooperation is generally understood by both parties to be important. Internal audit can be an effective sensing group, alerting external audit to developments that bear on external audit's total audit effort, including the assessment of control risk.

Although external audit is less likely to develop information that is useful to internal audit, there is the same need and the same mutual benefit in that reciprocal action. A particularly important input source here is the nonconfidential discussions that external auditors typically have with senior organization officers, and that can sometimes be made available to internal audit. However, many of these discussions may be highly confidential, and internal audit should not press their external audit counterparts for information that is not public in nature. More important, external audit can supply internal audit with information on such matters as new accounting and auditing standards.

(c) Use of a Common Methodology

In many situations, internal audit should try to follow technical and documentation procedures similar to those of their external auditors. The most common examples are the format and indexing schemes of workpapers, audit sampling procedures, and audit procedures followed for specialized audit areas. Alternative sampling approaches are discussed in Chapter 16, "Gathering Evidence through Audit Sampling." Some external audit firms have strong technical support in this area and may endorse one approach over another. Because that sampling approach may be supported by external auditor–supplied computer programs and other materials, it is often efficient for internal audit to use the same approach. One rationale here is that this makes it easier for external audit to review and utilize the work of internal auditors.

Some internal auditors, however, may view such common procedures as relatively unimportant. In any event, it must be recognized that internal audit's objectives are broader than those of external audit, and there is often a need for different approaches to specific audit tasks. Probably the best approach is to recognize that such a common methodology may be most useful in financial auditing situations, but that judgment needs to be exercised in its actual application. Certainly, common approaches should not be carried to such an extreme that they get in the way of individual efforts for developing meaningful and useful audit results. A common methodology is a tool to be used with reasonable care and caution.

(d) Collaborative Work Assistance

In some instances, external audit may request direct assistance from internal audit in performing its work. Here, internal audit does not share independent work efforts with the external auditors but works directly under the supervision of them, essentially as part of their staff. This was a more common practice in previous years, when the emphasis on the coordination effort was primarily to reduce external auditor hours and fees. In its lowest-level form, the internal auditors assigned might function as junior helpers. In a more sophisticated form, however, the two audit groups might work together under a single administrative head on a project such as an inventory observation, because of the need for tight audit coordination and control. This same situation might also exist in the case of a fraud investigation.

Any such collaborative work arrangement must be handled with extreme care. Internal auditors should generally resist any direct assignment that implies a second-class work status that is not in keeping with their own professional competence. The problem can be solved sometimes by having internal audit function serving as an assigned consultant, or with the clear understanding that the arrangement involves equals working on a temporary basis to meet a clearly recognized need. Another solution is to put the best qualified person in charge of the joint work effort, regardless of whether an external or internal auditor, and regardless of who is to ultimately be in possession of the workpapers involved.

(e) Cooperation and Collaboration in Auditor Training

Commonly, both the internal and external audit groups have training capabilities that are useful for both. External audit, which serves many clients, is especially likely to have developed various types of training programs, which can be useful to the internal auditors of their clients. In other instances, however, internal audit may be conducting training sessions or developing other training materials that are unique to the particular client organization. The external audit firm may want to utilize such materials for its staff members working on that particular audit. An example here might be when the training relates to special production processes or computer systems that need to be used by external audit. In actual practice, however, because internal and external auditors have different primary missions, it is often more advantageous for each to develop and administer its own training programs.

When training materials of one audit group are used by the other, such usage is usually provided with minimal charges because of the common interests served. Some external auditing firms also have developed training programs for internal auditors as a separate business venture. Such training programs are less directly linked to the audit coordination program. Internal audit should weigh these materials on their individual strengths and should always select the best source for internal audit training, even if delivered by another public accounting firm.

(f) Supportive Follow-Up of Audit Findings

Both external and internal audit develop findings and recommendations affecting the activities of the organization under review. Although the line organization personnel individually and collectively have the basic responsibility for the consideration of such recommendations and the related corrective actions, both audit groups have a common interest in the nature and scope of all reported deficiencies and in corrective actions. Both audit groups should be alert to all deficiencies and work in a coordinated manner to monitor corrective actions for the reported operational procedures. Also, the auditors should be very interested in the overall audit findings monitoring system and how effectively it is being administered.

The external audit's primary interest is in the fairness of the presentation of the organization's financial statements, and external auditors will not be involved with the underlying operational procedures in the same depth as internal audit. Hence, external audit will normally have fewer audit findings and recommendations pertaining to those operational procedures. In addition, an external auditor will be less involved in the follow-ups to audit recommendation than will internal audit. However, the particular findings and recommendations made by external audit normally have great visibility with the audit committee and organization management. As a result, the initiation of any findings and subsequent follow-up by external audit should be viewed with special concern by all parties of interest. External and internal auditors should cooperate in every possible way to share information on anything bearing on the current and evolving effectiveness of the organization's operational procedures, especially in the areas pertaining to the system of internal control. By working together, they best ensure the implementation of needed corrective actions.

(g) Joint Audit Project Planning

When internal and external auditors work cooperatively to achieve effective audit coordination, they will find that they need to sit down together to plan their respective audit programs in advance of the actual audit efforts. As discussed in Chapter 13, "Internal Audit Organization and Planning," the planning process involves the audit committee and the two audit groups. Typically, it may extend over a number of years and should be expressed partially in approved budgets. Although external audit will normally participate to some extent in that long-range planning process, its own plans focus more sharply on the need each year to develop the proposal for the following year's engagement, which requires the approval of the stockholders and the board of directors.

Chapter 13 discusses the planning process, where internal audit develops an audit universe of all entities or units subject to audit, performs a risk analysis against that universe to select candidates with the highest audit risks for review, and develops a current and long-range audit plan based on that risk evaluation. External auditors should perform a similar risk assessment based on the scope of their review at a given organization.

The concept of audit universe is different for external audit. Their universe will often be based on various balance sheet accounts or financial transactions, while the internal audit universe is usually based on operational areas or processes in the organization. However, these risk-assessment processes and audit plans based on the separate audit universes should be coordinated. The result of this coordination is a continuing planning process whereby audits for future years are added to the plan and activity in current years further refined to the extent practicable preceding the performance of actual audit work. Through joint planning, the needs of each audit group can be reconciled. However, internal audit determines risk-based audit plans with an understanding of external audit needs primarily for the next year.

External audit, then, makes its risk-based judgment of what needs to be done to satisfy the audit responsibilities, with consideration given to the support expected from internal audit. In making that judgment, proper weight should be given to the size of the internal audit staff, its demonstrated capabilities, and the extent to which it can be available for this audit work. The benefits derived from this coordination are essentially the same as those obtained from any kind of advance planning. Auditors, like any other managers, need to determine in advance what they want to accomplish and how they will make that desired future become reality. This is true irrespective of whether such agreed-on plans can and should be modified when changing conditions so require. The coordination of these risk-based audit plans results in the achievement of over-all audit objectives and provides the most essential foundation for an effective coordinated audit effort. This should be a standard practice in the well-managed internal audit organization.

Internal and external auditors have professional backgrounds that are very similar in many areas. This, together with the fact that they see a great deal of each other's work, provides a strong basis for effective coordination and cross-evaluation. Of course, as defined in SAS No. 65, external audit is expected to eval-uate the work of internal auditors when they rely on that work. Moreover, exter-nal audit's self-interest in having good internal auditing, combined with their close access to senior management, can help to get better organizational status and resources for internal audit. Internal audit should encourage cross-evaluation by external audit and make full use of it. The whole issue of internal and external audit coordination becomes more complicated today with the requirements of SOA Section 404 reviews. If internal audit is performing the Section 404 reviews for external audit attestation, there must be some independence between these two parties for these efforts.

Evaluation of the external audit effort by internal audit is also inevitable and useful, although it may cause some differences or problems. In some situations, external audit may not really welcome evaluation by the internal audit group. A more healthy attitude, however, is to recognize that there is always room for improvement and that very often internal audit can make a good, objective eval-uation. Moreover, the acceptance of constructive cross-evaluation is more consis-tent with the professional partnership approach described throughout this chapter. It can be expected that there will be more of the two-way evaluation in the future. This has been an accepted practice in many larger organizations, and may become a standard procedure in the future.

10.7 COORDINATION IN PERSPECTIVE

The common interests of internal and external auditors in their assessments of the adequacy of the system of internal control, as a basis for achieving their respective primary missions, provide substantial motivation to achieve an effec-tive coordination effort. Clearly, effective coordination makes good sense for all parties. Clearly also, effective coordination serves the overall interests of the organization. The challenge for all is to understand and support those factors that contribute to the achievement of effective coordination. For internal audit, it is important to understand the primary missions of each audit group while building on the strong common interests as foundations for the achievement of those primary missions. It is also important for internal auditors to demonstrate their compliance with standards of professional excellence to provide the needed basis for effective coordination between two mutually respected profes-sional partners. Only then can the coordination effort support the achievement of an integrated audit process for maximum organizational welfare. There is the need for an effort by all parties of interest—especially of the internal and external auditors themselves—to foster effective coordination. It needs also to be recognized that effective coordination is a continuous process. The potential rewards, however, clearly warrant the efforts that may be expended.

ENDNOTES

[1] American Institute of Certified Public Accountants, "Statement on Auditing Standards No. 65." New York: AICPA, 1991.

[2] Standards for the Profession Practice of Internal Auditing, Institute of Internal Auditors, Altamonte Springs, FL.

CHAPTER ELEVEN

Fraud Detection and Prevention

11.1 GROWING CONCERNS ABOUT MANAGEMENT FRAUD

The scandals at Enron, WorldCom, Adelphia, and others that came to light about the time of the enactment of the Sarbanes-Oxley Act (SOA) were all examples of financial fraud by senior corporate officers. Fraudulent activity can occur at all levels of an organization, but in the mid-2002, just days before and after the enactment of SOA, corporate officers appeared to be the real troublemakers in this slew of financial frauds. Despite the publicity condemning these senior corporate officers as the real troublemakers, fraud can take place at all levels. Just as a CEO, in cooperation with the CFO, may fraudulently manipulate earnings to boost reported corporate profits and their individual bonus compensation, a manager or even staff-level employee may take some fraudulent action for personal gain or just to "get even" with someone because of job frustration. Unfortunately, the publicity surrounding Enron and other incidents of fraud has created an almost everybody-does-it attitude in recent years. Ernst & Young, in its 2003 Global Fraud Survey,[1] reported that 85% of the worst frauds were caused by insiders on the payroll and over half of those frauds were initiated by members of management.

SOA and its strong emphasis on better internal controls did not change things. Early 2004 brought the $18 billion Parmalat fraud covering—of all things—a dairy company headquartered in Parma, Italy, which primarily distributed milk and cookies. As this book goes to press, we still do not have all the answers as to where the money went, but Parmalat ended up with a worldwide network of fictitious bank accounts.

The effective modern internal auditor needs to recognize potential fraudulent business practices as part of any audit and should recommend controls and procedures to limit exposure to this fraudulent activity. An important first step is to understand the dictionary or legal definition of fraud, whose common-law definition is the obtaining of money or property by means of false token, symbol, or device. In other words, someone improperly authorizes some document that causes an improper transfer of money. Fraud can be costly to any victimized organization, and effective internal controls are an organization's first line of defense against fraud. A comprehensive, fully implemented, and regularly monitored system of internal controls is essential for the prevention and detection of losses that arise from fraud, and internal auditors often find themselves very involved in fraud-related issues. When a fraud is discovered in the organization, internal audit is often one of the first resources called on to conduct an investigation to determine the extent of the fraud. In other situations, internal auditors discover a fraud in the course of a scheduled audit and then investigate and report the matter to the corporate consul or other legal authorities. However, both internal and external auditors historically have not regularly looked for fraud as part of their scheduled audits. This is changing.

Auditors today, both internal and external, are assuming a more important role in the detection and prevention of fraud. This chapter discusses controls to prevent and detect fraud and introduces the American Institute of Certified Public Accountants (AICPA) Statement on Auditing Standards (SAS) on fraud, No. 99, *Consideration of Fraud in a Financial Statement Audit*. While the SAS series has essentially gone away with the enactment of SOA and its Public Corporation Auditing Oversight Board (PCAOB), SAS No. 99 was a last but very important auditing standard. This chapter also discusses IIA initiatives here as well as procedures to detect and prevent computer systems fraud. Fraud has been with us from time immemorial, but auditors in the past have claimed that detecting fraud was beyond their responsibilities. Today, they are finding themselves with an increasing responsibility to detect fraud in the course of their review activities as well as to recommend appropriate controls to prevent future frauds.

11.2   RED FLAGS: FRAUD DETECTION FOR AUDITORS

Many fraudulent activities are easy to identify *after the fraud has been uncovered!* An employee of an organization who has been embezzling money over an extended time period may be caught through some slip-up that reveals the fraud. After such a fraud is discovered, it is often easy to look at the situation after the fact and say such things as, "But, she was such a good employee—she has not missed a day of work for nearly 2 years! How could she have done this?" or "Now that I think about it, I wondered how he could afford all of those long weekend trips to expensive places!" It is easy to analyze the facts after a fraud has been discovered as a "lesson learned," but auditors and management should look for indicators of possible fraudulent activities in advance with a skeptical eye. They should look for what are called "red flags."

Although there still was much to be resolved as this book was released, the first corporation as well as its CFO to be indicted for accounting fraud under

SOA was a health-care provider called HealthSouth Corporation. The then-largest U.S. provider of outpatient surgery, diagnostic and rehabilitative services, HealthSouth operated in approximately 1,900 locations in 50 states as well as some international facilities. It reported in excess of $1.4 billion of *fictitious* earnings over a 6-year period in order to meet analyst estimates and to keep the stock price high. As matters are now evolving, several of the company's financial and other officers have pleaded guilty, with more to come. While this accounting fraud had been going on at least since the early 1990s, there had been numerous "red flag" signs of possible fraud that were seemingly ignored by their external auditors and others:

- HealthSouth's year 2000 pretax earnings more than doubled to $559 million, although its sales grew only 3%. Pretax earnings for 2001 were nearly twice 1999 levels, although sales rose just 8%. While there is nothing wrong with fantastic earnings growth, analysts and others might have asked some hard questions.

- In late 2002, HealthSouth's internal auditors were denied access to key corporate financial records. Internal audit reported this to their outside auditors, who took no action. The audit committee evidently did not get involved either.

- The CEO seemed to be spending an excessive amount of attention on sports and popular music performers, flying his management staff off to events and bringing "sports stars" in to work with the company.

These are only examples of the activities that were occurring around the company that suggested possible fraud. Having fantastic percentage reported earnings gains does not mean fraud, but this can raise questions. Similarly, elaborate corporate-sponsored social events may only cause one to question how the organization is managing its resources rather than pointing to fraud. However, these kinds of activities should raise questions. At HealthSouth, an ex-employee even sent an e-mail to the external auditors suggesting they look in three specific accounts for fraudulent activity. This is more than a red flag; it is an attempt to blow the whistle. Based on this tip, some level of investigation was launched by the external auditors with nothing being found. Internal management pressure on a normally dominant CEO to back off from some fictitious financial reports eventually started a chain of events that soon exposed the fraud.

Red flags are normally the first indications of a potential fraud. Someone sees something that does not look right and then causes even a low-level investigation to be initiated. Auditors are often the very first people to become involved. Exhibit 11.1 lists a series of red flags that may point to potential financial fraud activities. None of these is an absolute indicator of fraud, but auditors should always be skeptical in their reviews and be aware of such warning signs. When an auditor sees evidence of one or more of these or other red flags, it may be time to dig a little deeper. Unfortunately, internal auditors often fail to detect fraud for one of the following reasons:

- *Unwillingness to Look for Fraud.* Based on their training and past experience, internal auditors have historically not actively looked for fraud.

They have often tended to view fraud investigation as a police detective type of activity and not a prime internal audit responsibility.

- *Too Much Trust Is Placed on Auditees.*   Internal auditors, in particular, try to maintain a friendly, cordial attitude toward auditees in their organization. Because they encounter these same people in the company cafeteria or at the annual company picnic, there is usually a level of trust here. Internal auditors quite correctly try to give their auditees the benefit of the doubt.

- *Not Enough Emphasis Is Placed on Audit Quality.*   Internal audit findings often point to some of the same red flags as mentioned in Exhibit 11.1. They are included as audit report findings pointing out such matters as missing records or accounts that were not reconciled. However, fraud-related issues were not raised in any quality review of the auditor's work.

- *Fraud Concerns Receive Inadequate Support from Management.*   The hint of possible fraud requires auditors to extend their procedures and dig a bit deeper. However, general and even audit management may be reluctant to give the auditor extra time to dig deeper. Unless there are strong suspicions to the contrary, management will often want the audit team to move on and stop spending time on what they feel is an extremely low-risk area.

- *Auditors Sometimes Just Fail to Focus on High-Risk Fraud Areas.*   Fraud can occur in anything from employee travel expense reporting to the treasury function's relations with offshore banks. There can often be a much greater risk in the latter, although auditors often tend to focus on the former. While it may be comparatively easy to find problems in travel expenses, there is always a need to focus on higher-risk areas.

Fraud is a word that can have many meanings, but we are referring to it in terms of fraud as a criminal act. There are over 300 references to fraud in federal criminal statutes, and the term appears throughout SOA. Most of those federal references are based on the federal general fraud statute:[2]

> Whoever, in any manner within the jurisdiction of any department or agency of the United States, knowingly and willfully falsifies, conceals, or covers up by any trick, scheme, or device a material fact, or makes any false, fictitious, or fraudulent writing or document knowingly the same to contain any false, fictitious, or fraudulent statement or entry, shall be fined not more than . . . or imprisoned not more than . . . or both.

Although stated in legalese, this is a strong statement. The auditor's word *material* is not included here and anything false, fictitious, or fraudulent could be considered a violation. There are multiple state statutes generally modeled after these federal rules, and an internal auditor should be aware of his or her state's rules.

To help detect fraud, auditors need to have an understanding of why people commit fraud. An organization can have the red flag environment described in the previous section, but it will not necessarily be subject to fraudulent activities

EXHIBIT 11.1

Financial Fraud Potential Red Flags

The following list represent "red flags" that may be warning signs for evidence of financial fraud:

- Lack of written corporate policies and standard operating procedures
- Based on interviews at multiple levels, lack of compliance with organization internal control policies
- Weak internal control policies, especially in the division of duties
- Disorganized operations in such areas as purchasing, receiving, warehousing, or regional offices
- Unrecorded transactions or missing records
- Counterfeit or evidence of alterations to documents
- Photocopied or questionable handwriting on documents
- Sales records with excessive voids or credits
- Bank accounts not reconciled on a timely basis or stale items on bank reconciliations
- Continuous out-of-balance conditions on subsidiary ledgers
- Unusual financial statement relationships
- Continuous unexplained differences between physical inventory counts and perpetual inventory records
- Bank checks written to cash in large amounts
- Handwritten checks in a computer environment
- Continuous or unusual fund transfers among company bank accounts
- Fund transfers to offshore banks
- Transactions not consistent with the entity's business
- Poor screening procedures for new employees, including no background or reference checks
- Reluctance by management to report criminal wrongdoing
- Unusual transfers of personal assets
- Officers or employees with lifestyles apparently beyond their means
- Unused vacation time
- Frequent or unusual related-party transactions
- Employees in close association with suppliers
- Employees in close relationship with one another in areas where separation of duties could be circumvented
- Expense-account abuse such as managers not following established rules
- Business assets dissipating without explanation

Source: Adapted from American Institute of Certified Public Accountants, www.aicpa.org.

unless one or more employees decide to engage in fraud. Exhibit 11.2 lists some typical reasons or excuses for committing a fraud. These are all reasons that apply where strong internal controls are in place and the fraud is only committed by one person. Fraud detection is much harder when there is collusion among multiple persons. In the HealthSouth fraud described previously, a very aggressive CEO assembled a top management team called "the company" to prepare

Exhibit 11.2

Reasons for Committing Fraud

- *Employee has desperate need for money.* This is probably the major motivator and type of fraud most difficult to detect. Whether it is a nasty divorce or a drug problem, the need for money can cause employees to resort to criminal actions.

- *Job frustrations.* Employees can become frustrated and feel that their company "doesn't give a damn" about them and feel free to act inappropriately. Job layoffs or pay grade freezes can foster such feelings.

- *"Everybody does it" attitude.* This type of situation is often common in a smaller retail type environment where an employee thinks that everyone else is stealing as well. This attitude can also develop when senior managers seem to be living extravagantly at the same time that the company is incurring losses.

- *Challenge of "beating the system."* This is a particular problem with would-be hackers in an automated systems environment. However, there can be many other cases where an employee, for example, tries to set up a fictitious customer account, perhaps with the employee's home address, to see if he can bill the company and receive cash in return.

- *Lax internal controls make fraud easy.* This is a basic motivation to attempt almost any fraud.

- *Low probability of detection.* Similar to the weak internal controls point. If an employee knows that chances of getting caught are nil, the temptation to commit fraud is greater.

- *Low probability of prosecution.* When a company seemingly never takes action to bring criminal charges against anyone, the word gets out, and people can view getting caught as an acceptable risk with little worry about prosecution.

- *Top management that does not seem to care.* Employees can often collectively determine when an employee seems to get away with little more than a slap on the fingers after breaking some rule, or when otherwise very appropriate behavior is not rewarded.

- *Low organizational loyalty or feelings of ownership.* In today's complex world, we often have situations where the owners of some business operation are a continent and many organizational layers away. It is easy to have the attitude that no one really seems to care on a daily basis.

- *Unreasonable budget expectations or other financial targets.* Organizations sometime establish expectations that are all but impossible to meet. This can create an environment where people will sometimes bend the rules to meet those targets.

- *Less-than-competitive compensation and poor promotion opportunities.* If they cannot receive what they feel are appropriate rewards through normal compensation, people may bend rules to benefit themselves.

the fraudulent financial reports. Members of "the company" at HealthSouth were highly compensated and received many incentives. The fraud did not become public until a member of "the company" began to have concerns about this growing accounting fraud. Whenever multiple people are involved in the same fraud, there is always a possibility that someone will break ranks.

While the detection of major frauds involving senior management participation are difficult to uncover, fraud that occurs at lower levels in the organization are often easier to detect with a proper level of auditor investigation. For example, a payroll process can present a wide range of opportunities for fraud through the use of such mechanisms as inflating the actual hours worked by an employee, generating checks for fictitious or terminated employees, or issuing duplicate checks for an employee. These are the classic types of issues that are part of many internal audit procedures. However, rather than just an internal control violation, an internal auditor should think of these items in terms of potential areas for employee fraud. Auditors have performed these procedures for years but sometimes just forget. In the HealthSouth fraud just discussed, it was later discovered that the external auditors did not do a classic bank balance confirmation with HealthSouth's banks. This is the test whereby the auditor asks the bank to independently confirm the bank balance as of a certain date. The Parmalat fraud discussed earlier included fraudulent bank confirmation letters that probably should have been detected sooner. In the promotion of audit efficiency over the years, auditors—particularly external auditors—have dropped many of these traditional procedures. It may be time to revisit some!

11.3 PUBLIC ACCOUNTING'S NEW ROLE IN FRAUD DETECTION

The external auditor's responsibility for the detection of fraud in financial statements has been an ongoing but contentious issue over the years. The very first AICPA Statement on Auditing Standards (SAS No. 1) provided:

> "The auditor has no responsibility to plan and perform the audit to obtain reasonable assurance that misstatements, whether caused by errors or fraud, that are not material to the financial statements are detected." In other words, the external auditor then was responsible to determine if the debits equaled the credits but had no responsibility to detect fraudulent activity. The public accounting profession stood by this position for many years. Even during the period of numerous financial frauds that led to the 1987 Treadway Commission Report on Fraudulent Financial Reporting (see Chapter 4, "Internal Controls Fundamentals: COSO Framework"), external audit standards did not include any responsibility for the detection of fraud.

Despite continuing pressure for change, AICPA audit standards regarding the external auditor's responsibility for fraud did not change until 1997 when this responsibility for fraud was restated in SAS No. 82:

> "The auditor has a responsibility to plan and perform the audit to obtain reasonable assurance about whether the financial statements are free of material misstatement, whether caused by error or fraud." This revised but tighter standard was released after much professional discussion but at about the peak of the dot-com bubble when the investing public was more concerned about their investments surging forward and not that much with fraud.

Moving to present times with Enron, WorldCom, and a host of others, concerns about fraudulent financial reporting has certainly changed. Given SOA and the new PCAOB, it was perhaps too late, but in December 2002 the AICPA released SAS No. 99 on the auditor's responsibility for detecting fraudulent financial reporting. With this new standard, the external auditor has become responsible for providing reasonable assurance that the financial statements are free of material misstatement, *whether caused by error or fraud*. We have used our italics here, because this is a major change in external auditors' responsibilities.

SAS No. 99 calls on financial auditors to take an attitude of professional skepticism regarding possible fraud. Putting aside any prior beliefs as to management's honesty, the audit team should exchange ideas or brainstorm on how fraud could occur in the organization they are about to audit. These discussions should identify fraud risks and should always keep in mind the characteristics that are present when frauds occur: incentives, opportunities, and ability to rationalize. Throughout the audit, the engagement team should think about and explore the question, "If someone wanted to perpetrate a fraud here, how would it be done?" From these discussions, the engagement team should be in a better position to design audit tests responsive to the risks of fraud. The guidance here is that the external audit team should *always* go into an audit engagement anticipating that there may be some level of fraudulent activity.

The external auditor engagement team is expected to inquire of management and others in the organization as to their perceptions of the risk of fraud and whether they are aware of any ongoing fraud investigations or open issues. The auditors should make a point of talking to all levels of employees, both managers and others, giving them an opportunity to "blow the whistle" and encouraging someone to step forward. It might also help deter others from committing fraud if they are concerned that a coworker may turn them in during a subsequent audit. During an audit, the external audit engagement team should test areas, locations, and accounts that otherwise might not be tested. The team should design tests that would be unpredictable and unexpected by the client. This represents a major change in external auditing standards!

SAS No. 99 also recognizes that management is often in a position to override controls in order to commit financial-statement fraud. The auditing standard calls for auditors to test for management override of controls on every audit. SAS No. 99 calls for a major external audit emphasis in detecting fraud, including procedures that external auditors are expected to perform in every audit engagement. This can be a major change from the "let's take the afternoon off and talk about things over a game of golf" approach that was common in many past external audit engagements.

In addition to imposing a very tough fraud detection auditing standard on its members, the AICPA has taken strong steps to bring external auditors up to speed regarding situations that encourage fraud as well as providing both educational materials and case studies. Its Web pages are filed with case studies, publications, CPE courses, and other references on management fraud issues. You do not have to be an AICPA member to access the site, but there are member and nonmember prices for purchasing items. As an example of the AICPA materials, Exhibit 11.3 shows a misappropriation of assets checklist for auditors. Moving from being an auditing and accounting professional organization that avoided getting involved in fraud prevention and detection over many years, the organization's SAS No. 99 standards as well as the AICPA's published anti-fraud guidance materials very much raise the bar for all CPAs. Given the enactment of SOA and other recent events, it is unfortunate that the release of these audit standards did not happen sooner.

EXHIBIT 11.3

Risk Factors Relating to Misappropriation of Assets

Risk factors that relate to misstatements arising from misappropriation of assets are also classified according to the three conditions generally present when fraud exists: incentives/pressures, opportunities, and attitudes/rationalizations. Some of the risk factors related to misstatements arising from fraudulent financial reporting also may be present when misstatements arising from misappropriation of assets occur. For example, ineffective monitoring of management and weaknesses in internal control may be present when misstatements due to either fraudulent financial reporting or misappropriation of assets exist. The following are examples of risk factors related to misstatements arising from misappropriation of assets.

INCENTIVES/PRESSURES

A. Personal financial obligations may create pressure on management or employees with access to cash or other assets susceptible to theft to misappropriate those assets.

B. Adverse relationships between the entity and employees with access to cash or other assets susceptible to theft may motivate those employees to misappropriate those assets. For example, adverse relationships may be created by the following:

   o Known or anticipated future employee layoffs

   o Recent or anticipated changes to employee compensation or benefit plans

   o Promotions, compensation, or other rewards inconsistent with expectations

OPPORTUNITIES

A. Certain characteristics or circumstances may increase the susceptibility of assets to misappropriation. For example, opportunities to misappropriate assets increase when there are the following:

   o Large amounts of cash on hand or processed

   o Inventory items that are small in size, of high value, or in high demand

   o Easily convertible assets, such as bearer bonds, diamonds, or computer chips

   o Fixed assets that are small in size, marketable, or lacking observable identification of ownership

B. Inadequate internal control over assets may increase the susceptibility of misappropriation of those assets. For example, misappropriation of assets may occur because there is the following:

   o Inadequate segregation of duties or independent checks

   o Inadequate management oversight of employees responsible for assets, for example, inadequate supervision or monitoring of remote locations

   o Inadequate job applicant screening of employees with access to assets

   o Inadequate record keeping with respect to assets

   o Inadequate system of authorization and approval of transactions (for example, in purchasing)

   o Inadequate physical safeguards over cash, investments, inventory, or fixed assets

   o Lack of complete and timely reconciliations of assets

   o Lack of timely and appropriate documentation of transactions, for example, credits for merchandise returns

   o Lack of mandatory vacations for employees performing key control functions

   o Inadequate management understanding of information technology, which enables information technology employees to perpetrate a misappropriation

   o Inadequate access controls over automated records, including controls over and review of computer systems event logs

---

Source: Copyright © 2002 by the American Institute of Certified Public Accountants, Inc. Reprinted with permission.

11.4 IIA STANDARDS FOR DETECTING AND INVESTIGATING FRAUD

Internal auditors are often in a better position to detect fraud than external auditors. While many external auditors do not visit a client much more often than around the quarterly and annual financial statement dates, internal auditors are just that—internal to the organization and at the organization on a daily basis. Just through observation, an internal auditor may be in a much better position to see a red flag that could easily be missed by an external auditor, despite the new AICPA fraud standard. The shipping supervisor who shows up at the annual holiday party in an expensive Italian suit and sporting an expensive brand-name wristwatch might raise a small blip on an internal auditor's radar screen that an external auditor might not see. There are many very valid reasons to justify this show of wealth, but it could be something to remember going forward.

Internal auditors run in to many such potential fraud issues in the ongoing course of their audits. They typically get involved in much more detailed, transaction-level reviews than their external audit counterparts and see questionable documents or transactions more frequently. If management feels that there may be a potential fraud in the organization, the first step is almost always to contact internal audit, who also will have some connection and communication with the corporate legal department. They can discuss any potential concerns there and get a quick opinion whether some concern requires more attention. If there are strong signs of an active fraud, corporate legal will almost always be ready to jump in to help address the matter.

IIA Professional Standards on due professional care and scope of work cover fraud in a very general sense, as discussed in Chapter 12, "Internal Audit Professional Standards." An internal auditor will be concerned about such matters as the possibility of wrongdoing and should consider evidence of any improper or illegal activities in an audit. However, the standards that provide specific guidance on fraud seem to follow the older external audit standards just discussed. Recognizing that it may be difficult to detect fraud, the revised 2004 IIA standard 1210.A2 provides the guidance, with our italics noted: "The internal auditor should have sufficient knowledge to identify the indicators of fraud *but is not expected to have the expertise of a person whose primary responsibility is detecting and investigating fraud.*" This is recognition that internal auditors may not have the expertise for uncovering fraud issues.

This same fraud standard is supported by an IIA Practice Advisory, 1210.A2-1, Identification of Fraud. Despite the statement in the standard that internal auditors are *not expected to have the expertise*, the supporting practice advisory provides an internal auditor with some guidance on detecting and investigating fraud. We have included an edited portion of this practice advisory:

> Deterrence of fraud consists of those actions taken to discourage the perpetration of fraud and limit the exposure if fraud does occur. The principal mechanism for deterring fraud is control. Primary responsibility for establishing and maintaining control rests with management.

Internal auditors are responsible for assisting in the deterrence of fraud by examining and evaluating the adequacy and the effectiveness of the system of internal control, commensurate with the extent of the potential exposure/risk in the various segments of the organization's operations. In carrying out this responsibility, internal auditors should, for example, determine whether:

- The organizational environment fosters control consciousness, and realistic organizational goals and objectives are set.
- Written policies (e.g., code of conduct) exist that describe prohibited activities and the action required whenever violations are discovered.
- Appropriate authorization policies for transactions are established and maintained.
- Policies, practices, procedures, reports, and other mechanisms are developed to monitor activities and safeguard assets, particularly in high-risk areas.
- Communication channels provide management with adequate and reliable information.
- Recommendations need to be made for the establishment or enhancement of cost-effective controls to help deter fraud.

When an internal auditor suspects wrongdoing, appropriate authorities within the organization should be informed. The internal auditor may recommend whatever investigation is considered necessary in the circumstances. Thereafter, the auditor should follow up to see that the internal auditing activity's responsibilities have been met.

This practice advisory does not really educate the internal auditor on "red flag" types of conditions that might suggest potential fraudulent activity. Rather, it suggests that if an organization does not have good policies and procedures or lacks a code of conduct, this could indicate an environment that encourages fraud. This is often true. But, the lack of a current code of conduct or poorly drafted policy statements should not be the major reason for an internal auditor to go on a hunt to for potential fraudulent activities. The "red flags" in Exhibit 11.1 are better indicators.

The IIA has not taken the strong position on detecting fraud that the AICPA has. An early 2004 search to the IIA Web site using the key word "fraud" just does not produce the same wealth of material as is now found on the AICPA site. There are references to articles on fraud in older issues of the IIA publication, *The Internal Auditor*, but not much more. Other fraud-related articles are listed but are only available to IIA members. The previously referenced practice advisory is an example. The IIA also has special conferences on the topic, but the AICPA is taking a stronger professional lead here in providing guidance to auditors.

The IIA, along with the AICPA, ISACA, the Association of Certified Fraud Examiners, Financial Executives International, the Institute of Management Accountants, and the Society for Human Resource Management, have collaborated and sponsored some fraud guidance material published as a supplement to SAS No. 99. Other professional organizations that participated in reviewing and developing fraud guidance include the American Accounting Association, the Defense Industry Initiative, and the National Association of Corporate Directors. However, the AICPA is clearly taking a lead role here, and interested professionals should visit the AICPA Web site (www.aicpa.org/antifraud).

11.5 FRAUD INVESTIGATIONS FOR INTERNAL AUDITORS

In addition to helping to build and review controls to prevent and detect fraud, internal auditors may sometimes become very involved in fraud investigations. While appropriate legal authorities should be used for many fraud investigations, internal audit can often play a key role in other, less major matters. Internal auditors should generally not play the role of Sherlock Holmes but can help to gather information for smaller investigations or provide supporting materials for larger matters. Internal audit often gets involved in a matter through some troubling information encountered during an audit or an anonymous tip through a call or e-mail.

When faced with potential fraud information, a first step for internal audit should always be to consult with the organization's corporate counsel. As a result of the nature of the allegation and the extent of the initial information, the matter may be turned over to legal authorities, such as the federal district attorney's or state prosecutor's office. In some cases, legal counsel will suggest that other authorities be involved in the matter at once. In smaller, seemingly less major matters, internal audit will often be asked to take responsibility for the investigation. In many instances, these types of investigations involve just a detailed review of documents. The evidence gathered from that document review will become the basis for any further action to be taken.

Fraud-related investigations cause an internal auditor to operate differently than he or she does during normal financial or operational internal audits. In any fraud-related review, an auditor should have three major objectives:

1. **Prove the Loss.** Fraud-related reviews usually start out with the finding that someone stole something. The internal audit–led investigative review should assemble as much relevant material as necessary to determine the overall size and scope of the loss.

2. **Establish Responsibility and Intent.** This is the "who did it?" step. As much as possible, the audit team should attempt to identify everyone who was responsible for the matter and if there was any special or different intent associated with the fraud action.

3. **Prove the Audit Investigative Methods Used.** The investigative team needs to be able to prove that their fraud-related conclusions were based on a detailed, step-by-step investigative process, not just an uncoordinated "witch hunt." The review should be documented using the best internal audit review processes. Of particular importance is that all documents used need to be secured.

There are many other procedures associated with a fraud-related examination. The objective of this book is not to describe the overall process of fraud examinations but to discuss the increased emphasis on fraud detection and prevention as outlined by new standards, particularly the AICPA SAS No. 99. Internal auditors interested in learning more about fraud investigations should explore the activities and publications of the Association of Certified Fraud Examiners at www.cfenet.com. In addition to the previously referenced AICPA materials, this professional organization has a variety of educational and guidance material as well as maintaining a formalized examination.

11.6 INFORMATION SYSTEMS FRAUD PREVENTION PROCESSES

Information systems or computer fraud covers a wide range of issues and concerns. In today's business environment information systems are virtually always a key component of any modern financial- or accounting-related fraud. Because information systems support so many areas and because they cross so many lines in the organizations, we can think of computer fraud in multiple dimensions ranging from the "minor" to significant fraudulent activities:

- *Improper Personal Use of Computer Resources.* An organization may establish rules stating that there should be no personal files or programs on its work-supplied systems. Such rules are frequently ignored by employees, who may use word-processing or spreadsheet resources to perform some personal work. An organization should emphasize to employees that they should not be doing personal business while at the workplace.

- *Internet Access Issues.* As with the personal use of computers, organizations often establish guidelines and sometimes controls to restrict Internet use. Again, such rules are frequently ignored by employees and sometimes bypassed by software that will allow them to get around firewalls in systems. There can be a much greater possibility of abuse here but there is also the potential for the organization to monitor employees' Internet usage through software-based monitoring tools.

- *Illegal Use of Software.* Employees will sometimes attempt to steal or download copies of company software or will install their own software on organizational computer resources. They are violating organizational rules and often putting their employers in violation of software license agreements.

- *Computer Security and Confidentiality Fraud Matters.* Employees can violate password protections and gain improper access to computer systems and files. Even if they are only trying to "see if it works," they are performing a fraudulent act by violating computer security rules.

- *Information Theft or Other Data Abuse Computer Fraud.* It is one thing to improperly access a computer system by violating password controls and another to improperly view, modify, or copy data or files. This can be a significant case of computer crime.

- *Embezzlement or Unauthorized Electronic Fund Transfers.* Stealing money or other resources through improper or unauthorized transactions is the most significant computer fraud issue. Whether this involves initiating a transaction to send an accounts payable check to one's home address or facilitating a major bank transfer, this can be a major area for computer fraud or crime.

The above examples run the course from what might be considered fairly minor to significant information systems abuses. We mention the more minor items to point out the range of items that can be considered computer fraud. If I am given a laptop computer for my work and am told it is only for business use, but I use it to write a book report as part of my child's homework, does this represent computer crime or fraud? The answer here is really yes, per the established rules. If the organization has set up rules, they were created for good reason and employees should not violate them. However, should internal audit launch a review to discover violations in this area? Probably not; there are more important high-risk areas on which to spend limited time and resources. A strong code of conduct and ethics program, as discussed in Chapter 9, "Whistleblower Programs and Codes of Conduct," should be the predominant control procedure in this case.

We have used the previous example to illustrate that there are many possibilities for computer fraud and abuse. It is often also a very complex area, where strong technical skills are needed to understand tools and methods. This is an area where the rules are changing continually. Individuals with a fraudulent intent are finding new ways to violate established automated controls, and skilled professionals are finding ways to detect and protect against this fraudulent activity. Chapter 19, "General Controls in an E-Business and Networked Environment," discusses information systems operations controls in a networked environment.

A related computer systems fraud detection area is computer forensics, the detailed examination of computers and their peripheral devices, using computer investigation and analysis techniques for finding or determining potential legal evidence in a fraud situation. The idea here is that essentially anything written in a computer file can be recovered, even if it has been erased through an operating system command. The evidence that one might need to find covers a wide range of areas such as theft of trade secrets, theft or destruction of intellectual property, fraud, and other civil cases involving wrongful dismissals, breaches of contracts, and discrimination issues.

Recovered computer data can often be a gold mine in a fraud investigation. Perpetrators often feel that they have covered their tracks by deleting files, but computer forensics tools often allow full recovery. Forensic examinations involve the examination of computer media, such as floppy disks, hard disk drives, backup tapes, CD-ROMs, and any other media used to store data. The forensic specialist uses specialized software to discover data that resides in a computer system, or can recover deleted/erased, encrypted, or damaged file information, and recover passwords so that documents can be read.

We have used this example of computer forensics as one approach to aid computer fraud investigations. This is an area that requires specialized tools and training, and an auditor will probably not have the skills to perform such an analysis without obtaining necessary help. The Web site www.forensics.com

provides a massive number of listings of consultants and other firms; this may be a good source for obtaining help in this area.

Other than direct testimony by an eyewitness, documentary evidence is usually the most compelling form of evidence, and paper trails have traditionally been a gold mine for investigators, especially where fraud is involved. In the past, documentary evidence was limited to paper, and where the best evidence rule applied, the original document was produced. However, documents are rarely typed today but are produced on personal computers. Some of these documents are no longer printed and are e-mailed or faxed to the recipient directly from the computer. Because of the change in the way that information is distributed and the way people communicate, copies of computer files are now as good as the original electronic document.

We have used computer forensics here as an example of new technology-based techniques for fraud detection. The use of firewall software to protect a system or user from entering transactions or accessing systems beyond a fixed region is another example. Virus protection software is a third. A full discussion of the computer fraud aspects of these and other areas is beyond the scope of this book. The internal auditor must just realize that computer fraud is a large and complex area.

11.7 FRAUD DETECTION AND THE AUDITOR

Fraud has always been with us, no matter how well we build strong attitudes of honesty through codes of conduct and the like, as well as build ever stronger controls to prevent it. Badly burned by the accounting scandals that led to SOA, the AICPA and external auditors have taken on the major task of better detecting fraudulent activities during their financial statement audits. Time will tell how effective the SAS No. 99 rules are on external auditors, but the standard calls for a new dimension to how auditors think when planning and conducting financial statement audits.

Internal auditors need to give greater consideration to fraud in their audit work as well. They have always been involved in some level of fraud investigation work when called on by management, but fraud detection and prevention considerations needs to become a more significant component of every internal audit. Internal auditors perhaps need to enter a new internal audit engagement by asking themselves some questions about where an auditee might commit a fraudulent act. Internal auditors should retain a level of skepticism about the potential for fraud in their ongoing work assignments.

ENDNOTES

[1] *Fraud, The Unmanaged Risk*. Ernst & Young 8th Global Survey, New York, 2003.
[2] The Federal fraud statute referenced is a series of rules such as 18 U.S.C. 1341 on mail fraud and 18 U.S.C. 1344 on bank fraud.

PART FOUR

Administering Internal Audit Activities

CHAPTER TWELVE

Internal Audit Professional Standards

12.1 IMPORTANCE OF PROFESSIONAL STANDARDS

Every profession requires a set of standards to govern its practices, general procedures, and ethics. These standards allow specialists performing similar work to call themselves professionals because they are following a recognized and consistent set of best practice standards. The key standards for internal auditors are the Institute of Internal Auditors' (IIA's) *Professional Standards for the Practice of Internal Auditing*, a set of guidance materials that has been known as "The Red Book" by many internal auditors in the past. These older IIA standards, last published in 1995, were lengthy and sometimes difficult to embrace. The IIA revised its standards in 2004 after comments derived from a lengthy exposure draft. This chapter will summarize these IIA standards as well as provide guidance on how to apply them to today's internal audit organization.

We will also revisit the IIA Code of Ethics for internal auditors, an important supporting foundation for internal auditors in today's world of frequent open questions regarding professional ethics, and will also consider the code of ethics for a related auditing organization, the Information Systems Audit and Control Association (ISACA). Although ISACA does not have the same level of standards as the IIA, their CobiT information systems internal control framework and information regarding their related professional group, the IT Governance Institute, were discussed in Chapter 7, "Internal Controls Frameworks Worldwide: CobiT and Others." Chapter 25, "Continuous Assurance Auditing, XBRL, and OLAP," will introduce another very important set of internal audit standards, the quality audit guidance and standards from the American Society for Quality (ASQ). ASQ's internal audit standards and its quality auditors represent a different dimension and discipline from the IIA's approaches and standards. They also represent an area that should be better represented and understood in the overall world of internal auditing.

The IIA's *Standards for the Professional Practice of Internal Auditing* represent a "must-know" set of information for internal auditors today. Our fifth edition had an extensive set of extracts from the often too detailed and difficult to implement older standards. While any standards are an evolving set of rules that may not exactly reflect all industry practices at a given point in time, they provide a set of guidelines for internal auditors worldwide to follow in their service to management. The new IIA *Standards for the Practice of Internal Auditing*, summarized here, are available from the IIA.[1] They represent an important source of guidance for today's internal auditor and should be in every internal auditor's professional library.

12.2 CODES OF ETHICS: THE IIA AND ISACA

The purpose of the IIA's Code of Ethics is to promote an ethical culture in the profession of internal auditing. This code of ethics is displayed in Exhibit 12.1. It is necessary and appropriate for a profession that depends on the trust placed on users of internal audit services on objective assurances about risk management, control, and governance. The IIA's current Code of Ethics was released in 2000 and is based on the principles of internal auditor integrity, objectivity, confidentiality, and competency. These are the behavioral norms expected of internal auditors and are intended to guide the ethical conduct of internal auditors.

The IIA Code of Ethics replaces an earlier and also rather lengthy 1988 version that had eleven specific articles defining preferred practices; that version, in turn, replaced a 1968 version with eight articles. The current 2000 version, with its highlighted emphasis on integrity, objectivity, confidentiality, and competency becomes much easier to understand and recognize than the rather detailed articles in prior versions. As a minor note, the 1988 version used the term "Members and CIAs" in each of its articles. The current code simply says "Internal Auditors," perhaps a better terminology. Any person performing internal audit services, whether or not a member of the IIA or a CIA, should follow this code of ethics. Professional certificates, including the Certified Internal Auditor (CIA) designation, will be discussed in Chapter 28, "Professional Certifications: CIA, CISA, and More."

This IIA Code of Ethics applies to both individuals and entities that provide internal auditing services. For IIA members and recipients of or candidates for IIA professional certifications, breaches of the Code of Ethics will be evaluated

EXHIBIT 12.1

Institute of Internal Auditors Code of Ethics

1. Integrity
Internal auditors:
1.1 Shall perform their work with honesty, diligence, and responsibility.
1.2 Shall observe the law and make disclosures expected by the law and the profession.
1.3 Shall not knowingly be a party to any illegal activity, or engage in acts that are discreditable to the profession of internal auditing or to the organization.
1.4 Shall respect and contribute to the legitimate and ethical objectives of the organization.

2. Objectivity
Internal auditors:
2.1 Shall not participate in any activity or relationship that may impair or be presumed to impair their unbiased assessment. This participation includes those activities or relationships that may be in conflict with the interests of the organization.
2.2 Shall not accept anything that may impair or be presumed to impair their professional judgment.
2.3 Shall disclose all material facts known to them that, if not disclosed, may distort the reporting of activities under review.

3. Confidentiality
Internal auditors:
3.1 Shall be prudent in the use and protection of information acquired in the course of their duties.
3.2 Shall not use information for any personal gain or in any manner that would be contrary to the law or detrimental to the legitimate and ethical objectives of the organization.

4. Competency
Internal auditors:
4.1 Shall engage only in those services for which they have the necessary knowledge, skills, and experience.
4.2 Shall perform internal auditing services in accordance with the *Standards for the Professional Practice of Internal Auditing.*
4.3 Shall continually improve their proficiency and the effectiveness and quality of their services.

Source: IIA Code of Ethics, Copyright 2004 by The Institute of Internal Auditors, Inc., 247 Maitland Avenue, Altamonte Springs, Florida 32710-4201 USA. Reprinted with permission.

and administered according to IIA bylaws and administrative guidelines. The IIA goes on to state that even if a particular conduct is not mentioned in this code, this does not prevent the conduct or practice from being unacceptable or discreditable. Violators of the code, whether a member, certification holder, or candidate, can be held liable for disciplinary action.

The Information Systems Audit and Control Association (ISACA), as well as its affiliated research arm, the IT Governance Institute is a professional audit organization that represents or speaks primarily for information systems auditors. ISACA was originally known as the EDP Auditor's Association (EDPAA), a professional group that was founded in 1969 by a group of internal auditors that then felt the IIA was not giving sufficient attention to the importance of computer systems and their related technology controls. We have almost forgotten that EDP stands for electronic data processing, an almost archaic term, and we now have ISACA. It is still leading the IIA on technology related issues. ISACA is also the professional organization that administers the CISA (Certified Information Systems Auditor) examination and program and is responsible for the CobiT internal control framework discussed in Chapter 7.

With its information systems audit and IT governance orientation, ISACA represents a somewhat different group of auditors. Historically, ISACA drew a large number of members from information systems audit specialists and public accounting external audit firms, and it has had a very strong international membership in some areas of the world. Many IIA members are also ISACA members, and while the two groups do not have many joint meetings or other endeavors, each represents an important segment of the audit community.

While ISACA—fortuitously—does not have its own set of professional standards, it does have a code of ethics, as shown in Exhibit 12.2. Because of its IT heritage, the ISACA code is more oriented toward technology-related issues. It is a set of professional standards that applies to and should be of particular value to information systems audit professionals. Although the wording is different, there is nothing in the ISACA code that is really contrary to the IIA code. Internal auditors, whether working primarily in information systems areas or with a more general internal controls orientation, should exercise strong ethical practices in their work.

EXHIBIT 12.2

ISACA Code of Professional Ethics

The Information Systems Audit and Control Association, Inc. (ISACA) sets forth this Code of Professional Ethics to guide the professional and personal conduct of members of the association and/or its certification holders.

Members and ISACA certification holders shall:

1. Support the implementation of, and encourage compliance with, appropriate standards, procedures and controls for information systems.

2. Perform their duties with objectivity, due diligence and professional care, in accordance with professional standards and best practices.

3. Serve in the interest of stakeholders in a lawful and honest manner, while maintaining high standards of conduct and character, and not engage in acts discreditable to the profession.

4. Maintain the privacy and confidentiality of information obtained in the course of their duties unless disclosure is required by legal authority. Such information shall not be used for personal benefit or released to inappropriate parties.

5. Maintain competency in their respective fields and agree to undertake only those activities, which they can reasonably expect to complete with professional competence.

6. Inform appropriate parties of the results of work performed; revealing all significant facts known to them.

7. Support the professional education of stakeholders in enhancing their understanding of information systems security and control.

Failure to comply with this Code of Professional Ethics can result in an investigation into a member's, and/or certification holder's conduct and, ultimately, in disciplinary measures.

Source: Control Objectives for Information and Related Technology (COBIT®), 3rd Edition, © Copyright 1996, 1998, 2000, the IT Governance Institute® (ITGI), http://isaca.org and http://itgi.org, Rolling Meadows, IL 60008 USA. Reprinted by permission.

12.3 INTERNAL AUDITING'S PROFESSIONAL PRACTICE STANDARDS

Internal auditors work in a large variety of organizations and are asked to perform internal audit reviews in a diverse number of operational and financial areas. Because of this diversity, internal auditors are faced with a wide spectrum of professional challenges, including that management expects internal auditors to perform reviews in a competent and consistent manner. As the key internal audit professional organization, the IIA, through its Internal Auditing Standards Board, develops and issues standards that define the basic practice of internal auditing. The *Standards for the Professional Practice of Internal Auditing* is designed to:

- Delineate basic principles that represent the practice of internal auditing as it should be.

- Provide a framework for performing and promoting a broad range of value-added internal audit activities.

- Establish the basis for the measurement of internal audit performance.

- Foster improved organizational processes and operations.

The standards aid in this process; they provide a guideline for management to measure their internal auditors as well as for internal auditors to measure themselves. The standards also set some constraints upon internal audit activity.

(a) Background of the IIA Standards

As stated in its own materials, the Institute of Internal Auditors first issued these Standards for the Professional Practice of Internal Auditing in 1978 "to serve the entire profession in all types of business, in various levels of government, and in all other organizations where internal auditors are found . . . to represent the practice of internal auditing as it should be . . . ." Prior to the approval of these standards, the most authoritative document was the "Statement of Responsibilities" of internal audit, originally issued by the IIA in 1947 and subsequently revised over the years until the current standards. The founding author of this book, Vic Brink, played a major role in the development of these first IIA standards. The foreword to the 1978 IIA standards describes them as "the criteria by which the operations of an internal auditing department are evaluated and measured." This foreword goes on to state, "Compliance with the concepts enunciated by the Standards is essential before the responsibilities of the internal auditor can be met."

The Standards were developed by the IIA's Professional Standards Committee based on their own professional expertise as well as comments received from IIA members and other interested parties. Because of the diverse group of participants who developed the standards, the final language has some overlap, compromise, and incompleteness. As a result, individual standards and guidelines may be subject to varying interpretations. These matters will be discussed in subsequent sections of this chapter.

An internal auditor today is expected to follow these standards. It would be a rare internal audit function that did not have an internal audit charter, as was discussed in Chapter 2, "Management Needs: Internal Audit's Operational Approach," and those charters will almost always strongly affirm adherence to the IIA's *Standards for Professional Practice*. Internal auditors may have also come from some other professional area, such as banking or an external audit firm. Many such disciplines have professional organizations with their own standards that, generally, will not be in conflict with the IIA Standards. They may use slightly different terminology, as was discussed with the ISACA Code of Ethics, but should follow audit practices that generally fit under the IIA Standards. As a matter of practice, however, the IIA's *Standards for the Practice of Internal Auditing* will govern the work of internal audit. When there appears to be a conflict and when the individual questioning that conflict is working as an internal auditor, the IIA's standards will take precedence over any conflicting professional standards.

The IIA has historically published these standards, with the above title, in a small publication known as the previously mentioned "Red Book." With a changing world and impressions of the role of internal auditors, these standards have changed over the years. There was a major update to them in 2001, and a revised set of standards was issued in 2004. This section will discuss the overall framework of the current standards as well as provide some background on the standards as they have developed over the years.

(b) IIA's Current Standards: What Has Changed

The fifth edition of this book contained a very extensive and sometime critical description of the IIA standards as they existed in 1999. For any internal auditor who has attempted to follow and understand those old standards, the current releases are refreshing in their simplification. The older standards were released in an almost impossible level of detail. An example of the new as well as the old standards explains this:

> **Current Standard: 2500 on Monitoring Progress.** There is one general Attribute and Performance standard here stating that the chief audit executive (CAE) should establish a system to monitor the disposition of the results of audits. This one general standard has one substandard for audit assurance related activity as well as one consulting activity substandard. As will be discussed below, the standards recognize that internal auditors will be involved in audit assurance as well as in consulting-related activities.

> **Previous Standard: 440 on Following Up.** Starting with a general standard similar to the current section 2500, this older standard had 23 individual sub- or sub-sub- clarifying standards following it. There was good guidance here, but this older standard was really far too specific. Substandard 440.01.12.a states that the "Director of Internal Audit" should establish the procedures for the time frame in which audit report responses are required. While certainly a valid guideline, it does little good to tell an auditee that IIA standards "require" that their audit report responses must be delivered in 7 days if their response is that it will take 10 days.

This is just one small example. The older standards were too detailed for effective internal audit management. The current IIA standards provide a much more realistic set of guidance materials to allow an internal audit function to perform effectively and efficiently.

The past standards were divided into five broad sections, ranging from old section 100 on overall internal audit standards for independence to some very detailed standards for managing the internal audit department in the old section 500. The current standards now consist of two broad sections, the 1000 series of what are called attribute standards, and the 2000 Series performance standards. Under each of these are more detailed implementation standards that are further split between standards covering internal audit assurance activities and others for internal audit consulting work.

The sections following describe the Attribute and performance standards in some detail as well as some of the descriptive implementation standards. Recognizing that internal auditors may be asked to just review internal controls or to act more as internal consultants, there may be multiple sets of implementation standards: a set for each of these major types of internal audit activity. The objective here is not, however, to just reproduce these IIA published standards but to describe how they have changed over recent years or are evolving. If not already in possession of them, all internal auditors should obtain from the IIA or at least gain access to these standards and develop a good understanding of their contents.

(c) Authority of the Internal Auditing Standards

The IIA standards provide a guideline for all internal auditors as well as their overall internal audit departments. These standards do not have the same legal authority as the public accounting auditing standards that were previously issued by the AICPA's Auditing Standards Board (ASB) or by today's PCAOB, but the IIA Standards represent the only widely recognized set of performance standards for internal auditors. Organizations' management will judge the professional adequacy of their internal audit function by its compliance with IIA standards, and board audit committees will often insist that the internal audit department *formally* adopt the IIA standards as part of its charter.

External auditors, when deciding to rely on the work of internal auditors, will include the internal auditor's compliance with the standards as a measure to help in that decision. This is documented in the AICPA's Statement on Auditing Standards (SAS) No. 65, "Internal Auditors' Relationships with Independent Outside Auditors," and discussed in Chapter 10, "Working with External Auditors." The IIA Standards do not apply *just* to members of the Institute of Internal Auditors. They provide a guideline for *all* internal auditors, although members of the IIA and certified internal auditors (CIAs), in particular, are expected to follow them. The CIA certification and other internal audit professional designations are discussed in Chapter 28.

All internal auditors should develop a general understanding of these *Standards for the Professional Practice of Internal Auditing.* While they will not tell an internal auditor how, for example, to review the internal controls surrounding an invoicing system, they provide good general guidance on how to perform effective internal audits. While differences may affect the practice of internal auditing in various business or national environments, compliance with these IIA standards is essential if the responsibilities of internal auditors are to be met.

If internal auditors are prohibited by laws or regulations from complying with certain parts of the standards, they should comply with all other parts of the standards and make appropriate disclosures.

12.4 CONTENT OF THE IIA STANDARDS

The standards consist of what are called attribute standards, performance standards, and implementation standards. The attribute standards address the characteristics of organizations and parties performing internal audit activities. The performance standards describe the nature of internal audit activities and provide quality criteria against which the performance of these services can be evaluated. While the Attribute and Performance Standards apply to all internal audit services, the Implementation Standards also apply to specific types of engagements and are further divided between standards for assurance and those for consulting activities. This split reflects that internal auditors sometime do strictly audit assurance-type projects, such as reviewing internal control effectiveness in some area, and sometimes do internal audit consulting-related work.

The attribute standards are numbered in sections as part of the number 1000 series of standards, while performance standards are classified in the 2000 series. Implementation standards, further designated as (A) for assurance or (C) for consulting are organized under each of these Attribute and Performance Standards. The sections that follow describe the Attribute and Performance Standards in some detail as well as some of the descriptive Implementation Standards. Recognizing that internal auditors may be asked to just review internal controls or to act more as internal consultants, there may be multiple sets of implementation standards: a set for each of the major types of internal audit activity. Implementation standards established for internal audit assurance activities are coded with an "A" following the *standard* number (e.g., 1130.A1), and those covering internal audit consulting activities are noted by a "C" following the *standard* number (e.g., *nnnn*.C1).

Our objective here is not to just reproduce these IIA published standards but to describe their content. The IIA Web site, theiia.org, is an official source for these IIA internal audit standards, and the reader is advised to consult that source.

(a) Internal Audit Attribute Standards

Attribute standards address the characteristics of organizations and individuals performing internal audit activities. Numbered from paragraph 1000 to 13000, they cover broad areas that define the attributes of today's modern internal auditor. Here, as well as with the performance standards given subsequently, we have listed and described these standards (listed by their standard paragraph numbers):

> **1000—Purpose, Authority, and Responsibility.** The purpose, authority, and responsibility of the internal audit activity should be formally defined in a charter, consistent with the standards, and approved by the board of directors. Separate implementation standards here state that internal auditing assurance and consulting services should be defined in the internal audit charter.

1100—Independence and Objectivity. The internal audit activity should be independent, and internal auditors should be objective in performing their work. Subsections under this discuss the importance of both individual and organizational objectivity as well as the need to disclose any impairment to internal audit independence or objectivity.

1110—Organizational Independence. While the IIA Standards do not specify that internal audit should report to the audit committee, that reporting relationship should be free from any interference in determining the scope of internal auditing, performing work, and communicating results. While we often think of internal audit as a key function in today's SOA corporate world with board audit committees, internal audit can operate in many different international locations or for many different types of organizations. Whether serving a not-for-profit organization in the United States or a governmental enterprise in a developing country, internal audit always must exhibit organizational independence.

1120—Individual Objectivity. This really repeats a basic principle of internal auditing: Internal auditors should have an impartial, unbiased attitude and avoid conflicts of interest.

1130—Impairments to Independence or Objectivity. If internal audit's independence or objectivity is impaired in fact or appearance, the details of the impairment should be disclosed as part of the audit work. This could be a management-imposed impairment or one due to the background or other circumstances surrounding an individual internal auditor. There are several Assurance and Consulting Attribute Standards here, but one summarizes this standard:

1130.A1—Internal auditors should refrain from assessing specific operations for which they were previously responsible. Objectivity is presumed to be impaired if an *internal* auditor provides services (assurance here but consulting a similar paragraph) for an activity for which the *internal* auditor had responsibility within the previous year.

This is an important standard! Because of their specialized knowledge, internal auditors are sometimes asked to go back to the group where they once worked to audit it. No matter how hard they may try to act to the contrary, they will not be viewed as objective by others.

1200—Proficiency and Due Professional Care. Engagements should be performed with proficiency and due professional care. There is an important proposed new implementation standard here:

1210.A1—The CAE should obtain competent advice and assistance if the internal audit staff lacks the knowledge, skills, or other competencies needed to perform all or part of the engagement.

1210.A2—An internal auditor should have sufficient knowledge to identify the indicators of fraud but is not expected to have the expertise of a person whose primary responsibility is detecting and investigating fraud.

As discussed in Chapter 11, "Fraud Detection and Prevention," this guidance is somewhat weak. The AICPA under SAS No. 99 is requiring external auditors to aggressively think about "red flags," indicators that might include the possibility of fraud, as well as to look for potential fraud in the course of their audits. Although this is certainly an IIA professional standards decision, we feel that internal auditors should maintain a greater awareness about the possibility of fraud in the course of their internal audits. Internal auditors are often the best investigators to find these circumstances. For example, an external auditor may have little contact with a remote sales office, but internal audit may visit that same office as part of a regularly scheduled internal audit.

1210.A3—Internal auditors should have general knowledge of key information technology risks and controls available technology-based audit techniques. However, not all internal auditors are expected to have the expertise of an internal auditor whose primary responsibility is information technology.

New with the current standards, we feel this is *a very important* change to internal auditing standards! Recognizing that there is a need for information systems audit specialists, the standard now states that *all* internal auditors *should* have an understanding of information systems risks and controls. In addition, a proposed new substandard here on due professional care specifies that internal auditors should consider the use of ". . . computer-assisted audit tools and techniques." Computer-assisted audit techniques have been part of the "tool kits" of many internal auditors.[2] While a good idea for all of these years, they now have risen to the level of internal audit standard.

1220—Due Professional Care. Internal auditors should apply the care and skill expected of a reasonably prudent and competent internal auditor. Due professional care does not imply infallibility. Another section of these standards goes on to state that in exercising due professional care, an internal audit should consider the:

- o Extent of work needed to achieve the engagement's objectives
- o Relative complexity, materiality, or significance of matters to which assurance procedures are applied
- o Adequacy and effectiveness of risk management, control, and governance processes
- o Probability of significant errors, irregularities, or noncompliance
- o Cost of assurance in relation to potential benefits

This internal audit really says that an internal auditor should be cautious in beginning and performing an internal audit. The first of these bullet points, the extent of work, says that an internal auditor, for example, should perform an adequate level of investigation and testing before just coming to a final audit recommendation. As one of the new standards released in 2004, computer-assisted audit techniques appear once again:

1220.A2—In exercising due professional care the internal auditor should consider the use of computer-assisted audit tools and other data analysis techniques.

1220.A3—The internal auditor should be alert to the significant risks that might affect objectives, operations, or resources. However, assurance procedures alone, even when performed with due professional care, do not guarantee that all significant risks will be identified. As discussed in Chapter 5, "Understanding and Assessing Risks: Enterprise Risk Management," risk assessment is becoming an increasingly important area for internal auditors. This guidance has been part of the IIA standards going back to the early versions and should be part of an internal auditor's procedures.

The standards continue in this section with 1230—Continuing Professional Development—a standard on the need for continuing professional education and development.

1300—Quality Assurance and Improvement Program. The CAE should develop and maintain a quality assurance and improvement program that covers all aspects of internal audit activity and continuously monitors its effectiveness. The program should be designed to help internal audit add value, improve the organization's operations and provide assurance that internal audit activity is in conformity with the IIA *Standards* and *Code of Ethics*. A new change here is the sentence, *"This program includes periodic internal and external quality assessments and ongoing internal monitoring."* This standards change emphasizes the importance of good quality assurance processes within internal audit. Quality assurance as well as quality audits are discussed in Chapter 26, "Internal Audit Quality Assurance and ASQ Quality Audits."

(b) Internal Audit Performance Standards

These standards describe the nature of internal audit activities and provide quality criteria against which the performance of these services can be measured. There are six performance standards, outlined below, along with substandards and implementation standards that apply to compliance audits, fraud investigations, or a control self-assessment projects. While we are summarizing the standard here for the purpose of describing internal audit processes, the interested professional should contact the IIA to obtain the standards in either computer downloaded or printed format.

2000—Managing the Internal Audit Activity. The CAE should effectively manage the internal audit activity to ensure it adds value to the organization. This standard covers six substandards covering Planning, Communication and Approval, Resource Management, Policies and Procedures, Coordination, and Reporting to the Board and Senior Management. These substandards generally describe such good internal audit management practices as 2040 on Policies and Procedures stating that the CAE should establish such guides.

2060 on Reporting to the Board and Senior Management contains guidance applicable to today's SOA rules: "The chief audit executive should report periodically to the board and senior management on the internal audit activity's purpose, authority, responsibility, and performance relative to its plan. Reporting should also include significant risk exposures and control issues, corporate governance issues, and other matters needed or requested by the board and senior management."

2100—Nature of Work. Internal audit activity includes evaluations and contributions to the improvement of risk management, control, and governance systems. One of the changes in wording here adds that these work processes should use "a systematic and disciplined approach." The previous IIA standards did not really address the important area of risk management. Risk management was discussed in Chapter 5 and is outlined in the standards as follows:

2110—Risk Management. Internal audit should assist the organization by identifying and evaluating significant exposures to risk and contributing to the improvement of risk management and control systems.

2110.A1—Internal audit activity should monitor and evaluate the effectiveness of the organization's risk management system.

2110.A2—The internal audit activity should evaluate risk exposures relating to the organization's governance, operations, and information systems regarding the COSO standards of internal control discussed in Chapter 4.

2110.C1—During consulting engagements, internal auditors should address risk consistent with the engagement's objectives and should be alert to the existence of other significant risks.

2110.C2—Internal auditors should incorporate knowledge of risks gained from consulting engagements into the process of identifying and evaluating significant risk exposures of the organization.

The 2120 and 2130 substandards cover control and governance. A standards change on governance is very appropriate and timely given SOA:

2130—Governance. The internal audit activity, consistent with the organization's structure, should contribute to the governance process by proactively assisting management and the board in fulfilling their responsibilities by:

○ Assessing and promoting strong ethics and values within the organization

○ Assessing and improving the process by which accountability is ensured

○ Assessing the adequacy of communications about significant residual risks within the organization

○ Helping to improve the board's interaction with management and the external and internal auditors

○ Serving as an educational resource regarding changes and trends in the business and regulatory environment

As discussed in the next section, IIA standards are very consistent with SOA requirements. Following these proposed new standards, internal audit should be able to very much follow the SOA principles of good corporate governance.

2200—Engagement Planning. Internal auditors should develop and record a plan for each engagement, including the scope, objectives, timing, and resource allocations. An important aspect of all internal audits, planning is discussed in Chapter 14, "Directing and Performing Internal Audits."

2201—Planning Considerations. In planning an audit engagement, internal auditors should consider:

- The objectives of the activity being reviewed and the means by which the activity controls its performance.

- The significant risks to the activity, its objectives, resources, and operations and the means by which the potential impact of risk is kept to an acceptable level.

- The adequacy and effectiveness of the activity's risk management and internal control systems compared to a relevant control framework or model.

- The opportunities for making significant improvements to the activity's risk management and control systems.

2201.A1—When planning an engagement for parties outside the organization, internal auditors should establish a written understanding with them about objectives, scope, respective responsibilities, and other expectations, including restrictions on distribution of the results of the engagement and access to engagement records. This is a revised section in the standards that really describe the engagement letter that should help launch all internal audits, as discussed in Chapter 14.

2201.C1—Internal auditors should establish, and generally document, an understanding with consulting engagement clients about objectives, scope, respective responsibilities, and other client expectations.

2210—Objectives should be established for each engagement.

2210.A1—Internal auditors should conduct a preliminary assessment of the risks relevant to the activity under review, and engagement objectives should reflect the results of this assessment.

2210.A2—The internal auditor should consider the probability of significant errors, irregularities, noncompliance, and other exposures when developing the engagement objectives. This is related to the risk assessment considerations discussed previously.

2210.C1—Consulting engagement objectives should address risks, controls, and governance processes to the extent agreed on with the client.

2220—Engagement Scope. The established scope should be sufficient to satisfy the objectives of the engagement.

2220.A1—The scope of the engagement should include consideration of relevant systems, records, personnel, and physical properties, including those under the control of third parties.

2220.A2—If significant consulting opportunities arise during an assurance engagement, a specific written understanding as to the objectives, scope, respective responsibilities, and other expectations should be reached and the results of the consulting engagement communicated in accordance with these consulting standards. This says that an internal auditor can begin an audit as a strictly assurance level of review, but may expand it to a consulting-level audit if there is a need or management request.

2220.C1—In performing consulting engagements, internal auditors should ensure that the scope of the engagement is sufficient to address the agreed-upon objectives. If internal auditors develop reservations about the scope during the engagement, these reservations should be discussed with the auditee to determine whether to continue with the engagement.

2230—Engagement Resource Allocation. Internal auditors should determine the appropriate resources necessary to achieve the audit engagement objectives. Staffing should be based on an evaluation of the nature and complexity of each engagement, time constraints, and available resources.

2240—Engagement Work Program. Internal auditors should develop and document work programs that achieve the engagement objectives. These work programs should establish procedures for identifying, analyzing, evaluating, and recording information during the engagement. They should be approved prior to their implementation, with any adjustments approved promptly.

2300—Performing the Engagement. Internal auditors should identify, analyze, evaluate, and record sufficient information to achieve an audit engagement's objectives and should base conclusions and engagement results on appropriate analyses and evaluations.

2330—Recording Information. Internal auditors should record relevant information to support the conclusions and engagement results.

2330.A1—The CAE should control access to engagement records, and should obtain the approval of senior management and/or legal counsel prior to releasing such records to external parties, as appropriate.

2330.A2—The CAE should develop retention requirements for engagement records that are consistent with the organization's guidelines and any pertinent regulatory or other requirements.

2330.C1—The CAE should develop policies governing the custody and retention of engagement records, as well as their release to internal and external parties. These policies should be consistent with the organization's guidelines and any pertinent regulatory or other requirements.

2340—Engagement Supervision. Engagements should be properly supervised to ensure that objectives are achieved, quality is assured, and staff is developed.

2400 and 2410—Communicating Results. Internal auditors should communicate their engagement results including the audit's objectives and scope as well as applicable conclusions, recommendations, and action plans, including the internal auditor's overall opinion and or conclusions.

2410.A2—Internal auditors are encouraged to acknowledge satisfactory performance in engagement communications.

2410.A3—When releasing engagement results to parties outside the organization, the communication should include limitations on distribution and use of the results.

2420—Quality of Communications. Communications should be accurate, objective, clear, concise, constructive, complete, and timely.

2421—Errors and Omissions. If a final communication contains a significant error or omission, the CAE should communicate corrected information to all *parties* who received the original communication.

2430—Engagement Disclosure of Noncompliance with IIA Standards. When noncompliance with the *Standards* impacts a specific engagement, communication of the results should disclose the:

- *Standard(s)* with which full compliance was not achieved

- Reason(s) for noncompliance

- Impact of noncompliance on the engagement

2440—Disseminating Results. The CAE is responsible for communicating the final results of audit work to appropriate *parties* who can ensure that the results are given due consideration.

2440.A2—If not otherwise mandated by legal, statutory, or regulatory requirements, prior to releasing results to parties outside the organization, the chief audit executive should:

- Assess the potential risk to the organization.

- Consult with senior management and/or legal counsel as appropriate.

- Control dissemination by restricting the use of the results.

2440.C1 and C2—The CAE is responsible for communicating the final results of consulting engagements to clients. During consulting engagements, risk management, control, and governance issues may be identified. Whenever these issues are significant to the organization, they should be communicated to senior management and the board.

2500—Monitoring Progress. The CAE should establish and maintain a system to monitor the disposition of results communicated to management as well as a follow-up process to monitor and ensure that management actions have been effectively implemented or that senior management has accepted the risk of not taking action.

2600—Resolution of Management's Acceptance of Risks. When the CAE believes that senior management has accepted a level of residual risk that *may be* unacceptable to the organization, the CAE should discuss the matter with senior management. If the decision regarding residual risk is not resolved, the CAE and senior management should report the matter to the audit committee for resolution.

These current IIA standards represent a significant improvement over the older and very lengthy standards that were in place through the 1990s. The standards conclude with a glossary of terms to better define the roles and responsibilities of internal auditors. Various glossary terms are introduced in other subsequent chapters, but one that is important for internal auditors is the definition of "independence." The word frequently appears in internal auditing literature, but the official definition of internal auditor independence is:

> Independence is the freedom from significant conflicts of interest that threaten objectivity. Such threats to objectivity must be managed at the individual auditor level, the engagement level, and the organizational level.

This is an important concept for today. We again emphasize that these past paragraphs are *not the verbatim IIA standards* but an edited and annotated version. Some of the more minor standards statements have been eliminated in this chapter, a few words in some cases have been changed, and descriptive comments have been added. As previously stated, internal auditors should obtain and understand the official version of these standard through the Institute of Internal Auditors at www.theiia.org.

(c) Revisions to the IIA Standards

The IIA from time to time publishes practice advisories (formerly Guidelines) to interpret the *International Standards for the Professional Practice of Internal Auditing* or to apply them to specific internal audit concerns. Although some of these practice advisories are applicable to all internal auditors, while others are designed to meet the needs of a specific industry, audit specialty, or geographic area, including guidance on topics such as environmental issues, information technology, government auditing, and guidance issued by other standard-setting bodies and adopted by appropriate committees of the IIA. Practice advisories address topics that currently require attention. They may have a limited life or may be elevated to standards level based upon importance, usage, and acceptance. In addition to gaining a working knowledge of the standards, internal auditors should be aware of any practice advisories that may impact an internal auditor's work.

12.5 IMPORTANCE AND RELEVANCE OF THE IIA STANDARDS

The IIA *Standards for the Professional Practice of Internal Auditing* provides an important set of guidance materials for any internal auditor. Because of the many different environments where internal auditors will work, the many different types of audits performed, and the varying demands for internal audit services, the typical internal auditor will perform many different day-to-day functions. However, whenever there are questions or uncertainties, an internal auditor should consult these Standards for guidance.

As stated, this chapter has provided a somewhat summarized, edited, and annotated version of the IIA standards. The editing changes are minor and include such things as using CAE for chief audit executive and combining a pair of A and C advisories when they both essentially say about the same thing. These standards are referenced throughout the book—particularly in Chapters 13 through 17 on organizing, directing, and performing internal audits.

ENDNOTES

[1]Standards for the Professional Practice of Internal Auditing, 2004, Institute of Internal Auditors, Altamonte Springs, FL.

[2]See Robert R. Moeller, *Computer Audit, Control, and Security*, John Wiley, New York, 1989. Note: The current edition is out of print, but a new edition is in preparation.

CHAPTER THIRTEEN

Internal Audit Organization and Planning

13.1 ORGANIZING AND PLANNING FOR THE INTERNAL AUDIT FUNCTION

Previous chapters have dealt with the foundations and standards of internal auditing, the nature of controls, and the operational approach of internal auditing. This chapter offers approaches to bring these concepts together for organizing and planning for an effective internal audit function. Many, if not all, organizations today have an internal audit function—the Sarbanes-Oxley Act (SOA) effectively requires internal audit in today's organization. Some smaller private or not-for-profit organizations today still may not have a credible internal audit function but need to organize one. Other corporations may be concerned about improving the effectiveness of their existing internal audit function. This chapter provides some guidance on options for establishing an effective internal audit function to better achieve internal audit's goal of service to management.

An effective plan of organization is a key component of a successful internal audit function. The leader of that group, the chief audit executive (CAE), is responsible for implementing the best solutions for an internal audit function with consideration given to the five components of the management process discussed in Chapter 2, "Management Needs: Internal Audit's Operational Approach": (1) planning, (2) organizing, (3) providing resources, (4) administering, and (5) controlling. This chapter discusses the specific application of this five-component management process for internal audit organizations. A series of high-level activities are discussed that must take place in order to achieve the overall goals and objectives of the internal audit effort.

We also consider approaches for overall internal audit organization planning, including: support for the audit committee, management at all levels of the organization, and the internal audit team. While some internal audit activities will be reactive in a response to a crisis situation, the effective internal function needs a well-organized plan that serves management needs providing service to the organization.

13.2 ORGANIZING THE INTERNAL AUDIT EFFORT

There is no single or optimal way to organize an internal audit function in a modern organization. A senior manager, and soon to be CAE, who has been given the challenge to establish a new internal audit function has a variety of options, depending on the organization's overall business, its geographic and logistical structures, the various control risks it faces, and its overall culture. The attention and interest of the audit committee and senior management can also be major factors. This section will discuss some of the elements required to build and manage an effective internal audit organization.

A key requirement for any effective organization is a strong leader; for internal audit, that leader is a CAE who understands the needs of the overall organization and its potential control risks as well as the contributions that internal audit can make. This person must have the support of both the audit committee and senior management. Most large organizations today have multiple units often spread across the world and with many different business units. Even if geographically positioned in only one location, the larger organization will almost always have multiple specialty functions with control risks potentially requiring separate internal audit emphasis. The effective internal audit department must be organized in a manner that serves senior management and the audit committee by providing the best, most cost-effective audit services to the entire organization. We will consider the benefits and difficulties in having a centralized or a decentralized internal audit organization as well as some alternative internal audit organizational structures.

(a) Centralized versus Decentralized Internal Audit Organizational Structures

Over one hundred years ago, many business organizations were managed and organized in a highly centralized manner. Major decisions often were made by a central authority, and lower levels in the organization did little more than pass materials up through the ranks for central office approvals. Perhaps the best, or most absurd, modern-day example of this form of a highly centralized organization would be the government of the Soviet Union before its collapse in the late 1980s. There, all planning and economic decisions theoretically were made by a limited number of central authorities. A plant wishing to order pencils as part of its needs for office supplies would have to put its requirements for pencils into an annual production plan. Assuming that plan was approved by the central authorities, the plant would then file supply requisitions in order to request its needs for pencils over the course of the planning cycle, often as long as five years. The central planning authority would look at all planned requests for pencils across the country and then decide both how many pencils were to be manufactured in order to supply everyone and even how many trees would need to be cut down to supply raw materials for those pencils.

This type of central planning once sounded very efficient to the student or idealist; however, most societies today know it just does not work! Large economic units find it difficult—if not impossible—to develop appropriate centralized plans to correctly define the requirements or set the rules for everyone. Too many persons spend time processing forms, and the ultimate users of the services do not see much value from the process. This centralized approach creates little more than bureaucracy! We also saw a similar example of the failure of central planning when the U.S. federal government tried to regulate prices and allocate the supply of gasoline in the late 1970s. The result was high prices, long lines due to local shortages, and an army of bureaucrats trying to write and rewrite rules. Prices went down and oil supplies increased only after central controls were abolished in the early 1980s. Today, many once highly centralized organizations have pushed decision-making authority down and have decentralized many of their processes. Many larger organizations today are extremely decentralized, with each operating unit responsible for making most of its business decisions, including securing its own financing.

Whether the internal audit function or the total organization—any organizational unit can be administered on a centralized or decentralized basis—the main question is the extent to which individual decisions should be made and actions taken at lower or local organizational levels, as opposed to those requiring clearance or approval by central organizational levels. For internal audit, the kinds of decisions and actions involved will include the modification of required audit procedures, procedures necessary to report given types of deficiencies, negotiations necessary to take actions on audit findings, the manner of reporting audit findings, and internal auditor's follow-up on the corrective action covering reported deficiencies. The arguments or benefits that support decentralization generally include:

- Freeing up higher-level personnel from minor decisions so that they can deal with other important matters. Senior management does not always need to review or approve all levels of organizational details. It can become mired in these lower-level details and miss making important overall management audit strategy decisions.

- Local unit personnel often have a better understanding of their local problems. Rather than summarizing problem situations and passing them up to higher levels for the decisions, local unit management can often act directly and in a more intelligent manner.

- Delays involved in passing decisions up for approval can be avoided. Local unit personnel are often better motivated to solve problems at their own level of the organization and will often have the opportunity to develop more appropriate decisions.

Local unit internal audit groups who are empowered, through delegations of authority, to make decisions are often viewed with more respect by other local unit personnel.

Despite these comments favoring decentralized organizational structures, there are strong arguments in favor of a centralized or corporate internal audit function where members from a single headquarters staff perform audits throughout the organization. Some of the arguments in favor of a highly centralized rather than a decentralized internal audit organization structure include:

- The COSO internal controls framework and SOA rules (see Chapters 3, "Internal Audit in the Twenty-First Century: Sarbanes-Oxley and Beyond," and 4, "Internal Controls Fundamentals: COSO Framework") very much promote the importance of "tone-at-the-top" messages from senior management at multiple levels. A centralized internal audit organization should be in a strong position to deliver such messages to the field audit organization and the units they are reviewing.

- Local or separate audit groups may not know the full implications of some corporate policies and decisions. This is particularly true where communication links to remote internal audit groups are weak. Decentralized organization field auditors may have problems explaining the rationale behind certain central policy decisions or have trouble adequately communicating those decisions. A centralized audit group may do a better job here.

- A centralized internal audit organization will generally find it easier to maintain uniform, organization-wide standards. This can be established through strong internal audit common policies and procedures and messages communicated via e-mails, conference calls, and other tools.

- A decentralized internal audit function may sometimes forge too strong a level of loyalties with their local reporting unit. The local audit manager could become more loyal to a plant or division manager where audit is located than to the CAE.

While this discussion assumes that an internal audit organization is either highly centralized or decentralized, there are numerous in-between positions possible where some matters are delegated and others not. Many internal audit functions can very successfully keep certain specialized functions at headquarters and reporting to the CAE with other more operational audit units at divisional or unit headquarters. It is not practicable to suggest a single best solution among these alternatives, and the CAE should have the responsibility for organizing internal audit in a manner that best suits the needs of the organization.

Complex organizational structures will often have an influence on the way that internal audit is organized. A special kind of decentralization of authority exists when separate internal audit groups exist as part of the overall organization and are not part of the regular or central internal audit function. These separate internal audit functions, which may be the result of a restructuring or an acquisition, often report directly to the management of individual subsidiaries and divisions. The responsibility of the central internal audit function here is often only to serve in an advisory capacity, and many of the administrative considerations discussed in this chapter are not directly applicable. This kind of situation can occur when an organization A owns perhaps 55% of organization B, with the other 45% held by other parties. Organization B will probably have its own audit committee and CAE. However, A's 55% ownership of B means that A's CAE has some responsibility for the audit function at B.

The CAE for the parent organization (A in the above example) should have a special professional concern as to the effectiveness of the semiautonomous internal audit groups that goes beyond the normal interest in the effectiveness of all organization operations. The special relationship to any semiautonomous internal audit groups will normally be indicated on a complete internal audit organization chart that shows these other groups as reporting to the central CAE on a dotted line basis. In these situations, the existence of the semiautonomous internal audit group's responsibility to local management does not preclude the regular or corporate internal audit department from making supplementary reviews of these subsidiaries and divisions, as deemed necessary.

The central internal audit organization cannot be responsible for organization-wide internal audit results unless it has both access and line control over all supplementary internal audit work. The central CAE has a responsibility to make any dotted line reporting relationships to other internal audit groups sufficiently strong or as weak as necessary given overall organizational considerations.

(b) Alternative Internal Audit Organization Structures

An internal audit function in a small organization presents a smaller number of organizational challenges. One person, the CAE, will be given responsibility for internal audit, and depending on the size of the staff needed, a group of managers or supervisors responsible for the staff internal auditors may report to that director. In a very small organization, all of the staff may report directly to that executive. While many of the internal audit planning and administration topics covered throughout this book still apply to the very small internal audit organization, the CAE of a very small audit organization does not need to give much consideration to internal audit organizational variations. All of internal audit will be reporting to that one director with not enough staff to provide many organizational variations.

Most organizations will have an internal audit function large enough to require the CAE to consider the best way to organize internal audit given a variety of factors affecting the overall organization. Although there may be many minor variations, internal audit functions are commonly organized following one of four overall approaches: the types of audits performed, internal audit conformance to the general structure of the organization, organization by geographical area, and combinations of the aforementioned approaches with a headquarters staff.

(i) Organization by Type of Audit. Internal audit functions are frequently organized by the types of audits to be performed. An audit department might be divided into three groups of specialists: information systems auditors, financial audit specialists, and purely operational auditors. This approach rests on the logic that individual internal auditors may be most effective if given responsibility for an area in which they have expertise and experience, recognizing that efficiency is often achieved through specialization. The problems and control risks pertaining to a particular audit area can often be best handled through the assignment of internal auditors who have the necessary special expertise. For example, an organization may have a great number of district and regional sales offices with the same kind of operations. That internal audit function may want to develop a special internal auditing group that does nothing but audit these sales offices. The practical benefits here can be substantial.

At the same time, internal audit management should recognize that there are disadvantages to this type-of-audit approach. Where several types of audits exist at a given field location, it may be necessary for each specialist internal auditor to travel to that location. This extra cost in time and money should be clearly offset by the added efficiency gained from the several specialist internal auditors. Exhibit 13.1 is an organization chart from this type of internal audit organization. It shows that specialized groups have been established for information systems, financial auditing, risk assessment, and several operational areas. A risk with this approach is that specialist internal auditors may spend too much time on their own specialty areas and miss the big picture in the process. This has been particularly true with technical, computer audit areas, which may spend too much time on technical control issues and miss significant control-concern risks in the process. It is often very difficult for the CAE to create a team of integrated auditors with this type of approach.

Although tight, specific definition of audit tasks can promote efficiency and allow for more effective, specialized audits, a variety of assignments keeps an internal auditor from getting in a rut and performing audit reviews in too mechanical a fashion. Here, the audit staff is alert and well motivated and can bring a fresh approach to old problems—something that frequently pays good

EXHIBIT 13.1

Specialty-Based Internal Audit Organization

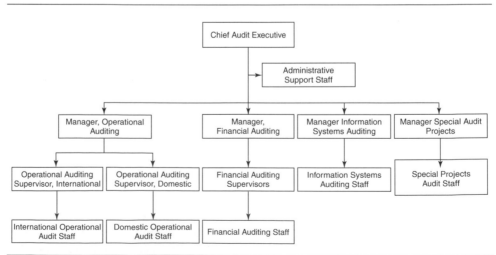

dividends. Mixed assignments for individual internal auditors lend themselves best to growth and professional development. They help to create *the integrated auditor.* This integrated audit approach promotes adequate education and training opportunities to all members of the audit staff.

On the balance, any gains through audit specialization may be more than offset by the factors just discussed. Internal audit management faces the danger that these gains will appear to be more substantial than they actually are. The specialist approach should be used cautiously and only when the organization has strong needs for auditors with unique abilities. In many instances, using the type-of-audit approach for an internal audit organizational structure is at odds with the objectives of achieving maximum quality of the audit effort, especially as the concern of internal audit moves further away from reviewing lower-level procedures and toward broader managerial issues.

(ii) Internal Audit Parallel to Overall Organizational Structure. In a large organization, a practical alternative is to align audit responsibilities along the same lines as the organizational structure. Individual internal audit groups can be assigned to specific organizational components such as operating divisions or affiliated subsidiaries. When these operating units are in specialized lines of business or geographical areas, internal audit may benefit from the previously discussed advantage of an understanding of audit and control issues for the particular types of operational activities and the related development of greater internal audit expertise. An example might be a large manufacturing organization that has a separate subsidiary responsible for financing equipment leases. Because of significant differences in control issues between manufacturing operations and those of the finance operations, internal audit management might find it effective to have two separate audit groups, one to cover manufacturing operations and the other for the financial subsidiary.

An advantage in this internal audit organizational approach is that management in charge of the various operations, and other operating personnel as well, can develop more effective working relationships with the responsible internal audit personnel. The separate internal audit groups should come to speak the language of the particular operation and can become more useful to the individual management groups. Internal audit can also develop more effective working relationships with responsible managers at all levels. There are often certain disadvantages to this separate form of internal audit organization structure, similar to those of the type-of-audit approach just discussed. Just as separate information systems and manufacturing auditors might travel to and perform audits of the same general area, here a manufacturing division and a finance division auditor might each be asked to review the same general area if multiple operating divisions are located there. Although organizational operating units are often separate and autonomous, this approach can result in duplication of field travel, diminished internal audit staff motivation, and reduced opportunities for management development. A given operating division can be considered to be less important to the overall organization, and members of the internal audit team assigned there may feel that their career opportunities are hampered. Another potential danger with this approach is that the separate internal audit groups can develop too close of an alliance with the particular divisional or staff personnel they audit, which can sometimes undermine the independence and objectivity of the individual internal auditors.

The effectiveness of this internal audit organizational structure approach is more controversial than it first appears and perhaps should be used cautiously. Even a very large organization, with many different operating units, may find it more effective to have a central group of *corporate auditors* who perform their reviews at all units, by line of business. The organization with multiple internal audit groups, each serving separate lines of business, may find it difficult to conduct audits throughout the organization that speak in the same voice, no matter how strong the central internal audit policies and procedures.

(iii) Geographical Approaches to the Internal Audit Organization. Under this approach, all organizational operations in a given geographical area are assigned to a designated group of internal auditors. In some cases, this geographical approach can automatically, to some extent, become a type-of-audit or organization-structure approach when particular types of operations are concentrated in separate geographic areas, but usually there will be some diversity of audit assignments in the individual areas. Exhibit 13.2 shows an internal audit function organized by geographical area.

The advantages and disadvantages of an area approach to an internal audit organization are reasonably well indicated by the evaluation of the first two organizational structures discussed. On balance, a geographic approach often seems to be best and is commonly used in practice. The number of separate audit offices to be established will depend on the scope of the organization's operations. In some organizations, there may be a number of separate audit offices within the United States, with international operations located in one separate office, often at a prominent offshore location. Organizations with a large, diverse number of international operations may have multiple international internal audit offices.

EXHIBIT 13.2

Geography-Based Internal Audit Organization

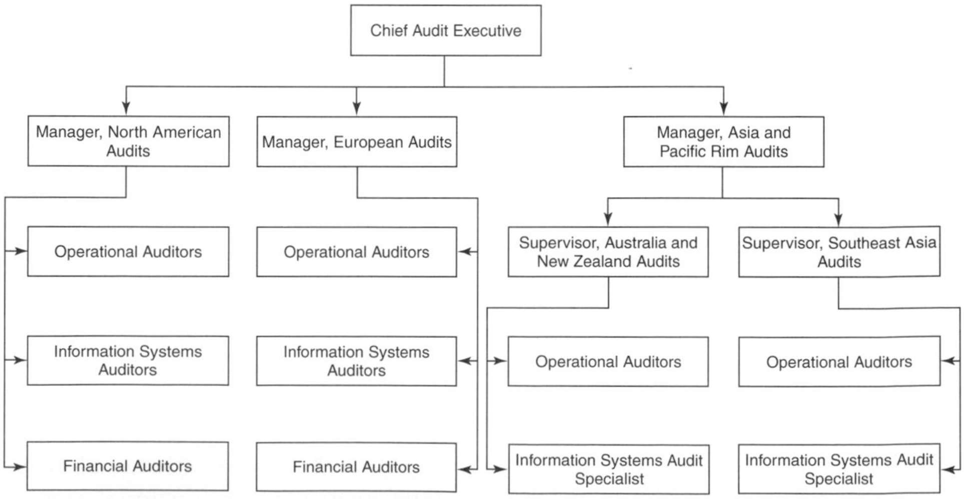

(iv)   Use of a Headquarters Internal Audit Staff.   The three approaches to the organization of internal audit field activities just discussed should always be supplemented by some kind of headquarters organization. Each of the organization charts shown in Exhibits 13.1 and 13.2 show some type of central internal audit staff support function. At its minimum, this headquarters will consist of the CAE and a very limited administrative support staff. Any expansion of the central internal audit organization above this minimum depends on what work is delegated to the line components and the types of internal audit services provided by the central unit. In a typical situation, all or almost all audit reports may be reviewed and approved at the central headquarters. Other matters requiring centralized attention, such as common internal audit policies and procedures, may be developed, or at least finalized and distributed, by the headquarters internal audit function. There may also be some planning and administrative work that either must be done, or is preferably done, at the organization's headquarters. Most of these activities will require some administrative support. Other activities may be performed in part by the CAE, but will usually require additional professional internal audit assistance, which might be provided by one or more headquarters internal audit managers or other planning and administrative personnel. Normally, the CAE will want one individual to have the authority to act in the audit executive's absence, thus ensuring a needed continuity of operations.

With a highly decentralized organization where most of the internal audit activity takes place by division, by type of audit, or by geographic area, this central internal audit function may be viewed as little more than a central "corporate overhead" type of function that contributes to expenses of the operating unit but provides little value. Although the CAE reports to the audit committee and speaks to senior management, both may question how familiar that audit executive is with field or operating-unit audit activities. A centralized internal audit function may not be particularly effective if the headquarters function does not add value to total internal audit efforts.

(v) Nonaudit and Informal Staff Assignments.   Internal auditors are frequently asked to carry out special financial or operational activities at the request of senior management, even though those activities are so much a part of the regular day-to-day organization activities that they do not satisfactorily meet the test of true internal auditing. These are often task force projects of limited duration, such as solving an overall inventory control problem. The internal auditors assigned may be pulled from their regular audit assignments to participate on the project and then return to internal audit when it is complete.

Although such activities may delay completion of the audit plan and because of various organizational control problems, these short-term special projects are generally good for internal audit as a whole and for the individual auditors assigned. Senior management's desire to have internal audit participate on a special project represents an endorsement of the professionalism of all members of the internal audit organization. The CAE should actively encourage these types of projects from time to time to give members of the staff additional experiences and potentially to groom them for other positions within the organization.

A different problem arises when management asks internal audit to assume some nonaudit function on a regular basis. Illustrative would be the responsibility for reviewing and approving current cash disbursements before those disbursements are actually made. Management may assume that because internal audit has certain special control skills, it is best suited to the organization to perform these special tasks. These types of ongoing special projects generally take resources away from regular internal audit activities and may even place internal audit in a position where its independence could be compromised. The CAE should strenuously object to such ongoing assignments. Assuming that internal audit has no alternative other than to accept such an assignment, the recommended organizational approach should be to segregate these additional activities from the normal internal audit activities, and to subject them to periodic reviews by the regular internal audit group. Wherever possible, this kind of a situation should be avoided. The dual responsibilities tend to infringe on the time for internal audit management activities. In addition, there is the very real danger that the dual responsibilities will weaken the image of the CAE to others in the organization.

The discussion of organizational arrangements in this chapter has dealt chiefly with formal types of structures and the essential guidelines for efficient operations. For many organizations, there may also be various kinds of interrelationships in the internal audit department that cut across the established organizational lines. Such interrelationships are informal and take place as necessary to meet current operational needs. They will exist under all types of formal arrangements. Within reasonable limits, these informal organizational arrangements serve a useful operational purpose and often point the way to needed formal organization modifications. If carried too far, however, they can undermine the effectiveness of internal audit's basic mission. The important thing, therefore, is to recognize their necessity but to keep them within sensible bounds.

It is always important to emphasize the changing nature of internal audit organizational needs along with the changing structure of the entire organization. As organization operations change, both in terms of size and function, the approach followed by internal audit also needs to be reappraised. Organizational arrangements in the last analysis are a means to an end, never an end themselves. Although this reappraisal can and should be made on a rather continuous basis, the preparation of the annual internal audit budget provides an especially good opportunity to carry out a more complete organization reevaluation. At this same time, consideration can be given to the matters of staff administration and control, which are discussed in Chapter 14, "Directing and Performing Internal Audits."

13.3 INTERNAL AUDIT ORGANIZATION PLANNING

Organizational planning is the process of organizing and matching goals and objectives with available resources to achieve the most effective utilization of those resources. For internal audit, these resources include the staff, budget, internal audit tools, and the softer concept of the reputation internal audit has earned among other organization personnel. These resources include both what internal audit actually has in hand and what it can reasonably expect to get as a result of additional management support. The CAE should always consider the environment in which the internal audit function operates, including the overall organization and the world of which the organization is a part. Within the organization, this environment includes management and other personnel at all levels, including executives responsible for the various operational components audited, intermediate managers, and all other personnel. A portion of these individuals will be supportive, some hostile, and many relatively indifferent. Some people will be in positions where these attitudes are very important, while in other cases, the relationship is more detached. As part of the planning process, internal audit must attempt to appraise this environment as it currently exists and as it might change over time. Through the study and evaluation of internal audit resources and of the environment, internal audit goals and objectives can be planned and formulated in an intelligent and effective manner.

Internal audit planning is vitally concerned with this process of formulating objectives, but it goes still further. Planning has to do with developing the supporting strategies, policies, procedures, and programs that will best assure that actions carried out currently will move the internal audit department toward the achievement of its future objectives. For internal audit, planning means projecting where to go in the future and devising the means that will help to best get there. Like every other functional manager, the CAE must be concerned about the present and future role of the internal audit function.

(a) Establishing Internal Audit Plan Goals and Objectives

Internal audit's role should be a dynamic one, continually changing to meet the needs of the organization as circumstances warrant. These changes may include the coverage of new areas, assistance to management in solving problems, and the development of new internal audit techniques. Planning is especially important in the face of uncertainty. While formal plans should be developed over extended time periods, the organization demands often make it important that internal audit must change plans as the needs arise. When management needs change, such as the requirements caused by an acquisition, internal audit must analyze these trends and have the flexibility to adjust to the new conditions.

An internal audit function must have a clear understanding of its objectives as a first step to formalizing its plans. What does management expect of internal audit? What types of coverage and findings are desired? The preceding chapters have considered the role that internal auditors could and should play in their organizations. These concepts should be defined in specific terms by the CAE as well as other individuals responsible for internal audit activities.

This high-level or conceptual planning of internal audit activities is not an easy task and hence is frequently not done adequately. However, the more carefully and sharply this planning is done, the more likely that planning for these activities will be carried out effectively. Additionally, the goals and objectives established through a planning process are not constant for all time. As conditions change, they should be reappraised and modified as is appropriate. The following internal audit-related planning issues should be considered:

- *Type of Managerial Assistance.* Will planned internal audit activities be limited to ascertaining compliance, and to what extent should efforts be made to search out and report possibilities for improvements? In the latter case, does improvement mean the operational efficiency of existing policies and procedures and/or the reappraisal of these underlying policies and decisions?

- *Level of Managerial Assistance.* What is the scope or the extent to which internal audit's reappraisal role will involve specific organizational levels? How far up in the organization should internal audit go in carrying out this review role? Internal audit may review controls at a field location level that may point to potential control problems within a more senior management group. Internal audit may have to seek support and assistance from various levels of management to follow up on this type of control problem. Senior officers often appreciate internal audit reviews of their organizations several levels down, but resent reviews that are too close to home.

- *Degree of Independence.* To what extent, both in terms of access to various parts of the organization's operations and in its authority to report on all matters pertaining to the organization's welfare, should internal audit seek independence? Internal audit usually does not want to be viewed quite like the external auditors, but has a unique reporting relationship with its direct lines to the audit committee.

- *Resources to Be Provided.* Goals and objectives should also include an identification of the kind of internal audit efforts necessary, its organizational structure, the size of the department, its composition in terms of people and their qualifications, and the level of budgetary support. These determinations will necessarily be linked to projections of the growth and profitability of the overall organization.

- *Quality of Service.* Internal audit should strive to improve the value of its audits in terms of such factors as the depth of coverage or quality of audit analysis. Compliance with the Institute of Internal Auditor's (IIA) professional standards, discussed in Chapter 12, "Internal Audit Professional Standards," will help to achieve this coverage. In addition, internal audit should experiment with new techniques and reexamine how best to satisfy management expectations.

- *Quality of Internal Audit Staff.* The selection and training of staff are crucial for productive and high-quality audit results. Internal audit goals and objectives must properly consider an appropriate level of staff development and training.

Internal audit should review the above considerations before it embarks on any level of organization-level planning. Of course, any internal audit plan must reflect the potential risks that internal audit will face. Risk analysis, which is an essential element in the internal audit planning process, was discussed in Chapter 5, "Understanding and Assessing Risks: Enterprise Risk Management."

(i) Developing a Planning Strategy. A managerial strategy is necessary to define the major operational approaches by which an organization's goals and objectives are achieved over time. Goals and objectives describe where one wants to go and are concerned with what is to be achieved, whereas strategies outline a means of accomplishing desired results. Strategies are sometimes also called *major policies*, the term *major* distinguishing these higher-level determinations from the more routine supporting policies pertaining to the implementation actions. Internal audit should consider the following strategies:

- *Manner of Organizing the Internal Audit Staff.* For many organizations, this is a question of the desired level of internal audit staff centralization or decentralization and physical dispersion discussed previously.

- *Staffing Policies.* At the highest level, staffing has to do with the qualification requirements as well as the required numbers of personnel. These considerations are discussed in more detail in Chapter 14.

- *Manner of Administering the Internal Audit Function.* Administration is a combination of issuing instructions, coordinating the efforts of individual persons, and providing effective leadership. The major strategy or policy issue here is the manner in which responsibilities are delegated within the organization. Today the trend is toward greater delegation and a more participative, democratic approach.

- *Extent of Formal Auditing Procedures.* Internal audit procedures should be formally documented whenever possible. Nevertheless, the nature of many internal audit activities is such that internal audit management must weigh the costs of developing formal documented procedures in a new area against management pressures to complete the task using just basic workpaper documentation.

- *Flexible Audit Project Planning and Programming.* Unforeseen audit requirements and management requests can create the need for changes in both audit programs and overall plans. Although these cannot be predicted with any accuracy, a flexible approach ensures maximum service with existing resources. Nevertheless, the CAE should not develop a plan and then abandon it shortly thereafter due to "other requests." The difficult decision is to decide what is necessary but to accomplish planning objectives.

- *Level of Aggressiveness.* The flexibility to be imaginative and innovative in audit reviews, and to press strongly for new and higher levels of management service, enables internal audit to maintain the highest standards. Even though certain levels of management may not request a review in a given area, internal audit may see a potential internal control problem and schedule a review. Such an aggressive review approach may face criticism on various levels.

- *Action on Recommendations.* Internal audit should be interested in the actions taken as a result of internal audit recommendations, beyond reporting the conditions leading to audit report recommendations. All too often, managers may thank internal auditors for their findings and recommendations but then take no positive actions to correct the problems and implement internal audit's recommendations. A well-written audit report serves no useful purpose unless it is used as a guide for appropriate action. Internal audit needs a strategy to ensure that actions are taken on reported audit findings and recommendations.

- *Identification of Time Periods.* All of the previously discussed aspects of internal audit goals and objectives need to be related to specific time periods, normally in months or years. In certain cases, the accomplishment of the individual goals and objectives should be sought in specific phases, a portion in six months, a second phase in two years, and the like.

Internal audit plans must be consistent with the goals and objectives of the audit committee and senior management. Agreement between management and internal audit is more likely to be achieved if internal audit first thinks through the issues carefully, considers the risks, and develops an organization-level audit plan. To the extent that management will not accept internal audit's views, two sets of goals and objectives then emerge: those accepted by management—which then become part of internal audit's published plan—and those temporarily held in abeyance by internal audit. The latter serve as a useful base point for subsequent negotiation with management as conditions change.

In some instances, the CAE may feel very strongly about an audit strategy that senior management or even the audit committee initially rejects. For example, the CAE may have some information indicating that certain officers of the organization are improperly accounting for personal and lavish travel expenses. The CAE may propose such an audit to a senior officer and be discouraged from initiating the review. Depending on the potential seriousness of these concerns and the nature of the management rejection, the CAE should next take the matter to the audit committee. As discussed in Chapter 8, "Internal Audit and the Board Audit Committee," the CAE has an SOA obligation to bring an issue to that level.

Objective measurements should be developed to report the progress of internal audit goals and accomplishments in reported periods. This type of reporting will enable internal audit to measure performance and evaluate progress to date. Specific projects should be developed, where feasible, to accomplish each of the internal audit objectives. Exhibit 13.3 is an example of a special report on the status of projects initiated as one internal audit objective.

(ii) Short- and Long-Range Internal Audit Planning. An internal audit plan cannot be developed solely on just such factors as last year's plan and current available resources, proceeding as if nothing has changed beyond the calendar. Many factors have an impact on the type of audit activities that should be planned, and various functions and individuals within the organization will have some input into that planning process. Some of the groups who will play an important influence on the development of the audit plan include:

- *Management Requests.* Organizational management at all levels can and should request internal audit assistance in various internal control-related areas. This request process was discussed in Chapter 2, on understanding management needs.

- *Board of Directors–Initiated Requests.* Even though internal audit will have a close relationship with senior management, SOA rules state that internal audit reports to the audit committee of the board of directors. That group may initiate high-level requests for internal audit services outside of normal management channels.

EXHIBIT 13.3

Progress Against Audit Objectives Special Report

MAXXAM CORP. INTERNAL AUDIT
SPECIAL TRAVEL ACCOUNTING AUDIT STATUS REPORT
March XX, XXXX
PERFORMANCE AGAINST AUDIT BUDGET

	PLANNED	ACTUAL
Operational Audit Hours	360	432
Information Systems Audit Hours	120	146
Financial Audit Hours	4	12
Total Hours	484	590

START AND COMPLETION DATES

Planned	Oct XX, XXXX	. to	Nov XX, XXXX
Actual	Nov XX, XXXX	to	Jan XX, XXXX

BUSINESS UNITS AND TRAVEL VOUCHERS REVIEWED

Planned	XXX	XXXX
Actual	XXX	XXXX

AUDIT OBJECTIVES ACHIEVED: XXXX

INTERNAL CONTROL ASSESSMENT: Adequate

COMMENTS:

- *External Auditor–Initiated Requests.* Internal audit should work closely with the organization's external auditors. In order to realize economies or to take advantage of internal audit's particular skills in performing operational reviews of key controls, the external auditors may often request internal audit assistance. SOA has caused many changes here, and this relationship is discussed in Chapter 10, "Working with External Auditors," as well as Chapter 6, "Evaluating Internal Controls: Section 404 Assessments," on SOA Section 404 rules.

In order to develop short- and long-range audit plans, internal audit needs to take into account these outside requests for internal audit services, along with information regarding audit needs based on the results of other audits, internal audit control assessments, and other inputs. A key factor in developing these organization-level plans is audit's assessments of control risk, discussed in Chapter 5. As noted, risk assessment allows internal audit to review various potential audit candidates throughout the organization and to allocate always limited audit resources to higher-risk areas.

(A) LONG-RANGE PLANNING

It is a normal practice in any well-run internal audit organization to develop a long-range audit plan. In its final form, this long-term audit plan represents the agreement among internal audit, the audit committee, and senior management as to the planned activities for each component of the internal audit organization, subject later to any changes in accordance with specified procedures. An internal audit long-range plan is an important tool to manage the internal audit function, to communicate planned internal audit activities to other interested parties, and to measure the performance of internal audit on a periodic basis. These plans are often prepared on two levels:

1. **Annual Internal Audit Plan.** A detailed plan should generally be prepared on a one-year basis to outline the planned audit activities for the upcoming year. The plan is limited by the current audit department budget and planned resource levels. Exhibit 13.4 is an example of an annual audit plan.

2. **Multiyear Future Periods Audit Plan.** Internal audit typically does not have the resources to complete audits for all higher-risk audits in a given year. In addition, they may perform a review in a given area with objectives to revisit that same area at some future period. A multiyear (usually five-year) audit plan outlines those future planned internal audit activities. Just as an annual plan is created at least once per year, the five-year plan is updated or rolled forward annually. Exhibit 13.4 shows a five-year plan. While there is no one correct format for an annual audit plan, it should be organized to show the audit committee and organization management the areas where internal audit plans to concentrate its efforts over an upcoming period. The plan should show the area to be reviewed for each planned audit, the relative risk assessed for the audit, the type of audit, its location, the planned hours, and any other planned costs. Depending on the size and complexity of the overall organization, the plan as shown can be summarized and broken into a variety of different sequences. This will allow various levels of management to understand the breadth and scope of audit coverage in their areas.

Prior to developing its annual plan, internal audit should request suggestions from both the audit committee and management for areas of audit emphasis. This request also should be directed to selected unit managers because of their familiarity with operations. Audit managers who have the responsibility for individual operational areas should also be requested to submit their proposals for audit coverage. In addition, other key members of the audit staff should also be contacted to obtain suggestions for audits based on their fieldwork observations. The preparation of the annual plan thus stimulates the staff to reexamine objectives and select those audits of most importance. Of course, scheduling a future internal audit should not be based just on some input suggesting it would be a good idea but should include some investigation and risk assessment of the area.

EXHIBIT 13.4

Internal Audit Annual Plan Example

EXAMPLECO CORPORATION 20X1 INTERNAL AUDIT PLAN

MAXXAM CORP 20XX INTERNAL AUDIT FIVE YEAR PLAN

Division	Audit	Risk Rank	Est. Start	Planned Finish	Est. Hours Oper.	Est. Hours I/S	Est. Hours Finan.	Total Hours	Travel Costs	Other Costs	Comments
ELECTRO	INV. PLANNING CNTRLS.	8.4	11/10/X1	03/05/X1	420	80		500	$1,200		CARRYOVER XX
ELECTRO	PHYS. INV. OBSERVATION	9.5	01/20/X1	02/15/X1	60		30	90	$2,200	$400	
ELECTRO	B-PLANT SECURITY	7.4	02/15/X1	03/31/X1	170	50		220	$900		
ELECTRO	MATERIALS RECEIVING	6.2	04/22/X1	05/25/X1	340	80	100	520	$1,200		
ELECTRO	PROCUREMENT CONTROLS	6.8	07/25/X1	10/05/X1	240	100		340	$200		
ELECTRO	NEW MARKETING SYSTEM	7.8	09/20/X1	01/15/X2	100	340		440			20X1 HOURS ONL'
ELECTRO	Q/A LAB. CONTROLS	5.9	04/15/X1	06/01/X1	210		80	290	$1,200		
DISTRIBUTION	EDI ORDER CONTROLS	9.1	03/25/X1	05/20/X1	240	180		420		$250	
DISTRIBUTION	WHSE. PHYSICAL SECURITY	7.9	08/10/X1	09/25/X1	90			90	$120		
DISTRIBUTION	FACTORY LABOR REPORTING	8.2	10/20/X1	11/15/X1	280	80	110	470	$50	$240	
DISTRIBUTION	PRODUCT INCENTIVE SYSTEM	5.8	04/25/X1	06/15/X1	80		120	200			
DISTRIBUTION	PROD. WARRANTY RETURNS	6.7	08/10/X1	10/15/X1	270		40	310			
DISTRIBUTION	LAN CONTINGENCY PLANNING	7.9	11/10/X1	12/15/X1	40	150		190			
DISTRIBUTION	A/R CONTROL PROCEDURE	9.2	11/05/X1	02/20/X1		120	320	440		$80	20X1 HOURS ONL'
ASIA PACIFIC	G/L SYSTEM INTEGRITY		05/20/X1	06/30/X1		180	180	360	$3,600		
ASIA PACIFIC	LABOR RELATIONS STDS.		06/10/X1	06/30/X1	180			180	$3,600		
ASIA PACIFIC	MFG. CONTROL SYSTEM		05/05/X1	06/30/X1	100	100	100	300	$3,600		
CORPORATE	GOVERNMENT RELATIONS DEPT.		10/15/X1	11/20/X1	150		100	250			
CORPORATE	EXT. AUDIT YR.-END SUPPORT		01/20/X1	04/12/X2		160	280	440		$400	20X1 HOURS ONL'
CORPORATE	CONSTRUCTION CONTRACTS		05/15/X1	07/25/X1	340	150	90	580			
TOTAL DIRECT INTERNAL AUDIT					3310	1770	1550	6630	$17,870	$1,370	
NON-AUDIT	HOLIDAYS AND VACATION							880			
NON-AUDIT	COMPANY AND STAFF MEETINGS							210		$500	
NON-AUDIT	TRAINING							160	$4,800	$3,400	
NON-AUDIT	AUDIT ADMINISTRATION							440		$1,500	
TOTAL PLANNED 20X1 INTERNAL AUDIT HOURS								8320			

EXHIBIT 13.5

Five-Year Audit Plan Example

MAXXAM CORP 20XX INTERNAL AUDIT FIVE YEAR PLAN

DIVISION	AUDIT	RISK RANK	20XX HOURS	20X1 HOURS	20X2 HOURS	20X3 HOURS	20X4 HOURS
ELECTRO	SYSTEM DEVELOPMENT CNTR.	9.7			250		250
ELECTRO	NEW SYSTEMS UNDER DEV.	9.5		500	500	500	500
ELECTRO	PHYS. INV. OBSERVATION	9.5	90	90	90	100	100
ELECTRO	ACCOUNTS PAYABLE SYSTEM	9.1			350		
ELECTRO	UNSCHEDULED OPERATIONAL	8.9		1200	1200	1500	1500
ELECTRO	UNSCHEDULED SYSTEM AUDIT	8.9		750	1000	1000	1000
ELECTRO	INV. PLANNING CONTROLS	8.4	500	80			200
ELECTRO	RAW MATERIALS SCHEDULING	8.3			200	80	
ELECTRO	EQUIPMENT FIXED ASSETS	8.2		250		250	
ELECTRO	NEW MARKETING SYSTEM	7.8	440				
ELECTRO	A-PLANT SECURITY	7.4		220			200
ELECTRO	B-PLANT SECURITY	7.4	220			200	
ELECTRO	PROCUREMENT CONTROLS	6.8	340				
ELECTRO	MATERIALS RECEIVING	6.2	520				500
ELECTRO	PLANT LABOR REPORTING	6.2		400	100		300
ELECTRO	R-PLANT SECURITY	6.2			150		
ELECTRO	Q/A LAB. CONTROLS	5.9	290		150		150
ELECTRO	PRODUCT SHIPPING	5.7		220			220
ELECTRO	PAYROLL AND PERSONNEL REVIEW	5.2		360			360
	TOTAL ELECTRO ANNUAL AUDIT COVERAGE		2400	4070	3990	3630	5280
DISTRIBUTION	INV. CONTROLS	9.3			300	100	
DISTRIBUTION	A/R CONTROL PROCED.	9.2	440	40			400
DISTRIBUTION	EDI ORDER CONTROLS	9.1	420		120		400
DISTRIBUTION	UNSCHEDULED OPERATIONAL	8.9		1200	1200	1500	1500
DISTRIBUTION	UNSCHEDULED SYSTEM AUDIT	8.9		800	800	1000	1000
DISTRIBUTION	DELIVERY SCHEDULING	8.2		450	100		450
DISTRIBUTION	FACTORY LABOR REPORTING	8.2	470		150		500
DISTRIBUTION	PHYSICAL INVENTORY OBSER.	8.1		90		90	
DISTRIBUTION	LAN CONTINGENCY PLANNING	7.9	190	40	40	40	40
DISTRIBUTION	WHSE. PHYSICAL SECURITY	7.9	90			100	
DISTRIBUTION	PRODUCT TESTING	7.5		240			200
DISTRIBUTION	PROD. WARRANTY RETURNS	6.7	310		300		200
DISTRIBUTION	PRODUCT INCENTIVE SYSTEM	5.8	200				

Benefits are also derived from coordinating with other audit groups. In addition to the external auditors, various government auditors may perform reviews of certain operational and financial matters. Information should be obtained, when possible, as to their reported areas of concern and planned future audits. The annual plan should be distributed to various management and audit groups. In selecting audits for the annual work program, the audit risk analysis should also be considered. Some criteria to be applied in reviewing potential audit areas include:

- *Prior Findings.* Deficiencies may have been reported in a prior audit, indicating the need for follow-up review. This is especially important where significant findings were reported in more than one prior audit.

- *Management Requests.* The chief executive officer or other senior officials may request specific audits. In addition, the audit committee may ask for coverage of various areas. These requests must, of course, be given priority. Also, various levels of management—such as department heads or branch managers—may ask for internal audit reviews.

- *Prior Audit Coverage.* Significant delays may have occurred in returning to an audit area because of higher priorities. As the time between audits increases, additional weight has to be assigned in these areas for future audit coverage, particularly if the prior reviews indicated internal control weaknesses.

- *Required Internal Audits.* Compliance with certain legislative or other governmental requirements may have been assigned to the internal audit department. Also, internal audit will often have a role in either performing the Section 404 work independently or providing assistance to the external auditors in its SOA Section 404 internal control assessment, as discussed in Chapter 6.

- *Sensitive Areas.* Sensitive areas may change in view of revised conditions, or may be inherent in the nature of the organization's operation. An example might be the review of conflicts of interest in the aftermath of some unfavorable publicity.

Internal audit should prepare a formal analysis as part of its annual planning process, showing accomplishments against the past one- and five-year plans. This document will allow internal audit to explain why a given audit project may have run over schedule due to expanded audit scope requirements and why others may have been dropped. While these matters are reported on a month-by-month basis, an annual report shows performance for the period and provides some support for the new multiyear audit plan. Exhibit 13.6 is an example of an annual plan performance report.

The audit plan examples described in Exhibits 13.4, 13.5, and 13.6 show audit projects along with their estimated time and expense requirements. A financial budget to support these plans may be of even greater significance. In order to support budget requirements, internal audit must estimate the costs involved with the total auditing program to be carried out over the year ahead. This will include how internal audit plans to implement its annual plan in terms of the number of personnel, travel, and supporting services required to perform the planned audits and to support other internal audit activities, such as staff training. Internal audit must justify both the overall validity of the proposed audit plan and the efficiency with which internal audit plans to carry out the program. Other questions necessary to build the budget include: What locations are to be covered? What kind of audit work is to be done? How long will it take to do the job? What staff will be required? What will be the travel costs? and, What supporting services need to be provided? The answers to these questions may require an in-depth analysis of the major factors pertaining to the operations of the internal audit department.

Internal audit plans, as finally approved and supported by financial budgets, provide a major basis for administering and controlling the day-to-day

EXHIBIT 13.6

Annual-Plan Performance Report

MAXXAM CORP 20XX INTERNAL AUDIT PERFORMANCE

DIVISION	AUDIT PROJECT	PLANNED END DATE	ACTUAL END DATE	COMMENTS	PLANNED HOURS	ACTUAL HOURS	COMMENTS	PLANNED TRAVEL/ EXP.	ACTUAL TRAVEL/ EXP.	COMMENTS	AUDIT STATUS
ELECTRO	INV. PLANNING CONTROLS	02/15/XX	02/12/XX		500	542		$2,585	$2,490		COMPLETE
ELECTRO	NEW MARKETING SYSTEM	03/22/XX	03/28/XX		440	385					COMPLETE
ELECTRO	B-PLANT SECURITY	01/15/XX	01/30/XX		220	245		$7,550	$6,954		COMPLETE
ELECTRO	PROCUREMENT CONTROLS	09/12/XX	11/09/XX	MGMT. REQ. DELAY	340		IN PROCESS	$5,370	$1,366		IN PROCESS
ELECTRO	MATERIALS RECEIVING	06/20/XX		DELAYED	520			$14,323	$0		DELAYED
ELECTRO	Q/A LAB CONTROLS	05/12/XX	07/30/XX		290	485		$8,459	$12,856	ADDED TRAVEL	
DISTRIBUTION	A/R CONTROL PROCEDURES	08/10/XX	08/22/XX		440	531		$100	$225		COMPLETE
DISTRIBUTION	EDI ORDER CONTROLS	06/15/XX	07/22/XX	RESOURCE PROBS.	420	452		$0	$0		COMPLETE
DISTRIBUTION	FACTORY LABOR REPORTING	11/10/XX		IN PROCESS	470			$14,865	$9,655		IN PROCESS

operations during the budget year. How tight that control will be depends on how much flexibility has been allowed in the final budget, and on the overall policies of the organization as to budgetary compliance. Under best practices, the budget should be viewed as a major guideline but one that is subject to change when it is agreed that new developments warrant such change.

CHAPTER FOURTEEN

Directing and Performing Internal Audits

14.1 ORGANIZING AND PERFORMING INTERNAL AUDITS

While the effective internal auditor serves as the eyes and ears of the audit committee and senior management, an internal auditor must do more than just review published documentation and procedures. Internal auditors must visit organization facilities where the actual work is performed and where records are maintained. The auditor can then observe and develop an understanding of the processes in place and design and perform appropriate tests to evaluate supporting internal controls. Chapter 4, "Internal Controls Fundamentals: COSO Framework," discussed the process of selecting areas for internal audit review through a formal risk analysis. Once higher-risk audit candidates have been identified and the audits planned, the next step is to organize and perform the audits. This chapter introduces procedures to direct and perform internal audits, including surveys, documentation of internal controls, workpaper documentation, and administrative controls for managing internal audits. These procedures are appropriate whether the audit of operational area such as manufacturing resource planning or a financial area such as an accounts payable function. The same procedures are also appropriate for specialized audits, such as reviews of telecommunications or information technology (IT) controls. The basic steps to perform internal audits discussed in this chapter—such as the preliminary survey to evaluate audit evidence and documentation techniques, with an emphasis on flowcharting—are useful for performing most internal audits.

The process of directing and performing internal audits discussed in the chapter are based on the internal audit professional standards, discussed in Chapter 12, "Internal Audit Professional Standards," as well as Chapter 13's guidance for organizing an overall internal audit function. More detailed information on preparing workpapers and communicating results through audit reports are discussed in Chapter 17, "Audit Reports and Internal Audit Communications."

Internal audit will be more effective if all members of the audit staff follow consistent, professional procedures in performing their reviews. They will be more effective in the eyes of management, who will come to expect a consistent, quality approach from internal audit in the ongoing performance of their work.

14.2 AUDIT PLANNING PREPARATORY ACTIVITIES

Every audit assignment should be planned carefully prior to its start as part of internal audit's annual planning and risk-assessment process, as discussed in Chapters 5, "Understanding and Assessing Risks: Enterprise Risk Management," and 13, "Internal Audit Organization and Planning." This audit project planning, however, is often a challenge. Despite plans for unscheduled or special reviews, other requests either may come from management or situations such as unfavorable results from other audits may cause changes in the audit planning process. While there often are pressures to begin such special audits immediately, a properly planned audit will almost always have better audit results. In addition, internal audit can obtain significant savings in time and effort with adequate advance planning and preparatory work.

Although some of the preparatory activities described in this chapter can be performed during the audit itself, most normally take place in advance of visiting the audit site or beginning the audit. These important preparatory activities include defining the objectives, scope, and procedures used in an individual internal audit. This is particularly important in larger organizations performing multiple, concurrent audits with different mixes of audit personnel assigned to each. The following sections discuss the steps required to plan and perform a typical internal audit. While no single audit is really typical, the planning outlined here normally is done well in advance. Relative risks, as discussed in Chapter 4, should have been considered, and based on this risk evaluation, a long-range audit plan would have been developed. The next step is to develop detailed individual audit plans, starting with the definition of specific audit objectives.

(a) Determining Audit Objectives

The need to establish specific audit objectives for each review is the most important aspect of audit planning. Objectives based on management's desires, the various audit approaches available, audit staff capabilities, the nature of prior audit work, available resources and time, and the specific objectives and limitations of an audit project should all be considered at the beginning of each assignment. General objectives are part of the overall audit plan and define high-risk areas for internal audit consideration. Based on this risk identification, broad audit objectives can be established. When the individual audits included in that long-range plan are scheduled, these stated original audit objectives should be reexamined and defined in more detail as necessary. The objectives also should be reviewed with management and others requesting the audit. For example, the original audit plan may have identified controls over an order-entry process to be a high-risk area considered for an audit. A new system with improved controls may limit the original need for the order-processing and -shipping review or change the potential emphasis of that review. Once an overall audit purpose is defined, the scope of specific audits can be established.

Internal audit management sets forth this scope, audit objectives and planned procedures in an engagement-planning memo. Although it may be altered later through a preliminary audit investigation process, a formal statement of scope and objectives communicates the general intentions of the planned audit to the staff members who will be assigned to the review. Exhibit 14.1 shows a sample audit planning memo.

(b) Audit Scheduling and Time Estimates

The annual internal audit plan, discussed in Chapter 13, should be used to decide which audits are to be performed in any given period. Key internal audit staff members and managers, should have participated in this planning process and be aware of ongoing needs for any subsequent plan adjustments. Preliminary time estimates are established and time frames set for performing each audit. However, changes are often made to this annual plan during the course of the year due to the increased resource requirements of other audits in progress, revised audit scopes, personnel changes, and other management priorities.

In addition to the annual plan and its revisions, individual audit schedules, based on this plan, should be prepared. Depending on the nature of the audits performed and audit staff size, these individual schedules may cover a month, a quarter, or even a longer period. For a larger internal audit department, detailed audit schedules should be prepared for both the entire audit department and the individual auditors and reviewed at least monthly to reflect changes or adjustments. For example, an internal audit specialist in a key area may be unavailable for several weeks or months. This might require an overall shift in audit department plans.

EXHIBIT 14.1

Audit Planning Memo Sample

Date: Mar 15, 20XXX

To: Workpaper Files

From: L. C. Tuttle, Audit Supervisor

Subj: Accounts Payables System Audit Planning Memo

The memo is to document the planned review of the accounts payables process at the ExampleCo Corp. manufacturing headquarters facility. The review is planned to begin on about April 15, 20XX and will be staffed with four members of the internal audit organization; Henry Hollerith for information systems controls, two regular or senior internal audit staff members, and L. C. Tuttle as project leader.

The review will include internal accounting controls at the headquarters accounting facility, controls over linkage with the purchasing system at multiple facilities, the management of the cash discount system, and overall controls surrounding the Electronic Data Interchange (EDI) function for receiving advices of shipments to the plants and for paying remittances due. The review will perform both manual and computer systems based tests to assess the overall process as appropriate.

The audit is scheduled to begin on about April 22, 20XX and has been budgeted to require a total of XX hours of time from the overall audit team. A detailed audit plan, including an estimate of expected hours by auditor, will be prepared prior to the actual start of the review.

The review will emphasize controls over the recently implemented Electronic Data Interchange (EDI) procurement processes at the specific request of the Supply Chain Management team. In addition, the review will include the preparation of documentation to support Sarbanes-Oxley Act Section 404 requirements covering this process. All audit findings and recommendations will be reported in a normal internal audit department report.

———————————————————

L. C. Tuttle, Audit Supervisor

———————————————————

S. J. Smyth, Audit Manager

Exhibit 14.2 shows a sample detailed schedule of audit activity for an entire department over a three-month period. The same type of plan can be reorganized to show project assignments for each auditor over a similar multimonth period. It can also be used to show scheduled vacations, supervisory and administrative time, and formal training. As a control device, a detailed audit plan can serve as a tool for the reconciliation of available auditor days with scheduled audit requirements. While an internal auditor can easily develop such a plan tailored to meet individual audit department needs using spreadsheet software, commercial software packages as discussed in Chapter 23, "Computer-Assisted Audit Techniques," are readily available.

Exhibit 14.2

Audit Plan Project Schedule Example

EXAMPLECO CORP. INTERNAL AUDIT DEPARTMENT
APRIL–JUNE AUDIT PROJECT SCHEDULE

PROJECT #	AUDIT	AUDITOR	ACTIVITY	APR	MAY	JUNE
A23-O6	AP— EDI REVIEW	H. HOLLERITH	TEST EDI CONTROLS	20	80	45
A23-O6	A/P—EDI REVIEW	J. JONES	DOCUMENT PAYMENT PROCEDURES	110	24	12
A23-O6	A/P—EDI REVIEW	T. SCHMIDT	TESTS OF TRANSACTIONS	36	80	8
A23-O6	A/P—EDI REVIEW	T. SCHMIDT	TESTS OF TRANSACTIONS	36	80	8
A23-O6	A/P—EDI REVIEW	L. TUTTLE	MANAGE AUDIT	12	18	12
A28-78	BRANCH SALES OFFICES	J. DOE	LOCATIONS G34, F21, R45	120	145	30
A28-78	BRANCH SALES OFFICES	M. LESTER	LOCATIONS E33, G34, N16	0	65	160
A31-01	JOB COSTING REVIEW	F. BUSHMAN	COMPLETE REVIEW/ISSUE REPORT	80	16	0
A31-01	JOB COSTING REVIEW	L. TUTTLE	RESOLVE ISSUES, MANAGE AUDIT	12	4	0
E04-00	FIREWALL SECURITY REV	H. HOLLERITH	TEST AND DOCUMENT CONTROLS	0	64	80
E04-00	FIREWALL SECURITY REV	J. HOOVER	REVIEW SECURITY PROCEDURES	0	40	60

The number and level of staff required for various audits depends on an evaluation of the nature and complexity of the audit projects as well as auditor abilities and time constraints. Audit projects should be broken down into individual tasks for making these audit project hour estimates. Overall estimates are then more reliable and can serve as a benchmark for comparing actual with budgeted audit performance. Of course, the plans developed at an early stage of the audit often are preliminary and must be adjusted once more information is obtained.

Auditor skills and developmental needs should be considered in selecting personnel for any audit project assignment. After deciding on the individual audit segments, the talents needed to perform the audit tasks must be determined. For example, one segment of a planned audit may require an information systems audit specialist to evaluate certain IT controls, while another may require an auditor with audit-sampling skills to construct and evaluate a statistical test.

(c) Preliminary Surveys

The annual and long-range audit plans discussed in Chapter 13, should be made with some knowledge of the expected area to be audited. For example, internal audit management would realize that a branch office review should take *about* X hours to complete based on past experience; however, risk analysis for annual audit planning is often performed at a high or overview level. Steps beyond those risk-analysis and annual-plan-hours estimates are taken before starting the actual audit. The first step should be a preliminary survey that gathers background materials regarding the entity to be audited. This survey is often the responsibility of audit management or the designated in-charge auditor and is followed by a "field survey" discussed in Section 14.3(b). Prior to starting actual fieldwork, it is essential that there be some review of an area's background and other pertinent materials covering the planned audit.

Some of this background information may be available from prior audit work-papers or correspondence. The following items should, generally, be reviewed if available during an internal audit preliminary survey:

- *Review of Prior Workpapers.* The prior audit objectives and scope, audit workpapers, and programs used should be reviewed to gain familiarity with approaches used and the results of those audits. Some internal audit groups prepare an audit critique at the conclusion of each review to better understand the approaches used and the alternatives available for future audits. Special attention should be given to any problems encountered in the prior audit and the suggested methods of solving them. The organization of workpaper permanent files, which often contains this material, is discussed in Chapter 15, "Workpapers: Documenting Internal Audit Activities."

    Knowing the amount of time that the prior audit took as well as any problems encountered can help internal audit to determine the planned resources needed. The results of prior tests performed should be reviewed, deciding whether any should be reduced, eliminated, expanded, or performed on a rotating basis in future audits. Prior work-papers may indicate that a large sample of test-count items was included as part of an inventory review, but due to generally good internal control procedures, few problems were encountered. Planning for the upcoming audit should focus on whether those same control procedures, if still in place, can allow sample sizes to be reduced.

- *Review of Prior Audit Reports.* Past audit findings and their significance should be considered, as well as the extent of management commitments to take corrective actions. To obtain leads to other sensitive areas, the auditor should also study reports on similar entities or functions in the organization. For example, if a branch-level audit is planned in a multi-branch organization, recent audit reports covering other branches may point to potential problem areas in the branch planned for review. Related findings in other areas may also be useful.

    Particular attention should be given if substantial corrective actions were required. Those planning the upcoming planned audit may want to include an examination of these areas. Attention should also be directed to any disputed items from a prior report. Although internal audit management should have an objective of clearing up all disputed items in an audit report, there may be situations where the auditor and auditee agree to disagree. These matters are discussed in Chapter 15. The auditor should note any such areas as a suggestion for a planned audit in an upcoming period.

- *Organization of Entity.* The auditor should obtain an organization chart of the entity to be audited to understand its structure and responsibilities. Particular attention should be given to areas where there may be a potential separation of duties problem. In addition, the number of employees and the names of key employee contacts by major departments or sections should be obtained. This should include, if possible, the name of a key liaison for contacts during the planned audit. If applicable, the entity's mission statement or similar functional descriptions should be obtained to better understand its objectives. Budgets and financial-performance data should be reviewed as background material. The audit manager may want to obtain this information through a telephone request or an e-mail note and should advise the auditee that the requested information is to help in the planning of the potential audit. The areas reviewed when gaining an understanding of the entity's organization will vary somewhat depending on the type of audit planned. In an operational audit of a manufacturing area, an internal auditor might want to gain an overall understanding of the manufacturing process. Similarly, a planned IT legacy computer system general-controls review would require the auditor to gain some background information about the type of computer equipment used, the telecommunications network, and the applications processed.

• *Other Related Audit Materials.* Supporting data from related audits completed, planned, or in process should also be studied. This may include audits by the external auditor, with an emphasis on any management letters, or any reviews by governmental regulatory auditors. The results of internal reviews by departmental or other organization officials, trip reports, and other related reports provide additional useful background material. Any indication of known problem areas from these reviews should be noted. In many instances, it is beneficial to review articles in the professional literature—such as the Institute of Internal Auditors' publications—to discuss successful approaches used by other internal auditors.

14.3 STARTING THE INTERNAL AUDIT

The first step in starting most internal audits is to inform the organization to be audited—the auditee—that an internal audit has been scheduled. This is often done through an informal telephone call or conversation followed by a formal engagement letter notifying auditee management of the planned review. This engagement letter should inform the auditee of *when* the internal audit is scheduled, *who* will be performing the review, and *why* the audit has been planned (a regularly scheduled, management or auditor committee request, etc.). This who, what, and why approach should be used for all engagement letters. A sample engagement letter is shown in Exhibit 14.3. This letter should notify auditee management of the following.

1. **Addressee.** The communication should be addressed to the manager directly responsible for the unit being audited.

2. **Objectives and Scope of the Audit.** The auditee should be clearly advised of the purpose of the planned audit and areas it will cover. For example, the letter might advise that internal audit plans to review internal controls over the shop floor labor data collection system, including main-plant shop floor operations.

3. **Expected Start Date and Planned Duration of the Audit.** As much as possible, the engagement letter should give the auditee some understanding of the timing of the audit.

EXHIBIT 14.3

Internal Audit Engagement Letter Example

March 15, 20XX

To: Red Buttons, Dept. 7702

From: Sam Smyth, Internal Audit

Subj: Accounts Payable System Audit

The internal audit department has scheduled a review of your accounts payable processes. Our review will include your general accounting procedures, communications and interfaces with the purchasing department, and the procedures for accepting cash discounts. We also plan to perform a detailed review of your EDI procedures. This review has been scheduled through our annual internal audit planning process and has also been requested by our external auditors.

We expect to start our review during the week of April 22, 20XX, and we plan to conclude our work, including the issuance of an audit report, in June. Lester Tuttle will be directly responsible for this review; he will contact you to discuss our review plans in greater detail. Lester will be assisted by two other members of our regular audit staff as well as by Herman Hollerith, who will do some EDI system detailed testing.

We will need access to your regular accounts payable records and accounting reports. In addition, please inform your EDI value-added vendor that we plan to perform some automated testing over ExampleCo files. Please arrange for systems access in advance of our visit. We will also require some working space in your office area.

Please contract me at ext. 9999 if you have any questions.

CC: G. Busch
        A. Ponzi, X, Y, & Z Co.
        L. Tuttle

4. **Persons Responsible for Performing the Review.**   At a minimum, the in-charge auditor should be identified. This will help auditee management to identify this key person when a team of auditors arrives on site.

5. **Advance Preparation Needs.**   Any requirements needed in advance of the field visit or at the audit site should be outlined. This might include obtaining copies of certain reports in advance of the visit. This is also an appropriate place to request field audit office space, computer systems network access, or access to key computer systems.

6. **Appropriate Engagement Letter Carbon Copies.**   Although the term "carbon copy" is outdated today, copies of the engagement letter should be directed to appropriate levels of management.

Financial, statistical, and other reports relating to the entity being audited should also be requested in advance. Reports of this nature can help identify trends or patterns. Also, comparisons can readily be performed between entities to determine any significant variances. Appropriate levels of management should also be copied on this engagement memo. Although it is usually appropriate to inform auditee management that an internal audit has been scheduled, there may be circumstances where no formal engagement letter is released. For example, if the audit is fraud-related, the review might be performed on a surprise basis and only scheduled through appropriate levels of senior management. Small retail locations are also good candidates for surprise audits. In most instances, however, auditee management should be informed of the planned audit visit and made aware of its planned objectives.

Some internal audit professionals have taken different stands on whether or not audits should be announced in advance. They argue that a surprise audit allows a review of actual conditions without giving the auditee the benefit of cleaning up records, documentation, and other matters. However, the arrival of an audit team for an unannounced audit can cause some serious disruptions to the auditee organization, with the possibility that the prime auditee may be on vacation or away at a seminar. Unless there is a suspected fraud or a need for a surprise cash count, unannounced audits should generally be avoided. There may be reasons to postpone or reschedule the review as announced in the engagement letter. For example, a key manager or technical support person may have a prescheduled vacation during the period of the planned audit. If that person is a key source of information and if there are no special reasons for the audit's planned time schedule, audit management should reschedule it to accommodate local management. In many situations, however, the unit management may inform internal audit that "this is a bad time," with no strong reasons for postponing the audit. Because internal audit has a comprehensive schedule of planned audits and its own scheduling problems, it is appropriate to refuse such requests for postponement and insist on initiating the audit as planned.

Once the audit has been scheduled and auditee management informed, the assigned audit team should be ready to begin work at the auditee site. This phase of the audit is called *fieldwork*, even though the audit may not take place at a remote site and possibly will just start down the hall from internal audit. The term fieldwork dates from earlier days when internal auditors often traveled to remote locations—the field—to perform their internal audit reviews. At this point, the internal audit team has gathered such background information as relevant policies and procedures. Internal audit would next perform a field survey to improve the assigned audit team's understanding of the areas to be reviewed as well as to establish preliminary audit documentation of those procedures.

(a) Internal Audit Field Survey

This survey is critically important in determining the direction, detailed scope, and extent of the audit effort; it is the first step taken at the audit site. An internal auditor cannot just rush in with no clear purpose or objectives and begin examining documents and observing operations. A field survey allows auditors to: (1) familiarize themselves with systems and (2) evaluate the control structure and level of control risk in the various systems to be included within the audit. If members of the audit team are unfamiliar with the audit location and its management, this is the point to make introductions and to clarify any questions that may have been raised through the engagement letter. It is also the appropriate time for the in-charge auditor to outline planned interview requirements and to establish a preliminary schedule. The following elements should be considered by the in-charge auditor and other members of the team during a typical field survey:

- *Organization.* During the field survey, the auditors should confirm that organization charts, including the names of key personnel, are correct. The auditor should become familiar with functional responsibilities and key people involved in the operations. Often, a title on an organization chart does not reflect the true responsibilities of that position. Formal position descriptions should be requested whenever they may be appropriate. If the function does not have prepared charts available at the time of the preliminary survey, the auditor should draft a rough organization chart and review its assumptions with auditee management.

- *Manuals and Directives.* Copies of applicable policy and procedure manuals, extracting data of interest for the audit workpapers, may be available through an online system, and appropriate access should be obtained. Applicable federal and state laws and regulations should be studied, as well as management directives to comply with them. Depending on the overall objectives of the audit, correspondence files should also be screened for applicable materials.

- *Reports.* Relevant management reports and minutes of meetings covering areas appropriate to the audit—such as budgeting, operations, cost studies, and personnel matters, and the results of any external inspections or management reviews as well as actions taken—should be analyzed. Examples might include manufacturing cost performance reports or a fire inspector's review of computer room physical security. Such reports may provide leads for the audit, as well as a summary of problems faced, recommendations made, and progress made in their implementation.

- *Personal Observation.* A tour or walkthrough of the activity familiarizes internal auditors with the entity, its basic operations, personnel, and space utilization. It also provides the audit team an opportunity to ask questions and observe operations. Auditors are sometimes guilty of visiting an operation, spending all of their time in an accounting or administrative office, and completing the audit without a clear understanding of the actual activity audited. This can result in serious omissions in the final audit work. The impressions gained from this tour should be documented in the audit workpapers as a narrative. Compliance with company procedures should also be observed and documented.

- *Discussions with Key Personnel.* Discussions with key personnel in the area being audited help to determine any known problem areas, the current results of the unit's operations, and any planned changes or reorganizations. Questions should be raised based on preliminary data reviewed or tour observations.

The field survey is the initial contact point with the auditees for any review; here, management meets the audit team and the assigned auditors have their first exposure to the entity to be reviewed. Problems or misunderstandings can potentially arise at this point. Although these matters should have been resolved at the time of the engagement letter release, unit management may not always understand what the internal auditors want, or they may not have a correct understanding of the entity, despite their preliminary planning. The result may point to a need to adjust the scope of the planned review, the planned audit procedures, or even the overall audit. If so, the assigned in-charge auditor should contact internal audit management for guidance.

This section has referred to both "the internal auditor" and "the in-charge auditor." Depending on the size of the overall internal audit staff and the audit engagement, the review may be performed by one or several internal auditors. One assigned auditor should always be designated as the "in-charge" auditor, with responsibility for making most on-site audit decisions. In-charge responsibilities are usually assigned to more senior members of the audit staff, but the responsibility should be rotated throughout the staff to give less experienced auditors some management experience.

(b) Documenting the Internal Audit Field Survey

Normally, the field survey will occupy the first day or two at the audit site. For large reviews, the survey can be performed during a separate visit in advance of the auditor's detailed testing and analysis work. In either case, the work performed and summaries of data gathered through the field survey should be documented in audit workpapers. Copies of key reports and published procedures should be obtained, summary notes and observations recorded from all interviews and tours, and flowcharts prepared for all systems or processes.

This section discusses procedures for documenting the understanding gained during the auditor field survey. These will be part of the auditor's workpapers discussed in Chapter 15. The auditor's field survey also serves as a means for identifying potential new and innovative approaches to performing the audit. Such new techniques should be considered in the light of changed procedures or operating conditions. For example, a function that was once processed manually may now be automated. Flowcharts should be prepared describing major processes, control risks, and internal control points. Through their graphic summary of the flow of operations and data, flowcharts illustrate the complexities and control points in a system or process. The old adage that "a picture is worth a thousand years" very much applies here!

The concept of developing flowcharts for all major transaction processes is important for documenting many audit processes and is essentially necessary for the SOA Section 404 documentation that was discussed in Chapter 6, "Evaluating Internal Controls: Section 404 Assessments." There are many variations and approaches to developing flowcharts, but flowcharts should attempt to show the relationships between different operational elements and where control points exist in a process. Once completed, these flowcharts become part of the auditor's permanent workpaper file for that entity. They also support requirements that organizations maintain documentation covering their internal controls.

In many instances, internal audit may have prepared flowcharts as part of an earlier review, and may need only to be updated. Sometimes, an organization will have prepared its own internal flowcharts to document procedures for ISO quality standards or for other purposes. These should certainly be used, although the auditor will want to determine that they are correct and current.

No matter what the source, process flowcharts should be assembled for all major processes in the area to be reviewed.

Despite the need to have flowcharts for major processes, they may not be needed for small or relatively simple operations. In some cases, the internal auditor can describe a process through abbreviated workpaper narrative notes. In most internal audit projects, however, flowcharts should be a standard method for audit documentation and should utilize any automated tools available.

Although the approaches to developing internal audit flowcharts are described here as part of the auditor's field survey procedures, flowcharting techniques are useful for supporting many other internal audit procedures as well. The successful internal auditor should develop strong flowcharting skills, which can be used throughout the internal auditor's career.

(i) Flowcharting Approaches. Flowcharts are a pictorial or symbolic representation of a process. They have been used for years by procedures analysts and computer programmers to describe how a given process or computer program will function. Useful in describing general business procedures, noninformation systems flowcharts generally follow one of three formats: process, procedural, or functional. The internal auditor should develop a general understanding of all three and use the one that best describes an area to be reviewed. A process flowchart describes the flow of information or the significant steps in various organization operations. For example, Exhibit 14.4 describes the steps necessary to process incoming mail. A similar process flowchart could be developed for manufacturing operations to show how materials move through various machines and combine with other assemblies to make the completed component. Process flowcharts are often used for describing automated systems.

Paperwork or procedural flowcharts track the manual flow of paperwork, including where copies are filed or who approves or amends a given copy. This type of flowchart was very common prior to the now almost universal use of automated systems with limited paper trails. Through the 1960s, larger organizations even employed what were called *systems and procedures specialists* to document these paperwork processes. Although rare today, this type of flowchart is still useful for documenting the flow of manual paper documents through a process. Exhibit 14.5 is an example of a paperwork flowchart showing the approval of employee travel expense forms. A functional flowchart documents the progress of a document through various departmental entities in an organization. It is really a special version of either of the above two flowchart types and places its emphasis on organizational boundaries. Exhibit 14.6 is an example of a functional flowchart showing the steps necessary for management to process an employee pay increase in an organization.

These three similar but somewhat different flowchart approaches raise the question of which style is best for internal auditors. Each has its uses, but an internal auditor may find the process flowchart style to be most useful for audit documentation. The paperwork flowchart is most useful when the auditor needs to describe a complex paperwork process with numerous document approval steps and filing requirements. The functional flowchart is useful when the auditor wants to describe procedures or operations across various organizational or

EXHIBIT 14.4

Process Flowchart: Opening of Business Mail

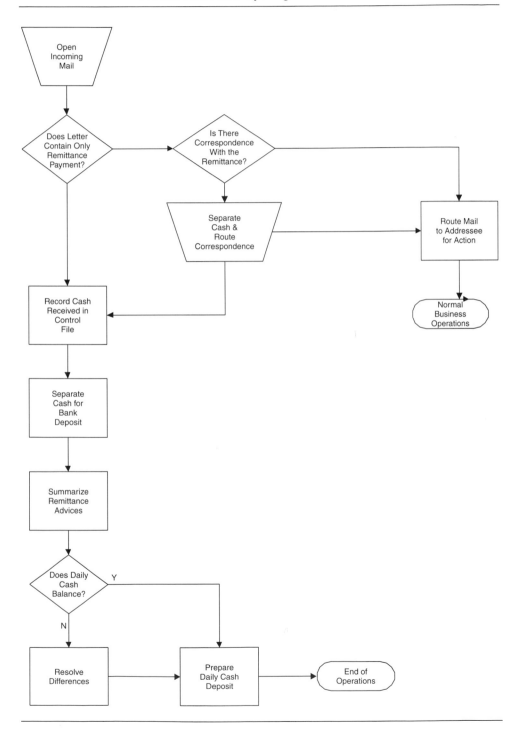

EXHIBIT 14.5

Procedural Flowchart: Travel Expenses

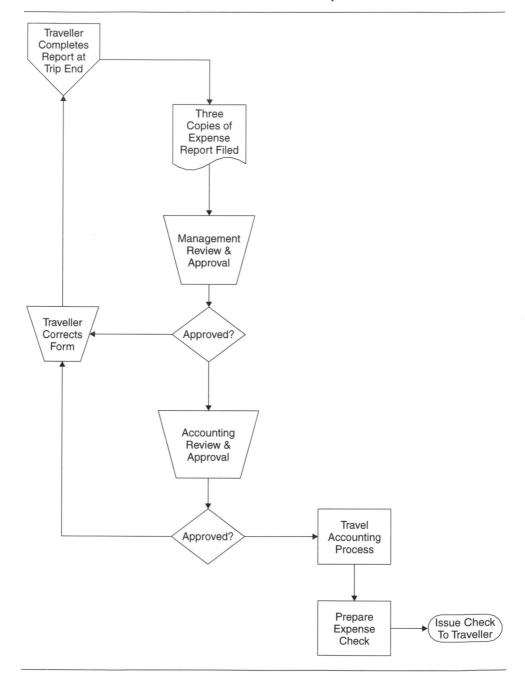

departmental boundaries. Paperwork may flow across various departments in the organization or data from a distributed system may actually leave the organization and return for subsequent processing. The functional flowchart also can be used to describe these paperwork steps and organizational boundary issues,

EXHIBIT 14.6

Functional Flow Chart Example—Process Pay Increase

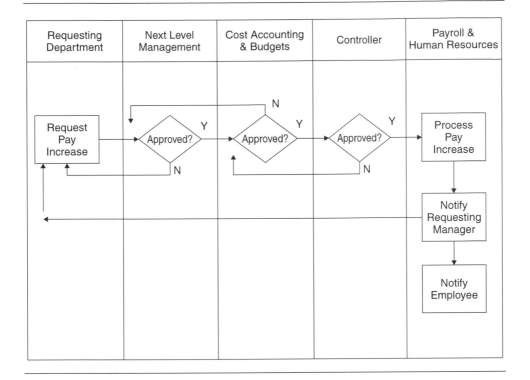

but the other two types are more effective when these issues are important. Two general approaches are commonly used for developing process-oriented flowcharts: the *method approach* and the *end-result approach*. The method approach places emphasis on the system, including an analysis of controls to prevent errors, rather than describe system outputs. Under this approach, the auditor describes and documents system processes; if there are acceptable controls, the assumption is that the end results are acceptable.

The end-result approach, however, starts with documenting from the final information product, such as an accounting month-end budget performance report. The data elements that feed into this report are traced back to their sources, and only data that affect the final product need to be identified. In a typical set of financial systems, it is not necessary to describe all information flows; the final product budget performance report is an example. In contrast, under the method approach, the flowchart describes all procedural steps, including some programs, decision branches, or reports that are irrelevant to the auditor's concerns over final budget performance. The end-result approach may save some time and money in researching and preparing the flowchart; however, an internal auditor faces a risk that other control issues may be missed.

An example might better explain these two approaches. A factory labor payroll system might collect timecard data from the factory floor with inputs going to payroll, personnel, external tax reporting, factory labor efficiency, and cost-accounting systems. A flowchart of this system following the method approach would document information flows to all of the subsystems along with the relevant controls for those supporting systems. An internal auditor may find it necessary to look at past audit history. For example, an audit of a job order-costing system might require a review of any past audit findings. In an end-result-oriented flowchart, where the auditor was only interested in the factory payroll system, the review might start with pay registers and just trace them back to their timecard sources. In an actual audit, each of these flowcharts could be much more extensive, but the method approach will almost always require more steps and areas for consideration than an end-results-style flowchart. Although an internal auditor should be aware of each of these flowcharting approaches, many internal audit departments will find the method approach the most useful for documenting operational procedures. The flowcharts may be modified, if required by circumstances, to eliminate the details of extraneous processes. Exhibit 14.4 is a process flowchart prepared for describing the controls over incoming customer mail receipts. Major control points illustrated in the flowchart are:

- The mail clerk lists cash received as a control for cash accountability.

- Remittance advices are used for recording receipts in a receipts cash book as well as inputs to the automated accounts receivable system, thus providing a control for entries made.

- Deposits are made on a daily basis.

- The automated system generates reports weekly on aging and extent of receivable balances to provide a control over collection activities.

- Receipted deposit slips and later bank statements provide control over final disposition of money received.

(ii) Flowcharting Symbols and Tools. The flowcharts in the preceding exhibits use fairly standard symbols as well as commentary to describe the various steps being documented. These symbols are recognized by many professionals. Exhibit 14.7 shows typical symbols used in preparing flowcharts for manual or automated processes. At one time, most internal auditors developed their flowcharts with pencil and paper using plastic symbol templates. While this was a convenient way initially to draw flowcharts, it was difficult to make changes or modifications to these manually prepared documents. As a result, auditors sometimes avoided preparing and then updating detailed flowcharts. Automation changed this. Just as most auditors now use automated spreadsheet software rather than pencils and 14-column paper forms, various automated tools are available to help develop auditor flowcharts. This software ranges from inexpensive or free Web-based tools to more sophisticated packages such as Microsoft's Visio® business graphics software. A variety of other computer system–based flowcharting tools may be available to internal auditors in many organizations. Most of these are used primarily by information systems departments for their own systems projects. These software tools are subsets of the computer-assisted systems engineering (CASE) tools used by many information systems

EXHIBIT 14.7

Common flowcharting Symbols

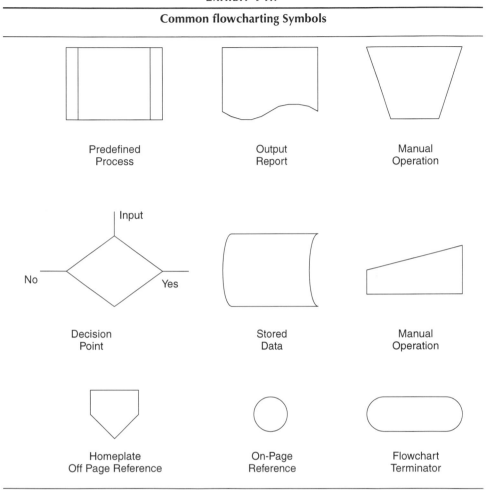

organizations. Internal audit should discuss its flowcharting needs with information systems management and then evaluate the applicability of any possible information systems department flowcharting tools for its potential use.

(c) Field Survey Auditor Conclusions

The purpose of an internal audit field survey is to confirm the assumptions gained from the preliminary audit planning and to develop an understanding of key systems and processes. Because the information that supports the preliminary audit planning is often imperfect, this is an important point where the assigned audit team can make adjustments to their planned audit scope and objectives. For larger audits, it is often a good idea for audit management to visit the team performing the field survey and review its results. This way, any necessary management-approved scope changes can be made. This on-site presence can clear up any potential questions that could be raised later.

An internal auditor may encounter instances where the information gathered from a field survey may cause the audit team either to adjust the planned audit scope substantially or even to cancel the detailed audit work. Sometimes, the audit team involved in the preliminary planning may call the auditee at a remote location and be advised that there are "no changes" in the area of the auditor's interest. When the audit team arrives, the field survey could point out significant changes, such as the introduction of a new information system, which changes the overall control environment and may require the internal audit team to add another specialist to the project, causing both staffing and audit test strategy adjustments. In other cases, the audit team may find that changes are so substantial that the planned audit should be canceled or postponed. In most instances, however, the field survey provides the audit team with additional data to help them adjust their planned procedures.

The materials gathered in an internal audit field survey should be used either to document or to update a workpaper permanent file. If a member of audit management is not on-site, the results of the survey should be summarized in written form, communicated through e-mail, and reviewed with internal audit management before proceeding with the audit. Exhibit 14.8 is an example of an internal audit report on field survey conclusions. This document is particularly important if the in-charge auditor feels there is a need to change audit scope or planned procedures.

14.4 USING AUDIT PROGRAMS TO PERFORM INTERNAL AUDITS

Internal audits should be organized and performed in a consistent manner with an objective of minimizing arbitrary or unnecessary procedures. Of course, an internal auditor will not recognize what those arbitrary or unnecessary procedures are until an auditor has gained some experience in performing reviews. To provide help and guidance, internal auditors should use what are called *audit programs* to perform audit procedures in a consistent and effective manner for similar types of audits. The term *program* refers to a set of auditor procedures similar to the steps in a computer program, instructions that go through the same program instructions every time the process is run. For example, a computer program to calculate pay will include instructions to read the timecard file of hours worked, look up the employee's rate stored in another file, and then calculate the gross pay. The same steps apply for every employee unless there are exceptions such as overtime rates coded into the payroll program. Similarly, an audit program is a set of preestablished steps that an internal auditor performs. An audit program is a tool for planning, directing, and controlling audit work and a blueprint for action, specifying the steps to be performed to meet audit objectives. It represents the auditor's selection of the best methods of getting the job done and serves as a basis for recording the work steps performed.

An effective internal audit department should have a series of generalized audit programs prepared for recurring audit activities. Many of these programs, such as one covering an observation of the taking of physical inventories, are often used from year to year and entity to entity with little change. In other situations, the auditor may only have to modify a standard program to adjust it to the

EXHIBIT 14.8

Field Survey Conclusions Audit Memo Report Sample

April 5, 20XX

To: Sandra Smyth, Audit Manager

From: Lester Tuttle

Subject: Accounts Payable Field Survey Conclusions

We have just concluded our preliminary meetings with local management as well as a review of documentation and an observation of operations over the ExampleCo accounts payable operations. While most of our preliminary audit plans to review accounts payable controls were correct, we identified two areas where our audit scope and planned audit procedures should be modified:

1. *Cash Discount System* We were advised that, with the low interest rates we have been experiencing in recent years, the company has found little advantage to taking cash discounts for prompt payment. As a result, we were advised this system is not normally used today.

   I suggest we reduce Jane Jones's planned 40 hours in this area to 20 hours and either utilize her for other matters or end her role early.

2. *EDI Controls* The use of EDI is much more extensive than anticipated, and A/P does not appear to be doing a very good job in handling this growth. A much more extensive effort at controls documentation and transaction testing is needed.

   I suggest we ask Hollerith to return for an extra week during the month of May. That would increase his hours for that month to 120. We discussed this, and he is open to changing his schedule.

Please advise if these proposed changes are acceptable.

Lester C. Tuttle

---

unique aspects of a particular audit. In some situations, a standard audit program will not be applicable. For example, the internal auditor may want to review controls in a new business entity with some unique control characteristics, or audit management may want to take a different approach because of problems encountered with similar previous reviews. Based on the planned audit objectives and data gathered in the preliminary and field surveys, the in-charge auditor may want to prepare a customized audit program for guiding the review. This may be little more than a standardized program with minimal local changes, or it may be a unique set of audit procedures based on the preliminary planning and the results from the field survey. In order to prepare this program, the internal auditor first should have an understanding of the characteristics of what constitutes an adequate audit program.

(a) Audit Program Formats and Their Preparation

An audit program is a procedure describing the steps, procedures, and tests to be performed by the auditor when actually doing the audit. The program should be finalized after the completion of the preliminary and field surveys and before starting the actual audit fieldwork. It should be constructed with several criteria in mind, the most important of which is that the program should identify the aspects of the area to be further examined and the sensitive areas that require audit emphasis.

A second important purpose of an audit program is that it guides both the neophyte and more experienced auditors. For example, management may request that an internal audit department observe the taking of the annual physical inventory. This type of review consists of fairly standard procedures to ensure, among other matters, that shipping and receiving cut-off procedures are proper. A less experienced internal auditor may not be aware of these procedural steps, and even experienced internal auditors may forget one or another step. An audit program outlines the required audit steps. An established internal audit department will probably have built a library of programs, established over time, for tasks such as a physical inventory observation or a review of fixed assets. When planning a review where such established programs exist, audit management needs only to use this established program with consideration being given to any changed conditions that have been discovered through the preliminary or field surveys. The audit program is revised as necessary, with the changes being approved by audit management prior to the start of the review.

For many internal audit departments, appropriate established audit programs may not be available for many areas. This is so because internal auditors are typically faced with a wide and diverse set of areas for review, but they will not have the time or resources to review every area on a frequent basis. Established programs prepared for prior audits often become out of date due to new systems or changed processes. The auditor responsible for the field survey or another member of audit management should update any existing audit program or prepare a revised set of audit program steps for the planned review. Depending on the type of planned audit, programs usually follow one of three general formats: a set of general audit procedures, audit procedures with detailed instructions for the auditor, and a checklist for compliance reviews.

Some examples may better illustrate these audit program types. Exhibit 14.9 is an audit program for a review of petty cash controls at a branch unit. It consists of general audit procedures to review cash at any unit of a multifacility organization. Petty cash controls are one of the smaller, less critical internal control concerns in many organizations. However, this is a step that an internal auditor will regularly perform in many cases. The program shows the rather simple steps that should be included in any such audit and illustrates an example audit program.

Exhibit 14.9 represents a typical internal audit program format. For each audit, the tasks are broken into numbered steps with space allowed for the initial and date of the internal auditor completing the audit step as well as a column for a reference to the workpaper that describes the audit step. For example, for the Step 1 start of this process, the internal auditor performing the procedure would describe the particulars of that cash count. Typically, an established internal audit function would have developed these general audit programs for many of its regular or periodic audits. The audit team visiting an organizational unit could then use standard programs to review internal controls in a consistent manner from one unit to the next. This is particularly important in a multi-unit organization where audit

EXHIBIT 14.9

Audit Program Standard Format: Review of Petty Cash Example

Audit: _____ Location: _____ Date: _____

AUDIT STEP	Initials & Date	W/P Reference
1. Prior to review, determine who is the cashier responsible for the petty cash fund balances, receipt requirements, replishment procedures, and guidelines for authorized disbursements.	_____	_____
2. Perform the petty cash review on a "surprise" basis. Identify yourself to the cashier, ask that the cashier function be closed during your intial review, and make a detailed count of the cash in the account as well as any personal checks included. Perform this count in the presence of the cashier and ask the cashier to acknowledge your results.	_____	_____
3. If personal checks were included that are over one day old, inquire why they were not deposited on a prompt basis. If the fund is being used as an employee short-term loan fund, with check held as collateral, assess the propriety of this practice.	_____	_____
4. Reconcile the cash count with the fund's disbursement register, noting any differences.	_____	_____
5. Determine that all disbursements recorded have been made to valid employees for authorized purposes.	_____	_____
6. Observe office security procedures covering the fund. Determine that the funds are locked or otherwise secured.	_____	_____
7. Review procedures for fund replenishments. Select a prior period, review supporting documentation, and reconcile to purchases journal.	_____	_____
8. Assess the overall control procedures, propriety, and efficiency of the petty cash process.	_____	_____
9. Determine that the function is used only for authorized small cash disbursements rather than as a change or short-term loan fund.	_____	_____
10. Document the results of the review and intiate corrective actions if any problems were encountered during the review.	_____	_____

management wants to have assurance that controls over the area were reviewed and evaluated in a consistent manner, no matter who the assigned auditor or which location. This sample audit program is shown as a printed document that would typically be developed and controlled by internal audit. In other instances, the in-charge auditor might prepare a custom program to evaluate certain special procedures encountered during the field survey.

An audit program with detailed instructions or procedures assumes that the auditor using it lacks some of the technical knowledge necessary to perform the review. These are often developed for a one-time review of some fairly specialized area and prepared by audit management, or so that a knowledgeable audit specialist with inadequate knowledge to plan all of the procedures outlined in a detailed, specialized audit program can perform the outlined steps given some guidance. This step-by-step audit program format is useful when a centralized audit management group with remote auditors in the field wishes to have all of those field auditors perform the same general procedures.

The checklist audit program was once internal audit's most common format. The auditor would be given an audit program composed of a long list of questions requiring "yes," "no," or "not applicable" responses and would complete these program steps either through examinations of documents or through interviews. Exhibit 14.10 is an example of a checklist format audit program for reviewing an organization's ethics and business compliance policies. Yes and no responses, when asked in an information-gathering context, are often appropriate. A checklist-format audit program has two weaknesses, however. First, while a series of auditee yes or no type interview responses can lead an experienced auditor to look at problem areas or to ask other questions, these same points may be missed when a less experienced auditor is just completing the questionnaire and not going beyond the yes and no answers, digging a bit deeper as to where they might lead. A procedures-oriented audit program better encourages follow-up inquiries in other areas where information gathered may raise questions.

The questionnaire format audit program also tends to cause the auditor to miss examining necessary evidential matter when just asking only the questions. The more inexperienced auditor can too easily check "yes" on the questionnaire without determining, for example, whether a yes response is properly supported by audit evidence. An example would be a question regarding whether some critical document is regularly approved. It is easy to ask the question, receive an answer of "yes," and never follow up to see if those documents were actually approved. Each of these audit program formats will work for different types of reviews provided the internal auditor gives some thought to the program questions. The key concern is that all audits should be supported by some type of audit program that documents the review steps performed. This approach allows audit management to recognize what procedures the auditors did or did not perform in a given review. Strong and consistent audit programs are an important step to improving the overall quality of the internal audits performed.

The reliability of the evidence to be reviewed and various types of other information available should also be considered when developing the final audit program. There is little value in keeping steps in an established audit program that call for reviews of systems and procedures no longer in use. An internal auditor,

EXHIBIT 14.10

Audit Program Checklist Format: Review of Business Ethics Example

Audit _____ Location _____ Auditor _____ Date _____

INTERNAL CONTROL CONCERN	YES	NO	N/A
1. Does the company have a written code of business ethics and business conduct?	_____	_____	_____
2. Is the code distributed to all employees?	_____	_____	_____
3. Are new employees provided orientation to the code?	_____	_____	_____
4. Does the code assign responsibility to operating personnel and others for compliance with the code?	_____	_____	_____
5. Are all employees required to acknowledge that they have read, understood, and agree to abide by the code?	_____	_____	_____
6. Are training programs delivered to all employees regarding compliance with the code?	_____	_____	_____
7. Does the code address standards that govern employee conduct in their dealings with suppliers and customers?	_____	_____	_____
8. Is there an effective mechanism in place to allow employees to confidentially report suspected violations of the code?	_____	_____	_____
9. Is there an appropriate mechanism in place to follow-up on reports of suspected violations of the code?	_____	_____	_____
10. Is there an appropriate mechanism to allow employees to find out the results of their reported concerns?	_____	_____	_____
11. Is compliance with the code's provisions a standard used for measuring employee performance at all levels?	_____	_____	_____
12. Is there a procedure in place to update the code on a periodic basis?	_____	_____	_____

in developing an audit program, should try to select audit steps that are meaningful and that will produce reliable forms of audit evidence. For example, the audit program often needs to call for detailed tests in a given critical, high-risk area rather than suggesting that the information can be gathered through interviews.

Advanced audit techniques should also be incorporated into audit programs wherever practicable. For example, computer-assisted audit techniques (CAATs), discussed in Chapter 23, can perform selected audit steps—similarly, the use of more advanced audit procedures such as statistical sampling procedures to allow the auditor to extract data easily from larger populations. Members of the audit staff who have information systems audit or other technical skills should be consulted when preparing these audit program steps.

There is no best or set format for an audit program; however, the program should be a document that auditors can use to guide their efforts as well as to record activities. This audit program will then be included in the workpapers to serve as almost a table of contents of the audit activities described in those workpapers. Word processing packages and other related software can be used to prepare audit programs.

(b) Types of Audit Evidence

As discussed in Chapter 12, IIA standards state that an internal auditor should examine and evaluate information on all matters related to the planned audit objective. The auditor should gather audit evidence in support of the evaluation, what internal audit standards call *sufficient, competent, relevant,* and *useful.* An audit program, properly constructed, should guide the auditor in this evidence-gathering process. An internal auditor will encounter multiple types of evidence that can be useful in developing audit conclusions. If an auditor actually observes an action or obtains an independent confirmation, this is one of the strongest forms of evidence. However, an auditee's often casual response to an auditor's question covering the same area will be the weakest. It is not that an auditor thinks the auditee is not telling the truth, but that actually observing some event is far superior to just hearing about it. Internal auditors will encounter different levels of audit evidence and should attempt to design their audit procedures to look for and rely on the best available audit evidence. Exhibit 14.11 provides some ranges of best evidence for different classifications of materials.

The field survey and the subsequent development of an audit program are preliminary activities to performing the actual audit. It is often more efficient to have supervisory personnel complete these preliminary steps before assigning staff auditors for the actual review. These supervisory auditors, either audit management or experienced in-charge auditors, usually have the experience to make quick assessments of field situations and to fine-tune the overall audit approach. However, once the survey and final audit program are complete and have been reviewed and approved by internal audit management, internal audit is faced with the challenge of performing the actual audit to meet the desired audit objectives. The preparatory work from the survey will play an important

EXHIBIT 14.11

Internal Audit "Best Evidence" Classifications

Evidence Classification	Strongest	Weakest
Audit Technique	Observation/Confirmation	Inquiry
Origin of Evidence	Corroborative	Underlying Statistics
Relationship to Auditee	External Department	Internal
Form of Evidence	Written	Oral
Sophistication of Evidence	Formal/Documented	Informal
Location of Evidence	Actual System	Derived/Supporting System
Source of Audit Evidence	Personal Audit Work	Others

role in ensuring the audit's success; however, the internal auditor will now be faced with the day-to-day problems of performing the actual audit.

The actual audit steps performed will depend on the characteristics of the entity audited. A financially oriented audit of a credit and collection function will be quite different from an operational review of a design engineering function. The financial audit might include independent confirmations of account balances, while the operational audit might include extensive interviews with management and supporting documentation to assess key internal controls. Despite these differences, all internal audits should be performed and supervised following a general set of principles or standards. This will ensure that internal audits are properly directed and controlled.

14.5 PERFORMING THE INTERNAL AUDIT

This section discusses the general steps necessary to perform any internal audit, and should be used in conjunction with the specific audit procedures discussed throughout this book. While a preliminary survey is often the first preliminary step, an engagement letter, shown in Exhibit 14.3, is the important first step in announcing the planned audit, its objectives, the assigned audit team, and the approximate time periods. A single engagement letter is usually sufficient; however, in some audit situations there may be a considerable time interval between an initial field survey and the actual audit. A second engagement letter would then be useful.

Even though a separate letter may have been released for the earlier field survey, the engagement letter outlines the arrangements for the formal audit. As discussed previously, unannounced audits may be justified in cases where there is a suspicion of fraud or when a unit is very small, with records that can be easily altered. In most instances, however, audit management should start the review with this formal engagement letter to alert local and line management of the planned review, allowing them to adjust their schedules as appropriate. In some instances, auditee management may request a postponement for any number of reasons. With the exception of a potential fraud situation, internal audit management should always try to be flexible.

The auditors assigned also have some advance work prior to actual fieldwork. If there was a separate field survey, those results should be reviewed, as should any audit permanent file workpapers. For larger audits with multiple auditors, program assignments should be made in advance. Travel and lodging arrangements should be made in accordance with organizational policies. Travel costs can be a major expense for an internal audit department, particularly if there are numerous, scattered audit locations, either domestic or worldwide. Significant travel savings can often be realized by taking advantage of discount airfares and making other cost-effective travel arrangements. Internal audit management must recognize, however, that travel always will be a major budget expense and should not eliminate trips to higher-audit-risk locations just because of the cost of travel. Internal audit has a responsibility to the audit committee and senior management to report on the status of the organization's internal control structure. Field visits should not be postponed or eliminated because of the cost of travel to remote locations.

(a) Internal Audit Fieldwork Procedures

An audit can cause interruptions and problems in the day-to-day operations of the auditee organization. The in-charge auditor and members of the audit team should begin by meeting with appropriate members of auditee management to outline preliminary plans for the audit, including areas to be tested, special reports or documentation needed, and personnel to be interviewed. This also is an appropriate time for the internal audit team to tour the unit and to meet other personnel in the unit to be reviewed. The auditors should request that management contact all affected members of the auditee organization to provide them with an auditor-prepared tentative schedule of the planned audit work. This will eliminate potential problems in securing the cooperation of auditee personnel.

Problems can still occur while conducting the audit. For example, a key section supervisor may claim to be too busy to talk to internal audit and may not supply necessary information. Similarly, a cycle from key computer system file that was to have been saved for audit tests may have been deleted. These types of problems can either slow progress or require a revised testing and analysis strategy. Any problems should be detected early in the assignment and solved as soon as possible. Difficulties in obtaining cooperation of one department's personnel, for example, may slow work in that area and delay the completion of the entire audit.

The in-charge auditor should meet with auditee management to discuss any problems and to find solutions. If local management appears to be uncooperative, the in-charge auditor may have to contact internal audit management to resolve the problem at a different level. If a key component of the planned audit is missing, such as a missing data file, audit management should develop a revised strategy to get around the problem. This might include:

- Revising audit procedures to perform additional tests in other areas. This type of change, however, should only be performed with care. If there was a strong reason for selecting the now missing file—such as the need to tie it to some other data—it may be necessary to reconstruct the missing balances.

- Completing the audit without the missing data file. The workpapers and the final report would indicate internal audit's inability to perform the planned tests. The in-charge auditor should always gain approval from internal audit management for this approach.

- Complete other portions of the audit and reschedule a later visit to perform tests. (This is only an option if the missing data file cannot be reconstructed or if a different cycle of data would be sufficient.) Management should be informed, of course, of audit budget overruns because of this problem.

These or similar types of problems can be encountered in this manner for many field audits. It is important that the problems be detected and resolved as early in the audit as possible. If the internal audit team faces a total lack of cooperation, management should be informed at appropriate levels to resolve the matter. Both the internal auditors and auditee's should always remember that both parties are members of the same overall organization with common general interests and goals.

The actual audit fieldwork should follow the established audit program. As each step is completed, the responsible auditor should initial and date the audit program. Documentation gathered from each audit step, as well as any audit analyses, should be organized and forwarded to the in-charge auditor, who performs a preliminary review of the audit work. The in-charge auditor monitors the performance of the audit work in progress and reviews workpapers as they are completed for each step. Exhibit 14.12 shows a field audit point sheet where the in-charge auditor has signed off on key audit program steps and suggested areas for additional work. This type of document is useful for all larger audits.

The results of many audit steps will not yield specific audit findings but may raise questions for further investigation. The conditions in many areas reviewed

EXHIBIT 14.12

Internal Audit Findings "Point Sheet" Example

Name of Audit: **Physical Inventory Reconciliation**   Date:_____

Potential Finding #: **3**   Title: **Excess Inventory Write-Offs**   W/P Ref:_____

  Source of Audit Concern Where Were Conditions Found:
   Audit adjustments at end of year

  Statement of Audit Condition Observed:
   Inventory write-offs during current year increased by XX% of previous year

  Potential Cause of Error:
   Computer system errors, poor physical security, and inventory location errors

  Effect of Audit Errors:
   Production shortages, excessive insurance claims, erroneous interim reports

  Preliminary Audit Recommendation:
   See W/P_____

  Results of Discussion with Management:
   See W/P_____, which discusses acceptance of preliminary findings

  Comments and Recommended Final Disposition:

can be subject to explanations or interpretations by local management. Rather than just writing them up, the field audit team should generally discuss preliminary audit observations with the persons responsible for the area. The auditor can sometimes misinterpret something that is easily resolved. If questions still remain, the matter may become a preliminary audit finding, as discussed in the following section.

(b) Audit Fieldwork Technical Assistance

The field survey or the audit program development process should have identified any need for specialized technical help to perform the audit; however, other complex problems requiring technical support may arise in the course of the audit fieldwork. For example, the assigned auditor may question the accounting treatment of a certain set of transactions and want to get better information about normal practices for them. Similarly, the auditors may encounter a specialized computer application, with unique control considerations, that was not sufficiently identified or described in the survey.

If a technical issue is not familiar to the audit team, the in-charge auditor should seek technical assistance as soon as possible. An internal audit supervisor or specialist may have to research the audit or technical issue in order to provide the answer. In other instances, it may be necessary to bring an internal audit expert in the area in question to the field site to resolve the concern or problem. However, a typical internal audit department does not have resident experts in the audit department, ready to travel out to the field site to resolve a problem. If at all possible, the matter should be resolved through telephone calls, e-mails, or exchanges of documentation.

The important message that audit management should communicate to staff is that all technical audit problems should be brought to the attention of the in-charge auditor for resolution as soon as possible. Any cost and extra time requirements resulting from these technical problems should be documented. If the technical problem cannot be promptly resolved, it may be necessary to reschedule the audit or to revise the strategy, as described above.

(c) Audit Management Fieldwork Monitoring

Supervisory visits by internal audit management should be made frequently to review an audit's progress and provide technical direction. These reviews supplement the ongoing reviews made by the in-charge auditor, who is part of the field staff. The frequency and extent of these visits will depend on the criticality of the review, the experience of the assigned staff, and the size of the review. A medium-sized review headed by an experienced in-charge auditor and covering familiar areas may not require a management review if communication lines are good. However, if the audit covers a critical area, if a new program or new techniques are used, or if the assigned in-charge auditor has limited experience in the area reviewed, an experienced member of audit management should visit the fieldwork project periodically.

The purpose of these visits should be to review the work in progress and to help resolve problems encountered. While audit management may feel that this is also an appropriate time to take the assigned field staff out to lunch or dinner to thank them for their efforts, all should realize this is not the purpose of audit field visits. Audit management should take this opportunity to understand any evolving issues in the audit and to suggest changes as appropriate. This is also a good time for management to start the review of completed audit workpapers, as discussed in Chapter 15.

Audit workpapers document the work performed and provide a link between the procedures documented in the audit program and the results of audit tests. Because they will become the basis for findings and recommendations in final audit reports, the workpapers should appropriately document all audit work. While the in-charge auditor should have been reviewing and commenting on workpapers for larger audits and audit point sheets (as illustrated in Exhibit 14.12), smaller reviews without a separate auditor will not have this type of feedback. The member of audit management visiting the field site should spend some time reviewing and approving the workpapers and preliminary finding sheets.

These workpaper-review comments should be documented, cover such areas as additional work or explanations required, and suggest adjustments to the audit program if appropriate. The management review should typically not result in major changes to the audit approach. However, internal audit management can often bring some additional guidance or understanding to the audit in process.

The review comments should be documented in a review comment sheet that references pages or items in the workpapers where the management reviewer has questions or has identified missing items of audit documentation. Based on these review comments, the staff auditors should perform the additional audit work required and make the necessary changes to the workpapers, indicating the action taken on the review sheet. After completion of internal audit's comments, the additional work done, or corrections, the supervisor indicates on the review comment sheets his or her clearance of all items as well as any further actions to be taken.

(d) Potential Audit Findings

Whenever the internal auditor discovers a potential audit deficiency, a brief summary of the conditions and possible findings should be prepared. This summary is sometimes what is called an *audit preliminary findings sheet*. Whether or not the conditions described in such a document result in a final audit report finding depends on the results of additional review and analysis. A point-sheet deficiency would not necessarily become an audit finding in the final report, but the sheet can be used to document potential audit report findings. A point sheet describes any deficiency or an opportunity for improvement identified during the audit fieldwork. These matters must be documented by the auditors in the field as soon as there is an indication that a potentially substantive audit issue exists. This facilitates bringing these issues to the attention of both internal audit and auditee management at an early point in the review. It also serves as a control to ensure that all leads are followed up. In addition, the various auditor point sheets, developed by individual staff members, may bring out a number of minor issues that fall into a pattern, indicating a more serious overall condition.

The use of point sheets also starts the preliminary report-writing process early in the audit, and helps to ensure that the essential facts for developing an audit report finding have been obtained. Although the contents of a specific point sheet can vary depending on the needs of the individual internal audit department, a point sheet typically has the following elements:

- *Identification of the Finding.* This is just an identification number for the audit and a description of the potential findings.

- *The Conditions.* The description is generally brief but sufficient to give local management an understanding of the conditions found.

- *References to the Documented Audit Work.* The audit point sheet should contain cross-references to the step in the audit program that initiated the comment, as well as where it is documented in the audit workpapers.

- *Auditor's Preliminary Recommendations.* Audit report space should be used to document the nature of the potential audit finding, and what was wrong. This might become the basis for a potential future audit report finding. Some notes on potential auditor-recommended corrective actions might be included here.

- *Results of Discussing the Finding with Management.* The in-charge auditor should discuss all potential findings on an informal basis with the manager directly responsible for the matter. The results of this conversation should be documented in the point sheet

- *Recommended Disposition of the Matter.* On the basis of the conversation with management, the in-charge auditor should include comments on the recommended disposition of the finding. It might be recommended for inclusion in the audit report, dropped for a variety of reasons, or deferred until more information can be gathered.

Audit point sheets are a good method of documenting potential audit findings. Some audit organizations may even have a space on this document for the auditee to respond to the auditor's suggested finding and recommendation. Both can be published in the final audit report, as covered as part of the overall discussion on audit reports in Chapter 17. Point sheets should always be supported by and cross-referenced to the specific audit workpapers, and the status of the points raised should be documented to show their eventual disposition. If developed into a finding, the point sheet can also be cross-referenced to that audit report finding. If the point-sheet potential finding is dropped during the fieldwork or later, the reasons should be documented.

(e) Audit Program and Schedule Modifications

The audit program is the overall guide for conducting the audit. Developed from preliminary survey data and from past internal audits on file, they may be subject to adjustment during the course of the review. Auditors must be responsive to new evidence, changes in supporting systems, and other changes in conditions. In the early stages of an audit, it may be necessary to redirect some of the planned audit staff assignments as well as to modify some audit program steps. The in-charge auditor should always obtain approval from audit management before making any such changes.

The need for audit program modifications is most common when internal audit has developed a common audit program for use in reviews of similar but not identical units. For example, an audit program may have been developed to cover controls over the purchasing function for an organization with multiple independent manufacturing units, each with separate purchasing functions. Those purchasing function audit programs should reflect both organization policy and general internal control principles. Due to local differences, however, this audit program may contain steps that are not applicable to one or another specific purchasing area under audit. Any such steps that are bypassed on the individual audit program should be approved and documented as to the reasons.

Changes are often required in the audit schedule and plan as work progresses. Some flexibility should be factored into plans to meet unforeseen requirements. During the field audit assignment, situations may be encountered that affect the progress of its audit, such as an unexpected problem or event, the need to modify or drop an audit program segment, the discovery of a new area for review, or changes in audit personnel. In other instances, there may be slippage in the plan due to additional time requirements to finish an audit program step. In these circumstances, revised budgets are needed. Proper approvals for these changes should always be obtained from internal audit management.

(f) Reporting Preliminary Audit Findings to Management

A major area of emphasis in any audit is the identification of areas where the unit reviewed is not in compliance with internal controls practices procedures, or where improvements are needed. These areas would have been documented during the course of the audit through the use of a point or findings sheet type of document. Although these potential audit items should have been discussed with the supervisors directly responsible, the audit team should also review them with unit management before leaving the field audit assignment.

Potential audit findings should be reviewed with unit management during the audit to determine if they are factual. Depending on the scope and size of the audit, these potential findings should be reviewed at several points during the course of the review. If an audit is scheduled over multiple weeks, the in-charge auditor might schedule a meeting with unit management at the end of each week to discuss all findings that developed over the course of that week. If the findings are of a minor, procedural nature, management can take necessary corrective actions at once. They can then be deemphasized or deleted in any final audit report. For other findings, the in-charge auditor should review proposed findings to ascertain that cost savings are indicated and properly reported and that findings are related to operational effectiveness.

Even though the audit's duration may be too short to have weekly status meetings, the field audit team should almost always review all potential findings with management before leaving the location. This will allow internal audit to present its preliminary findings and recommendations to local management to obtain their reactions and comments. It also gives both parties an opportunity to correct any errors in the preliminary audit report findings before internal audit leaves the location.

14.6 PLANNING AND CONTROLLING INTERNAL AUDIT FIELDWORK

Internal audit projects should be managed in the same manner as any large project requiring personnel time and other resources and resulting in a defined deliverable. Both personnel resources and other costs should be planned and budgeted on a detailed level. The actual performance should be recorded and measured against established time and cost-based budgets to analyze and correct for any significant variances. Significant project milestones, such as the completion of fieldwork or of the draft audit report, should also be tracked against plans.

Chapter 13 discussed the development of the annual audit plan, and this chapter considers the need for detailed plans for individual audit projects. All aspects of audit projects should be budgeted with time and other costs measured against those plans. No matter how large or small the internal audit function, an audit project performance-reporting system should be established. For audits greater than about two-weeks duration or those performed in multiple locations at the same time, progress reports should be required on a weekly or biweekly basis. These reports should be based on the time summaries from the assigned audit staff as well as commentaries from the in-charge auditor at the location. They can include such information as budgeted and actual time to date, estimated time to complete, and a summarized description of progress against the audit program. This data can be gathered by the supervising auditors at field sites and transmitted to the central internal audit department. The in-charge auditor should take responsibility for explaining any significant variances in audit actual versus budget performance. In addition to reporting on a single field audit project, this report also provides input to the audit department's project status system, as was discussed in Chapter 13.

The time expended on individual audit projects should be further summarized by internal audit management to provide an overview of all audits planned or in process. A three-month period is often a good time period for planned future activities, given the various senior management requests and other factors that can impact an internal audit plan. This type of report is used to provide control over audits scheduled or in process while a separate, more detailed report can be completed for each individual audit to ensure that they are started and completed on a timely basis. The rolling three-month report can be a useful tool for communicating with the audit committee.

Any increases in audit time budgets should be carefully monitored, identifying reasons for the variance as well as any corrective action plans. Audit project monitoring indicates any not started on time or that are outside of budget parameters. In some cases, the problem may be inaccurate budgets; in others, the problem may lie in auditor performance. Close control of the audit will prevent slippage caused by inadequacies in staff, delays in solving problems, insufficient supervision, and excessive attention to detail.

Chapter 13 outlines how internal audit should make use of automated techniques to develop and maintain this reporting and control system. Spreadsheet or database packages can provide a powerful structure for building such systems. Many paper-based reports can be eliminated, and the field auditors can transmit their time summaries and status report information to a central internal audit project-reporting system.

As discussed throughout this book, internal auditing is a large and complex process with many activities. The most important values the internal audit process provides to the Audit Committee and management are the detailed audits performed in the field or as part of overall operations. Gathering initial evidence, performing the audit, and reporting initial findings to management are all part off the process. Exhibit 14.13 summarizes these steps for performing internal audits up through the completion of the fieldwork. Once the fieldwork has been completed, the next step will be the preparation of the actual audit report, as discussed in Chapter 17.

Exhibit 14.13

Internal Audit Process: Summarized Steps

The Internal Audit Process—Through Fieldwork
I. Perform risk analysis to identify potential control risks.
II. Based on results of risk analysis and audit resource constraints, develop overall annual and long-range plans to perform audits.
III. Schedule audit and allocate resources.
IV. Prepare engagement letter for auditee.
V. Perform field survey covering area of audit.
VI. Prepare or refine workpapers based on department standards and field survey.
VII. Begin fieldwork and perform audit procedures.
VIII. Document procedures and perform audit tests of key controls.
IX. Develop point sheets covering potential audit findings.
X. Complete fieldwork and review proposed findings with auditee.

CHAPTER FIFTEEN

Workpapers: Documenting Internal Audit Activities

15.1 IMPORTANCE OF WORKPAPERS

Workpapers are the written records kept by an internal auditor that contain the documentation, reports, correspondence, and other sample materials—the evidential matter—gathered or accumulated during the internal audit. The term *workpaper* is a rather archaic auditor expression that describes a physical or computer file that includes the schedules, analyses, and copies of documents prepared as part of an audit. The common characteristic of all workpapers is that they are the evidence used to describe the results of an internal audit. They should be formally retained for subsequent reference and substantiation of reported audit conclusions and recommendations. As a bridge between actual internal audit procedures and the reports issued, workpapers are not an end in themselves but a means to an end. Workpapers are created to fit particular audit tasks and are subject to a great deal of flexibility. They must support and document the purposes and activities of an internal auditor, regardless of their specific form. Thus, workpaper principles and concepts are more important than just their specific formats.

Internal audit workpapers may also have legal significance. In some situations, they have been handed over, through court orders, to government, legal, or regulatory authorities. When scrutinized by outsiders in this context, inappropriate workpaper notes or schedules can easily be taken in the wrong context. They form the documented record of both those who performed the audit and those who reviewed that work. Internal audit workpapers are the only record of that audit work performed, and they may provide future evidence of what did or did not happen in an audit at some point in time.

This chapter provides general guidance for preparing, organizing, reviewing, and retaining workpapers. While once organized in bulky legal-sized paper folders, audit workpapers today are often stored as computer-based folders or as a combination of paper- and computer-format documents. This chapter will provide guidance for the beginning internal auditor on what and what not to collect for workpapers and also will suggest workpaper good practice strategies for internal audit management. As a side note, this chapter as well as other chapters will use the term *workpaper.* Other people have used *working paper* or *work paper.* All mean the same thing.

15.2 FUNCTIONS OF WORKPAPERS

As discussed in Chapter 1, "Foundations of Internal Auditing," internal auditing is an objective-directed process of reviewing selected reports and other forms of business documentation as well as interviewing members of the organization to gather information about an activity gather evidence to support an audit objective. The internal auditor then evaluates the materials examined or information gathered from interviews to determine if the objectives of the audit are being met, such as whether various standards and procedures are being properly followed. Based on this examination, the auditor forms an audit conclusion and opinion that are reported to management, usually in the form of audit findings and recommendations published in an internal audit report, as discussed in Chapter 17, "Audit Reports and Internal Audit Communications." An internal auditor, however, should not just flip through some reports or just casually observe operations to give management some impressions of what was found. The audit evidence, documented in the auditor's workpapers, must be sufficient to support the auditor's assertions and conclusions.

The overall objective of workpapers is to document that an adequate audit was conducted following professional standards. The auditor can perhaps better understand the overall role of workpapers in the audit process by considering the major functions these papers serve:

- *Basis for planning an audit.* Workpapers from a prior audit provide the auditor with background information for conducting a current review in the same overall area. They may contain descriptions of the entity, evaluations of internal control, time budgets, audit programs used, and other results of past audit work.

- *Record of audit work performed.* Workpapers describe the current audit work performed and reference it to an established audit program (see Chapter 14, "Directing and Performing Internal Audits," on preparing audit programs). Even if the audit is of a special nature, such as a fraud investigation where there may not be a formal audit program, a record should be established of the auditing work actually carried out. This workpaper record should include a description of activities reviewed, copies of representative documents, the extent of the audit coverage, and the results obtained.

- *Use during the audit.* In many instances, the workpapers prepared play a direct role in carrying out the specific audit effort. For example, the workpapers can contain various control logs used by members of the audit team for such areas as the controls over responses received as part of an accounts receivable customer balance independent confirmation audit. Similarly, a flowchart might be prepared and then used to provide guidance for a further review of the actual activities in some process. Each of these would have been included in the workpapers in a previous audit step.

- *Description of situations of special interest.* As the audit work is carried out, situations may occur that have special significance in such areas as compliance with established policies and procedures, accuracy, efficiency, personnel performance, or potential cost savings.

- *Support for specific audit conclusions.* The final product of most internal audits is a formal audit report containing findings and recommendations. The documentation supporting the findings may be actual evidence, such as a copy of a purchase order lacking a required signature, or derived evidence, such as the output report from a computer-assisted procedure against a data file or notes from an interview. The workpapers should provide sufficient evidential matter to support the specific audit findings that would be included in an audit report.

- *Reference source.* Workpapers can answer additional questions raised by management or by external auditors. Such questions may be in connection with a particular audit report finding or its recommendation, or they may relate to other inquiries. For example, management may ask internal audit if a reported problem also exists at another location that is not part of the current audit. The workpapers from that review may provide the answer. Workpapers also provide basic background materials that may be applicable to future audits of the particular entity or activity.

- *Staff appraisal.* The performance of staff members during an audit—including the auditor's ability to gather and organize data, evaluate it, and arrive at conclusions—is directly reflected in or demonstrated by the workpapers.

- *Audit coordination.* An internal auditor may exchange workpapers with external auditors, each relying on the other's work. In addition, government auditors, in their regulatory reviews of internal controls, may request to examine the internal auditor's workpapers.

In some respects, audit workpapers are no different from the formal files of correspondence, e-mails, and notes that are part of any well-managed organization. A manager would keep files of incoming and outgoing correspondence, notes based on telephone conversations, and the like. However, these files are based on just good practices and may vary from one manager to another in an organization. The manager may generally never be called on to retrieve these personal files to support some organizational decision or other action.

Internal audit workpapers are different in that they may also be used to support or defend the conclusions reached from the audit. They may be reviewed by others for various reasons. Members of an internal audit organization may work on common projects and need to share workpapers to support their individual components of a larger audit project or to take over an audit performed previously by another member of the audit staff. It is essential that an internal audit department have a set of standards to assure consistent workpaper preparation.

(a) Workpaper Standards

Institute of Internal Auditors (IIA) professional standards, outlined in Chapter 12, "Internal Audit Professional Standards," provide high-level guidance in the preparation and use of audit workpapers through the 2330[1] standard:

> Internal auditors should record relevant information to support the conclusions and engagement results.

This very broad standard is supported by a series of practice advisories that provide additional supporting information on internal audit workpaper issues such as their preparation, control of the documentation, and retention requirements. The actual style and format of workpapers can vary from one internal audit department to another and, to a lesser extent, from one audit to another. An internal audit department should develop its own workpaper standards that are consistent with the IIA standards. The organization's external auditors also may suggest standard workpaper formats that are consistent with theirs; however, internal audit should always recognize the differences between the financial statement attestation work of external auditors and the operational aspects of internal auditing. There may often be no compelling reason to adopt external audit workpaper standards to meet the operational needs of internal audit.

Workpapers are not designed for general reading or as noninternal audit management reports. They are primarily designed to support individual internal audits and will be used by other members of the internal audit function, including management and quality assurance, as well as external auditors and corporate legal functions. The workpapers should follow a consistent set of standards and be able to stand alone so that an authorized outside party, such as an external auditor, can read through them and understand the objectives of the audit, the work performed, and any outstanding issues or findings. From a workpaper standards standpoint, internal audit workpapers should be concerned with the following areas:

- *Relevance to audit objectives.* The workpaper's content must be relevant to both the total audit assignment and the specific objectives of the particular portion of the review. There is no need for materials that do not contribute to the objectives of the specific audit performed.

- *Condensation of detail.* Condensation and careful summarization of detail reduces the bulk of workpapers and makes their later use more efficient. An audit may make use of computer-assisted audit techniques (CAATs), as discussed in Chapter 23, "Computer-Assisted Audit Techniques," to confirm balances on a data file, but it is often not necessary to include the entire CAAT-produced output in the workpapers. A totals summary with test results, some sample details, and a copy of the computer program used may be sufficient.

- *Clarity of presentation.* To present clear and understandable material, auditors and their supervisors should review workpaper presentations on an ongoing basis and make recommendations for improvements.

- *Workpaper accuracy.* Workpaper accuracy is essential for all audit schedules and other quantitative data. Workpapers may be used at any time in the future to answer questions and to substantiate later internal audit representations.

- *Action on open items.* Questions are frequently raised during an audit, as part of the internal auditor's workpaper notes, or information is disclosed that requires follow-up. There should be no open items in workpapers on completion of the audit. All workpaper items should either be cleared or formally documented for future audit actions.

- *Standards of form.* For workpapers to accurately describe the audit work performed, they must be prepared in a consistent format within any audit workpaper and from one to another within the internal audit department. An internal audit manager should, for example, know where to find the auditor hours schedule covering the review in any workpaper reviewed. The standards of form should include:

    o *Preparation of headings.* Individual workpaper pages should have a heading with the title of the total audit, the particular component of that total audit assignment contained in a given workpaper sheet, and the date. A smaller heading on one side should indicate the name or initials of the person who prepared the workpaper and the date of preparation.

    o *Organization.* The use of appropriate headings, spacing, and adequacy of margins facilitates reading and understanding. The auditor might think of this organization along the lines of the manner in which a textbook is organized.

    o *Neatness and legibility.* These qualities not only make the workpapers more useful to all readers, they also confirm the care that went into their preparation.

    o *Cross-indexing.* All workpapers should be indexed and cross-indexed. Cross-indexing provides a trail for the auditor and ensures the accuracy of information in the workpapers, as well as in the subsequent audit report.

(b) Workpaper Formats

As mentioned, workpapers were once lengthy manual documents, handwritten by auditors with samples of any reports and other exhibits included in the package. With the almost pervasive auditor use of laptop computers to develop and document internal audit work, those older manual workpapers are far less common today. Exhibit 15.1 shows a manually prepared workpaper page from an operational audit of a physical inventory observation. Although the exhibit is in a text font that implies manual, handwritten preparation, the same page can be developed through word-processing software. The important point here is this is a brief auditor description of an internal auditor's observations. This form can stand on its own. The workpaper reader can determine the entity it covers, who did the work and when, and how this workpaper sheet relates to others in the audit. This basic format will be used in other figures in this chapter and in examples throughout the book. The internal auditor must be particularly careful to document all work steps and all audit decisions. For example, if an audit program had a work step that the in-charge auditor determined was not appropriate for a given review, the auditor should explain why that step was deleted rather than just marking it "N/A." In some situations, the initials of the audit supervisor who approved the change should also be included. Similarly, if the auditor was following up on a matter from a prior audit, the workpapers should document the manner in which the problem was corrected or else who advised the auditor that it had been fixed. It is not sufficient just to mark it "corrected" with no further references.

The auditor should always remember that situations may change, and the auditor's workpapers may be called into question many years after they have been prepared. It is not unusual for a regulatory agency, such as the Securities and Exchange Commission (SEC), to demand to see a set of workpapers prepared years ago as part of an investigation. They might ask further questions or take other steps based on the audit work and observations recorded in those quite old workpapers. Memories often fade, and in this type of situation the audit workpapers may be the only credible record.

EXHIBIT 15.1

Manually Prepared Workpaper Example

	Exampleco Internal Audit	*RRM*
Ar-2-5.1	*Audit: MAXXAM Plant Inventory Observation*	*3/4/05*
	Location: South Bluff Date: March 4, 2005	

Internal audit observed the taking of finished goods physical inventory at the MAXXAM division plant in South Bluff, OH. We reviewed the physical inventory instructions issued by the plant controller's office (See X-Ref 01) and found them to be complete and satisfactory. Plant personnel started the inventory at 8:00 A.M. on March 3. Internal audit observed that all other activities were shut down during the inventory taking, and that the counting proceeded in an orderly manner.

Worksheets for recording the counts were prepared by ExampleCo's inventory system—they listed the parts assigned to designated store locations but with no actual quantities (See X-Ref 02). A representative from the plant controller's office headed the control desk, issued the count sheets, and logged them in upon receipt.

As part of this inventory observation, internal audit selected a series of random stock keeping numbers and independently took test counts. We compared these counts to the counts recorded by the inventory team. Test counts and results were summarized on X-Ref 02. We generally found . . .

15.3 WORKPAPER CONTENT AND ORGANIZATION

As discussed, internal audit workpaper formats will generally be based on word-processing-based files and folders or may be organized as 8½×11–inch sheets secured in three-ring binders. Some may even use the much older format of folders prepared for legal-sized sheets and bound at the top. Today, most internal auditors prepare their workpapers on their laptop computers where many of the auditor commentaries and schedules are maintained in secure files and folders. Regardless of page size or media, the purpose of a workpaper sheet is to provide a standard framework for documenting internal audit activities. As discussed previously, workpaper pages should be titled, dated, initialed by the preparer, and prepared in a neat and orderly manner. While Exhibit 15.1 is a representative workpaper sheet illustrating substance and format standards, an internal audit has many requirements where that example workpaper format will not work. The sections that follow expand on the basic workpaper format.

(a) Workpaper Document Organization

A typical audit will involve gathering a large number of materials to document the audit process. With the wide range of operational activities reviewed and the equally wide range of audit procedures, the form and content of those individual workpapers may vary greatly. The major categories depend on the nature of the audit materials and the work performed. For most internal audits, the workpapers can be separated into the following broad audit areas:

- Permanent files
- Administrative files
- Audit procedures files
- Specialized computer-assisted audit procedures files
- Bulk files of voluminous materials
- Audit reports and follow-up matters

An internal audit department's workpaper standards should be built around these types of files. This chapter refers to these as *files*, while the term *folders* is perhaps more appropriate today, and some internal audit departments still use the older term *binders* to refer to these different workpaper groupings. Just as in any manual filing system, workpaper materials are classified by their basic type and grouped together in a file or bound together in a binder in a manner that aids in their retrieval.

(i) Permanent Files.
Many audits are performed on a periodic basis and follow repetitive procedures. Rather than capture all of the data necessary every time each audit is performed, certain data can be gathered from what is called a permanent workpaper file, which contains data of a *historical or continuing nature* pertinent to current audits. Some of this data may include:

- Overall organization charts of the audit unit
- Charts of accounts (if a financial audit) and copies of major policies and procedures

- Copies of the last audit report, the audit program used, and any follow-up comments
- Financial statements about the entity as well as other potentially useful analytical data
- Information about the audit unit (descriptions of major products, production processes, and other newsworthy matters)
- Logistical information to help the next auditors, including notes regarding logistics and travel arrangements

A permanent file is not meant to be *permanent* in that it will never change; rather, it provides the auditor starting a new assignment a source of background material to help plan the new audit. Chapter 14 discussed the need to review permanent files when planning a new audit. Over the course of a new audit, the supervising auditor may come across other materials to update or include in the permanent file. The permanent file is a source of continuity to tie audits together over time. Exhibit 15.2 shows an index or table of contents from an audit permanent file binder.

Auditors are sometimes guilty of loading up their audit permanent files with materials that do not deserve permanent file status—for example, copies of various procedures that will have changed by the time of the next audit. Materials readily available at the time of the next audit need not be retained in permanent files unless certain ongoing procedures were based on those earlier materials. Similarly, internal auditors sometimes fill up permanent files for out-of-town locations with maps and menus of local restaurants. These units will change as will both individual auditor preferences and department policies. This administrative planning material should be kept to a minimum.

(ii) Administrative Files. Although a separate workpaper administrative file may not be necessary for a smaller audit, the same general administrative

EXHIBIT 15.2

Workpaper Permanent File Index

	ExampleCo Internal Audit MAXXAM Plant Division Permanent File Index	RRM 04/01/05
INDEX	PERMANENT TILES	DATE
A-13	MAXXAM Div. Audit Reports & Responses – 2003	02/01/03
A-14	MAXXAM Div. Audit Reports & Responses – 2004	02/02/04
B-02	MAXXAM Accounting Policy	09/06/99
B-17	MAXXAM Section 404 Documentation Standards	11/06/01
C-01	Product Descriptions – MAXXAM Division	05/02/04
E-12	Press Releases – MAXXAM Division	11/13/04
G-02	Internal Audit Plant Visit Background Notes	09/12/04

workpaper materials should be incorporated somewhere in all audit workpaper sets. If only a single auditor or limited review, this material may be incorporated into the single workpaper.

(iii)   Audit Procedures Files.   These files and folders record the actual audit work performed and vary with the type and nature of the audit assignment. For example, a financial audit may contain detailed spreadsheet schedules with auditor commentary on tests performed. An operational audit may contain interview notes and commentary on auditor observations. This file is generally the largest for any audit. Most internal audit procedure files contain the following elements:

- *Listings of completed audit procedures.*   Workpapers are a central repository documenting the audit procedures, and include copies of the audit programs along with the initials of the auditors and the dates of the audit steps. Commentary notes may be on the programs or attached as cross-referenced supplementary notes. Exhibit 15.3 shows a completed audit program filed in the workpapers.

- *Completed questionnaires.*   Some internal audit functions use standard questionnaires covering particular types of internal control procedures. These questionnaires normally provide for *yes* and *no* answers and appropriate supplementary comments.

EXHIBIT 15.3

Workpaper Audit Program Example		
	ExampleCo Internal Audit Audit: Headquarters Direct Sales	JAS
B25	AUDIT PROGRAM—CASH	10/31/04
Ref.	Audit Procedure	Disposition
1.a	Review sources of reducing difficult-to-control cash conditions.	W/P B.32—JAS 10/30/04
1.b	Determine physical safeguards for providing adequate cash at all stages.	
1.c	Review procedures to keep cash on hand—in all forms and levels.	
2.a	Determine that petty cash and branch funds are utilized and operated on an imprest basis.	W/PB.27—JAS 10/30/04
2.b	Assess adequacy of documentary support for petty or miscellaneous cash disbursements.	
2.c	Review controls surrounding issuance and use of company credit cards.	
3.a	Determine that all employees who handle or have direct or indirect access to cash are adequately bonded.	

- *Descriptions of operational procedures.* Workpapers frequently describe briefly the nature and scope of a specific type of operational activity. This description can provide a basis for later audit management probing and evaluation. It can be in flowchart or narrative form. The auditor should always note on the workpaper the source of information to develop this description. A member of auditee management may have described the process or the auditor may have gathered this information through observation.

- *Review activities.* Many operational audit workpapers cover specific investigations that appraise selected activities. These can include testing of data, observations of performance, inquiries to designated individuals, and the like. This is perhaps the most common type of workpaper prepared by the internal auditor. It follows no one form but only serves to describe the audit activities performed and the results. Exhibit 15.4 shows a workpaper covering tests of an audit of travel and entertainment expenses.

- *Analyses and schedules pertaining to financial statements.* In a financially oriented audit, a special variety of workpapers relates to attesting to the accuracy of financial statement or account balances. This type of workpaper schedule is an appropriate documentation for the Section 404 reviews discussed in Chapter 6, "Evaluating Internal Controls: Section 404

EXHIBIT 15.4

Travel Audit Workpaper Example

	ExampleCo Internal Audit	
	Audit: Headquarters Travel & Entertainment	RRM
Z12.4.	Location: Headquarters Date: October 14, 2005	10/14/05

Internal audit reviewed a sample of employee travel and entertainment reports filed during the third quarter. During that period, 987 reports were filed. We selected a sample of 45 reports for our review based on the following criteria:

✓ All reports for the 6 senior officers—16 reports reviewed

✓ Reports involving international travel—2 reports reviewed

✓ All other reports having total reported expenses > $2,000—7 reports reviewed

✓ A sample of the remaining reports filed—27 reports reviewed

Our review was based on ExampleCo travel and entertainment procedures dated 11/11/05 (See X-Ref Z-12-2.3). We reviewed the sample reports for the following criteria:

♦ Reported expenses within policy guidelines

♦ Use of the company credit card where appropriate

♦ Use of company designated air and rental cars

♦ Appropriate levels of management approvals

The results of this review were summarized on . . .

Assessments." Exhibit 15.5 is such a workpaper schedule. Fairness and accuracy statements may also include:

o Schedules relating to particular general ledger accounts

o Analyses of individual accounts, such as accruals

o Details of backup data and supporting physical counts

o Results of specific kinds of verification

o Explanations of adjustments to accounts

o Notes as to pertinent supplementary information

o Summaries of statement balances and adjustments

- *Organizational documents.* There are often basic organization documents such as organization charts, minutes of meetings, particular policy statements or procedures, copies of contracts, and the like. While some of these might be more appropriate for the permanent file, others are unique to a particular audit. However, the internal auditor often does not have to not include all material in the workpapers. For example, it may be sufficient to include a table of contents and have relevant extracts rather than incorporating an entire procedures manual in the workpapers. The purpose of these documents is to help future auditors in their decisions or processes.

- *Findings point sheets or drafts of reports.* Point sheets describing the nature of the audit finding as well as reference to the detailed audit work should be included in audit procedures files even though a copy has been forwarded to the administrative file. A workpaper point sheet is shown in Exhibit 15.7. For smaller audits that do not have an administrative file, several draft versions of the written report should be included. These drafts can be annotated to show major changes, the persons responsible for authorizing those changes, and in some cases the reasons for the changes.

- *Supervisor's notes.* During an audit, the in-charge auditor or audit supervisor prepares review comments that may require explanation by the auditor. In some cases, further audit work may be needed. Exhibit 15.8 is an example of such a review sheet.

- *Audit bulk files.* Internal audits often produce large amounts of evidential materials, which should be retained but not included in the primary workpapers. For example, internal audit may perform a survey that results in a large number of returned questionnaires. These materials should be classified as workpapers but should be retrieved from the bulk file as necessary.

Workpapers are the method of documentation for communication within the audit department from one audit or auditor to the next. They are also a means of communication with the organization's external auditors. An internal audit department should establish some overall standards covering the style, format, and content of the workpapers used in various audits. Some specific details do

EXHIBIT 15.5

Financial Audit Workpaper Example

MAXXAM, Inc.
Working Trial Balance—Balance
Sheet
December 31, 20XX

Prepared by: RRM   Date: 2/10/X1
Reviewed by: LCT   Date: 2/18/X1

W/P Ref.	Acct. No.	Description	Ledger Bal. 12/31/X0	Ledger Bal. 12/31/X1	Adj. Ref.	Debit (Credit)	Final Balance 12/31/X1
					Adjustments		
A–23	153	Cash	392,000	427,000	Z22	50,000	477,000
B–12	170	Marketable Securities	52,200	62,200			62,200
B–14	181	Receivables (net)	1,601,400	1,715,000	Z23.1	(50,000)	1,665,000
C–02	240	Inventories	2,542,500	2,810,200	Z32	133,000	2,943,200
D–12	275	Prepaid Expenses	27,900	19,500			19,500

not need to be "frozen" given the various types of audits performed and evolving audit automation procedures, as discussed later. However, workpaper contents should be prepared consistently for all audits. The audit procedures workpaper file, for example, should contain materials covering each of the above areas.

(b) Computer-Assisted Audit Techniques Workpapers

Workpapers for computer-assisted audit techniques (CAATs) usually take a different approach than that for more conventional internal audits. While there are many different approaches to use automated procedures and to perform audit tests, the approaches discussed in Chapter 23, "Computer-Assisted Audit Techniques," represent some of the more typical types of CAATs. With a CAAT, a series of specialized, auditor-developed routines is being used to survey files, perform recalculations, or perform some other audit test and analysis procedures. This work should be workpaper documented in the same manner as any other internal audit procedures.

CAATs require a specialized auditor-developed or -controlled software routines to analyze some other automated files or records. The integrity of the results from any CAAT is highly dependent on the internal auditor being able to assert that a controlled and properly tested version of the auditor's software was used for the audit work. For very simple audit-retrieval software, the workpapers could contain a listing of the actual program code used as well as some evidence, such a clip from the file Properties[2] description of all files used in the CAAT. This should support the internal auditor if there are any questions about the results of the CAAT procedures.

The CAAT workpapers should have a fairly detailed description of when the CAAT was run, any problems encountered during the processing and the analysis performed to ask questions or verify the results from the CAAT tests. There should always be narrative workpaper descriptions of the overall CAAT process. Exhibit 15.6 lists some considerations for documenting internal audit CAATs.

EXHIBIT 15.6

Computer-Assisted Audit Techniques Workpaper Requirements

1. Provide a description of the application and process being tested. A flowchart from the Section 404 documentation would support this.

2. Describe the software tool used for the computer-assisted audit techniques (CAAT). If it is standard vendor software, the name and version should be sufficient. If it consists of internal audit–developed routines, include detailed documentation.

3. Describe the audit objectives of the CAAT, including files to be accessed and key cutoff dates.

4. Document the CAAT software for audit workpaper purposes. Include program code, macro instructions, sample screen prints, and other materials necessary to describe procedures.

5. Provide documentation of CAAT tests performed.

6. Provide a schedule of the actual CAAT processes with documentation to support the claim that proper files and versions were used.

7. Include examples from the actual CAAT outputs, including reconciliation to determine that correct input files were used.

8. Include cross-references from CAAT procedures to any other related internal audit work.

In many respects, the internal audit documentation of computer-assisted procedures should follow the same general workpaper preparation and documentation processes described throughout this chapter.

Just like regular audit workpapers, CAAT workpapers should be able to stand on their own. This is often a more difficult task for the specialist preparing them, because they may contain technical matters not readily understood by outsiders. The internal auditor must exercise care to describe and document all CAAT procedures properly.

15.4 WORKPAPER PREPARATION TECHNIQUES

Much of the process of preparing workpapers involves drafting audit comments and developing schedules to describe audit work to support audit conclusions. This is a detailed process that requires that an internal auditor follow the overall audit department standards for the preparation of workpapers, and also to make the workpapers easy to follow and understand. An important aspect is to ensure that all members of the internal audit staff have an understanding of the purposes and the criticality of their audit workpapers. They will be reviewed by internal audit management and others, who may question the type and extent of the work performed based on whatever is documented in the workpapers. This section discusses some of the basic techniques needed for preparing adequate workpapers. These comments are largely based on the more common laptop-prepared workpapers of today but also include the older, manually prepared workpapers used by auditors in many past years. Whether prepared manually or using a computer-based system, audit workpapers should be prepared with certain indexing and notation standards that will allow for easy review by other interested audit professionals.

(a) Workpaper Indexing and Cross-Referencing

Similar to reference notations in textbooks, sufficient cross-references and notations should allow an auditor or reviewer to take a significant reference and trace it back to its original citation or source. For example, a workpaper document describing a financial review of fixed assets might mention that the automated system that calculates depreciation has adequate controls. It is sufficient to provide a cross-reference so that the interested reader could easily find those depreciation computation controls when reviewing the workpapers.

Index numbers on workpapers are the same as volume and page numbers in a published book. Exhibit 15.1 shows a workpaper page with an index number, often placed in the upper-left corner. That number should also tie into a table of contents, which usually appears on the first page of the workpaper folder or manual binder. The number identifies the specific page in the specific workpaper binder. References to this number elsewhere in the audit allow an auditor to select immediately the correct workpaper binder and page. The system used for index numbers in a set of workpapers can be as simple or complex as desired. Many internal audit departments adopt the same general indexing system used by their external auditors so that all members of the audit staff can understand the correct reference to a volume in a given workpaper set. A method for indexing manually prepared internal audit workpapers might follow a set of three digits so that "AP-5-26" would mean the

26th page section of the 5th step in a given set of audit procedures. If multiple pages were required for page 26, they would be expressed as AP-5-26.01, -26.02, and so forth. Any numbering system should be easy to use and adaptable to change.

Cross-referencing refers to placing other reference workpaper index numbers within a given workpaper schedule. For example, a workpaper schedule may discuss controls over fixed-asset additions and state that all additions above some specified limit receive proper approval by management. That workpaper statement would parenthetically reference another workpaper index number denoting fixed-asset tests and indicating evidence of management approvals. Cross-reference numbers are particularly important in financial audits where all numbers on various schedules should be tied together to ensure consistency.

(b) Tick Marks

Going back to the days of manually prepared audit workpapers, auditors often prepare a financial or statistical schedule and then selected various numbers from that schedule to perform one or more additional tests. For example, an auditor may review a sample of purchase orders to determine if they (1) represent vendors on the approved list, (2) are subject to competitive bids, (3) are computed correctly, and so forth. Rather than list this sample of purchase orders on multiple workpaper sheets for each of the tests, auditors normally use one schedule and employ what are called *tick marks* to footnote various tests performed.

Tick marks are a form of auditor manual or pencil shorthand notation that have evolved over the years, particularly for financial audits. An auditor can develop a particular check mark to indicate that a given value on the financial schedule cross-foots to other related values and another tick mark to indicate that it ties to the trial balance. The auditor need only note somewhere in the workpapers the tick mark used for each. Rather than asking the auditor to develop a legend, many internal audit departments used a standard set of tick mark symbols in all workpapers. For example, a check mark with a line through it may mean that the workpaper item was traced to a supporting schedule and the numbers tied. These standard tick marks should be used by all members of the audit staff for all audits.

Standard tick marks improve communication because audit management can easily review and understand workpapers. Exhibit 15.7 illustrates a set of

EXHIBIT 15.7

Workpaper Auditor Tick-Marks Examples

✓-	Agreed to mm/dd/yy workpapers
≋	Confirmed with maker of transaction—no exceptions
✓	Examined during audit procedures
ℱ	Footed
ℱℱ	Footed and cross-footed
∧	Traced to ledger balance
CR	Traced to cash receipts deposit slips
ℒ	Verified computation

traditional tick marks that were used in the pencil and paper days. Today, these same symbols may not be available through Microsoft Word, but similar special characters can be designated for the same purpose. In developing these tick marks, the internal audit department might want to adopt the notation used by its external auditors. Of course, the auditor might develop another mark to indicate some other type of cross-check performed in the course of an individual audit, which would then be clearly explained.

(c) References to External Audit Sources

Internal auditors often record information taken from outside sources. For example, an auditor may gather an understanding of an operational area through an interview with a member of management. The auditor would record that interview through workpaper notes and rely on what was told to the auditor as the basis of further audit tests or conclusions. It is always important to record the source of such commentary directly in the workpapers. For example, a workpaper exhibit could show how the auditor gained an understanding of a sample system. The source that provided that information to the auditor should be documented.

Auditors may need to reference an external law or regulation to support their audit work. Similarly, they may perform a vendor-related review and access a telephone book to verify vendor existence. It is usually not necessary to include in the workpapers a copy of what may be a voluminous regulation, nor a copy of a page from the telephone book. However, workpapers should clearly indicate the title and source of all external references, including the net address, if appropriate. Extract page copies can be included to make a specific point when necessary, but a reference notation is normally sufficient.

(d) Workpaper Rough Notes

When conducting interviews, internal auditors often make very rough notes, often written in a personal form of shorthand easily readable only by the auditor. Auditors subsequently should rewrite or reenter these rough notes into the workpaper commentary. Because there may be a reason to re-review them, these original note sheets should also be included in the workpapers, placed in the back of the workpaper manual binder or even in a separate file.

Historically, most workpapers were prepared in pencil. Schedules were recorded on accounting spreadsheet forms, commentaries were written in longhand, and any exhibits were attached. Many internal audit departments have now automated their workpapers through the use of spreadsheet and word-processing software. This automation does not change the workpaper standards; it usually makes the workpapers easier to read and to access. The typical workpaper today may use a mix of manual and automated schedules and audit commentaries. However, today's workpaper is usually a computer systems folder with some references to paper documents.

Technology is rapidly changing, and we may be seeing different formats of audit evidence supporting audit workpapers in future years. Digital image scanners are very common today. They can be passed over a paper document, creating a digital image of that document for later audit evidence retrieval. Similarly, some computers are now equipped with a pen stylus for the user to "write" directly on the computer screen. The data is captured in computer files. These and other evolving technologies offer opportunities for audit workpaper automation. Evolving technologies and the internal auditor of the future are briefly discussed in Chapter 30, "Future of the Modern Internal Auditor."

15.5 WORKPAPER REVIEW PROCESS

All workpapers should go through an independent internal audit review process to ensure that all necessary work has been performed, that everything is properly described, and that audit findings are adequately supported. The chief audit executive (CAE) has the overall responsibility for this review but usually delegates that work to supervisory members of the internal audit department. Depending on the size of the audit staff and the relative importance of a given audit, there may be multiple reviews of a set of workpapers, one by the in-charge auditor and another by a more senior member of internal audit management.

Evidence of this supervisory review should consist of the reviewer's initials and dates on each workpaper sheet reviewed. Some internal audit functions prepare a memorandum or workpaper review checklist to document the nature and extent of their reviews. In any case, there should be documented evidence that all workpapers have received a proper level of supervisory review. In addition to initialing completed workpapers, the supervisory reviewer should prepare a set of review notes with any questions raised during the review process to give to the responsible auditor for resolution. Some of these review points or questions may simply highlight clerical errors such as missing cross-references. Others may be of a more significant nature and may require the auditor to do some additional follow-up work. Review questions should be cleared promptly, and the reviewer should take the responsibility to ensure that all open questions are

EXHIBIT 15.8

Workpaper Supervisor Review Example

A.4.2	ExampleCo Internal Audit Audit: Axylotl Plant Production Control Workpaper Review Notes	RRM 11/08/05
W/P Ref.	Supervisor Review Notes	Auditor Action
B-12, C-21	Missing W/P X-references.	Corrected
B-16	Schedule does not crossfoot to D-02 Summary. Please revise or correct.	OK—See D-02.1
D-20	Does the ref. point to a larger control problem?	
D-21	W/P sheet was not signed or dated.	Corrected
D-36	Evidence does not support your recommendation—clarify!	See D36.3
D-41 to 5	Missing W/P X-references.	Corrected
—	Where is the X-Cat software located?	See XCM binder

resolved. This workpaper review process should *always* take place prior to the issuance of the final audit report. This will ensure that all report findings have been properly supported by audit evidence as documented in the workpapers. Exhibit 15.8 is an example of an audit supervisor's workpaper review notes. This exhibit shows a manual type of paper report, but such a report today may be done through Word files using its change-tracking facilities.

15.6   WORKPAPER OWNERSHIP, CUSTODY, AND RETENTION

Audit workpapers are the property of the overall organization and the audit committee, but they should generally remain under the custody of the internal audit department. Access to these workpapers should be controlled by the internal audit department and be limited to only authorized individuals. Management and other members of the organization may request access to workpapers to substantiate or explain an audit finding, but that workpaper should only be reviewed in a supervised manner. Internal audit can share copies of certain documentation with others but never give them the complete workpaper folder to copy or modify. In other instances, noninternal auditors may wish to utilize documentation prepared in the workpapers for other business purposes. In all events, however, the internal audit department should approve these requests and maintain control over the process.

Internal and external auditors will typically grant access to each other's audit workpapers. While this access should always be approved by both sets of audit management, it is often a useful way to increase overall audit efficiency. There is often no reason, for example, for the external auditor to review a given area if such a review has been adequately performed by internal auditors and if the external auditors can rely on that work through a workpaper review. These matters were discussed in Chapter 10, "Working with External Auditors," on coordination with external auditors.

As discussed previously, there may be circumstances when legal or regulatory authorities request access to audit workpapers or reports. Prior to any release, internal audit should obtain formal approval from senior management and/or legal counsel as appropriate. This type of potential exposure illustrates the importance of internal audit workpapers to the organization and why they should be prepared with due care. Internal audit will most frequently encounter this legal requirement when there is some type of lawsuit against the auditor's organization and the other side obtains the right to perform a discovery review of various items of documentation. The organization may be faced with a court order to hand over copies of all workpapers, correspondence, and other documentation covering a certain matter. While this process is more common with external auditors, internal audit also must comply with such a court order. It can make copies but must otherwise turn over files for legal review.

When internal audit is forced into this situation, the importance of workpaper quality and appropriate supervisory reviews becomes evident. Internal auditors may be subsequently asked to testify, under oath, why they made a statement or ignored an obvious error documented in their workpapers. Audit managers may be asked to explain why they initialed workpapers containing a probable limited review or what later appear to be obvious errors. Formal internal audit retention policies for all audit workpapers should be consistent with the organization's guidelines and any legal or other requirements that affect the organization. Care should be taken that older workpapers can be fairly easily retrieved and are given adequate protection from fire or other hazards.

Audit workpapers, along with the resultant audit reports, are the key tangible output products of internal auditors. Because the workpapers support the final audit reports, adequate audit reports are not possible without adequate supporting workpapers. Internal auditors often encounter auditees who have failed to document some system or process. This often results in an audit report finding. The same internal auditor, however, may be guilty of a similar type of control weakness by failing to prepare adequate audit workpapers. This will be revealed if the internal audit department goes through a quality assurance review, as discussed in Chapter 26, "Internal Audit Quality Assurance and ASQ Quality Audits." However, the best way to establish a level of confidence that workpapers are prepared adequately and in accordance with department standards is to ensure that internal audit management performs adequate levels of reviews of all internal audit workpapers.

ENDNOTES

[1] IIA standards are summarized in Chapter 12, "Internal Audit Professional Standards," and complete information regarding them can be obtained through www.theiia.org.

[2] Properties are a Microsoft Word option that show where a file resides, its size, and when it was created, modified, and last used.

CHAPTER SIXTEEN

Gathering Evidence through Audit Sampling

16.1 AUDIT SAMPLING TO IMPROVE RESULTS AND EFFICIENCY

Internal auditors make assessments about audit issues or satisfy their audit objectives through detailed reviews of the audit evidence. That evidence sometimes consists of a limited set of files or reports where the internal auditor reviews the entire set or population of data to develop audit conclusions. A review of equipment contracts for a small manufacturing organization may not involve more than a very limited number of items where the auditor can perform a 100% review of the audit evidence, the equipment contract records. This approach is much more difficult when internal audit is faced with a large population of items to examine—hundreds, thousands, or even more.

In the early days of internal auditing, 100% examinations of transactions or documents were commonly performed to test compliance with control procedures. As organizations grew larger and more complex, this 100% examination approach was often not feasible, so auditors examined a portion of the transactions. Because of the large computerized files of invoices, reports, inventory items, and other documents to be reviewed, internal auditors would typically select a sample to develop an audit conclusion. In addition, they needed some way to review these large masses of computerized data. There is a major internal audit challenge here. Internal audit needs a consistent approach to statistically sample a portion of a large population of data and then to draw audit conclusions based on the results of that limited sample.

This first audit sampling challenge requires having procedures that allow an internal auditor to extract a sample representative of the entire population. If there are 100,000 transactions and if an internal auditor only looks at 50 of them, finding 10 exceptions (20% of the sample), can the auditor conclude that 20% of the entire population of transactions, or 20,000, are exceptions? This audit conclusion is true only if the sample of 50 drawn is representative of the entire population. Audit sampling techniques can help an internal auditor determine an appropriate sample size and develop an opinion for this type of audit task.

Audit sampling has two major branches: statistical and nonstatistical. Statistical sampling is a mathematical-based method of selecting representative items that reflect the characteristics of the entire population. Using the results of audit tests on the statistically sampled items, an internal auditor can express an opinion on the entire group. For example, an auditor could develop a statistical sample of items in an inventory, test those items in that sample for their physical quantity or value, and then express an opinion on the value or accuracy of the entire inventory. Nonstatistical sampling, also called judgmental sampling, is not supported by mathematical theory and does not allow an auditor to express *statistically precise* opinions on the entire population. Nevertheless, nonstatistical or judgmental sampling is often a useful audit tool.

16.2 AUDIT SAMPLING DECISION

When planning an audit that includes the examination of a large number of transactions or other evidence, an internal auditor should always ask the question, "Should I use audit sampling?" The correct answer here is often not just a simple yes or no but may be complicated by such factors as the number or nature of items to be sampled, a lack of technical expertise or computer software availability to do the sampling, a "fear" of the mathematical focus of sampling, and the potential nonacceptance of sampling results by management. "Sampling" also is an expression that is often misused by auditors. All too often, an internal auditor will be faced with a file cabinet filled with hundreds of documents to review. The auditor will pull out one or two from the front and perform audit procedures based on this limited selection. This very examination of two items may be certainly all right. However, the auditor often should not try to draw conclusions for the entire population based on that limited sample. To effectively perform this type of examination, auditors need a process where they:

- Understand the total population of items of concern and develop a formal sampling plan regarding the population of items

- Draw a sample from the population based on that sampling selection plan

- Evaluate the sampled items against audit objectives

- Develop conclusions for the entire population based on audit sample results

These steps represent the process of audit sampling. Another very good definition of audit sampling can be found in a somewhat old and now out of print AICPA handbook:[1]

> Audit sampling is the application of an audit procedure to less than 100 percent of the items within an account balance or class of transactions for the purpose of evaluating some characteristic of the balance or class.

Audit sampling is really a formal process of pulling a sample and drawing some form of conclusion for the entire population based on the sample's audit results. Audit sampling can often be a very attractive and effective option for internal auditors.

Why use audit sampling? Internal auditors often hear reports on the results of statistical sampling techniques in consumer research, government studies, or in the quality-control testing on a production assembly line. Audit sampling can be a very effective tool for internal auditors as well. While 100% examinations of audit evidence work for limited amounts of audit evidence is possible, internal audit almost always finds itself looking at a sample—either very large or small—of the audit evidence. The internal auditor then draws an audit conclusion based on the results of the sample. With formal audit sampling, internal audit can draw a conclusion along the lines of, "Based on the results of our audit sample, we are 98% certain the true inventory balance is between X and Y." This type of statement and process will be discussed in greater detail in the paragraphs following.

Formal audit sampling can be a powerful tool. With education and some practice, internal auditors can easily and effectively begin to use audit sampling. Whenever an internal auditor needs to draw conclusions based on a population of multiple items but does not want to examine the entire population, audit sampling can introduce better and more efficient audits. The following are reasons that encourage the use of audit sampling and statistical sampling in particular:

- *Conclusions May Be Drawn Regarding an Entire Population of Data.* If a statistical sampling method is used, information can be accurately projected over the entire population without performing a 100% check on the population, no matter how large. For example, an internal auditor may be interested in the occurrence of some error condition in a large volume of incoming product freight bills. The auditor could select a statistical sample of these freight bill documents, test the sample for the error condition, and then be able to make a 98% certain type of estimate about the occurrence of that error condition in the entire population of freight bills. This technique typically will result in a strong audit position and significant audit savings.

- *Sample Results Are Objective and Defensible.* Internal control errors often occur on a random basis over the total items subject to error, and each error condition should have an equal opportunity of selection in a random sample. An audit test based on random selection is thus objective and even defensible in a court of law. Conversely, a sample based on auditor judgment could be distorted due to intentional or unintentional bias in the selection process. An auditor looking for potential problems might examine only the larger or sensitive items, ignoring others.

- *Less Sampling May Be Required with the Use of Audit Sampling.* Using mathematics-based statistics, auditors need not increase the size of a sample directly in proportion to increases in the size of the population to be sampled. Even though a sample of 60 items may be needed to express an audit opinion over a population of 500 items, that same sample of 60 may still be sufficient for a population of 5,000. An internal auditor who does not use statistical approaches often will oversample large populations because of the incorrect belief that larger populations require proportionately larger samples. As a result of using statistics-based sampling procedures, less testing may be required.

- *Statistical Sampling May Sometimes Provide for Greater Accuracy than a 100% Test.* When voluminous amounts of data items are counted in their entirety, the risk of significant clerical or audit errors increases. However, a small sample will typically receive very close scrutiny and analysis. The more limited sample would be primarily subject only to sampling errors resulting from the statistical projection.

- *Audit Coverage of Multiple Locations Is Often More Convenient.* Audits can be performed at multiple locations with small samples being taken at individual sites to complete an overall sampling plan. In addition, an audit using comprehensive statistical sampling may be started by one auditor and subsequently continued by another. Each of their sample results can be combined to yield one set of audit results.

- *Sampling Procedures Can Be Simple to Apply.* In years past, an internal auditor often was required to use tables published in sampling manuals or to use complex computer systems to develop a sampling plan and sample selection. With the availability of laptop-computer-based software packages, audit sampling has been simplified. The sampling tools and techniques discussed in this chapter should help to explain the process for internal auditors.

Despite the advantages of audit sampling, an internal auditor must keep in mind that *exact information* cannot be obtained about a population of items based on just a sample, whether it be judgmental or statistical. It is only through making a 100% test and following good audit procedures that an internal auditor can obtain exact information. With nonstatistical, judgmental sampling, information is only obtained about those items examined. With statistical sampling, regardless of the number of items examined, positive information can be obtained about all of the items in the population within a level of statistical confidence. The sections following will discuss both judgmental and statistical audit sampling—both important internal audit tools. In addition, the discussion on statistical sampling provides guidance on attributes, monetary unit, and variables sampling techniques as well as other techniques for internal auditor use.

16.3 INTERNAL AUDIT JUDGMENTAL SAMPLING

Although this book promotes a more statistical audit sampling approach for many internal audits, nonstatistical judgmental sampling often is a very appropriate internal audit procedure in many situations. As its name implies, this approach requires an internal auditor to use his or her best judgment to design and select a sample. No statistical decision rules are used and the auditor only selects a sampling plan approach that will provide a large enough sample to test the audit objectives, such as whether the internal controls reviewed are operating properly or if the procedures examined are being followed. Judgmental sampling requires an internal auditor to select a representative sample of items in a population of data or transactions for audit review. The sample is something less than 100% of the entire population of items included in the review but should be sufficient for internal audit to report on overall audit conclusions based on those sample results. For internal auditors, the methods for a judgmental sample selection may take many forms, including:

- *Fixed Percentage Selection.* An examination of a fixed percentage—such as 10%—of the items or dollars in an audit population. These sample items are then often selected haphazardly, with the auditor opening a file drawer, for example, and selecting every one or two account files until the desired sample size is met.

- *Designated Attribute Selection.* A selection of all or part of the items active during a time period, such as one month in an audit covering a year's transactions. Alternatively, an auditor could select all items having a common characteristic, such as all accounts ending in a particular letter of the alphabet, as part of a review of vendor invoices.

- *Large Value Selection.* A selection for audit review of just those items with large monetary or other significant balances.

- *Designated Area Selection.* An examination of only items readily available, such as those stored in a particular file drawer. Such sample items may be selected because they looked "interesting."

- *Other Selected Attribute Selection.* A review of only sensitive items or items with some other attribute of audit concern. In a review for inactive or obsolete inventory items, an auditor might select for review only those items that appear to be dusty or located in out-of-way locations in the inventory stores area.

Although useful data may be obtained from judgmental samples, the results can be misleading or inaccurate regarding overall conclusions about the whole population or account. An internal auditor may look at the accuracy of finance charges for the largest 10% of some accounts under the assumption that these are the most significant. Even though no significant problems were found for the 10% sampled, the auditor will not know of any significant control problems over the remaining accounts representing the other 90%. Similarly, an internal auditor can select a dusty corner of a storage space in a search for obsolete inventory. The items found in that area are probably candidates to scrap and an audit comment, but they cannot be assumed to represent the level of obsolescence throughout the facility.

When planning a review based on judgmental samples, an internal auditor must make three audit judgmental sampling decisions. First, the internal auditor must develop a method of selection, and decide what types of items to examine. Internal auditors can be subject to criticism if problems are encountered later that were not included in the sample selection. An examination of all account names starting with the arbitrary first letters A and M will not reveal a problem for an account with an account name starting with S.

The size of the sample is the second audit judgment decision. Auditors sometimes incorrectly select only two or three items located off the top of the deck, review them, and develop conclusions on the audit results are based on this very limited and unrepresentative audit sample. This can be misleading, and the managers who receive internal audit report findings often assume that a far larger sample was reviewed. The sample size should be reasonable compared to the entire population. Too small of a sample will not represent the overall population, while a too large sample may be too time-consuming or otherwise expensive to evaluate.

The third decision is how to interpret and report the audit results from the limited judgmental sample. An internal audit review of excess and obsolete inventory that selects 20 dusty and dirty items from the stores area, and finds that 10 are obsolete, should not then conclude that 50% of the entire inventory is obsolete based on that sample. The bulk of the stores inventory may be active and appear to be clean. If those active items were not considered in the selection, conclusions from the judgmental sample may be inaccurate. Even though 50% of the dusty and dirty items examined may be obsolete, this does not mean that *the entire* inventory is obsolete. The results from a judgmental sample must be stated very carefully. Exhibit 16.1 provides examples of some ambiguous audit report conclusions based on incomplete judgmental samples. All of these examples point out that the findings were based on some level of judgmental sample. The problem here is that auditors frequently refer to their audit sample and draw conclusions from the results even though there has been little statistical support for these sample conclusions.

(a) Judgmental Sampling Example

Judgmental sampling is often an effective audit technique because there are often instances where it is impractical to take statistically correct samples. Time and other logistical constraints may prevent a true random sample where every item in the population class should be given an equal chance of selection. A

EXHIBIT 16.1

Judgmental Sampling Problem Audit Findings

Finding 1: Based on our sample of inventory items, we found three items that were incorrectly labeled. Controls need to be improved to …

What's Wrong Here: No reference to the number of items in the inventory, the size of the sample, or the implications of the sample results.

Finding 2: Based on our statistical sample of accounts receivable accounts, we found …

What's Wrong Here: No reference to what is meant by a "statistical sample" and how the conclusion was developed.

Finding 3: We found seven incorrectly valued items in our sample of fixed asset items; based on the results of our sample, we recommend …

What's Wrong Here: Again, no clarification on what is meant by "items in our sample."

well-thought-out judgmental sample allows an internal auditor to draw meaningful conclusions based on a limited sample.

As an example where a judgmental sample is often particularly appropriate, consider an internal auditor working for a large convenience store chain called Quick Bite Stores, with 1,400 units located throughout the United States and Canada and where about 15% of the units have relatively large sales volumes. All units, both large and small, are widely scattered geographically, with some in such places as Hawaii, Alaska, Puerto Rico, and Nova Scotia. The demographics of these units are described in Exhibit 16.2. Although the stores are organizationally divided into nine separate regions, many controls and procedures are administered centrally from the Phoenix, Arizona, headquarters. Corporate-developed internal control procedures are the same, whether for a large or small unit. Due to some reported internal control problems, management has requested that internal audit test store compliance with certain procedures at

EXHIBIT 16.2

Quick Bite Store Demographics

Region	Total Units	Large Units
NW U.S. & Alaska	131	12
SW U.S. & Hawaii	239	122
Mountain States	194	6
SE U.S. & Puerto Rico	86	36
Midwest U.S.	162	0
New England	249	23
Western Canada	168	9
Central Canada	103	0
Eastern Canada	68	2
	1400	210

various remote locations and provides the results of its audit at an upcoming board meeting.

From past audits, internal audit knows that individual store compliance with various centrally directed procedures will vary. Those units close to headquarters receive more frequent management visitors, and store compliance is often well implemented. Those in remote locations may not always follow the rules as closely. To comply with management's request, internal audit would want to review a representative sample of all units throughout the United States and Canada. One approach would be to take a statistical sample from a population of all of the units. First, internal audit could decide on a sample size and then randomly select the units to be visited. This approach has several potential problems if internal audit wants to present some meaningful conclusions to Quick Bite management:

- Although management has requested that all units be reviewed, internal audit knows that more attention should be given to the 210 larger units. If a true random sample selection approach is used, the sample selection might not include enough of the larger units to satisfy management. While there are formal statistical justifications to resolve this, service to management concerns call for internal audit to design a sample that emphasizes the larger units.

- Audit travel and time logistics must be considered when selecting the units to review, and a random draw might include some of the more difficult-to-reach locations (such as both Alaska and Puerto Rico in the same random draw). Although geographically distant locations might be eliminated, internal audit still might want to review a representative sample across all of Quick Bite's territories. While there are statistical approaches to stratify the population across locations as well as by size, the statistical selection mathematics becomes complex.

Given the above situation, an internal auditor might develop a sampling plan that would examine an arbitrarily selected judgmental sample. The internal auditor might arbitrarily decide to visit 4% (or 56) of the total Quick Bite units, with six or seven units reviewed in each of the nine regional areas in the United States and Canada. Geographically distant locations, such as Hawaii and Alaska, would be eliminated from potential selection for logistical reasons. Internal audit might then decide to visit two larger units in each of the regions where there are larger units. Having developed this sampling plan, internal audit should discuss this plan with management to make certain they understand and accept the sampling approach. There is no statistical precision behind this selection approach, just good auditor judgment.

There could be true random draw in the selection of larger units from each of the regions with larger units by placing names of each larger unit within a region in a box and drawing two. Some judgmental bias could technically be introduced into this process. Assume that there are three larger units in the Seattle area with another nine scattered throughout the northwest United States and Alaska. If the random draw by region happened to select two of the larger

Seattle units (possible with a true random draw), internal audit might reject one of the Seattle units and select another to give a more representative selection from this region. The point to remember is that this is a *judgmental sample.* If the internal auditor assigned to the Midwest region has relatives in the Minneapolis area, there would be no harm in selecting Minneapolis as one of the sites to visit, allowing the assigned auditor to spend an evening with relatives, provided that there is no other reason not to select Minneapolis.

Next, internal audit could select four smaller units from each of the regions where the larger units were selected, as well as six from the two regions with no larger units. Here, auditor travel logistics should be considered. If one larger unit was selected in Seattle and one in the Portland area for the northwestern draw, it might be best to select smaller units that are easily visited as part of a visit to the selected larger units. Random selection techniques might choose a small Quick Bite northwestern-region location (such as eastern Montana or Sitka, Alaska), but it would not be cost- and time-efficient to visit either of these smaller units while also visiting the larger ones in Seattle and Portland; instead, internal audit could take a judgmental sample of two smaller units in each region that are nearby the larger unit selected. Exhibit 16.3 shows this judgmental sampling plan for the northwest and Alaska region.

Internal audit would then use the judgmental sample to perform the planned audit procedures. Although the results will not be based on a truly random sample that can be projected across all of the stores with statistical accuracy, management will generally understand when internal audit makes some arbitrary decisions when developing its sample, such as rejecting certain geographically remote units from the population to be selected, as long as the sample appears to represent the population. Exhibit 16.4 shows some sample findings from this Quick Bite audit report based on these judgmental sampling results. Internal audit has been careful in this example report to qualify the results of the findings and to not suggest they can be easily projected across the remainder of

EXHIBIT 16.3

Quick Bite Northwest Region Judgmental Sample Plan			
Location	Large	Small	Judgemental sample selection
Seattle area	4	29	1 Large + 2 Small
Spokane area	1	13	
Other WA	0	9	
Portland area	4	21	1 Large
Other OR	0	12	
Boise area	1	8	
Other ID	0	6	
Anchorage	2	9	2 Small
Other AK	0	12	
	12	119	2 Large + 4 Small

EXHIBIT 16.4

Quick Bite Stores Audit Findings (Based on a Judgmental Sample Selection)

1. **Store Inventory Controls Need Improvement.** Quick Bite procedures require that each store should take a detailed count of perishable inventory items on a daily basis and should use the summarized results for monthly reporting. We reviewed these procedures at 56 different units throughout the U.S. and Canadian regions. Our sample was judgmentally selected to represent both large and small Quick Bite units. Based on the units visited, we found that perishable inventory procedures are generally not being followed.

2. **Federal Labor Notices Are Not Posted.** The U.S. government requires that certain notices about overtime rules and minimum wages must be posted in all workplaces. We visited two of the 122 large units and four of the 239 small units in the Southeast and Puerto Rico region and found that these signs were generally not posted. While other units in that region may be in compliance with the law, our limited sample indicated that these requirements are not being followed for the region. We did not encounter this problem in the other regions visited.

3. **Cash Count Procedures Are Weak.** Quick Bite procedures call for a formal cash count, including a reconciliation of any differences, for all units. We visited 56 units throughout the organization, including a total of 14 larger units. Based on the units selected, we found that cash count controls are generally good for the larger units but are weak for the others.

the population. Management often is not interested in the statistical integrity of the sample as long as the results appear to represent the entire population. Nonstatistical sampling is useful for many audit situations. However, internal audit should take care to not claim that their audit results are based on a "statistical sample," a term that implies much more precision.

16.4 STATISTICAL SAMPLING: AN INTRODUCTION

Despite the ease of use of nonstatistical sampling, internal auditors often want to project the results of an audit sample over the entire population with a strong degree of accuracy and confidence. This is where statistical sampling becomes a powerful internal audit tool. Based on the rules of probability, statistical sampling is more than simply taking a sample on a random basis, and it requires the use established mathematical selection techniques. The results of statistical sampling can be then projected over the entire population in a manner that will be accepted by the courts, government regulators, and others. Statistical sampling is unfortunately one of those topics that many auditors encountered in an undergraduate college course, finishing the class and hoping to never encounter that subject again!

Statistical sampling was once a fairly complex process for most internal auditors, requiring a high degree of mathematical and computational skills. Today, the process is easier with software tools available to eliminate much of the computational difficulty once encountered. The following sections discuss some of the statistical concepts supporting statistical sampling as well as more common approaches to internal audit statistical sampling. Examples are presented to help an internal auditor more effectively use statistical sampling.

(a) Statistical Sampling Concepts

An important first step for using statistical sampling is to have a general understanding of probability and statistical concepts. While this chapter does not attempt to be a statistics textbook, some basic statistical concepts and terminology are discussed. Although an internal auditor can draw a statistical sample just by following the rules and without the need for an in-depth understanding, interested persons should consult a book on statistical auditing.[2] Some concepts are fairly easy and are used in examples discussed in this chapter. This general understanding is important!

We start with some of the important statistical sampling terms. First, a *random sample* is a process of taking a sample where each unit in a population has an equal probability of selection. When a sample is selected on a random basis from a group or population of transactions, it represents one of many groups of samples that could be selected from the same population. The characteristics of one random sample drawn by an auditor may be different from a sample from the same population drawn by another. To determine how far a sample result differs from that of a 100% test, an internal auditor should have an understanding of the behavior of all possible samples that might be drawn from a population.

It is important to understand the measures of central tendency over data. In audit sampling or statistics, specialized terms such as *average value* are used to describe or measure data. These data measurements are considered in terms of both an example and the mathematical descriptions. While auditors typically encounter much larger populations, consider a population of 25 accounts receivable balances with a total value of $86,345.24 as shown in Exhibit 16.5. Six different measures are commonly used by statisticians to look at the central tendencies of this data or the degree that the various values are dispersed around a central average. The most common measure for looking at data is the statistical measures called the *mean, median*, the *mode*, the *range of data values*, the *variance*, the *standard deviation*, and the *skew-ness of the data*. Although the calculation of these central-tendency measures can be performed today by pressing a function key on the auditor's business calculator, an internal auditor should understand their meaning, use, and how they are calculated.

(i)   The Mean.   The mean is the simple average of the values of items in a population. It is calculated by adding up the total amount in the population of interest—in this example, 25 individual balances for $86,345.24—and then dividing this total by the total number of observed items in the population. The Greek μ symbol is often used to report the mean. In this example, the mean or μ is 86,345.24/25 = $3,453.81.

(ii)   The Median.   The median is the middle amount value when all of the items in the population are ranked by size. Exhibit 16.5 contains a column on the right side, rank, which shows the ranking of each item by its value or size. Item 21 has been ranked as number 1 because it is the smallest value in the population at $35.87. Item 22 is ranked as number 2 because it is the next smallest. The median is calculated by counting the number of individual items in the population

Exhibit 16.5

Sample Population of Accounts Receivables Balances

Item#	A/R Balance	Rank
1	$275.00	3
2	$1,059.25	8
3	$2,564.78	15
4	$9,032.00	22
5	$1,750.00	12
6	$17,110.40	25
7	$1,713.99	11
8	$6,245.32	20
9	$534.89	5
10	$534.89	6
11	$2,564.78	16
12	$1,122.05	9
13	$3,025.88	17
14	$514.99	4
15	$10,554.58	24
16	$1,988.63	13
17	$7,026.50	23
18	$978.00	7
19	$1,654.54	10
20	$3,066.00	18
21	$35.87	1
22	$78.99	2
23	$2,003.00	14
24	$6,995.41	21
25	$3,915.50	19
	$86,345.24	

and selecting the one where 50% are larger and the other 50% are smaller. In this example, item 16 has been ranked as number 13 and $1,988.63 is the median for this population. Twelve items are smaller and twelve larger. The median is rarely the same value as the mean. Here, the median value is smaller than the mean because there are more items of smaller value in the population.

(iii)   The Mode.   The mode is the amount or value that occurs most frequently in a population. In this example, two items—numbers 9 and 10—each have a value of $534.89. The mode is generally not a very meaningful measure of statistics. While sometimes useful with a larger population with many items bunched around the same general values, a mode is more useful when the data is summarized into a histogram. The Exhibit 16.6 histogram for this sample shows that the most common value for the sample data is less than $500.

(iv)   The Range.   The range is the difference between the largest and the smallest values in a population. In this example, the range is the difference between item 6 ($17,110.40) and item 21 ($35.87 or $17,074.53). This measure is primarily useful as an indicator of the breadth of the population data. The range will also be discussed as part of measuring dispersion through what is called the standard deviation.

(v)   Variance.   The variance is a measure of how spread out a distribution is. It is computed as the average squared deviation of each number from its mean. The symbol σ^2, or sigma squared, is often used for the standard deviation For example, for the numbers 1, 2, and 3, the mean is 2 and the variance is the square root of this standard deviation calculation:

$$\sigma^2 = \frac{(1-2)^2 + (2-2)^2 + (3-2)^2}{3} = .667$$

(vi)   Standard Deviation.   Each of the measures discussed until now—such as mean and median—should be fairly easy to understand for most professionals,

EXHIBIT 16.6

Accounts Receivables Balances Histogram

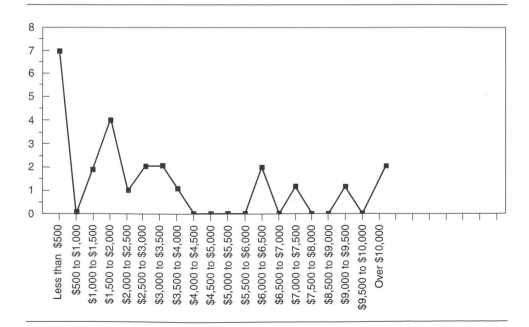

even those who have not had much background in statistics. In contrast, many find the concept of standard deviation more difficult even though it is an important measure of the dispersion or distribution of data around a central mean.

The standard deviation is a measure of the *variability* of values for individual items in a population. The symbol σ, or sigma, is often used for the standard deviation where:

$$\text{Standard Deviation} = \sqrt{\dfrac{\sum\limits_{i=1}^{n}(X_i - \bar{X})^2}{n}}$$

Standard deviation tells the auditor how much variation of values exists around the mean or central point. (See Exhibit 16.7.) One column in Exhibit 16.7 shows the $x_i - X$ differences, and the next shows differences as squared values of those differences. Following the above formula, dividing the sum of these squared differences by the population size minus one (a correction because this is a sample) to compute the standard deviation of $4,045.78.

The properly skeptical internal auditor may ask "What is all of this good for?" Standard deviation, which will be used later in this chapter, is a measure of the central tendency of a normally distributed population of data. Thus, the standard deviation shows how far the items in a population are from the mean or central point. A population of 50 items all with values of about $1,000 each as well as a population of another 50 with average values of less than $1 would have about the same mean value as a different population of 100, with 50 items around $450 and the other 50 of around $550. Although the mean for each would be around $500, they would be very different populations of data, and the standard deviation would help to explain those differences.

(vii) Normal Distributions. A normal distribution is the bell-shaped diagram used to show data; often organized with a few values very high, a few very low, and most in the middle. If a large supply of small pebbles were to be dropped, one by one, onto a flat surface, the pebbles would form in a mound the shape of a bell curve. Much of the data that internal auditors deal with also follows this bell-curve shape. If we look at the population of an average large city and plot the number of people by age, a few will be either very old or newborn at any point in time—with perhaps an equal number less than five years and greater than 90 years—but the average, or mean, age may be about 45. These ages will be distributed into a bell-curve shape or what is called a normal distribution. The assumption that most populations follow a normal distribution is important for internal auditors involved in sampling. Populations of data may take other shapes. In Exhibit 16.8, the distribution marked as A follows this normal distribution where the mean, median, and mode are all the same. Distribution D does not follow that normal curve in shape, while the other two here are skewed either to the right or left.

Standard deviation is a measure of how many items in a population will be disbursed around the central or mean point in a standard distribution. Statistical theory says that 68.2% of a normally distributed population will reside plus or minus one standard deviation around the mean; 95.4% will be within two

EXHIBIT 16.7

Standard Deviation Example Calculations

n	x_i	$x_i - \overline{X}$	$(x_i - \overline{X})^2$
1	275.00	(3,178.81)	10,104,833.02
2	1,059.25	(2,394.56)	5,733,917.59
3	2,564.78	(889.03)	790,374.34
4	9,032.00	5,578.19	31,116,203.68
5	1,750.00	(1,703.81)	2,902,968.52
6	17,110.40	13,656.59	186,502,450.43
7	1,713.99	(1,739.82)	3,026,973.63
8	6,245.32	2,791.51	7,792,528.08
9	534.89	(2,918.92)	8,520,093.97
10	534.89	(2,918.92)	8,520,093.97
11	2,564.78	(889.03)	790,374.34
12	1,122.05	(2,331.76)	5,437,104.70
13	3,025.88	(427.93)	183,124.08
14	514.99	(2,938.82)	8,636,662.99
15	10,554.58	7,100.77	50,420,934.59
16	1,988.63	(1,465.18)	2,146,752.43
17	7,026.50	3,572.69	12,764,113.84
18	978.00	(2,475.81)	6,129,635.16
19	1,654.54	(1,799.27)	3,237,372.53
20	3,066.00	(387.81)	150,396.60
21	35.87	(3,417.94)	11,682,313.84
22	78.99	(3,374.82)	11,389,410.03
23	2,003.00	(1,450.81)	2,104,849.66
24	6,995.41	3,541.60	12,542,930.56
25	3,915.50	461.69	213,157.66
Sum	86,345.24		392,839,570.23
Average,	3,453.81		16,368,315.43
$\overline{X}$		Std. Dev.	4045.78

standard deviations. How the items in the population are distributed around those central measures of mean and standard deviation is often of interest to the internal auditor. Is there an equal distribution of large and small values around the central measures? At times, a population will *not* follow this normal

EXHIBIT 16.8

Normal and Other Distribution Examples

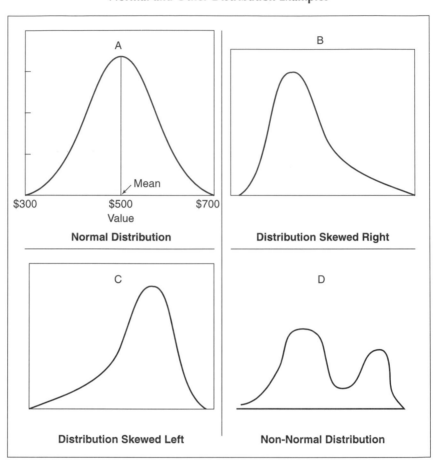

or symmetrical shape. If plotted by age, the population of a retirement community would be heavily weighted to older persons. We would say that this distribution by age is *skewed*. Curves B and C in Exhibit 16.8 are examples of skewed populations—skewed to either the right or left. Many accounting populations follow the B type of distribution, with a few items with very large values. It is important for internal auditors to understand if a population of data is skewed to either the right or left. Audit testing and evaluation procedures are often modified by this distribution of skewed data.

Because of its rather complex-looking formula, the importance of standard deviations does not seem that apparent, and the calculation of standard deviations may seem rather difficult or at least tedious. Various tools are available to perform these calculations, ranging from the audit software discussed in Chapter 22, "Infrastructure Service- and Support-Delivery Controls," to spreadsheet software to handheld calculators. An internal auditor who needs a better understanding of standard deviation concepts should reference one of the statistical textbooks mentioned earlier. Exhibit 16.9 shows the concept of standard deviations around a mean value and the included percentages.

(b) Developing a Statistical Sampling Plan

As a first step for audit sampling, an internal auditor should develop a sampling plan that will allow each item in a population to have an equal probability of selection. This involves a much more precise approach than that used in the judgmental sampling plan selections discussed previously. The plan should attempt to remove any bias in the selection of items to ensure that they are representative of the total population. An internal auditor is often faced with a challenge here in understanding any large amount of data, whether inventory records, accounts receivable payment histories, actual physical locations of assets, or other types of audit evidence. Statistical sampling allows an internal auditor to pull a

---

EXHIBIT 16.9

Percentage of Observation Around a Standard Deviation

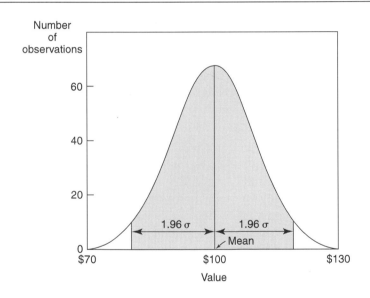

Distance from mean in terms of ± standard deviations on both sides of mean.	Percentage of observations included.
±1.00 std. deviations	68.26%
±1.65 std. deviations	90.00%
±1.96 std. deviations	95.00%
±2.33 std. deviations	98.00%
±2.58 std. deviations	99.00%
±3.00 std. deviations	99.73%
±3.30 std. deviations	99.90%

representative sample of this data that will allow an audit conclusion to be drawn for the entire population of data. However, an internal auditor must understand the nature of the data to be reviewed when developing this sample selection strategy or audit plan, including:

- *The population (or universe or field) to be sampled must be clearly defined.* The *population* is the total number of units from which a sample can be drawn, including the scope or nature of items to be reviewed, such as *all accounts payable vouchers for a year* and the specific characteristics of audit interest. An example would be a large number of accounts payable vouchers where internal audit is only interested in materials purchases. Payables covering other areas—such as travel reimbursements or telecommunications charges—would not be included in this example audit population.

- *The population should be divided or stratified into groups if major variations exist between population items.* A population such as a materials inventory often includes a few items of very high value and many of smaller values. Such a population would not follow a normal distribution. When a population covers a few very large or significant items and many others with very small amounts, statistical conclusions based on the entire population will often not be as valuable. Internal audit may be more interested in whether the large items are fairly valued but only have a general interest in the other, smaller value items. With a wide diversity in the population, internal audit should consider stratifying the sample by placing the smaller set of high-value items in one population and the balance in a separate population. Separate samples could be drawn from each.

- *Every item in a population must have an equal chance of being selected in the sample.* Every attempt should be made to eliminate bias in a sample selection when there is limited availability or even lack of availability of particular items of interest. Auditors are sometimes guilty of bias when deciding to restrict some items from the sample selection even though the audit's conclusions are expressed in terms of the total population. They may decide arbitrarily to ignore some items in a population because of lack of easy access. They will pull the sample from readily available items and then state their audit conclusions as if they had looked at the entire population. If certain items must be ignored for logistical or other valid reasons, internal audit should always reveal that fact when reporting results.

- *There should be no bias in making the sample selection from the population.* Similar to the above situation, an auditor may be faced with a population of items stored at both local and remote facilities and then only look at ones in the local facility. The auditor can then draw an audit conclusion based only on the items stored locally. Those items stored in remote warehouses that have been ignored may have different attributes than the central warehouse items. Sample result conclusions from the local items reviewed may not represent the remote warehouses.

The sampling plan to be used should be clearly documented and discussed with management as part of the audit planning process. Often, members of management who understand the items to be reviewed suggest adjustments to the sampling plan for internal audit consideration. The development of a sampling plan is an important step for any audit sample.

(c) Selecting the Items to Be Sampled

There are four common methods for selecting an audit sample: *random number, interval, stratified,* and *cluster selection.* The latter two are also often referred to as types of sampling, but they are more properly identified as optional selection techniques. The following sections discuss very briefly each of these techniques. The modern internal auditor should have a general understanding of the most appropriate technique for a given audit situation.

(i) Random Number Selection. Items here are selected *at random,* with each in the population having an equal chance to be selected as a part of the sample. In theory, an internal auditor would place all the items from a population in a container, or numbers to identify them, mix them thoroughly, and independently draw the individual items for the sample from the container. Since this is generally not feasible, the auditor must find other means to draw the random sample. In the past, auditors used random number tables published in statistical sampling books. The process to use those past tables was often time-consuming and somewhat complex.

Today, an auditor can use any of a large number of computer tools to select random numbers. An Internet search for *sampling random numbers* will reveal a wide variety of quite adequate software tools, some free or others selling for a small amount. The idea is to have a starting and ending number for all items in the population, determine the sample size, and then select random numbers based on that sample size. This process is easy with, for example, a population of 1,000 invoices where it is easy to identify each by number.

With larger or more complex populations, each item in the population to be sampled must be identified with a unique identifying number, such as the voucher number on a paper document, the part numbers for an inventory, or some sequential number. For example, if the population is described on a multiple page mainframe type of computer-generated report, items can be identified on the basis of page number and line number per page. An inventory of 1,625 items could be printed on a 30-page report with about 55 lines per page. Since the individual inventory items in such a computer-generated report generally will not be numbered, they can be identified by their placement on this report. The items on page 1 would range from page 1, line 1 (or 0101 to 0155), followed by 0201 to 0255 for the entries on page 2. This scheme will define the items in the population subject to selection.

The sample size for such a selection should be large enough to recognize that some items cannot be selected and must be replaced. In our example of a population based on printed report page and line numbers, where the highest number in a series would be 0155, might draw the random number of 0199. Since that item does not exist based on the scheme used, the item number should be rejected and another random number drawn.

Although public accounting firms have developed a theoretical minimum sample size for their tests (often 60 or even 30), internal auditors generally should use *no minimum sample size* for use in an audit. An internal auditor may conservatively select a very large sample on the basis of better results, with management more apt to accept the results of a large sample. Alternatively, a small sample size may be sufficient to arrive at adequate conclusions based on a limited amount of work. These internal audit sample-size decisions are made strictly on the basis of audit judgment and the objectives of the audit without regard to formal statistical sampling rules. Since they are formal and often very mathematical, sampling theory rules are beyond the scope of this book and can be found in an audit sampling text.

A random-number-based population selection assumes that most populations follow a standard bell-curve distribution. Many actual populations do not follow such a normal distribution, raising a question on the feasibility of using audit sampling. Often, a population contains a small but significant group of very large items with the remainder having small balances distributed over a wide range. In other cases, most items, whether as errors or not, may be all nearly equal with respect to the audit attribute to be examined. They do not follow a standard distribution even though the basis of many of the statistical sampling methods discussed assumes that the distribution is in the form of a normal distribution. While there are mathematical techniques to get around non-normal distribution and to still take a valid sample, they are mathematically complex and not necessary for the typical internal auditor. However, a good method of assuring more accurate results when a sample is drawn from a badly skewed population is to increase the sample size. Mathematical theory says that as the sample size gets larger, the shape of the sampling distribution becomes closer to a normal distribution.

(ii) Interval Selection. Another technique for selecting sample items in a statistically sound manner is through what is called *interval selection* or *systematic sampling*. This requires the selection of individual items based on uniform intervals from the items in the total population. This technique is especially useful for monetary unit sampling, as discussed in Section 16.6, or when the particular population does not have an assigned value that makes it practicable to work from the items selected on the basis of random table numbers. In an interval sample, an internal auditor would develop a sample by selecting every *n*th item in the population, such as an inventory listing. It is necessary that there be a reasonably homogeneous population, in terms of type of item, and no bias in the arrangement of the population, which would result in the interval approach coming up with a sample that is not statistically representative.

Interval selection should be related to the size of the sample and the total population. Where necessary, the population can be estimated. The planned sample size divided into the population size then establishes the interval. Thus, a population of 5,000 and a needed sample of 200 would yield an interval requirement of 5000/200, or 25. An internal auditor would then examine every 25th item in the population series with the starting point in the first interval group established on a random number basis. In the event that the actual population turned out to be larger than was estimated, a practical solution would be to increase the sample by extending the interval selection on the same basis. If the actual population were less than estimated, it would be necessary to complete the sample through a new interval selection based on the number of items short in relation to the total population size. This problem can be avoided by always having a safety margin through using a larger than needed sample estimate.

An interval selection where every nth item is selected is perhaps the easiest way to draw a sample from a population; however, the very nature of the method introduces the possibility of bias in the sample selection. For example, in a sample of daily transactions with an interval selection of every 30 days, if the starting random number pointed to the beginning of the month, a compliance error that normally took place later in the month might not be detected. The internal auditor could select day five of month one, then move forward on the interval of 30 to perhaps day six of month two and so on. Based on this start, items from day 15 to about 30 will never be selected. Because of this bias, intern auditors should use caution before using this technique.

(iii) Stratified Selection. Here, a population is divided into two or more subgroups or strata, with each subgroup handled independently. Stratified selection is an extension of random or interval selection techniques because either can be applied to the smaller strata of the population. In some cases, one of the strata may be examined 100%, while the other strata would be subject to random selection. The justification for stratification may be that one stratum has significantly different characteristics, and internal audit wishes to evaluate that subgroup on a more individual and precise basis. Through reducing variability, stratification can decrease the standard deviation, and help to reduce sample sizes.

The data presented in the Exhibit 16.5 example show where stratification might be useful. Internal audit might decide that 100% of items in the population with balances greater than $10,000 should be examined. In a purely random selection, using a random number table and a sample size of five, none of the three large items might be selected. Using stratification, internal audit could divide this population into two strata: items over $10,000 and items under. The strata less than $10,000 would be subject to random selection, as discussed previously. The strata greater than $10,000 would receive 100% selection.

The most common populations requiring stratification are those that have a few items of very high value, such as inventories, accounts receivable, or invoices. Since these high-value items have much greater significance, internal audit may wish to subject them to higher standards of scrutiny. In other cases, the need for stratification may arise from the fact that individual subgroups are processed in different ways, or by different groups, and the nature of the items may call for different standards of audit scrutiny, such as certain inventory subject to theft. Under these conditions the larger variability in the total population makes a single type of testing and evaluation inapplicable.

These stratified sampling principles have long been recognized. Their importance in audit sampling is that stratification provides more meaningful statistical measures together with the possibility of smaller sample sizes. Once the stratification selection technique has been adopted and the subgroups subjected to different standards of audit scrutiny, the results of each evaluation can be used independently, based on the sampling of the separate populations, or brought together to support a consolidated conclusion relative to the total population.

(iv) Cluster Selection. In the sampling approach called *cluster selection*, the sample is made by systematically selecting subgroups or clusters from the total population. Cluster selection is useful when items are filed in shelves or in drawers, and it is physically more convenient to select subgroups based on the physical shelf area or individual file drawers. The rationale is that the items on particular portions of the shelf areas or in designated drawers is substantially similar in their nature and that a sample thus selected will be representative. However, the variability *within* the individual samples is frequently less than the variability *among* the samples. Hence, it is customary to use a larger sample when using the cluster selection approach to offset this lesser variability. A variation of the cluster selection approach, called *multistage sampling,* involves sampling the individual clusters instead of examining the sample as a whole.

Assume a population of 60,000 warehouse items located on 2,000 feet of shelves. If internal audit decides to review a sample of 600, the plan might be to divide the population into 20 clusters where each cluster would have 30 items. Since the average number of items on the shelves is 30 per linear foot (60,000/ 2,000), each cluster would cover an area of 1 foot (30/30). These individual clusters would then be selected at intervals of 100 feet (2,000/20) and with a random start. Of course, the validity for this type of sample selection is dependent on the consistency of the population. That is, random number selection or regular interval selection would presumably assure a better representative sample. While sometimes useful, cluster sampling generally must be used with care.

16.5 AUDIT SAMPLING APPROACHES

An internal auditor can take several approaches to complete an audit sampling project, depending on the audit objectives, whether internal audit wants to performs tests of compliance or wants to verify balances such as in a financial statement, and on any special conditions. The three most common approaches are called: *attribute sampling, variables sampling* (including monetary unit sampling), and *discovery sampling. Attribute sampling* is an approach used to measure the extent or level of occurrence of various conditions or attributes—in other words to assess internal controls. For example, an internal auditor might want to test for the attribute of whether invoice documents have received proper approval signatures. An invoice will either be correctly approved or not—a yes or no qualitative condition. Normally, the attribute measured is the frequency of an error or other type of deficiency. The extent of the existence of the particular deficiency, such as improperly approved documents, determines the seriousness of the situation and how internal audit will report its findings and recommendations. Attributes or characteristics can be applied to any physical item, financial record, internal procedure, or operational activity. Attribute sampling often deals with compliance with a designated policy, procedure, or established standard.

The key point is that attribute sampling is a test for internal controls. A control is either determined to be working or not working. "Sort of working" is not an appropriate determination! The auditor tests conditions in the selected items and then assesses whether the overall population is in compliance with the control attribute.

Variables sampling deals with the size of a specified population, such as an account balance, and tests of balances in individual sample items. Here the auditor's focus is on "how much" as opposed to the "yes or no" focus of attribute sampling. The objective of variables sampling is to project total estimated quantities for some account or adjustments to the account on the basis of the auditor's statistical sample. Illustrative would be a sample to estimate the total value of an inventory based on sample results. Variables sampling is concerned with absolute amounts as opposed to the number or extent of a particular type of error.

Two important variations to variables sampling are *stratified sampling* and the now very common *monetary unit sampling*. Variables sampling procedures are closely related to attribute sampling, but include additional concepts and calculations. Because of the more complicated nature of the variables sampling approach, a step-by-step analysis is given below for single-stage variables sampling. The example is based on a simplified manual estimate of the standard deviation when computer support tools or other information on the standard deviation are not available.

The third type of statistical sampling, *discovery sampling*, in many respects is similar to the nonstatistical judgmental sampling discussed earlier. Discovery sampling is used when an internal auditor wants to pull a sample from a large volume of data without the statistical and mathematical controls associated with variables and attribute sampling. The following sections discuss all of these sampling methods in some detail; however, the information contained in this chapter may be just enough to make an internal auditor "dangerous." That is, this chapter provides a discussion of these sampling methods but does not equip an internal auditor with enough information to fully master statistical sampling concepts. Appropriate additional training, experience, and specialized books and computer software tools are necessary.

(a) Attribute-Sampling Procedures

The purpose of attribute sampling is to estimate the *proportions* of items in a population containing some characteristic or attribute of interest. For example, an internal auditor may be interested in the rate of occurrence of some monetary error or compliance exception that might exist in a population of accounts payable disbursement vouchers. The auditor would be interested in the number of items that have some type of significant error, not the total monetary value of all of the errors. This type of test is very appropriate for assessing the level of internal control in a population such as an account. This can be a very important approach for Sarbanes-Oxley Act Section 404 internal controls tests. The starting point in attribute sampling is to estimate an expected rate of errors—that is, how many errors can internal audit and management tolerate? Depending on the items sampled and the culture of the organization, this expected error rate may be as little as 0.01% or as large as 5% or even more. Even if senior management states that "no errors" will be allowed in some highly critical operation, all parties often recognize that there may be a small or very small possibility of an error, and depending on the criticality of the operation, such a very small error rate will be accepted. An expected error rate is the recognition that certain types of operations contain errors no matter how good are the other controls and procedures. If internal audit were to perform a 100% examination of an account but only find a small number of errors—say, 0.5%—it might be difficult to convince management that its controls are weak. Management might expect and tolerate a 1% error rate and not express much concern at internal audit's findings. In an attribute-sampling test, internal audit must estimate the expected rate of errors in the population sampled. This can be based on management's stated expectations, other audit tests, or just internal audit assumptions.

Along with estimating the expected error rate, internal audit must decide on the acceptable precision limits and the degree of wanted confidence for the sample. In other words, an internal auditor would like to be able to say, "I am 99% confident that the error rate of this account is less than 1%." These estimates will allow an internal auditor to determine the size of a sample that will provide a reliable conclusion regarding the condition tested. This determination is made through statistical methods and can be obtained from various statistical software packages or even from manual tables found in the old statistical sampling books. These factors provide an initial basis for the size of the sample to be reviewed. The internal auditor now selects this sample and examines the items sampled to determine the number of errors that exist in the sample.

As can be expected, the error rate in a sample is normally higher or lower than the previously estimated acceptable error rate. If lower, the internal auditor has established that the condition tested is safely within the limits selected. If the sample shows a higher error rate, the auditor must determine whether the results are satisfactory and what further action, if any, is needed. Conceivably, the sample can be expanded, but internal audit will often feel that there is an adequate basis for arriving at a conclusion. The key to meaningful attribute sampling is to take an appropriate sample and properly develop an audit conclusion based on the sample results.

Attribute sampling, once commonly used by both internal and external auditors, is now used less frequently because of the computational requirements and statistical knowledge required. However, it remains an effective tool to report to management on the status of some control procedure. While this section will describe attribute sampling in some detail, the internal auditor who wishes to obtain a greater understanding is encouraged to seek out a detailed book on the subject.

(i) Performing the Attribute-Sampling Test. An attribute-sampling test is useful for an internal auditor who is faced with a rather large number of items to be examined and wants to test whether certain controls are working or not working. An attribute sample can be performed following four basic steps:

1. Understand the nature of the items to be sampled.

2. Establish statistical parameters for the attribute-sampling test.

3. Select the sample and perform audit procedures.

4. Evaluate the results of the attribute-sampling test.

Each of these steps, of course, has many additional substeps. This type of sampling, for example, is used by governmental regulatory agencies, and its results are acceptable in a court of law. Although the process takes more work than the nonstatistical procedures discussed previously, when properly performed, this relatively easy-to-use technique will allow an internal auditor to express an opinion over the presence of some condition with a high degree of statistical authority.

As with an operational audit, an internal auditor must first define what is to be evaluated or tested before embarking on any audit sampling. An internal auditor should first carefully define the objectives of the audit. In the case of attribute sampling, an internal auditor needs to understand the specific nature of the compliance tests to be performed, the nature of the sampling units, and the population. Each of these is critical for performing an attribute-sampling test and includes the following considerations:

- *Define the Nature of the Compliance Tests to Be Performed.* As discussed, a compliance test is a yes/no type of audit test. That is, the attribute sampled must either be correct or incorrect. There can be no measures of "'almost correct" or "'close enough." In a test of the completeness of travel report approvals, organizational procedures may state the responsible manager must approve all travel reports greater than $100. Thus, any voucher not approved by the responsible manager would be considered a compliance or control error. Internal audit should carefully define the types of tests to be performed as well as the acceptance and rejection rules. Exhibit 16.10 contains examples of typical attribute-sampling tests. All tests should be carefully defined. While it is possible to separately sample for two or more different attributes, each statistical test should concentrate on compliance with one such test criteria. If multiple ones are

EXHIBIT 16.10

Attribute-Sampling Test Examples

1. In a test of expense account documents, the auditor may want to test whether all reports have been approved by a person at least one level above the person submitting the report. In this audit, anything that has not been so approved would be classified as an error.

2. If computer security rules require that all passwords must be changed every 30 days or sooner, any password that had not been changed within the 30-day limit would be treated as an error in an attributes test. Even if a password had been changed after 31 or 32 days, it would still be considered an error for attributes test purposes.

3. Internal auditors reviewing control procedures in manufacturing production environment may be asked whether controls over that area are adequate or are not adequate. Although there may be many shades of gray in such a real-life situation, an internal auditor would be required to make a yes/no decision for an attributes test of these controls.

used in a single test, the failure of any one would mean that the entire item sampled is out of compliance. Considerations necessary to launch an attributes test include:

- *Understand the Population to Be Sampled.* Internal audit should have a clear understanding of the number and location of the items to be sampled. If initial plans are to sample *all* travel accounting reports, those reports must be available or readily accessible. If some items are filed at a remote, international location, internal audit may not be able to sample *all* such reports unless it gains access to the remote, international reports as well as the items filed centrally. Otherwise, internal audit should reduce the scope of the population sampled and look at only domestic travel accounting reports. The size of this population will have an impact on the number of items to be sampled. In addition, any audit results should clearly disclose that international travel reports were not sampled.

- *Define the Sampling Unit.* If the population of interest is travel expense reports and the audit test performed is whether these expense reports have approved, the sampling unit is the individual travel expense report. In some instances, this can be a more complex measure. For example, if testing to see whether certain codes have been correctly entered on a purchase order, the audit test may be to check on two different purchase order codes. An internal auditor can define each purchase order to be an individual unit with the test whether both codes are correct. However, internal audit could define the two codes tested on a purchase order separately, making each purchase order two units. A single purchase order could have one, two, or no errors. This latter approach of performing separate attribute tests against the same overall population is usually not very practical or effective.

(ii) Establishing Statistical Parameters for the Attribute-Sampling Test. The auditor must first make some preliminary estimates, based on observations and other audits, of what is expected from the sample results and, second, evaluate the results of an actual audit sample based on those expectations. If a fairly high level of errors in the population is expected, the auditor should select a sample that is sufficient to confirm or refute those initial expectations. Internal auditors need to estimate the maximum tolerable error rate, the desired *confidence level* of the sample, the estimated population error rate, and then the initial sample size. These parameters are:

- A. Maximum Tolerable Error Rate
- B. Desired Confidence Level
- C. Estimated Population Error Rate
- D. Initial Sample Size
- E. Selecting the Sample to Perform Audit Procedures
- F. Evaluating the Results of the Attribute-Sampling Test

(A) MAXIMUM TOLERABLE ERROR RATE

Statisticians also call this estimate the *desired upper precision limit*. This is the error rate that an internal auditor will allow while still accepting the overall internal controls. The idea is that a typical population may have some errors. In the previously discussed audits of travel expense reports, which were reviewed for departmental management approvals, a realistic internal auditor recognizes that there may be *some* errors, such as vouchers that have not been correctly coded. This is an error an internal auditor might accept but still feel that internal controls are generally adequate.

The maximum tolerable error rate is normally expressed as a percentage that can vary based on the nature of the items reviewed. In the above example, an auditor might accept a 5% tolerable error rate or upper precision limit. In other instances, a smaller or larger estimate can be used. However, for internal audits this estimate should never be more than 10%. Such an estimate indicates major internal control problems, and the resultant attribute sample may provide little further information. If an internal auditor knows that internal controls are very bad, it is of little value to take an attribute sample to verify what internal auditor has already determined through other audit procedures. Similarly, an internal auditor should normally expect some errors and establish some reasonable value for this rate, perhaps 1% or 2%.

(B) DESIRED CONFIDENCE LEVEL

This is a measure of the auditor's confidence on the results of a sample. That is, internal auditors usually would like 95% or 98% certainty that the results of the sample are representative of the actual population. An internal auditor will never be 100% certain that a condition exists unless the auditor reviews essentially 100% of the items in the population. If a population of 100 items contains one error, an auditor might look at a sample of 10 items and find no errors. He or she may look at 20, 30, 50, or even 90 items and still not find that one error. The only way to be 100% certain that the population contains a 1% error rate is to look at 100% of the items. However, based on the laws of probability, an internal auditor can look at a much smaller sample and still state that he or she is 95% or 98% certain that the error rate is no more than 1%.

The assumed confidence level value, usually 95% or 98%, along with the estimated population size discussed previously, will determine the size of the sample needed to test the estimated population. Too large of a confidence level may require too large of a sample. Too low of a confidence level may reduce the size of the sample, but the results may be questionable. Management typically would not accept an internal audit finding that states they are "75% confident" that some condition is true.

(C) ESTIMATED POPULATION ERROR RATE

In attribute sampling, an internal auditor estimates the level of errors in population and then takes a statistical sample to confirm or refute those assumptions. In order to calculate the sample size, the internal auditor also needs to estimate the expected rate of occurrence of errors in the population. This estimate, together with the confidence level and the maximum tolerable error rate, determines the size of the sample. For example, if the confidence level is 95% and the maximum tolerable error rate is 5%, the auditor should look at a sample of 1,000 items in a very large population if the estimated population error rate is 4%. A smaller estimated population error rate will reduce the sample size. Given the same parameters, an estimated population error rate of 1% will drive the sample size down from 1,000 to 100 items. If the expected population error rate is very large— greater than 50%—the required sample size will become very large. Generally, the larger the difference between the maximum tolerable error rate and the estimated population error rate, the smaller the necessary sample size.

(D) INITIAL SAMPLE SIZE

The previous three factors, along with some other correction factors, determine the necessary sample size. Although a statistical textbook will provide the formulas, internal auditors normally use audit software to develop attribute-sampling plans. A Web search for *attribute sampling software* will provide a wide range of options. Accessing such a statistical sample software package, an internal auditor only needs to provide the (1) maximum tolerable error rate, the (2) confidence level, the (3) estimated population error rate, and the (4) approximate sample size. The software will then provide the required sample size for the attributes test. Exhibit 16.11 contains some attribute sample sizes estimated using these values. The exhibit illustrates that if the confidence level is 99%, the maximum tolerable error rate is not over 5%, and the estimated error rate is 4%, an internal auditor should examine 142 items for an attributes test over a population of about 500 items.

   This is a brief introduction to the process of selecting a sample size when performing an attribute test. The real difficulty for auditors here is that sample sizes tend to be large. Because judgmental tests often sample perhaps only 50 items, it may be difficult to justify the larger sample sizes needed to perform a statistically correct attribute test. While in some instances an internal auditor can modify the sample size by modifying sampling assumptions, this becomes part of the overall audit conclusions. In the Exhibit 16.11 illustration, the 142-item sample for a 500-item population with the previous assumptions goes down to a sample size of 102, or 30%, if the confidence level is lowered from 99% to 95%. In such cases, there is the possibility that management may question audit findings with a 95% certainty, particularly when the auditee disagrees with the findings and is looking for a way to refute the sampling results.

(E) SELECTING THE SAMPLE TO PERFORM AUDIT PROCEDURES

Having made some audit sample assumptions and determined the sample size, the next step is to pull the actual items for review. The random number tables described previously or some similar means can be used to pull the number of items called for through the sample calculations. Reserving extra audit items through the random number selection can reduce the possibility of drawing duplicate random numbers or finding that an actual item does not legitimately exist within an otherwise valid range of items. Multiple attributes can be tested using the same set of sample items. The concept to remember is that the internal

EXHIBIT 16.11

Sample Sizes for Sampling Random Sample Attributes

Confidence Level 99%
Expected Error Rate Not Over 5%

Population Size	Sample Size for Reliability of:					
	±1%	±1.5%	±2%	±2.5%	±3%	±4%
200						99
250						110
300						119
350					175	126
400					187	132
450					197	137
500					206	142
550				263	214	145
600				274	221	148
650				284	228	151
700				293	234	154
750				302	239	156
800			397	310	244	158
850			409	318	248	160
900			420	324	252	162
950			431	330	256	163
1000			441	336	260	165
1050			450	341	263	166
1100			459	346	266	167

auditor will be performing a separate yes/no type test for each of the individual attributes on each of the items in the sample.

Workpaper documentation should describe all items selected as part of the attribute test. Spreadsheet software is useful here for recording the results of the audit tests, but the internal audit procedures should be performed with great care. If an audit fails to recognize an error condition in the selected sample items, that fact will throw off the conclusions reached as part of the overall sample. With a large population, each sample item may speak for hundreds or even thousands of actual items. Each sample item should be evaluated carefully and consistently against the established attributes. An assessment of "close enough" should not be used. If some attribute measurement is too stringent for certain items, internal audit should consider reevaluating the entire sample set. An internal auditor may be looking for several error conditions but then find another error not included in the original test design. If it is significant, internal audit may want to redefine the overall attribute test.

(F) EVALUATING THE RESULTS OF THE ATTRIBUTE-SAMPLING TEST

As discussed, prior to actually selecting and evaluating the sample items, the internal auditor has made some initial assumptions regarding the maximum tolerable error rate, the reliability, and the level of confidence, as well as about how many compliance errors would be tolerated while still maintaining that controls are adequate. The next key step is to evaluate the sample results against those assumptions to determine if an internal control problem exists. Recall that an upper precision limit or maximum tolerable error rate and a confidence level formed the standards used to determine the sample size and perform the sampling test. The auditor should now assess the actual error rate of the sampled items and calculate an upper precision limit based on those sample errors. That precision limit, computed on the basis of the actual sample, should be less than or equal to the desired precision limits established at the beginning of the sample exercise in order for the auditor to report favorable results from the sample.

Normally, if the results of the sample do not meet the preliminary criteria, the internal auditor has a major finding. These audit criteria should have been well thought out and approved by auditee management before beginning the test. However, sometimes internal audit or management may decide that the original assumptions were too conservative. A new upper precision limit or confidence level could be used and the sample results measured against it. This approach should only be used with the greatest caution. In effect, the auditor here is attempting to justify some bad results. Were the matter ever to reach a court of law, internal audit would have a tough time justifying why it had altered its assumptions to make the sample results look good. A better approach when the results are unfavorable is to expand the sample size.

When attribute-sampling results turn out unfavorably, management sometimes may claim that internal audit only looked at some *very unusual* items and that the remainder of the population is not that bad. An increase in the sample size will have the effect of decreasing the computed upper precision limit, assuming that the auditor does not find a substantial number of additional errors. Both internal audit and management should weigh the relative costs and benefits of this approach. A better approach is to report the internal control problem based on the current results and to expand the sample size in a subsequent audit review. Management should, hopefully, take steps during the interim to improve internal controls in the area of interest.

Attribute sampling is a very useful technique for assessing one or several internal controls in an area of audit interest. Because estimates of such things as the maximum tolerable error rate are made in advance, it is difficult to dispute the audit test assumptions when compared to sample results. Similarly, because random number or similar techniques are typically used to select the sample items, it would be difficult to claim auditor bias in the selections. To better explain the attribute-sampling process, an example follows.

(b) Attribute-Sampling Audit Example

This section discusses an example of attribute sampling at Gnossis, Inc., a large research and development organization. Management has asked internal audit to assess whether the controls over its human resource records are correct. Certain employees have complained that they did not receive their scheduled increases on a timely basis, and Gnossis was recently fined in a court action when human resources records deficiencies were found during a legal discovery action. Senior management has asked internal audit to review payroll department internal controls.

Gnossis has about 4,000 employees, and internal audit has decided to perform an attributes test to assess the internal controls covering human resource records. The Gnossis human resources function uses two computer systems for employee records—one for pay calculations and one for benefits—and maintains a centralized manual system for all employees where such matters as health insurance declarations are filed. Through a review of the human resources record keeping process, internal audit found some 30 different record keeping control issues, ranging from such major matters as whether pay is properly withheld for tax purposes to more minor items such as whether monthly deductions to pay for an employee credit union contribution are correct. Internal audit could combine all of these 30 record keeping issues as a single attribute. Then, an attribute sample test could check for all of these as a single yes/no test. The problem here is that a few minor problems would force internal audit to conclude that internal controls are not working even though no problems were found over the major issues. This will often be difficult to communicate to management.

A strategy is to test Gnossis human resources records for separate attributes. Although internal audit could have tested separately for all 30 attributes, a better approach is to decide which are the most significant and to only test for those separate attributes. Assume that internal audit has decided to test human resource records for the following five attributes:

1. Pay grade and status on the automated system should be the same as in manual files.
2. Authorizations for withholdings should be signed and dated by employees.
3. Preemployment background checks should have been completed.
4. If there were no life insurance deductions, employee-signed waivers should be recorded.
5. Pay increases are according to guidelines and are properly authorized.

These items are certainly not all of the areas where audit can test to determine if controls are adequate; however, in this example, internal audit has determined that it will statistically test employee record internal controls based on these five attributes. Internal audit first discusses this approach with Gnossis management to obtain their consent. The next step is to establish sampling parameters and develop a sample plan. Based on the prior year's experience and staff projections for the coming year, it is estimated that there are approximately 4,000 employees in Gnossis payroll records. Using statistical sampling software, internal audit assumes an expected error rate of 2%, a desired precision of 1.25%, and a 90% confidence level to select a sample size of 339 items. The item of interest is an employee payroll file, and internal audit will separately review employee files for each of these five attributes.

■ 383 ■

Internal audit's next challenge is to select the 339 plus, perhaps 40 extra, payroll files for audit inspection. The physical records are stored alphabetically in the human resources department, and the eight-character employee numbers are not sequential but assigned when an employee joins the organization. Because of turnover over the years, internal audit was not able to directly select the sample by matching selections from a random number table to a list of employees in sequence by their employee number. Rather, the sample employees are selected from a printed list of employees, a report 75 pages long and with about 55 items per page, using four-character random numbers 0101 through 0155 by page to 7555.

The sample items selected are listed on spreadsheets, as shown in the Exhibit 16.12 example, with space to list the results of each attribute test. Although largely manual procedures were used to select the sample, internal audit could have made this selection using automated procedures as follows:

1. Use a random number program to generate 379 numbers for the 339-count desired sample size, along with 40 extras. The range of the random number should be between 1 and 4,000.

2. Output the selected random numbers to a file and sort them in ascending order.

3. Using a utility program, match the sequential random numbers with the record counts on the employee master file. Thus, if the first random number is 0137, the program would select the 137th record on the employee master file.

4. Output the selected record data to a spreadsheet file similar to the data shown in Exhibit 16.13.

This automated approach to attributes sample selection will take more initial effort but will reduce auditor clerical time. This type of approach is best if internal audit also contemplates using additional audit sampling procedures against the employee records files. Once the statistical sample is selected, these attributes are tested by pulling the designated employee personnel file. The procedures here are essentially the same as for any audit. The internal auditor checks each employee record selected against each attribute and then indicates on the worksheet whether the attribute is in compliance. After reviewing these attributes for the 339 sample items, the final step is just to tabulate the exceptions or error rates. For Attribute 1 as described previously, internal audit finds that 10% of the employees in the sample had data errors between their manual payroll files and automated payroll records. At the 90% confidence level, this represents 7.3 to 13.3% of the total number of employees at Gnossis. Because sample results show an extensive error rate for this one important attribute, the results are immediately disclosed to management without the need for further sampling.

Summary information on the results of these five attributes tests is provided to management in a formal audit report. Only minor or insignificant problems appear for three of the five attributes tested, while for the other two, Attributes 1 and 3, significant internal control problems are found. In internal audit's opinion,

EXHIBIT 16.12

Attribute Test Worksheet for Human Resource Test of Records

Random Number Selected	Matching Employee #	Employee Name	Audit Attribute Test Result					Auditor Initials	Date Reviewed
			# 1	# 2	# 3	# 4	# 5		
0137	0266812	Archer, James Q.							
0402	0342201	Aston, Robert							
0988	0466587	Djuruick, Mary Jo							
1003	0502298	Eggbert, Katheran P.							
1256	0629870	Fitzgerald, Edward K.							
1298	030029	Gaddi, Emron							
1489	0687702	Horen, Rupert D.							
1788	1038321	Issac, Stanley L.							
1902	1189654	Jackson-Smith, Susan							
2263	1250982	Jerico, John							

EXHIBIT 16.13

Attribute Test for Human Resource Internal Controls

Random Number Selected	Matching Employee #	Employee Name	Audit Attribute Test Results					Auditor Initials	Date Reviewed
			# 1	# 2	# 3	# 4	# 5		
0137	0266812	Archer, James Q.	OK	OK	OK	OK	OK	RJK	11/16
0402	0342201	Aston, Robert	NO - 12,3	OK	NO - 14.02	OK	OK	RJK	11/17
0988	0466587	Djuruick, Mary Jo	OK	OK	NO - 14.12	OK	OK	RJK	11/16
1003	0502298	Eggbert, Katheran P.	OK	OK	OK	OK	OK	RJK	11/16
1256	0629870	Fitzgerald, Edward K.	OK	OK	OK	OK	OK	RJK	11/16
1298	030029	Gaddi, Emron	OK	NO - 13.2	NO - 14.32	OK	OK	RJK	11/16
1489	0687702	Horen, Rupert D.	OK	OK	OK	OK	OK	RJK	11/16
1788	1038321	Issac, Stanley L.	OK	OK	OK	OK	OK	RJK	11/16
1902	1189654	Jackson-Smith, Susan	OK	OK	OK	OK	OK	RJK	11/16
2263	1250982	Jerico, John	NO-12.5	OK	OK	NO - 25.23	OK	RJK	11/16

the internal control breakdown over these two attributes is sufficient to suggest major problems within the human resources record keeping process. Based on these internal audit recommendations, management has the responsibility to analyze the entire file to determine the extent and frequency of these and other attribute errors throughout the system.

(c) Attribute-Sampling Advantages and Limitations

When there is a need to review a large number of items, attribute-sampling procedures can provide a statistically accurate assessment of a control feature or attribute. Although statistical theory requires a relatively large sample size, internal audit can review some control or condition within a sample of that data and then can state that it is confident, within a preestablished confidence value or percentage, that the number of errors in a total population will not exceed a designated value or that the control is working. Attribute sampling is not useful for determining the estimated correct value on an account such as an inventory book value but is an extremely useful tool for reviewing control procedures in a variety of operational areas. Some auditors feel the technique has some impediments to its use, including:

- *Attribute-sampling computations are complex.* This chapter has only introduced some very basic attribute-sampling concepts. The actual review and analysis of sample results can be very complex and require the use of complex sampling software. An internal auditor needs to have a good understanding of the process or could be in danger of interpreting results incorrectly.

- *Generating appropriate definitions of attributes may be difficult.* In the previous human resources records example, the internal auditors sampled and evaluated controls on five attributes selected from a set of 30 actual attributes. The selection of attributes to be tested was based on either auditor judgment or management requests. However, an auditor may have missed one or another important attribute when analyzing the data.

- *Attributes sample results may be subject to misinterpretation.* Properly presented, the results of an attributes sample should be stated very precisely, such as, "We are 95% confident that the percentage of error items in the account is between 2 and 7.3%." Despite this precision, people may hear these results and interpret them incorrectly, such as "There is over a 7% error rate in the account." That is not what was communicated, but many listeners prefer easier answers.

- *Imperfect data requires corrections.* The basic theory surrounding an attributes sample assumes that the population of data follows a normal distribution, with no other unusual complications. While nonstandard data distributions can be corrected through adjustments in the sample size selection and evaluations, non-normal distributions complicate the process.

Despite these problems, attribute sampling equips internal audit with a very powerful tool to assess internal controls in a large population of data through the evaluation of a limited sample. While the technique is too time-consuming or complex for many audit problems, the modern internal auditor should develop a basic understanding of attribute sampling and make use of it when appropriate. The technique is particularly appropriate when the initial, judgmental results of an internal controls review indicate problems in an area and when management disputes the preliminary results from audit's limited, judgmental sample as being "unrepresentative." A follow-up attributes sample will allow internal audit to take another look at the data and come back making a stronger statement about the status of internal controls surrounding the area in dispute.

16.6   MONETARY UNIT SAMPLING

Attribute sampling measures the extent of some condition and variables sampling estimates the value of an account. Variables sampling can be further divided between the more traditional stratified sampling methods, discussed briefly in this chapter, and what is called *monetary unit sampling*. Monetary unit sampling is a technique to determine if a financial account is fairly stated. It is a particularly good method for estimating the amount of any overstatement of accounts. This technique is alternatively called monetary unit sampling, dollar unit sampling, or probabilities proportional to size (PPS) sampling. The concept here is that every dollar or unit of currency in an account is treated as a member of the population and each has a chance of selection. A $1,000 voucher for an account will have 1,000 units of population while a $100 voucher for the same account will have 100. Thus, a $1,000 item in a population has a thousand times greater chance of selection than a $1 item has. This has been a very popular form of sampling, particularly for external auditing firms, and although various texts and sources use different names, we will here call this approach monetary unit sampling.

As stated, the sampling unit is *each dollar* rather than a physical unit, such as an invoice or payroll checks. For example, if purchases are being tested for a year, the monetary unit sampling population will consist of the total dollar value of purchases made, and the sampling unit will be each dollar of purchases. If errors are found in the invoices, they are related to individual dollars in these invoices using various evaluation methods. Although monetary unit sampling is discussed in many sampling books, an older book by Leslie, Teitlebaum, and Anderson[3] provides one of the more detailed descriptions of this process. The authors can be considered the fathers of monetary unit sampling for auditors.

(a) Selecting the Monetary Unit Sample: An Example

Assume that internal audit wants to review a series of accounts receivable balances to determine if they are fairly stated or recorded. There are 1,364 items or customer balances in this account, with a total recorded balance of $54,902.25. The balances range from some large to others very small, with the first 30 of them listed in Exhibit 16.14. Assume that internal audit has initially decided on a sample size of 60, or to look at only 60 individual dollars and the items these dollars represent. With this sample, the auditor can look at $54.902.25/60 = 915.034 or every 915th dollar in the account balance. Each time the items included in one of those dollars are selected, the auditor will examine that entire item.

EXHIBIT 16.14

Monetary Unit Sampling Selection Example

Acct. No.	Balance	Cum. Total	Start	Int. Tot.	-I-Mus Selects			-II-
1	$123.58	$123.58	37 +	124 =	161			
2	$754.22	$877.80	161 +	878 =	1039 SELECT	1039 –	915 =	124
3	$588.85	$1,466.65	124 +	589 =	713			
4	$2,055.95	$3,522.60	713 +	2056 =	2769 SELECT (2)	2769 –	1830 =	939
5	$341.00	$3,863.60	939 +	341 =	1280 SELECT	1280 –	915 =	365
6	$855.20	$4,718.80	360 +	855 =	1215 SELECT	1215 –	915 =	300
7	$12.55	$4,731.35	300 +	13 =	313			
8	$89.00	$4,820.35	313 +	89 =	402			
9	$250.00	$5,070.35	402 +	250 =	652			
10	$1,099.30	$6,169.65	652 +	1099 =	1751 SELECT	1751 –	915 =	836
11	$87.33	$6,256.98	836 +	87 =	923 SELECT	923 –	915 =	8
12	$788.99	$7,045.97	8 +	789 =	797			
13	$5,892.10	$12,938.07	797 +	5892 =	6689 SELECT (7)	6689 –	6405 =	284
14	$669.90	$13,607.97	284 +	670 =	954 SELECT	954 –	915 =	39
15	$24.89	$13,632.86	39 +	25 =	64			
16	$123.00	$13,755.86	64 +	123 =	187			
17	$123.00	$13,878.86	187 +	123 =	310			
18	$6.00	$13,884.86	310 +	6 =	316			
19	$540.90	$14,425.76	316 +	541 =	857			
20	$100.50	$14,526.26	857 +	101 =	958 SELECT	958 –	915 =	43
21	$66.89	$14,593.15	43 +	67 =	110			
22	$39.00	$14,632.15	110 +	39 =	149			
23	$35.00	$14,667.15	149 +	35 =	184			
24	$89.00	$14,756.15	184 +	89 =	273			
25	$100.00	$14,856.15	273 +	100 =	373			
26	$53.90	$14,910.05	373 +	54 =	427			
27	$436.09	$15,346.14	427 +	436 =	863			
28	$237.76	$15,583.90	863 +	238 =	1101 SELECT	1101 –	915 =	186
29	$209.91	$15,793.81	186 +	210 =	396			
30	$28.89	$15,822.70	396 +	29 =	425			

Starting Random Seed = 37

Interval Selection = 915

Total Sample Items Selected = 10

Exhibit 16.14 has columns for the account numbers (here numbered from 1 to 30), the balance for each of these accounts, and the cumulative total. The additional columns in this exhibit show the process of making a monetary unit selection, as follows:

1. Although the auditor will select every 915th dollar, a starting point is needed somewhere between $1 and $915. To select this, a starting random number between 1 and 915 was selected; in this case, the number was 37.

2. The starting random number, 37, is then added to the first invoice of $123.58 or rounded to 124 to yield 161. All values have been rounded to avoid pennies. Since 161 is less than 915, the next item, 754, is added to the accumulated value to yield 1,039. Here, the auditor will encounter the 915th dollar, and this item will be selected for review.

3. A new starting number is now needed, and 915 is subtracted from 1,039 to compute a starting number for the next item of 124. This is added to the third item of 589 to yield 713, not enough for selection.

4. The fourth item in this sample is large, 2,056. The interval of 915 appears twice in this stream of dollars ($915 \times 2 = 1830$) and the item is selection for two of the sample items.

5. The sample selection procedures are shown in Exhibit 16.14. The auditor can walk through these calculations using a pocket calculator.

The selection of items for a monetary unit sample is generally just as easy as that shown in Exhibit 16.14. An auditor can select a sample using a spreadsheet software package or even through a manual calculation using a desk calculator. The purpose is simply to determine the monetary interval based on the calculated sample size. Two key points and limitations of monetary unit sampling should be mentioned here. First, monetary unit sampling is only useful for testing for the presence of *overstatement*. In the extreme, monetary unit sampling will never select an account that has been incorrectly recorded at a zero value. If the auditor has selected dollars in a population that is understated, the selection method may never find those dollars. Second, the selection method described does not handle credit amounts correctly. The sample selection procedure would not work correctly if the account included a large number of credit items. The best solution here is to pull out all recorded credit balances and treat them as a separate population to be evaluated. If there are only a small number, they might be ignored. Despite these limitations, monetary unit sampling is an effective way to evaluate the recorded balance in a large monetary account.

(b) Performing the Monetary Unit Sampling Test

The number of dollars to be examined in a population determines the auditor's sample size. Similar to attribute sampling, a monetary unit sampling test requires that four things be known regarding the account to be sampled:

1. The maximum percentage of the recorded population value that the auditor will tolerate for errors. This is the same upper precision limit discussed previously for attribute sampling.

2. The expected confidence level.

3. An expected error rate for sampling errors.

4. The total recorded value of the account to be evaluated.

The first of the above is the dollar value of the populations that may contain allowable errors divided by the recorded book value of the population. This is the same estimate discussed previously for attribute sampling, an error rate that an internal auditor could tolerate and still accept the overall controls in the system. Using public accounting terminology, an internal auditor should first think of the total amount of *material errors* that would be accepted. Although this can be calculated, generally a small percentage rate of perhaps 2% is used.

The estimated confidence level follows the same general rule for attributes. An internal auditor cannot really say that he or she is *100% confident* unless the sample size is 100%. Too low of a confidence level, such as 80%, will cause management concern. Often 98% or 95% are good assumptions.

These factors provide data to determine the recommended sample size, which again, can be obtained from a table or from statistical sampling software. The values in Exhibit 16.13, based on a 95% confidence level, can be used here. As discussed previously, this is also an area where some public accounting firms have used a fixed sample size of 60, arguing that the mathematics does not require larger sample sizes.

The monetary unit sample size is then used to calculate the monetary interval by dividing the recorded book value of the account by the sample size to determine the every *n*th dollar interval. This interval sets a selection limit for larger items and all items greater than or equal to this interval will be selected. Exhibit 16.11 shows the process for selecting items through monetary unit sampling. Each item represented by a selected dollar is then evaluated by the auditor to determine if it is correctly stated. The auditor calculates the correct amount for each selected account and records both that amount and the correct audited amount. This will point out how much each account is overstated.

(c) Evaluating Monetary Unit Sample Results

Monetary unit sampling is a popular approach for evaluating account balances to determine if they have been overstated. Since every dollar in every item in an account will be subject to sample selection, overstated items may be discovered during the sampling process. The evaluation of the monetary unit sampling results to estimate the total error in the account is a more complex process. The basic idea is to document the recorded amounts and the audited amounts for each item selected and then to calculate the error percentage for each. Upper precision limits are calculated for each error item to determine the suggested amount of any audit adjustment.

The computations for a formal monetary unit sample evaluation have a series of statistical or theoretical options that go beyond the scope of this chapter. The process is often of more interest to external auditors, who can use this to propose a formal adjustment to a client's audited financial statements. For internal auditors, it is often sufficient to use the results of items selected through monetary unit sampling to gain an overall assessment as to whether an account is correctly stated. Books such as Leslie, Teitlebaum, and Anderson's, referenced previously, can walk the interested internal auditor through this formal sample evaluation process.

(d) Monetary Unit Sampling Advantages and Limitations

The most important advantage of monetary unit sampling is that it focuses on the larger-value unit items in a population. A purely random sample could bypass large-dollar-value items based on a random selection. Because monetary unit sampling selects sample items proportional to their dollar values, there is less risk of failing to detect a material error since all the large-dollar-value units are subject to selection based on the size of each. Any item in a population that is larger than the monetary interval will *always be selected.* Even though management will expect internal audit to take unbiased, random samples, it might express concern if an audit bypassed certain large-value items using other sample selection techniques. Monetary unit sampling ensures there will be a greater coverage of the large-value items in a population. Another advantage is that if no errors are found in an initial sample and a very low expected error rate is established, relatively small sample sizes may be used. An internal auditor can readily determine the maximum possible overstatements and restrict the sample sizes in these circumstances. As discussed, public accounting firms often limit their monetary unit sample sizes to either 60 or 30 items. In addition, an internal auditor obtains the benefits of unlimited stratification by use of a monetary sampling unit.

Monetary unit sampling is also attractive because the item selection is computationally easy. As illustrated in the previous example, an internal auditor can effectively select a sample from a relatively large population using a spreadsheet program or even a pocket calculator, making it a good choice when at a field location and lacking computer-assisted audit tools. The main disadvantage of monetary unit sampling is that the procedure does not adequately test for financial statement understatements. Missing documents or transactions are a common problem in poorly controlled systems, and if items are missing from a population, dollar unit sampling procedures will not detect the missing items. They cannot be sampled. Accordingly, an internal auditor cannot project a value of the population using monetary unit sampling. A drawback to this method is that zero or negative values cause problems because there is no chance such items will be sampled. Another problem is that a total book value must be known in order to make interval calculations. The method cannot provide estimates of unknown population values. Finally, because monetary unit sampling is a relatively new concept for internal auditors, there is less training materials available than for traditional methods such as attribute sampling.

Despite these concerns and limitations, monetary unit sampling is often the best method for auditing errors in some recorded book value. It can also be useful as a selection method for an internal control attributes test when all items in the population have some recorded monetary value. The approach is often superior to the random number selection previously discussed and will result in a very appropriate selection.

16.7 VARIABLES AND STRATIFIED VARIABLES SAMPLING

Variables and stratified variables sampling are methods of audit sampling where the auditor's objective is to test the detailed items that support some account total in order to assess whether that total is fairly stated. Although discussed separately because of its characteristics, monetary unit sampling is a type of variables sampling. In a variables sample, an auditor selects individual *items* in a population and estimates the total population based on whether the items selected were fairly valued. A variation of pure variables sampling is called *stratified sampling* where a population is divided into various levels by their values or extended values. As in the discussion on attribute sampling, items here within each strata are selected, often with differing sampling plans for various strata. The highest-value strata may have 100% inspection, while the selection for lower-value strata will be based on random selections.

Variables sampling, particularly when using stratification, can require some daunting mathematical calculations. It saw limited auditor use until computer systems and software became available to simplify sample selections and calculate the projection of results. Stratified sampling allows internal auditors to place a greater concentration on larger items in a population when they are included as separate strata. However, by placing them in a separate population subject to random selection, the auditor is not forced to examine all of these items with the major advantage of improving the efficiency of the testing. When the population variability or standard deviation is high, sample sizes may be reduced for the desired levels of precision and reliability by using stratified random sampling. If a sufficient number of strata are selected, the sampling error can often be reduced substantially. With the use of modern statistical sampling software, this becomes a very feasible internal audit approach. Another advantage is that emphasis can be given to sensitive areas that require audit. Often, an internal auditor's preliminary analysis will disclose areas with potential errors or problems. These can be classified in separate strata and audited 100% or on a sampling basis, as warranted. Stratification provides an internal auditor with a tool for reviewing sensitive areas in a very systematic manner. The computation to perform stratified variables sampling properly is complex and usually supported through computer software.

With the discussion of how mastering the mathematics of variables sampling is often difficult, the internal auditor reader may ask, "Why should I care about this?" A practical example might help. Some years back, this author was involved in an audit of the manufacturing inventories of several large facilities. For defense contractual and other reasons, these was pressure by senior management and the external auditors to take a full end-of-year physical inventory although plant management resisted, saying their local inventory cycle counting procedures were strong. An internal audit procedure was developed to survey and stratify inventory records by their extended item values. A variable sample was pulled, test counted by internal audit, and the results projected over the total inventory value. The end result was that internal audit was able to report they were some 99% confident the plant inventories were between plus or minus X dollars and consistent with the recorded inventory book values. Internal audit saved the plants from taking full physical inventories.

We have talked about computer statistical sampling software in a general manner here, not recommending any package over another because software and related technology change so fast that any package recommended could soon be obsolete. For suggestions on appropriate software to use, the internal auditor might contact The Institute of Internal Auditors or an external audit firm.

The real strength of variables sampling comes from the auditor's ability to suggest a projected book value for the account sampled. As discussed in the previous example, internal audit can perform a stratified variables sample of an inventory and then report the results to management, stating, "We are 95% confident that the correct book value of the inventory should be between X_{LOW} and Y_{HIGH}. Since the recorded book value of the inventory at the time of our sample was Z, we recommend an adjustment of plus or minus W dollars." This is a very powerful internal audit decision tool.

Using variables sampling, an internal auditor can decide how to report the projection of dollar amounts, whether for adjustments or for estimates of the effect of a particular deficiency. The projection is normally stated as a range of values for a given confidence level. Management, however, often prefers a specific dollar amount or point estimate. The point estimate is calculated by multiplying the samples mean times the number of items in the universe. This estimate is generally used when the range of values, or confidence interval, around the point estimate is small. For example, the point estimate based on a statistical projection of the results of audit is $100,000. The precision at a 95% confidence level could be stated as plus or minus $4,000, giving a range of final audit results between $96,000 and $104,000. Under these circumstances, management will accept such a range, and the use of the point estimate would generally be warranted.

If the calculated range were between $60,000 and $140,000, management would probably never accept these results and an internal auditor would have to either increase the sample size or use a different method of reporting. One method of reporting here would be to state: "We estimate with a probability of 95% that the recorded inventory value of $2.5 million is overstated between $60,000 and $140,000, and is most likely overstated by $100,000." The projected results can be presented in terms of the upper limit, where the internal auditor reports the assurance that the amount of error or deficiency is *not greater than* this amount. In a statistical review of equipment on hand, an internal auditor could project, at a 95% confidence level, that the maximum overstatement of the equipment is $30,000. Since this amount is not material in relation to the $5 million of equipment owned by the organization, the auditor can conclude that the amount of error is not significant.

However, the auditor could also analyze the causes of errors found in the sample to determine procedural weaknesses that required correction. The upper limit is frequently used by internal audit to determine the validity of account balances for financial statement purposes. A tolerable error rate is first determined for the population. If the projected error rate using the upper limit does not exceed the tolerable error rate, the account is considered reasonably stated for financial statement purposes.

A one-sided confidence limit also can be used to demonstrate that the total universe value *is not less than* some amount at a given confidence level. For example, in a statistical sample of fixed asset acquisitions, it is found that equipment costing over $1,000 was being expensed rather than capitalized. The projection shows a 95% confidence that the amount expensed in error is at least $150,000. Audit samples are typically based on the amounts of individual inventory items. Frequently, it is more practical to deal with the differences between the book and actual (as determined by an internal auditor). Under this approach, a similar procedure is followed but all of the samples and computations pertain to the differences data. The advantage is that smaller amounts (and thus smaller standard deviations)—and, therefore, smaller samples—will be required to achieve the same levels of confidence and precision.

It is, of course, possible that the differences will be as great or almost as great as the absolute values and, therefore, the advantages may disappear. However, the use of differences is a good technique and can often be used as a first approach. A second type of evaluation is the ratio estimate. Here, the auditor works with ratios instead of absolute values. Computations of the standard deviations under this method are more complicated, but computers can affect significant timesavings. The ratio estimates method is preferable to the use of the difference estimates method when the errors found are related in size to the value of individual items being tested.

This discussion of variables sampling has been very brief and does not describe many of the mathematics typically required in such an exercise and also typically embedded into statistical sampling programs. For more information, an internal auditor should consult some of the previously referenced statistical sampling books. See Exhibit 16.7 for examples of standard deviation calculations.

16.8 OTHER AUDIT SAMPLING TECHNIQUES

A fair amount of study, training, or experience is necessary to gain more than a minimum level of proficiency in any of these audit-sampling methods. Attributes, monetary unit, and variables sampling—probably in that order—are the more important tools for internal auditors to understand and use. Sampling is a broad area with many other approaches as well, and other methods can be used under certain circumstances. The following sections briefly describe some of these other sampling methods.

(a) Multistage Sampling

This technique involves sampling at several levels. A random sample is first selected for some group of units and then another random sample is pulled from within the population of the units first selected. For example, each of 200 retail stores maintains its own inventory records, sending only summarized results to a headquarters office. Internal audit, interested in the age or condition of the inventory, might first select a sample of the stores and then at each store select a random sample of their inventory items. When all locations are examined with a sample selected at each location, the result can be treated as a variables or attribute sample.

Multistage sampling assumes that each primary sampling unit is homogeneous, but that assumption can sometimes cause problems. If the auditor assumes that all of the previously discussed Quick Bite example stores are essentially the same, and the auditor subsequently finds that one or two of the units are very different from the others, such a failure to consider those unusual stores in the overall audit test can bias any overall sample projection. This technique can be useful for a retail chain store environment. However, the formal mathematics for calculating sample sizes and reliability, and in particular for estimating the sampling error, are complex. While practical for the chain store situation, the method can break down if the internal auditor wants to project the results of the sample test statistically.

(b) Replicated Sampling

This is a variation of multistage sampling in that it requires the drawing of one overall random sample of size X, composed Y separate random subsamples of size X/Y. If a sample of 150 items is to be taken from a very large population, rather than drawing a single sample, the auditor would select 15 samples of 10 items each. These primary samples from the overall population would be pulled from a series of random numbers. Then the same random numbers that were used to select each of the primary items would be used to select subsamples for items within those groups. The first random number would be assigned to subsample 1, the second to subsample 2, and so forth until a sufficient number had been apportioned.

Why would an internal auditor want to use replicated sampling rather than the multistage sampling previously described? The main reason is that the mathematics is easier. Again, this chapter has not devoted space to a detailed discussion of this sampling procedure, but this is a technique that may be useful to internal auditors in some situations.

(c) Bayesian Sampling

A technique rarely used or even mentioned in the audit sampling literature but which appears to have great potential promise is *Bayesian sampling*. The procedure is named after the mathematician Thomas Bayes (1702–1761), and is based on revised probabilities of sample sizes and the like, based on what are called *subjective probabilities* acquired from the results of prior tests. Very simply put, Bayesian sampling allows an auditor to adjust sample assumptions and probability factors based on the results of a prior audit. In other words, even though the size of the population is the same and the auditor's risks are unchanged, the sample can be modified based on the results of past audit work. While auditors tend to do this as a matter of course, Bayesian sampling allows an auditor to *formally* modify the sampling plan based on the results gathered in past audit tests.

The purpose of this section is only to mention these audit-sampling concepts. The modern internal auditor will probably not encounter Bayesian sampling either in many other internal audit publications or by contact with external auditors. However, the evolving internal control model, defined in the COSO report and as described in Chapter 3, "Internal Audit in the Twenty-First Century: Sarbanes-Oxley and Beyond," may make a Bayesian sampling approach potentially attractive. Internal auditors will probably encounter Bayesian sampling in the future!

16.9 MAKING EFFICIENT AND EFFECTIVE USE OF AUDIT SAMPLING

Audit sampling is a key, important part of the internal auditor's "tool kit," but should not be viewed as an essential requirement to be included in all audits. An internal auditor may or may not decide to test transactions in performing an audit. The auditor may, for example, either decide on the basis of overall comparisons and other auditing procedures that a test of transactions is unnecessary, or that the amounts involved are not sufficiently material to warrant testing. However, an internal auditor is often faced with situations that require sampling of transactions. The best of control systems cannot eliminate errors resulting from system breakdowns, and overall reviews or tests of a few transactions may not be sufficient to disclose whether internal controls are operating effectively.

An organization's procedures may appear to be adequate, but an internal auditor generally must test actual transactions to determine whether the procedures have been followed in practice. If tests are made, audit sampling should be considered as a basis for arriving at more valid conclusions. If the test of transactions generated through the audit sample indicates that operations are acceptable, no further work may be required. Where errors are found, an internal auditor is generally faced with the decisions described below in order to arrive at an audit conclusion:

- *Isolating Errors.* Through a review of the types of errors and their causes, an internal auditor may be able to isolate the total amount of errors. For example, one vendor may be submitting erroneous invoices, and a review of all of the vendor's invoices may pinpoint all the errors. As another example, a particular automated system may appear to be causing the errors, and a special review of that system may be required. Either type of analysis can determine the amount of deficiency as well as the basic cause.

- *Reporting Only on Items Examined.* When an internal auditor encounters significant errors, it may only be necessary to report the results of the tests to operating personnel. The nature of the errors will strongly encourage operational managers to strengthen procedures and determine the magnitude of errors. As part of this review, an internal auditor should attempt to determine the causes for the condition and make specific recommendations for corrective action. Unless an internal auditor projects the results of a statistical sample, management is provided only with errors or amounts pertaining to the items examined.

- *Performing 100% Audits.* Although an internal auditor is not expected to perform a detailed examination of all transactions, in some instances there may be a need for an extended examination when significant errors are found. An example is where certain recoveries are due from vendors but where specific vendors and amounts have to be identified in order to file the claims. If not a 100% examination, the auditor's sampling plan must be based on a very high confidence level, perhaps greater than 99%, and a low risk level of perhaps 1%. The result will be a very large sample but with a very high acceptability of sample results. This large sample size or 100% examination may not be justified in terms of the costs involved, and a more conventional statistical sampling plan may suffice.

- *Projecting Results of Sample.* If the selection of items for the test is made on a random basis, the results can be evaluated using statistical tables. The number and dollar amount of errors can be projected to determine the range of errors in the entire field at a given confidence level. The projection can be used to make an adjustment, or as a basis for decisions of the kind described in the preceding paragraphs.

- *Alternative Sampling Results.* Internal auditors often experiment with audit sampling, such as in the review of equipment operating records to ensure effective utilization, or tests of purchase requisitions to determine the timeliness of filling requests. An internal auditor often uses such procedures as inquiry, observation, vouching, confirmation, computation, and analysis. As a basis for extending the use of audit sampling, internal audit can review areas in which testing was performed in prior reviews along with an analysis of the objective of each test, the period covered, the effective use of judgmental or audit sampling, the number of items in both the field and the sample, the results of these tests, and the feasibility of using these audit sampling procedures in subsequent audits. A review of this nature can have the following benefits:

  o The analysis may pinpoint areas where auditors have been overauditing with larger-than-necessary judgmental sample sizes. An internal audit analysis should discover common weaknesses, for example where testing has been performed for short periods, such as one month, even though the audit report issued implied a period of the entire year.

  o The analysis can examine areas where auditors have not been testing the entire population and only concentrating on sensitive or high-dollar items; this is only a problem when the audit report implies that the entire population has been reviewed.

  o Identify areas where audit sampling is practicable in light of the objectives of the test, number of items in the population, and results of the prior testing performed. This type of detailed analysis makes more efficient and effective use of audit sampling techniques. A strong internal audit quality-assurance process, as discussed in Chapter 25, is often the best time to identify opportunities for the extended use of audit sampling procedures. Of course, internal auditors should become familiar with these procedures and incorporate them as part of the planning process rather than waiting for the quality-assurance function to catch the audit exceptions for any failure after the audit work has been planned and completed.

16.10 HUMAN RESOURCES INTERNAL CONTROLS ATTRIBUTES TEST

For many years, audit sampling was a difficult process both to understand and to use. Auditors needed to refer to published handbooks filled with extensive tables and then to use that data to perform fairly detailed sample selection and test result evaluation calculations. The process was comparatively difficult and certainly was not understood by many auditors. Computerized sampling software has changed all of that. It simplifies the necessary calculations, eliminating the need for reference to formulas or tables. In addition, it facilitates the use of sophisticated techniques, thus enabling an internal auditor to obtain more precise and unbiased results. An internal auditor can, of course, use the time-consuming manual calculation procedures to determine the sample size and to evaluate results in the rare situation when a computer is not available. Today, an auditor can usually take a laptop computer to the site, or the auditee may have a computer available for the auditor's use. In other cases the data may be transmitted or mailed to a central location. When the modern internal audit embeds audit-sampling procedures into other general audit procedures, a better, more effective audit review results. Computer-based sampling software techniques will facilitate audit sampling through the following procedures:

- *Combine Audit Steps.* Savings in audit time can be achieved if various audit steps are performed as part of the same statistical sample. This can be done by testing for as many attributes or characteristics as possible in the sample. For instance, in a review of purchases, the primary audit objective may be to determine whether there is adequate documentary support. In addition, an internal auditor may decide to include tests as part of the statistical sample, to determine whether excess materials are being acquired.

- *Use a Preliminary Sample.* Auditors can devote considerable effort to developing a sampling plan based on an estimated confidence level, precision, and expected error rate or standard deviation; however, in many cases there is insufficient information on which to develop the sampling plan—as, for example, in a first audit. By taking a preliminary sample of from 50 to 100 items, an internal auditor is in a better position to make decisions on the extent of sampling required. The preliminary sample can then be included as part of the final sample. Also, the results of the preliminary sample may lead an internal auditor to conclude that no further testing is required.

- *Perform Interim Audits.* When a sampling plan is prepared in advance—such as for the year—the items to be tested can be examined on a monthly or other interim basis without waiting until the end of the year. Thus, staff auditors can be utilized when available to perform the audit sampling on an interim basis. For example, if the sample plan calls for examination of every hundredth voucher, these can be selected for examination as the transaction is processed.

- *Enlarge the Field Size.*   A basic consideration in audit sampling is that the sample size should not vary to a great extent with an increase in field size. Thus, savings can be obtained by sampling for longer periods of time, or from a field composed of more than one department or division. In some cases an internal auditor may decide to test a particular account for a two-year period, with selection of items during the first year on an interim basis as part of that two-year test.

- *Use a Mix of Attribute and Variables Sampling.*   In some cases, an internal auditor does not know in advance whether variables sampling is required. Since variables sampling is often more complex to apply, the auditor may pick a random sample for attributes, evaluate the results, and decide at that point, on the basis of dollar errors, whether variables sampling is required. If it is, the sample can then be projected or incorporated in an extended sample selected for variables. The important point is that once a sample is taken on a random basis, it can be evaluated using different sampling methods.

- *Apply Simple Audit Sampling Methods.*   Some auditors believe that they must use complex methods of sampling and spend considerable effort and study in arriving at the method to use. In most instances, a simple estimation sample will provide adequate results, without the need for techniques that are difficult to understand, apply, and explain. This does not mean that an internal auditor can overlook judgment in the audit tests. Sensitive items should be examined in addition to a random selection of items, if required. These can be examined on a 100% basis or sampled as part of a separate stratum.

- *Achieve an Effective Balance of Audit Costs and Benefits.*   An internal auditor should take into account the costs of examining each sampling unit when considering extending a sample. The costs of additional work should be compared with benefits from obtaining increased confidence or precision in the final results. As an internal auditor first tries and then effectively uses some of the audit sampling techniques discussed in this chapter, the auditor should subsequently find other useful areas in which to use sampling in the course of operational audit, including:

  - *Production Activities.*   The production function in the modern organization has always been one of the major areas for statistical applications. One of the most common of these is the use of statistical tests by quality-control groups that show which individual manufacturing units are completing particular parts or processing operations in accordance with desired specifications. The same problem exists in connection with purchased parts, materials, and partial assemblies. Other applications include the forecasting of machine capacity needs and continuing maintenance needs. The same procedures can be applied as either a review of production functions or as an independent test.

  - *Inventory Management.*   While variables sampling can be used for such things as the valuation of an inventory, attribute sampling is useful for testing inventory-related internal controls, such as whether estimates for inventory obsolescence are correct, or testing to determine if needed inventory levels by individual items are correct.

○ *Marketing.* Combined with various types of statistical analysis, marketing functions sometimes use attribute-sampling procedures to measure and evaluate consumer preferences. Major applications include the evaluation of advertising approaches, promotional activities, sales techniques, and the like.

○ *Personnel or Human Resources.* Common attribute sampling in this area includes the analysis and evaluation of record keeping requirements, recruitment policies, training methods, employee turnover, compensation policies, and other compliance tests. As illustrated by the example earlier in this chapter, attribute sampling can be useful for testing compliance with various procedural requirements.

○ *Finance-Related Attributes Tests.* Variables sampling is much more common in financial areas because it is normally used to test the value of an account or the like. However, there is also a strong need for attribute sampling as part of the auditor's assessments of internal control procedures. Attribute sampling can include reviews of pricing policy, capital project evaluations, and all types of cost and revenue projections.

Audit sampling is a powerful tool that is all too often ignored by some internal auditors. At one time some auditors did not use audit sampling because it was viewed as too difficult or too theoretical. Auditors then found it easier to say, "You have a problem here" rather than saying, "Based on our audit sample, we are 95% certain that we have identified a control problem." Findings based on appropriate audit samples allow internal auditors to express concerns or opinions on a more solid basis. Computer tools now make statistical sampling a simpler task. In the old days, auditors relied on extensive tables of values and difficult formulae. Today, the effective modern internal auditor should learn the basics of audit sampling and use them when appropriate.

ENDNOTES

[1] *Audit Sampling.* American Institute of Certified Public Accountants Audit and Accounting Guide, New York, 1983 (out of print).

[2] Dan M. Guy, D.R. Carmichael, and O. Ray Whittington. *Practitioner's Guide to Audit Sampling*, New York: John Wiley & Sons, 1998.

[3] Leslie, Donald A., Albert D. Teitlebaum, and Rodney J. Anderson, *Dollar-Unit Sampling: A Practical Guide for Auditors*, Copp Clark Pitman, 1979.

CHAPTER SEVENTEEN

Audit Reports and Internal Audit Communications

17.1 AUDIT REPORTS FOR EFFECTIVE INTERNAL AUDIT COMMUNICATIONS

An audit report is a formal document where internal audit summarizes its work on an audit project and reports its *findings* and recommendations based on that work. Audit reports are perhaps the most important element of the internal auditing process and the major means to apprise people both inside and outside the organization of internal audit's work. Audit reports constitute an enduring type of evidence about the professional character of internal audit activities and allow others to evaluate this contribution. Effective audit reports, of course, must be supported by high-quality audit fieldwork, but that same audit field-work can be nullified by poorly written or prepared reports. Preparation of clear and effective reports are a major concern for internal auditors at all levels, from the chief audit executive (CAE)—who is ultimately responsible for the internal auditing—to staff members of the auditing team who did the detailed work and wish to report their audit results.

Good reporting is more than just report preparation and appearance. Audit reports should reflect the basic philosophy and related concepts of the organization's total audit approach, including its underlying review objectives, supporting strategies and major policies, procedures covering the audit work, and the professional performance of the audit staff. Internal audit reporting provides a good opportunity to integrate total internal auditing efforts and to provide a basis for overall appraisal.

While the audit report is the major means of communication, the modern internal auditor will be less effective if communications with the rest of the organization are limited only to published reports. Communication with other members of the organization must be effected daily through interviews during the course of fieldwork, closing meetings when audit findings are first presented, meetings with senior management to apprise them of the results of audits, and many other contacts throughout the organization. All members of the internal audit organization must be effective communicators in both their written and spoken words. Audit reports and audit communications are particularly important today for communicating with the audit committee of the board, given the requirements of the Sarbanes-Oxley Act (SOA). This chapter will discuss the purpose and presentation styles of audit reports, including various formats and methods of presenting the results of audit work to management and others in the organization. Audit reports are a major component of internal audit communication.

17.2 PURPOSES AND TYPES OF AUDIT REPORTS

Internal audit reports have several important functions, which should always be considered when completing audit work and communicating the results. Whether a formal written document circulated to senior and board level management or an informal or even verbal presentation at the end of the audit fieldwork, internal audit reports should always have four basic objectives:

1. **Disclosure of Findings.** The audit report should summarize and outline the conditions observed or found, both good and bad, and can thus be viewed as a source of information to management concerning the operations of some segment of the organization.

2. **Description of Findings.** Based on the conditions observed and found by internal audit, the audit report should describe what, if anything is wrong with the conditions found, as well as why it is wrong. The term "wrong" here includes internal control weaknesses, violations of company procedures, and any of a wide variety of other internal audit concerns. These are also called gaps.

3. **Suggestions for Corrections.** Audit reports should include recommendations, based on the findings, to serve as a framework for action for correcting

the conditions and their causes. The objective of these report suggestions is to improve operations.

4. **Documentation of Plans and Clarification of Views of Auditee.** The auditee may wish to state mitigating circumstances or provide a clarification of issues for any reported matters in disagreement. Depending on the report format, this is also a place where the auditee can formally state plans for corrective actions in response to the audit findings and recommendations.

This four-step process—(1) what is wrong? (2) why is it wrong? (3) what should be done to correct the matter? and (4) what will be done?—forms the basis of virtually all audit reports. Internal auditors should always keep these four steps in mind when drafting audit reports and the separate audit findings that provide the basis of them.

(a) For Whom Is the Audit Report Prepared?

While internal audit organizations often spend considerable time in preparing their audit reports, they sometimes lose sight of who is the report reader. At first glance, the answer seems very simple: It is being prepared for management. But management exists at all levels, including the management of the organizational component reviewed and at the higher levels to which the component is responsible, as well as the audit committee at the highest level. Each management group has special needs and interests, and the question becomes one of which needs best serve overall organizational interests. In more specific terms, the question comes down to what internal audit's respective responsibilities are to the direct auditee versus to the auditee's bosses.

The auditee—that is, the organizational staff and the management group that has been audited—will be motivated by a combination of organization and local entity interests. Direct auditee management knows that its ultimate welfare is closely related to total organizational success but knows also that these rewards are largely determined by its own performance. This perception of performance is a combination of the operational results achieved and how upper-level management thinks the directly responsible managers are actually contributing. In everyday parlance, local or unit management strives to look good to upper-level management. What this all means in terms of internal audit is that the local managers often want help, but want it on a basis that does not discredit them with more senior levels of management. Ideally, they might like to have internal audit work with them on a private consultant basis but not report finding any "dirty linen" to senior management. While the internal audit professional standards discussed in Chapter 12, "Internal Audit Professional Standards," recognize that internal auditors will sometimes act as consultants that is not internal audit's prime role.

Internal audit tries to help local management do a more effective job and knows that in order to identify internal control problems and recommend potential solutions, internal audit must have the full cooperation and a near-partnership relationship with local management. However, this cooperative attitude can place pressure on internal audit if it is asked to pull its punches in audit reports with copies to senior management. Internal audit may feel that its reported concerns will be implemented sooner if it does not criticize local management too harshly in its published audit reports. However, internal audit has a major responsibility to report conditions found or observed. While providing service to local management, internal audit's obligations reach all the way up to the audit committee of the board.

As a starting point for resolving these potentially conflicting demands, all management levels must be provided with a comprehensive understanding of each other's needs and internal audit's responsibility to serve them. There is often a need to increase the level of tolerance and flexibility by raising the level of findings and issues considered sufficiently significant to warrant inclusion in an audit report. This way, internal audit can eliminate many of the more minor matters that should be, and can be, finalized at the local level without involving higher-level managers. A determined joint effort is needed between the local managers and internal audit to work out needed follow-up actions during the course of an internal audit.

The general effect of all these actions is to push internal audit more toward a "service to local management" concept in their work and away from being viewed as headquarters spies. This approach must continue to recognize that internal audit always has its important reporting responsibility to senior management and the audit committee.

17.3 PUBLISHED AUDIT REPORTS

Although audit reports have been discussed as almost a single concept, they can take a variety of different formats and styles in either a "soft" computer-format or a hard-copy paper style. In either case, an audit report is a formal report document outlining internal audit's concerns and recommendations following the four objectives discussed previously. In past years, management sometimes placed restrictions or constraints on internal audit that almost limited it from preparing effective audit reports. For example, some senior managers, in the past, may have declared that all audit reports must be one page or less in size. This type of request sometimes occurred in the past because internal audit functions got too carried away with writing up pages and pages of audit report findings that may have seemed significant to the internal auditor but not to senior management.

Audit reporting attitudes also have changed after SOA. In the congressional hearings leading to the act, there was criticism directed at audit committees receiving only summarized reports, at best, and not receiving any level of detail regarding audit findings—whether from internal or external auditors. With SOA, audit committee members, and, of course, senior management are to receive or have access to full copies of all audit reports. While it is their right to request summarized reports as well, they are still responsible for receiving and understanding all reported audit findings. Internal control findings must be clearly described in an internal audit report. This section will discuss formal published audit reports as well as alternative mechanisms for internal audit reporting.

(a) Approaches to Published Audit Reports

The form and content of internal audit reports can vary widely. An audit report covering a review of internal controls may appear different from a report on the adequacy of business continuity controls or one on fraud investigation procedures.

However, no matter the subject of the internal audit, formal audit reports should always cover a similar general format, starting with a cover page, a description of the work performed and then internal audit's findings and recommendations. We are describing an audit report in the sense of an older, multipage type of document. Today, a report would typically be in a software document format that may never even be formally printed. However, just as the words in a printed book can not be changed once printed, software copy versions of audit reports should be protected in a manner that no one but the author—internal audit—can change them after release or publication.

Just as a traditional book will begin with a cover page and preface, an audit report should begin with an introductory page. Exhibit 17.1 is an example of audit report introductory page of formal audit report covering a review of the purchasing function in a manufacturing organization. This report's introductory page or pages should have the following elements:

- *Report Addressees and Carbonees.* An audit report should always be addressed to one person responsible for drafting report responses, often someone usually at least one organizational level above the auditee. There should also be a selected list of carbonees, as determined by internal audit. The latter will include the auditee's manager, members of

EXHIBIT 17.1

Formal Audit Report Introductory Page

EXAMPLECO

INTERNAL AUDIT DEPARTMENT
AUDIT REPORT

HEAVY IRON DIVISION PURCHASING FUNCTION

To: Malcolm Muddle, Director of Operations

CC: Amos Arrons, Heavy Iron Finance
        Cecelia Clark, ExampleCo Controller
        Sam Sneed, Heavy Iron Purchasing
        Tom Abacus, Debits & Credits, CPAs

The ExampleCo internal audit department has performed an internal controls review of the Heavy Iron Division purchasing function. The objective of our review was to assess the quality of the control environment in place and the control procedures operating over the Heavy Iron purchasing function. Our work was restricted to Heavy Iron purchasing activities at their headquarters facility in Burning Stump, NE, and did not include purchasing activities at their facilities in Brazil and Nigeria. We completed fieldwork for this audit on October 10, 20XX.

Our review included an assessment of the adequacy of Heavy Iron Division purchasing procedures and their compliance with both those and ExampleCo corporate procedures. We performed detailed tests of procedures, as we felt appropriate, and also reviewed controls over the Heavy Iron purchasing department information system. In addition, we performed a detailed confirmation and quality assurance assessment of a sample of Heavy Iron vendors.

We generally found the internal controls over the Heavy Iron Division purchasing function to be adequate. We did find some areas where we feel corrective actions are necessary to improve the internal control structure. These audit findings and management's planned corrective actions are included in this report.

Samantha Smith
Internal Audit, Nov. 7, 20XX

---

senior management, and other interested persons such as the partner in charge of the external audit team. (As an aside, we are using an archaic term here—carbonee—even though carbon copy paper has all but disappeared. Of course, we mean those receiving additional copies.)

- *Title of Report and Objectives of Review.* A brief, definitive title tells the reader what is contained in the audit report and also will be useful for various summary reports. Similarly, an audit report should have a brief but clear statement of the objectives of the review.

- *Audit Scope and Date of the Fieldwork.* Usually included with the statement of audit objectives is some abbreviated information on the general scope of the audit and the approximate date of the audit fieldwork. A statement that a given report covers a review of the "purchasing function for electronic components at the XYZ division" will lead the report reader to expect a different report than a statement that the audit covered just the "purchasing function."

- *Locations Visited and Timing of Audit.* Because of potential timing delays in wrapping up audit reports due, time may pass between the time of the fieldwork and the final published audit report. The report cover page should clearly state when the audit fieldwork was performed and also mention the locations visited.

- *Audit Procedures Performed.* A brief paragraph describing the audit procedures performed is often very helpful to the report reader. This information is particularly useful if internal audit has performed some special testing procedures in order to arrive at its opinion.

- *Auditor's Opinion Based on the Results of the Review.* An internal audit report should *always* have some fairly general assessment of the overall adequacy of the controls or other concerns in the area reviewed. For example, the opinion statement might be worded as follows:

  ○ "We found the controls in the area reviewed to be adequate except for . . ."

  ○ "We found that most controls were good and were operating as installed . . ."

  ○ "We identified significant control problems in the areas reviewed. Our findings . . ."

The statement of the auditor's opinion can take many forms. However, it generally points to the detailed audit findings and recommendations, which follow these first pages of the full audit report. Exhibit 17.2 contains some examples of other auditor findings, including an opinion statement. No one form is "right" and the audit department's style should be consistent with audit commitee and senior management's wishes.

Internal audit reports often follow one of several common approaches. Given the type of organization, its overall management style, the skills of the internal audit staff, and many other factors, each of the audit report formats described has its own merits as well as disadvantages. Internal audit wants to communicate what it did, what it found, and what needs to be corrected in a manner that will gain the attention of key managers in the organization. All professionals are faced

EXHIBIT 17.2

Informal Memo Format Audit Report Example

MEMO

To: Sam Sneed, Purchasing Dept.
From: Samantha Smith, Internal Audit
Date: Thursday, October 10, 20XX
Subject: Audit of Purchasing, Interim Report

ExampleCo Internal Audit has completed its review of the Heavy Iron Division purchasing function. Our fieldwork was started on September 5 and included visits to the Heavy Iron offices and additional testing as we found necessary. We have concluded our fieldwork for this review as of October 5, and this memo represents an interim audit report covering said fieldwork. A formal audit report, requiring your plans for corrective actions, will be released after we complete certain additional audit work, including purchase order confirmations.

We generally found internal controls over Heavy Iron purchasing function operations to be adequate. However, we also found certain internal control weaknesses requiring additional Heavy Iron Division investigation and correction actions. Although these comments may be subject to revision when we complete all of our audit work in this area, we have initially identified the following control weaknesses.

- Despite frequent, multiple use of certain parts, blanket purchase orders allowing for price/volume discounts are not used.

- There appears to be little effort to seek bids from multiple vendors for some common commodities. Multiple vendors might yield lower prices.

- Security over purchasing files is weak. Although the function is largely automated, many product lines still use substantial paper records. There is no effort to protect those records during nonbusiness hours.

- The automated purchasing system needs an upgrade or overhaul. The system now in use is over 15 years old, has poor documentation, and cannot interface with several other key systems.

These comments are very preliminary and will be discussed in greater detail, along with our recommendations for corrective action, in our draft audit report to be issued after the completion of our final audit work. If there are any questions during the interim, please contact me.

---

with a barrage of paper documents as well as electronic communications, which they are asked to read, understand, and act on. Internal audit wants to provide the readers of its reports with enough information to explain the issues but not so much that members of management will place the report on an office credenza or e-mail in-box with little more than good intentions of reading it later. Without enough information, the reader may not know if a serious problem or other issues requiring action exist given the summarized report format. In an overly detailed report, the reader may miss significant points given the large volume of the materials presented. Alternative approaches to developing and issuing internal audit reports include:

- *Audit Reports with "Encyclopedic" Coverage.* Some internal audit reports strive to present a great deal of information about the activity area reviewed. Their objective is to provide an in-depth reference source to the report user. The information can be of a historical nature or pertain to the current situation. It may cover operational practices and results or may deal with financial information. An example here might be a review of a complex finance-oriented automated system or a description of a complex manufacturing process.

- *Description of the Audit Procedures Performed.* Audit reports sometimes provide a great deal—sometimes too much—of information about the audit procedures actually performed. Audit steps may be described in some detail, as might the scope of actual verification and testing. Sometimes, this audit report coverage almost repeats the materials contained in audit procedural manuals, as discussed in Chapter 13, "Internal Audit Organization and Planning." With this type of audit report, there may be a question as to how interested the reader of the report is in these procedural details and what purpose they really serve. Most users of audit reports should be willing to rely on the competence of internal audit for those technical dimensions. Detailed descriptions are only of value when internal audit needs to describe a complex area such as the decision logic forming an opinion based on audit statistical sampling parameters. On balance, such detailed accounts of technical procedures should be excluded, or at least minimized.

- *Detailed Explanations of Audit Findings.* Some internal audit reports go into fairly voluminous detail about the results of the various audit efforts. Although the coverage here may look impressive, it is doubtful whether an extensive amount of detail describing the audit findings serves a useful purpose. With a very large audit report "book," the reader may be turned off and thus miss the important materials. Audit reports should give only a necessary and sufficient amount of information about audit findings and allow the reader to understand the detailed issues involved.

- *A Highly Summarized Report.* In the other extreme, some internal audit departments have released very summarized reports that only provide information that internal audit has reviewed some topic area and usually found no control exceptions of significance. This same style of report often mentions that control exceptions were found and they were corrected, with no detail. These reports often do little more than state that internal audit has reviewed an area and found some minor items, which were not included in the report even though they might be interesting to a reader. Unless these summarized reports support a longer, more detailed report, they are not effective for most internal audit reporting needs. In addition, the summarized report may put the audit committee reader at risk by glossing over a potentially significant internal control weakness and are not providing the details required under today's SOA rules.

- *Focus on Significant Issues.* The more common report format—often the best—is one that focuses only on "significant issues," those that have potentially important bearing on internal controls weaknesses, policies, operational approaches, the utilization of resources, employee performance, and the results achieved or achievable. More senior organizational managers are interested primarily in problems that are of such a nature and scope, and they typically wish to be informed and given the opportunity to contribute to solutions. If these significant issues relate to completed actions, the issues would have to be still more significant to merit the reporting. The advantage of this focus on significant issues is that senior managers can get the information they need without wading through excessive detail.

The actual audit report format and method of presentation will vary from one organization to another. Exhibit 17.2 shows examples of positive sounding audit report. Although this is a memo format report, only one page in length for purposes of this book, multiple-page reports should follow the same general style. While audit reports were once hard-copy typed documents, word-processing software has changed the style and format of audit reports today. Audit reports can now be issued with interesting typeface fonts, with supporting graphics, or in a totally electronic format over a proprietary intranet. However, no matter what the basic format, an audit report should always contain the elements of what internal audit did, when they did the work, and what they found. A very key portion of an internal audit report should be the auditor's findings and recommendations.

(b) Elements of an Audit Report Finding

During a review, the internal auditors assigned to the project may encounter exceptions or internal control weaknesses in some of the areas to review, as outlined in the established audit program. (See Chapter 14, "Directing and Performing Internal Audits," on how to prepare an audit program.) Those audit programs identified exceptions as well as other internal audit observations are the subject of the audit report findings. For example, the audit program may direct the auditor to review a sample of travel expense vouchers to check that they are properly approved and to verify that the reported expenses are consistent with published travel policies. If internal audit finds that some of the sample selected are not properly approved or are not in compliance with travel policy, internal audit will have one or more potential audit findings to report.

Auditors will encounter a large number and variety of these exceptions in the course of almost any review. Some may be relatively important—such as the discovery of significant numbers of vouchers submitted for payment but lacking proper approval signatures. Others may be relatively minor—such as the discovery of an employee who reported $25.50 for meal expenses when policy requires that such expenses must be less than $25.00. While the latter is a violation of policy, senior management may not be too interested in an audit report that is filled with these relatively minor infractions. This is not to say that an internal auditor should look the other way at such "minor" internal control items. Such smaller internal control exceptions should be documented and discussed with management at the conclusion of fieldwork but they may not necessarily be the type of issues to report to senior management through a formal audit report unless a series of them represents a trend. Then, internal audit might consider reporting them through a summarized finding covering the overall condition.

An internal auditor must analyze the bits and pieces of information gathered during a review to select findings and recommendations for inclusion in the final report. At the conclusion of the audit fieldwork, internal audit should always ask itself whether there was sufficient information to develop an audit finding, and, if so, how these matters of audit concern should be presented. Options for the latter range from informal discussions with local management to a formal presentation in the audit report.

Audit report findings presented in a common format allow the report reader to understand the audit issues easily. No matter what the nature of the audit work or the finding, readers should be able to scan an audit finding and quickly decide what is wrong and what needs to be corrected. While important to both the internal auditors who drafted a finding and to report readers, audit report findings are sometimes not that well constructed. Poorly drafted audit findings often make the report reader question what the problem is, and why they should be concerned. Good audit report findings should contain the following:

- *Statement of Condition.* The first sentence in a report finding should usually summarize the results of internal audit's review of the area of concern. It can give a comparison of "what is" with "what should be." The "what is" summarizes the condition or appraisal made by internal audit based on the facts disclosed in the review. The purpose is to capture the report reader's attention. Examples of audit report finding statements of condition include:
  - "Obsolete production equipment is being sold at bargain rates and in a manner that does not follow fixed asset disposition policies."
  - "The backup and contingency plan for the new customer billing system has not been tested and does not follow organizational security standards."
  - "The ABC division work-in-process inventory is not correctly valued according to generally accepted accounting principles."
- *What Was Found?* The finding should discuss both the procedures and the results of those procedures. Depending on its complexity, the finding can be summarized in little more than one sentence or may require an extensive discussion describing the audit procedures. This "what was found" statement can be as simple as, "Based on a sample of employee expense reports filed for fourth quarter 20XX, the preferred organization rental car agency was not used in over 65% of the expense reports reviewed." Often, this portion of the finding will be much more extensive, as internal audit describes the procedures performed and what was found. Examples can be found in the Exhibit 17.3 sample audit report findings.
- *Internal Audit's Criteria for Presenting the Finding.* The finding should always have a criterion, or a statement of "what should be" to be used in judging the statement of condition. Without strong criteria there cannot be an audit finding. Criteria vary according to the area audited and the audit

EXHIBIT 17.3

Audit Report Findings and Recommendations Examples

I. *BLANK PURCHASE ORDERS*

Blanket purchase orders would allow the organization to receive supplies of frequently used common parts without the need to issue a separate purchase order for each commodity replenishment. Company purchase department policies allow and even encourage the use of these blanket orders, at buyer discretion. We found that several buyers of small commodity parts have never used the blanket purchase order concept. They generally advised us they thought they could get better prices by negotiating each purchase separately.

We reviewed the pattern of purchase orders for several frequently purchased commodities and found opportunities for potential savings. For example, separate purchase order arrangements with different vendors were made for certain electronic switch units. Vendor prices varied up or down by about 5% over the nine months reviewed. A blanket purchase order might have provided a guaranteed price, based on total aggregate quantities purchased.

Recommendation. A program of blanket purchase orders should be initiated for frequently used commodity type parts. Price versus total quantity agreements should be negotiated with key supplying vendors. The purchasing department should monitor the cost savings and other benefits from the program.

II. *PROFESSIONAL TRAVEL EXPENSES*

The company travel policy specifies that all employees should work with the company travel agent to find the lowest airfares for business travel. In addition, policy specifies that travelling employees should always attempt to be at their business destinations by 12:00 noon on the first business day of their trips. We found that this travel policy is largely ignored by employees in certain company departments. For example, almost all air travel arrangements for employees of department 22-88 were made individually by employees, ignoring the travel agent. Expenses were charged to corporate charge cards with no evidence of efforts to seek minimal air travel cost. Similarly, in our review of travel records over the past six months, we found over 5% of employees ignored the lowest-cost recommendation of the agent and selected higher-cost air tickets. Frequently, these same employees made air travel arrangements that brought them to their destination late on the first day of the trip.

Recommendation. Policies should be strengthened to encourage least-cost air travel. A revised policy statement should be developed and issued to all travel-mode employees, emphasizing the need for lowest-cost travel. When employees do not accept the travel agent's least-cost recommendation, the fact should be printed on the air ticket travel itinerary included with the employee's expense report. Departmental managers should be assigned first-tier responsibility to reduce their employee's air ticket travel expenses.

III. *AFTER-HOURS OFFICE SECURITY*

Company policy specifies that all office employees should clear their desks of all reports, memos, and other business papers at the end of the business day and also should sign-off from their desktop computers. In a review of office areas on three successive evenings during the period of our fieldwork, we found numerous desks covered with work materials and numerous computer systems still left running. These practices compromise company security due to the possibility of unauthorized persons viewing materials left in desk areas.

Recommendation. All employees should be reminded of after-hours desktop policies. The security department should visit office areas from time to time in the evening. Persons not in compliance with after-hours policy should be reminded with a desktop security department note.

---

objectives. The criteria may be the policies, procedures, and standards of an organization. In some instances, internal audit must develop the criteria. In an audit of the effectiveness of some procedure, there may not be preestablished targets or measurements that can be used as indicators and standards may be couched in general or vague terms. Internal audit should consider the following:

○ *Criteria of Extremes.* Clearly inadequate or outstanding performance is relatively easy to appraise. However, when performance moves closer to the average, it becomes more difficult to judge. Internal audit can sometimes use extreme cases of inadequate performance as criteria for the report finding. This might cause internal audit to state that some observed condition was "almost as bad as . . ."

○ *Criteria of Comparables.* Comparisons can be made between similar operations or activities, determining their success or lack of success and causes for the differences. While it is never good to state specifically that Department A is X% worse than Department B, the report might compare the conditions found to average or typical conditions throughout the organization.

○ *Criteria of the Elements.* In some cases, internal auditors incorrectly state their performance criteria with such broad terms that it is impossible to evaluate the reported condition. This is the type of vague criteria that states "all managers should make good decisions." While ideal, we all know exceptions exist. The reported measure should be broken down on a functional, organizational basis, or by elements of cost related to specific activities.

○ *Criteria of Expertise.* In some cases, internal audit may find it useful to rely on other experts to evaluate an activity. These experts may be outside the organization or may be part of the audited organization's staff. This type of supporting reference often strengthens the overall audit finding.

• *Effect of the Reported Finding.* Internal audit should always consider the question of "How important?" when deciding whether to include an item in the audit report. Internal audit must weigh materiality—if the finding is of no significance, it may not be a finding at all. Once the decision has been made to include it as a finding in the audit report, the effect of the reported condition should be communicated. Findings that will result in monetary savings or that affect organizational operations and achievement of goals are always of special interest to management.

• *Cause or Reason for the Audit Deviation.* The answer to the question "Why?" is especially important to management when reading an audit report. The reasons for a deviation from requirements, standards, or policies should be explained as well as possible. Identifying a cause for the condition gives a basis for taking needed management action.

• *Internal Audit's Recommendation.* Audit report findings should conclude by recommending appropriate corrective actions. This is the audit finding's conclusion of "What should be done?"

Although internal audit's description of objectives, audit procedures performed, and the opinion of the controls as a result of the review are all important elements in an internal audit report, members of management will evaluate the quality of the report on the basis of the reported findings and recommendations. If any facts reported in an audit finding are incorrect, no matter how close to the real truth, the auditee will typically challenge the credibility of the overall audit report. Any misstatement can place the entire audit report into question. Internal audit should *take extreme care* to report its audit findings factually and accurately. Otherwise, a significant amount of good internal audit work can be ignored. Care should also be taken in developing strong, meaningful, and realistic recommendations. The recommendations should generally give some consideration to the costs and benefits of various alternative recommended actions. Of course, if the audit finding is highlighting a potential violation of the law, the recommendation should always be to take prompt and complete corrective action.

(c) Balanced Audit Report Presentation Guidelines

If part of internal audit's efforts is to evaluate the efficiency, economy, and effectiveness with which management has accomplished its objectives, then internal audit has a responsibility to disclose both satisfactory and unsatisfactory conditions found during an audit. While conditions needing improvement should always be described, communication here should minimize the description of audit findings in totally negative terms. Rather, internal audit should strive to encourage management to take needed corrective action and to produce results. An internal audit report cannot be fully successful if the auditee is not receptive to the results of the audit, but a report with findings that just talks about what was right also provides little help to management. Consequently, internal audit should adopt a positive reporting style that is balanced with a mixture of favorable as well as appropriate unfavorable comments, that always present matters in perspective, and emphasizes constructive rather than just negative comments.

To provide a level of balance, internal audit must sort through the various positive and negative data gathered during the course of a review and ask itself the question, "What should be the type and extent of favorable comments to be reported as a result of this audit?" The answer cannot be laid down in precise terms. The same criteria used in identifying significant findings can be used to report items considered significant based on standards of performance. For example, assume that an audit objective was to evaluate the timeliness of completing purchase requisitions. Comments in a report finding should relate to the organization's ability or inability to complete these purchase requisitions in a timely manner and ignore other unrelated issues. Some techniques to provide better audit report balance are:

- *Provide Audit Reports with Perspective.* Internal audit should avoid the temptation to cite only those factors that support internal audit's conclusions and to ignore those that distract from it. Perspective is always added when listing the monetary effect of a finding as well as the value of the entire account under review. A $1,000 error sounds much more severe when it is part of a $100,000 account than it does for a $10,000,000 account. The report finding should disclose, as appropriate, the total monetary amount audited or recorded in relationship to the total value of errors encountered. The significance of the finding is made evident by this procedure. Also, when deficiencies are disclosed in only part of the area examined, balance will be added to the report by identifying those areas examined that did not contain deficiencies. This practice should be in accordance with an internal audit policy of disclosing accomplishments as well as deficiencies.

- *Report Auditee Accomplishments.* Since the evaluation process involves weighing both satisfactory and unsatisfactory aspects of auditee operations in light of the audit objectives, mentioning auditee accomplishments in improving controls or correcting errors together with the noted deficiencies or aspects in need of improvement can add much to the usefulness of the audit report as a management tool. The auditee accomplishments should be disclosed in the summary of the report when the conclusions of the audit may be affected by their significance and in the findings when a detailed disclosure of the accomplishments is desired or necessary.

- *Show Planned Actions.* In situations where the auditee has taken, or has made plans to take, corrective action prior to the completion of the audit, the audit report should disclose this fact. In addition, other steps taken by the auditee in an attempt to correct a reported deficiency may not be so obvious but nevertheless should be considered as a positive reportable action. For example, the auditee may have contracted with an outside consultant to help implement the internal controls needed in a computer system covered in an audit report. Such arrangements should be included in the report along with those control weaknesses.

- *Report Mitigating Circumstances.* Mitigating circumstances generally consist of factors relating to the problems or conditions discussed in the audit report over which management has little or no control. Since these factors lessen management responsibility for the condition, they should be reported as part of cause. Mitigating circumstances, for example, may include the very short time frame in which a program was required to be implemented, business conditions requiring immediate changes, or a lack of adequate budget funds for adding personnel or other resources to accomplish objectives.

- *Include the Audit Responses as Part of the Audit Report.* The auditee's response to a finding may contain information that provides additional balance to an audit report. In addition to planned corrective action, the auditee may indicate other related accomplishments or cite additional facts and other circumstances. In instances where agreement has not been reached on the finding or recommendation, the auditee should be given the opportunity to explain the basis for nonoccurrence.

- *Improving Audit Report Tonal Quality.* The use of positive and constructive words and ideas rather than negative and condemning language will give a positive tone to the report. Unless deserved, audit reports should avoid phrases indicating that the auditee "failed to accomplish," "did not perform," or "was not adequate," and should state audit report ideas in a positive and constructive manner. Audit reports phrased to a positive and constructive tone, and negative titles and captions should be avoided since they do not add to the finding and may even misrepresent the actual situation. Thus, a negative-sounding title for a finding such as "Inadequate Controls over Company Cash Controls" might be replaced by "Cash Controls Improvement" or "Cash Collection Procedures."

These comments are not meant to suggest that all audit reports should be sugarcoated and that internal audit should never make strong critical statements about auditees. An audit and its subsequent audit report can often be a very critical process where internal audit investigates an area that perhaps has not received much management attention. If internal audit finds serious problems in the area reviewed, it should clearly identify problems that might be significant unless prompt corrective actions are taken. When possible, however, internal audit should give credit where due and discuss either positive or mitigating circumstances as would be appropriate. Exhibit 17.4 contains some examples of negatively and positively toned audit report findings.

EXHIBIT 17.4

Audit Report Negative and Positive Statement Examples

Negative Audit Findings	Positive Audit Findings
1a. We found that controls in the area were generally poor.	1b. We identified areas where controls need improvements.
2a. Little management attention has been given to keeping documentation current.	2b. The documentation was not current and other priorities have prevented it from being updated.
3a. The failure to reconcile these accounts was caused by a lack of management attention.	3b. We observed that these accounts had not been reconciled for several past periods.
4a. Documentation was either out of date or nonexistent.	4b. We found only minimal current documentation in this area.
5a. The new inventory system is poorly designed.	5b. The inventory system has some major control weaknesses. More attention should have been given to its design.
6a. This failure to protect passwords could result in a management fraud.	6b. Poor password controls are a weak internal control.
7a. No attention has been given to protecting stockroom inventories.	7b. Better controls should be established over stockroom inventories.
8a. The responsible manager did not seem to understand company procedures in this area.	8b. Training in the use of these procedures needs to be strengthened.
9a. The department failed in several of its training program operations.	9b. Several opportunities exist for strengthening controls in training program operations.
10a. The budgetary system was not adequate to assist management in the control of project funds.	10b. The establishment of a proper budgetary system would assist management in the control of project funds.

(d) Alternative Audit Report Formats

With today's technology, audit results can be reported in a wide spectrum of formats. While the standard written audit report format described here is certainly the most familiar and best way to describe audit work, internal audit can use other approaches to describe the results of their audit findings and recommendations. That standard report becomes a record of corporate governance activity allowing an organization to certify what internal audit did, what they found, and what was recommended. In our litigation-prone society, it is essential that an organization and its audit committee have formal, secure records of its internal audit activities. However, internal audit should consider some alternative approaches, particularly for interim audit results reporting. Some of the less formal and more abbreviated alternative means by which internal audit can report the results of its work include:

- *Oral Reports.* In some situations, internal audit may want to report the results of its work and any recommendations on an oral basis. This reporting mode should always occur, at least on an interim basis, when the on-site audit team reports the results of their work at an end of audit fieldwork closing conference. In other cases, an oral report may be the result of emergency action needs, and an oral presentation may also be a prelude to a more formal written report. To some extent there may always be oral reporting as a means of supplementing or explaining written reports, especially when individuals being served have special needs. Oral reporting is often useful but only should be a supplementary form of audit reporting.

  An oral report should not be a substitute for the formal written report because there generally is no permanent record beyond meeting notes. The auditor may think that local management agrees to correct some problem, but management may not really say that. As a result there are more likely to be later misunderstandings unless detailed, contemporaneous notes are taken for workpaper documentation or if the meeting is taped. However, the appearance of a tape recorder or video unit usually causes distrust. Oral audit reports should be used carefully and not in lieu of later written reports.

- *Interim or Informal Memo Reports.* In situations where it is deemed advisable to inform management of significant developments during the course of the audit, or at least preceding the release of the regular report, internal audit may want to prepare some kind of interim written report. These reports may only pertain to especially significant problems where there is a need for prompt corrective action, or the reports may be a type of progress report. A memo report should be used, at a minimum to describe the results of an oral presentation, as discussed previously. An interim or memo report is often released to record the results of an oral presentation and to call local management's attention to a potential audit finding. The material discussed in this example report will eventually be included in a more formal audit report discussing the total results of an internal audit.

- *Questionnaire-Type Audit Reports.* The usual procedure is that some kind of a written report is prepared at the completion of an individual audit assignment. A questionnaire type of report can be a useful interim summary to the formal audit report or serve as an appendix to the formal report document. This format works best where the scope of the audit review deals with reasonably specific procedural matters, and usually at a fairly low operational level. This type of report usually has a limited range of overall usefulness. Exhibit 17.5 is an example of a questionnaire-style audit report. It is perhaps best used as an educational tool to inform management of internal audit's concerns.

- *Regular Descriptive Audit Reports.* In most audit assignments, the work should be concluded with the preparation of a formal descriptive audit report. The exact form and certainly the content of such written reports will vary widely, both as between individual audit assignments and individual internal audit departments. They may be short or long and presented in many different formats, including differing approaches for quantitative or financial data presentations. The whole idea is that they represent a documented record of internal audit's work on an assignment.

- *Summary Audit Reports.* Internal audit functions frequently issue an annual or a more frequent report summarizing the various individual reports issued, and describing the range of their content. These summary reports are often primarily prepared for the audit committees or other members of senior management. Exhibit 8.4 shows an example of this

EXHIBIT 17.5

Questionnaire-Type Audit Report Example

ExampleCo Heavy Iron Division Audit of Purchasing, October 29, 20XX Summary of Internal Control Strengths and Weaknesses	Result
1. Are departmental operating procedures current and adequate?	**YES**
2. Are purchasing requirements properly specified by requesting departments?	**YES**
3. Are multiple bids sought for all regular, non-custom purchases? *Multiple bid procedures are regularly ignored.*	**NO**
4. Do requesting groups regularly send specifications with purchase requests?	**YES**
5. Are blanket purchase orders used for volume use parts? *Although procedures exist, blanket purchase order procedures are often ignored.*	**NO**
6. Have dollar-based authorization limits been set for all P/Os and are they followed?	**YES**

Note: The above is only a sample of what would be a much larger "Yes" and "No" type of audit questionnaire report. Additional sheets could be attached to better explain "No" control weakness responses.

type of summary report as part of the Chapter 8, "Internal Audit and the Board Audit Committee," discussion on serving the audit committee of the board. Summary reports are especially useful to top-level managers, but they must be only cover pages for the senior managers and board members who have an SOA responsibility to have access to the full reports. In a larger internal audit organization, summary reports also allow the CAE to see the total reporting effort with more perspective, and on an integrated basis.

17.4 AUDIT REPORTING CYCLE

Starting in the early stages of an audit, it is often desirable to develop a framework for the final report, filling in as much detail as possible as the audit moves along. Information and statistics on the area to be audited can be gathered during the survey stage and included in the workpapers as discussed in Chapter 14. This will ensure that needed information is obtained early in the audit, and it will prevent delays in the final report-writing process. In addition, the objectives and scope of the review, defined at the start of the audit, should be fine-tuned as the audit moves along.

As findings are developed and completed, they can be inserted in the proper sections of the report, together with any comments by the auditee. The completed audit report is just one step—though a very important one—in internal audit's overall process of evaluating and commenting on the adequacy of internal controls in order to serve management's needs. The audit report process starts with the identification of findings, the preparation of a draft report to discuss those findings and their related recommendations, the discussion of the audit issues identified with management along with the presentation of the draft report, the completion of management responses to audit report findings, and the publication of the formal audit report covering the area under review. Exhibit 17.6 outlines the critical phases and action steps for the preparation of an audit report. Although a given internal audit department may alter some of these steps slightly to modify its own needs, this generally should be the process necessary to issue an appropriate internal audit report.

EXHIBIT 17.6

Audit Report Preparation Steps

A. Outline Audit Findings
   a. Determine if there is sufficient support to warrant the findings.
   b. Review the findings to determine where additional evidence may be needed.
   c. Ascertain that the causes and effects of findings have been considered.
   d. Determine whether there is a pattern of deficiencies requiring procedural changes or whether the findings represent isolated cases.

B. Preparation of Audit Report Draft First Draft
   a. Review findings drafts for adequate development.
   b. Ascertain whether the findings are stated in specific rather than in general terms.
   c. Ensure that figures and other facts have been checked and cross-referenced in the workpapers.

EXHIBIT 17.6 *(CONTINUED)*

Audit Report Preparation Steps

    d. Review workpapers supporting all findings for adequacy of support and disclosure of items of significance.

    e. Check for adequacy of tone, punctuation, and spelling (Note: Do not rely just on Microsoft Word spell-checks!).

    f. Ascertain whether there is sufficient support for the expression of the auditor's opinion or whether a qualification is needed.

    g. Determine whether the cause, effect, and recommendations are adequately developed.

    h. Discuss methods of improving content and writing style with internal audit team.

C. Discussion with Management

    a. Determine whether management was aware of the problem and already was taking corrective action.

    b. Find out management's reasons for the conditions.

    c. Ascertain whether there are facts or mitigating circumstances of which the auditor was unaware.

    d. Determine management's ideas on how to correct the conditions.

    e. Ensure that management is aware of all significant items that will be present in the report.

    f. Ensure that efforts are made to obtain management's agreement on the facts and conditions.

D. Preparation of Final Audit Report Draft

    a. Ascertain that all prior recommendations for changes in report have been made.

    b. Ensure that management's viewpoints have been adequately considered.

    c. Determine that the report is well written and easily understood.

    d. Ascertain that summaries are consistent with the body of the report.

    e. Ensure that recommendations are based on conditions and causes stated in the findings.

    f. See that management's viewpoints are fairly stated and adequately rebutted, if necessary.

    g. Review the report for use of graphics, tables, and schedules to clarify conditions presented.

    h. Ensure that auditors who wrote the findings agree with any changes made.

E. Audit Report Closing Conference

    a. Ensure that management has had an opportunity to study the final report.

    b. Attempt to obtain agreement on any points of difference.

    c. Consider any suggestions for changing content of report, as well as specific wording.

    d. Obtain current plans for follow-up action from management.

F. Issuance of Final Report

    a. Ensure that final changes are made in accordance with the closing conference.

    b. Check the report once again for typographical errors.

    c. Review the report for a balanced presentation, with positive comments included on results of audit when applicable.

    d. Make a final reading of report for content, clarity, consistency, and compliance with professional standards.

As findings are developed, the internal audit team at the audit site should review them with members of auditee management, soliciting their perspective's on the finding's validity. Possible causes for the audit finding should also be discussed and additional information gathered to prove or disprove the potential audit report condition. In some instances, organizational personnel will assist in obtaining information to develop the findings. They will often provide useful feedback as to whether internal audit's facts are correct or whether they are on the right track. Areas of disagreement can be pinpointed and resolved. Discussing findings with organizational personnel at a staff level helps to get agreement and encourages implementing actions. When agreement is reached, internal audit may be able to limit the amount of detail included in the audit report findings, thus shortening the audit report.

(a) Draft Audit Reports

Once the audit fieldwork has been completed and internal audit has discussed its proposed audit findings with the auditee, a draft audit report should generally be prepared. We have used the term "generally" since sometimes a draft report will not be necessary if a special, investigative report is to be made for presentation to management. For example, internal audit would typically not prepare a fraud investigation draft report to review with persons involved in the potential fraud. In other cases, internal audit should prepare a report draft with their proposed findings and recommendations along with a space for management responses. The draft is then sent to the manager directly responsible for the area that was audited. This is the party who responds and outlines the corrective actions to be taken. Internal audit will then combine these auditee responses with the original report header pages and the draft findings and recommendations to produce the final audit report, as is shown in the Exhibit 17.7 example. This final draft report is typically presented as a last opportunity for the auditee to read and understand the tone and contents of the audit report to be issued.

Closing meetings and a draft report are important steps to validate the adequacy and accuracy of the reported findings and the soundness of the related recommendations prior to the release of the final audit report. While the major foundation for this validation is the audit work performed by the internal audit staff, work needs to be supplemented by the review and confirmation of the auditee personnel. The benefits of this supplementary validation are twofold. First, this provides a cross-check on the accuracy, completeness, and quality of the audit work. Important facts may have been overlooked or erroneously interpreted. There may also be other factors affecting some particular matter that are known only to certain people. The exposure to the auditee thus provides an important check on whether the findings and recommendation will stand up under later scrutiny. The second benefit is to help promote a partnership relationship with local management that will create both a cooperative spirit and a commitment to working out adequate solutions.

While this above-mentioned type of validation should go on during all stages of a review, one of the most important ways this is affected is through the presentation of the draft report to auditee management. Depending on the nature of the audit objectives and the complexity of the audit findings, the draft report can be presented at either the closing conference at the end of the fieldwork, just preceding the departure of the field audit personnel, or delivered to the auditee after the completion of the fieldwork. Strategies for the timing of the draft report delivery include:

- *At the Exit Conference.* Internal audit will generally find it difficult to deliver full draft audit reports at the end of fieldwork exit conference. Most audits are just too complex; there may be too many final questions/clarifications or needed editorial skills to allow draft audit reports to be delivered at the time of the exit conference. This draft report delivery at the exit conference strategy typically only works for compliance-type audits of smaller field or branch locations where the recommendations are to correct less significant problems, such as mispriced goods at a local retail branch.

- *Before Departure of the Field Audit Team.* Here, the audit team has discussed its concerns with local management in a formal exit conference and then prepares the draft report, including any additional comments or clarifications that may result from that conference. In most situations, this approach is more realistic than presenting the draft report at the time of the exit conference. However, the pressure to wrap up the audit work and "get home" may cause the audit team to take shortcuts in their desire to complete the field engagement. This strategy only works best with relatively simple audit assignments.

- *After the Completion of Fieldwork.* With this strategy, the audit team has its exit conference but returns to the home office to draft the final audit report over the next few days or even weeks. Many internal audit organizations find that this approach works best. Audit management has an opportunity to review the field team's work and to make adjustments, as appropriate, to the draft audit report. The risk here is that the internal audit team responsible for the review will be pulled in other directions and will not complete the draft audit report in a timely fashion.

Audit exit or closing conferences should include members of the audit team and the local management responsible for the area reviewed. At the conference, major findings and proposed recommendations are reviewed and, to the extent that an agreement has already been reached between audit and local organization on particular matters, an opportunity is provided to inform responsible management in the area reviewed and to secure further agreement on audit findings and recommendations. The closing conference provides internal audit with a major opportunity to confirm the soundness of the audit results and to make any necessary modifications to the audit report draft as justified. This is also a major opportunity to demonstrate the constructive and professional service that internal audit can provide. These meetings, although sometimes contentious, can be a major means for building sound partnership relations with the auditee. The objective should be to get as much agreement as possible so that the audit report can indicate the completed actions.

In many situations, the draft report is forwarded to the local management for their review and corrective action comments prior to the finalization of the formal or final report. Local management and the actual auditees will typically be given a limited amount of time to review this draft report, to suggest changes to its overall tone or to specific findings, and to prepare their audit responses. While internal audit should encourage auditee management to request changes to the draft report, the emphasis should be on the substantive issues in the draft report rather than on its wording.

Internal audit should request formal responses within perhaps 14 days after the receipt of the draft report. Although this is a relatively short time period given the time that the audit team often has spent on its fieldwork and draft report preparation, auditee management should be in a position to develop a rather rapid response, since they are aware of the findings and suggested recommendations from the exit conference. However, both internal audit and auditee management should try to operate in the same general time frame. That is, if internal audit spends an inordinate amount of time preparing its draft report, it should give auditee management a greater amount of time to prepare its audit report responses.

The submission of draft reports to auditee management at a later stage has merit through the demonstration of genuine consideration for the auditee. However, internal audit should work with auditee management to avoid excessive delay in finalizing the report. A major part of the effectiveness of the report is the extent to which it is issued promptly.

(b) Audit Reports: Follow-Up and Summarization

Once management has submitted its audit report responses, internal audit should combine them with its draft findings and recommendations to release the final audit report. This report will be addressed to management at least one level above auditee management, with copies to the board audit committee and other appropriate officers of the organization. A representative example of such a brief but complete audit report is shown in Exhibit 17.7.

Once the final audit report has been issued, internal audit should schedule a follow-up review to ensure that needed actions based on the audit were actually taken. In some cases, management may request this procedure. While the desirability of follow-up action in itself is very clear, questions can be raised as to whether this is the proper responsibility of internal audit, and whether such action by internal audit will undermine the basic responsibilities of the managers in charge of the particular activities. Although internal audit standards call for follow-up reviews, they can put internal audit more in the role of a police officer and could conflict with its ongoing partnership relationship with the auditee.

Internal audit should play only a limited specific role after the audit report has been released, such as making itself available to respond to questions, and to review again the situation at the time of the next scheduled audit in the area. Many organizations have adopted an intermediate type of approach where the coordination for audit report recommendation follow-up is placed in the hands of another office—usually within the controller's organization or some more neutral administrative services group. The corrective actions are then initiated by the responsible line or staff manager, but responses are made to the coordinating group. If there are undue delays in dealing with the recommendation, the coordinating office can issue a follow-up status report. Under this approach, copies of these responses can also be supplied to internal audit for information, or internal audit can maintain a liaison with the coordinating group. There is no single best answer as to how this follow-up effort should be handled, but on balance it seems best to subordinate internal audit's formal role in it. Internal audit's help can always be requested on a special basis, either by the coordinating office or by individual managers. In addition, any lack of action can be highlighted at the time of the next scheduled internal audit review.

Internal audit has a responsibility to produce audit reports that are readable, understandable, and persuasive. The objective is to issue reports that will command the attention of the managers who have the responsibilities for the various operational activities, and to induce them to take appropriate corrective action. A secondary objective is for audit reports that will build respect for the internal auditing effort.

Internal audit receives a final payoff in its knowledge of the actions taken by auditees based on the internal audit report recommendations. A combination of internal audit technical skills and the ability to communicate results to people in a way that will best ensure their acceptance and active support are elements of good audit reporting. The importance of this part of internal audit's work underlines the need to give audit reports careful attention. It means that the CAE should be actively involved in the report process, and all levels of the internal

---

EXHIBIT 17.7

Final Audit Report Example

April 20, 20X2   Report No. X2-36

Mr. Bruce R. Weston, General Manager
Bright Products Division
The Wonder Corporation

Dear Mr. Weston:

The corporate audit department has completed an operational review of the internal control structure for the Bright Products Division engineering organization. Bright Products engineering has a FY 20X2 budget of $13,000,000 and is responsible for technical research, product design, and development of the Whatzit product line. As of March 30, 20X2, engineering had 1,018 employees, of which 916 were direct.

The objective of our review was to evaluate the controls over equipment resource planning and utilization, compliance with policy, and the effectiveness and efficiency of the current plan of organization. Our audit included, but was not limited to, reviews of the following.

- General organization controls over engineering projects
- Controls over company utilization of capital equipment
- Controls over the accuracy of the reporting of indirect labor charges
- Departmental expenses, including a review of travel expense reports

This review covered operations during the period January 1 to December 31, 20X1. The review was made by Roger G. Wilson and his assistant, Connie Rodriguez, during the period February 13 to March 31, 20X2.

Our review found that the Bright Products engineering department is well managed, with generally good controls over its resources. However, we found that controls over capital equipment inventory should be strengthened. Our audit findings and Bright Products Division's plans for corrective actions are summarized below.

The internal auditing department wishes to express its appreciation for the very fine cooperation received during the review by the divisional management and personnel.

Respectfully submitted,
Charles W. Reiber, general auditor

EXHIBIT 17.7 *(CONTINUED)*

Final Audit Report Example

The Wonder Corporation
Findings and Recommendations

CAPITAL EQUIPMENT INVENTORY

Capital equipment is not under proper administrative control within the Bright Products engineering organization. The Equipment Capitalization Report, maintained by property accounting, is not used by the engineering organization on a regular basis. Although engineering has responsibility for the assets assigned to them, they have not taken a capital equipment inventory of that equipment for over one year.

We selected 50 units from the most current Equipment Capitalization Report and found the following:

- Three units with an original capitalized value of $119,402 could not be located during our fieldwork. One of these was found after the release of our draft report.

- Nine units were found to have no capital equipment serial number identification tags.

The cause for these expectations is the lack of sufficient capital equipment inventory verification procedures and the failure to consistently use serial number identification tag procedures.

RECOMMENDATIONS

Engineering should utilize the existing property accounting reports to better control its capital equipment. All section managers installing engineering capital equipment should be reminded of the need to properly install identification tags on all newly installed equipment. In addition, engineering should take a full wall-to-wall inventory of its capital equipment and schedule period limited inventory reviews on an ongoing basis.

MANAGEMENT RESPONSES

Copies of the Equipment Capitalization Report will be circulated to responsible managers on a regular basis. Procedures have been issued to remind engineering managers of the need to review that report and to assure that identification tags are properly installed.

A full inventory of installed capital equipment will be taken in June 20X2. Procedures will be developed to regularly cycle-count installed capital equipment.

---

audit staff should think in terms of ultimate report needs. In this connection, the problems of report development should also be given proper attention in internal audit training programs. The reports become a statement of internal audit's credibility when reports are subsequently circulated, referred to, and implemented. Audit reports are usually the major factor by which the reputation of an internal audit department is established.

(c) Audit Report and Workpaper Retention

Internal audit's formal audit reports and their supporting workpapers are important documents supporting internal audit's activities. Procedures should be implemented to retain the records for each audit performed as part of regular corporate records storage procedures. While storage of these records was once treated more informally as just an audit function decision, SOA rules have changed things! As discussed in Chapter 3, "Internal Audit in the Twenty-First Century: Sarbanes-Oxley and Beyond," because of the Enron document destruction by their then external auditors, SOA rules require that all records *must be maintained* for a period of seven years. While these rules were aimed at external auditors, they should apply to internal audit as well.

All audit reports and supporting workpapers should be deposited in the corporate records storage facility. While some organizations have their own procedures for this storage, many use outside providers who place these documents in secure areas for later retrieval as required. While these external sources provide references to aid any later retrieval, internal audit should establish its own internal procedures to cross-reference their audit work with the storage titles of the stored items.

While we often think of stored internal audit records as paper binders of workpaper files and other supporting materials, most internal audit work today should be developed in computer records. This material should be scanned or copied and then downloaded to a secure storage media. Material on laptop audit computers should be "burned" on to CD-ROM disks or some other more permanent storage devices. For internal audit materials located on corporate servers or legacy systems, internal audit should make arrangements with the information systems organization to download and store internal audit records following the same procedures used for other centralized systems.

17.5 EFFECTIVE AUDIT COMMUNICATIONS OPPORTUNITIES

Communications are an important element of every phase of internal audit activities. Internal auditors communicate with others through formal audit reports, through face-to-face encounters in audit fieldwork or meetings, and through a wide range of other formal and informal communications. When there is a misunderstanding or conflict on an audit assignment or when the auditor's recommendations are not correctly understood, an analysis of the difficulty usually points to some type of communication problem. Internal auditors should always keep in mind that communications are a basic ingredient of almost every type of audit activity. All internal auditors should understand how to maximize job satisfaction, improve communications, and handle organizational conflicts.

(a) Maximizing Internal Audit Job Satisfaction

Job satisfaction comes first from expected things such as reasonably pleasant working conditions, fair compensation (including reasonable benefits), and qualified supervision. Because these are *expected*, they are not major motivating factors to internal auditors; but if not provided, they can be a major source of irritation and dissatisfaction. The second kind of job satisfaction comes from higher levels of self-expression and self-fulfillment. Included here would be the assignment of greater job responsibilities, more authority, the opportunity to learn and develop the opening of broader career opportunities, and being given greater freedom to achieve results without burdensome restrictions. This second kind of job satisfaction is achieved through strong managerial competence in its planning, organizing, administering, and controlling activities, and in the way it provides resources. Employees—or whom we often call associates today—typically take pleasure in being part of an organization that is well managed, as evidenced by its above-average reputation, profitability, and growth. They also associate such organizations with offering expanded opportunities for qualified people.

At lower organizational levels, efforts to provide maximum job satisfaction are often called "job enrichment." The worker in an automotive assembly line who attaches a small part as the partially assembled car moves down the line provides a classic example of a job that can be boring and potentially disturbing. Job enrichment comes when a worker is given other duties that provide some variety and that expand the nature and scope of his or her responsibilities. Unfortunately, there are limitations to that job enrichment because some cost savings are more often directly dependent on automated production processes. When a worker joins in the planning of the work and in the development of policies and procedures by which that work is actually accomplished and administered, the potential benefits can affect both employer and employee. All levels of the organization can benefit through the input that comes from experience and firsthand exposure to actual operations.

Participative management can be successful in all phases of the management process—planning, organizing, providing resources, administering, and controlling—especially in having some inputs to key decisions about goals, policies, and procedures. If a participative management effort is perceived by the lower-level associates as being superficial—for example, when views submitted are not fairly or adequately considered—then the entire managerial approach can be harmed. Internal auditors should keep participative management concepts in mind when making audit recommendations and when organizing their own internal audit organizational efforts.

The establishment of proper standards for rewards and related penalties is an essential part of the management of people. The rules governing those rewards and penalties must be defined, properly interpreted, and administered throughout the organization. Internal auditors need to recognize the importance of these standards in human relations and the need that they be administered in a manner that demonstrates genuine concern and fairness to all participants. Some of these issues were discussed in Chapter 9, "Whistle-blower Programs and Codes of Conduct." Because of the sensitive nature of any human relations system of rewards and penalties and the varying objectivity of individuals in evaluating fairness, there are bound to be differences of opinion and some resulting dissatisfaction surrounding any system. Individuals will tend to judge the system in terms of the impact on them, and their criteria will be the fairness of the system as designed and as administered.

(b) Effective Internal Audit Communications

Effective communication both on a person-to-person basis and with larger groups is a key component to internal audit success. The modern internal auditor should have a good understanding of some of the problems associated with effective communications and an understanding of how to cope with those problems. Situations continuously arise in an organization when two individuals need to communicate with each other. These include giving an oral instruction to a staff auditor, discussing an operational problem during an audit exit meeting, counseling a subordinate, interviewing a prospective employee, and conducting a staff performance review. All of these situations involve differing personal relationships, but consist of a continuing two-way flow of messages. An internal auditor should understand this process in order to identify the kinds of problems that can distort or actually prevent effective communication. These problems affect all steps in the communication process and include:

- *Not Giving Proper Consideration to the Power Relationships of Message Senders and Receivers.*   Communication with a line supervisor will often be different than with a corporate senior officer.

- *Ignoring Temporary Emotional Stress by Either the Sender or Receiver.*   An audit exit meeting can often turn into a situation filled with conflict and stress unless the internal audit communicator takes care to consider these potential emotional issues.

- *Failing to Properly Evaluate the Capacity of the Recipient to Receive and Understand the Message.*   If internal audit encounters a severe control problem in a technical area in the course of its work, those issues must be communicated properly.

- *Use of Words That Can Have Multiple Meanings or Can Convey Unintended Meanings.*   We have discussed this problem in our discussion on preparing audit reports. This is all the more critical in verbal communications.

- *Undue Haste in the Transmission of Messages That Undermine Clarity and/or Credibility.*   Messages often need to be communicated slowly so all parties will understand them.

- *Perception That the Sender Wishes to Satisfy Personal Needs, Thus Inducing Emotional Resistance and Blocks.*   Often an internal auditor will be viewed by others as having a personal agenda. Others quickly recognize this and communication may become blocked.

- *Failure to Build Needed Foundations for the Core Message and Related Bad Timing.*   Internal audit concerns are not effectively communicated when they are just thrown in the lap of the auditee.

- *Lack of Clarity or Conviction Because of a Reluctance to Cause the Receiver Dissatisfaction.*   While an internal auditor must build a case to describe a concern convincingly, the auditor should never mince words to avoid describing a problem situation but should always clearly communicate a control concern.

- *Impact of Nonverbal Actions Such as Tone of Voice, Facial Expressions, and Manner of Communication.*   In some parts of the world, for example, a crossed leg with the sole of the foot pointing to the listener can be viewed as an extreme insult.

- *Not Giving Consideration to the Perceptions and Related Feelings of the Recipient.*   Auditors should try to understand how messages will be received and decoded by their receivers.

All of these problems are part of the larger need for an internal auditor to put himself or herself in the receiver's perspective and to consider how a message will be received. When done with some empathy, the result should be effective two-way conversation. The communicator must do everything practicable to understand how the receiver thinks and feels and then to communicate in a manner that gives all possible consideration to that knowledge. While the communicator often has conflicting higher-priority needs that prevent fully satisfying the receiver, it is still important to have a good understanding of the total communication process in order to make choices that are most consistent with overall organizational welfare.

Both parties—especially the main activator—learn from the questions and comments made by the receiver in response to a series of messages. This is called "feedback." Part of effective two-way communication is to induce feedback so that an auditor has the best possible basis for determining whether managerial objectives are achieved. Different approaches may be necessary to induce and utilize good feedback. A related component—listening—is important in order to utilize any feedback better and to demonstrate interest in the other person's views. Otherwise, the result can be to create an emotional response that significantly blocks the receiver's acceptance and understanding of the sender's intended message.

(c) Conflict and Organizational Change

People's varying needs relate alternatively to competition, conflict, and cooperation. Traditionally, conflict has been viewed as destructive and undesirable. However, when properly administered, conflict can be useful in achieving organizational welfare. Internal auditors need to learn to utilize conflict to the point where it is constructive but to control it when it threatens to get out of hand. Internal audit's responsibilities unavoidably generate situations that create competition and potential conflict. Both organizational units and individuals continuously compete in terms of job performance, recognition, management support, and other needs. That competition should induce imaginative and sound thinking and high-level work performance. At the same time, the forces generated can be so intensive that the competitors seek any means to win, irrespective of the questionable propriety and legitimacy of those means. At that point, competition ceases to benefit the organization and appropriate corrective actions are needed. Management thus has a challenge to exploit the benefits of competition and healthy conflict in a legitimate professional sense but to control the process to avoid excesses. Internal audit becomes very much part of this set of competition and conflict concerns. In the course of their reviews, auditors often find themselves in conflict with various elements of an organization. Auditors can cause auditees to lose a level of competitive standing within their organizations, and auditees may disagree with internal audit on just that basis. In the course of a review, conflict often occurs, and the effective auditor should use this conflict to communicate with management and convince it to take appropriate actions. However, the effective auditor needs to understand how to control that conflict.

Although the achievement of an immediate goal to win is an important and desirable motivation, it is the responsibility of every manager to make subordinates understand that there are other things more important than that particular victory. Put in other terms, people need to understand that how one wins is more important than the fact of winning. These principles also need to be reinforced continuously by the rejection of approaches that are not in the common interest. This means that internal audit must both be continuously alert and watch for red flags that indicate potential problems. When problem situations are observed, decisive actions may be necessary. Rules may be amended, particular individuals disciplined, and personnel assignments readjusted. Ideally, conflict should not be allowed to develop to the point where these more dramatic direct actions are necessary. There is a challenge to utilize this conflict but not to let it get out of control to such an extent that it is counterproductive.

In the typical organization, there is a continuing need for properly balancing stabilization and change. Management seeks stabilization through developing policies and procedures whereby operations are standardized to improve internal controls and to ensure the best handling of recurring similar types of events. However, changing conditions call for amended policies and procedures. The problem is to find a proper balance between stabilization and needed change. This is complicated because the perception and resolution of changes are often very difficult and sometimes controversial—that is, the factors involved are usually hard to analyze and measure. One obstacle to change is that organizations often become used to the existing policies and procedures and tend to become biased in their favor, thus making them unaware of and unresponsive to need for change. Internal audit often encounters this when it recommends many policy or procedural changes. Additionally, people typically do not like to accept change even when the need for it is reasonably clear. Somehow, convenience tends to triumph over objectivity. This means that internal auditors often face a great deal of resistance when suggesting changes, irrespective of the changes' real merits.

At the highest level, the need for change may involve new strategies, new business ventures, changes in products, or new supporting policies. Related changes may involve new organizational structure, relocation of plants, new production processes, or changes in people, but internal auditors typically do not make recommendations for change at that level. In some cases, these changes involve only established habits or convenience, while others require more substantial adjustments. There is often some built-in resistance to change ranging from minor attitudes to deliberate defensive action—including, in its most extreme form, sabotage. The managerial challenge is that when a decision involving change has been properly made, any resistance, whatever it may be, should be minimized, eliminated, or at least reasonably controlled.

When making their recommendations, internal auditors should understand how the organization will deal with the change. How can internal audit achieve needed changes in a manner that will best serve higher-level organizational welfare? In all cases, the nature and scope of the necessary actions depend on the significance of the particular recommended change. Because individuals place such a high priority on their freedom of action, the design and implementation of controls is an area where human considerations are especially important. Since all managers are responsible for internal controls and at the same time are subject to them, the impact of recommended control improvements on people should be carefully considered. Perhaps in no phase of the management process is an understanding and consideration of people so critical.

(d) Understanding the People in Internal Auditing

This discussion of human relations has focused on the interests of all internal auditors in connection with their relations with management and to each other. While all of this is of interest to internal auditors as a part of their review and analysis of internal controls, it should also be of interest in the management of internal audit. Some unique and specific problems confront internal auditors in their activities, including an image problem. To some extent, this image problem is due to the term "auditor" that is often thought of as focusing excessively on detail and compliance or control issues and is viewed as threatening. As has been discussed in earlier chapters, this image may have been earned in the past because of the manner in which internal auditors were once used in organizations. To some extent, the image has also resulted because some internal auditors today do not do enough through their audit work and mode of personal relations to build a better image.

The modern internal auditor faces some serious problems in changing this image. Internal audit is charged with certain protective responsibilities that tend to make others in the organization see them as an antagonist or police officer. Internal audit's total role goes far beyond the narrow role of providing protective service. The modern internal auditor today is no longer the "police officer" or the person with the green eyeshade who is buried in detail. Instead, the modern internal auditor should be concerned with total organizational welfare at all levels and in relation to all organizational activities. In all aspects, communications and relations with people are continuing challenges that involve a target for internal audit that is always moving forward. Internal audit's success in meeting that challenge provides one of the greatest available opportunities to serve the organization and to achieve its maximum welfare.

PART FIVE

Impact of Information Systems on Internal Auditing

CHAPTER EIGHTEEN

Business Continuity Planning and Disaster Recovery

18.1 IMPORTANCE OF INFORMATION SYSTEMS CONTINUITY PLANNING

Most organizations today would not be able to function without their information systems and the supporting communication networks, data repositories, and technical personnel. Focusing on computer files and programs, organizations have regularly established procedures for keeping backup versions of older files in off-site, secure locations along with processes for restoring those backup data files if some sort of disaster has limited access to current versions. While earlier backup processes were based on those fairly simple system configurations, today's larger-scale integrated systems have made backup and recovery much more complex. However, until recently, many organizations have limited their information systems backup procedures to little more than saving key files.

Information technology (IT) professionals, and certainly internal auditors, have raised questions over the years on what would happen to an organization if it lost its entire information systems resources. Information systems resources in the early days were typically based on centralized data centers. Starting in the 1980s, improved information systems disaster recovery planning and backup processing strategies were an answer to these concerns, frequently including arrangements with a remote disaster recovery data processing facility. Key backup files and programs were stored at off-site locations, and the plans called for the IT staff to shift to that alternate facility in the event of a disaster event. Professionals thought of information systems disasters in terms of fires, floods, or some other bad weather situation. In the earlier primarily mainframe systems days, organizations even took what today sounds like rather bizarre actions for developing their IT disaster recovery plans. These included signing reciprocal agreements with nearby locations having similar IT resources so that each could move to that other location for processing in the event of an emergency at either. Others established raised floor vacant space at one of their facilities and secured an agreement with their computer system hardware and network providers to quickly move in a replacement system in the event of an emergency. Computer hardware vendors will still agree to replace equipment in the event of an emergency. In fact, this is easier today as computer hardware if usually off-the-shelf rather than being almost custom manufactured as was common in the past. Reciprocal agreements between two chief information officers sounded good in theory, but they have never really worked beyond low-level, almost humanitarian help. That nearby reciprocal agreement site might be out of service for the same weather-related disaster or probably would not be interested in someone else running their systems in off-shift time periods. As a final impediment, corporate legal consul would have a dozen reasons to say no to a reciprocal agreement.

Those disaster recovery plans of the 1980s and early 1990s were not sound, and a series of specialized disaster recovery vendors arose with fully equipped computer systems sites operating at idle or what is called "hot sites." Organizations contracted to use those sites in the event of a disaster and both ran periodic tests and kept key backup files there or at some other secure site. Even though technology changes caused some challenges to these disaster recovery operations, these specialized "hot site" backup vendors provided the primary IT backup solution for many organizations moving into the twenty-first century.

September 11, 2001, frequently referred to as 9/11, changed everything. Two terrorist led airliners crashed into the two 100+-story New York World Trade Center towers, among other targets, causing those buildings to collapse. In addition to a massive loss of life and property, these events triggered activation of a series of organization IT disaster recovery plans. The World Trade Center was populated with a large number of IT systems–based financial institutions, virtually all with some form of disaster recovery plan in place, and most of those disaster recovery plans were later found to be wanting. In the immediate aftermath of the disaster, telephone lines were clogged, bridges to get out of Manhattan were closed, and airlines were shut down. Many of the IT disaster recovery plans in place just did not work, and only a limited number of organizations had disaster recovery plans that were effective.

This chapter discusses both procedures for building an effective IT continuity and disaster recovery plans and areas for internal audit attention in the wake of what was learned after the 9/11 disaster. This chapter also focuses on business recovery rather that just the recovery of IT systems and operations. While in past years internal audit often was one of the few organizational functions raising disaster recovery concerns, it is an important aspect of an organization's internal control foundation today. Effective information systems continuity programs are increasingly becoming part of U.S. federal regulation requirements, and management at all levels generally should recognize the need for effective information systems recovery provisions. Along with other groups or functions in the organization, internal auditors have a key role in the review, testing, and evaluating their organization's continuity planning.

18.2 BUSINESS CONTINUITY PLANNING TODAY

An organization today faces numerous risks around its information systems assets. There typically is not one major or central computer facility for handling major automated applications, but a wide range desktop of devices, servers, and other computer systems connected through often very complex communications, storage management networks, and links to the Internet. Organizations do not have all of their information systems resources tied around one or several central data centers, and management is more interested in keeping its information systems up and running rather than in worrying about the risk of losing a central computer systems facility. The concept of information systems disaster recovery planning, going back to the 1970s, was based on having processes in place to resume operations if some single disaster made the computer center inoperable.

The language and strategic approaches to IT disaster recovery planning has changed. While we certainly cannot deny that the events of 9/11 represented a major disaster, professionals today more typically think in terms of a business continuity plan (BCP), the plans and processes necessary to restore overall business operations. The user of an online order-processing system doesn't care about whether the server is operating, but only if a customer order, submitted through an Internet site, can be processed properly and efficiently. The information systems should be restored and operating as quickly and efficiently as possible but the key objective is to support and restore the business processes.

In addition to concerns about restoring operations in the case of some disaster or continuity-requiring event, today's organization should also be concerned about the continued and high availability of its IT resources. Any form of computer systems downtime can be very costly to an organization. For example, the Disaster Recovery Institute[1] has estimated that the average hourly impact of an hour of systems downtime is $89,500 for an airline reservations system or $2.6 million for a credit card authorization provider, among others. Beyond just estimates, eBay's Internet auction site went down for 22 hours in August 1999. This caused $4 million in lost fees and a $5 billion drop in eBay's market value.[2] The message here is that high systems availability is very important to an organization, and internal auditors should continually look for areas where they can suggest BCP and information systems availability improvements.

(a) Emergency Response Planning

With older IT disaster recovery plans, after an extensive project to build the recovery plan, the materials were often published in thick books located on the desks of a few key managers in the organization. The idea was that in the event of some emergency event, people would pull out their disaster recovery manuals and be able to look up such key data as the telephone number of the designated backup site in order to report the emergency or the instructions for other emergency procedures. The material in these thick books might work in theory if the manuals were always kept up to date and the nature of the crisis event allowed time to review the manual first and then react. Many real-life events are much more crisis-oriented with little time to dig out the disaster recovery manual and read its documented information. When the building is on fire, for example, human nature says that one should get out of the building as soon as possible, not spend time studying the published evacuation instructions. Organizations need to think through these various possible situations in advance. They need an *emergency response plan*.

Two types of emergency incidents are significant. The first is the fire-in-the-building type of emergency incident. The supporting emergency response plan here would include posted fire exits and frequent fire drills. This type of emergency response plan should cover all organizational operations, not just information systems and should be regularly tested. The second level of emergency response plan, however, covers specific individual incidents that may or may not turn out to be significant, but must be corrected at once followed by an investigation and a plan of corrective action to prevent further incidents. These are called emergency *incidents*, and they often include such matters as security breaches or the theft of hardware or software. A good emergency incident response plan should be acted on quickly to minimize the effects of any further breaches. It should also be formulated to reduce any negative publicity and to focus attention on quick reaction time.

The emergency incident response plan can be separated into four sections:

1. **Immediate Response Activities.** Whether a security breach, a theft of assets, or physical intrusion, resources should be in place to investigate the matter and take immediate corrective action.

2. **Incident Investigation.** All reported matters should be fully investigated to determine the situation that caused the emergency and possible future corrective actions going forward.

3. **Correction or Restoration.** Resources should be available to correct or restore operations as necessary. Since emergency incidents can cover a wide variety of areas, these resources may include information systems security specialists, building security managers, or others.

4. **Emergency Incident Reporting.** The entire emergency incident and the actions subsequently taken should be documented along with an analysis of lessons learned and any further plans for corrective actions.

Emergency incident responses must be decisive and executed quickly. We initially put water on an active fire, not build short-term strategies to prevent it from burning further. Quick actions are needed with little room for error in most cases. By staging fire-drill-like practice emergencies and measuring response times, it is possible to develop a methodology that fosters speed and accuracy. Reacting quickly may minimize the impact of resource unavailability and the potential damage caused by any future systems or facility compromises. An organization faces many emergency incidents or other threats beyond the massive 9/11 type of emergency or overall failure of its computer systems resources. While the focus should always be on more major contingency-planning issues, an organization needs to have mechanisms in place to respond to every level of unexpected emergency event.

Internal auditors should look for appropriate emergency response plans as a component of many internal audit reviews. These plans may exist at a total facility level, as does a fire escape plan, or at an individual level, as does a plan to respond to a security breach. In many areas of the organization, auditors should ask are appropriate emergency response plans are in place, are they regularly updated and current, and have they been tested?

(b) Business Continuity Planning

A BCP is an outline of the steps necessary to help an organization recover from major service disruptions, whether a fire emergency, a computer equipment or network equipment failure, or any other form of major disruption. The goal of a BCP is to help an organization reduce the impact of a disaster outage or extended service interruption to an acceptable level and to bring business operations back. A BCP represents a change in emphasis from what IT professionals formally called a disaster recovery plan. That older emphasis was to get data processing operations working while the BCP emphasizes needs of the business unit.

This section outlines some of the steps necessary to build such a BCP. While information systems organizations have had disaster recovery plans in place for some time, those older approaches were often not that effective in actually getting key business processes operating again. Just as there are key separate steps necessary for planning and for conducting an internal audit, there are some key steps necessary for an effective BCP. Several professional organizations such as the U.S.-based Disaster Recovery Institute and the London, England–based Business Continuity Institute have adopted a frequently published and well-recognized set of 10 BCP recommended professional practices as outlined in Exhibit 18.1. These have become the universally accepted standards in the industry for the key steps or components in a BCP. The following sections will discuss these steps in greater detail. An effective BCP is critical for an organization, and management is responsible for the survivability and sustainability of total operations to serve customers and service recipients. Many companies and most government organizations are required by law to develop these continuity and contingency plans. In other

EXHIBIT 18.1

Business Continuity Planning Recommended Professional Practices

The following recommended professional practices or steps were initially developed by the Disaster Recovery Institute:

1. *Project Initiation and Management.* BCP processes should be managed through formal project management processes and within agreed time and budget limits.

2. *Risk Evaluation and Control.* A formal BCP risk evaluation process should be used to determine events that can adversely affect the organization and its facilities with disruptions as well as major disasters, the damage such events can cause, and the controls needed to prevent or minimize the effects of potential loss. This should include a cost-benefit analysis to justify investments in controls to mitigate these risks.

3. *Business Impact Analysis.* Managers should understand the overall impacts resulting from disruptions and disaster events that can affect the organization as well as techniques that can be used to quantify and qualify them. This requires identifying critical functions, their recovery priorities, and interdependencies such that recovery time objectives can be set.

4. *Developing Business Continuity Strategies.* One single BCP is not applicable for all circumstances, and management should develop an appropriate strategy to determine and guide the selection of alternative business recovery operating strategies for recovery of business and information resources within the recovery time objective, while maintaining the organization's critical functions.

5. *Emergency Response and Operations.* Emergency procedures should be in place to respond to and stabilize the situation following an incident or event, including establishing and managing an Emergency Operations Center to be used as a command center during the emergency.

6. *Developing and Implementing Business Continuity Plans.* The BCP should be developed, documented, and implemented using a formal, best practices based process that provides recovery within established recovery time objectives.

7. *Awareness and Training Programs.* Processes should be in place to make all appropriate members of the organization aware of the appropriate BCP procedures in place with training programs in place on their usage.

8. *Maintaining and Exercising Business Continuity Plans.* The BCP and its key elements should be kept up to date with periodic testing of critical plan elements. Processes should be implemented to maintain and update the BCP in accordance with the organization's strategic direction.

9. *Public Relations and Crisis Coordination.* Processes should be in place to communicate all events surrounding a contingency event and to

EXHIBIT 18.1 *(CONTINUED)*

Business Continuity Planning Recommended Professional Practices

> communicate with and, as appropriate, provide trauma counseling for employees and their families, key customers, critical suppliers, owners/stockholders, and corporate management during crisis. All stakeholders should kept informed on an as-needed basis.
>
> 10. ***Coordination with Public Authorities.*** Processes should be in place for coordinating continuity and restoration activities with local authorities while ensuring compliance with applicable statutes or regulations.

Source: Robert R. Moeller, *Sarbanes-Oxley and the New Internal Auditing Rules,* © copyright 2004, John Wiley & Sons. Used with permission.

instances, legislation indirectly effectively requires a BCP. The Sarbanes-Oxley Act (SOA) Section 409, for example, requires registered organizations to be able to report their financial results in a timely manner. A systems failure is not an excuse, and an effective BCP will help to support the organization here.

18.3 CONTINUITY PLANNING AND SERVICE LEVEL AGREEMENTS

An information system function cannot just arbitrarily establish a series of BCP guidelines for all business process and application areas. It must have a strong buy-in from the users and application owners as well as their joint assurances of expectations and service delivery. If a senior executive in a specific user department feels that some of her business processes must *always* be operational with a full backup capability for significant transactions, that department should negotiate with information systems to provide that level of continuity service and must recognize the necessary costs of additional hardware and software to provide that capability. In the past days of downloaded tape copies being periodically shipped to a remote location, anything close to an immediate backup was only a theoretical concept. A transaction had to be written first in the main system and its database and then copied to a backup facility. There was always a delay, ranging from weekly or daily backup files to almost immediate real-time systems approaches. Newer storage management approaches, called mirroring, can provide immediate backups. These techniques are described in the following sections. They are very effective but certainly more expensive.

While the details of the BCP must be established as outlined below, key user departments should negotiate their recovery expectations through formal service level agreements (SLAs). A SLA is a contract between the business process owner and the provider of IT services for specified service objectives. SLAs are discussed in greater detail as part of the ITIL (Information Technology Infrastructure Library) service delivery best practices in Chapter 22, "Infrastructure Service- and Support-Delivery Controls," and are fundamental to business continuity activities. SLAs should be used to define minimum levels of expected computer systems backup and recovery. They are a contract between information systems and key user areas to support both normal day-to-day operations as well as the actions to be taken in the event of a serious service disruption. SLAs describe expected and promised levels of continuity services and are basic building blocks for establishing effective continuity plans.

SLAs are encountered most frequently when a contract is made for the services of an outside provider. For example, a computer services vendor may agree to handle the processing of some application at a rate of x cents per transaction and will also agree to process these transactions within a specified turnaround time. The organization pays for these services based on the transaction rate and recognizes adjustments if expected turnaround time standards are missed. Similar SLA arrangements between users of services and information systems should be made within the organization, but the internal costs are normally based on internal budget amounts. For a BCP-related SLA, the befitting user business function will specify its backup needs and will accept a periodic budget charge for those information systems and related services. If promised SLA targets are missed, a budget credit would be issued. Even though these SLA debit and credit amounts are based usually on internal "funny money," they can become an important measure of management performance.

Business recovery SLAs are frequently structured to cover most if not all departments or functions in the organization. As part of these charges, they are also receiving an information systems function commitment or promise to provide an agreed on level of continuity services. When a business area has specific needs, special or unique SLAs should be created. Internal auditors should be aware of the importance of SLAs when reviewing continuity planning and the organization's BCP. This is the type of contract that sets appropriate rules and expectations.

18.4 NEW BUSINESS CONTINUITY PLAN TECHNOLOGIES: DATA-MIRRORING TECHNIQUES

Internal auditors frequently assess whether key files are backed up on a regular basis when reviewing systems or applications controls. However, many systems backup procedures to download copies of critical transactions to tape cartridges or disk files are not effective in today's world of constant streams of real-time transactions. Full file or database backups taken every week, every day, or even every hour, along with captured streams of interim transactions are just not effective in our world of constantly updated applications. When a system shuts down because of some emergency, it is necessary to go back to the most recent database backup as a benchmark or starting point and then reprocess all of the transactions that had been submitted after the last backup to the present. However, when the business process is very active, such as for high-volume trading or ordering, it is almost impossible to get caught up reprocessing past transactions without shutting down the actual application. An airline-ticketing and -scheduling system is an example. In order for the enterprise to survive, the system must be operational virtually at all times around the clock and at a high-level availability rate. For an organization

EXHIBIT 18.2

High-Availability Percentages		
Availibility	Number of 9's	Estimated Down Time
99%	Two 9's	87 hours a year
99.9%	Three 9's	8 hours a year
99.99%	Four9's	52 minutes a year
99.999%	Five 9's	5 minutes a year
99.9999%	Six 9's	Less than one minute a year

to state that it is operating and available nearly 100% or 99.99% of the time, it can only be out of operation, or "down," less than one hour per year. Exhibit 18.2 outlines these high-availability percentages, and many modern organizations seek to assure themselves and their stakeholders that they are nearly 100% available.

Legal and regulatory mandates for business continuity now make this high availability a top priority, and an organization needs to move and copy its data in order to rapidly recover critical business operations in the event of data loss, data corruption, or disaster. Fortunately, there have been many new technology advancements over recent years that allow rapid and frequent backups. A technology known as RAID (redundant array of independent disks) is often used where data is simultaneously copied to multiple locations on one or more disk files to create redundancy. Exhibit 18.3 shows this concept in a configuration called RAID 1. There are numerous variations of the technology with names of RAID 0, 1, 2, and so on. It is not an objective of this chapter to provide a detailed technical description of RAID, but to describe this concept, known in general as mirroring. Internal auditors usually do not need a detailed understanding of this type of technology but should have enough knowledge to ask some appropriate questions as part of a review.

EXHIBIT 18.3

RAID 1 Data Mirroring Concepts

Multiple discs are established such that all data, A through P in this example, are mirrored on duplicate discs, creatig 100 percent redundancy.

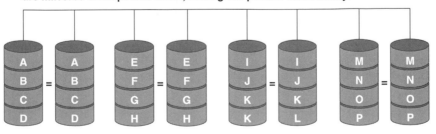

Source: Robert R. Moeller, *Sarbanes-Oxley and the New Internal Auditing Rules,* © copyright 2004, John Wiley & Sons. Used with permission.

RAID technology provides 100% redundancy of application data such that there will be no need to rebuild the disk files structure in the event of a disk failure. We encounter RAID at a very basic level on a desktop computer using Microsoft's XP operating system where, if a power failure or the like occurs, a restored version of disk files is retained. While of no help in a total disk "crash," this technology provides perhaps the most efficient level of backup and recovery for desktop computer systems.

While RAID technology allows the data center to have multiple disks side by side to provide recovery from any "crash" type failures, the technique is particularly valuable when transaction data is mirrored to a remote facility, connected through a wide area network (WAN). The solution to managing this multiple-disk, multiple-location backup and recovery is really a storage vendor hardware and software solution. Although several vendors have efficient storage management products on the market, we are highlighting one here as an example, EMC Corporation's SRDF solution.[3] The letter S in the SRDF name stands for EMC's Symmetrix high-speed multiple disk storage device, a kitchen-refrigerator-sized device holding many individual linked disk drives with a capacity of many terabytes of storage data. Thus, the Symmetrix Remote Data Facility is a mirroring storage device that allows the transfer of data between multiple Symmetrix storage management systems at very high speed using public or private networks. Mirroring is just what the name implies. If we set two glass mirrors on the table in front of us at 45-degree angles and look at them, we will see two images of our self at once. Mirroring data achieves the same results. Pressing the Enter key for a computer transaction immediately writes it to two more mirrored storage devices.

Exhibit 18.4 shows this type of configuration. A computer system uses a Symmetrix storage device for regular processing with all transactions that are

EXHIBIT 18.4

EMC Symmetrix Data Mirroring Example

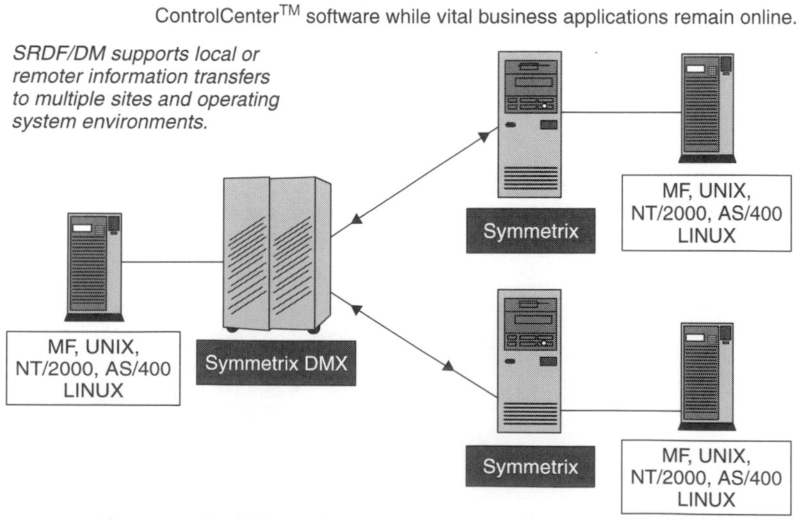

ControlCenter™ software while vital business applications remain online.

SRDF/DM supports local or remoter information transfers to multiple sites and operating system environments.

MF, UNIX, NT/2000, AS/400 LINUX

Symmetrix DMX

Symmetrix

MF, UNIX, NT/2000, AS/400 LINUX

Symmetrix

MF, UNIX, NT/2000, AS/400 LINUX

Source: Copyright 2000 EMC Corporation, Hopkinton, Massachusetts, Reprinted with permission.

recorded on the prime storage device also being mirrored over high-speed lines to another Symmetrix storage system. The exhibit shows two redundant systems. This mirrored operation creates multiple copies of the same data configurations, making for easy restoration of services in the event of an emergency. This product has been highlighted because it distinguished itself during the 9/11 World Trade Center terrorist attack. Better than its competitors at that time, essentially no data was lost on computer systems when those two buildings were destroyed. Businesses picked up on operations at remote sites as soon as they were able to get to those sites, with essentially no loss of data.

As mentioned several times in this book, storage management is an evolving and important information systems direction. Properly employed, it will very much improve the reliability and backup capabilities of information systems. An internal auditor who has been involved with more traditional information systems hardware components should learn and better understand storage management processes. EMC has been mentioned as a provider of products here, but others, such as Veritas and Legato, also provide some excellent software tools for backup and storage management.

18.5 ESTABLISHING EFFECTIVE CONTINGENCY POLICIES: WHAT ARE WE PROTECTING?

Effective policies should underpin an organization's overall approach to contingency and disaster recovery and determine the fundamental practices and culture throughout the organization. BCP policies are usually linked closely with information systems security policies because both address basic requirements to ensure the stability and continuity of an organization. It is essential therefore that BCP policies exist, are up to date, comprehensive in their coverage, and that they are understood by all interested parties. In the old days of centralized computer systems and primarily batch processing, it was fairly easy to delineate IT contingency and recovery responsibilities. User functions delivered transactions to input/output (I/O) desk function and systems users expected the data processing function to handle all required tasks, including building controls in the systems, backing up files, and initiating recovery efforts in the event of some disaster contingency event. With modern systems, the world has very much changed with many "dotted lines" in today's organization, and many stakeholders often not sure who is responsible for contingency policies in various areas of operation. Effective organizational contingency policies are needed!

One level of policy may simply state that the *owners* of an application are responsible for making arrangements for backups and other contingency-processing arrangements. That said, they usually must make these arrangements with information systems through a formal SLA where the information systems function outlines its contingency-processing capabilities and the relative costs for various options. If an application owner wants full transaction mirroring, as discussed in Section 18.4, that owner will have to absorb the cost of this added-value service with overall costs being distributed to other users of the applications. That is, if the sales department wants one-hour backup recovery for its sales transactions, information systems should agree to provide that level of service at a designated cost, and sales would charge this back to other benefiting users such as marketing or the controller's function. This sounds easy but can become a complex accounting issue coupled with much negotiation.

The matter can often be resolved through formal SLAs, as mentioned previously and discussed with the ITIL materials in Chapter 22. The SLA typically spells out measures for performance and consequences for failure. Some SLAs may look like detailed legal documents containing a massive number of provisions and details and thus may be most appropriate for an outside vendor provider, but an organization's marketing function is not going to bring legal action against its information systems function, for example, and the SLA should point out levels of expected service as clearly and simply as practicable. A typical SLA might include:

- A description of the types of information systems services covered.

- Published measures of performance and problem review mechanisms.

- Recovery commitments in the event of an extended interruption in normal services.

- Volume assumptions for the service (particularly if there are large variable costs involved).

- Reliability, availability, and performance (RAP) requirements.

- Minimum staffing levels or other minimum resource levels such as computer sizes, storage commitments, and bandwidth.

- Methods of dealing with operational problems (escalation, help desk, hotline, and agreed-on severity levels).

- Conditions of use or change of use conditions/restrictions.

- Any dates/deadlines where specific deliverables are due at initial switch on, ramp-up, ramp-down, or upgrade of service. For example, year-end, implementation dates, delivery of upgrades, legislation changes.

- The method of delivery (e.g., paper/fax/personal delivery/electronic means/source or object code).

- Time after which the deliverables must be consumed or tested and still supported (obsolescence limits).

- Documentation/manuals and standards.

- Definition of what is considered a service failure and what is considered an enhancement to the service (e.g., what is a software bug and what is an enhancement).

This list is not necessarily all-inclusive, but it illustrates content of a typical SLA between user departments and information systems. Care should be given to considering all resource areas that are important in the service arrangement between information systems and the user group. This includes areas such as responsibility to telecommunications service providers, controls over purchased software, and responsibilities for documentation. The SLA often becomes the basis for establishing a contingency-planning policy.

In our era of strong ethical standards and SOA requirements, these SLAs should be shared with key levels of management and the board to outline the overall plans for reacting to a contingency event. All parties should be aware of these arrangements as well as the plans to build an effective BCP. If an organization does not have an effective system of SLAs between its information systems function and other key business units, internal audit might bring up this issue in its discussions with management, particularly with the organization's chief information officer (CIO). The lack of effective SLAs can be considered a general control weakness.

18.6 BUILDING THE DISASTER RECOVERY BUSINESS CONTINUITY PLAN

As mentioned in the first two sections of this chapter, what were once called disaster recovery plans were often published in thick notebooks that were out of date almost as soon as they were distributed. In addition, they focused on the recovery of information systems operations from a disaster event but not primarily on the recovery of the business and its key operations. Many organizations have established some form of disaster recovery plan for good business and internal control reasons, and government regulations are now requiring disaster recovery plans in an increasing number of areas. However, organizations that have established disaster recovery plans following those old rules probably do not have an effective BCP in place today.

This section outlines steps to build an effective BCP for an organization. Internal auditors can play a key role in this process with their knowledge of business systems, and the internal control requirements of the Committee of Sponsoring Organizations (COSO) or Control Objectives for Information and related Technology (CobiT) frameworks, as outlined in Chapters 4, "Internal Controls Fundamentals: COSO Framework," and 7, "Internal Controls Frameworks Worldwide: CobiT and Others." Although the words disaster recovery or BCP are not found specifically in the SOA legislation, the astute board audit committee or CFO should realize that an organization must have an effective BCP in place and working both in order to attest the internal controls are effective as required in SOA Section 404 and to release its financial results in a timely manner.

If an organization already has an existing BCP for part or all of its business activities, this BCP needs to be reviewed to determine whether that existing plan can effectively meet projected *business* contingency needs—and we have emphasized the business recovery aspect of the plan. All too often, organizations have taken their old-style disaster recovery plans and just renamed them, giving minimal thought to their business continuity requirements. That BCP should be current or have been regularly updated. It should have a detailed section on incident and risk assessment covering all key business activities and include a strategy for recovery of all significant business processes including applications, communications resources, and other information systems assets. There should be assignments for disaster and business teams as discussed below. The BCP should contain detailed instructions for the business recovery process, including the overall project organization with notification and reporting procedures.

Once any existing BCP has been reviewed and an assessment made of its adequacy, the existing BCP should be enhanced and updated as required.

If no BCP exists or if the current version is very much in need of help, a project should be launched to create a new BCP with a designated project manager appointed to lead the effort. This individual should have good leadership qualities, an understanding of business processes, skills with information systems security management, and strong project management capabilities. An ideal candidate might have Project Manager Professional (PMP) credentials.[4] For some organizations, the information security officer may possibly be an ideal candidate for this role. In other cases, internal audit specialists can assume a major role here. The objectives and deliverables for such a BCP project need to be clearly defined to enable the assigned overall BCP project team to ensure that their work is consistent with original project expectations.

A BCP project's principle objective should be for the development and testing of a well-structured and coherent plan that will enable the organization to recover normal business operations as quickly and effectively as possible from any unforeseen disaster or emergency that interrupts normal information systems services. There should be subobjectives to ensure that all employees fully understand their duties in implementing the BCP, that information security policies are adhered to within all planned activities, and that the proposed contingency arrangements are cost-effective. The BCP deliverables should consist of:

- Business risk and impact analysis
- Documented activities necessary to prepare the organization for various possible emergencies
- Detailed activities for initially dealing with a disaster event
- Procedures for managing the business recovery processes, including testing plans
- Plans for BCP training at multiple levels in the organization
- Procedures for keeping the BCP up to date

Each of these BCP major components will be discussed in the following sections. A major objective here is to allow the organization to restore business operations as quickly and effectively as possible in light of a disaster event. This is an activity that requires active participation on many levels, and one where internal audit should take a major role in helping to ensure the effectiveness of the BCP.

(a) Risks, Business Impact Analysis, and the Impact of Potential Emergencies

The identification and analysis of risks, as discussed in Chapter 5, "Understanding and Assessing Risks: Enterprise Risk Management," is an important internal tool. Risk or business impact analysis is a particularly important process for determining what applications and processes to include in the overall BCP. The thinking here is different from that in the "old days." In the past, recovery analysts and internal auditors focused too much on the subjective probabilities of some event occurring. That is, there were extensive discussions covering the potential probability of a tornado, an earthquake, or some other catastrophic event at a data center location. Those analyses tended to focus on the loss of the main data center but not on recovery of the business applications.

Today's BCP should include a descriptive list of the organization's key business areas, typically ranked in order of importance to the business, as well as a brief description of the business process and its main dependencies on systems, communications, personnel, and data. If the organization already has prepared an assessment of its key business processes, this can be an excellent time for the BCP team to update that documentation and to evaluate the relative importance of each. It should be noted that this is an inventory of *business processes*, not just critical IT application systems. While the two are often one and the same, it is important that they be considered as the key processes to keep the business operating.

A next step here is to look at those key business processes in terms of potential business process, outage failure impacts. Exhibit 18.5 shows this type of analysis in an Excel worksheet. Each separate key business process would be listed in the column on the left with risk of failure factors considered for each key business process such factors as the Impact on Customer Services, Loss or Customers, and the like. Within each of these risk factors, the criticality of the impact of various levels of outages should be considered. Factors such as a specified application failure of less than two hours that will Impact Customer Services but will cause a minimal Loss of Customers and essentially no risk of Exposure to Possible Litigation could be noted on the chart. While monetary values can be added to such a worksheet, this can be equally effective as just a worksheet to highlight key time-based exposures. The concept behind these results in an outages analysis table and the steps necessary to get back in operation is that they are components of what is usually called a business impact analysis (BIA). A newer term in the world of disaster recovery and continuity planning, BIA is the process of defining the key business process risks that will have an impact on business operations as a result of a loss of services.

Based on the outage risks, the BCP team should study and document its recovery requirements for their key business processes. This includes business process procedures, automated systems, and hardware plus software requirements. In addition, existing backup and recovery procedures should be documented within the BCP, including any off-site data storage arrangements or existing arrangements with disaster recovery hot or cold site vendor. This data and information will provide the organizational background material to construct an effective BCP. Again, the emphasis should be on recovering business operations, not just on getting the automated systems reloaded and operating again.

(b) Preparing for Possible Contingencies

Once the BCP project team has reviewed business processes, completed its initial processes, and assessed the business risks, they should next take steps to minimize the effects of potential emergencies. An objective here is to identify ways of preventing an emergency situation from turning into an even more severe disaster for the organization due to the lack of preparedness. The BCP project team should focus on activities that are essential to the continued viability of the business and the types of backup and preventive strategies appropriate for these key

EXHIBIT 18.5

Business Failure Analysis Impact

Business Process	Customer Service Impact	Loss of Customers	Loss of Additional Recovery Revised Cost	Penalty Clause Exposures	Possible Litigation	Loss of Key Information	
						> 6 days	
						2–5 days	
						24–48 hours	
						2–24 hours	
						< 2 hours	
					> 6 days		
					2–5 days		
					24–48 hours		
					2–24 hours		
					< 2 hours		
				> 6 days			
				2–5 days			
				24–48 hours			
				2–24 hours			
				< 2 hours			
			> 6 days				
			2–5 days				
			24–48 hours				
			2–24 hours				
			< 2 hours				
		> 6 days					
		2–5 days					
		24–48 hours					
		2–24 hours					
		< 2 hours					
	> 6 days						
	2–5 days						
	24–48 hours						
	2–24 hours						
	< 2 hours						

Source: Robert R. Moeller, Sarbanes-Oxley and the New Internal Auditing Rules, © copyright 2004, John Wiley & Sons. Used with permission.

business activities. The BCP team needs to next develop appropriate backup and recovery procedures for the identified critical applications. The complexity and related cost of these backup continuity procedures will depend on the identified business process restoration needs as outlined in the Exhibit 18.5 business failure impact analysis.

Organizations have a variety of options for establishing a backup strategy. Larger organizations often have the resources to do much of this on their own although many rely on an outside vendor to provide backup processing services. An organization will generally commit to one of the following strategies:

- *Fully Mirrored Recovery Operations.* This is the approach discussed previously in Section 18.4. This strategy requires the maintenance of a fully mirrored duplicate site with mirrored linkages between the live site and the back up, alternate site over broadband lines. This requires specialized storage management hardware and software and is almost always the most expensive option. Fully mirrored strategies will provide the greatest level of recovery assurance.

- *Switchable Hot Site Facility.* Here arrangements are made with a vendor who will guarantee to maintain an identical site with communications to enable the transfer of all data processing operations to this hot recovery site within an agreed-on time period, usually less than 1 to 2 hours. Because of the need to keep the equivalent of an exact duplicate site in waiting, the costs here can be almost as high as a fully mirrored arrangement.

- *Traditional Hot Site.* Here the organization will contract with a disaster recovery vendor, who will guarantee to maintain a compatible site to enable the switching of data processing operations to that site within an agreed-on time period, usually less than 8 hours after notification. This once was a very common recovery approach that was very much challenged after the 9/11 events. There were just too many organizations in distress contacting the same hot site vendors that did not expect so many to have a disaster event simultaneously.

- *Cold Site Facility.* This was a more frequent approach when disaster recovery sites were viewed as being very expensive, and organizational information systems management wanted some possible solution. This strategy involves establishing emergency site space to allow the organization to begin processing as well as a standby arrangement with a vendor to deliver a minimum hardware configuration. This strategy also goes back to the days of classic mainframe computers that required air-conditioning and water-cooling operations located under raised floor computer room sites. In theory, those specialized cold sites could be operational within 2 to 3 days.

- *Relocate and Restore.* This is the weakest level of backup strategy. It involves the identification of a suitable location, hardware, and peripherals, and the reinstallation of systems and backed up software and data *after* an emergency has occurred. Some managers have been guilty of advocating this approach. They have backed up their software and data with no firm plans for making arrangements if a disaster event actually happens. This strategy is inadequate for today's business processes.

- *No Strategy.* Almost unheard of today, there are still some organizations that have no backup and restore strategy for their information systems operations. This is often an, "I'll get to building my BCP later, I'm too busy right now!" type of approach. This approach carries the highest risk of all with no regular off-site backups of systems or data. In the event of some disaster, this option usually ends up with the organization going out of business. The internal auditor that encounters this situation should communicate a strong warning of these business risks to the audit committee.

One of the most important aspects of the BCP is the selection of an appropriate strategy for the backup and recovery of an organization's information systems. These procedures, especially for key business processes, should be designed to get systems back in operation per management requirements. While in some instances, an organizational decision to go to a hot site strategy will be the major direction for almost all applications, an individual but highly critical process may require full mirroring capabilities. Such a mixed mode of backup strategies can be appropriate if the organization decides that full mirroring is only justified for that one highly critical process, while the others will rely on an adequate but appropriate hot site strategy.

An organization may have a mixed set of backup strategies with some being stronger than others. However, all key processes in an organization should have some level of backup and restoration policy that allows the overall business to remain in operation. While not all processes may require full mirroring, for example, all should be part of a consistent, comprehensive approach that will allow the overall business to get back in business in the event of a serious disruption. The cost of recovery can be a major factor here, and the BCP team should outline cost options and get the application owners to buy into an option through an appropriate SLA. Internal audit, in its periodic reviews of BCP procedures throughout the organization, should highlight any discrepancies encountered here.

The BCP should have a high-priority objective to provide an adequate level of service to all customers throughout an emergency. Critical customer service activities should be included in the BCP, ordered in a priority sequence with restoration steps outlined in some level of detail. There are business managers who understand customer needs, but they may not necessarily be part of the recovery site BCP team, particularly if it would be operating at a remote hot site. Documentation describing key customers and customer service activities should be essential components of the BCP. The emphasis should be on getting the organization back in operation!

No matter what backup strategy is used, key files, and documents should always be stored in secure off-site locations. Disaster recovery and business recovery teams should be designated and trained, with periodic tests to assure their ongoing familiarity with processes. Most important, the BCP implementation team should reflect, in general, on the lessons learned from the 9/11 World Trade Center event or from other disaster events. A search of material from the previously referenced Disaster Recovery Institute can be of help. While a small number of 9/11 sites with full mirroring capabilities were able to get back in operation, many lacking this capability had severe problems. Immediately after the 9/11 attacks, bridges around Manhattan were closed and even after they opened, airlines were shut down for a short time.

(c) Disaster Recovery: Handling the Emergency

Building a BCP is a relatively easy process when the team sits in a closed room, brainstorms, and talks through and plots a contingency recovery strategy. It suddenly becomes more difficult when alarm bells ring signifying that an emergency event has occurred. One of the first tasks is to determine to what level the emergency situation requires activation of the full BCP and notification of the emergency response team. This notification should normally be communicated in a pre-agreed-on call-list-driven format with members of the disaster recovery team instructed to assemble at a designated off-site location. In addition, management and key employees should be kept informed of developments affecting the BCP activation and its impact on their areas of responsibility. The BCP project team leader would be responsible for this notification activity.

This is the phase of the BCP with the objective to get back in operation. It almost always involves contacting the designated alternate processing site, activating communications lines, making arrangements to get the team to that site, and otherwise taking steps to restore operations. Assuming that the team is using a hot site vendor, the disaster recovery team should arrive at a backup site, get operating systems versions and key databases loaded, and begin production operations. These steps are often far easier said than done, and it is sometimes a challenge to get communications lines connected and up and running in the new environment. This is processing that must be handled in a tight time frame and under considerable organizational pressure. But the objective is to have as many as possible critical business processes restored and operating quickly.

For the BCP and the resultant recovery to be effective, the recovery team must carefully consider and plan for the potentially complex series of activities needed to recover from a serious emergency. A planned approach is likely to result in a more coherent and structured recovery. It is likely that a serious disruptive event will produce unexpected results, which may differ in some ways from the predicted outcomes contained within this plan. The recovery team should review any predefined procedures or strategies in the light of the actual situation arising following the emergency event and modify these procedures as appropriate.

(d) Business Continuity Plan Organization Training

Extensive BCP processes and published documents are of little value unless people in the organization responsible for executing those BCP processes are regularly trained in their use. While many traditional disaster recovery plans were published in thick books full of data with the idea that team members would look up critical references, telephone numbers, and the like after a disaster event, this approach really was not very practical in a 9/11 type of disaster where the entire building has suddenly collapsed into dust. Secure, online plans will provide some help here, but what is needed is a BCP team familiar with the emergency response plans discussed earlier and trained in the general processes necessary in the event of an extreme emergency. Certain BCP team members must know enough about the plan so they will react almost instinctively in the event of a severe emergency situation.

In order to act without having to flip through a published plan to decide the next step, the BCP project team needs to launch a contingency-planning training program for members of the organization on many need-to-know levels. Having four levels of BCP training is an effective approach:

1. **BCP Level 1 Training. General Management Overview.** This training should provide a broad understanding throughout the organization that a BCP exists, how it will work, and how it is maintained and tested. This is the type of training that would be given to a wide range of people, starting with the audit committee, to outline the overall strategy for recovery in the event of an emergency event and to describe expectations of how the organization would operate in a contingency environment.

2. **BCP Level 2 Training: Key Application Systems Users.** Beyond the senior-level overviews, training should be focused on recovery procedures for critical applications. In many instances, critical applications should function in a business as usual sense except that processing will take place at the alternate hot site. However, some normal resources such as user help desks often will not work in the same manner. The training here should be oriented toward the designated critical applications and how they are planned to operate. This training should operate in a case analysis mode whereby users can review BCP processes for their applications and hopefully ask detailed questions or point out areas where corrective action may be needed.

3. **BCP Level 3 Training: IT Operations and Systems Staffs.** The information systems staff, both operations and systems, are the persons who usually will be most affected by a contingency that requires operations in a recovery mode. Training here should emphasize and reemphasize key elements of the BCP; it should take the format of regular and periodic fire drills. In some instances, this training can be based on actual BCP tests while game-type simulation may be effective in others.

4. **BCP Level 4 Training: BCP Team Members.** The smaller team who launched and are responsible for the business continuity plan development, testing, and other related activities are the persons with the greatest familiarity with the established BCP. Nevertheless, their knowledge of these processes needs to be refreshed and updated on an ongoing basis. The BCP project manager typically would be charged with leading a training effort to review BCP status to date, changes in process and potential future strategy changes.

18.7 TESTING, MAINTAINING, AND AUDITING THE BUSINESS CONTINUITY PLAN

A published BCP is of little value until it receives an appropriate level of testing. Organizations will assemble a team and implement a BCP as discussed. Often, these documents are comprehensive and well thought out, but the plan is of little value unless it both is well maintained and current and is periodically tested. Meeting this BCP maintenance challenge is relatively easy. It means that every time there is a change to a critical—or any—element in the BCP, the plan must be updated to reflect those changes. In the "old days" when disaster recovery plans were thick published notebook documents, plan maintenance was difficult because resources were just not available to keep the BCP current. Today, with well-thought-out automated office procedures and information technology asset control processes, BCP maintenance should be relatively easy and can be prepared and conducted at three levels:

1. **The Software, Hardware, and People Level of BCP Maintenance.** The equipment environment supporting any set of information systems is almost constantly changing. New equipment is added while other gear is retired, and other technology changes or updates affect such areas as communications facilities. Many BCP maintenance changes should take place almost automatically with the BCP maintenance links described previously. That is, the upgrading of a software component or the addition of a new staff member should flow into the BCP's automated links as described earlier. However, those changes must be constantly reassessed and reevaluated. That someone has accepted a new position as an analyst to cover for someone who resigned does not mean that the new person will understand the BCP and his or her associated responsibilities in that area.

   The BCP team should review all changes to the plan on a regular basis with a more detailed review perhaps quarterly. Hardware and communications links should be evaluated to determine that they still work in the same manner as identified in the initial BCP, with changes being made to the plan as appropriate. That same effort is true for software, and critical elements should be tested as required. New or different people who have been added to the BCP should be interviewed to ascertain that they understand their roles and responsibilities. In some instances, repeating the training described earlier will be necessary.

2. **BCP Changes to Contingency and Recovery Arrangements.** An organization usually will have made arrangements with outside vendors to support their BCP backup processing needs, including the hot site vendor or communications provider. These arrangements should be reviewed and updated on at least a quarterly basis. This is not a portion of the overall BCP where changes are frequent, but there is value in determining that all terms and conditions are up to date. A hot site vendor, for example, may have made a small change in its arrangements that was not included in the organization's BCP. This quarterly review gives the BCP implementation team an opportunity to affirm that everything is still up to date.

3. **Business Criticality BCP Maintenance.** This portion of BCP maintenance focuses on the key business processes that were identified and described following the Exhibit 18.5 worksheet. That original exercise required a review all critical business processes and an analysis of recovery requirements, including relative priorities. The BCP team should go through this schedule probably once per quarter to add or delete new

applications, to rethink recovery needs, and to generally reorganize this set of critical applications. Potential changes to this business criticality document may cause substantive changes in the overall recovery plan. The BCP team should be aware of the types of issues that can cause changes here.

(a) Business Continuity Plan Testing

All of the effort that goes in to building a BCP, arranging for backup processing, training team members, and planning for business recovery may be of little value unless the BCP, or at least portions of it, are tested on a regular basis. The tests must be carefully planned and often work best when only a component of the overall environment is tested. A BCP test is somewhat like a fire drill in an office building where security management plans the drill, clears it with appropriate levels of management, and schedules the fire drill for an appropriate time. While an actual fire could happen at any time, it is not a good idea to set off the fire alarms concurrent with the CEO's quarterly employee meeting to report results or on the afternoon before a long holiday weekend. Otherwise, such a test can be a career-limiting factor for the manager that instigated the unannounced test. Although back in the legacy system mainframe days, this author recalls an IT manager of a European unit of his then employer who decided to "test" his disaster recovery plan by personally cutting off power to computer systems operations center and announcing this was just a test but everyone still had two minutes to clear out of the facility. His test proved that his unit's disaster recovery plan was not working and also ended the manager's career.

BCP tests should be planned well in advance and be structured as a rehearsal for various portions of the BCP. Internal audit can often be a useful resource to help plan and observe these tests. Some portions of a test are relatively easy, such as the operations at a remote hot site. Vendors offer testing time as part of their contracts, and organizations should regularly use their allotted time slots here to make certain that the operating software, database backups, and other supporting programs can be brought up to operations at the remote site. These types of tests are usually planned well in advance with the hot site vendor and with the information systems organization.

A more realistic dimension of the BCP hot site test would be for the responsible organizational manager to inform the information systems staff that at some time in the next month there will be a hot site test and then to confidentially make arrangements with the vendor for the test. The BCP manager could then announce the test on a "surprise" basis for a certain segment of operations, with the BCP team required to access backups from off-site storage, initiate arrangements to travel to the hot site, and to begin operations. Computer systems operations would continue as normal, but the BCP team would be charged with determining that certain portions of systems can be loaded and brought into operation at the hot site. The ongoing results of such a test should be documented, and internal audit might be informed in advance to observe and help document the testing process here.

A much more difficult—but very important—aspect of BCP testing is business systems recovery. It is difficult because we are testing key operational systems such as an online order processing operation that the organization expects to be up and in operation in a 24 hour, 7 days a week operation. A test of this sort would require loading supporting systems at the hot site, working with the telecommunications provider to set up a dummy network for starting up operations at a test site. A selected group of operations people would be involved here as well to process test orders and other transactions. An objective of this type of test would be to measure how long it took for the business to be restored for the key business process. The organization will have multiple key business processes, but such a test should focus on restoring the operations of a very limited number of them.

Testing can be a very important portion of the BCP training discussed at the beginning of this section. It can also be a useful process for internal audit to evaluate the effectiveness of the organization's BCP readiness. While a BCP test will never totally simulate an actual disaster, such as the 9/11 events, an effective program of testing will allow the organization to assess its readiness for a potential contingency event. This testing can be expensive and take staff away from important regular activities. Before embarking on any such type of test, the BCP project manager along with senior IT management should define the specific objectives for each test, establish a set of operating rules for the tests, and involve a limited set or participants and observers for each test scenario. The results should be documented for a lessons-learned analysis and a program of continuous BCP improvements.

(b) Auditing for the Effectiveness of the Business Continuation Plan

Internal audit can and should play an important role in the BCP's development as well as its testing processes. Internal audit might offer its resources to observe and comment on the results of BCP tests, to suggest testing scenarios, or to offer consultative advice on the progress of the BCP development. While internal audit can be part of these BCP processes, they should periodically step back, assert their independence, and schedule audits regarding the adequacy of BCP processes and business recovery procedures in general. Audits should be planned and scheduled as part of internal audit's regular risk assessment and audit-planning process.

While internal audit may play the role of observers in the BCP testing process, formal internal audits should be scheduled to periodically assess all aspects of BCP readiness and the adequacy processes in place. Internal audit must be careful not to cross the fine line between acting as an advisor to the BCP team and auditing their processes, where the audit committee may be the party interested in the overall adequacy of the BCP process for the continuance of the corporation. Internal audit's review of organization BCP processes should be based on such matters as the adequacy and currency of its BCP documentation, the results of scheduled tests, and a host of other issues. Exhibit 18.6 contains review points for an internal audit review of organization BCP processes. While every organization is different, the exhibit points out some general areas that should be considered in an internal audit review of organization BCP procedures. These focus on an audit of one self-contained set of resources and processes but could be expanded for a larger, multilocation organization.

The establishment of adequate contingency processes is an important component of an organization's internal control structure. That internal control structure was discussed in Chapters 4, "Internal Controls Fundamentals: COSO Framework," and 6, "Evaluating Internal Controls: Section 404 Assessments," on COSO and SOA Section 404 internal controls. Internal audit should communicate the results of its reviews to senior organizational management as well as the audit committee. The results of the BCP audit should be included in the internal materials that would be part of the organization's Section 404 assessment of internal controls.

EXHIBIT 18.6

Contingency Plan Audit Review Points

1. Review the existing BCP with the responsible manager.
   1.1. Does the plan appear to be current and up to date?
   1.2. Does the BCP cover all areas of the organization or just IT operations?
   1.3. Are there open BCP issues to be resolved?
   1.4. Has the BCP been reviewed with key members of management?
   1.5. Has the plan been reviewed with external auditors?
2. Examine the contents and format of the BCP.
   2.1. Based on the internal understanding of organization operations, does the BCP appear to cover key business processes?
   2.2. Are there adequate levels of business impact analysis and risk assessments as part of the BCP documentation?
   2.3. Does the plan appear to cover appropriate procedures for backups and off-site storage?
   2.4. Does the BCP carry step-by-step outlined procedures for executing it in the event of an emergency?
   2.5. Are call list chains included in the BCP?
   2.6. Does the BCP include key vendor and emergency supply contacts?
   2.7. Does the BCP document contacts for fire, police, and external media contacts?
   2.8. Is there a process in place to provide for regular and automatic updates of the BCP?
3. Determine overall training and understanding of the BCP.
   3.1. Discuss the BCP with several members of the team designated to execute the plan to determine their understanding.
   3.2. Do members in IT operations and systems appear to understand their roles and responsibilities?
   3.3. Based on discussions with key persons in critical business process areas, do they appear to have a general understanding of their business recovery roles?

EXHIBIT 18.6 *(CONTINUED)*

Contingency Plan Audit Review Points

    3.4. Based on an interview with the CFO or designee, assess whether there is adequate understanding of the BCP and how it will operate.

    3.5. Review BCP training records to determine if the training appears to be adequate, timely, and regularly scheduled.

4. Review the results of recent BCP tests.

    4.1. Is there a formal program of testing critical BCP elements?

    4.2. Are testing results documented in a lessons-learned format?

    4.3. Does BCP testing cover both business recovery as well as IT functions?

5. Review of BCP backup procedures.

    5.1. If a remote hot-site vendor is used, review the contract and related documentation for currency.

    5.2. Review the documented results of hot-site tests.

    5.3. Review the adequacy of other backup vendor or location procedures.

6. Prepare internal audit documentation assessing the overall adequacy of the organization's BCP.

Source: Robert R. Moeller, *Sarbanes-Oxley and the New Internal Auditing Rules,* © copyright 2004, John Wiley & Sons. Used with permission.

18.8 CONTINUITY PLANNING GOING FORWARD

As organizations have become ever more dependent on their automated business systems, procedures to keep those processes in operation in light of some emergency or other disaster have become increasingly important. The organization's staff can no longer get by with pulling out their No. 2 pencils and complete old paper forms as backup processes. Automated systems today are tied to complex in-house and Internet-based databases where those old procedures are no longer applicable. Going forward, the 9/11 World Trade Center terrorist event proved that many older contingency procedures were just not applicable. The mirroring processes discussed earlier in this chapter point to a direction for future business continuity planning.

The old "disaster recovery" rules have changed as well. It is no longer sufficient for information systems operations to move to a hot site backup location to begin processing and assume that the organization will soon be back in operation. Processes must focus on restoring business operations in light of an extended interruption in information systems services. Business requires the ability to get all of its processes back in operation with minimal delay. Internal auditors have an important role here in helping management to implement effective BCP processes and regularly assess their operations and controls.

ENDNOTES

[1] Disaster Recovery Institute International, Falls Church, VA (www.dri.org).
[2] Technology on the Web, *Forbes*, March 29, 2004.
[3] In interest of full disclosure, Robert Moeller, the author, previously worked for EMC Corporation helping to launch its then Operations Management Consulting group.
[4] PMP is an examination- and experience-based qualification administered by the Project Management Institute (www.omi.org).

General Controls in an E-Business and Networked Environment

19.1 IMPORTANCE OF INFORMATION SYSTEMS GENERAL CONTROLS

Auditors became involved with computers and data processing controls as manual and punched card accounting applications were first installed on early computer systems. These early systems were often impressively installed in glass-walled rooms within corporate lobbies. Those early applications were not particularly sophisticated, and internal auditors often unfamiliar with data processing technology would "audit around the computer." That is, an internal auditor might look at input controls procedures and the application's outputs, and then check whether the inputs balanced to the output reports. This was a time when there was little question about accuracy and controls if a report was produced by a computer system. The auditor would just go around the actual computer program processing procedures.

    Things changed in the early 1970s. There was a fast-growing California-based insurance company, Equity Funding Corporation, which seemed to be almost growing too fast. Although it was an almost unheard-of audit technique at the time, their external auditors decided to try a new technique at that time and run their own audit software programs against Equity Funding's computer system files. The result was the discovery of a massive fraud with invalid data recorded on system files. Under management's direction, fictitious insurance policy data was entered in computer files. Equity Funding's public accountants had previously audited around that computer system, relying on printed and output reports from those computer systems, and did not use procedures to verify the correctness of supporting computer programs and files. A massive fraud was discovered here, and in the aftermath of the Equity Funding affair, organizations such as the American Institute of Certified Public Accountants (AICPA) and the Institute of Internal Auditors (IIA) began to emphasize the importance of reviewing what were then called data processing operations and application controls. A new professional specialty, then called *computer auditing,* was launched!

In those early days of business data processing, most computer systems were expensive and considered to be "large." Fairly standard sets of auditor control objectives and procedures were developed for reviewing controls. While many are still applicable for computer systems today, internal auditors must look at these information systems control objectives from a somewhat different perspective when reviewing controls in the modern information systems environment. The internal audit profession began to think of information systems controls in terms of those within a specific information systems application and what are called general controls, the pervasive controls surrounding all information systems operations.

This chapter emphasizes general controls for information systems; application controls are discussed in Chapter 21, "Reviewing and Assessing Application Controls." General controls cover all information systems operations and include:

- *Reliability of Information System Processing.* Good controls need to be in place over all computer systems' operations. These controls often depend on the nature and management of the specific size and type of computer system used. These general controls are discussed throughout the remainder of this chapter.

- *Integrity of Data.* Processes should be in place to ensure a level of integrity over all data used in various application programs. This is a combination of the operations controls discussed in this chapter and the specific application controls discussed in Chapter 21.

- *Integrity of Programs.* New or revised programs should be developed in a well-controlled manner to provide accurate processing results. These control issues are discussed in Chapters 20 and 21.

- *Controls of the Proper Development and Implementation of Systems.* Controls should be in place to ensure the orderly development of new and revised information systems. These control issues are discussed in Chapter 22, "Infrastructure Service- and Support-Delivery Controls."

- *Continuity of Processing.* Controls should be in place to back up key systems and to recover operations in the event of an unexpected outage— what was called disaster recovery planning and is often known today as business continuity planning. These control issues are discussed in Chapter 18, "Business Continuity Planning and Disaster Recovery."

This chapter discusses general controls over information systems operations. The following sections are divided between controls over the older large mainframe computer systems operations and small systems, ranging from client/server systems to desktop operations. While there are differences between the sizes and management of these different types of computer systems, all should be subject to the same general control needs. In addition to discussing general controls procedures, this chapter also discusses some related computer hardware types and characteristics. This discussion will hopefully encourage an internal auditor to ask or look for the correct information in an information systems environment.

19.2 MAINFRAME, LEGACY SYSTEM COMPONENTS, AND CONTROLS

The UNIVAC II, one of the first successful business information systems computers, was introduced in 1951 and helped predict the results of the 1952 U.S. presidential election. It required a huge amount of physical space, weighed 15 tons, and cost $1.3 million (in 1950 dollars). Its central processing unit (CPU) had doors on both sides of the device so a technician could walk through the CPU to make any required repairs. A "bug" in those days referred to an insect that got into the CPU cabinet and perhaps blocked a relay tab. In contrast, a $1,000 or lower priced personal computer system today has at least 50,000 times the memory and speed of the UNIVAC II—or more. Was the UNIVAC II a "large" computer system? In today's terms, although it was large, based on its cost or the floor space it occupied, with respect to its memory, speed, and functional capabilities, the answer is no. Defining the term *large* as it applies to computer systems becomes even more difficult today. Once described by their manufacturers as "minicomputers," those same systems may appear to be "large computers" to an auditor because they support a large variety of peripheral equipment such as multiple workstations, disk and storage devices, and the many other devices attached to the system—called peripheral devices. The large system computer hardware may also be supported by a big operations staff and will handle many varied processing tasks. Different professionals each have their own definitions for a large computer system. The technical programmer may define a large computer system in terms of the central processor's internal design or architecture. Management may define the same computer system's relative size in terms of what the equipment cost and the size of the information systems staff necessary to support the system. Some auditors not familiar with computer systems may observe an older, or what is now called a legacy computer system located inside a secure facility with a raised floor and, on that basis, will conclude that it must be large. This is particularly true if the auditor's experience is limited to small laptop or desktop machines.

Auditors have typically been interested in the size of the computer system to be reviewed because it will impact internal audit's approach and the audit control procedures. This has changed with the rush forward of technology developments, and there is not always a direct relationship between machine size and audit complexity. Nevertheless, some of the controls that internal audit would expect to find in a very large computer center operation would not necessarily apply to a small business computer system. For example, a technical or systems programming staff, responsible for monitoring performance and maintaining a large computer's operating system, is often not necessary for a smaller and more modern computer system.

(a) Characteristics of Large Information Systems

Large systems usually have some common characteristics, whether they are classic IBM mainframes requiring chilled-water cooling or several interconnected UNIX file server processors. While all information systems internal control characteristics may not apply to every large computer system, the following list of system attributes should help an internal auditor understand the characteristics of large business information systems:

- *Physical Security Controls.* A large computer center with significant data files is usually located in a facility with locked access controls and no windows to the outside. This security helps to protect the equipment as well as programs and data. Locked doors to the computer room prevent unauthorized persons, both employees and outsiders, from entering the area to pick up reports, to ask distracting questions of the operators, or to cause malicious damage.

  While all business operations are subject to terrorism, fires, or floods, a large system computer center has a particular vulnerability because the equipment cannot easily handle these stresses. Because of the type and extent of data processed in the modern large-scale computer system, their operations should be located in unobtrusive locations and built to minimize exposure to fires, floods, or other acts of God.

- *Environmental Control Requirements.* Specialized electrical power systems as well as dedicated air-conditioning or water-cooling chiller systems are often necessary because miniature electrical components operating at full power generate a considerable amount of heat. Because of these special needs and because computer systems consist of multiple pieces of equipment connected by communications cables, large systems are located in specialized rooms with dedicated environmental monitoring controls and false floors that provide space for power cables and ventilation. Large systems, vulnerable to electrical power outages or fluctuations, are almost always equipped with emergency power supplies that can smooth out power fluctuations or provide a source of emergency power to allow the computer system an orderly shutdown.

  Some systems may even be supported by independent generators to provide power over an extended period in the event of an outage. Weaknesses in environmental controls can potentially result in failures in the operation of key information systems applications. Internal audit should always be aware of control procedures in this area and make recommendations where appropriate.

- *Separate Storage Media Libraries.* The storage or library areas for magnetic cartridges and tapes are typically adjacent to the computer equipment rather than on racks in the machine area. This separation provides extra protection for the magnetic media and for more efficient mounting and backup of tape cartridges. Automated tools are often used to schedule and call up cartridges for mounting as well as to write internal labels onto tape files and to schedule them for backup rotation. Earlier generations of magnetic media files were often rotated to another library storage facility so that, in the event of a fire or other disaster within the computer room facility, these key backup files can then be recovered for transfer to an emergency backup processing site.

- *Multitask Operating Systems.* Virtually all computers use some type of a master program or operating system to control the various programs run by the computer and other tasks such as reading disk files or supplying report data to print server facilities. Typically, these operating systems can run many programs during the same time intervals and can handle many other tasks. A multitasking operating system on a large computer must be managed and usually requires specialized personnel, called systems programmers, to maintain the operating system.

- *In-House Programming Capabilities.* Organizations with small staffs may purchase the majority of their applications as packages from software vendors or have all of their systems supplied by the organization's headquarters staff. Organizations with large computer systems are often supported by an in-house systems and programming department ranging in size from a group of perhaps several hundred or more employees to others with limited in-house programming capabilities. Programmers are different as well. Until the early 1990s, many systems used the COBOL language, but programmers today may just develop parameters for specialized purchased software packages or may do some custom work in languages such as C++ or Visual BASIC. In-house programmers almost never write custom standard applications such as inventory control or payroll. A large organization with its own programming and systems analysis staff should have a fairly formal systems development methodology (SDM) or System Development Life Cycle (SDLC) procedures, to develop and implement new applications. SDLCs are discussed in Chapter 21. There should be specialized library files to control computer programs as well as technical documentation covering the programmers' work.

- *Extensive Telecommunications Network.* Virtually all modern systems have an extensive telecommunications network to support multiple online terminals, located throughout the organization, and connected either directly to the central computer system or to external networks. Telecommunications networks will be discussed in Section 19.3 (ii). The network may also require specialized technical personnel within the information systems organization to manage telecommunications.

- *Very Large or Critical Files.* Although a computer system may be rather small in many respects, it may have one or more applications that maintain critical data on very large databases or files. In older computer systems, these critical files often consisted of many reels of magnetic tape.

Today, disk-oriented database management systems are used. Because of the criticality of such large databases or files, the computer system—whatever its actual hardware size—takes on characteristics of a large system. The need for backup copies and the integrity of critical files are crucial to the information systems function. The organization should require strong file backup procedures and database administrators to help ensure the accuracy, integrity, and completeness of the database.

- *Input-Output Control Sections.* Although not as common today with telecommunications interconnections, some organizations still have an input-output control section to receive any batch input data (such as tapes mailed from remote sources), to distribute any inputs, and to schedule and set up production jobs. In the earlier days of information systems, when most production jobs were run in a batch mode, such control functions often balanced input batches to system outputs and resolved many problems. Today, users generally take responsibility for their own data, submitted through terminals in user areas with outputs transmitted back to them.

  Input-output sections may exist to receive any manually submitted transactions that are still processed in batch mode and to take responsibility for distributing key reports produced on data center high-quality laser printers, staging work, and scheduling production jobs in the computer room. Specialized software is used to support this equipment scheduling.

- *Specialized Staff Positions.* The size of a computer system may be defined by all of the previously discussed measures. However, management may have staffed the information systems organization with other specialized personnel such as data security professionals, telecommunications analysts, or quality-assurance specialists. When organized in such a manner, internal audit may want to structure their review procedures similarly to those they'd use for a large computer system.

The previously discussed characteristics, although not that specific or precise for the large legacy system, provide some guidance to determine if the auditor is working with a large information system. There are many variations in what can be defined as either a large or small computer system. While internal audit's control objectives will remain essentially the same for both, control procedures will differ. Techniques for auditing small systems are discussed in Section 19.2. If an internal auditor has doubts whether an information systems review should be tailored to a large or small system, the safest approach is to treat the system as a large, complex one.

(i) Classic Mainframe or Legacy Computer Systems. Large information systems organizations typically have their own unique control characteristics. Although much as been published about today's client/server and desktop systems, significant changes have also taken place over the years for large, mainframe computer operations. For internal auditors, internal controls issues that were once frequent audit concerns are now an almost accepted part of large computer systems operating procedures. Other, newer control issues have now become part of the internal audit's review process. In the early days of mainframe computer systems, a common internal audit concern was that computer operators should neither have access to computer programs nor the knowledge to change them if they somehow gained access. Similarly, the reasoning was that if programmers could operate the equipment, they could improperly modify or run unauthorized programs. Checklists and audit programs were published—including those in earlier editions of this book—that directed auditors to attest that, among other matters, computer operators did not program and programmers did not operate the equipment. Because of the complexities of modern, large information systems operating systems and the high production demands within the machine room today, this separation of duties generally exists in the large organization, but it still can be a concern in the small organization or computer systems environment, as will be discussed later in Section 19.3 (a). Of course, internal audit should always confirm that there is an adequate separation of responsibilities within any information systems function.

There is no typical hardware configuration for the modern large information systems organization. Often, the inexperienced auditor will be given a tour through a room filled with central processors, servers, storage devices, and other equipment and may complete the tour with little understanding of what was seen. Because of the miniaturization of electronic components, the modern computer center increasingly takes less space than was previously required. The IBM large legacy mainframe system is an example. Up until the mid-1990s, these large machines required water-cooling systems with a requirement for extensive plumbing. Advances in technology have eliminated the need for many of these elaborate, large, and expensive systems.

In addition, there have been significant changes in the design of some computer peripheral components. Magnetic tape drives have been now all but replaced, for example, by cartridges that are much smaller and have a much higher capacity. Disk drives are configured as arrays of small disks with considerably greater data storage capacity. Output printing is done on remote printers, although large, high-speed laser printers, which can replicate traditional paper forms at a very high speed, are now found in some computer operations. An internal auditor should gain an understanding of the types of equipment in a computer center scheduled for a general controls review by requesting a hardware configuration chart from operations management. While internal audit will probably not be in a position to determine if the computer center has, for example, the correct models of disk drives, such a chart will indicate that management has done some planning in their computer hardware configuration. These charts are often filled with model numbers rather than explanations of the equipment. The internal auditor should always ask questions about the nature of this equipment.

While the number and type of disk drives, printers, and other equipment will vary, an internal auditor can expect to find similar characteristics in all operating facilities. The previously mentioned characteristics for a mainframe operation suggest what an internal auditor can expect to find in such a large computer system, no matter what model of computer is actually being used. These characteristics should help internal audit to develop procedures to test the appropriate controls. When auditors first started to review information systems general controls, they often looked for such things as locked computer room doors, fire extinguishers, and proper batch controls. These controls are now in place as a matter of course in large computer centers. While internal audit should always keep them in mind, other general control objectives and procedures must also be considered.

(ii)   Operating Systems and Software.   Early business computer systems had little more than a basic master program—what came to be called an operating system—to load the application programs into the hardware circuitry, with the application programs taking care of their own utility functions, such as tape file label checking or sorting data. The IBM 1401 computer of the mid-1960s had only 8K (8,000 bytes) of memory to contain its operating system as well as all other program requirements. The basic 1401 operating system did little more than load programs and communicate with input and output devices. Modern operating systems software are much more complex and capable of handling many users and systems functions. Some of the types of operating software that an internal auditor will encounter in a large, legacy computer system are discussed in the following sections.

(A) OPERATING SYSTEM SOFTWARE

Computer operating systems are the basic software tools that provide an interface among computer system users, the application programs, and the actual computer hardware. In addition to the basic operating system, the auditor will encounter various software monitors and controllers in this class of software, including specialized software to schedule jobs or to handle logical security. Operating system software can be classified in four broad categories:

1.   Central operating system

2.   Operations control programs

3.   Systems programming aids

4.   Application-related support software

The auditor should have a general understanding of the various types of operating systems software that may be installed on a given system. While not all of these will be candidates for internal audit procedures, the auditor should be aware of the control risks associated with each:

- *Central Operating Systems.*   The operating system (O/S) supervises the processing of all systems resources and programs. IBM's older large computer MVS operating system, as mentioned previously, is an example. Because they were often so closely tied to the hardware they control, operating systems traditionally have been unique by computer vendor and sometimes even by model. Today, there is a trend toward common operating systems. The UNIX operating system, for example, has been implemented on virtually all sizes and models of computer systems. Although less common on large mainframes, UNIX is found on many small to midsized computers and is a major controller for Internet systems. UNIX provides common user interface functions with the hardware where it is installed. There are other versions of UNIX, which differ slightly. In addition, the open source operating system, LINUX, is becoming increasingly common today.

- *System Monitors.* There are a variety of basic operating system support software products that help schedule jobs into the machine, monitor systems activities, and help solve operator problems or system errors. These products are very closely tied to the basic operating system but are usually sold and installed separately. Monitors provide internal signals to other operating system functions—that is, they are similar to a semaphore signal once found on a railroad track. Once a train enters a stretch of track, the signal detects the train and raises various semaphores to signal other trains that one is already on the track. Some monitors just log operating system activity for historical purposes. An example is IBM's SMF (System Maintenance Facility) utility, which monitors virtually all systems activities, including which programs are processed and the various disk file and other resources used. Operating system memory dumps are another example of a monitor. Here, the contents of the affected system memory are reported when a program goes into an error status.

- *Network Controllers and Teleprocessing Monitors.* These are specialized operating system programs that supervise and control transmissions between the host computer system and peripheral devices. These devices allow the multiple applications processing on a host computer system to communicate with multiple and differing network connections. Software programs that support the interaction between online terminals and the host computer also fall into this class of operating software. IBM's online monitor, often called "kicks" or CICS (Customer Information Control System), allows user terminals to access and process online programs. An internal auditor may find the name CICS somewhat curious because this utility is generally used for much more than customer information applications. CICS was originally developed by IBM in the early days of its old 360 series computers for a specific customer who needed a method to access a central system in an online manner. IBM did not have such an online software product at the time, although its mainframe computer system competition did. So, it created CICS as a special product. It has since become IBM's basic online processing control product, and many have forgotten what the acronym CICS really means.

All of these special names or acronyms can cause an auditor some communication problems. Computer systems users may know what the product does but may forget what the acronym really represents. As long as the systems specialist and the auditor understand the functions of a software product, there is little need to worry about the specific meaning of the acronym. The modern internal auditor should not become discouraged by this "foreign language" of specialized computer software terms and names. When information systems technical personnel speak in their own techno-jargon, an internal auditor should always ask for clarification when not certain what is meant.

(B) Application Software Administration and Control

A large class of system software products is responsible for controlling access to system resources, monitoring application program computer resource usage, and supervising other resources such as tape files. Online documentation tools, which provide program reference listings as well as document machine problems, can be also classed in this category of application control software. Examples of these administrative control application control systems include:

- *Access Control Programs.* These are the password-based logical security software programs that protect system resources. For a large IBM machine, product names include Computer Associate's ACF-2 and IBM's RACF logical security software. Access control software, which is typically centrally administered and controls the access to all applications, should be an important risk concern area for internal auditors. An internal auditor should understand how this software is administered for the entire organization as well as its use on individual applications.

- *Job Accounting Software.* Information systems operations should have a means to measure the level of computer resources used by each job processed. Specialized job accounting software provides this facility by linking back into the operating system and tracking the amount of resources each application program uses. If an organization measures computer resource usage and allocates these charges to its users, an error in the job accounting software can cause users to make improper decisions regarding the cost of their applications. Many organizations use their job accounting software to charge benefiting users for their proportionate use of computer system resources. Although not discussed in this chapter, audits of computer billing and pricing systems are an important area where internal auditors can combine their knowledge of internal accounting controls with the technical considerations of a computer resource pricing system.

- *Library Control Software.* Media library control software logs and tracks tape or cartridge files to verify they have proper logical identification labels. This software typically defines parameters to prohibit an application from processing data if the logical tape file label is incorrect. However, the same control software can also be set to bypass this control or can allow individual user groups to establish their own label rules. A tape or removable cartridge library control system is an example of operating software that lies between the application program and the operating system. If not controlled properly, this type of software can present significant security and control risks. Internal audit reviews of either specific applications or operating system integrity often ignore these software products, assuming that they have adequate controls.

- *Online Documentation Tools.* Two types of software are usually included here. First are system software utilities that create and maintain listings of data names, cross-reference files, and computer operator support information. The second are information logging facilities that allow operators to record machine problems for later resolution. These utilities are several levels removed from the operating system but have the ability to access otherwise protected files in order to develop the required reference listings and, thus, are useful for audit review purposes. However, because this software is so common and used by many users, auditors typically do not review controls over this type of software. Information-logging facilities have replaced the manually prepared shift reports and problem reports that once existed in many data centers. An example is the online facilities used to log console operator problems. While auditors once looked for extensive handwritten notebooks, operators can now enter their activities through an online screen. This has a distinct advantage over older, paper-based versions in that various historical trends and statistics can be summarized and reviewed by information system management. Auditors who have asked to review paper-based logs in the past should at least become familiar with these various new documentation tools.

This very brief list of application support software tools illustrates the massive need for internal auditors to understand the functions and controls risks surrounding this specialized and essential large system software. Because limited time and resources create difficulties for scheduling separate reviews of these various software elements, internal auditors should be aware of the control risks associated with these products and periodically perform specialized, controls-oriented reviews.

(C) SYSTEMS PROGRAMMER SUPPORT TOOLS

Software is available to help system programmers to monitor operating system problems and to make any necessary changes. Because this software allows highly technical system programmers to take certain shortcuts, and because they may not formally document their work on the same level of detail often found for application programs, this software presents special audit risks. This class of system software can be further classified into:

- *Operating Systems Utilities.* Utility programs allow systems programmers to make operating system program adjustments easily. IBM's SMP/E (System Modification Program Extended), for example, is used to apply corrections to the MVS operating system. IBM may notify its customers of a small, noncritical fix and ask them to add the corrections with SMP/E. Internal audit should find out which utilities have been installed. While many are designed to perform useful functions not included in the main operating system, some may present security, integrity, or control risks. Although these products were designed to solve problems, they can be used by computer operations to get around one or another system control.

- *Performance-Management Software.* Specialized software monitors the performance of the operating system in such areas as response times, error rates, and application job load requirements. For example, Candle Computer Corp's Omegamon product is used primarily on MVS-type systems to monitor and correct operations problems. Performance-management products sometimes have powerful attributes that can modify operating system functions as well.

- *Capacity-Planning Software.* Separate software products can also monitor performance CPU (central processing unit) utilization, DASD (direct access storage device) response times, and I/O (input/output) performance. The systems programmer uses these to adjust file buffer sizes, mixes of jobs, and other variables with an objective to improve overall system performance. Many capacity-planning packages produce extensive graphical reports showing various measures of system performance. Internal auditors can find these reports useful in reviewing the overall operations-management procedures used to monitor computer systems capacity.

The modern large computer center will also have a variety of language processors, such as C++ or Java, and other specialized control programs to access files and the database-management system. These include numerous special programs called *utilities* to sort data, copy files, and correct file problems. Some utilities are quite powerful.

(b) Mainframe System General Controls Reviews

In the older, traditional information systems organization, the computer operations area was often internal audit's prime area of internal control concern. The computer operator had considerable power to make changes or to bypass system controls such as overriding tape label controls or change-program processing sequences, or inserting unauthorized program instructions into production applications. While this is still possible today, the complexity of large computer operating systems as well as the sheer volume of work passing through the modern computer operations center make this difficult. Internal audit has greater risks to consider.

Many earlier audit recommendations regarding information systems operations controls are no longer feasible. For example, auditors traditionally recommended that someone review computer console logs on a regular basis. Older business data center computers had a console printer attached to record all operator actions. These logs were useful for tracing problems and also recorded any inappropriate operator activities. Today, console activity is recorded onto log files, and its data extracted only for special purposes. The sheer volume of that data would make a periodic human review of console log reports all but totally unrealistic; other tools and controls are available to help internal auditors understand operations controls. Internal audit should initially gain an understanding of the information systems organization, its established control procedures, and specialized duties and responsibilities.

The distribution of control procedures in the modern information systems organization will have an impact on how internal audit develops its procedures and the areas that internal audit may want to emphasize during a particular review. Many large organizations with specialized mainframe-type computer systems have developed information systems groups with some persons responsible for application development, others for computer operations, and still others for such technical areas as telecommunications management, database administration, and computer systems logical security. Just as in the financial controls area, internal audit should always look for a separation of duties over such key functions. However, internal audit must first understand the information systems organization.

Formerly called the data processing department, this function has come to be called *information systems* as computer-based systems have become much more critical to the modern organization. While there can be many variations in an information systems organizational structure, internal audit should look for a separation of functions between systems and programming, computer operations, and technical support functions. The technical support function will often include storage management administration and telecommunications control along with systems programming. However, these groups are sometimes set up as separate organizations reporting directly to the chief information officer (CIO). Although once organized as a single function, security and contingency planning are often separate functions in today's IT organization.

End-user or client/server systems are another function that did not appear on earlier organization charts. This function helps users to develop their own applications on the personal microcomputers configured in local area networks (LANs) and located throughout the organization. End-user, client/server computing is sometimes attached to the application-development function or may be separate. Internal audit should be aware of how end-user computing is managed and controlled, even if it happens to be outside of the classic information systems organization. The service support and delivery functions discussed in Chapter 22 provide some insights on these functions today.

The person responsible for information systems, today usually called the chief information officer (CIO), should report to an appropriate senior management level. Before its rise in importance, information systems historically reported to financial controllers, since most computer applications were accounting oriented. Because it now typically supports manufacturing, purchasing, marketing, and many other types of applications, the modern information systems function now typically reports at a higher level in the organization, and the CIO is part of the senior management team.

A variety of other functions may be attached to the modern information systems department. Some support office automation equipment and related functions, while others are responsible for both voice and data telecommunications. These activities will typically be part of the technical support or the systems programming functions. Modern information systems departments are taking on these additional responsibilities because of their overall responsibilities for organizational information. Information systems management, data security, and integrity controls and procedures need to be established whether a critical document is on the mainframe computer or is transmitted through a departmental fax machine. Quality assurance (QA) sometimes acts as an internal audit function within information systems; it may be a staff function attached to the director or attached to systems and programming. Management controls—including published policies and procedures, documented position descriptions, and programs for staff training and career development—should be as least as good as those found in the rest of the organization. That is, if the organization has overall policies and procedures, internal audit should determine that they are also followed within information systems, or should point out the deficiencies.

An important step in the review of information systems operations general controls is to clearly define the review's objectives. All too often, a member of management or the external audit firm may ask internal audit to "review the computer systems controls" in the data center. Memories do not fade very fast and that request may be based on IT controls as they once existed in older systems. The modern internal auditor should consider the following questions when planning the review:

- What is the purpose of the information system operations review?
- Which specific controls and procedures are expected to be in place?
- How can evidence be gathered to determine if controls work?

Based on the results of this exercise, internal audit should develop a set of control objectives specifically tailored for the planned review rather than just use a standard set of internal control questions. This should be a standard approach, even though internal auditors use standard lists of objectives for information systems reviews more frequently than for other operational and financial types of reviews. Whether information systems or any other review, the audit objectives identified depend on the purpose of the review.

If management has requested a review of the costs and efficiency of data center operations, the audit procedures might include such areas as the charge-back and the job-scheduling systems. An outside auditor–requested review of the same data center might pay little attention to the charge-back system but would emphasize change-control procedures over program libraries. General controls reviews of computer center operations can take several forms, but are typically organized as:

1. Preliminary reviews of information systems controls
2. Detailed general controls reviews
3. Reviews of specialized controls area
4. Reviews of compliance with laws or regulations

Although a general controls review can have a variety of purposes, it will often fit into one of these four following review types:

1. **Preliminary Reviews of Information Systems Controls.** This is the type of review that outside auditors sometimes call a *preliminary survey* or an *assessment of control risk.* Its purpose is to gain a general understanding or overview of the information systems controls environment. Internal audit asks questions, observes operations, and reviews documentation, but there typically is only very limited testing, if any. For example, internal audit might inquire about the procedures for updating production program libraries and might review the forms used for the approval process. However, the auditor would probably not select a sample of the programs in the production library to determine if the department had followed proper library updating procedures.

   A preliminary review can help determine the need for a more detailed general controls review or extended control risk assessment at a later date, or can gather preliminary controls information for a specific applications review. This type of review is limited in scope and may not cover all aspects of the information systems organization. Some areas where a preliminary review would be appropriate might include:

- A preliminary controls review of information systems operations at a new acquisition

- A follow-up review after a very detailed controls review from an earlier period; the review here would emphasize changes in control procedures as well as actions taken on prior audit recommendations

- An outside auditor's request for internal audit to review and document a general understanding of information systems controls

Although they can change with the specific purpose of the preliminary review, audit procedures in Exhibit 19.1 can be used for a preliminary review of information systems general controls. An internal auditor is gaining information here about the general structure of the information systems organization, how it plans and organizes resources, its management reporting tools, and procedures for security and contingency planning. These audit steps might be used when the organization is considering the acquisition of another company and management has asked internal audit to assess its information systems control environment. These audit steps will not help in assessing the types of systems in place, but will assess how that information systems function is organized and managed. Instead of presenting a formal report with its findings and recommendations, internal audit would simply give management an assessment of information systems general controls.

2. **Detailed General Controls Reviews of Operations.** A comprehensive, detailed review of information systems general controls will typically cover all aspects of operations, including systems programming, telecommunications controls, and database administration. A detailed general controls review should also include tests of controls over program libraries, made by running specialized programs to compare source versions with production program versions. A detailed general controls review requires good planning in order to make it effective and also requires internal audit to spend considerable fieldwork time in both the information systems operations and development functions. While the preliminary review can sometimes be performed by a less experienced auditor with limited information systems audit skills, a detailed general controls review is best performed by a more senior audit staff member with a good understanding of information systems controls and procedures.

Based on a preliminary review or walkthrough of information systems operations, internal audit should develop an understanding of the control procedures over information systems operations. The detailed audit procedures performed can be modified based on this preliminary information. Questions internal audit might pose could include:

- *How is work scheduled?* Some computer operators do little more than initiate jobs from a production job queue file, while others have considerable

EXHIBIT 19.1

Information Systems General Controls Preliminary Survey

1. Obtain basic information about the environment through initial exploratory discussions with information systems (IS) management.

2. Review the organizational chart to determine that appropriate separation of functions exists. Discuss any potential conflicts with IS management.

3. Obtain job descriptions of key IS personnel and review them for adequate and appropriate qualifications, task definitions, and responsibilities. Ensure that security and control accountability are appropriately assigned to key personnel.

4. Based on discussion within management both inside and outside the IS organization, assess whether the organizational structure is aligned with business strategies to ensure expected IS service delivery.

5. Review IS policies and selected procedures for completeness and relevance with specific emphasis on security, business continuity planning, operations, and new systems development.

6. Inquire whether responsibilities have been assigned to keep the policies and procedures current, to educate/communicate them to staff members, and to monitor compliance with them.

7. Based on discussions with senior IS management, assess whether strategic, operational, and tactical IS plans are in place to ensure alignment with the organization's overall business plans.

8. Determine the existence of an IS steering committee and review this committee's functions through a limited review of steering committee meeting minutes.

9. Ensure that a formal methodology is used in the development of new systems or major enhancements to systems in production. The methodology should include formal steps for definition, feasibility assessment, design, construction, testing, and implementation as well as formal approvals at every stage.

10. Assess the uses of system development efficiency and effectiveness tools, including joint application design (JAD), rapid application design (RAD), code generators, CASE tools, and documentation generators.

11. Determine that a process is in place for making changes to application programs in production, including testing and documentation sign-off, and formal approvals to implement the change.

12. Ensure that responsibility for physical and logical security has been appropriately apportioned and that appropriate documented procedures exist.

13. Review procedures in place for operating and maintaining the network, in terms of device configuration and software parameter changes, and ensure that procedures for allocating and maintaining the network configuration are performed on a scheduled basis and under proper change management.

14. Review the business continuity plan to ensure that detailed plans for recovery of operations have been prepared and that the plans are documented, communicated to the appropriate personnel, and properly tested on a periodic basis.

15. Review both the IS budget and the actual costs as well as performance against those measured to assess financial performance. Discuss the reasons for any variances.

authority in deciding which jobs to run. In the latter situation, internal audit might want to spend time reviewing control log reports and operator instructions. If these procedures have been automated, internal audit may want to consider a specialized review of the production control software area.

○ *How is storage media managed?* Automated tools are often used here. In addition, some operations have a separate library facility where production cartridges or tapes are mounted. When automated tools are not used for controlling tape libraries, there is a greater chance for mount errors. Even when software has been installed, computer operators often can bypass label controls and introduce incorrect files into a production environment.

○ *What types of operator procedures or instructions are used?* Large systems operations documentation can take a variety of formats; internal audit should have a general understanding of this documentation format and content. This will help in the design of specific audit tests.

○ *How is work initiated and how does it flow through operations?* In many large computer system operations, production is initiated through remote job entry user terminals. In others, the production-control function funnels all necessary input data to machine operations. Some functions rely on users to initiate most inputs through their online terminals. The type and nature of internal audit's tests will depend on the customary procedures.

The basic idea is for internal audit to understand how information systems operations function. The effective internal auditor should go through a set of these types of questions prior to each review. A large systems operations function may install new procedures from time to time, changing or adding complexities to the control structure. The audit procedures to be performed in a detailed review of general controls for a legacy computer system can be extensive, depending on the size and scope of the audit. Exhibit 19.2 contains a limited set of control objectives for this type of review.

3. **Specialized or Limited-Scope Reviews.** Because of management requests and perceived risks, auditors often perform limited reviews over specialized areas within an overall information systems function. These specialized reviews can be limited to one function, such as storage administration, or even to one specialty area, such as output report distribution. Often, management will request that internal audit perform this type of a review due to some identified problem, such as a well-publicized security violation.

An audit of a highly specialized or technical area of information systems operations often takes considerable internal auditor creativity in planning the work. Management may be concerned about the equity of the computer charge-back system and may ask the audit department to look at it. Internal audit will need to gain a general understanding of the system used, spend time planning the additional procedures and tests to be performed, and then return to the actual testing.

EXHIBIT 19.2

Large System General Controls Review Objectives

1. Determine that the computer equipment is located in a secure, environmentally controlled facility.

2. Discuss physical and environmental control procedures with information systems management to determine current policies and future plans.

3. Tour computer operations facilities and observe physical security strengths and weaknesses, including:
   a. The existence of locking mechanisms to limit computer room access only to authorized individuals
   b. The placement of computer room perimeter walls and windows to limit access
   c. The location of power transformers, water chiller units if appropriate, and air-conditioning units to provide proper protection
   d. The general location of the computer room facilities within the overall building to minimize traffic
   e. The existence of fire detection equipment, including zone-controlled heat and smoke detectors
   f. The existence of a zone-controlled, overall fire protection system, including local extinguishers

4. Review computer room temperature, humidity, and other environmental controls and assess their adequacy.

5. Briefly review maintenance records to ascertain that physical and environmental controls are regularly inspected and maintained.

6. Production processing should be scheduled to promote efficient use of computer equipment consistent with the requirements of systems users. Through interviews with operations management, develop an overall understanding of computer processing demands, including online and batch production work as well as any end-user computing.

7. Also through interviews, describe the telecommunications network surrounding the computer system, including connections to workstations, computer centers, and the outside.

8. Review procedures for scheduling regular production jobs, including the use of automated job-scheduling tools.

9. Match a limited number of scheduled production jobs against actual completion times to determine whether actual schedules are followed.

10. Determine that operating system job classes or priority codes are used to give proper priority to critical production jobs, and evaluate procedures for rush or rerun jobs.

11. Review documentation standards for production applications to determine that they provide operators with information regarding:
   a. Normal operations, including instructions for special forms, tape files, and report disposition
   b. Application restart and recovery procedures

12. Review procedures, automated or manual, for turning new applications or revisions over to production to determine if there is a review by operations following standards.

13. Determine that policies prohibit computer operations personnel from performing programming tasks or running unauthorized jobs.

14. Determine that production source libraries cannot be accessed by operations personnel.

15. Assess information systems procedures for periodically reviewing the contents of log files or otherwise monitoring improper operator use of computer equipment.

EXHIBIT 19.2 *(CONTINUED)*

Large System General Controls Review Objectives

16. Review and document procedures for changing production programs or procedure libraries when emergency situations require special handling.

17. Determine that all emergency processing activities are properly documented and are subject to subsequent management review.

18. Select several documented emergency program fixes and determine that the necessary changes were added to production processing libraries and were documented.

19. Determine that an automated system is in place to log all computer systems activity, including all jobs and programs run, any reruns, abnormal terminations, or operator commands and data entered through system consoles.

20. Determine that computer activity logs are reviewed periodically, that exception situations are investigated, and that the results of investigations are documented.

21. Determine that files produced from the computer operating system's log monitor are retained long enough to allow investigation of unusual activities.

22. Review procedures for logging problems to determine that all abnormal software and hardware operating conditions are documented.

23. Determine that schedules exist for the submission of critical input batch files and that procedures exist to follow up on missing data.

24. Review procedures to prohibit unauthorized input or access to production files and programs.

25. Review a limited sample of production batch applications to determine that appropriate system control techniques are used.

26. Determine whether users or information systems personnel are responsible for reviewing output controls and assess whether those control reviews are being performed.

27. Assess procedures for reviewing distributed output reports to determine whether they are complete.

As information systems departments grow in complexity and importance to the organization, auditors can expect to perform more of these specialized, limited reviews. With the information systems function a major resource in many organizations, it may be inappropriate to attempt to review *all* information systems general controls in *all* operational areas as one single detailed review. This would be the same as if internal audit attempted to perform a review of "manufacturing" in a major plant environment. Rather than cover all manufacturing functions, internal audit might review production control one year and receiving and inspection the next, and eventually cover most significant functions. For a specialized review of a specific information systems control area, such as memory media library management, internal audit should expand on the procedures developed for a general controls review in that area and add additional audit tests as necessary.

4. **Reviews to Assess Compliance with Laws or Regulations.** One of the major objectives of internal control, as discussed in Chapter 4, "Internal Controls Fundamentals: COSO Framework," on internal control fundamentals,

is compliance with laws and regulations. Internal auditors should always be aware of objectives in this area and include appropriate tests in their reviews. Auditors working with governmental agencies or in organizations that do extensive governmental contracting may often be required to perform information systems-related compliance audits to determine if appropriate laws and regulations are being followed. These will differ very much from agency to agency and from one political division to another.

A compliance-related information systems review can often be combined with a preliminary or detailed general controls review, but auditors must be aware of the relevant procedures and regulations, such as those published by the governmental agency requiring the audit. Most bank-examination agencies, for example, have published information systems controls guidelines. When operating in this type of environment, internal auditors must become aware of the regulatory environment as well as any published procedures.

19.3 CLIENT/SERVER AND SMALL INFORMATION SYSTEMS

Auditors traditionally have had problems evaluating controls in small information systems organizations, ranging from client/server systems to small organization desktop systems. These problems arise because small systems are often installed with limited staffs in a more "user-friendly" type of environment. Internal auditors, however, typically look for controls in terms of the more traditional, large mainframe information systems environment—that is, strong physical security, good revision controls, and proper separation of duties among members of the information systems organization often just do not exist or are only partially implemented in the typical small systems environment. This approach was perhaps adequate when these small business or desktop systems were used primarily for single-office accounting or similar low-audit-risk applications. The large capacity and capability of small systems today, the growth of telecommunications networks including the Internet and intranets, and the transition to client/server computing has made these small systems important parts of the information systems controls framework. When faced with evaluating controls in these small computer systems settings, internal auditors have sometimes reverted to the traditional, almost "cookbook" types of controls recommendations. That is, they have recommended that desktop systems be placed in locked rooms or that a small, two-person information systems development staff is expanded to four in order to ensure proper separation of duties. While there may be situations where such controls are appropriate, they often are not applicable in a small business setting. Internal audit can easily lose credibility if its control recommendations are not appropriate to the risks found in the small computer systems setting.

Organizations are implementing increasing numbers and networks of smaller systems to support business units, support specific departmental computing, or provide information systems for the entire organization. Despite their small size, these systems often can represent significant control concerns. The following sections discuss information systems controls in the small system business information systems environment, including control procedures for local area networks (LANs) and client/server computing systems.

This chapter began with a discussion of the differences between general, interdependent controls and application controls in large systems. These differences are equally applicable for small business systems including Internet-based systems and client/server configurations. Internal audit should understand the general controls surrounding a small computer system. Adequate general controls are necessary in order to place reliance on specific application controls.

(a) General Controls for Small Business Systems

Although some internal auditors once thought of small business computers and client/server systems as one generic computer system class (as opposed to large, mainframe computers), technological and organizational changes have caused significant differences in control procedures and internal audit concerns among them. Small systems can be implemented in a variety of ways, depending on the type of system and the size of the organization. The modern internal auditor should be able to recognize these differences and develop appropriate general internal control procedures to review them. Subsequent sections of this chapter will discuss these general controls in terms of small business computer systems, Internet and networked systems, and client/server systems controls.

Internal audit may encounter all of the above types of small computer systems in a single modern organization. Small business computer systems provide total information systems support for a small business function or unit, but these systems may also support unit or departmental computing functions in a large organization in support of central computer systems resources.

Client/server systems, defined in greater detail later in Section 19.3(a)(iii), are often a combination of various types and sizes of interconnected computer systems and may be found in all types and sizes of organizations. Process, or nonbusiness, systems include the numerous types of small computers used increasingly for manufacturing, distribution, and other various operational control applications. Internal audit will frequently find these specialized control machines in many areas of an organization's operations.

(i) Small Business Computer System Controls. This chapter began with a definition of large computer system in terms of their hardware equipment and information systems organizational attributes. If a computer system is located in a secure facility, has a multitasking operating system, or has a large programming staff, internal audit should probably consider it to be a "large" computer system for purposes of audit planning and should be reviewed for appropriate large system general controls procedures. While not particularly precise, this definition would have covered the typical major computer system. The same type of attribute-based description can be more difficult to apply in the small system environment. A strict computer hardware architecture definition often does not help internal audit to decide when to apply small system control procedures. For example, small desktop computers can be coupled together with attached peripheral devices to provide more computer power than some traditional mainframe machines. When reviewing controls in such an environment, internal audit should consider these linked computers to be the same as the large, legacy mainframe systems discussed previously. Another problem in identifying a small computer is that they often look like a large processor. For example, IBM's AS/400 system was first implemented in the 1980s as what was then called a minicomputer. The AS/400 product line and the individual machine capacities have been expanded to make many of these systems effectively operate as classic mainframe systems.

Small systems, once known as minicomputers, have been used for business applications since about the late 1960s. They are a product of the increased miniaturization of electronic components as well as of different approaches used by computer engineers. Because they were relatively inexpensive, easy to use, and did not require elaborate power or air-conditioning support, minicomputers were used by many small business organizations as well as for specialized information systems applications. Long before the introduction of today's desktop systems, they brought information systems capabilities to organizations that could not afford the large investments required by classic mainframe systems.

Desktop or laptop systems (also known as personal computers) have had a rapid growth curve. Hobbyists began building their own what were initially called microcomputers using newly available integrated circuit chips in the mid-1970s; things really got started in the late 1970s when Apple Computer Corporation was formed and produced the Apple II microcomputer. Although the machine was initially viewed as a curious toy by many, a spreadsheet software package, VisiCalc, introduced about a year later, made the Apple II a serious tool for business decision making. In the early 1980s, IBM introduced its personal computer and legitimized the microcomputer as a serious business processing tool. Many of the machines are still said to be "IBM compatible" even though IBM is a relatively minor player in that industry.

Today, personal computers, often connected into networks, are used for many business information systems applications. They are often the only computer system resource for a small company or a division of a large organization, and often have replaced small mainframe systems. They may also be used for specialized departmental computing even though there may also be a large, mainframe computer capability within the organization. In particular, these specialized computers are used for such applications as research laboratory or manufacturing process control rather than for pure business information systems. These same machines may also be used for some business processing applications in addition to their intended specialized purposes.

Ever-increasing speed and capacity has done much to promote the use of small systems. When the first Apple II was released, it had an internal memory of 42K, or 42,000 memory locations. By the mid-1990s, in contrast, off-the-shelf machines typically come with 32,000,000 memory locations, or 32 megabytes. Virtually every other measure, whether it is processing speed, capability of running multiple tasks, or disk file memory capacity, has changed dramatically. Even the term "microcomputer" has become obsolete. The former "microcomputer" is now known as a desktop or laptop computer, with legacy devices having their own special names.

These machine-size-based definitions of computer systems often cause difficulties for internal auditors because they are used for so many types of business-related applications. Internal audit may be directed by management to review the general controls surrounding "all" computer systems in the organization. Clearly, this type of directive covers the mainframe computers and free-standing divisional smaller systems. The directive may also cover the organization's departmental desktop computers, sometimes free-standing but more often connected to the Internet. However, internal audit may wonder if such a directive really covers the specialized workstation computer in the engineering laboratory used for recording test results or the microcomputer at the end of the distribution line that weighs the package and routes it to the correct shipping dock. These definition problems will only get worse as such things as embedded systems take a greater role in controlling business processes. Embedded systems are the computers that reside behind such things as the dashboard of a car or on the control panel of a video recorder or even in the kitchen microwave. As consumers, we press these flat panel screens and generally do not think we are submitting computer system commands. However, embedded systems will take greater roles in business processes as their capacities and applications increase.

While all of the above are computer systems in accordance with a management request to review all systems, internal audit's reviews should emphasize the computer systems used for *business information systems* purposes. To follow the above example, the processor at the end of the distribution line probably uses a standard set of embedded software that cannot be modified by the local staff. It was very possibly purchased from an outside systems vendor and, after initial installation and testing, it simply works, with no programmer interaction. Such a machine generally has limited business or control risk implications.

Internal audit will often work in an environment where only small business system computers are used, particularly when the auditor's organization is relatively small or does not require extensive computer systems power. An example would be a not-for-profit organization whose only systems needs are to support direct mailing and limited accounting-related applications. While these can be handled today by a network of individual small computers, the organization may have purchased a classic minicomputer some years ago, when that represented the best technical solution. Although it is not the most current or modern, internal audit still has an obligation to review the internal controls surrounding that older system provided that it falls within internal audit's risk parameters. Internal audit should review the controls over such a smaller computer operation as if it were either a small business system or a classic, large organization mainframe system. While the underlying concepts and objectives of internal control will not vary, the scope and nature of the internal audit review will. When internal audit has doubts, the controls review should be conducted as if it were a large system. The following is a summary of typical small business information system characteristics:

- *Limited Information Systems Staff.* The small business computer system, whether personal computers on a LAN or an older minicomputer, will have a very limited dedicated information systems staff, if any. A desktop computer used to provide accounting reports for a small company may be maintained by a single person. A small business or LAN system may have a manager/LAN administrator, a programmer, and perhaps one or two operators as its total information systems department. The nature of the equipment, the applications processed, and the size of the total organization tend to limit information systems staff size. This small operation creates a control risk because no one person may be required to perform such functions as backing up critical files. However, a small staff size will not in itself always cause an organizational controls concern. Internal audit should be able to look for compensating controls just as it does when reviewing a small accounting department where a classic separation of duties is lacking.

- *Limited Programming Capability.* The typical small business computer system makes extensive use of purchased software packages. The few programmers in the department, if any, are responsible for updating the purchased packages, maintaining operating system tables or parameters, and writing simple retrieval programs. If internal audit finds a large programming staff or extensive in-house development activity, some of the control procedures discussed previously for large systems development functions should be considered.

- *Limited Environmental Controls.* Large mainframe computer systems require specialized power, temperature, and other environmental controls such as water-cooled chillers for the central processors. Small business computer systems tend to be just the opposite. They can generally be plugged into normal power systems and operate within a fairly wide range of temperatures. Because of these limited requirements, small systems are sometimes installed without important, easy-to-install environmental controls such as backup drives or electrical power surge protectors. While some small business computer installations or file servers may be housed in formal, environmentally controlled computer rooms, this is not a necessary attribute of these systems.

- *Limited Physical Security Controls.* Because of less need for environmental controls, these systems are often installed directly in office areas. The level of auditor concern regarding physical security controls depends on the type of computer equipment and the nature of the applications being processed. Internal audit may sometimes recommend that physical security be improved, particularly where a file server is involved or if critical applications are being processed. In many other instances, this lack of physical security controls should not present a significant control problem.

- *Extensive Telecommunications Network.* Only a limited number of desktop systems today are free-standing devices. Most are tied together in a local network or to the Internet. The typical individual network supports anywhere from a few to hundreds or more devices with most residing locally in the same general building or facility. These systems may also be linked to a mainframe as part of a distributed processing network where files are both uploaded and downloaded. All of these issues add different levels of control considerations to the system under review.

The previous characteristics certainly do not *define* a small business computer system, but only explain some common system attributes. However, they should help internal audit to better decide on the control procedures to be used. As noted, when in doubt, internal audit should consider the system to be a larger, more complex one.

(ii) Small LAN Systems in Large, Traditional Organizations. LANs have been discussed as a type of computer system often found in small businesses as opposed to the large organization's classic mainframe system with its centralized processor and the network of connected terminals. In our rapidly changing information systems environment today, this configuration is no longer always true. Separate LANs are often found at a departmental or separate operating division level in the large organization. These may operate as dual systems, separate from the mainframe central system, used for a specialized departmental database or information system necessary for that unit's operations. Often, this dedicated LAN may have evolved through one or several groups placing their unique applications on an office desktop computer system when they were unable to get priorities for a mainframe system development. As other departmental users saw the value of such a local application, the organizational unit may have established its own departmental LAN, separate from the traditional mainframe system. Today, that same LAN as well as client/server architecture will be used as almost a first choice to avoid the time and expense of placing a new application on the information systems department–administered classic mainframe.

Because the departmental LAN is separate from traditional mainframe-based systems and often does not follow the standards established by the central information systems organization, internal audit should treat these operations reviews similarly to those in a separate, small business type of system. LANs were initially implemented as part of traditional large organization, mainframe computer system networks. The centralized computer system would have its network of attached terminals as well as multiple attached LANs. Today's workstations on LANs may be used for local, microcomputer-based data processing as well as for communication with the centralized computer system. Each of the LAN workstations sends and receives its mainframe-based transactions through the LAN server and then to the mainframe system. Although this computer system has some of the characteristics of the small business systems described previously, it is very much a component of a large computer system, and internal audit should consider the general controls over a LAN connected to a large system mainframe essentially the same as the controls in any large computer system.

(iii) Client/Server Computer Systems. The term *client/server* first appeared in information systems business literature in the late 1980s. For non-information-systems specialists, including many auditors, it is one of those specialized information systems terms that are often difficult to understand, let alone describe. However, client/server architecture has become a very popular information systems configuration in all sizes of organizations and all types of modern computer systems. In a local network environment, for example, each of the workstations on the network is a *client.* The centralized LAN processor, which contains common shared files and other resources, is called the *server.* The workstation user submits a request from the user's client machine to a server, which then serves that client by doing the necessary processing and then fulfilling the request.

This client/server architecture, however, goes beyond just a workstation and a LAN server. An application that queries a centralized database can be considered the client, while the database that develops the view of the database is the server to all workstations requesting database service. Similarly, an application program can request services from an operating system communications server. Exhibit 19.3 shows a client/server system sample configuration where a single server handles requests from multiple clients across a network, and Exhibit 19.4 outlines control procedures for a client/server, networked environment. This discussion of client/server architecture, though very general, represents the typical computer systems configuration of today. Internal auditors also should consider control objectives here similar to those found in large computer systems along with a strong telecommunications network, as discussed in Exhibit 19.2.

(iv) Nonbusiness Specialized Processor Computer Systems. In many organizations today, other systems can be found in areas beyond information systems operations. Special-purpose machines may be located in engineering laboratories, manufacturing control operation, marketing departments, and many other areas.

EXHIBIT 19.3

Client/Server Simplified Architecture

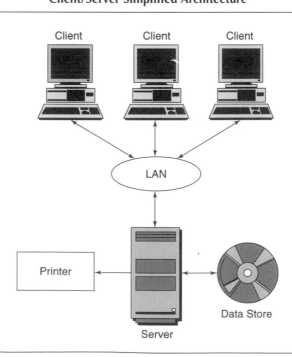

EXHIBIT 19.4

Audit Procedures for a LAN, Client/Server Environment

---

1. Determine if there is a complete inventory of all systems hardware, including the servers, printer(s), and communication controllers, as well as a complete inventory of all application and system software.

2. The network hardware inventory report contains unique identification numbers or model numbers for the various hardware devices. Through review of a limited sample, determine if items on the network inventory report correspond to the physical equipment and that network hardware components contain an asset number or other ownership identification mark that cannot be removed or altered.

3. Review policies for storing unused equipment and disposing of obsolete or badly damaged communications equipment. Does the policy require management approval of equipment disposal?

4. Determine that hardware devices and documentation are located in a secure facility and that the file server components (keyboard lock and power on password) are restricted to the systems administrator.

5. Observe the file server facility and verify that it is physically secured, and observe the LAN file-server computer and verify that it is secured in a manner to reduce the risk of removal of computer components or the computer itself.

6. Verify that file server facility temperature and humidity controls are adequate, static and electric surge protectors are in place, and fire extinguishers are nearby.

7. Observe the storage methods and media for backup diskettes and tapes, verifying that they are protected from environmental damage.

8. Review the procedures in place for restricting, identifying, and reporting authorized and unauthorized users of the network. Determine that users are required to use passwords and that passwords are changed periodically, are internally encrypted, and not displayed on the computer screen when entered.

9. Review procedures for monitoring the access and use of the network. Evaluate a sample of LAN users' access/security profiles to ensure access is appropriate and authorized based on an individual's responsibilities.

10. Where the LAN is connected to an outside source through a modem or dial-up network, determine what controls are in place to secure these outgoing connections. In particular, does the security firewall function for these connections?

11. Determine that backup copies of all LAN files created at intervals are adequate, current, and for disaster recovery purposes. Ensure that LAN applications have been prioritized and scheduled according to their sensitivity and importance.

12. Select a sample of LAN application software and verify that they are supported by a written contingency recovery plan and are prioritized by their level of sensitivity and importance. In addition, verify that all the sensitive applications sampled have been subject to a test of the backup files.

13. Review the log of LAN downtime for the last six months. If frequent downtime has been recorded, determine if adequate short- and long-term measures have been implemented to resolve the problem.

14. Interview the LAN administrator to assess whether this person is knowledgeable and properly trained.

15. If available, obtain the LAN application operating schedule and assess whether key LAN-based financial and operational applications, such as any payroll or accounts payable, have adequate processing coverage.

16. Interview a sample of LAN users and determine if they are satisfied with response time and LAN availability.

The computer systems may be used for process control, automated design work, statistical analysis processing, or for many other applications. Some are totally dedicated to specific applications, while others may be used for a variety of tasks within their assigned functions. This multitude of information systems machines has come about in many organizations because of the relatively low cost of such machines, the familiarity of many professionals with information systems techniques today, and the inability of traditional information systems departments to support specialized information systems needs.

Although these systems are not used for traditional business information needs, such as maintaining accounts receivable records, they often support critical applications for the organization. For example, an engineering system may support new product computer-aided design (CAD) work. Systems backup and integrity concerns in this environment may be equally as great as in the typical business information systems center. Internal audit's role in regard to specialized information systems operations will vary with both management's direction and internal audit's review objectives. While some audit organizations will have little involvement with reviews over specialized computer systems, information systems controls reviewed here can often play an important role in support of internal audit's understanding of control procedures and in other operational audit activities.

Before attempting any review of such a specialized computer system, internal audit should obtain a rough familiarity with the functions of that operation. For example, an internal auditor who plans to review a dedicated computer-aided design and manufacturing (CAD/CAM) computer operation needs a general understanding of the terminology, general workings, and objectives of CAD/CAM.

Reviews of specialized computer systems are not recommended for the less experienced internal auditor. In order to find control analogies from normal business information systems situations and translate them to specialized controls environments, an auditor must be fairly experienced in reviewing business information systems computer centers, whether large or small operations. Over time, internal audit will encounter more of these specialized computer operations. The creative internal auditor can make increasing contributions to management by performing operational reviews over these computer centers on a periodic basis.

(b) Small Systems Operations Internal Controls

As discussed, internal auditors have traditionally looked for a proper separation of duties as a first procedure for evaluating information systems general controls. This organizational control is also often lacking in a small business information systems function. While good information systems control objectives call for a proper separation of responsibilities between users, programmers, and operators, such strict organization controls are often difficult to establish in a small department. When auditors first began to review general organizational controls in these small information systems departments and tried to apply large mainframe system control remedies, those recommendations often were hard to sell to a cost-conscious management; they would be treated with derision today.

The responsible manager of the small client/server or LAN-based information system today may also be the principal programmer and operate the equipment when the need arises. Because much of the programming involves manipulating simple retrieval languages, many users have some programming knowledge. The separation of duties controls found in a large shop just does not exist in this small environment, but there should be compensating controls, including:

- *Purchased Software.* Nearly all small computer systems today operate with purchased software packages where "programmers" do not have access or have very limited access to source code. A major task may be to just install vendor software upgrades on the local system.

- *Increased Management Attention.* Although the management in an organization supported by a small business computer system may have very little knowledge of information systems techniques, they often give considerable attention to the key computer-generated reports. In a small company, it is not unusual for top management to review, for example, an accounts receivable aged trial balance in detail and on a regular basis.

- *Separation of Input and Processing Duties.* In virtually all modern small business computer systems today, users submit data inputs through their individual workstations and receive outputs on their terminals or remote printers.

Even with these compensating organizational controls in the modern, small business computer system, internal audit should also be aware of potential control risks and weaknesses. Information systems departments continue to exist in which the responsible manager implements many of the applications, has responsibility for the network management, controls all passwords, and appears to be the only person in the organization who understands the information systems applications. While a limited staff may be acceptable in some circumstances, the organization faces a risk if all information systems knowledge is vested in only one person. Other control weakness symptoms in the small information systems organization that do not typically exist in the large department include:

- "Loyal" employees who do not take their vacations or time off
- The use of special, undocumented programs known only to the information systems manager
- Direct information systems department participation in system input transactions, such as adjustments to the inventory system

Control risk may be a major consideration when audit procedures have identified significant control weaknesses in these small business systems. In large organizations, auditors often look for documented position descriptions as evidence of good management controls over the information systems function. Many small organizations do not have such descriptions for *any employee.* An internal auditor will not be effective in suggesting that such position descriptions be drafted just for the information systems function while ignoring the rest of the organization when overall control risk is minimal because of the small size of the organization.

As discussed, the plan of organization and related management practices are often among the strongest control procedures in a large information systems organization. In the small organization, the size and informality typically associated with such a small group will tend to weaken controls. Senior management should have a good understanding of the information systems function, its plans, and its objectives. A very important general control for the small information systems organization is adequate documentation over its systems and procedures. Management can be very vulnerable if systems, programs, and operating procedures are not properly documented.

There have been instances where both members of a two-person information systems organization suddenly resigned due to a disagreement or better employment offer. Without adequate documentation, it is very difficult for someone else suddenly to take over. This is even true if the organization primarily runs packaged software, since there may be many special procedures associated with those packages. The risk is equally high if the organization uses desktop systems where users do much of their own work. The network administrator who configures the system and backs up files has a key control responsibility.

Sometimes, the small information systems organization is located at an operating unit of a large organization with other centralized information systems facilities. Even though the small information systems organization is entirely free-standing, it may receive central direction as to appropriate standards and procedures. In order to ensure compliance with these standards, internal audit should have a general understanding of them and the level at which these corporate standards are expected to be followed. Sometimes, a large organization will issue mandatory standards applicable to all of its operating units, no matter their size, even though the standards may not be practicable for smaller units. While central management may look the other way regarding local compliance with these standards, internal audit often feels compelled to bring up violations found at a small unit. If such problems exist, internal audit should discuss these concerns with the central information systems management group responsible for the standards. Very little is accomplished if a field internal auditor brings up a violation of a corporate standard found at a remote unit when that central management really does not expect full compliance. This may be a topic more for a centralized review of standards!

(c) Small Systems Operations Internal Audit Activities

A small computer system may provide information systems support for the total organization or for a separate operating unit of a large organization. Such systems may have many of the attributes of a large, mainframe computer system, including a limited but formal information systems organization, production schedules, and a responsibility for implementing new applications. However, the small computer system organization often has no other specialized functions. Internal audit will encounter a variety of computer hardware "brands" or product names in a small systems environment, but most will be "open systems" with a common operating system such as Microsoft's Windows that can operate no matter what brand of hardware is used. This is different from classic mainframe computers, where the manufacturer generally built the computer hardware as well as an operating system. Numerous vendors supply such small business computer systems with both improved functionality and price performance, and internal auditors will be more effective in reviewing small business computer system controls if they have an overall knowledge of some of their capabilities.

Despite the small and more informal nature of a typical small business computer system, internal audit should still expect to have some of the same general organizational control objectives discussed for large systems, although some procedures may be modified due to the more informal nature of these small systems. The following sections discuss some of these control concerns.

(i) Small System Controls over Access to Data and Programs.   When unauthorized persons are allowed to access and modify computer files and programs, general controls are very much weakened. However, internal audit should consider access to data and programs to be *the major general controls objective* when reviewing the small information systems organization. This is true whether the information systems department uses packaged software products or software developed in-house.

Controls over access to data can be considered in terms of both specific applications and general controls. However, in small computer systems, general controls often have a greater importance than specific application data access controls because applications operating on a single small business computer system will typically all operate under the same set of data access controls. In a small system, data can be improperly accessed and modified through improper data access attempts through user terminals, unauthorized use of specialized utility programs, or invalid information systems requests. Of course, there may also be other ways to access data such as improper access through uncontrolled dial-up telephone lines.

(ii) Improper Data Access through User Workstations.   Small systems, whether a LAN-based desktop systems or a powerful server-type system, often do not have the sophisticated security controls found on many large mainframe systems. Rather, these small systems have a user logon/password identification coupled with menu-based information security. A systems user typically enters the assigned logon or User ID identification code into the terminal and receives a display of a menu screen with the applications available for that code. The user can only then access the applications assigned to that menu. For example, a small business computer system may have a series of accounting applications that some users can update and others can only view. Two series of logon ID codes would be assigned: The first would display a menu of programs to update these various accounting applications and the second would display only the files.

This type of menu-based security, historically found in systems such as an IBM AS/400, can provide a fairly effective control against improper access attempts. However, these controls can tend to break down due to the informality of many small organizations. Logon codes are often not changed on a regular basis, one general menu is given to virtually all employees, or terminals with more privileged IDs are left on for virtually all to use. Because users are generally not aware of potential data sensitivities and vulnerabilities, management may give only minimal attention to such security issues. In order to review controls in this area, internal audit should first gain a general understanding of the data security system installed. Such security ranges from good password-based systems and highly structured menu systems to rudimentary sets of procedures. The next step is to understand how that security system has been implemented in the system under audit. Finally, internal audit should determine how that system is being used. The latter step implies that the auditor should spend some time reviewing the use of the application and its controls in user areas.

A small business computer system may not have the logging mechanisms to monitor invalid access attempts. Instead, internal audit should review the overall administration procedures covering the security system. These can include reviewing how often logons are changed, who has access to the system administrator's menu, and what local management's general appreciation is of information systems access controls.

(iii)   Unauthorized Use of Utility Programs.   Modern small systems often are equipped with powerful utility programs that can easily change any application data file. These programs are designed to be used for special problem-solving situations, and they often produce only a limited audit trail report. All too often, these utilities serve as substitutes for normal production update programs or are used by an information systems manager for these special updates, and sometimes are even given to users. For example, an organization may have installed an inventory status system. While the system normally provides proper stock-keeping records, the inventory status may become misstated from time to time due to a variety of reasons. In order to help users correct these inventory status record keeping problems, the information systems manager or LAN administrator may have developed the practice of correcting inventory balances through the use of a utility program. While the information systems manager may be following proper management direction in the normal use of such a program, there may be no audit trails of its use.

These utility programs go by a variety of names depending on the type of computer operating system used. For example, in a UNIX operating system environment, the *su* (superuser) command has some powerful attributes that should be protected. Internal audit should understand the types of standard utility programs available for the system under review. The usage of the particular program can best be determined through inquiry and observation.

(iv)   Improper Information Systems Data and Program Access Requests.   The informality of small organizations often allows data to be accessed improperly through normal information systems operations procedures. For example, someone known to the information systems function may initiate a special computer run, which results in an improper access to confidential data. In large, more formal organizations, such a request would often require some type of special management permission, but small, more informal organizations often waive such requirements. This type of access may be a greater control risk than access through use of improper programs.

Internal audit should look for controls to prevent such casual information systems requests. The best control could be a formal "request for data services" type of form, approved by management. In addition, logs should be maintained listing all production information systems activities as well as the name of the requester and the report recipient. Many of the control concerns over improper access to data also apply to small system program libraries. Small business systems typically do not have the sophisticated software control tools over program libraries found in large, mainframe systems. However, many do have menu-based systems that offer some security types of controls. Without such a proper menu type of security system to limit improper access, it can often be relatively easy for someone with a little knowledge to locate and potentially modify program library files.

Internal audit may also find weak controls over program library updates. The one or two information systems personnel in a small information systems department who act as network administrators typically can update program libraries with little concern for documenting those changes or for obtaining any type of upper management authorization. While some of these changes may be justified in order to respond to user emergency requests, others may not be properly authorized. It is difficult, if not impossible, to install separation-of-duties organizational controls over small business system program libraries. In addition, it probably will not work for internal audit to suggest that management formally review and approve all program library updates—they will neither be interested in nor have the technical skills to perform such reviews. The best control method here might be to install procedures that require the logging of all changes or software package updates to the production program library, with such logs subject to periodic internal auditor reviews.

This type of control takes advantage of the fact that many small business computer system program compilers maintain a hash[1] total count of the program size in bytes and also have the ability to retain some form of date or version number within the program name. Internal audit might then suggest a small business computer system program library control as follows:

1. Establish program naming conventions that include the date or version number included with the program name. When not available in commercially purchased software, a separate control file with this data can be established. This feature is becoming increasingly common; for example, it can be implemented within the Windows XP operating systems.

2. Have the persons authorized to make program changes log in the version number, date, program size, and reason for the change in a manual listing subject to periodic management. If the application was developed in-house, the source code should contain comments explaining the change.

3. Maintain at least one backup copy of the program library and rotate a copy of the program library file to an off-site location at least once per week.

4. Strengthen access controls such that unauthorized personnel cannot easily access program library files.

5. Perform an internal audit review of the library change log on a periodic basis. That review should match logged program versions, dates, and sizes with data reported on the program library file.

These steps will not provide internal audit with complete assurance that all program changes have been authorized; however, if internal audit periodically reviews logged changes and questions any discrepancies, programmers will probably take care to document and log any production program changes.

(d) Small Systems Operations Controls

Traditional information systems operations control concerns, such as a review of console log files, are not practical in the modern large data center. Internal audit questions about console log reviews are typically not appropriate because of the complexity of large systems. Such control concerns may still be applicable in the small computer system. Computer operators or network administrators can represent a significant control risk in the small information systems operation. Operators can often bypass system controls or can insert incorrect run parameters through console log entries, and small computer systems often do not have the software and hardware tools to monitor such operator activities. Internal audit, nevertheless, should have similar control objectives for small business systems and related network operations as for those discussed previously in Section 19.3(a)(ii) as operational controls in large systems. Because of the lack of hardware and software control tools, internal audit should spend much more time reviewing and understanding individual computer or network operations procedural controls.

Many small computer hardware and operating systems software packages are designed such that a traditional systems programmer function is not necessary. For example, the IBM AS/400's operating system is designed effectively to "tune" itself better than could be accomplished by most system programmers. Small computer systems do, however, require some type of technical person to back up files, to reset passwords, and to install program library upgrades. This type administrator is often a very key person in a networked, small systems environment.

A prime control concern in the small computer system is often just whether the information systems organization is keeping the operating system and related software products properly updated. Both computer and software vendors will regularly supply upgrades for their products. If such upgrades are not installed on a fairly regular basis, the system can quickly become out of date and unreliable.

ENDNOTE

[1] A hash total is a summation of the numeric and alphabetic values for some computer value. It is used as a control total.

CHAPTER TWENTY

Software Engineering, the Capability Maturity Model, and Project Management

20.1 CAPABILITY MATURITY MODEL AND PROJECT MANAGEMENT

The U.S. federal government has been a major contractor over the years for a wide number of information systems projects. Agencies of the government generally contracted for this work from many different vendors. However, they frequently found that the contractors selected for a given project missed their cost or schedule estimates or delivered otherwise poor-quality software products. Faced with continuing software vendor performance frustrations over the years, the federal government entered into a contract with the Software Engineering Institute (SEI), a federally funded research and development center sponsored by the U.S. Department of Defense and operated by Carnegie Mellon University (CMU)® in about 1999 to develop a better approach and process to measure and assess a software development group.

SEI took a design-engineering approach to this challenge. That is, an engineering team designing a new tool, such as a production component or a military weapons system, takes a very structured approach in developing the product. The design steps are tightly controlled and documented with good procedures over such areas as revision control. The well-run design-engineering organization will have its processes so well defined and managed that they can easily pick up a new assignment and deliver it in a high-quality manner.

SEI contrasted the well-ordered procedures in many design-engineering functions with the often almost chaotic processes found with software development. It developed a model, called CMM, or the Capability Maturity Model[®,1] that allows an organization to assess themself and to determine where they stand in their software development maturity.

CMM is a model for organizational improvement. It takes the application of process management and quality improvement and creates a model for organizational excellence. The CMM model is based on five levels of software maturity, where a systems development function will initially start at what is called Level 1, where processes are unpredictable and poorly controlled and will move up to a Level 5, where the software development process is based on a focus of continuous improvements. These CMM levels will be discussed in greater detail in the sections that follow.

Some internal auditors will ask why this concept of a technical process for improved software development is important. On one level, CMM is just a set of software development processes at a time when many business organizations today do not do that much of their own development work. However, it is also a very good model to measure the overall processes in place in an information systems organization. Many information systems functions set their own internal goals to move their organizations up through the levels of CMM maturity, and an internal auditor working with information systems organizations should develop an understanding of this very important CMM model.

20.2 THE CMM MODEL

CMM is in reality a basis for measurement for a development organization that wants to assess where it is today and what it needs to do to improve its processes. CMM defines what is called software process maturity in terms of five distinct levels of development maturity with distinct expectations for each of these levels. The CMM model starts with what is called Level 1, where processes are unpredictable and poorly controlled. Internal auditors have seen this Level 1 type of maturity in many organizations where nothing is documented all that well, where systems development controls are weak, and where the software development group is operating in some form of near chaos.

The CMM model says that if a system development organization installs some better key processes, it will improve its operations to move to a next higher level of maturity. That is, an organization can initially move from the initial and unpredictable processes of Level 1 up to Level 2, where processes tend to be repeatable. These five levels of CMM processes are shown in Exhibit 20.1 and the sections that follow will describe each process in greater detail. Information systems management is often interested in where they stand on the CMM evaluation

EXHIBIT 20.1

CMM Software Process Maturity Levels

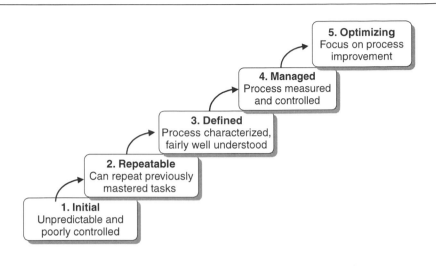

scales, and internal auditors will find this a useful measure to assess where a systems development organization stands in terms of its peers.

(a) CMM Level 1: Unpredictable and Poorly Controlled Processes

In the early days of information systems, virtually all systems development efforts and other procedures were run on an ad hoc, "seat of the pants" basis where there were very few formal procedures. This was the era when a data processing manager might encounter a key user near the coffee machine and informally request some systems change. Rather than using a formal process for requesting new information systems projects, that user might just ask data processing for a new system or report. Often little was documented. The data processing manager perhaps made a quick note regarding the request, assigned it to a programmer or analyst, and often never discussed the new project with the requestor until it was complete. The requested report or system may or may not have met the user's needs and almost never met the requestor's user's complete expectations. In addition, there were generally no development standards in place.

This type of scenario was characteristic of many early information systems functions. There were often no established procedures, very little documentation, and minimal revision controls, creating what was often an almost chaotic overall information systems environment. This was the era of the mid-1960s through the 1970s, when information systems were a new technology with few established standard practices. Seemingly, everyone was trying to accomplish lots of things with limited resources.

Over the years, things got better. IBM published the concept of the Systems Development Life Cycle (SDLC) for developing new applications. Although not widely adopted at first, this 1960s standard procedure became the accepted way to design and develop almost all new applications worldwide. The terminology and steps have varied over time; Chapter 21, "Reviewing and Assessing Application Controls," discusses this SDLC application development process. Other procedures such as revision control, programming standards, and quality-assurance standards were later developed and became widely accepted as the information systems application development profession matured.

Unfortunately, some information systems functions today have not matured all that much. Although new systems are seldom, if ever, requested and designed over the water cooler, procedures such as development standards and software revision controls are often still not that good in some information systems organizations. These information systems functions lack many, if not most, good operating procedures, and systems often are developed and operated in an almost chaotic manner. Using CMM terminology, these are described as Level 1 organizations with unpredictable and poorly controlled processes. The overall philosophy in this type of information systems organization is to "just do it" to produce results rather than going through any level of planning or establishing development processes.

Information systems organizations today often like to brag that they are at CMM Level 2, Level 3, or higher. No one wants to admit that their information systems function is operating at a CMM Level 1 chaotic state. Nevertheless, many are still there, with unpredictable or poorly controlled procedures. An internal auditor can quickly assess when an information systems function can be classified as a Level 1. There will be few standardized procedures and those that are documented are often not regularly followed.

CMM Level 1 is known as the Initial phase of the overall CMM model. The Carnegie Mellon SEI guardians of CMM probably felt that Chaotic was too strong of a name, and the term Initial is appropriate for an information systems development group starting at this beginning level and generally growing and improving to reach higher levels in the overall CMM model. Each CMM level is often described in terms of (1) the activities performed by the organization, (2) the activities performed by the information systems projects, and (3) the resulting process capabilities of the systems development group. These descriptions better describe an information systems group at each level of its relative maturity.

Level 1. Activities Performed by the Systems Development Organization

- The systems development group lacks sound management practices.

- Good software-engineering and development practices are undermined by ineffective planning and reaction driven commitments to deliver requested services.

Level 1. Activities Performed in Systems Development Projects

- During a crisis of any nature, project leadership tends to abandon planned procedures.

- The lack of sound systems development management practices tends to defeat even strong software-engineering development processes.

Level 1. Resulting Software Process Capabilities

- Software processes are ad hoc with unpredictable results because development processes are constantly changed or modified as the work progresses.
- There are few stable software development processes in evidence.

This CMM Level 1 organization can be the type that internal auditors of another age "loved." That was often because it was so easy to come up with internal auditor findings and recommendations. It did not take all that much work for the auditor to write up a set of findings and recommendations. Often, these were repeated from a similar audit in a previous period. The auditor knew things were chaotic, information systems management knew something had to change, but the proper procedures were never implemented.

The world is changing! With so much information published about CMM and its recommended approaches, information systems managers and even more senior managers are asking questions about the quality and maturity of their information systems organization. Many organizations have tried to get around this chaotic, unpredictable information systems environment by ending all in-house development and relying on purchased software. This really does not solve all of the problems. Purchased software packages can eliminate some problems, but those same packages must be implemented and maintained in an orderly manner. While many information systems groups may never rise much above Level 2 or some aspects of Level 3, many organizations will strive to get above Level 1. Through recommendations and advice, internal audit can help an information systems organization to make its processes controlled and predictable.

(b) CMM Level 2: Repeatable and Consistent Processes

A systems development function should strive to move from the chaotic, unpredictable Level 1 to Level 2. The key defining word for this level is *repeatable*. Rather than doing things in an ad hoc manner, a systems development organization should begin to establish repeatable operating practices. Exhibit 20.2 shows the difference between CMM Level 1 and Level 2. Rather that just acting, the systems development organization should devote more attention to planning its activities and then should evaluate its results with an objective of process improvement.

Systems development organizations do not make an immediate jump from Level 1 to 2 but essentially go through a slow process of adapting various Level 2 processes. The idea with CMM is to gradually improve systems development operations as an organization becomes more mature in terms of its processes. In line with the three points raised previously, Level 2 can be described as follows:

Level 2. Activities Performed by the Systems Development Organization

- The systems development organization has established software development policies and procedures, as will be discussed later in Section below.

EXHIBIT 20.2

CMM Level 1 to Level 2 Differences

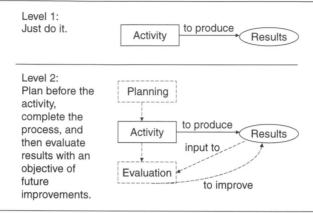

- ○ Although various specific systems development projects may differ, the systems development function should institutionalize effective project management processes to allow the repetition of successful project management practices developed in earlier specific projects.

Level 2. Activities Performed in Systems Development Projects

- ○ Realistic project commitments should be made based on previous project results and current project requirements.
- ○ Processes should be in place to track software costs, schedules, and functionality to identify any problems meeting commitments.
- ○ Control requirements and work products should ensure that project standards are being complied with.

Level 2. Resulting Software Process Capabilities

- ○ The software process capability should be disciplined such that there are stable project-planning and -tracking processes in place and that earlier successes can be repeated.
- ○ The project management process should be under the effective control of a project management system following realistic plans.

Level 2 and beyond require the effective installation of a series of what CMM calls as Key Process Areas (KPAs). These define the detailed processes necessary to get to Level 2 and beyond. Level 2's KPAs are:

- • CMM Level 2 requirements management processes
- • CMM Level 2 software project planning
- • CMM Level 2 software tracking and oversight
- • CMM Level 2 software quality assurance
- • CMM Level 2 software configuration management
- • CMM Level 2 software subcontract management

(i) CMM Level 2 Requirements Management Processes. Requirements management is a software development process that covers both the technical and customer specifications of software about to be developed and implemented. It is not unusual for an application development group to develop and implement a software application without a full understanding of what the application is supposed to accomplish as well as its overall expected functional specifications. The CMM requirements management process call for the information systems organization to install a formal process for defining the requirements of its information systems development efforts with the following KPA objectives:

- To ensure that the requirements for software products—both new applications being developed and other software tools—are defined and understood

- To establish and maintain agreement on the requirements with all information services requestors: users, customers, and other interested parties

- To ensure that the requirements are met

Requirements should be documented and controlled to establish a basis for software development and project management use. Changes to requirements should be documented and controlled to ensure that plans, deliverables, and all related activities are consistent with these requirements. Good project management practices are discussed as part of the process descriptions provided later in this chapter.

(ii) CMM Level 2 Software Project Planning. In addition to the project management processes, discussed in Section 20.4, as part of CMM Level 2, the project planning key process area calls for processes to be in place to develop documented estimates of the size, cost, and schedule for use in planning and tracking all software development projects. All affected groups or individuals involved in a software development effort should receive information on commitments and agreements regarding the project. In addition, the project should follow a formal management process for project planning with adequate tracking and status reporting, including the measurements for the completion of milestones.

The CMM project management KPA calls for a much higher level of detailed project planning and tracking than is used by many information systems organizations. Internal auditors should consider using this area as a high-level standard for assessing the progress of information systems development when reviewing the management of selected information systems projects. Exhibit 20.3 is a questionnaire for an internal audit review of information systems project management key processes.

(iii) CMM Level 2 Software Tracking and Oversight. The purpose of a formal project-tracking process is to monitor the project's actual progress against its plan. Monitoring is accomplished by collecting significant information about the schedule, resources, costs, features, and quality and comparing this information

EXHIBIT 20.3

Review Schedule for Review of CMM Project Management KPAs

1. Determine estimates are in place and documented for planning and tracking all information systems projects.

2. Processes should be in place for documenting activities and commitments surrounding all significant project activities.

3. All affected groups involved in the project development process should provide commitment agreements regarding their projects.

4. Project planning should follow documented and approved organizational project planning policies.

5. Measurement processes should be in place to track the status of all project-planning activities.

6. All project cost and schedules actual results should be tracked and compared with estimates in project plans.

7. Processes should be in place to initiate corrective actions when results differ significantly from project plans.

8. Project progress should be regularly tracked against the planned schedule, effort, and budgets.

9. Senior management should regularly review the project-tracking statue on a regular basis and make adjustments as appropriate.

to the original and currently approved project plan. The objectives of the CMM Software Tracking and Oversight KPA include:

- The process should include the information needed to conduct periodic project-planning status meetings and reviews.

- Project managers and management should be provided with sufficient information to make data-based business decisions.

- The tracking process should provide information to assist future projects in their estimation and planning efforts.

In many respects, the project-tracking process is a by-product of the project management review KPA process.

(iv) CMM Level 2 Software Quality Assurance. The purpose of this process is to provide management with appropriate visibility into the processes being used and software products being built. This KPA involves the reviewing and auditing of software products and activities to ensure that they comply with applicable procedures and standards. The objectives of the Software Quality Assurance KPA includes:

- All software quality-assurance activities should be planned, with the plans being reviewed and approved by the appropriate levels of management.

- Software products and activities should adhere to applicable standards, procedures, and requirements.

- Software quality noncompliance issues that cannot be resolved with a given project should be addressed by senior management.

(v)   CMM Level 2 Software Configuration Management.   The purpose of the Software Configuration Management KPA is to establish and maintain the integrity of all software process products throughout the software life cycle. The scope of configuration management involves identifying and controlling configuration items and units. This is similar to the ITIL configuration management process discussed in Chapter 22, "Infrastructure Service- and Support-Delivery Controls." In addition, the scope of this KPA includes systematically controlling all changes to active configurations as well as maintaining the integrity and traceability of configurations throughout their software life cycles. The goals of this KPA are:

- Software configuration activities should be planned.
- Changes to software work products should be formally identified and controlled.
- Configuration baselines should be established, and affected groups and individuals should be informed of their status and content.

(vi)   CMM Level 2 Software Subcontract Management.   The purpose of the Subcontract Management KPA is to select and effectively manage qualified subcontractors. The scope of this KPA includes processes for selecting appropriate software subcontractors, for establishing commitments with them, and for tracking and reviewing the subcontractors' performance and results. The goals of this KPA are that the information systems organization, as the prime contractor, should:

- Select only qualified software subcontractors.
- The prime contractor and the subcontractors should formally agree to their commitments and obligations to each other.
- The prime contractor should track actual results and performance against commitments.

(c) CMM Level 3: Defined and Predictable Processes

As we move up the systems development process improvement chain, CMM Level 3 calls for the organization to use the lessons it has learned to provide inputs to the planning and evaluation processes as well as to improve results. Called the Defined level, this improved level of systems development has the following characteristics:

Level 3. Activities Performed by the Systems Development Organization

- ○ Strong documentation should be in place for the organization's standard processes for maintaining and developing software.
- ○ Processes should be in place to integrate project management and software-engineering/systems development processes to exploit effective system development processes.
- ○ There should be ongoing support for each of the KPAs within this and other levels including a training program to ensure skills development.

Level 3. Activities Performed in Systems Development Projects

- ○ Projects should custom-tailor the organization's standard software processes to develop their own well-defined project software processes.
- ○ Because the software process has become well defined, management should have good insights into the technical progress of all projects.

Level 3. Resulting Software Process Capabilities

- ○ This software process capability should be standard and consistent because both software-engineering and software management activities are stable and repeatable.
- ○ Costs, schedule, and functionality should be under control, with the software quality tracked.

Although Level 3 calls for more common activities such as cost and schedule management, many find the move from Level 2 to Level 3 a difficult step. CMM Level 3 calls for a software development organization to achieve a much higher level of organizational coordination. Few organizations are able to achieve CMM Level 3, which also encompasses the following KPAs:

- CMM Level 3 organizational process focus
- CMM Level 3 organizational process definition
- CMM Level 3 training programs
- CMM Level 3 intergroup coordination
- CMM Level 3 peer reviews
- CMM Level 3 integrated software management
- CMM Level 3 software product engineering

(i) CMM Level 3 Organizational Process Focus.   This KPA calls for the overall organization to raise the importance of the software development process function throughout the organization. All too often internal auditors encounter shrugged shoulders and answers along the lines of, "I don't know . . . that was an Information Systems decision." When asking such questions as why certain application controls are not performing with adequate control considerations. The scope of this KPA involves developing and maintaining an understanding of software development and related project processes throughout the organization. To operate at a CMM Level 3, there should be coordination throughout the organization to assess, develop, maintain, and improve these processes.

(ii) CMM Level 3 Organizational Process Definition.   Very similar to the Process Focus KPA, the purpose of this KPA is to integrate project software-engineering and software management activities that improve software process performance and provide a basis for cumulative, long-term benefits. The goal is to develop and maintain a standard software development process, where data surrounding those development activities are collected, reviewed, and adjusted for ongoing improvements. As step beyond the normal software development process, attention should be devoted to ongoing improvements.

(iii) CMM Level 3 Training Programs. This KPA calls for an ongoing software development training program to enhance the skills and knowledge of individuals so they can perform their roles effectively and efficiently. This training activity should be planned to support training needs of the projects, the organization, and individuals.

(iv) CMM Level 3 Intergroup Coordination. This KPA requires the disciplined interaction and coordination of the several project and software-engineering groups within the organization. Customer or end-user requirements should be recognized and agreed to by all groups. All related issues should be identified, tracked, and resolved on an intergroup basis.

(v) CMM Level 3 Peer Reviews. Sometimes difficult to launch, peer reviews involve the methodical and systematic examination of work products by other members of a software development team to identify defects as well as areas where changes are needed. The goal here is to establish a process that will identify defects in the software development process early and efficiently.

(vi) CMM Level 3 Integrated Software Management. This KPA calls for aggressively integrating the organization's software-engineering and management activities into coherent and well-defined software processes tailored to the organization's software assets. Although defined as a separate CMM KPA, this really says that an organization should give particular attention to software development planning and coordination.

(vii) CMM Level 3 Software Product Engineering. The software development process should consistently perform software development activities as a well-defined engineering process that integrates all software development activities in a manner to produce correct, consistent software products effectively and efficiently. While CMM is tailored to the consulting groups or software development organization that wishes to release a range of high-quality products to outside customers, these same concepts should exist for internal information systems groups just as well. The goals should be to develop and implement high-quality software in a consistent manner.

(d) CMM Level 4: Managed, Measured, and Controlled Processes

CMM becomes a very difficult challenge to a software development organization as it moves beyond Level 3 and up to Levels 4 and 5. Level 4 calls for an organization to begin predicting the results needed and creating opportunities to get those results. Exhibit 20.4 describes CMM Level 4, where a software development organization should attempt to predict needed and expected results and then to create opportunities to get those results.

Similar to the descriptions of activities by systems development organizations and projects, and the resulting software process capabilities for Levels 1, 2, and 3, the activities and attributes of Level 4 are:

Level 4. Activities Performed by the Systems Development Organization

    o The systems development organization should set quality goals for both software products and processes.

EXHIBIT 20.4

CMM Level 4 Activities

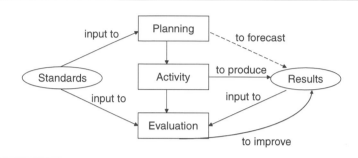

- ○ There should be measures of productivity and quality for all important software process activities across all projects as part of an organizational measurement program.

- ○ The organization should provide a foundation for quantitative evaluation.

Level 4. Activities Performed in Systems Development Projects

- ○ Projects should achieve control over their products and processes by narrowing the variation in their process performance to fall within acceptable boundaries.

- ○ The risks of moving up the learning curve if a new application domain are known and carefully managed.

Level 4. Resulting Software Process Capabilities

- ○ Software process capability is predictable because the process is measured and operates within measurable limits.

- ○ Allowances should be made for predictive trends in process and quality within quantitative bounds to allow for corrective action when any limits are exceeded.

Just as with the introduction and discussion of specific KPAs for Levels 2 and 3, two specific areas have been identified at this level: qualitative process management and software quality management. The emphasis of these is to integrate software development activities throughout the organization.

(e) CMM Level 5: Optimizing Processes

Level 5 is the maximum, best practices level of CMM. It is very difficult to implement and achieve. It calls for an organization to install self-correcting mechanisms that are implemented in such a manner that activities will be constantly and continuously improved. The emphasis is very much on defect prevention through the organization and the aggressive and active management of changes with the following activities and expected capabilities:

Level 5. Activities Performed by the Systems Development Organization

○ The entire organization should be focused on continuous process improvement with the goal of defect prevention.

○ Data should be used for cost-benefit analysis of new technology and new process changes.

○ Innovations in systems development and software-engineering practices should be transferred to the entire organization.

Level 5. Activities Performed in Systems Development Projects

○ Project teams should analyze defects and determine their causes.

○ Project teams should evaluate processes to prevent known types of defects from recurring.

Level 5. Resulting Software Process Capabilities

○ The software process capability should be continuously improving because the organization improves the range of capability and process performance of software development projects.

○ Improvements occur both by incremental advancement of existing processes and by innovations using new technologies and methods.

20.3 AUDIT, INTERNAL CONTROL, AND CMM

The CMM model describes a process for improving the quality of software development for organizations. While some aspects of CMM and the published materials describing it often seem more tailored to the software development organization developing products for external customers, with an emphasis on major governmental contractors, the CMM model provides an effective way to think about how an organization is performing and what steps it should take to improve its processes. Even though a group is not directly focused on CMM, an internal auditor can use this model to evaluate current performance and to recommend areas for future improvement.

What does an organization need to do to claim that it is operating at some CMM level? The chapter describes some of the specific and important KPAs required to make any such claim. However, an organization must go through some extensive process improvement along with maintaining supporting documentation to assert that it is operating at some CMM level. To achieve certification at some level, an organization must contract with a certified outside registrar to review processes and to certify the CMM level. This is really not necessary for most non-government-contracting organizations. These CMM guidelines should simply be used as standards for improvement.

20.4 INFORMATION SYSTEMS PROJECT MANAGEMENT

Information systems development efforts have always been run as projects—going back to the very early days. However, there was seldom a consistent approach to how these projects were defined, organized, and managed. While some professionals with a military- or government-contracting background introduced high levels of structure in their project management activities, others just labeled their efforts as "projects" with little consideration given to good project management techniques. Project numbers were assigned to the effort, progress was sometimes reported in bar chart formats, but the systems work often continued in a fairly unstructured manner. Often, the work necessary to build the project was loosely defined, and there was no monitoring of the progress against the plan.

The whole concept of project management has changed in recent years. A well-recognized professional organization, the Project Management Institute[2] (PMI) has organized and described project management best practices in what they have called the *Project Management Book of Knowledge* (PMBOK). PMI has really established a project management profession with a well-recognized professional designation, the Project Management Professional (PMP), which is awarded to otherwise experienced project managers who are able to pass a qualifying examination and meet continuing professional education requirements. In many organizations today, information systems projects are managed with a much more professional approach than in the past.

Today's internal auditor should gain an understanding of these newer project management techniques in order to see if they are being used appropriately in systems development work under review. While many may not be PMP certified, an internal auditor should look for evidence of the generally good and acceptable PMBOK tools and techniques, discussed in the material that follows, when performing reviews of any information systems project area. Space limitations prevent a detailed overview of the PMBOK model, but it breaks the project management process in to a series of separate knowledge areas:

- Project integration management
- Project scope management
- Project time management
- Project cost management
- Project quality management
- Project human resource management
- Project communications management
- Project risk management
- Project procurement management

The idea is that the professional project manager should understand the inputs, tools, and techniques, and the outputs for each of these areas and how they relate to each other. The PMBOK model takes each of these knowledge areas and describes its supporting processes in some detail. We have introduced the project integration process as an example, but the project management professional should consider and devote a similar degree of attention and detail to each of these project management knowledge areas.

(a) Project Management Integration Management

Integration management includes the processes required to ensure that various elements of a project are properly coordinated. An internal auditor will see this need for coordination management when faced with many large projects. For example, how should necessary activities be organized to ensure completion of the SOA Section 404 requirements that were discussed in Chapter 6, "Evaluating Internal Controls: Section 404 Assessments,"? After determining the scope of such activity, internal audit would need to develop a plan that will organize such a review, which includes all necessary areas and locations in the organization.

Similar to other PMBOK elements, Project Integration Management consists of three major processes:

1. Project plan development
2. Project plan execution
3. Overall change control

These processes interact with each other and with processes in other knowledge areas as well. Within a project, each process may involve effort from one or more individuals or groups of individuals. These processes are broken in to detailed elements, based on their inputs, tools and techniques, and process outputs. This set of Project Integration Management elements is shown in Exhibit 20.5. The module, like the others in PMBOK, is divided into the three elements of development, execution, and change control.

Each of these elements should be considered in terms of project plan development, execution, and change control for that module. PMBOK then defines inputs, outputs, and tools and techniques for each. The PMBOK model does not specifically define what should be included in Project Integration Management, but that the outputs of plan development, for example, should include a project plan and reporting covering the supporting detail.

EXHIBIT 20.5

Project Integration Management Elements

PMBOK PROJECT INTEGRATION MANAGEMENT

4.1 Project Plan Development
    4.1.1 Inputs
        4.1.1.1 Other Planning Outputs
        4.1.1.2 Historical Information
        4.1.1.3 Organization Policies
        4.1.1.4 Constraints
        4.1.1.5 Assumptions
    4.1.2 Tools and Techniques
        4.1.2.1 Project Planning Methodology
        4.1.2.2 Stakeholder Skills and Knowledge
        4.1.2.3 Project Management Information System (PMIS)
    4.1.3 Outputs
        4.1.3.1 Project
        4.1.3.2 Supporting Detail

EXHIBIT 20.5 *(CONTINUED)*

Project Integration Management Elements

4.2 Project Plan Execution
4.2.1 Inputs
    4.2.1.1 Project Plan
    4.2.1.2 Supporting Detail
    4.2.1.3 Organization Policies
    4.2.1.4 Corrective Action
4.2.2 Tools and Techniques
    4.2.2.1 General Management Skills
    4.2.2.2 Product Skills and Knowledge
    4.2.2.3 Work Authorization System
    4.2.2.4 Status Review Meetings
    4.2.2.5 Organizational Procedures
4.2.3 Outputs
    4.2.3.1 Work Results
    4.2.3.2 Change Requests

4.3 Overall Change Control
4.3.1 Inputs
    4.3.1.1 Project Plan
    4.3.1.2 Performance Reports
    4.3.1.3 Change Requests
4.3.2 Tools and Techniques
    4.3.2.1 Change Control System
    4.3.2.2 Configuration Management
    4.3.2.3 Performance Measurement
    4.3.2.4 Additional Planning
    4.3.2.5 Project Management Information System
4.3.3 Outputs
    4.3.3.1 Project Plan Updates
    4.3.3.2 Corrective Action
    4.3.3.3 Lessons Learned

20.5 PROJECT MANAGEMENT AND THE INTERNAL AUDITOR

Internal auditors should gain an understanding of good project management techniques, with the PMBOK model being a good example of best practices. Internal auditors will find this valuable on two levels. First, internal auditors frequently encounter "projects" within their organization related to a large variety of organizational efforts, whether new information systems, facility moves, or any of a large number of project-type efforts. Organizations frequently call these efforts "projects," but they are sometimes lacking the elements of good project management. When an internal auditor reviews any area that involves a formal project, the auditor should ask the following general questions:

- *Have you built a work breakdown structure?* The work breakdown structure is the first step required to build a project plan. The ideal is to define all of the work elements that will be required to implement the project. An auditor can just think about this as a fairly detailed list of all of the tasks that will be necessary to complete the project.

- *Have you prepared a formal project plan?* A project plan describes the work elements necessary to complete the effort, showing linkages between various work elements and the start and completion elements for each. The project planner has to take the elements from the work breakdown definition and decide how they should be linked together.

- *Have resources been assigned for the project?* The project planner must define who will be assigned to the project as well as any other resources necessary. The idea is that you cannot complete a project without resources to complete the effort.

- *Is there plan versus actual performance reporting for the project effort?* A project is almost certain to fail unless a project manager is monitoring performance against that project plan. An internal auditor should look for this type of plan versus actual reporting to monitor the progress of any project.

Internal auditors should be sensitive to these elements of successful project management. All too often, an internal auditor will find a project that is not all that well managed and lacks the elements of good project management as defined in the PMI's PMBOK. It provides an important set of audit criteria for any review of a project-related effort. While this is an important criterion for reviewing the controls surrounding all projects in the organization, internal audit projects also should be managed with this same project management discipline. The result should be a more efficient and more effective internal audit function in the organization.

ENDNOTES

[1] The Software Engineering Institute (SEI) is a federally funded research and development center sponsored by the U.S. Department of Defense and operated by Carnegie Mellon University.

[2] Project Management Institute (PMI), Four Campus Boulevard, Newton Square, PA 19073-3299.

CHAPTER TWENTY-ONE

Reviewing and Assessing Application Controls

21.1 IMPORTANCE OF INFORMATION SYSTEMS APPLICATION INTERNAL CONTROLS

Information systems applications drive many if not most of today's organization processes. These applications will range from the relatively simple, such as an accounts payable system to pay vendor invoices, to the highly complex, such as an enterprise resource planning (ERP) system, an interrelated set of database applications to control virtually all business processes. Many of these applications are based on vendor-supplied software, some are developed by in-house development teams, and many others may be based on spreadsheet or database desktop applications. While the internal control procedures discussed in previous chapters apply to the entire information systems function, specific controls are also associated with each of these applications. In order to perform internal control reviews in specific areas, such as accounting, distribution or engineering, internal auditors must have the skills to understand, evaluate, and test the controls over their supporting information systems applications. Reviews of specific application controls can often be more critical to achieving overall audit objectives than reviews of general information systems controls.

Application controls, however, are very dependent on those general information systems controls, discussed in Chapters 19, "General Controls in an E-Business and Networked Environment," and 22 "Infrastructure Service- and Support-Delivery Controls." For example, if there are inadequate controls over the program library update process, it will be very difficult for an internal auditor to rely on the controls built into a specific application. Even though internal audit may find that an order-entry system is properly screening sales orders for valid credit approvals, the surrounding general controls must also be considered. Without program library update controls, for example, the order-entry system's programs could be changed, without management's authorization, perhaps to override established credit approval controls.

A typical organization may have a large and diverse number of production information systems applications. They will support a wide variety of functions within the organization, starting with accounting but including such areas as manufacturing, marketing, engineering, and others. These supporting application systems are implemented using a variety of information systems technologies, such as centralized systems with telecommunications networks, Internet-based network systems, client/server applications, and even older mainframe batch-processing systems. Some of these applications may have been developed in-house, but increasingly large numbers of them are based on purchased software packages. In-house-developed applications may be written in a language such as C# (also called C sharp) or Visual Basic, a database report-generator language such as SQL, or the object-oriented language Java. Application documentation may range from very complete to almost nonexistent. Despite the best efforts of internal audit to suggest improvements, the same can often be said about application controls.

Management is typically interested in audit findings covering specific application control reviews. For example, while an audit finding on general controls over computer operating system program libraries may not generate management interest, a finding of an incorrect discount calculation based on a foreign currency conversion problem in an accounts payable application is sure to draw attention. However, because of the relative complexity of many information systems applications and because their controls often reside both within the application and in supporting user areas, audits of many information systems applications can be a challenge to the modern internal auditor.

This chapter discusses how internal auditors can effectively review internal accounting controls in information systems applications, including how to select applications for review, developing an understanding of application controls as well as evaluating and testing those controls, and techniques for reviewing new applications under development. These application-review activities can then be used to support an overall review of selected operational areas and to support Sarbanes-Oxley Act (SOA) Section 404 internal controls assessments as discussed in Chapter 6, "Evaluating Internal Controls: Section 404 Assessments."

21.2 COMPONENTS OF AN INFORMATION SYSTEMS APPLICATION

An internal auditor should understand the components or elements of a typical computer system application. People not familiar with information systems sometimes think of a computer application just in terms of the system output reports or the data displayed on terminal screens. However, every application, whether an older mainframe system, a client/server application, or an office productivity package installed on a local desktop system, has three basic components: (1) the system inputs, (2) the programs used for processing, and (3) the system outputs. Each of these has an important role in an application's internal control structure.

Early computer system applications could easily be separated into these three components. The traditional computerized payroll system used timecards and a personnel paymaster file as its inputs and a set of programs to calculate pay and benefits as well as to update pay history records. The outputs from that payroll system were the printed checks, payroll register reports, and updated paymaster files. Today, that same payroll system might accept inputs from an automated plant badge reader that controls office entry accesses and tracks attendance, a shop floor production system that performs incentive pay calculations, various other online inputs, and a human resources database. A series of computer programs, some located on a mainframe computer system and others distributed to remote workstations, would do the processing. In many cases today, much of the payroll processing may be handled by an outside service function that does most of the processing activities. The modern payroll system's outputs might include credit transactions to transmit to employee bank accounts, pay vouchers mailed to employees, input files for various tax and benefit sources, various display screens, and an updated human resources database.

While the input, output, and computer processing system components may not be clear to an auditor performing an initial review, the same three elements exist for all applications; however complex the system may be, the auditor should always develop an understanding of the application by breaking down its input, output, and processing components. The following sections briefly discuss some of the control aspects of these application components to provide an overview of modern information systems applications. The internal auditor unfamiliar with information technology (IT) concepts should consider taking an introductory systems-related course at a local college. All internal auditors should have, at the very least, a general understanding of information systems applications and their supporting processes.

(a) Application Input Components

Every computerized application needs some form of input, whether it is separate transaction vouchers or data supplied from some other automated system. Think of a common handheld calculator: the device will generate no results unless data of some sort is input through the keyboard. Although the computer programs in an application determine the outputs and have a major impact on controls, an internal auditor should always understand the nature and sources of them. In traditional, batch-oriented systems, this was a fairly easy process because inputs often were sequential records recorded in a magnetic tape file or even as punched cards. Today, inputs are often generated from various automated sources, including wireless data collection devices and specialized bar code readers.

(i) Data Collection and Other Input Devices. As mentioned, the very early computer systems used punched cards as their input source. One of these paper punched cards carried 80 or 90 columns of alphanumeric encoded data. Users entered their transactions on data collection sheets for keypunching onto one of these card formats. The original data collection sheet was the first step in the input chain. Auditors reviewed controls to determine that all transactions were keypunched correctly. These cards were then machine sorted or otherwise manipulated prior to entry into a computer system, being either read directly into a computer program or copied to magnetic tape for subsequent processing on a batch basis. That is, 500 lines of transactions may have been prepared on data collection sheets and processed as a batch. The need for all transactions to be correctly keypunched and subsequently read into the computer program, made input transactions controls a key component of an application's overall internal controls.

Technological improvements have eliminated those punched cards and separately keypunched input records. Batch-type transactions that must be entered into a computer application are typically not entered by a specialized "keypunch" or data-entry department. Rather, operational departments use online terminals to enter their transactions for collection and subsequent processing. Following a processing schedule, these transactions may be all collected and updated in a batch mode. The data-entry programs used to capture them often have some transaction-screening capabilities to eliminate any low-level errors common to earlier batch input systems. In many other situations, the entry of a transaction updates files in a real-time mode.

Transaction input data comes from many sources. A retail store captures sales inputs through a combination of sales entries entered on the point-of-sale (POS) terminal and product sales are entered through bar code readers. Similarly, data is captured on a manufacturing shop floor through various tickets and badges that are entered in readers by workers directly on the shop floor. A small computer chip embedded on the label of the component may provide inputs as to the products purchaser or subsequent movements. (These chips are called radio frequency IDs [RFIDs] and are discussed in Chapter 19.) These are all input devices generating transactions for updating to some type of application. Input transactions are increasingly generated not from within the organization but from applications located in other physical locations and controlled by others. Organizations today receive a wide variety of data transactions through the Internet or electronic data interchange (EDI) systems, also discussed in Chapter 19. Here, another organization may submit purchase order transactions, accounts payable remittances, or other significant business transactions. Individuals initiate sales transactions, trade securities, and perform other business through their home computers via the Internet. All of these represent input transactions to various IT applications. Each has its own unique control considerations.

An internal auditor reviewing input controls over these types of applications should always look for the same basic control elements found in all computer systems. First, there should be some means of checking that only correct data is entered. A computer program that, through its supporting validation tables, can verify that a part or employee number is or is not valid, cannot easily verify that the current quantity should have been entered as 100 as opposed to 10. The older batch systems had hash total checks to help check for these possible errors. A hash total is a nonmonetary value such as the "sum" of all account numbers. Modern systems need reasonableness checks built into their data-collection procedures, and the programs processing the transactions need controls to prevent errors or to provide warning signals.

(ii)   Inputs from Other Automated Systems.   Computer applications are often highly integrated, with one application generating an output file of data for processing by other applications. The transaction entered into one system may impact a variety of other interrelated applications. Thus, an error or omission of an input at one point in a chain of applications may affect the processing of another connected application. In addition to understanding the sources of the transactions feeding to an application, an internal auditor should understand the nature of all other automated inputs to that same application. For example, a modern payroll system may receive inputs from a sales performance system to calculate sales commissions. The sales performance file that feeds the payroll system is another input. The input controls there are based on the input, processing, and output controls of the sales performance system. If sales performance data represent a significant input to the payroll system, an internal auditor needs to be concerned about the controls over it, as well as over any other supporting applications.

A large network of interconnected applications can present a challenge to the auditor attempting to review the input controls for just one of these. An internal auditor may be interested in understanding application input controls for application X. However, files from applications A, B, and C may provide inputs to X, while D and E provide inputs to A and C, respectively. In order to review input controls, an internal auditor typically does not have the time or resources to review all of these processes and must decide on the most critical of them and assume that the other less critical supporting applications are generating appropriate transactions.

(iii) Files and Databases.   Although usually generated by some other supporting application or updated by the application under review itself, an application's files and databases represent important inputs. In some instances, these files represent tables of data used for the validation of program data. As part of gaining an understanding of an application, the internal auditor should understand the nature and content of all supporting application files. The software that controls these files generally has various record-counting and other logical controls to determine that all transactions are correctly written onto and can be retrieved from the magnetic or electronic media. Files also have their own dating and label-checking controls to prevent them from being improperly input, such as in the wrong processing cycle or to an incorrect application.

Once written as streams of sequential records on magnetic tape, today's files are input onto higher-density tape cartridges, diskettes, or magnetic disk memory cards. However, the internal auditor needs a general understanding not only of the type and nature of inputs to a computer application but also of the source of the file data and any controls over it, as will be discussed in greater detail in Section 21.4.

Database files can represent a particular challenge to an internal auditor. Although the term *database* is often misused to refer to almost every type of computer file, a database is in fact a method of organizing data in a format such that all important data elements point or relate to each other. In past years, many mainframe computer systems used what were called *hierarchical databases,* where data was organized in a "family-tree" type of structure. IBM's older mainframe product called IMS (Integrated Management System) was once the most popular type of this software. In a manufacturing organization, each product might be organized as a header record that would point to each of its parts. Those components in turn would each have a hierarchy of records comprising its individual parts. File integrity is very important here because a program error that breaks one of the connecting chains would make it difficult to retrieve the lost data.

The relational database is a much more common file structure today found on all types and sizes of computers. A relational database is like a multidimensional Excel or Lotus spreadsheet. That is, the user can retrieve data across various database rows, columns, and pages rather than having to go to the head of each tree and then search down through that tree to retrieve the desired data. In addition to being a very effective way to organize data input to application systems, these databases allow for easy retrieval of end user–oriented reports. The DB2 database products offered by IBM as well as all Oracle Corporation database products use this very efficient relational database model.

(b) Application Programs

Applications are processed through a series of computer programs or sets of machine instructions. The payroll system example in this chapter consists of a series of computer programs. One of the programs perhaps reads the employee's timecard data, stores the number of hours worked, and then uses the employee identifying number on the input timecard to look up the employee's pay rate and scheduled deductions. Based on this match, the program looks up the employee's rate of pay and multiplies this by the number of hours worked to calculate the gross pay.

A computer program is a set of instructions covering every detail of a process. The process of writing a program is simply a process of writing detailed instructions and then following them to the letter. As an auditor experiment, to comprehend the details required to write a larger computer program, the reader can write down each step to follow in the morning from the time the alarm goes off until your arrival at the office. Do this one day, documenting all normal actions as well as alternate decision paths, such as whether to have fruit or cereal. The following morning, use these same instructions *exactly* as they are written, to get up, wash and dress, and then go off to work. Most will arrive at work missing an item of clothes or worse. This is the difficulty in writing detailed computer programs! It is usually not necessary for internal auditors to know how to write formal computer programs today beyond the simple audit-retrieval applications discussed in Chapter 23, "Computer-Assisted Audit Techniques," but the effective internal auditor should understand how computer application programs are built and what their capabilities are, to define appropriate control procedures.

(i)   Traditional Mainframe Programs.   Mainframe, or what we often call legacy-type computers today, have been used extensively for business applications since the early 1960s. These computer systems were first programmed with the actual electronic computer "machine language" of binary 1s and 0s, before computers were generally used for business applications. Machine language is called the first-generation language, while assembly language—a symbolic language with codes to represent instructions (such as those to add or to store a value)—was called the second generation.

Third-generation languages soon followed. They used actual English-like instruction statements such as "ADD A TO B" to describe the actions to be taken. Programs called *compilers* translated these instructions into machine language. Although a large variety of these third-generation, or compiler, languages were introduced in the 1960s, COBOL became the almost standard language for business data processing well into the 1980s. Illustrating its English-like character, Exhibit 21.1 shows an example of COBOL. It is still in use today for classic mainframe systems; however, specialized database and report-generator languages as well as object-oriented languages are making ever-increasing inroads.

The manner in which COBOL business programs are written has changed over the years as well. Earlier programs followed almost no standards. A programmer might insert a variable value such as an overhead rate into the COBOL code. When that rate changed at a later date, a programmer had to search through the program listing because the language often provided insufficient index cross-references. Early programs were sometimes written with program logic that was difficult to follow and where control errors were possible. Today, computer systems should be

---

EXHIBIT 21.1

Computer Programming Elements: A COBOL Example

I. COBOL is an English-like language using verbs to describe actions to be performed and alphanumeric symbols to describe data fields. For example, employee hours worked might be carried in a data item called HOURS-WORKED and pay rates might be called just that, PAY-RATES. While pay rates would be carried in a table for all employees, the pay calculation here would be:

MULTIPLY HOURS-WORKED BY PAY-RATE GIVING GROSS-PAY ROUNDED

The above statement calculates a rounded value for GROSS-PAY which is then used for further pay processing.

II. COBOL program statements are organized almost as text where sets of instructions are grouped by paragraphs. The set of instructions to the pay calculation might be called PAY-CALC. A program can get back to these paragraph names by what is called a GO TO instruction. The very last two lines of the above pay calculation might be:

PRINT FINAL-PAY.
GO TO PAY-CALC.

These final two instructions would complete the pay calculation of pay for one employee and go back to the beginning of the paragraph for the next. However, GO TO statements can cause a problem for complex COBOL programs, with program code instructions pointing a variety of different ways.

III. A better way to organize COBOL is through what is called *structural programming*.

Here, sets of instructions are organized as subroutines. The example program would call up the pay calculation subroutine by stating PERFORM PAY-CALC. Then, all of the calculations for pay would be grouped together, and rather than ending with a GO TO, the subroutine would simply terminate with an END. This would return the program control back to the statement following PERFORM PAY-CALC, perhaps PERFORM PRINT-CHECKS.

While they can be very simple, COBOL programs can also be very complex and difficult to read and understand. A strong set of programming standards should help make this process more manageable.

---

designed and developed using the software-engineering principles discussed in Chapter 20, "Software Engineering, the Capability Maturity Model, and Project Management."

A wide range of computer languages are used today, with names such as Visual Basic or Java. In addition, many applications are developed through English language–like report generator languages that reside on top of the supporting computer language. Besides having the skills to write an audit-retrieval request, as discussed in Chapter 23 on computer-assisted audit techniques, an internal auditor today often does not need to have programming skills in one or another language.

(ii) Modern Computer Program Architectures. While in past years a business application under review would almost always be written in COBOL, today most programs are developed as either object-oriented or fourth-generation programs, where reports and database manipulations take place using almost English-like instructions. An internal auditor today with only a fundamental knowledge of a language such as Visual Basic, COBOL, or C may have some initial difficulties understanding how client/server-based applications are programmed and constructed. Often, they consist of many very small program code modules that pass data to one another, sometimes over remote telecommunications lines. An internal auditor should rely on the overall application program standards in place as well as on other programming development and maintenance controls, and rather than looking for these in each given application reviewed, should review the general systems development controls in the information systems organization. These might be included in a general review of information systems operations, as discussed in Chapter 19. Exhibit 21.2 contains some internal audit procedures for a review of an applications development or programming organization.

(iii) Purchased Software. Most computer applications today are based on purchased software. An outside vendor will supply the basic programs, and the information systems development organization only has the responsibility of building custom tables, file interfaces, and output report formats around the purchased application. The actual program source code for the purchased software is often protected by the vendor to prevent improper access and changes. Both the internal auditor and IT management should be concerned that the software vendor has a reputation for high-quality, error-free software. If there is any doubt that the software vendor lacks stability, arrangements should be made at the time of the software purchase contract to place a version of the vendor's source code "in escrow" in the event of a vendor's business failure. A bank or some other agency would hold a version of the protected source code for release to customers if the software vendor were to fail. Audit procedures for reviews of newly purchased software applications are discussed in Section 21.6. The internal auditor should have as good an understanding of the internal controls surrounding these purchased software applications as of any other in-house-developed application.

Large, integrated packages such as the ERP systems mentioned previously can have a major impact on all aspects of an organization. These database application

EXHIBIT 21.2

Procedures for Auditing Systems Development Controls

1. Are formal requests for new or revised applications submitted with proper authorizations?

2. Has a to-be-completed projects list been prepared and a schedule implemented for accomplishing such tasks?

3. Do the application development objectives fit within the long-range scheduled plans of the organization?

4. Have responsibilities for systems development been assigned and sufficient time allotted to complete the assignments?

5. Is there a sufficient division of responsibilities within the application development function?

6. Does the application development process contain enough user interviews to obtain an understanding of needs?

7. Does the applications implementation process give sufficient attention to controls, such as audit trails and security?

8. Are cost/benefit analyses regularly prepared as part of application designs?

9. Is the overall application development project management process adequate and are all interested parties represented in key decisions?

10. Are there adequate controls to ensure that all application data originates from approved sources?

11. Is there adequate planning to determine that hardware and software will be sufficient when placed into production?

12. Has sufficient attention been given to the backup and storage of the media used by the application?

13. Are there adequate controls to provide assurances regarding the integrity of the data processed and the outputs from those applications?

14. Does the application provide adequate tools for the identification and correction of processing errors?

15. Does the application have an audit trail to indicate that all transactions go to their present state?

16. Has adequate documentation been prepared for all applications systems and programming activities?

17. Has test data been prepared according to a predefined test plan, outlining expected results, and have user groups participated in the test transaction?

18. For a conversion from an existing application, have good control procedures been established over this conversion process?

19. Has internal audit been invited to participate in a preimplementation review of all critical systems?

20. Is there a formal signoff or approval process as part of systems implementation?

packages may include production, purchasing, inventory, human resources, accounting, and all other business applications implemented as a linked series of databases. Data introduced to one application component, such as a revised standard cost for a manufactured part, will connect to other connected systems as necessary. For example, that revised standard cost will be reflected in inventory and financial systems among others.

(c) Information Systems Output Components

In addition to the brief discussion about computer application inputs and the programs to process that input data, no discussion of an application system would be complete without a description of its outputs. These usually consist of output screens or updated files as well as printed reports. This is an important area to survey in an application review, because, in many instances, the controls of internal audit concern in an application are contained on the output screens or in control files.

Older applications produced large volumes of output reports indicating the results of the processing and any control or error problems. The sheer volume and frequency of these output reports prevented users giving adequate attention to many reported control problems, unless some other type of problem was discovered. Internal auditors frequently have been able to identify control concerns that users could have identified by just reviewing their output reports.

Today's application produces far fewer if any paper-based output reports—instead, the results of processing are often reported on online data-retrieval screens. In some cases, special online reports signal control problems and data errors; while in others, the user is responsible for calling up the appropriate screen to review any problems. All too often, this step may be ignored and processing errors can go undetected. Internal auditors should always review the scope of application output reports and their user dispositions. Reports or screens are not the only output. Often, an application that produces report-format outputs also passes transactions or updated files to a variety of other applications. This is essentially the same situation as was discussed previously regarding integrated application inputs. Just as a modern application system may receive its inputs from a highly integrated set of feeding application systems, it may be one more link in a chain to still others. Again and always, the internal auditor should develop a good understanding of the application reviewed as well as all of its inputs and outputs.

21.3 SELECTING APPLICATIONS FOR INTERNAL AUDIT REVIEW

While all major computer operations and key applications should be subject to regular reviews, the typical internal audit organization does not have the resources or the time to regularly review the controls for all of its IT applications. There will be just too many given the limited time, the relative risks, and audit resources available. In addition, many of these applications represent a minimal level of control risk. As part of a specific operational review or as part of a general information systems control review, internal audit should select only the more critical applications for review.

The audit process for selecting these applications should be again based on relative risk following the selection procedures outlined in Chapter 5, "Understanding and Assessing Risks: Enterprise Risk Management." Because information systems applications are so critical to all organization operations, internal auditors often receive specific requests to review application controls. Some of the factors that may affect internal audit's decision to select one specific application over another may include:

- *Management Requests.*   Internal audit is often asked by management to review the controls in newly installed or other significant information systems applications due to reported problems or their strategic importance to the organization. These management requests are not always made for the correct reasons. For example, sales analysis reports may appear to be incorrect due to bad data submitted from a reporting division, but management may consider the incorrect reports to be a "computer problem" and request an internal audit application review. Internal audit may not initially be aware of such user input problems and may perform normal review procedures. When internal audit is aware of such mitigating circumstances, audit test strategies should be modified prior to starting the review.

- *Preimplementation Reviews of New Applications.*   In many instances, internal audit should become involved in reviewing new applications before they are placed in production. This is true whether an application is an in-house-developed application or a purchased software package. Strategies for internal audit preimplementation reviews are discussed in Section 21.8 (a) of this chapter.

- *Postimplementation Applications Reviews.*   For some critical applications subject to a risk analysis, auditors may also want to perform a detailed applications review some time shortly after the actual system implementation. If an application has sufficient financial and operational control significance, internal audit may want to schedule at least limited control reviews on an ongoing basis.

- *Internal Control Assessment Considerations.*   Chapter 6 discussed the need for evaluating and testing internal controls as part of the SOA Section 404 process. A computer application control assessment is an important part of that overall Section 404 evaluation. Internal auditors are often given the responsibility for understanding, documenting, and testing specific information systems application controls. The results of that internal audit work will provide a basis for the external auditors in their SOA attestation processes.

- *Other Audit Application Selection Criteria.*   There are many other reasons why internal audit may select one application over another for a detailed, internal control–oriented review. These are in addition to those discussed here and in Chapter 5, on audit risk, and may include some of the following considerations:

  - Does the application control significant assets?
  - Does the application's performance represent a significant risk exposure for the organization?

○ Is the application a strategic system for organizational decision making?

○ Does the application support a function that will be reviewed later as a scheduled internal audit operational review?

○ Have significant changes been made to the application system that were not part of any preimplementation audits?

○ Have there been significant personnel changes in the departments or functions using the application?

Internal audit is typically faced with requests for reviews of a large number of application candidates at any time, and care should be taken in documenting the reasons for selecting one application over another. This will help if internal audit is questioned subsequent to completing a series of reviews. Audits of the controls over representative IT applications are sometimes included as part of a general control review of the information systems function. Internal audit should develop a detailed understanding of the general controls surrounding information systems operations as discussed in Chapter 19, and then review the controls surrounding one or more selected applications.

Internal auditors often perform reviews of the specific applications that support an overall functional area. For example, internal audit may schedule a combined operational and financial review of the purchasing department. This may also be the appropriate time to review the application controls for the major automated purchasing systems supporting that department. In this integrated audit approach, internal auditors can concentrate on both the more technical issues surrounding the applications and on other supporting operational controls.

21.4 PERFORMING THE APPLICATIONS CONTROL REVIEW: PRELIMINARY STEPS

Once an application has been selected for review, internal audit should gain an understanding of the purpose or objectives of that application, the systems technology approaches used, and the relationship of that application to other automated or significant processes. It may be necessary for the assigned internal auditor to do some background reading and study special technical aspects of that application. This auditor understanding can often be accomplished through reviews of past audit workpapers (if available), interviews with IT and user personnel, and reviews of application documentation. While prior audit workpapers can be very helpful and the interview process will allow an auditor to ask relevant control-related questions, a review of application documentation is often a useful first step in reviewing and evaluating the controls over an information systems application. As the second step, internal audit should perform a "walkthrough" of the application to better understand how it works and how its controls function. These preliminary steps will allow an internal auditor to develop specific audit tests of the application's more significant controls.

(a) Documenting Key Application Components

In the early days of computerized applications, documentation often consisted of detailed program and system flowcharts, record layouts, and little else. This helped the programmer, but was of little use to the application's users or internal auditors attempting to understand the application's controls. In addition, these early flowcharts were often hand prepared and became quickly out of date. When one relatively small change was subsequently added to a complex system flowchart, designers were often reluctant to erase or to redraw their pencil-and-paper-based charts. They may have remembered the changes but other interested persons reviewing this documentation, such as internal auditors, would not be aware of them.

Over time, application documentation evolved into a more text- and functional chart–oriented format. Decision tables and logic charts described the functions of individual programs, while text described the overall system. Although this type of documentation was more functional and less technical, it also had a tendency to become quickly out of date. Programmers and system designers often would not take the time to incorporate later changes into this system documentation. Powerful documentation tools are now available, including flowchart generator packages. A real strength of these automated documentation tools is that detailed flowcharts can be combined into summarized versions with changes introduced on one chart updating all others.

Internal audit can expect to find various types and quantities of application documentation, depending on the relative age of the application to be reviewed. Due to poor information systems management procedures, complex in-house-developed applications may have very limited documentation. The published documentation covering some of the popular outside vendor–supplied insurance or banking application systems, however, will sometimes cover many dozens of volumes of descriptive text. Users will treat such documentation as almost encyclopedic reference materials. A review of the published documentation should be a first step to gaining an audit understanding of an application. If aspects of the documentation are missing or out of date, the internal auditor will probably have a finding at the conclusion of the review. However, this lack of documentation should not necessarily prevent an internal auditor from performing an application review. When performing the review, internal audit should normally look for the following documentation elements:

- *Systems Development Methodology (SDM) Initiating Documents.* These refer to the initial project requests, any cost/benefit justifications for the project, and the general systems design requirements. Although many initial assumptions may have changed during the system design and implementation process, these documents will help internal audit understand why the application was designed and controlled in the manner it is.

- *Functional Design Specifications.* This documentation should describe the application in some detail. Each of the program elements, database specifications, and systems controls should be described. If major changes have been made to the application since its original implementation, these changes should also be reflected in the design documentation. Their purpose is to allow the information systems department analyst to be able to make changes or to respond to user questions regarding the application.

- *Program Change Histories.* There should be some type of log or documented record listing all program functional changes within an application. Some information systems departments keep this with the application documentation, while others maintain it in a central file cross-referenced to the program source code. While this type of documentation is an essential element to control program changes, it will also provide internal audit with some feeling for the application's relative stability. A large number of ongoing change requests for a given application may mean that the application system is not achieving user objectives. Revision service support controls are discussed in Chapter 22.

- *User Documentation Manuals.* Along with the technical documentation, some form of user documentation should be prepared for the application. With a modern, online system, much of this user documentation may be in the form of HELP or READ ME types of online screens. However, this documentation should be sufficiently comprehensive to answer user questions. It should also be supported by evidence of a user-training program, as appropriate.

Internal audit should review this documentation to gain an understanding for the application control review to be performed and may want to use these materials to develop questions for later interviews. Copies of key or representative sections should also be taken for workpaper documentation. However, internal audit should normally not attempt to copy the entire documentation file for workpaper purposes. This is all too often incorrectly done by auditors. While adding considerable bulk to workpaper files, the practice does little to accomplish audit objectives!

(b) Conducting an Application Walkthrough

Once internal audit has reviewed prior workpapers and the application documentation, and interviewed users and information systems personnel to clarify any questions raised through the application documentation's review, a next step is to verify internal audit's understanding of the application by a *walkthrough*. This term refers to the same internal audit process as is used prior to the initial review of an operational facility, where the auditor requests a tour of the facility, such as a production floor. The purpose of this walkthrough is to confirm internal audit's general understanding of how the operational facility or computer system application operates. Its purpose is to preliminarily test application controls through sample transactions.

An example of a system to be reviewed might better help to explain the application walkthrough process. Assume that internal audit has been asked to review the controls over an older in-house-developed online accounts payable application on an older mainframe computer. The organization, however, is a manufacturing firm with other fairly sophisticated information systems applications. This accounts payable application was installed several years before but was never reviewed when it was under development. Now, management has asked internal audit to review the application's internal controls as part of the SOA Section 404 review. Based upon the review of application documentation, internal audit has determined that the application receives inputs from the following sources:

- Purchase order commitments from the manufacturing material requirements planning purchasing system.
- Notifications of goods received from the materials-receiving system.
- Various online terminal payment transactions for indirect goods and services that are not recorded through the materials-receiving system.
- Payment approval transactions entered through an input screen.
- Miscellaneous payables journal transactions entered as batch data. Application data is recorded on a relational database along with tables of values for validating purchase terms, including the calculation of cash discounts. Based on the review of documentation, application outputs include:
  - Accounts payable electronic fund transfer transactions as well as paper checks
  - Transactions to the general ledger application
  - Transactions to cost-accounting applications
  - Various control and accounting summary screens and reports

The prime system users are general accounting department personnel as well as members of the purchasing department who set up automatic vendor payments under pre-agreed-on terms. The example application flowchart in Exhibit 21.3 also describe this applications walkthrough and will also be referenced in other examples in this chapter. The steps for performing an application walkthrough for the example online accounts payable application are:

1. **Briefly Describe the Application for the Audit Workpapers.** Based on internal audit's review of the application's documentation, a brief description of the application should be prepared for later inclusion in the audit workpapers. This workpaper documentation follows the general format of the walkthrough description, except that there should be greater detail, and it should identify key subsystems, input screen formats, key data file names, and output report formats. (For a discussion of audit workpapers, see Chapter 15, "Workpapers: Documenting Internal Audit Activities.")

2. **Develop a Block Diagram Description of the Application.** This diagram represents an abbreviated auditor-level systems or functional level flowchart for the application. It should reflect the above-written description and also illustrate some application flow concepts. This hand-drawn document will help increase auditor understanding of the application reviewed. Exhibit 21.3 is an example of such a system block diagram. Internal audit can use this diagram to confirm an understanding of the system with key information systems and user personnel.

EXHIBIT 21.3

Accounts Payable Application Block Diagram Example

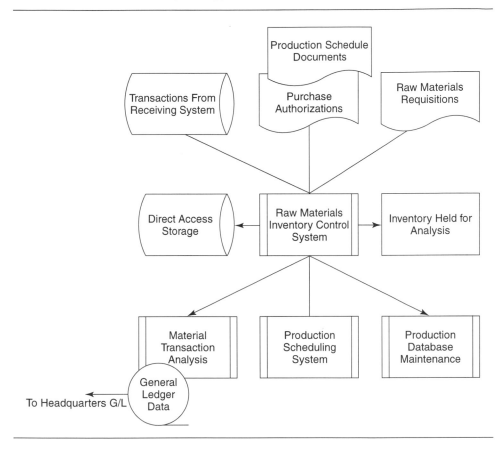

3. **Select Key Transactions from the System.** Based on the previous steps, one or several representative transactions should be selected to walk or to trace through the application. This selection would be based on discussions with users and fellow members of the audit team. In this example of an accounts payable system, the auditor may select the automated transactions that the receiving system should match against the payables purchase order records to initiate payment.

4. **Walk a Selected Transaction through the System.** In the days of manual or simpler information systems applications, a walkthrough amounted to just what the words say. That is, an auditor would take an input transaction form and would walk it through each of the clerical desks or steps normally used to process the transaction to verify the processing procedures. In a modern application, this walkthrough process typically requires recording a transaction as it is entered into a terminal, making "screen shot" prints, and then following that particular transaction through subsequent system steps. In this accounts payable example, the walkthrough transaction is a

receiving report entry indicating that a valid open purchase commitment had been received. Internal audit would then review the open commitments module of the system to determine whether the transaction was recorded on a transaction report or screen. It would then be traced to a properly computed accounts payable check or to a funds-transfer transaction and then to transactions given to the general ledger system for the net amount as well as for any cash discount taken.

This type of applications testing is often called *compliance testing.* That is, internal audit is verifying that the application is operating in compliance with preestablished control procedures. If internal audit wished to verify that all accounts payable checks had been input to the general ledger through a comparison of account balances or other methods, this would be called *substantive testing,* or a test of financial statement balances. Tests in support of SOA Section 404 controls should typically tie the single item test to financial statement general ledger accounts.

5. **Modify the System Understanding as Required.** Since the purpose of an application walkthrough is to develop a basic understanding of its functions and controls, a walkthrough review does not allow internal audit to determine whether *all* transactions are working as described. However, if internal audit discovers that the walkthrough transactions are not working as assumed, the preliminary auditor-prepared application documentation may need to be revised. Once revised, internal audit may want to repeat the previous steps to determine that internal audit has a proper understanding of system transaction flows.

These application walkthrough steps are summarized in Exhibit 21.4. The walkthrough allows internal audit to gain a preliminary understanding of not only the application and its controls, but also its relationship with other automated systems. Limited compliance testing allows the internal auditor to confirm that the application is operating as described. While not a substitute for detailed, substantive application testing, the walkthrough allows an internal auditor to identify major control weaknesses as well as to gain an understanding of the application sufficient to define control objectives for subsequent, detailed audit testing and evaluation procedures.

(c) Developing Application Control Objectives

After the review of documentation and walkthrough compliance testing, the internal auditor should next develop detailed audit objectives and procedures for completing the application review. This depends upon the type of review planned, the characteristics of the application, and the results of the preliminary review steps. A given review might be concerned with the level of control risk and the ability of the application to support financial statements correctly. The procedures associated with these audit objectives would be tests of the financial statement balances built up from detailed application transactions.

An internal auditor could have other objectives in reviewing an information systems application. Management may have asked internal audit to review an

EXHIBIT 21.4

Application Walkthrough Auditor Steps

1. Develop a general understanding of the application, its inputs and outputs, and steps requiring manual intervention.

2. For an application with a large number of steps requiring manual processing, select a sample of transactions to be processed from a normal production cycle. For workpaper documentation purposes, document identifying numbers for the transactions and work with the initial persons in the group who will be handing these transactions off to another workstation.

3. Observe the processing of each selected transaction at each workstation step, noting situations where a transaction is:

   • Input to another system or passed on to another workstation.

   • Held for further analysis or rejected for errors or other reasons.

4. Follow the selected transaction through each step in its processing, noting instances where the documented control procedures are not being followed or where the transaction causes unusual difficulties.

5. At the end of the walkthrough, discuss with the administrators any unusual or unexpected problems and document internal control status.

6. For a fully automated application with no paper trail, follow essentially the same procedure. However, make appropriate inquiries online to determine if the application is processing as expected. Resolve any differences or questions and document the results of the walkthrough test.

application to determine if it is making efficient use of database file resources or to review another application to determine if related discount and interest calculations associated with accounts payable are correctly performed. The walkthrough compliance testing may have identified significant problems, and the auditor may want to do little more than to confirm those preliminary, but troubling observations. Before proceeding any further with the review, the internal auditor should now confirm or revise the specific review objectives.

Specific application review audit objectives should be clearly defined. The auditor responsible for the detailed review might wish to summarize these objectives for the review and approval by appropriate members of management. This may help prevent an internal auditor from devoting resources to testing an area not considered significant. In the previously mentioned accounts payable system, the internal auditor may have established several specific objectives for this review:

   • The accounts payable system should have adequate internal controls, such that all receipts recorded from the receiving system are correctly matched to vendor files before the preparation of disbursements.

   • Vendor terms should be correctly computed with controls to eliminate potential duplicate payments.

   • Controls should be in place to prevent or at least flag improper or unusual disbursements.

   • All system-generated disbursements should be recorded on general ledger files using correct account numbers and other descriptive codes.

Depending on management's direction, internal audit might develop other objectives for performing such a review. For example, the review could focus on database integrity or on control procedures over miscellaneous disbursements. Any review may have multiple objectives. For example, if management had asked internal audit to review the accounts payable system to ensure that no illegal or improper payments have been made, internal audit would probably also want to add a general objective to assess control risk and to determine that the system of internal controls is adequate. Exhibit 21.5 describes a set of model control objectives for internal audit to consider when developing application review audit procedures.

Before actually starting any detailed application review, internal audit should document the specific objectives of the review and discuss them with the management requesting the application review to determine if the planned review approach is on target and will satisfy the audit request. This same procedure should take place even if the application review has been initiated by internal audit as part of a total review of an information systems function. Exhibit 21.6 lists potential objectives for application reviews.

EXHIBIT 21.5

Model Internal Audit Application Control Objectives

The following are generic test objectives that an auditor might establish when launching an application review. An understanding of the application to be reviewed is essential.

1. Determine that all transactions are accounted for in the applications—the number of transactions input in any cycle must be traceable to output files or reports.

2. Procedures should be in place to screen for processing errors, to hold errors for correction or disposition, and to reprocess as appropriate.

3. If the application receives input or provides output to other applications, transaction and record count controls should exist between these interfaces.

4. Monetary or other mathematical calculations in the applications should work properly, with good controls for such things as rounding.

5. If the nature of the information processed has legal or accounting standards implications, the application should operate in a compliant manner.

6. If the application uses tabled data for its processing, table files must be current, secure, and regularly updated.

7. The application should be protected with appropriate physical and logical security controls.

8. Adequate application documentation at a developer or user level should be provided to describe key processes and to aid in the answering of questions.

9. Processes should be in place to revise the application or install upgraded vendor software per user requests, as appropriate.

10. Appropriate procedures should be in place to back-up key files for restoration in the event of an unexpected contingency; contingency planning processes should be regularly tested.

11. The processing performance of the application should be consistent with the other information systems standards and any problems should be monitored regularly.

EXHIBIT 21.6

General Applications Review Control Objectives

1. Develop a general understanding of the application to be reviewed: its principle business purposes, inputs and outputs, and technology environment.

2. Based on this general understanding of the application, develop a general process flowchart that identifies key process decision points and internal controls.

3. Develop an understanding of general controls surrounding the application and its processing environment. General controls include access and program revision controls covering the information systems environment where the application is housed. Poor general controls can negate all other detailed application controls.

4. Discuss the application with systems users responsible for systems operations as well as with members of the information systems organization to understand any concerns or planned issues surrounding the application.

5. Develop a testing plan for the application that emphasizes:

   a. Identification of the significant transaction, accounting and business-related controls within and surrounding the application.

   b. Identify control objectives covering each of those significant controls. That is, what are the areas of auditor concern that should satisfy the auditor in order to determine that a key control is effective?

   c. Develop testing and sampling approaches for each of the key controls.

6. Gather evidence to test key application controls. Testing evidence might include:

   a. Copies of key files and extracts of transactions to re-perform application functions.

   b. Special application transactions to test application controls.

   c. Specialized software tools to check application transactions or other processing functions.

   d. Manual or paper documentation that will support application control testing.

7. Schedule and perform tests of key application controls using the test materials gathered.

8. Evaluate all test results in a pass / fail context and communicate the results of this testing with key systems users and the information systems organization.

9. Maintain copies of all testing evidence and document results of testing in internal audit workpapers.

10. Develop a corrective action plan with information systems, other entities supplying data to the application or users to correct problems identified as part of the applications review.

21.5 COMPLETING THE INFORMATION APPLICATION CONTROL AUDIT

Usually more difficult to define than the audit's objectives, detailed information systems application audit procedures vary and depend on (1) whether the application uses purchased or in-house-developed software; (2) whether the application is integrated with others or a separate process; (3) whether it uses client/ server and other more modern technologies or older, legacy computer system methods; and (4) whether its controls are largely automated or require extensive human intervention actions. The exact nature of an application can also vary considerably. Although internal auditors once reviewed controls over primarily accounting-related applications such as accounts receivable, accounts payable, or fixed-asset systems, today's internal auditor may review applications over other areas as well, such as manufacturing resource planning or loan portfolio analysis. Any of these areas requires a knowledge of its specific attributes as well as the supporting technologies. That is, an internal auditor should understand how the application works by first documenting the information systems applications, then defining specific audit test objectives, and finally performing a series of audit tests to verify that the application controls are in place and working as expected.

(a) Understanding and Documenting Information Systems Applications

Besides the review of documentation and the walkthrough, discussions with key user personnel and responsible systems personnel can aid the auditor's understanding. The amount of effort spent here depends both on the type of application reviewed and the number of users who can be of help. For example, a capital budgeting decision support application will probably have a small group of key users who have a thorough understanding of its procedures. A logistical support system, such as factory floor data collection, may be used by a large group, where it may be difficult to identify the key system users.

The next step is to complete the documentation of the application for audit purposes. Internal audit should have been making workpaper notes throughout. The documentation procedure here is largely one of summarization where workpapers describe the understanding gained and include notes for potential follow-up review work.

(b) Clarifying and Testing Audit Control Objectives

The previous section discussed the importance of establishing test objectives as part of an applications review—the types of controls an auditor would expect to be in place for an application. A next step, clarifying the objectives of the review, is often a major area where internal audit has been known to fail. Management may expect internal audit to review accounting controls but the internal audit review may have only concentrated on logical security controls and ignored the established control objectives. This misunderstanding of audit objectives becomes especially critical when the review is not typically in the auditor's more common realm of accounting applications. For example, if management has asked internal audit to review a new manufacturing resource planning system, its objectives could include validating internal accounting controls, or reviewing for materials parts flow efficiencies, or checking for system compliance with applicable regulations, or a combination of these. These should be summarized into a brief statement and discussed with both audit management and application-user management.

Although meeting the need for a clear statement of review objectives may appear an obvious early step, auditors often omit it. Of course, the objectives of an application review may change if internal audit encounters evidence of other control problems during the course of a review that would suggest audit scope or procedure changes. In the manufacturing resource review just discussed, the initial objective of affirming the adequacy of the system's application's internal controls might change to one of fraud detection if potentially invalid transactions were encountered.

Internal audit should next test the key control points within the application. Having already done limited compliance testing as part of gaining an understanding and the walkthrough, these test procedures can now be expanded to make a more definitive assessment of the application's controls. In older and simpler batch-oriented systems, this task was fairly easy. Internal audit looked for input data acceptance controls, any computer-processing decision points, and output data verification controls. Since there may have been only a few programs associated with such an older batch application system, this identification of test procedures could often be accomplished with minimal analysis.

More modern applications with online updating, close integration with other applications, and sophisticated programming techniques all combine to make identifying test procedures difficult. Other factors include:

- Inputs to the application may have been generated by external sources, such as EDI transmissions, or from other computerized applications at partner organizations.

- Controls once performed by data input personnel are now built into programs.

- Modern optical scanning input devices and output documents with multidimensional bar codes make visual inspection difficult.

- Database files may be shared with other applications, making it difficult to determine where a change or transaction originated.

- The application may make extensive use of telecommunications and will appear to be paperless to internal audit.

There are numerous other reasons why an internal auditor may have difficulty initially identifying audit test procedures in a modern IT application. However, the application description, along with key user discussions, should help to identify some of these controls. As a rule of thumb, an internal auditor should look for points where system logic or control decisions are made within an application and then develop test procedures to verify that those decision points are correct. These points include such areas as checks on the completeness of transactions or on the accuracy of calculations. They often represent the key controls within an application. Exhibit 21.7 lists some typical test procedures oriented both to more classic batch applications and to modern, integrated, online ones. The application description and the interviews can help determine which of these test procedures may be applicable.

(i) Tests of Application Inputs and Outputs. In the very early days of computer system and information systems auditing, many audit-related tests were little more than checks to verify that all inputs to a program were correctly accounted for and that the correct number of output transactions was produced

EXHIBIT 21.7

Sample Application Test Procedures

Note for the internal auditor: The following are test procedures that an auditor might use when assessing application controls. These may not apply to all applications; an understanding of the application is essential.

✓ Foot key files. Using computer-assisted audit techniques (CAATs), test that the data files are the same as the printed reports by using CAAT software to recalculate key file values and fields.

✓ Test key application calculations. Using a sample transaction, determine that the results and totals are the same as predicted.

✓ Run a special audit-only update. Prepare a set of test transactions covering all aspects of the application and arrange to run a special audit-only update. Review the results of the update for controls and processing correctness. Remove the audit-updated application from the production cycle.

✓ Transaction balancing. Using the transaction totals production process, independently calculate and reconcile the control totals to the reported application totals.

✓ Application logical security. Review the application's embedded security levels to determine if employees are allowed the proper levels of read and write access.

✓ Document controls. Test for controls in key documents (ID #s, etc.) for determining that updates can be traced back to the point of origination.

✓ Unauthorized changes. By counting the total number of characters or through other controls, determine if the application program versions on production libraries are the same as those retained in documentation files.

✓ Contingency planning provisions. Depending on audit risk, review the contingency planning setup; give special attention to the last contingency test results.

based on these inputs. An auditor's review of an automated payroll system would be an example. The auditor would test to determine that all timecards input were either accepted or rejected and that the number of output checks produced could be reconciled to those system input timecards. This is a test of system inputs and outputs.

Although automated applications have become much more complex, many audit test procedures today are often little more than those same tests of inputs and outputs. An internal auditor will examine the outputs generated from an application, such as invoices produced by a billing system, to determine that the input data and automated computations are correct. This type of audit test is limited in nature and will not cover all transactions or functions within an application.

The purpose of a control risk assessment or compliance test is to determine if application controls appear to be working. If all transactions or all data are to be reviewed, substantive testing procedures or tests of financial statement balances should be used. (See Chapter 16, "Gathering Evidence through Audit Sampling.") The extent of this testing depends upon the audit objectives. For example, an external auditor will tend to perform compliance tests over those aspects of an application which cover financial statement–related internal accounting controls. An internal auditor may also want to perform compliance tests over other areas, such as the efficiency of administrative controls.

For older applications, tests of inputs and outputs are often quite easy to perform. The auditor would select a sample of input transactions and then determine that the number of inputs was equal to the count of processed items plus any rejected or error items. This type of audit test is not nearly as easy for today's applications, where the auditor often will not encounter a one-to-one relationship between inputs and outputs.

Test transaction approaches, discussed later in this chapter, are often much easier to perform and even more meaningful. Nevertheless, tests of inputs and outputs are sometimes useful for reviews of applications. Audit procedures for this type of more traditional test are outlined in Exhibit 21.8.

(ii) Test Transaction Evaluation Approaches. An internal auditor may want to ascertain that transactions entered into a system are correctly processed. For example, when reviewing an online manufacturing application, an internal auditor might record several shop materials transactions as they are entered on manufacturing floor terminals. After a typical overnight processing cycle, the auditor can verify that those transactions have correctly made adjustments to inventory records and that work-in-process cost reports have also been properly updated. This verification can take place by reviewing the output reports generated by the system or by running special retrieval reports against data files. As part of the test transaction process, an auditor can also test whether error-screening controls are operating as described. The emphasis here should be on the testing of the error-verification routines within the application. Internal audit can select transactions

---

EXHIBIT 21.8

Automated Purchasing System Compliance Tests Example

1. Select a series of purchase orders generated by the system and trace them back to either requirements generated by the manufacturing system or by authorized, manual purchase inputs. All new purchase order transactions should be properly authorized.

2. From the same sample above, trace the purchase orders back to established records for vendor terms and prices. Resolve any differences.

3. Trace a cycle of automated purchase orders to EDI control log records to determine if all documents were transmitted on a timely basis.

4. Using sample purchase orders that are transmitted via EDI, determine if vendors are covered by signed, current agreements.

5. Select a sample or receiving report and determine if the system is working properly by matching receipts to open purchase orders and accounts payables.

6. Select a sample of recent accounts payables checks generated for parts and materials. Trace transactions back to valid receiving reports and purchase orders.

7. Using sample transactions that were either held upon receipt for noncompliance with terms or for improper timing, verify that transactions are handled correctly, per established procedures.

8. Balance a full cycle of purchase transactions—from the manufacturing system providing inputs to control logs over both EDI transactions and printed purchase order documents.

input to an application that appear to be invalid and then trace them through the application to determine that they have been properly reported on exception reports. Internal audit can also consider submitting test error transactions to a system to verify that they are being properly rejected by the application.

(iii) Other Application-Review Techniques. The computer-assisted audit software discussed in Chapter 23 can be useful in reviewing application system controls. All too often, internal auditors use computer-assisted software to test some accounting control such as an accounts receivable billing calculation but not to evaluate other significant controls. Audit software can match files from different periods, identify unusual data items, perform footings and recalculations, or simulate selected functions of an application. Other useful techniques are:

- *Reperformance of Application Functions or Calculations.* This type of test is applicable for both the automated and the manual aspects of application systems. For example, if a fixed-assets application performs automatic depreciation calculations, internal audit can use a CAAT to recalculate depreciation values for selected transactions as a compliance test.

- *Reviews of Program Source Code.* Internal audit can verify that a certain logic check is performed within a program by actually verifying the source code. However, this type of compliance test should be used with only the *greatest amount of caution*. Because of the potential complexity of trying to read and understand program source code, it is very easy to miss a program branch around the area being tested. There are specialized programs available to compare program source code with the compiled versions in production libraries.

- *Continuous Audit Monitoring Approaches.* Internal audit can sometimes arrange to build embedded audit procedures into production applications to allow those applications to flag control or other application exception problems. These techniques are discussed in Chapter 23, on computer-assisted audit techniques, often called CAATs. This approach goes beyond just auditing an application and adding procedures to make it self-auditable on an ongoing basis.

- *Observation of Procedures.* This type of observation may be of use when reviewing an automated application as well as a manual process. For example, a remote workstation receiving downloaded data from a central system may require extensive manual procedures in order to make the proper download connection. Internal audit can observe this on a test basis to determine if these manual procedures are being correctly performed.

(c) Completing the Application Control Review

Although compliance tests are powerful methods to test application controls, internal audit should be aware that their level of assurance is not absolute. There is a risk that an internal auditor may test an application control and find it to be working when, in fact, it does not normally work as tested. Because of the risks associated with such compliance tests, therefore, internal audit should always be careful to condition its audit report to management with a comment about the risks of incorrect results due to limited audit tests. Sometimes, the controls tested do not appear to be working correctly because internal audit does not understand some aspects of the application system. Internal audit may want to review the application description and identification of controls to verify that they are correct. It may be necessary to revise internal audit's understanding of application controls and then to reperform the audit risk assessment procedures.

If internal audit finds, through compliance testing, that the application controls are not working, it will probably be necessary to report these findings. The nature of this report very much depends on the severity of the control weaknesses and the nature of the review. For example, if the application is being reviewed at the request of the external auditors, the identified control weaknesses may prevent them from placing any level of reliance on the financial results produced by the application. If the control weaknesses are primarily efficiency-related or operational, internal audit may want to just report them to information systems management for future corrective action.

Applications can be primarily financial or operational. They can be implemented using purchased software, can be custom-developed applications located on mainframe systems using extensive database and telecommunications facilities, or can operate in a client/server environment or exist in numerous other variations. As noted, this diversity makes it difficult to provide just one set of audit procedures for all applications. While internal audit can develop a general approach to reviewing most data processing applications, it is usually necessary to tailor that approach to the specific features of a given application. The following sections describe how an internal auditor might perform a review of two different data processing applications. The first is a mainframe database application with interfaces to several other mainframe applications. The second is a client/server system using purchased software with telecommunication links through a network connection to a larger server machine.

21.6 REVIEW EXAMPLE: MAINFRAME ACCOUNTING APPLICATION

As an initial example, consider a database online purchasing system with interfaces to manufacturing resource planning, receiving, and an accounts payables system that uses electronic data interchange (EDI) techniques (discussed in Chapter 19). This system is implemented on a larger mainframe computer in a highly automated manufacturing organization. Assume that internal audit has reviewed general controls within the IT organization and found them to be generally adequate. Now, internal audit plans to perform an applications review of the automated purchasing system as well as of its interfaces with other systems.

Although implemented several years ago, the system was not reviewed while it was under development. The system is of major accounting significance, but internal audit scheduling problems prevented a preimplementation review. In addition, the application's title of "New Purchasing System" on data processing development schedules did not attract audit attention. However, management has asked internal audit to review the application's controls. The system has several paperless features that attracted their attention.

This example electronics assembly company purchases fairly high volumes of many small parts and components. Its purchasing department issues blanket purchase orders with many vendors to supply periodic shipments of parts with quantities specified by a just-in-time scheduling system. The purchasing department makes price and terms agreements with vendors in advance such that unit prices will drop as the total quantities purchased increases. To promote operational efficiency, this example system was implemented to minimize paperwork. It operates as follows:

1. Vendor purchase order price and terms agreements are input to a purchasing database. The blanket purchase orders are entered annually, and others are input as required.

2. The automated manufacturing resource planning system determines parts requirements. These are automated inputs to the purchasing database along with any other manual data inputs.

3. The system generates purchase orders on a daily basis, which, after review, are simultaneously transmitted to vendors using EDI or Internet-based communications and input to the automated receiving system.

4. When goods are received, the open purchase order data is called up from the receiving database. The quantities received are entered, and the data received is automatically entered by the system.

5. The material receipts data is automatically input to the inventory system and sent back to the purchasing database. If the receipt is in compliance with purchase order terms, the receipt is set up for payment.

6. Parts vendors are encouraged not to send invoices. For parts receipts in compliance with purchase order terms, the purchasing system will send records to the accounts payable system authorizing an electronic funds transaction or check to be issued. If the shipment arrives early or incomplete, the payment amount or timing will reflect this. If the vendor sends an invoice, it will be essentially ignored.

The automated purchasing system described in this example is a fairly complex, paperless type of application system using EDI—a methodology or approach found in many larger organizations. Because this application has some fairly tight ties to other applications (including manufacturing resource planning, receiving, and accounts payable), an application review presents internal audit with the dilemma of where to draw the review boundaries. For example, should the receiving or the accounts payable system be included in any automated purchasing applications review because they are so closely tied to that system?

Internal audit will do best to limit the scope of such an applications review. In this case, internal audit might only review the automated purchasing system and its interfaces with other applications. Internal audit can verify that the issuance of a purchase order correctly initiates a transaction to the purchasing system and that, when the receiving system indicates a receipt, a transaction is received by the automated purchasing application. However, it is not necessary to review controls within the purchasing system here—that can be the subject of another applications review.

Internal audit's objectives in a review of this sort can be many and varied. The external auditors may primarily want assurance that a receipt of goods is properly recorded as an accounts payable item. A more technically oriented internal auditor may want assurance that the purchasing system database properly maintains vendor terms and conditions. As always, objectives should be carefully defined and discussed with all parties interested in internal audit's review. An abbreviated set of controls objectives for a review of this purchasing system follow:

- Purchasing should have good controls over both inputs of purchase order and vendor terms data.

- The database should maintain purchasing data in an accurate and complete manner.

- There should be controls to prevent an improper purchase order from being created and transmitted.

- There should be adequate audit trails over transactions to or from such interface systems as manufacturing resource planning, receiving, and accounts payable.

- Only transactions for authorized and correct vendor payments should be sent to the accounts payable system.

(a) Reviewing Automated Purchasing System Documentation

The first review step—that of obtaining a good understanding of the overall application through discussions and a review of documentation, discussed above—can be fairly extensive in a system as comprehensive and integrated as this example. Internal audit may want to review purchasing department procedures, special control procedures over the use of the purchasing database system, and the application's systems and other user documentation. In performing this documentation review, internal audit may want to also review workpapers from any past audits of related applications and recent reviews of general controls in such areas as database administration. If this is internal audit's first review of an EDI-based application, the assigned audit team should become familiar with EDI controls (which are discussed in Chapter 19). Although interface applications may not have been reviewed previously, internal audit still may want to postpone any detailed reviews of them at this time. Any potential control questions regarding these interface systems can be documented on a "to do" list prepared in conjunction with this purchasing system review. Internal audit would expand the review to these others only if there appear to be potentially significant control problems.

(b) Identifying Automated Purchasing Internal Controls

Internal audit's next step is to describe or document the automated purchasing system using verbal and pictorial flowcharts, as discussed previously. In this case, the flowchart should be broken down into smaller subprocesses, such as one for setting up new vendor price and terms agreements. There are many potential internal controls issues associated with such a large database application as this purchasing system. In keeping with internal audit's review objectives, many of the control concerns here deal with the interaction of this application and interrelated ones such as receiving and accounts payable. Others deal with newer technologies such as the application's use of telecommunications for the EDI transmission of purchase orders.

Audit procedures based on the preliminary set of objectives as well as the understanding gained from the documentation review phase should be in the same general format as the audit procedures shown in Exhibit 21.7. Because this is a larger application, more controls points should be identified here.

Internal audit next would develop a tailored set of audit procedures for each portion of the example automated purchasing system. When building these specific sets of audit procedures, internal audit may want to consult with information systems or other specialists if appropriate. For example, this application receives inputs from a manufacturing resource planning system. If an internal auditor is unfamiliar with such applications, their unique characteristics should be discussed with other members of the audit team or user personnel to gain a general understanding.

Once controls have been identified in the example application, internal audit should discuss these with management and others, such as external auditors, who may have an interest in the audit. This review of planned objectives with outside parties may help prevent internal audit from attempting to perform controls tests that would be extremely difficult or that might only yield inconclusive results.

(c) Testing and Evaluating Automated Purchasing System Controls

The final audit steps—the tests of controls—follow the procedures identified previously. Compliance or walkthrough testing will not give internal audit an absolute assurance that the application controls are working as tested. Depending on the overall scope of the planned review, internal audit may want to test all of the controls identified in its applications overview. This decision may depend on the audit budget and the overall criticality of the application. In any event, internal audit should attempt to perform a walkthrough type of compliance test on what appears to be the application's more significant controls. When deciding which controls to test initially, it is perfectly proper to base the testing strategy on comments received from users or information systems personnel on potential control problems.

These individuals will frequently make comments during an auditor interview along the lines of, "The system would work fine except for . . . ." Such comments will often point internal audit to potential control weaknesses. Audit compliance tests involve such things as reverification of computations, comparisons of transactions, and the like. Detailed compliance testing can be a fairly time-consuming process if a large number of application controls are to be evaluated. The experienced auditor may want to have an audit department assistant help perform these detailed testing procedures.

21.7 APPLICATION–REVIEW EXAMPLE: CLIENT/SERVER BUDGETING

As a second example, internal audit has been asked to review the controls over a capital budgeting system based on client/server architecture. The financial-planning department has developed the capital budgeting analysis portion of the application using a popular desktop spreadsheet software package. Although built around a purchased software spreadsheet package, the users have coded a series of macro instructions for running the programs. The workstation portion of the system communicates with a server file containing mainframe budgeting system data.

Internal audit has been asked by management to review general controls over both local networks and their client/server computer operations. Following audit procedures in Chapter 19, internal audit found that general controls in these areas were adequate. That is, users documented their desktop applications, adequate backups of files and programs were performed on server files, password procedures limited access to only authorized personnel, and other good control procedures were followed. Among internal audit's recommendations was to place stronger controls over telecommunications access to the local network and to install virus-scanning procedures.

Some time after that general control review, this capital budgeting system was implemented on the administrative office network. Because this system provides direct input to the corporate budgeting system, management has asked internal audit to review its application controls. After discussing this review request with senior and information systems management, internal audit developed the following review objectives:

- The spreadsheet capital budgeting system should have good internal accounting controls.
- The system should properly make capital budgeting decisions based upon both the parameters input to the system and programmed macro formulas.
- The system should provide accurate inputs to the central or corporate budgeting system through the local file server.
- The capital budgeting system should promote efficiency within the financial-planning department.

These objectives represent the general format for objectives for this type of application. Management will often not state their objectives in quite these words and often may be looking for performance or features objectives. It is the responsibility of internal audit to listen to management's requests and to translate them to review objectives, as in the preceding example.

(a) Reviewing Capital Budgeting System Documentation

Internal audit first reviews the documentation available for this example capital budgeting system. Since the application is built around a commercial spreadsheet software product, internal audit might expect to find or should ask for some of the following:

- Documentation manuals or online files for the spreadsheet software package.

- Documentation for the programmed spreadsheet macro procedures, using, perhaps, a "spreadsheet" auditor type of software, which documents spreadsheet formulas.

- Procedures for uploading capital budget data to the mainframe budgeting application through network server files.

- Operations procedures for accepting the input data to the mainframe information systems function.

- Procedures to ensure the integrity of the data resident on network server files. Internal audit will probably not find documented procedures covering exactly all of the above five elements. However, there should be documentation covering the software product used, the interfaces with other applications, and the necessary manual procedures.

These materials can be reviewed by internal audit to determine that they are complete and that internal audit has gained a general understanding of the overall application.

(b) Describing the Capital Budgeting Client System

After reviewing the capital budgeting system documentation and discussing the application with its financial planning users, internal audit should then describe the system for audit workpaper documentation purposes. Since the application is built around a spreadsheet software product, this description primarily covers its manual interfaces. Control descriptions over file server applications and their network connections to client systems have been covered as part of the previously mentioned general control review.

Auditors often find it convenient to describe such an application in the form of a flowchart, although a written description may be just as adequate. The purpose of this type of description is to provide internal audit with workpaper documentation of the application and to provide a basis for the identification of significant control points.

(c) Identifying Capital Budgeting Application Key Controls

Although a rather simple but compact application, this example capital budgeting system has some critical control points. For example, if the spreadsheet macro procedures are incorrectly calculating capital costs, present values, and such related factors, management may very well take incorrect actions regarding their investment decisions. If data is incorrectly transmitted to the mainframe budgeting system, financial statement records may be incorrect. If the application is not properly documented, a change of key users in the financial-planning department may make the system nearly inoperable.

Based on internal audit's understanding of this example system, key system controls are now defined and documented. Here, because internal audit has recently performed a general control review, it is not necessary to reconsider those general controls during the application review. The audit review procedures can now be developed similar to those shown in Exhibit 21.9.

(d) Perform Application Tests of Compliance

For the final step in this application review, internal audit should perform tests of these established audit procedures. Depending on management's and internal audit's relative interest in the application, it may not be necessary to test all of the controls as listed. Many are related to one another. If no problems or weaknesses

---

EXHIBIT 21.9

Capital Budgeting Application Input and Output Audit Tests

---

1. Develop a detailed understanding of all significant input transactions to the application—their nature, timing, and source.

2. Develop a strong understanding of transaction error correction procedures, both the nature of the tables used for verification as well as any built-in program logic. Determine that some formal turnaround procedure exists to hold error items.

3. Using documentation or database descriptions, trace all input to output data flows within the application showing how many input elements (e.g., an order from inventory) will change or modify other system elements (the order may cause inventory to be reduced, sales and accounts receivable to increase, etc.). Document this understanding through audit data flow diagrams.

4. Determine that controls exist for comparing the number of items input to those that have either been accepted or rejected. Review error identification procedures to determine if users can easily understand the nature of these errors.

5. Review procedures for the correction and resubmission of rejected items. Determine if errors are held in a suspense file allowing analysis and correction.

6. Develop a detailed understanding of all significant system output control totals, consider nature of controls for any single update cycle and for cycle to cycle.

7. Select an input update cycle for review. Determine if the number of items input, less any rejected errors, ties into system output control totals.

8. For reviewing the test cycle, determine if all error items from this cycle have been corrected and resubmitted or else properly disposed.

9. Review control totals in the subsequent processing cycle to determine if file totals have remained consistent from one cycle to the next. Investigate any discrepancies.

10. Review existing error suspense files to determine if all error items are investigated and corrected in a timely manner. Investigate any items remaining in the error recycle for more than a selected number of processing cycles. Determine reasons for delay.

---

are identified in one control area, internal audit may decide to pass on the related control areas. Some of the tests of application controls might include:

- *Reperformance of Computations.* Capital budgeting is based on some very specific computations, such as the estimation of the present value of future cash flows based on discount factors. Using another spreadsheet tool or even a desk calculator, internal audit could select one or several present value computations generated by the system and recalculate them to determine the reasonableness of system processes. Any major differences should be resolved.

- *Comparison of Transactions.* Internal audit can select several sets of system budget schedules and trace them through LAN file servers to the mainframe budget system to determine that they have been correctly transmitted.

- *Proper Approval of Transactions.* Before any system-generated budget schedule is transmitted to the official mainframe budget system, it should have had proper management approvals. Internal audit should select a sample of them for review.

There are numerous other similar compliance tests that can be performed for such a system. The imaginative auditor will be able to perform these according to the nature of the audit and the objectives of management. Control weaknesses should be reported to management for corrective action.

21.8 AUDITING SYSTEMS UNDER DEVELOPMENT

Many internal auditors recognize that it is much more efficient to review an information systems application for its internal controls while it is being developed and implemented rather than after it has been placed into production. The role of the internal auditor in this case is similar to that of a building inspector reviewing a new construction project: It would be difficult to make constructive recommendations regarding the completed building. Even if some problems were found, the inspector would be under considerable pressure not to identify problems that would require significant portions of the building to be torn down and rebuilt. Rather, the building inspector identifies problems during construction and suggests how they can be corrected before completion. Similar to that building inspector, the effective internal auditor should also suggest corrective actions to improve system controls along the way. It is easier to implement changes during an application's implementation process than after it has been completed and the system placed into production.

To continue with the analogy, an internal auditor must be careful not to take responsibility for *designing* the new application's controls. The building inspector points out problems but certainly does not take responsibility for the controls' construction. The discussion on the foundations of internal auditing, in Chapter 1, "Foundations of Internal Auditing," emphasize that it is internal audit's task to review and recommend but not to design or build the controls in any area reviewed. When reviewing new applications under development, an internal auditor should point out internal control weaknesses to the applications' developers but only recommend that they implement those recommendations.

Application development groups, user management, and auditors all tend to agree that, in reviewing new information systems applications under development, internal audit provides "another set of eyes" to look at the new and soon-to-be-implemented application. This section offers approaches to reviewing new applications under development as well as a discussion of some of the pitfalls internal audit may encounter when attempting to audit them.

(a) Objectives of Preimplementation Auditing and the Obstacles

When the concept of preimplementation reviews was first proposed by the then new profession of "EDP auditors" in the early 1970s, traditional internal auditors often were opposed to the approach. Traditionalists argued that if an auditor reviewed an application in advance of its implementation, it would be difficult to come back later and review that same application after implementation. The concern was that if an internal auditor had "blessed" the internal controls of a system under development, how could that same auditor come back later and perform a critical review? Over the years, internal auditors have grown to accept the concept of preimplementation reviews. However, there are four major obstacles when reviewing new applications under development:

1. **"Them versus Us" Attitudes.** Although internal audit and general management may both accept the concept, information systems management may often express a wariness or even resentment when internal audit announces its plan to review an application that is under development and still has many details yet to be worked out. The announcement, "Hello, I'm from internal audit, and I am here to help you" may not be received all that favorably. Good preimplementation review procedures can establish respect for internal audit's role and add value in the development process. An internal auditor who spends many hours reviewing a complex new application with some potential control-related issues and who concludes only that "documentation needs to be improved" as a final recommendation will not be viewed as having added much value to the process.

2. **Internal Auditor Role Problems.** The auditor's role must be clearly understood by all parties and might be defined as one of the following:

   o *An Extra Member of the Implementation Team.* The systems design team invites the auditor to various design review meetings. However, that internal auditor will be more of an observer than a normal member of that design team. The auditor's objective is to gather data regarding key controls and processing procedures for a subsequent audit report.

   o *A Specialized Consultant.* Sometimes, an internal auditor can become so involved in the systems design and development process that the auditor is viewed as just another design team consultant making recommendations during the course of the implementation process. Internal audit should take care to not be viewed in that light. An internal auditor should act primarily as an independent reviewer providing help to the team, not as a specialized consultant who is part of the design process.

- ○ *A Control Expert.* In any review, internal audit should always make certain that a review of controls is included in the new project. However, the auditor should not be the primary designer of those controls. Otherwise, an auditor may have problems reviewing the completed application and its controls at some later date.

- ○ *An Occupant of the "Extra Chair."* Sometimes, an internal auditor does not do a proper level of preparatory work as part of a preimplementation review. Systems management may request an auditor to review various materials and attend design review meetings. An internal auditor who does not prepare but simply attends these meetings provides no real contributions. Nevertheless, if problems occur in the future, management may say, "But internal audit was there!"

3. **State-of-the-Art Awareness Needs.** New system applications often involve new technologies or business processes. A general understanding of new technologies may require additional auditor homework, to read vendor manuals and other documentation.

4. **Many and Varied Preimplementation Candidates.** The typical larger organization may have a significant number of new application projects that are potential candidates for preimplementation reviews. These projects will all have different start times, durations, and completion dates. An internal auditor needs to perform an ongoing risk assessment to select the most appropriate new review candidates.

Despite these potential obstacles, there are strong reasons for an internal audit function to become actively involved in preimplementaion reviews of new applications before they are placed into production. This is particularly true in today's era of major enterprise-wide applications that require detailed planning and testing in all areas of the organization.

(i) Preimplementation Review Objectives. The most important objective of application preimplementation auditing is to identify and recommend controls improvements such that they can be potentially installed during the application-development process. However, rather than just assuming that a new information systems project is a given and then reviewing its controls, internal audit should also have an objective of reviewing the justification and definition of the new development project. There should be a good project-management system in place that properly plans development steps and measures actual progress against those planned steps. For major projects, internal audit can evaluate the adequacy of project development controls used for the particular application.

The preimplementation phase also is an excellent time for an internal auditor to gain an understanding of the new application sufficient to design automated audit tests at some future time. In addition, this is the best time to define the computer-assisted audit techniques discussed in Chapter 23. Whether an in-house-developed system or the implementation of a vendor package, internal auditors reviewing new applications under development should gain an overall understanding of all aspects of that application project.

In addition, some internal auditors are faced with a statutory requirement for reviewing new applications under development. Several U.S. states and other countries have legislation requiring that all new significant state agency applications be reviewed by their internal audit departments for controls prior to implementation. Auditors in state government environment can expect such legislation to appear in their own states in the future.

(ii) Preimplementation Review Problems. Preimplementation reviews often present internal audit with some very serious implementation problems, including a frequent challenge of too many review candidates given limited internal audit resources. Internal auditors sometimes make the mistake of announcing their intention of reviewing *all* new applications and all major modifications prior to their implementation. In a larger organization, there may be dozens or even hundreds of user requests for new or major revision applications projects initiated regularly. Internal audit will find no time for comprehensive preimplementation reviews and only time for little more than nominal "rubber stamp" approval signatures. To overcome these difficulties, internal audit should consider the following:

- *Selecting the Right Applications to Review.* Auditors are faced with the problem of selecting only those applications of audit significance. Rather than rely on a simple value judgment or an arbitrary process, auditors should follow a risk-based, structured selection method for identifying those applications to review, similar to what was discussed in Chapter 5. A development group, for example, maybe working on applications A, B, and C. Given the relative application risks as well as limited audit time and resources, internal audit may decide to perform preimplementation reviews only for application B. However, if significant postimplementation problems appear in C, management might later second-guess internal audit and ask why system C had not been selected for review. An internal auditor with a consistent selection approach will be able to justify the decision to review B rather than C.

- *Determining the Proper Auditor's Role.* As discussed, when an application has been selected for preimplementation review, internal audit can all too often become overly involved in its system development and implementation processes. Particularly for applications based on vendor software or developed with rapid application development methods, new information systems projects require extensive user and systems development team efforts, with numerous design review meetings. While internal audit will often be asked to participate in these design review meetings, they may cause an auditor role problem. After being actively involved in the typical design review meetings where design compromises may be negotiated, internal audit may find it difficult to comment on these same decisions later as audit points. However, if internal audit is excluded from design meetings, it may have a hard time performing the review. To be effective in reviewing new applications under development, the internal auditor's role needs to be carefully defined.

- *Review Objectives Can Be Difficult to Define.* When an internal auditor informs the information systems department that a given application has been selected for preimplementation review and requests supporting documentation, the auditor may receive hundreds of pages of requirements studies, general design review documentation, meeting minutes, and other materials. Internal audit may then be asked to review and comment on this mass of materials. An audit objectives and control procedures approach can help an auditor choose the relevant materials to review.

Multiple implementation projects and new technologies present some major challenges to internal audit to perform effective information systems application preimplementation reviews. However, whether for new applications developed in-house or installed purchased software, internal audit preimplementation reviews will add value to the internal controls environment in the organization. In addition, auditors who have been accused in an old joke as being the ones who "join the battlefield after the action is over to shoot the wounded," can now play a proactive role in the application development process through preimplementation reviews.

(b) Preimplementation Review Procedures

Many of the same audit procedures used in other reviews should be followed for reviews of new applications under development. All too often, internal auditors argue that applications under development are somehow "different." However, as fluid and subject to ongoing developmental change as applications under development are, many of the same control objectives and procedures discussed previously for information systems applications are still quite appropriate for these reviews. Auditors should tailor their preimplementation reviews to correspond to the various phases of a new project's development starting with initial project initiation and moving to requirements definition, to development and testing, and finally to implementation. These same basic steps apply whether the application is an in-house-developed major application, a vendor's software package, or a user-initiated set of desktop applications. There will only be a difference in emphasis, depending upon the application's development approach.

When internal audit has selected a given application for preimplementation review, an important first step is to review the overall planned audit program with information systems management so that there is an understanding of what the internal auditor expects to find, as well as the review approach. Some procedures may be tailored to fit a given application, but the following objectives should apply for most preimplementation reviews.

(i) Application Requirements Definition Objectives.
When possible, internal audit should get involved in a preimplementation review in this early development phase. Here, internal audit should review the detailed requirements study

to determine the overall control status of the new application. If control concerns are identified during this phase of the applications development, it will be relatively easy for system designers to address and correct them.

Exhibit 21.10 is a set of audit procedures for the requirements definition phase of any project. Internal audit should look for similar requirements no matter how the new application is developed. Some of these procedures, of course, may require modification if the application under review is composed of specialized technologies or it will be a major modification to an existing system. However, internal audit should perform control procedures necessary to satisfy all of the control objectives listed here.

EXHIBIT 21.10

Preimplementation Review Requirements Definition Checklist

AUDIT STEP	INTIALS	W/P
1. Obtain a general understanding of the I/S department's Systems Development Methodology (SDM) standards for developing a requirements definition study.	_____	_____
2. Obtain feasibility study and other documentation authorizing the detailed system design.	_____	_____
3. Review the system's documentation to determine that it is generally consistent with SDM standards and the nature of the feasibility study; look for specific documentation rather than vague narratives.	_____	_____
4. Determine if any special skills are needed to review application controls, such as a new database platform or development approach. If appropriate, arrange for members of the audit staff to learn the new area through seminars or documentation.	_____	_____
5. Identify and review significant controls surrounding new application. Discuss these controls with both the requesting users and I/S management and develop audit testing procedures.	_____	_____
6. If significant portions of the application involve in-house-developed modules, assess whether appropriate consideration was given to commercial package alternatives.	_____	_____
7. Assess whether the impact of non-system manual aspects of the application have been considered as part of the requirements definition.	_____	_____
8. Review the preliminary project plan estimate surrounding the study. Determine if estimate appears complete and realistic.	_____	_____
9. If the application appears to be a candidate for computer-assisted audit procedures, begin preliminary audit planning.	_____	_____
10. Review the extent of user sign-ups on the requirements study documents. Based on selected interviews, assess whether users understand the new application and its ramifications.	_____	_____

Internal audit may need to decide if any special skills are required to complete the review. If the application involves the use of new or unique systems technologies and specialized supporting software, internal audit may want training on the software product to be used—such as participating in classes offered by the vendor to the development staff—or internal audit may bring in someone with specialized skills or training. For example, with some large projects that take years to develop and implement, it can be effective to add a specialist to the staff to cover just the review of such a large project. At the completion of this phase, internal audit might write an informal audit report outlining any preliminary observations and concerns. In addition, workpapers should be started to document the new application control's procedures.

(ii) Detailed Design and Program Development Objectives. This is typically the longest phase of a new applications project, and internal audit may want to schedule several reviews during this phase. While each of the periodic reviews should probably focus on a specific area of the new application development project, the overall purpose should be to satisfy some of the following questions:

- Does the detailed design comply with the objectives of the general requirements definition?

- Do users understand the controls and objectives of the new application under development?

- Has proper consideration been given to application controls and security?

- Is the application being developed according to the information systems department's own systems development standards?

- Have any earlier audit recommendations been incorporated into the detailed design?

During this phase, care should be taken not to become too buried in detail. Some information systems organizations may attempt to use internal audit as almost a quality-assurance function for the project. However, overall audit effectiveness will be diminished if internal audit's time is spent reviewing such things as compliance with detailed programming standards.

Reviews of this nature should be limited to periodic testing. Any control-related concerns encountered should be brought to the attention of management so that corrective action can be taken in a timely manner. If the new application is purchased software, there will often be limited in-house design and programming requirements. However, the information systems organization may have to build file-conversion programs or interfaces with existing systems or table files or report-generator definitions. These can represent major efforts, and internal audit still should review controls over the purchased software before it is installed and implemented.

(iii) Application Testing and Implementation Objectives. This phase includes testing of the new application, completion of documentation, user training, and conversion of data files. Internal audit often will be able to see if system controls appear to be working as expected and will want to test any embedded audit modules incorporated into the application. Exhibit 21.11 contains procedures for this phase to help internal audit recommend whether the new application is ready for final implementation. Significant system control problems, coupled with management pressures to implement the application as soon as possible, can make this phase difficult. Information systems often promises to correct control problems in the new application during what is often called a "phase two." Auditors often find that because of other priorities, phase two never seems to occur. Internal audit should consider the severity of such control problems and either document them for follow-up review or inform management of the need for corrective action during the current implementation.

At the conclusion of the application testing and implementation phase, the responsible auditor should prepare a final report that documents significant control issues identified by internal audit and subsequently corrected by the information systems development function. This report should also outline any outstanding control recommendations that have not been implemented. While

EXHIBIT 21.11

Preimplementation Review Application Testing Checklist

AUDIT STEP	INITIALS	W/P
1. Determine if a formal test plan exists, including an outline by application modules detailing the data condition, the business rule tested, the type of test, and the results for each element tested.	_____	_____
2. Review the results of several recent unit tests to determine if results have been mapped to the test plan, exceptions researched, and errors corrected as appropriate.	_____	_____
3. Determine if the application being tested satisfies original system design requirements. If exceptions exist, determine if they were properly documented and reviewed by key users.	_____	_____
4. Interview several key users to understand their participation in the testing process. Where participation is lacking, discuss the need for user participation to assure a successful application.	_____	_____
5. Review the extent of overall system testing including key interfaces with other applications and outside service providers.	_____	_____
6. If any original requirements have not been achieved by the completed application, assess procedures in place to determine whether to add procedures later or to otherwise allow for discrepancies.	_____	_____
7. If appropriate, initiate a series of internal audit-developed test transactions that emphasize key controls defined in earlier review steps; review the test results and assess performance.	_____	_____
8. Summarize the results of the testing activity and make an internal audit recommendation for the appropriateness of the application implementation.	_____	_____

reports up to this point have been informal, this final report should follow normal audit department reporting standards.

(iv) Postimplementation Review Objectives. Although the new application is no longer in development, this phase of a preimplementation audit is still important. The postimplementation review should take place shortly after a new application has been implemented and has had time to settle down. In other words, internal audit should perform the review after the users have had an opportunity to understand the application and information systems has had time to resolve any final implementation difficulties. The postimplementation review determines if application design objectives have been met and if established applications controls are working. It also should look at project controls to determine if the application was completed within budget. Ideally, this review should be performed by another member of the audit staff to provide an independent assessment of the new application.

(c) Preimplementation Audit Reports

Many internal audit departments have a fairly formal procedure for issuing audit reports. Draft reports are prepared, auditees prepare their responses after some discussion and negotiation on the draft report words, and a final audit report is issued, with copies distributed to various levels of management (see Chapter 17, "Audit Reports and Internal Audit Communications"). This audit report format is often inappropriate for reviews of new applications under development. An individual internal controls problem with a particular program or output report, which may be identified by an auditor when performing a preimplementation review, can be corrected by the applications developer almost at once. There is little need to discuss such a finding in the format of a formal audit report draft. The control concern should have been corrected long before the audit report was issued. Audit and general management, who might expect the more formal audit report with its findings and recommendations, should both understand the special report format used for preimplementation reviews.

Informal, memo-type reports should be issued after each phase of the preimplementation reviews. These memo reports should discuss the scope of review activities and document any audit concerns. If some of the prior concerns have been corrected, the actions taken and current status of the controls issue should be discussed. Exhibit 21.12 is an example of a memo-format preimplementation audit report. Of course, internal audit should also develop workpaper documentation covering these review activities, which will serve both to document preimplementation activities and to provide a basis for later applications reviews.

At the conclusion of the preimplementation review, internal audit should issue a formal audit report following audit department standards and the report formats discussed in Chapter 12, "Internal Audit Professional Standards." Where appropriate, this report can discuss preimplementation audit findings and corrective actions taken. However, the main function of this final report is to highlight outstanding control issues that still need to be corrected within the new application system.

Exhibit 21.12

Preimplementation Review Memo Report Example

MEMO

July 15, 20XX

To: Bob Cratchit, Excess Division Controller
        Tom Watson, Information Systems Director

From: ExampleCo Internal Audit

Re: Reporting 20XX Financial Consolidation System

Internal audit has completed a preimplementation review of the Reporting 20XX Financial Consolidation System being developed by the Excess Division. The purpose of our review was to assess the adequacy of both the system and project development controls surrounding this new application.

As part of our review, we assessed the controls built into the new application as well as the project development controls in place. We measured these project development controls against ExampleCo systems development procedures. Our review was completed in June 20XX, at a time when the application was still in its final phases of testing and development.

We found that the Reporting 20XX Financial Consolidation System is generally being built with good application controls and following good project management methods. However, we found two areas that we feel need to be addressed prior to the system's implementation:

- *Inadequate firewall protection.* The application is linked to both plant facilities and ExampleCo headquarters through the ExampleCo intranet. We found that the firewall protection over this application was generally inadequate, leading to the risk of unauthorized data access and manipulation. Prior to implementation, procedures here need to be improved.

- *Weak project management cost controls.* We observed that minimal attention was given to recording the time spent on various project tasks. As a result, the costs of the completed application will be inconclusive. As much as practicable, attention should be given to reconstruction of records to assess the development costs of this project.

After attention has been given to rectifying the above two issues, internal audit sees no reason why the new application cannot be implemented as scheduled..

21.9 IMPORTANCE OF REVIEWING APPLICATION CONTROLS

The effective internal auditor should place a major emphasis on reviewing the supporting information systems applications when performing operational audits in all areas of the organization. Even though good general or interdependent information systems control procedures may often be in place, individual applications controls may not all be that strong. An organization's applications may have been developed through a series of compromises among users or without any level of proper quality assurance. To evaluate information systems application controls properly, internal audit needs a good understanding of both information systems procedures and the specific control and procedural characteristics of each application area.

The effective internal auditor should spend a substantial amount of audit effort reviewing and testing controls over specific information systems applications as well as new applications in the development process. Such reviews will provide assurance to general management that applications are operating properly, and to information systems management that their design and control standards are being followed, allowing them to place greater reliance on the output results of such applications. Reviewing and assessing application controls should be a key component in the modern internal auditor's skill set.

CHAPTER TWENTY-TWO

Infrastructure Service- and Support-Delivery Controls

22.1 IMPORTANCE OF INFORMATION SYSTEMS INFRASTRUCTURE

Once called just computer operations, professionals today use the term infrastructure to describe all of the supporting processes that make an information technology (IT) department or function work. An IT function has developers to install new applications or to manage existing production operations. It also needs hardware devices, such as servers and network controllers, as well as skilled operations staff functions to operate those systems. In addition to technology-driven areas, an IT infrastructure organization needs processes to support and deliver services to the users of IT—its customers. This very broad area includes teams necessary to manage and maintain operating systems, people to manage capacity and configurations, and even a support desk function to help IT users with questions or to provide password resets. This area is known as the IT infrastructure, a service-driven and service-support area where the focus is less on technology and more on customer satisfaction.

This chapter will consider IT infrastructure controls and their importance in the audit and internal controls environment. The focus here is very much on processes that support the customers of IT processes, whether external or internal to the overall organization. If a production system is temporarily not in service due to a capacity problem on a server, that represents a breakdown in services to the end-user customer. Perhaps even worse, a severe breakdown in services occurs when the system is down but end-user customers have not been informed. An organization should be very concerned about providing adequate levels of IT services that align with customers' expectations, that are consistent over time, and that are provided at a reasonable cost.

This chapter will look at IT infrastructure services and controls from an internal audit perspective. In our world of acronyms that often become names, we will look at the ITIL (Information Technology Infrastructure Library) set of service-support and service-delivery processes. In addition to IT operations issues—such as how to investigate and solve reported problems called in to the operations "help desk"—our focus is to provide background information to better help the modern internal auditor to understand and review controls in these IT infrastructure areas.

22.2 ITIL BEST PRACTICES MODEL

ITIL (Information Technology Infrastructure Library) is a set of best practices first developed in the 1980s by the British government's Office of Government Commerce (OGC)—formerly called the Central Computer and Telecommunications Agency. It is a vendor/supplier-independent collection of best practices that has become widely observed in the IT service industry, first in United Kingdom, then in the European Union community (EUC), next in Canada and Australia, and is now increasingly common in the United States. ITIL is a detailed framework or description of a number of significant IT practices, with comprehensive checklists, tasks, procedures, and responsibilities, which are designed to be tailored to any IT organization. Dividing key processes between those covering IT service delivery and those for service support, ITIL has become the de facto standard for describing some fundamental processes in IT service management such as *change management*.

ITIL processes cover the IT infrastructure, the supporting processes that allow IT applications to function and deliver their results to systems users. All too often, auditors and others focus too much attention on the new application development side of IT and ignore important supporting service-delivery and service-support processes. An organization can put massive efforts, for example, in building and implementing a new budget-forecasting system, but that application will be of little value unless there are good processes in place, such as problem and incident management, to allow customers of IT or the users to report systems difficulties. Also needed are good capacity and availability processes to allow the new application to run as expected. These processes are all part of what is called the IT infrastructure. A well-designed and well-controlled application is of little value to the ultimate users without strong service-support and service-delivery processes in place. The modern internal auditor should have a good understanding of these service processes in their organization. ITIL provides a good general best practices model to follow.

While fairly common elsewhere in the world, ITIL processes are just now becoming more widely recognized in the United States. These ITIL best practices have been defined in professional publications and several books,[1] but are just now becoming more common. The sections that follow will provide an overview of some ITIL processes, including such areas as capacity or service-level management. This material should give an internal auditor some guidance on how IT functions, such as a help desk, should operate effectively, as well as support for recommending improvements in these very important IT process areas.

(a) ITIL Service-Support Processes

ITIL processes are split between those covering service support and those for service delivery. Service-support processes help make an IT application operate in an efficient and customer satisfying manner. The service-delivery processes, discussed in Section 22.2(b), cover areas to improve the efficiency and performance of IT infrastructure elements. There are five ITIL service-support best practice processes, ranging from release management, for placing a process in to production, to incident management, for the orderly reporting of IT problems or events. ITIL service-support processes cover good practices for any IT organization, whether a centralized operation using primarily classic legacy mainframe systems, as its IT central control point, to highly distributed operations. Because of the many variations possible in the structure and organization of an IT operations function, ITIL does not prescribe the details of "how" to implement service-support processes such as configuration or change management. Rather, it suggests some good practices and ways to manage inputs and relationships between these processes. There is no order or precedence among each of these processes. Each can be considered and managed separately but all of them are somewhat linked to one another.

In this section, we will discuss each of ITIL's five defined service-support processes. ITIL suggests preferred approaches for an IT operations function to organize and operate its productions systems in a manner that will promote efficient operation and will deliver high-quality services to the ultimate user or customer of these services. These are particularly useful for an internal auditor performing a review and making recommendations in an IT operations area. Many auditors have a good understanding of selected individual system controls as well as new application development controls and procedures. Those same internal auditors frequently do not give sufficient attention to the supporting infrastructure controls.

When observing and reviewing internal controls within an IT function, it is very useful to think in terms of these separate processes. For example, the first process discussed is Incident Management or what has traditionally been called the "help desk," a facility where systems users or customers can call in with a question or problem. While these types of functions can be very useful, they are often a source of grousing when, for example, a similar problem is called in repeatedly with no evident efforts to analyze things and initiate a solution to the problem. Going beyond just seeing a casual help desk and thinking of this as an overall process where matters are reported to other supporting processes will improve performance here and the overall quality of IT operations.

(i) Service-Support Incident Management.

The incident management process covers the activities necessary for restoring an IT service following a disruption. By a disruption, we mean any type of problem that prevents some user or IT customer from receiving adequate services, whether an overall system failure, the user's inability to access the application for any of a wide variety of reasons, a password failure due to a "fat fingers" typing error or other problems. The reported problem is called an *incident*, some type of deviation from standard operations. We will use this terminology and refer to incidents throughout our discussion of ITIL. Using another ITIL expression, the *service desk* is usually the owner for this process although all service-support groups across the IT organization may have a role. Although many IT functions have a function called a help desk, a customer support group, or and any of other names; we will refer to this general function as the *service desk*.

The objective of Incident Management is to restore to normal operations as quickly as possible in a cost-effective manner with minimal impact on either the overall business or the user. How quickly is quickly should not be subject to interpretation. Restoration time frame standards are defined in what are called Service Level Agreements (SLAs) between IT and the customer or just as good customer service practices. Effective SLAs are an important component of the IT infrastructure and are discussed in the material that follows as one of the ITIL service-delivery processes. The first component of the ITIL incident management process is the detection and documentation of the incident by the service desk, as a single point of contact. These incidents can include such matters as a user calling in some specific application problem to IT operations informing the service desk of an application processing problem.

Once received, the service desk should classify the incident in terms of its priority, impact, and urgency. The definition of a reported incident's priority is one of the more important aspects of managing IT incidents. Every person who calls in an incident thinks that his or hers is the most important, and the incident management function has the difficult task of defining the relative priority of the reported incident, its importance and impact on the business. Exhibit 22.1 shows the life cycle of an incident from the initial call through resolution and closure. A formal SLA, as part of the service-level management process, should define the priority with which incidents need to be resolved, the effort put into the resolution of and recovery from incidents depends on:

- *The Impact or Criticality of the Incident on the Reporting Entity or Overall Organization.* Incident management should assess, for example, how many users will suffer as a result of a reported technical failure of a hardware component. Similarly, a call regarding a problem with the month-end closing process should be assigned a higher level of criticality than a problem with the system that generates purchase orders.
- *The Urgency of the Reported Incident.* Urgency refers to the speed necessary to solve an incident of a certain impact. A high-impact incident does not, by default, always have to be solved immediately. An incident call that reports some user group can't work at all because of some service outage is often of greater urgency than a senior manager calling to request a functionality change.
- *The Size, Scope, and Complexity of the Incident.* The incident management team should investigate the reported incident as soon as possible to determine its extent. A reported failure of some component may just mean that a device is out of service or might indicate that a server is down. Those types of incidents often are not that complex and can be repaired relatively easily. A telecommunications failure that might impact multiple international units and thus might delay the monthly financial close can be much larger in size and scope.

Once an incident has been logged in, the process of investigation and diagnosis should begin. If the service desk cannot solve the incident, it should be assigned

EXHIBIT 22.1

IT Incident Management Life Cycle

```
┌──────────────────────────┐
│                          │         ┌──────────────────────────┐
│                          │◄───────►│   Incident detection     │
│                          │         │   and recording          │
│                          │         └────────────┬─────────────┘
│                          │                      │
│                          │         ┌────────────┴─────────────┐
│                          │◄───────►│   Classification and     │
│  Ownership, monitoring,  │         │   initial support        │
│  tracking, and           │         └────────────┬─────────────┘
│  communication           │                      │
│                          │                  ◄ Service ►──────► ┌──────────────────────────┐
│                          │                    Request          │  Service Request procedure│
│                          │                      │              └──────────────────────────┘
│                          │         ┌────────────┴─────────────┐
│                          │◄───────►│ Investigation and diagnosis│
│                          │         └────────────┬─────────────┘
│                          │         ┌────────────┴─────────────┐
│                          │◄───────►│  Resolution and recovery │
│                          │         └────────────┬─────────────┘
│                          │         ┌────────────┴─────────────┐
│                          │◄───────►│   Incident closure       │
└──────────────────────────┘         └──────────────────────────┘
```

to other support levels for resolution. However, all parties that work on the incident should keep records of their actions by updating a common incident log file.

Some incidents can be resolved through a "quick fix" by the service desk, others by a more formal problem solution, or in the case of more significant problems, by a work-around to get things back in partial operation coupled with a formal request for change (RFC) to systems, to a vendor, or whatever parties are needed to correct such a more significant problem. In any event, efforts should be marshaled to correct the problem, with the incident management function retaining ownership of the matter until resolution. Solid documentation should be maintained to track the incident until its resolution. The incident can be formally closed once matters have been fixed, of if not easily resolved, the incident should be passed to the problem management process function as discussed below.

All ITIL processes are somewhat related to one another, but in many instances, incident management represents the first line between users of IT services and IT itself. Properly organized, incident management should be much more than the help desks of an earlier time when users called in with problems that did not go much help beyond perhaps password resets. Incident management is a first point of contact between the customers—users—and the overall IT function. Incidents, the result of failures or errors within the IT infrastructure, result in actual or potential variations from the planned operation of services.

Sometimes, the cause of these incidents may be apparent and can be addressed or fixed without the need for further investigation. In other situations, there may be a need for a hardware or software repair, a matter that often takes some time to implement. Short-run solutions may be a work-around, a quick fix to get back in operation, or a formal RFC to the Change Management process to remove the error. Examples of short-term work-arounds might be just instructing a customer to reboot a personal computer or resetting a communications line, without directly addressing the underlying cause of the incident.

Where the underlying cause of the incident is not identifiable, it is often appropriate to generate a problem record for the unknown error within the infrastructure. Normally a problem record is generated only if investigation is warranted, and its actual and potential impact should be assessed.

Successful processing of a problem record will result in the identification of the underlying error, and the record can then be converted into a known error once a work-around has been developed, and/or an RFC. Exhibit 22.2 shows the relationship and logical flow between customers, incident management, problem management, work-arounds to correct known errors, and other ITIL processes to be discussed in the sections that follow.

(ii) Service-Support Problem Management. When the incident management process encounters a deviation of any sort with an unknown cause or reason, that incident should be passed on to *problem management* for resolution. The objective here is to minimize the total impact of problems through a formal process of detection and repair as well as taking actions to prevent any reoccurrence. The problem management process is the next step in the criticality of some reported incident and should be considered in terms of three subprocesses: problem control, error control, and proactive problem management. ITIL defines a "problem" as an unknown underlying cause resulting from one or more incidents, and a "known error" is a problem that has been successfully diagnosed and for which a work-around has been identified. The idea is not to necessarily create a second administrative function in an IT organization to take reported help desk incidents, but to identify when and how some help desk reported incidents should be passed on another person or authority to better diagnose the reported matter and treat it as a problem. An effective problem management process can do much to improve overall IT customer service.

Inputs to the problem management process, as defined by ITIL, are:

- Capturing the incident details from the incident management process discussed previously. Incident management is the first point of contact for reported IT problems. If the incident management resources cannot easily and efficiently diagnose and solve a problem, those details should be reported to a problem management function.

EXHIBIT 22.2

Logical Flow of Problem Resolution from Incident Management

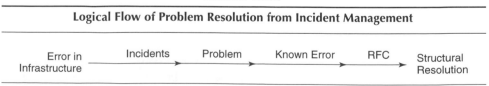

- An effective configuration management database (CMDB), as discussed in the following section, should become a key tool to better understand the problem's background and environmental details such as the software versions used, past problem history, and any other configuration details.

- Incident management often tries to fix a reported matter through an informal work-around procedure. Where these do not resolve things, the matter is passed on to problem management who should use this work-around data to help diagnose the problem.

In addition to resolving any single incident that was *bumped-up* to the problem management process, IT should try to establish processes for better problem and error control, including maintaining data to help identify trends and suggesting improved procedures for the proactive prevention of problems. Data should be maintained on solutions and/or any available work-arounds for a resolved problem, and closed problem records. In many instances, problem management may encounter a situation where it is necessary to go a step further and file a formal Request for Change (RFC) document either through the IT development function or through a hardware or software vendor.

The problem management process focuses on finding patterns among incidents, problems, and known errors. A detailed review of these patterns allows an analyst to solve the problem by considering the many possibilities and narrowing things down to a solution, what is called "root cause" analysis. There are many good techniques for resolving and correcting problems, often caused by a combination of technical and nontechnical factors. An internal auditor reviewing the problem management process should look for a set of formal and structured procedures to support problem analysis and resolution.

The problem management process is a good area for internal audit to diagnose IT service-delivery processes in order to better understand the overall health of IT operations. Areas where internal audit may ask some questions include:

- The number of RFCs raised and the impact of those RFCs on the availability and reliability of the overall IT services covered

- The amount of time worked on investigations and diagnoses for various types of problems by organizational unit or vendor

- The number and impact of incidents occurring before a root problem is solved or a known error is confirmed

- The plans for resolution of open problems with regard to people and other resource requirements as well as related costs and budgeted amounts

The ITIL service-support problem management process is an important area for internal auditors to consider and understand when assessing the overall health of IT infrastructure operations. An efficient incident management process is necessary to receive customer calls and take immediate corrective actions, but an effective problem management process will go a step further to analyze and solve the problem, initiating RFCs where necessary and otherwise improving IT customer satisfaction.

(iii) Service-Support Configuration Management.   Despite their relative size, IT operations functions are complex with multiple types and versions of systems components that must work together in an orderly, well-managed manner. This is certainly true for a major corporation with classic mainframe systems, "farms" of servers, and a multitude of storage devices and communications gear, but small computer systems operations can be complex as well. A formal *configuration management* function is an important service-delivery process supporting the identification, recording, and reporting of IT components, their versions, constituent components, and relationships. Items that should be under the control of configuration management include hardware, software, and associated documentation. Configuration management is not the same concept as the depreciation accounting process for asset management, although the two are related. Asset management systems maintain details on IT gear above a certain value, their business unit, and their location. Configuration management also maintains relationships between assets, which asset management usually does not. Some organizations start with asset management and then move on to configuration management.

The basic activity of the configuration management process is to identify the various individual components in IT operations, called configuration items (CIs), and then to identify key supporting data for these CIs, including their "owners," identifying data, and version numbers, as well as systems interrelationships. This data should be captured, organized, and recorded in what is often known as a configuration management database (CMDB). The team responsible for configuration management should select and identify these configuration structures for all the infrastructure's CIs, including establishing relationships between each CI and connected components in the overall IT infrastructure configuration. Going beyond just entry on the CMDB, the process should ensure that only authorized CIs have been accepted and that no CI is added, modified, replaced, or removed without an appropriate change request and an updated specification.

An internal auditor can think of the importance of the configuration management process in terms of desktop applications in the audit department. Every internal auditor probably has a laptop computer, but unless each has consistent versions of software, there may be difficulties in their systems communicating with one another. This is where configuration management is important. It is really more important when attempting to have an understanding of the various versions or even types of software and equipment found in a large IT operation.

The configuration management process also includes some control elements. A series of reviews and audits should be implemented to verify the physical existence of CIs and check that they are correctly recorded in the configuration management system. Although we have used the word "audit" here, this is not an internal audit process but a task of the IT team responsible for the configuration management process. Configuration management should also maintain records for CI status accounting to track the status of a CI as it changes from one condition to another, for instance from being under development, to being tested, going live, and then being withdrawn.

A CMDB does not have to be a complex, specialized application. An organization can have some level of CMDB by just using spreadsheets, local databases or even paper-based systems. In today's large and complex IT infrastructures, however, configuration management requires the use of physical and electronic libraries along with the CMDB to hold definitive copies of software and documentation. The CMDB should to be based on database technology that provides flexible and powerful interrogation facilities. It should hold the relationships between all system components, including incidents, problems, known errors, changes, and releases.

The existence and controls supporting a CMDB can be a good point for internal audit to understand the configuration management process and its supporting controls. If the organization does not have a good CMDB, internal audit can anticipate seeing strong internal control problems throughout the IT infrastructure. Exhibit 22.3 outlines for audit procedures for reviewing an organization's configuration management process.

The configuration management process interfaces directly with systems development, testing, change management, and release management to incorporate new and updated product deliverables. Control should be passed from the

EXHIBIT 22.3

Audit Steps for Configuration Management Database Processes

1. Review and understand existing configuration management practices as well as their interfaces to the service management processes, procurement, and development.

2. Assess the knowledge and capability of existing IT functions and staff in terms of controls and processes for the configuration, change and release management processes.

3. Review the extent and complexity of existing configuration data held in hard-copy form, in local spreadsheets or in configuration management databases (CMDB), and develop an understanding of that database and its retrieval tools.

4. Select a production application and understand its definition on the CMDB in detail, including interfaces to change management, release management, other service management processes, procurement, and development.

5. Using the CMDB reporting tool, define the inventory of configuration items for one system and physically trace reported CIs to actual configuration components.

6. Determine processes are in place to link configuration management business processes and procedures with the CMDB tools.

7. Test the CMDB and other support tool(s) to determine that key components, software, and documentation have been implemented and controlled on the CMDB.

8. Review adequacy of facilities to provide secure storage areas to manage CIs (e.g., cabinets, controlled libraries, and directories).

9. Assess the adequacy of processes to communicate and train the staff in the importance and use of configuration management.

10. Review problem management processes to determine the extent and appropriateness of their use of the CMDB for resolving problems.

11. Determine that appropriate access and updating controls are in place to prevent unauthorized or inappropriate use of the CMDB.

12. Determine that the CMDB receives adequate backups and that it is part of the continuity plan key resources backup and recovery procedures.

project or supplier to the service provider at the scheduled time with accurate configuration records. In addition, the CMDB can be used by the service-level management process to hold details of services and to relate them to the underlying IT components. The CMDB can also be used to store inventory details supporting CIs, such as supplier, cost, purchase date, and renewal date for a license. An additional bonus is the use of the CMDB to cover the legal details associated with the maintenance of licenses and contracts.

(iv)   Service-Support Change Management.   The problem management process, discussed above, often results in the need for IT changes. In addition, many other changes can come from programs to increase business benefits such as through reducing costs or improving services. The goal of the ITIL change management process is to utilize standardized methods and procedures for the efficient and prompt handling of all changes, in order to minimize their impact on service quality and the day-to-day operations of the organization. A broad range of components should come under the change management process, including:

- IT hardware and system software
- Communications equipment and software
- All applications software
- All documentation and procedures associated with the running, support, and maintenance of live systems

The last point above is important and often of particular concern to internal auditors. All too often IT hardware and software are upgraded or revised with little concern given to changing the supporting documentation. Changes to any IT components—for example, applications software, documentation, or procedures—should be subject to a formal change management process.

Internal auditors often encounter IT functions where the change management process is haphazard at best. Examples here are changes to applications without thinking through their implications on the overall IT infrastructure, incident management fixes that create other changes, or senior management requests for changes to solve short term or immediate problems. A formal change management process that reviews and approves any proposed changes will almost always improve IT and organizational internal control processes. The change management process should be tightly linked to configuration management, discussed previously. This process is responsible for ensuring that information regarding the possible implications of a proposed change is made available, and any possible impacts are detected and presented appropriately.

Change management processes should have high visibility and open channels of communication in order to promote smooth transitions when changes take place. To improve this process, many organization IT functions have instituted a formal change advisory board (CAB), made up of people from both IT, and other functions within the organization, to review and approve changes. A CAB is a body that exists to approve changes and to assist in the assessment and prioritization of changes. It should be given the responsibility of ensuring that all changes are adequately assessed from both a business and a technical perspective. To achieve this mix, the CAB should consist of a team with a clear understanding of the customer business needs as well as the technical development and support functions. Chaired by a responsible change manager—often whoever is responsible for the change management process—CAB membership should comprise IT customers, applications developers, and various experts/technical consultants as appropriate, and any contractor or third parties' representatives if an outsourcing situation exists.

The CAB should meet on a regular basis to review and schedule proposed changes. However, such a function should not act as an impediment to IT operations but should exist to provide an orderly scheduling and introduction of all types of IT infrastructure changes. When major problems arise, there may not be time to convene the full CAB, and there should be several responsible people with the authority to make emergency decisions.

Efficient overall service management processes require the capability to change things in an orderly way, without making errors and making wrong decisions. An effective change management process is indispensable for an effective IT infrastructure. When reviewing IT internal controls, internal auditors should look for an effective change management process. The benefits of this type of process include:

- Better alignment of IT services to business requirements
- Increased visibility and communication of changes to both business and service-support staff
- Improved risk assessments
- A reduced adverse impact of changes on the quality of services
- Better assessments of the costs of proposed changes before they are incurred
- Fewer changes that have to be backed out, along with an increased ability to manage this more easily when necessary
- Increased productivity of IT customers—through less disruption and higher-quality services
- A greater ability of IT to absorb a large volume of changes

An effective change management process is an important component of IT infrastructure controls. The process must align tightly with other key processes in the IT infrastructure: change, configuration, capacity, and release management. Exhibit 22.4 shows the relationship of change management to other key ITIL processes.

(v) Service-Support Release Management. IT customers and the IT function itself need effective processes to ensure that changes are introduced to all impacted parties in an orderly and well-controlled manner. The release management process covers these introductions of authorized changes to an IT service. A release will typically consist of a number of problem fixes and enhancements to the service, including new or changed software and hardware needed to implement

EXHIBIT 22.4

Relationship of Change Management to Other ITIL Processes

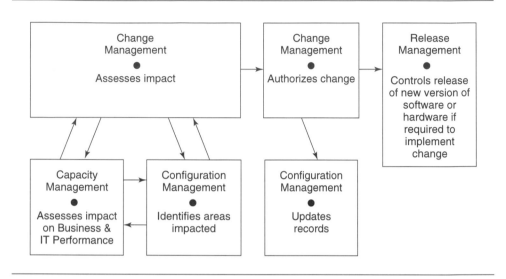

the required approved changes. Releases can take one of three formats or levels of release:

1. **Full Release.** All components in the release unit are built, tested, distributed, and implemented together. This eliminates the danger that obsolete versions of CIs (discussed previously in the "Service-Support Configuration Management" section) will be incorrectly assumed to be unchanged and used within the release. With a full release, all components supporting some application area or system are released as a single component.

   With all new and existing components bundled together, any problems are more likely to be detected and rectified before entry into the live environment. The disadvantage is that the amount of time, effort, and computing resources needed to build, test, distribute, and implement the full release will increase. Although in some circumstances the testing of a delta release, as discussed next, may need to be as extensive as that for an equivalent full release, the amount of building effort required to test a delta release is normally far less than for a full release.

   An example of a full release could consist of the complete release of a new version of a major component of an enterprise resource planning (ERP) software package. The full release concept is applicable to both software and hardware, although the full release of IT hardware is normally limited to major components and not the total system.

2. **Delta Release.** A delta, or partial, release is one that includes only those CIs that have actually changed or are new since the last full or delta release. For example, if the release unit is the organization's set of manufacturing control systems, a delta release would contain only those modules that have changed, or are new, since the last full or delta release of

the program of the modules. There may be occasions when the release of a full unit cannot be justified. In such cases, a delta release may be more appropriate. A decision should be made on whether to install or not install a delta release. There is no single correct choice, and a decision to do a delta release should be made on a case-by-case basis, with the CAB making the recommendation. Items to be considered when deciding whether to launch a full or delta release include:

- Size of a delta release in comparison with a full release, and hence the resources and effort required
- Urgency of the need for the facilities to be provided by the release
- Number of CIs (below the release unit level) that have changed since the last full release—a very large number will suggest a full release
- Possible risk to the business if compatibility errors are found in the release (e.g., would it be preferable to wait for a full release rather than to risk interface problems arising with a delta release?)
- Resources that are available for building, testing, distributing, and implementing the delta release (e.g., if implementation is to be via non-technical staff, is it easier to implement a complete new release than a delta release?)
- Completeness of impact analysis information, to make an informed and objective decision

3. **Package-Level Releases.** A package can contain an initial version of a new service, several new versions of batch programs, and a number of new and initial versions of individual modules, together with the release of a complete new desktop system (both hardware and software). Package releases can reduce the likelihood of old or incompatible software being wrongly kept in use and can help to ensure that all changes will be made concurrently.

There are normally dependencies between a particular version of software and the hardware required for it to operate. This will drive the packaging of software and hardware together to form a new release of the service, along with any related functional requirements. For example a new version of an application software system may require an upgrade to the operating system or some other hardware change may require a fix to some application. Changes of this sort should be bundled into, and one or other of these two changes could require a hardware change, for example, a faster processor or more memory. The release management process is concerned with changes to define IT services. These can be implemented by rolling out a combination of the new applications software with upgraded or new hardware, or simply changes to the service hours or support.

The modern internal auditor often will not be directly involved in this release management process. However, the controls and procedures surrounding new hardware and software releases will have a major impact on the overall IT infra-structure control environment. An internal auditor should become sufficiently familiar with these processes to better understand controls and procedures sustaining IT service support.

(b) Service-Delivery Best Practices

The preceding paragraphs have outlined the five ITIL service-support processes. Although there is no order as to which should be first, the following sections outline five additional ITIL service-delivery processes. Service support covered the accurate processing of IT applications and components ranging from receiving a reported incident to defining the problem to introducing the change and then releasing it in to production. The equally important ITIL service-delivery processes cover areas more closely aligned with the smooth and efficient operation of the overall IT infrastructure. Some of these, such as the continuity management process have traditionally been near and dear to the hearts of many internal auditors. Others, such as Service Level Agreements that define performance and expectations between IT and its customers, also should become familiar to internal auditors who encounter similar arrangements in other areas.

(i) Service-Delivery Service Level Management. Service-level management is the name given to the processes of planning, coordinating, drafting, agreeing, monitoring, and reporting on formal agreements between both IT and the providers and recipients of IT services. These agreements are called Service Level Agreements (SLAs), and they represent formal agreements between IT and both providers of services to IT as well as IT end-user customers. When the first ITIL service-level best practices materials were published in 1989, few organizations had SLAs in place. Today many organizations have introduced them—although with varying degrees of success—and internal auditors should become familiar with SLA concepts when reviewing internal IT infrastructure controls.

When IT contracts for services with some outside provider, such as for disaster recovery backup services, the arrangement will be covered by a formal contract where the disaster recovery provider agrees to provide certain levels of service, following a response-time-based schedule, and IT agrees to other terms. The governing contract here is a SLA between IT and the providers of services to them. Perhaps even more important, from an internal control perspective, are the SLA agreements between IT and its customers. We have used the term customer here for the older and still common term for IT users. There are many groups in an organization that use IT services, and they are all customers of those services expecting certain levels of service and responsiveness. This arrangement is defined through a SLA, a written agreement between the IT function and its customers, defining the key service targets and responsibilities of both parties. The emphasis should be on a partnership agreement, and SLAs should not be used as a way of holding one side or the other for ransom. A true partnership should be developed between the IT provider and the customer in a mutually beneficial manner; otherwise, the SLA could quickly fall into disrepute, and a culture of blame could prevent any true service quality improvements from taking place.

An SLA is a formal agreement in which IT promises to deliver services per an agreed-upon set of schedules and understands that there will be penalties if service standards are not met. The goal here is to maintain and improve on service quality through a constant cycle of agreeing, monitoring, reporting, and improving the current levels of IT service. SLAs should be strategically focused on the business and maintaining the alignment between the business and IT.

Exhibit 22.5 outlines the contents of a typical SLA. This should not be the type of document that an internal auditor might find as part of a mortgage house closing. Rather, the IT customers should negotiate the service requirements that they are seeking, such as an average response times no more than . . . or financial systems closing processing completed by . . . or a variety of other factors. To temper expectations and show what could be available, the IT function—as part of the service-level management process—would describe their capabilities and options in a service offerings catalog. The customer requirements will be prepared per specifications and customer needs and, after some negotiation, formal SLAs will be established. Performance against these SLAs should be monitored on an ongoing basis with performance reported regularly. Failure to meet these SLA standards could result in additional negotiations and SLA adjustments.

EXHIBIT 22.5

IT Service Level Agreement Sample Contents

There is no one form or format to describe an SLA. The following lists a sample set of contents:

INTRODUCTION

- Parties to the agreement.
- Title and brief description of the agreement.
- Signatories.
- Dates: start, end, review.
- Scope of the agreement; what is covered and what is excluded.
- Responsibilities of both the **service** provider and the **customer**.
- Description of the **services** covered.

SERVICE HOURS

- Hours that each service is normally required (e.g., 24x7, Monday to Friday 08:00–18:00)
- Arrangement for requesting service extensions, including required notice periods (e.g., request must be made to the **service** desk by 12 noon for an evening extension, by 12 noon on Thursday for a weekend extension).
- Special hours allowances (e.g., public holidays).
- Service calendar.

AVAILABILITY

- Availability targets within agreed-on hours, normally expressed as percentages—measurement period and method must be stipulated. This may be expressed for the overall service, underpinning services, and critical components, or all three. However, it is difficult to relate such simplistic percentage availability figures to service quality, or to customer business activities. It may be better to try to measure service in terms of the customer's inability to carry out its business activities.

RELIABILITY

- Usually expressed as the number of service breaks, or the mean time between failures (**MTBF**) or mean time between **system** incidents (**MTBSI**).

EXHIBIT 22.5 *(CONTINUED)*

IT Service Level Agreement Sample Contents

SUPPORT

- Support hours (where these are not the same as service hours).
- Arrangements for requesting support extensions, including required notice periods (e.g., request must be made to the service desk by 12 noon for an evening extension, by 12 noon on Thursday for a weekend extension).
- Special hours allowances (e.g., public holidays).
- Target time to respond to incidents, either physically or by other method (e.g., telephone contact, e-mail).
- Target time to resolve incidents, within each incident priority—targets vary, depending upon incident priorities.

THROUGHPUT

- Indication of likely traffic volumes and throughput activity (e.g., the number of transactions to be processed, number of concurrent users, amount of data to be transmitted over the network).

TRANSACTION RESPONSE TIMES

- Target times for average, or maximum, workstation response times (sometimes expressed as a percentile—e.g., 95% within 2 seconds).

BATCH TURNAROUND TIMES

- Times for delivery of input and the time and place for delivery of output.

CHANGES

- Targets for approving, handling and implementing RFCs, usually based upon the **category** or **urgency**/priority of the change.

IT SERVICE CONTINUITY AND SECURITY

- Brief mention of IT service continuity plans and how to invoke them, and coverage of any security issues, particularly any responsibilities of the customer (e.g., backup of free-standing PCs, password changes).
- Details of any diminished or amended service targets should a disaster situation occur (if no separate **SLA** exists for such a situation).

CHARGING

- Details of the charging formula and periods (if charges are being made). If the **SLA** covers an **outsourcing** relationship, charges should be detailed in an addendum because they are often covered by commercial confidentiality provisions.

SERVICE REPORTING AND REVIEWING

- The content, frequency, and distribution of service reports, and the frequency of service review meetings.

PERFORMANCE INCENTIVES/PENALTIES

- Details of any agreement regarding financial incentives or penalties based upon performance against service levels. These are more likely to be included if the services are being provided by a third-party organization. It should be noted that penalty clauses can create their own difficulties.

The SLA and the service-level management process provide the following benefits for the business and the IT organization:

- Because IT will be working to meet negotiated standards, IT services will tend to be of a higher quality, causing fewer interruptions. The productivity of the IT customers will improve as well.
- IT staff resources will tend to be used more efficiently as the IT organization provides services that better meet the expectations of its customers.
- With SLAs, the service provided can be measured and the perception of IT operations will generally improve.
- Services provided by the third parties are more manageable with the underpinning contracts in place, and any possibility of negative influences on the IT service provided is reduced.
- Monitoring overall IT services under SLAs makes it possible to identify weak spots that can be improved.

The SLA process is an important component of IT operations. If an organization does not use formal SLAs, internal auditors reviewing IT operations should consider recommending formal SLA processes. SLAs can create a totally new environment with an IT organization. All parties will better understand their responsibilities and service obligations, and the SLA can become a basis for resolving many issues. Internal audit can use it as a basis for assessing internal controls in a variety of areas and for making strong control improvement recommendations.

(ii) Service-Delivery Financial Management for IT Services. In its earlier days, the IT function in most organizations was operated as a "free" support service with its expenses handled through central management and with no costs allocated to benefiting users. There was not much attention to costs in those early days. If a department wanted some new application, they would pressure management to purchase the package and add any additional necessary people to manage it. Over time, IT organizations began to establish charge-back processes, but these were too often viewed as a series of "funny-money" transactions, where no one paid too much attention to the actual costs and pricing of IT services.

Today, the costs and pricing of IT services is or should be a much more important consideration. The well-managed IT function should operate like a business, and financial management is an important and key ITIL process to help manage the financial controls for that business. The objective of the service-delivery financial management process is to suggest guidance for the cost-effective stewardship of the assets and resources used in providing IT services. IT should be able to account fully for its spending on IT services and to attribute the costs of the services delivered to the organization's customers. There are three separate subprocesses associated with ITIL financial management:

1. *IT budgeting* is the process of predicting and controlling the spending of money within the organization. Budgeting consists of a periodic, usually annual, negotiation cycle to set budgets along with the ongoing day-to-day monitoring of current budgets. Budgeting ensures that there has been planning and funding for appropriate IT services and that IT operates within this budget during the period. Other business functions will have

periodic negotiations with IT to establish expenditure plans and agreed-on investment programs; these ultimately set the budgets for IT.

2. *IT accounting* is the set of processes that enable IT to account fully for the way its money is spent by customer, service, and activity. Many IT organizations do not always do a good job in this area. IT functions have a wide variety of external costs, including software, equipment lease agreements, telecommunications costs, and others. However, these costs are often not that well managed or reported. They have enough data to pay the bills and evaluate some specific area costs, but IT functions often lack the level of detailed accounting that can be found in a large manufacturing organization, as an example. The manufacturing cost accounting– or activity-based accounting model has applicability here. There are many good books on manufacturing activity-based accounting systems, but it is beyond the scope of this book to suggest a good accounting approach for IT operations.

3. *Charging* is the set of pricing and billing processes to charge customers for the services supplied. This requires sound IT accounting and needs to be done in a simple, fair, and well-controlled manner. The IT charging process sometimes breaks down in an IT function because billing reports of IT services are too complex or technical for many customers to understand. IT needs to produce clear, understandable reports of the IT services used so that customers can verify details, understand enough information to ask questions regarding service, and negotiate adjustments if necessary.

Financial management for IT services provides important information to the service-level management process, discussed previously, about the IT costing, pricing, and charging strategies. While generally not operated as a profit center, the financial management process allows both IT and its customers to think of IT service operations in business terms. The financial management process may allow IT and overall management to make decisions about what, if any, functions should be retained in-house or outsourced to an external provider.

The financial management process allows accurate cost-benefit analyses of the IT services provided and allows the IT organization to set and meet financial targets. It also should provide timely reporting to the service-level management process so that customers can understand the charging and pricing methods used. Of all of the ITIL service-support and -delivery processes, financial management is one that frequently gets short shrift. IT people have a technical orientation and tend to think of financial management as an *accounting issue*, a concept almost beneath them. On the other side of the coin, finance and accounting resources tend to look at IT financial issues as too technical beyond such simple transactions as equipment lease accounting or facility space charges. Internal auditors should use their financial skills as well as IT knowledge to review and assess financial management process internal controls.

Exhibit 22.6 provides some audit procedures for an internal audit review of the costs and pricing of IT processes and services. This is often not a common review area for internal audit, but given the large costs distributed to customers as well as the importance of an organization's IT resources, this should be an important audit area.

EXHIBIT 22.6

IT Costs and Pricing Internal Audit Review Steps

1. Develop and document a general understanding of the cost structure for IT operations, including the costs of equipment supplies and salaries.

2. Review and understand the costing philosophy for IT operations—is it an overhead function, cost recovery, or revenue generating?

3. Review processes for costing and pricing IT services:
   a. Are all IT costs covered?
   b. Based on interviews with IT users, does the costing and pricing system appear to be understandable?
   c. Is there a process in place to administer the costing process and to make adjustments if necessary?

4. Review the negotiation process with IT users to understand pricing process—are expected costs included in SLAs?

5. Select pricing reports during a period for several processes and check to determine the prices are included in SLAs.

6. Review the appropriateness of the adjustment process of over a period to determine the corrections are investigated and applied when appropriate.

7. Review data processing services billed for one accounting period and determine whether they cover all actual IT costs. Investigate and report on any differences.

8. For a selected accounting period, trace IT pricing charges to appropriate accounting system entries.

(iii) Service-Delivery Capacity Management. The capacity management process is designed to ensure that the capacity of the IT infrastructure is aligned to business needs and to maintain the required level of service delivery at an acceptable cost through appropriate levels of capacity. Through gathering business and technical capacity data, this process should result in a capacity plan to deliver cost-justified capacity requirements for the organization. In addition to a prime objective to understand an organization's IT capacity requirements and deliver against them both in the present and the future, capacity management is also responsible for understanding the potential advantages that new technology could have and assessing its suitability for the organization.

The capacity management process is generally considered in terms of three subprocesses covering business, service, and resource capacity management. Business capacity management is a long-term process to ensure that the future business requirements are taken into consideration and then planned and implemented as necessary. Service capacity management is responsible for ensuring that the performance of all current IT services falls within the parameters defined in existing SLAs. Finally, resource capacity management has a more of a technical focus and is responsible for the management of the individual components within the infrastructure. The multiple inputs to these three capacity management subprocesses include:

- SLAs and SLA breaches
- Business plans and strategies
- Operational schedules as well as schedule changes

- Application development issues
- Technology constraints and acquisitions
- Incidents and problems
- Budgets and financial plans

As a result of these inputs, the capacity management process—often under a single designated capacity manager—will manage IT processes, develop and maintain a formal capacity plan, and make certain that capacity records are up to date. In addition, the capacity manager must be involved in evaluating all changes to establish the effect on capacity and performance. This capacity evaluation should happen both when changes are proposed and after they are implemented. Capacity management must pay particular attention to the cumulative effect of changes over a period of time that may cause degraded response times, file storage problems, and excess demand for processing capacity. Other roles where there are capacity management responsibilities include some duties of the network manager, application, and system manger. They are responsible for translating the business requirements into the required capacity to be able to meet these requirements and to optimize IT performance.

The implementation of an effective capacity management process offers IT the benefits of an actual overview of the current capacity in place and the ability to plan capacity in advance. Effective capacity management should be able to estimate the impact of new applications or modifications as well as provide cost savings that are in tune with the requirements of the business. Proper capacity planning can significantly reduce the overall cost of ownership of a system. Although formal capacity planning takes time, internal and external staff resources, and software and hardware tools, the potential losses incurred without capacity planning can be significant. Lost productivity of end users in critical business functions, overpaying for network equipment or services, and the costs of upgrading systems already in production can more than justify the cost of capacity planning. This is an important ITIL process. The modern internal auditor should look for an effective capacity management function when reviewing IT infrastructure controls and processes.

(iv) Service-Delivery Availability Management. Organizations are increasingly demanding that their IT services be available on a 7 days per week 24 hours a day basis. When these IT services are unavailable, in many cases the business stops as well. It is therefore vital that an IT organization manage and control the availability of their IT Services. This can be accomplished by defining the requirements from the business regarding the availability of its IT services and then matching them with the possibilities of the IT organization.

Availability management depends on multiple inputs to be able to function well. These include requirements regarding the availability of the business, information regarding reliability, maintainability, recoverability, and serviceability of the CIs, and information from the other processes, incidents, problems, SLAs, and achieved service levels. The outputs of this process are:

- Recommendations regarding the IT infrastructure to ensure its resilience
- Reports about the availability of the services

- Procedures to ensure availability and recovery are dealt with for every new or improved IT service
- Plans to improve the availability of the IT services

The activities within the availability management process can be described as planning, improving, and measuring. Planning involves determining the availability requirements to find out if and how the IT organization can meet them. The service level management process, discussed previously, maintains contact with the business and will be able to provide the availability expectations to the availability management process. Business units sometimes may have unrealistic expectations with respect to availability and an incomplete understanding what this means in real terms. For example, they may want 99.9% availability yet not realize that this will cost about five times more than providing 98% availability. It is the responsibility of service-level management and the availability management process to manage these expectations.

An IT organization can either design for "availability" or "recovery." When the business cannot afford to have a particular service be down for any length of time, the IT organization will need to build resilience into the infrastructure and ensure that preventative maintenance can be performed to keep services in operation. In many cases, building "extra availability" into the infrastructure is an expensive task that can be justified by business needs. Designing for availability is a proactive approach to avoiding downtime in IT services.

When the business can tolerate some downtime of services or the cost justification cannot be made for building in additional resilience into the infrastructure, designing for recovery is the appropriate approach. Here, the infrastructure will be designed so that in the event of a service failure recovery will be "as fast as possible." Designing for recovery is a reactive management approach for availability. In any event, processes such as incident management need to be in place to recover as soon as possible in case of a service interruption.

The main benefit of availability management is a structured process to deliver IT services that are delivered according to the agreed-on requirements of the customers. This should result in a higher availability of the IT services and increased customer satisfaction.

(v) Service-Delivery Continuity Management. As businesses have become ever more dependent on IT, the impact of any unavailability of IT services has drastically increased. Every time the availability or performance of a service is reduced, IT customers cannot continue with their normal work. This trend towards a high dependency on IT support and services will continue and will increasingly influence direct IT customers, managers, and decision makers. That is why it is important, that the impact of a total or even partial loss of IT services be estimated and continuity plans be established to ensure that the business, and its supporting IT infrastructure, will always be able to continue working.

ITIL calls for an appropriate strategy to be developed that contains an optimal balance of risk reduction and recovery options. This calls for some of the same business continuity and disaster recovery strategies as discussed in Chapter 18, "Business Continuity Planning and Disaster Recovery." Using the approaches outlined there, an IT organization can implement an effective set of service continuity processes. However, internal auditors should refer to Chapter 18 to better understand and evaluate continuity and disaster recovery planning processes.

22.3 ITIL PROCESSES IN PERSPECTIVE

The ITIL service-support and service-delivery processes introduce an expanded and improved approach for looking at all aspects of the IT infrastructure. These processes are not independent and free-standing. While each process can operate by itself to some degree, each process depends on the input and support from other related processes. We have tried to show these interdependencies in several of the process descriptions. Exhibit 22.4 provides a good example where the change management process is dependent upon and supports other related processes.

Exhibit 22.7 puts these ITIL processes in a jigsaw and shows them covering an even larger perspective. Service-delivery and service support are two interrelated and side-by-side elements. They support the management of the IT infrastructure and management of the organizations. IT applications are in the center of this puzzle and a key central area of internal controls concern.

EXHIBIT 22.7

ITIL Jigsaw Puzzle

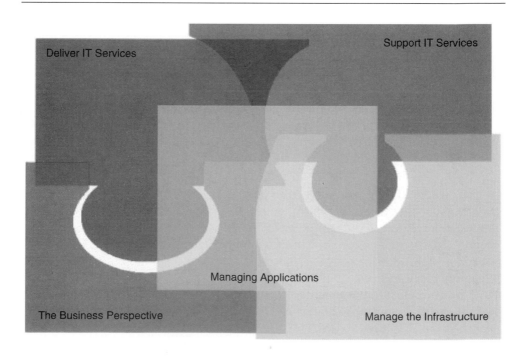

22.4 INFRASTRUCTURE IT STAFF SUPPORT

Our previous discussions of problem management, incident management, and change management among others tend to imply a very large IT organization with multiple levels of staff and management teams. An internal auditor might ask how these ITIL standards apply to the auditor's organization that perhaps has always been much smaller and has recently gone through a further downsizing. Our answer here is very much of a *no!* In order to be ITIL-compliant an organization does not need multiple levels of support staff. Rather, it needs to think of the various service-support and service-delivery processes included in ITIL and outlined in this chapter. A small IT function may not need to establish separate incident management and problem management functions, but it must think of each as separate processes with unique control procedures. Using this example, even a very small IT function should implement these various separate areas for IT process improvement.

Internal auditors should give this area particular care when making recommendations. The size and scope of the area being audited and the scope of operations should always be considered. This author thinks of the early days of information systems controls, back when many applications were developed in-house for production applications. To promote adequate separation of duties, many audit guidance materials recommended there be a separation of duties between people who operated the computer hardware and those who programmed it. Otherwise, in those days of much simpler systems, there was a risk that an individual with fraudulent intent might change an application program— to write an unauthorized check, for example—and then produce this personal check when operating the system. This was good control in the early days of IT, but it is not as relevant today. Internal auditors should think about the adequacy and appropriateness of IT controls in terms of those built into individual applications as well as the infrastructure process controls discussed in this chapter.

We have introduced the ITIL service-support and service-delivery standards at a very high level. The previously referenced ITIL publications will provide some very excellent best practices guidance on how to build and manage these important processes. However, materials are available through various other IT sources that can help to guide the internal auditor. The important area to consider is not the specific content of the organization's CMDB, for example, but that it has an adequate tool in place to control and manage the configuration of all IT assets, including hardware components, operating and application software, and supporting documentation. An internal auditor should look for these tools or supporting processes and assesses their adequacy in terms of the overall environment in the organization.

The IT infrastructure area is an important area for internal audit reviews. All too often internal auditors have concentrated their attentions on the applications controls and general IT controls of the past. In today's world of complex processes supporting the IT infrastructure, the ITIL processes described in this chapter outline some excellent areas for internal audit attention. When reviewing internal controls for any IT organization, whether a major corporate-level IT operation or the smaller function found in many of today's organizations. The effective internal auditor should concentrate on reviewing controls over key infrastructure processes.

ENDNOTE

[1] *ITIL Service Support,* June 2000, and *ITIL Service Delivery,* April 2001, Office of Government Commerce, London.

CHAPTER TWENTY-THREE

Computer-Assisted Audit Techniques

23.1 DEFINITION OF A COMPUTER-ASSISTED AUDIT TECHNIQUE

Internal auditors gather evidence from an organization's books and records to support their conclusions. This audit evidence includes the actual paper-based documents, evidence that these documents or supporting transactions were properly recorded in a timely manner, and contains appropriate authorizing signatures or notations. With automation, most of those documents are paperless today, and internal auditors have a challenge to review and understand those paperless document and procedures to support their audit conclusions. While internal auditors often rely on the internal controls surrounding those automated systems, they need tools to better understand and evaluate the completeness and accuracy of the data stored in the files and databases for today's automated applications. While internal audit can gather data by selecting and reviewing items from application output reports and display screens, it is often more efficient to use automated techniques to examine all recorded items on the supporting computer files. To gather information from automated systems, internal auditors often either reviewed the results of an existing printed report or output screen or requested the information technology (IT) function produce a special report to satisfy information requirements. However, internal auditors also can act with greater independence by developing their own specialized file retrievals. This audit analysis of data is accomplished through the use of what are called computer-assisted audit techniques (CAATs), independent-auditor-controlled software.

An internal auditor has a fundamental requirement to obtain evidence on the validity of accounting and operational data. However, large volumes of data or the lack of paper documents often make this review of evidence difficult or almost impossible in many cases. This chapter describes audit approaches to testing, analyzing, and gathering detailed evidence from data contained on automated applications through the use of internal-auditor-controlled CAATs. These techniques allow an auditor to review the contents of computerized applications data in files, ranging from accounting systems on large mainframe computers to smaller systems residing on departmental desktop systems. Although some CAATs require specialized data-processing skills, many can be performed by the typical internal auditor, with no particular programming skills, through the use of powerful audit software tools.

A CAAT is a specialized computer program, controlled by internal audit, which is used to test or otherwise analyze data on computer files. In the early days of data-processing systems, auditors often just relied on the printed outputs from automated systems and used conventional audit procedures to test and analyze this computer-generated data. As computer systems became more pervasive, with large data files, auditors needed an approach to adequately evaluate controls in large information systems. In the earlier days of automated systems, some pioneering internal auditors used CAATs to read and analyze financial data on large computer files. However, many auditors continued to use conventional manual techniques and relied on the printed report results of automated systems.

The necessity for CAAT procedures first became very evident with the now long forgotten Equity Funding fraud in the early 1970s. Equity Funding Corporation, an insurance company, was reporting very significant growth from the late 1960s up through the early 1970s. It was later determined, however, that Equity Funding's growth was based on a massive management fraud in which fictitious insurance policies were entered on Equity Funding's computerized records. The external auditors at that time relied on the printed reports output by the Equity Funding computer systems rather than on the data recorded on computer files. Had the external auditors looked at the contents of those computer files, they might have detected the fraud. Equity Funding did not have a significant internal audit function; an Equity Funding employee eventually revealed the fraud.

After the fraud was discovered, many professionals pointed out that it could have been detected much earlier had the computer files been analyzed by the auditors. A review of computer reports only was not sufficient. The auditors needed independently both to review computer procedures and to analyze the contents of the computerized records. The Equity Funding fraud launched what was then called computer auditing—now information systems auditing—and the use of CAATs.

A CAAT is an auditor-controlled computer program that can be run against a production data file to analyze and summarize the data and perform other audit tests. Before the days of powerful desktop software tools, a CAAT was an "advanced" technique. End users typically relied on their data-processing departments to write special retrieval programs to give them the various reports requested. Both internal and external auditors later began to use what was called generalized audit software to develop their own programs independently for testing and analyzing data. This generalized software became the basis for CAATs, discussed throughout this chapter. The term "CAAT" is used to define specialized computer systems and procedures to assist internal audit. Others, such as some external audit firms, may use the term *computer-assisted audit procedures* (CAAP). The two expressions mean the same thing and can be used interchangeably.

An example might better clarify the concept of a typical CAAT. Assume that internal audit is interested in testing the accuracy of the aging from an automated accounts receivable system; however, most calculated data for that system is only stored on computer files, with no significant paper reports describing these calculations. Internal audit is concerned that receivables, as reported on the aged trial balance report, may not be properly aged as to the number of days due. Thus, the receivables account balances may be over- or understated. Internal audit can test these agings using any of three approaches.

First, internal audit could use traditional, manual approaches where items are selected from a computer output report and then are traced back to any original source documents that may exist. Internal audit can then determine if the items selected are properly entered on computer system records and if the aging calculations are correct. Although tedious, this will work if paper records are available. However, because of the volume of receivable records in a typical automated system, internal audit can only selectively trace and test these items. Some exception conditions may be missed with such a manual test. In addition, internal audit might not be able to easily determine if the dating of transaction-based agings is functioning correctly.

A second approach is to perform a controls review over the automated accounts receivable system. The idea is that if controls over the application are found to be good, internal audit can rely on system reports. This approach is discussed in Chapter 21, "Reviewing and Assessing Application Controls." A review of systems documentation and perhaps of a selected program source code determines whether the system is properly aging receivables. Internal audit would then test those controls by, for example, running some test transactions into the system, either as manual transactions or through another CAAT. This is the general audit approach discussed in Chapter 4, "Internal Controls Fundamentals: COSO Framework." Properly performed, this review can detect significant internal control problems as well as determine whether the system is generally working in a correct, well-controlled manner. However, internal audit would only be able to estimate the total extent of the financial statement adjustments necessary due to any account aging errors, and so, in conjunction with this test, internal audit must determine that controls over data entry and error correction are adequate.

The third approach is to use a CAAT to recalculate independently all of the agings in the accounts receivable system, develop totals for the accounts receivable balance, and produce a listing of any unusual exception items. Internal audit might perform this third, CAAT-oriented approach through the following steps:

1. **Determine CAAT Objectives.** Internal audit should not just "use the computer" to test a system without a clear set of starting audit objectives for any CAAT. In the previous examples, internal audit would have an objective of determining if accounts receivable agings are correctly stated.

2. **Understand the Computer Systems.** Internal audit should review IT systems' documentation to determine how accounts receivable agings are calculated, where this data is stored in the system, and how items are described in system files.

3. **Develop CAAT Programs.** Using generalized audit software, other retrieval packages, or a computer language processor, internal audit would write programs to recalculate accounts receivable agings and to generate totals from accounts receivable files.

4. **Test and Process the CAAT.** After testing the programs, the internal auditor would arrange to have the CAATs processed against production accounts receivable files.

5. **Develop Audit Conclusions from CAAT Results.** Similarly to any audit test, audit conclusions would be drawn from the results of the CAAT processing, documented in the workpapers and discussed in the audit report, as appropriate.

This is the general approach to developing and processing CAATs. It follows the same steps that internal audit would use for establishing audit objectives and performing appropriate tests on any system or process. As previously discussed, a CAAT is a specialized set of computer programs or procedures that are under the control of internal audit. The CAAT can be developed through generalized audit software programs run on the production computer system, specialized software run on the auditor's own laptop computer, or specialized auditor-use-only program code embedded in an otherwise normal production application. These various CAAT approaches are discussed later in Chapter 25, "Continuous Assurance Auditing, XBRL, and OLAP." The modern internal auditor should have a good understanding of when CAATs should be used to enhance the audit process, the types of software tools available to an internal auditor, and how to use a CAAT in an audit. Although some CAATs require an internal auditor to have specialized programming knowledge, most can be implemented by an auditor with only a general understanding of information systems. This chapter should give internal audit an introduction to defining, developing, and using CAATs.

23.2 DETERMINING THE NEED FOR COMPUTER–ASSISTED AUDIT TECHNIQUES

CAATs are powerful tools that can enhance both the audit process and internal auditor independence. However, these procedures can sometimes be time-consuming to develop and will not always be cost-effective. Internal audit needs to understand when a CAAT might increase overall audit efficiencies and when it will not. This section discusses areas where CAATs will enhance an audit and areas to consider when developing and implementing a CAAT. Other sections will discuss alternative CAAT approaches and procedures for implementing them as well as some problems with this approach.

Before developing a specific CAAT, an internal auditor must first determine if the planned approach is appropriate. All too often, a member of management may have attended a seminar about audit efficiencies and then will ask the internal audit team to "do something" to improve audit efficiency by using the computer in audits. This is particularly true today as management expresses concern about the costs associated with Sarbanes-Oxley Act (SOA) Section 404 reviews, as discussed in Chapter 6, "Evaluating Internal Controls: Section 404 Assessments." This type of improved audit efficiency directive often may result in disappointments for all parties. Similarly, a highly technical auditor may sometimes develop a CAAT as part of an audit even though it really does not support the objectives of that review. The result may be interesting but will not contribute to the overall effectiveness of the internal audit's objectives. The decision to develop and implement a CAAT in support of an internal audit will depend on the nature of the data and production programs being reviewed in the audit, the CAAT tools available to internal audit, and the objectives of the audit. Internal audit needs an overall understanding of CAAT procedures in order to make this decision, and should consider the following:

- *The Nature or Objectives of the Audit.* Internal audit should initially evaluate the data to be reviewed in the audit and how it is maintained. Audits based on values or attributes of computerized data are typically good candidates for CAATs. For example, the above-mentioned accounts receivable audit is a good CAAT candidate because there is generally a large volume of transactions but minimal paper records. Many of the operational and financial audit areas discussed throughout this book are good candidates for CAATs. However, a business ethics policy audit, as discussed in Chapter 9, "Whistleblower Programs and Codes of Conduct," requires an examination of records usually only maintained in published procedures and may not be a good candidate for a CAAT. While a computerized database can summarize the ethics policy data, it provides only indirect support for the prime audit procedures.

- *The Nature of the Data to Be Reviewed.* CAATs are most effective when both data and most decision-dependent information about that data are based on automated systems. For example, a manufacturing inventory system will have most of the descriptive information about its inventory on automated system files. Inventory-related data is input directly, and inventory status information is based on computer reports or output screens. There are only limited paper-based original records. Internal audit procedures for inventory here might include an analysis of manufacturing costs, and inventory system attributes can be summarized and analyzed through a CAAT. Other computer systems comprise little more than log files, which organize otherwise manual records. An engineering project authorization system might have summary data stored in a systems file but most of the information about the projects may be in manual, paper-based files. CAATs might not be all that effective in these areas because internal audit would also need to review the manual data. Only audits over areas where there is heavy dependence on computerized data are good potential candidates for a CAAT.

- *The Available CAAT Tools and Audit Skills.* Internal audit must develop its CAATs using the automation tools available within the audit department or IT function. If internal audit does not have or has not budgeted for specialized CAAT software, an internal auditor cannot develop a CAAT that requires such software. Internal audit needs to consider the types of audit software available before embarking on any CAAT projects. That availability may be based on both audit budget constraints and product limitations.

Auditor skills must also be considered. Although training materials are available, the in-charge auditor must assess whether technical audit specialists are needed and are available for the CAAT-development project. The above three points are stated in very general terms, but they are areas to be considered when planning the overall strategy for using CAATs.

These comments point to many areas where a CAAT will be difficult or not particularly cost-effective. However, internal audit should keep an open mind and always consider using CAATs to enhance audit effectiveness. Given the lack of paper-based audit trails in many automated systems today, an internal auditor has little choice but to use computer-assisted audit procedures. The challenge to internal audit is to identify appropriate areas for CAATs.

Computer systems technology has changed extensively over the years. The batch-oriented systems of not that many years ago have been replaced by online, database-oriented systems. Large centralized computer hardware has been replaced, in many respects, by networked client-server workstations. Despite these changes, however, the auditor's basic approach for defining CAATs has not really changed. For example, in 1979 the American Institute of Certified Public Accountants (AICPA) published an Audit Guide, *Computer-Assisted Audit Techniques*,[1] which provided some basic direction on the use of CAATs. Although now out of date and out of print, it contains a good list of the types of audit procedures that can be performed through the use of CAATs. Adapted for internal auditors, this set of procedures contains the following:

- *Examining Records Based on Criteria Specified by Internal Audit.* Because the records in a manual system are visible, internal audit can scan for inconsistencies or inaccuracies without difficulty. For records on computer data files, internal audit can specify audit software instructions to scan and print these records that are exceptions to the criteria, so that follow-up actions can be taken. Examples of specified areas are:
  - Accounts receivable balances for amounts over the credit limit
  - Inventory quantities for negative and unreasonably large balances
  - Payroll files for terminated employees
  - Bank demand deposit files for unusually large deposits or withdrawals

- *Testing Calculations and Making Computations.* Internal audit can use software to perform quantitative analyses to evaluate the reasonableness of auditee representations. Such analyses might be for:
  - The extensions of inventory items
  - Depreciation amounts
  - The accuracy of sales discounts
  - Interest calculations
  - Employees' net pay computations

- *Comparing Data on Separate Files.* When records on separate files should contain compatible information, audit software can determine if the information agrees. Comparisons could be:
  - Changes in accounts receivable balances between two dates, comparing the details of sales and cash receipts on transaction files
  - Payroll details with personnel files
  - Current and prior period inventory files to assist in reviewing for obsolete or slow-moving items

- *Selecting and Printing Audit Samples.* Multiple criteria may be used for selection, such as a judgmental sample of high-dollar and old items and a random sample of all other items, which can be printed in the auditor's workpaper format or on special confirmation forms. Examples are:
  - Accounts receivables balances for confirmations
  - Inventory items for observations
  - Fixed-asset additions for vouching
  - Paid voucher records for review of expenses
  - Vendor records for accounts payable recircularizations

- *Summarizing and Resequencing Data and Performing Analyses.* Audit software can reformat and aggregate data in a variety of ways to simulate processing or to determine the reasonableness of output results. Examples are:
  - Totaling transactions on an account file
  - Testing accounts receivables aging
  - Preparing general ledger trial balances
  - Summarizing inventory turnover statistics for obsolescence analysis
  - Resequencing inventory items by location to facilitate physical observations

- *Comparing Data Obtained through Other Audit Procedures with Computer System Data Files.* Audit evidence gathered manually can be converted to a machine readable form and compared to other data files. Examples are:
  - Inventory test counts with perpetual records
  - Creditor statements with accounts payable files

Although the above were originally developed for external auditors and date before the days of integrated database files, these techniques are generally still applicable for internal auditors. The number and sophistication of these CAATs increases as the individual internal auditor becomes more experienced in their use.

23.3 TYPES OF COMPUTER AUDIT SOFTWARE

In the early days of computer systems, most systems users had to submit a request to the programming department for a special report or analysis program. Programming was difficult and controlled by specialists in the IT department. Auditors were often suspicious of that approach. Just as an auditor interested in some manual records account balance would not ask the auditee for the balance but would examine the records to calculate the total, their preference was to use programs controlled by internal audit to analyze computer-based data. This led to the development of what has been called generalized audit software. There are several common standard categories or types of computer audit software:

- Generalized audit software products
- Report generator languages
- Test data techniques
- Specialized audit test and analysis software
- Expert systems and inference-based software
- Embedded audit procedures

Depending on the overall data-processing environment and the objectives of internal audit, one or more of these tools may be used in a given audit situation. Some require specialized technical skills, but most can be implemented by the generalist internal auditor. Some type of audit software should be used by any effective internal audit department operating in today's highly computerized environments. With technology advances, some approaches that were common in the past are seldom used or available today.

(a) Generalized Audit Software

In the early days of information systems auditing, most applications were written in older programming languages such as COBOL. Students today work in languages such as Visual Basic and should recognize that COBOL and other similar languages, such as assembly languages, date back to an earlier era. Auditors then usually had neither the technical skills nor the time required to write their own retrieval programs to independently access data. When an auditor wanted to test or review the contents of a large data file, it was usually necessary to give a request to what was then called the data-processing department to produce that report. The auditor would be dependent on some programmer to produce this report and could not fully act independently. This lack of auditor independence problem was solved in the early 1970s by the major public accounting firms, who developed simple audit-retrieval programs. In addition to convenient data retrieval capabilities, this software often contained other common audit functions such as sequence number gap detection or audit sampling procedures.

This software eventually began to be marketed as generalized audit software (GAS). It was originally based on older mainframe systems although several good products are still on the market today. Generalized audit software today offers internal auditors some of the following advantages:

- *Increased Independence from Information Systems.* GAS allows internal audit to perform tests of an application without asking the IT function to write the necessary retrieval software, giving auditors an extra level of independence.

- *Increased Audit Efficiencies.* GAS software can perform such routines as to confirm accounts receivable records or to produce confirmation letters more efficiently than traditional audit procedures. In addition, such a CAAT will almost certainly be used over multiple years, so its development costs can be spread over time.

- *Opportunity to Observe Other Controls.* By using an independent set of programs on the auditee's systems operations, internal audit can observe and develop a better understanding of other information systems controls. For example, internal audit may observe procedural weaknesses in work schedules or tape cartridge retrievals from the data center library. While not related to the planned tests of given data files, these observations can often point to areas for subsequent audit work.

Exhibit 23.1 shows some information systems planning steps to develop a CAAT to test balances and interest rates for a financial institution loan file. Generalized software program code is generally much more easily constructed

EXHIBIT 23.1

Programming Steps to Developing a CAAT

1. Define overall audit objectives—What do we want to test and why?

2. Identify files and cycle dates that will test the audit objective.

3. Identify an audit software tool for performing the test.

4. Identify specific files and their format data contents that will be tested.

5. Code audit retrieval software to perform the desired audit test.

6. Test audit software against sample set of production files. Modify audit software until the audit test appears to be working correctly. If problems exist, correct audit program coding.

7. Determine availability and perform actual audit test.

8. Follow up on any unusual or unexpected results. Make further corrections as necessary.

9. Report audit results.

10. Document results of audit test.

than a conventional program written in a language such as Visual Basic or C. This type of programming code is usually easy to learn. Generalized audit software was originally introduced in the mainframe computer era where there were few other easy-to-use retrieval packages available. Today, auditors can also use other software retrieval language tools, which are available on many computer systems.

(b) Report Generators Languages

When information systems departments used compiler-based languages, such as COBOL, end users did no hands-on applications development and relied on the information systems department for all reports. This former dependency on COBOL-type languages has very much changed in today's modern information systems department. Today, end users with minimal training regularly produce special reports or perform complex file manipulations in addition to conventionally programmed applications with report-generator languages. Internal audit needs an understanding of the types of generalized retrieval languages available at the auditee location. They are generally available for most types and sizes of vendors' hardware, from legacy mainframes to laptop computers. Some of these software products are designed to operate only as a query language for a given database or vendor's application software package. These are called *report-generators* or *query languages*.

Others are quite general and can be used with many applications. The most general and flexible of these are computer languages where only very general instructions are necessary to produce a desired report rather than the detailed steps in a complete computer program. For example, the program's author need only specify a list of items to be selected to produce a fairly professional looking output report. These retrieval languages take care of most other report-editing and -formatting functions.

Software that comes with some form of a query or report-generator language can satisfy the many reporting needs of typical end users. For example, a fixed-assets control application may have a report-generator subsystem to allow customized fixed assets reports. Auditors should consider the use of these same report generators for audit-retrieval purposes. Many are easy to use. Otherwise, vendors will provide training in the use of the software at the time it is installed. Even if internal audit plans to use generalized audit software or other retrieval tools, these report-generator products can be very helpful for special analysis projects.

Since the early 1980s, there have been numerous data retrieval type products, some for end-user report-retrieval purposes and others primarily for use by the IT function such as overall applications generators. Any can be a powerful tool for auditor developed CAATs. While there is no one single definition of these auditor friendly retrieval languages, most exhibit one or more of the following characteristics:

- *Nonprocedural Language.* Earlier programming languages required the programmer to follow a fixed sequence of instructions to accomplish a given task. For example, a COBOL program producing an output report must first open and read the input file, then select and sort items of interest to finally produce the report. This same sequence of steps is not required with a retrieval language. The same example report could be produced with the single instruction, "List data sorted by . . ." This facility makes the software easy to learn.

- *Environmental Independence.* Many retrieval languages can be used on a variety of different computer systems. They are portable from laptops to mainframes, operating under different types of computer hardware, operating systems, and telecommunications procedures such as Internet connections.

- *Powerful Application-Development Facilities.* Although not necessary for internal auditors, most retrieval languages have powerful facilities to help application developers to design entire systems, including the methods for database access, "paint" procedures to develop retrieval screens, and graphical features for outputting reports.

A modern retrieval language offers considerable flexibility and ease of use. However, such software products may be expensive and difficult to justify only for internal audit use. Internal audit should investigate and consider using similar tools installed elsewhere within the organization. This software is typically licensed to the overall organization, and internal audit would be one additional user. If such tools are not in use, internal audit may recommend their consideration and use in conjunction with a review of information systems applications (see Chapter 21).

Generalized retrieval software can almost always be used for audit-retrieval purposes. It has the disadvantage that it does not have such built-in audit software functions as statistical sample selections or serial number gap detection. However, it will work quite well for item selections, recalculations, file-matching, or data-reporting purposes. Many specialized audit functions can generally be coded into the retrieval language with little difficulty.

Many software products come delivered with some type of vendor-supplied retrieval package. For example, accounting software packages for general ledgers often come with their own report-retrieval packages. Even specialized commercial software today, such as a system to control inventory in a computer center media library, comes with its own specialized retrieval software. These are often useful to an internal auditor for accessing and analyzing the particular data records.

A major disadvantage with the various retrieval products included in other commercial software is that an internal auditor, in a larger organization, may be required to learn the report-generation language from multiple software products, none of which may follow a consistent syntax. There may be one or several installed on the centralized computers, with additional ones on divisional servers or local workstations. Even though the learning curve for writing audit retrievals with these products is typically short, internal audit may encounter both training and logistical difficulties. Mainframe-based generalized audit software, discussed previously, or lap or desktop system audit packages, discussed in the next section, can provide internal audit with a single software retrieval product for use throughout the organization. However, audit objectives will determine what type of audit software is best used.

(c) Desktop Computer Audit Software Tools

The desktop computer has had a very significant impact on information systems since the introduction of the Apple II and IBM personal computers in the early 1980s. These computer systems are found in most organizations either as free-standing devices or, more typically, networked to central servers. The desktop computer can also be a useful tool for developing CAATs. Several very excellent audit-retrieval products are available to aid internal auditors here. While perhaps designed more with the external auditor in mind, these audit-retrieval packages are also very useful to the typical internal auditor. In addition, other certain standard desktop software products can also be used for audit-retrieval purposes. All of these audit tools are designed to access or download data from larger computer systems to bring them to internal audit's laptop computer. We have used the terms desktop and laptop here to refer to the same general type of auditor-friendly computer system.

Internal auditors often wish to examine and analyze the contents of data files located on various remote computer systems within the organization where generalized audit software or other retrieval tools are not available for processing at each of these remote locations. For example, due to software license restrictions or computer system incompatibilities, internal audit's generalized audit software may only be usable on the central computer system. Data files from other locations would have to be transported to that central site using the organization's communications network. Even if retrieval languages were available at all locations, it might be necessary for internal audit to spend increased travel time and additional resources processing CAATs at these remote locations. Desktop-based computer audit software tools can solve many of these problems.

Desktop computer audit software is a type of generalized audit software with many of the functions and features typically found on older mainframe systems but implemented on a business computer. It is not designed to perform audit retrievals against other systems but against original or extract files from larger computer system applications. This software was originally developed for external auditors who are faced with the need to access files from many different clients and computer systems, and therefore, many products currently on the market have an external auditor emphasis. Public accounting firms have developed software, which they sometimes make available to their clients and commercial vendors market others. One software product that this author has found to be quite useful in an internal audit department is called Audit Command Language (ACL).[2]

Internal audit often must extract and analyze data from very large files on mainframe systems with thousands or millions of records. Although an internal auditor needs to access these larger files, sometimes it is more convenient for internal audit to process this data on an audit department system rather than directly on mainframe systems. This larger volume of data can be processed on a typically much smaller audit desktop computer equipped with a very high-capacity hard disk. The audit computers also need a mechanism to read files from mainframe systems, using a modem or other communications port to access the mainframe processors. This will be effective provided the mainframe files are not too large or the laptop system has a sufficient hard disk capacity. An alternative and often better approach is to equip the audit computer with a memory stick or cartridge drive. These devices are not extremely expensive and can be a good addition to a centralized internal audit department machine. The audit computer can then read from mainframe tapes to process data for the computer audit test. Although many larger data centers have now converted to cartridge formats, tape formats will continue to be used for some time.

The actual audit software programs used for the computer-assisted audit procedures have similar functions and capabilities as the mainframe-based generalized audit software discussed in Section 23.3(a). Most types of CAAT procedures discussed previously, such as testing agings or recalculating balances, can be used with audit departmental computers. The only limitation sometimes is the memory and storage capacity of such smaller systems. Thus, if a large number of data files are to be compared as part of the CAAT, a laptop system will not be that efficient because only one tape drive would typically be available.

Exhibit 23.2 illustrates the programming instructions necessary to develop a CAAT application using the ACL product. In this example, an internal auditor would have secured a copy or extract of the organization's accounts receivable master. Using the audit command language, internal audit can easily perform this common financial audit task. The idea here is not to show how to write such a program but to illustrate that it is a relatively simple and easy-to-learn task.

(d) Test Data or "Test Deck" Approaches

The term "test deck" is an old computer audit–related term dating back to the earliest days of information systems, when applications operated in a batch

EXHIBIT 23.2

ACL Programming Example

ACL is a conversational easy-to-use interactive command audit language that the auditor can load onto the microcomputer to access a fairly universal set of computer file structures. Files can be accessed either through an online connection or from a tape file, extracted from the data center that the auditor would access through a special, 9-track tape drive.

As an example of using ACL, assume an internal auditor wanted to recalculate taxes payable account for a situation where the tax rates would be 20, 30, or 50% depending upon the income level. Income less than $5,000 would result in no taxes, and the other income breaks are $10,000, $30,000, and above. An audit analysis program to recalculate those taxes would first require codes to indicate where annual income was located on the tax file. The taxes payable could then be calculated with the following ACL command statements:

```
TAXES_PAYABLE_COMPUTED

0                                          IF INCOME < 5000
                  .2    *   (INCOME – 5,000)    IF (INCOME < 10,000)
1,000      +      .3    *   (INCOME – 10,000)   IF (INCOME < 30,000)
7,000      +      .5    *   (INCOME – 30,000)
```

These four commands would read through the file and produce an audit total.

---

mode and used punched cards as input media. In order to test a computer application, internal auditors developed a series of test transactions that achieved known results. These transactions were prepared on a set of input punched cards or a "test deck." The term *test deck* is obsolete given today's technology but it describes a very useful CAAT approach where an internal auditor submits a series of test transactions against a live production system to determine if controls are adequate. (A better expression for this approach is *test data*, although we will continue to use the traditional name of test deck.)

For example, internal audit might use a test deck CAAT to test controls in a batch payroll system. Internal audit would submit transactions for known employees showing standard hours of work, for others showing some overtime hours, and for a third group showing an excessive number of hours that should trigger an error report. A special, controlled run of the payroll system would then be arranged using these test transactions. Internal audit would subsequently verify that the pay was correctly computed, the files were correctly updated, and all expected error and transaction reports were correct. The audit test transactions would then be purged from the updated files. Through this test deck, internal audit could gain a level of assurance that the payroll system was working correctly.

Test deck approaches fell into disuse by auditors as systems ceased to be batch oriented and became more complex. However, this approach—which calls for the submission of audit test transactions to a copy of a live application—is still a viable CAAT tool for testing modern information systems applications. An actual deck of test transaction cards is not necessary. Test decks—or, more properly, test data approaches—can be very useful for gathering audit evidence. Even though an internal auditor will almost certainly not prepare a deck of test cards for the modern computer application, the approach uses a predetermined set of online transactions as the test deck. The CAAT approach allows internal audit to input a series of test transactions through an application input screen to achieve the following objectives:

- A general understanding of the program logic associated with a complex system
- A determination that valid transactions are being correctly processed by the application
- A determination that invalid or incorrect transactions are being correctly identified and flagged by the application's program controls

There are limitations in this testing approach. If a given transaction type has not been prepared for the test, internal audit cannot affirm that the application works correctly in respect to that transaction. If the documentation is incomplete or incorrect, internal audit may miss a key transaction test.

Test data CAATs can also be developed by tracing user-initiated transactions through a normal production cycle or by inputting a series of audit test transactions through a special test run of the application. There are advantages and disadvantages to each of these approaches.

(i) Tracing User-Initiated Transactions. An internal auditor sometimes must review and gather evidence of transaction controls for complex, online information systems applications. For example, internal audit may want to verify that a manu-facturing resource planning (MRP) system is operating with proper controls. Such a system generally has numerous programs to:

- Control the receipt of materials into the plant
- Place them in inventory
- Later retrieve them from stores and assign them to manufacturing work orders
- Add labor and other parts to complete the manufacturing process

These numerous and various transaction types, which update or affect mul-tiple programs, are difficult to assess through sample processing. When faced with a complex application, an internal auditor will often be unable to identify single points in the application process to develop comprehensive CAATs. A for-mal test data approach, where internal audit sets up a separate system process, is also difficult due to the overall complexity of the system.

The most reasonable approach to testing may be to trace a representative sample of normal transactions initiated through the production application. Fol-lowing the example of a manufacturing MRP system, an internal auditor should first identify key control points in the overall system. The next step is to observe and record transactions being entered at each of these points so that they can be subsequently traced to the appropriate online screens or reports. As part of this observation, internal audit may also want to ask users to input certain invalid transactions to ascertain that they have been correctly rejected. Exhibit 23.3 shows this user test data CAAT approach.

The tracing of user-initiated transactions is similar to the transaction walk-through approach for computer applications described in Chapter 21. The differ-ence here, however, is that an internal auditor captures a more substantial number of normal transactions for tracing and verification. This approach is not a true CAAT. However, it can often be combined with the use of other CAATs at key points in the application to gain a better understanding of the application's pro-cessing procedures and of its controls. For example, internal audit can trace inventory transactions input through the online screens of a manufacturing sys-tem. Combined with a CAAT, these could then be used to compare beginning and ending period inventory status files to highlight the differences caused by the production online transactions.

This procedure is more of a manual testing technique than a true CAAT. It also places emphasis on transaction input processing and the resultant outputs around the computer system rather than the actual operations of the component programs. It is often not the best way to gain positive assurance that an applica-tion is working with all of the proper controls. However, it can be an effective approach to gaining a level of assurance that the application appears to be work-ing with no obvious errors. While individual programs can be tested in some detail, this may be the only way to test an entire operational application.

(ii) Application Tests Using Test Data. This CAAT approach uses auditor-prepared test data transaction or test files. If an application has only one key input point, auditor-initiated test data entered through that point for processing in a

Exhibit 23.3

Test Data Computer-Assisted Audit Approach—User-Initiated Transactions

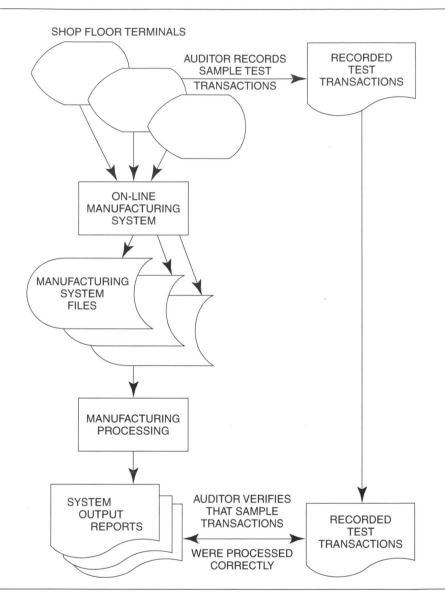

special run can often be an effective CAAT. For example, an organization may have an online labor hours collection system where employees input hours on a single-screen format for recording time and allocating the hours to various projects. Internal audit may be interested in verifying the integrity and correctness of the output data here.

An approach to testing this type of system is to build an audit file of representative test transactions for input to a special test run. These transactions represent differing valid and error conditions to allow internal audit to test as many conditions as possible through a special run of the application under review.

Live files or copies of live files can be used for all processing. The auditor's file of test transactions is input to this test run, and internal audit subsequently verifies the results of the systems processing. The test data approach can be an effective type of CAAT to gather evidence about smaller, self-contained information systems applications. Rather than using audit software to develop retrieval reports showing file contents, this technique allows internal audit to test program logic by passing test transactions against a set of live data files and production programs to verify the correctness of application processing. While the user-initiated transaction approach discussed previously has an internal auditor reviewing the results of an actual production transaction, this approach allows the auditor to develop a series of "can't happen" transactions to determine how systems controls are working in these extraordinary situations. The approach has some limitations:

- Data processing operations will sometimes object to internal audit's request to process a special run of one of their production applications for fear that the audit test data will somehow become intermingled with and corrupt the normal production data.

- Test data can only effectively test one cycle of an application. Due to the information systems operations disruptions this CAAT generally causes, it is usually difficult to schedule multiple test cycles.

- The approach is really only cost-effective for more self-contained applications, since it is difficult to design test data covering multiple input points.

- The preparation of a comprehensive set of test data often can be more time-consuming than the preparation of a conventional CAAT retrieval program.

Despite these limitations, a test data approach is often useful when internal audit reviews an application that has been implemented at multiple locations within the organization. By developing a standard set of test data and using it at each of the locations, internal audit can verify, among other things, that there have been no unauthorized changes to the application programs at the various remote locations.

(e) Specialized Audit Test and Analysis Software

Internal audit often has a need to review specialized computer files, such as those associated with the computer operating system or online transaction log files. This requires a very different type of CAAT than internal audit would develop for financial and operational application audit tests. Because computer operating systems and related files generally are very complex, generalized audit software will often not work. Generalized audit software works best with conventional files defined in fixed record and field lengths; this is often not true for systems software files that use very specialized file format structures.

An internal auditor is sometimes interested in monitoring the integrity of the mainframe computer's operating system or related parameter files. For example, IBM's older MVS operating system, once extensively used on their legacy system computers, contains numerous library files and parameter tables, which could be improperly manipulated to allow security and integrity violations. Specialized audit-analysis software can be used both to access these files and to identify potential operating system integrity exposures.

There are other specialized software tools today that a creative and technically skilled auditor can use to develop unique CAATs. Many are not specifically designed for auditors but for normal computer systems developers or end users. However, internal audit can often make very effective use of them including:

- Manufacturing production and materials scheduling software packages often contain ad hoc reporting subsystems to analyze these manufacturing files. Internal audit can use them to extract a sample of production part numbers for further testing.

- Software to control the movement of computer storage media in and out of a library often has an ad hoc reporting capability. With minimal training, an internal auditor can use these report-generator packages to test library operational and media management controls.

- Application programmers frequently use computer-aided systems engineering (CASE) software tools to help them build more effective new applications. CASE software can also be a very effective audit tool for developing process flowcharts and documenting applications.

Although typically not considered as CAAT software, there are numerous ad hoc retrieval or analysis software packages that can aid internal audit. Because such software is often easy to learn and use, internal audit need only to ask if such software is available when reviewing a specialized area or application. In other instances, internal audit may need to acquire certain specialized software tools to support audit efforts.

(f) Embedded Audit Procedures

Most conventional CAATs require an internal auditor to initiate some action to start the testing process. The CAAT will identify the condition only when it is processed as part of a scheduled, periodic audit. However, auditors often are interested in monitoring exception transactions within an application on an ongoing basis. Embedding audit software into a production application can provide continual monitoring for activities of interest and to report them for immediate or subsequent audit analysis. Earlier audit literature has referred to one of these approaches as the System Control Audit Review File (SCARF) method.

A second, related approach is called an Integrated Test Facility (ITF), an internal audit–established, built-in test data facility. Both might be better known as embedded audit procedures. In many respects, a continuous, embedded audit monitor is similar to the error- or exception-reporting mechanisms built into many conventional applications. It is also similar to the log file approach used for monitoring activities through a computer operating system. The major difference is that conventional application exception reports usually log all such problems and system log files record all activities. A continuous audit monitor only logs and reports items of predetermined audit interest. Also, application exception reports and system logs typically have a wide distribution while the audit monitors are reports for the exclusive use of internal audit. This general continuous audit monitor approach is discussed in Chapter 27, "Control Self-Assessments."

Both continuous audit monitors and ITFs allow internal auditors to have access to certain automated system conditions on an ongoing, continuous basis. Internal audit needs management support and commitment to devote audit resources to this type of effort. If audit management decides to implement these types of embedded audit procedures, they will have an expanded role in the organization's overall system of internal accounting controls.

(i) Continuous Audit Monitor Design and Implementation. As an example of a continuous audit monitor, assume that an auditor is working in a multi-branch financial organization with numerous transactions between these branches. Internal audit has reviewed the significant financial applications to test internal controls and has used generalized audit software to test key elements of the financial applications. However, the internal auditor is interested in monitoring and following up on certain exception transactions that may be initiated by various branch users from time to time.

The example application has a large number of exception reports for user follow up; internal audit is only interested in reviewing certain interbranch transactions above a specified dollar limit. While normal operational personnel also follow up on such transactions, internal audit is interested in the nature of such transactions and the level of follow-up activity. A continuous audit monitor CAAT can allow internal audit to review these ongoing exception transactions.

A continuous audit monitor CAAT is special, auditor-defined program code or software that gathers continuous evidence about transaction exceptions or potentially unauthorized items that may require auditor follow-up. This type of a monitor will not allow internal audit to perform detailed tests of an application but will collect the transaction data for subsequent testing and analysis. Because it must be built into a production set of programs, a continuous audit monitor CAAT should be installed only where internal audit has a strong, ongoing review interest.

Continuing with the above example, an internal auditor gains a detailed understanding of the application and identifies where the interbranch transactions of interest can be captured in the application. The information systems function then inserts program code into the application to monitor and capture all such transactions of interest. These are normally written into a protected log file for later audit review and analysis. Exhibit 23.4 illustrates how such a continuous audit monitor might be constructed.

Because a continuous audit monitor is an embedded set of program code, it cannot be easily changed. Internal audit should carefully design the objectives and selection criteria associated with any such monitor. Properly constructed, however, it can be an effective tool to independently monitor applications where internal audit has an ongoing interest. There are, however, some potential problems with this approach. First, internal audit is generally not able to implement such a

EXHIBIT 23.4

Continuous Audit Monitor Computer-Assisted Audit Approach

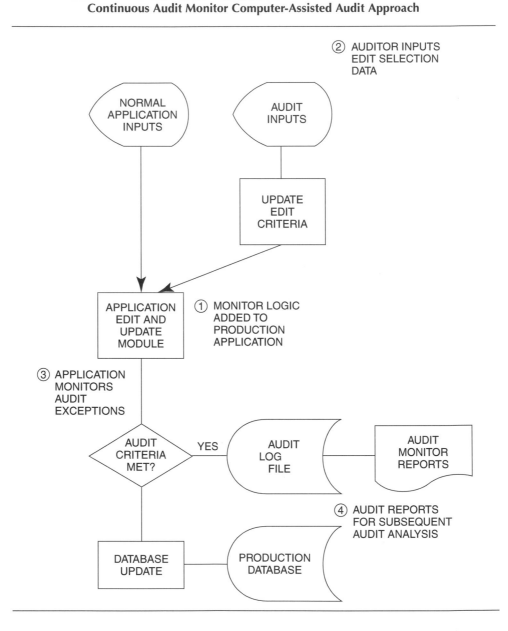

procedure independently, and needs the assistance of the IT department to build the monitor into a production application.

The other CAATs discussed previously in this chapter can often be established fairly independently by internal audit. Given an understanding of file structures, internal audit can use generalized audit software to perform various tests. Similarly, many test data procedures can be established independently. This is not true for many types of continuous audit monitors, which must be embedded into a normal production application. It is usually necessary for internal audit to work with the IT application development function to define the requirements of a monitor that can then be incorporated into the production application design. The most efficient time to suggest the implementation of such a monitor is when an application is being developed.

If appropriate, an internal auditor can request that a continuous audit monitor to be installed as part of the auditor's review of the system under development. Installing a continuous audit monitor in an application already operational is more difficult because it will require an application modification often requiring changes to all associated procedures. Internal audit should also recognize that because the IT function installs such a monitor, they will be aware of it and potentially have the ability to bypass its monitoring functions. Nevertheless, a continuous audit monitor can be a powerful tool to review certain exception items associated with critical transactions. Although the example cited was for a financial application, the procedure is also applicable to many other types of nonfinancial applications. In a manufacturing organization, internal audit could install such a monitor to log and report, for example, all scrap disposals above a specified limit.

(ii) Integrated Test Facilities. An integrated test facility (ITF) is an embedded audit module that allows an auditor to test an application on an ongoing or random basis. It differs from the continuous audit monitor, which records all production transactions of a certain activity or type. An ITF records only special test transactions that internal audit has independently input to the application. An example might better explain how an ITF is constructed and used. Similar to the continuous audit monitor example, assume that internal audit is interested in reviewing controls over a central financial system covering a large, multidivision organization. That central financial system receives transactions from its operating entities for both internal and interdivision financial entries. Each division included in the financial application is identified by a unique division code. In addition, the central organizational accounting function initiates transactions that affect all operating entities. An internal auditor may be interested in the controls over these various transactions as well as in any potentially improper accounting items.

An ITF allows internal audit to review this application on an ongoing basis. Internal audit might set up a dummy division number—such as "Division Code 99"—in the application's authorization files. All system reports for this Division Code 99 are then routed to the audit department. Internal audit inputs test transactions against this Division Code 99 to test the accuracy of the system and to verify program integrity. In addition, if other normal transactions impact all divisions, internal audit would be able to review them on their Division Code 99 reports. Exhibit 23.5 illustrates how such an ITF might be constructed. An ITF can be an effective test data type of CAAT for many forms of applications.

A special test run is not normally required as auditor transactions are entered with other normal transactions. Just as with other audit test CAATs, however, ITF transactions can then be compared to predetermined processing results in order to gather evidence about the application being tested. Internal audit can construct an ITF using two alternative approaches. First, the basic

EXHIBIT 23.5

Integrated Test Facility (ITF) Computer-Assisted Audit Approach

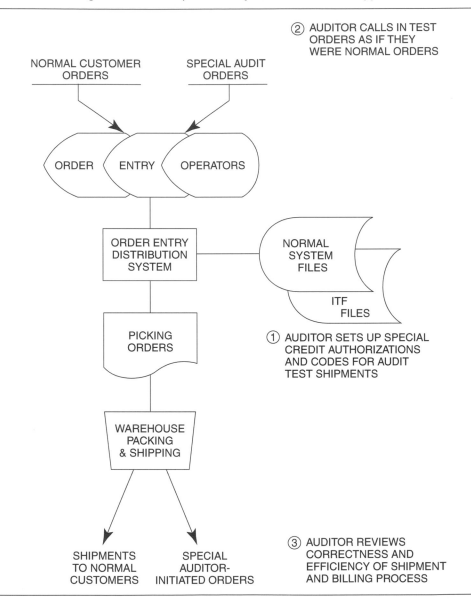

information systems application can remain unchanged, with auditors only inputting transactions against the designated auditor code—such as the Division Code 99 mentioned previously. It is then necessary to purge these transactions from the system only after the testing has been completed. For an accounting application, this can sometimes be as simple as entering reversal transactions to the system. However, this reversal process is often much more complex. For example, many accounting systems have allocation processes that may affect all balances in the system; it is important that internal audit's ITF test data does not cause other account balances to be altered. A second approach to building the ITF is to add a program or modify existing programs to filter out any audit transactions. This way, internal audit's test transactions can be transparent to other users of the system. The problem with this method is the special programming required to build the filter. If the IT department is one of the functions being examined, the integrity of the tests potentially could be compromised.

In either event, an ITF is an advanced approach to testing and gathering evidence about an automated application. Because of the program coding and logistics required to establish an ITF, the technique is difficult to establish and should be used only when internal audit has a strong, ongoing interest in reviewing an application. In addition, an internal auditor responsible for implementing the procedure should have a thorough understanding of all aspects of the target application before starting the ITF. Otherwise, internal audit's ITF transaction activities may have unintended effects.

Several other areas of caution should be considered before constructing an ITF. In some regulated industries—such as financial institutions—auditors may be in violation of state or federal statutes by establishing fictitious accounts in financial applications. Internal audit should discuss any ITF plans with the organization's consul, if appropriate. Internal audit should also take care to make certain that only a limited number of personnel are aware of the ITF. If it is generally known, for example, that Division Code 99 is internal audit's number, anyone making improper transactions will see that this code is bypassed. In a very general sense, any program developed or controlled by internal audit is a type of audit software. However, internal audit generally does not want to develop programs in a language such as C^{++} because of the development time requirements.

Because of concerns with efficiency, internal audit should use generalized audit software, such as the previously discussed ACL, or similar retrieval software for many of its CAATs. Which approach to use depends very much on the computer hardware and software environment, the current availability of software tools, auditor technical knowledge, and, most important, internal audit's CAAT objectives. In a larger information systems environment with centralized computer systems, generalized audit software is often the preferred alternative. It offers some of the following advantages:

- *Fast Learning Curves.* Auditors with even limited IT knowledge can easily build audit test and retrieval applications.

- *Preprogrammed Audit Functions.* The software generally has functions of audit interest, such as gap sequence number checking, built into the software.

- *Limited Coding Requirements.* Although the software is primarily designed for simple, "quick-and-dirty" retrieval reports, these can be produced with very few coding steps.

- *Specialized File-Processing Capabilities.* Many generalized audit software packages have the ability to read specialized system's files, such as the SMF log files found on large-scale IBM systems.

As can be expected, there are also some severe disadvantages in the use of generalized audit software, mostly because it was originally developed for larger, mainframe types of computer systems using batch-oriented simple file structures. The software often cannot easily read more complex file structures. Other disadvantages include:

- *Limited Equipment and Software Availability.* In addition to the unavailability for some computer operating systems, the software often cannot directly access many types of database systems.

- *Relatively High Cost.* A generalized audit software package may cost an audit department from $15,000 to $20,000, or more, with an annual maintenance fee from $5,000 to $8,000 per year. If only limited usage is planned, this may seem too expensive.

- *Limited Transportability.* Auditors in many larger organizations are faced with multiple computer sites that have differing operating environments. Equipment differences or software license restrictions may prevent transporting the audit software package to multiple sites.

A report generator is often the most cost-effective mainframe-oriented audit software tool for many audit organizations today. Internal audit can use and share the costs of a software package used in various other parts of the organization. Often, the report generator retrieval tool can accomplish most of internal audit's CAAT objectives despite its lack of specialized audit functions.

Desktop system audit software provides some unique advantages in many situations. Files can be downloaded to an auditor's computer within the audit department rather than having an internal auditor work directly in information systems operations. Although this tool was developed for external auditors, new computer hardware and audit products are making it increasingly attractive for internal auditors.

The decision of which CAAT software to use depends very much on overall audit objectives. Internal audit should consider the appropriate type of audit software, depending on overall audit objectives, the equipment environment, auditor information systems skill levels, and budget constraints.

23.4 STEPS TO BUILDING EFFECTIVE CAATS

Internal auditors should follow the same approach for developing CAATs whether using generalized audit software, a report generator retrieval language, or data downloaded to an auditor's laptop computer. This approach is similar to the systems development methodology (SDM) approach discussed in Chapter 21. The difference here is that an internal auditor may develop a CAAT for a one-time or limited-use effort rather than for an ongoing production application. Because internal audit often draws conclusions and makes rather significant recommendations based on the results of a CAAT, it is important to use good systems practices to design and test CAATs. The following is a four-step approach to developing a CAAT:

1. **Determine Audit Objectives of the Computer-Assisted Audit Application.** It is not sufficient for internal audit just to audit the automated accounting system. All too often an internal audit manager will just direct

a staff auditor to write a CAAT for some audit without fully defining its objectives. The desired audit objectives should be clearly defined; this will make the subsequent identification of testing procedures a much easier task. Once internal audit has defined CAAT objectives, file layouts and systems flowcharts should be obtained to select the appropriate data sources for testing. Sometimes at this point, an internal auditor encounters technical problems that might impede further progress. A CAAT documentation file or workpaper should also be started along with this step.

2. **Design the Computer-Assisted Application.** The CAAT software tool used must be well understood, including its features, the overall program logic, and its reporting formats. Any special codes or other data characteristics must be discussed with persons responsible for the computer application. Consideration should also be given to how internal audit will prove the results of audit tests by, for example, balancing to production application control totals. These matters should be outlined in the documentation workpapers.

3. **Program or Code and Then Test the Application.** This task usually follows Step 2 very closely. Programming is performed using the generalized audit software or some other selected software tool. Once the CAAT has been programmed, internal audit should arrange to test it on a limited population of data. The results must be verified for both correctness of program logic and the achievement of desired audit objectives. This activity should also be documented in the workpapers. Correctness of program logic means the CAAT must *work*. Sometimes an error in coding will cause the application to fail to process. The failure to achieve audit objectives is a different kind of problem. For example, in a CAAT to survey conditions in an inventory file, an auditor may make too broad of a selection, producing an output report of thousands of minor exceptions. Such CAAT logic should be revised to produce a more reasonably sized selection.

4. **Process and Complete the CAAT.** Making arrangements for processing the CAAT often requires coordination between internal audit and IT operations. Internal audit is often interested in a specific generation of a data file, and it is necessary to arrange access to it. During the actual processing, internal audit must take steps to ensure that the files tested are the correct versions.

Depending on the nature of the CAAT, an internal auditor should prove the results and follow up on any exceptions as required. If there are problems with the CAAT logic, internal audit should make corrections as required and repeat the steps. The CAAT application workpapers should be completed at this point, including follow-up points for improving the CAAT for future periods.

Computer-assisted audit techniques are powerful tools that can be used by any auditor, and should not be solely the responsibility of a computer audit specialist. Just as end users make increasing use of retrieval tools for their own information systems needs, all members of an audit department should gain an understanding of available audit tools to allow them to develop their own CAATs.

Of course, as more and more automated processes become paperless, the auditor's need to build and use CAATs will increase. That is, the traditional paper trails that auditors use to trace and validate transactions are reduced or even eliminated in today's modern automated system. Audit tools ranging from generalized audit software to continuous audit monitors will increasingly become the only options available to test and gather evidence about these paperless systems. Many operational systems today have some very strong paperless elements. For example, both electronic data interchange (EDI) systems and the automatic teller machines (ATMs) used by financial institutions have very limited paper trails, and the only way to effectively audit such applications is through the use of CAATs. An internal auditor must be creative when designing a CAAT to gather evidence regarding these paperless applications, and many of the techniques described in this chapter apply.

23.5 IMPORTANCE OF CAATS FOR AUDIT EVIDENCE GATHERING

Internal auditors often do not give sufficient attention to the need to gather evidence when reviewing automated applications. It is often an interesting and challenging audit task to gain an understanding of an automated application and to evaluate its internal controls. However, detailed confirmations of account balances or other types of evidence-gathering tests are sometimes viewed by some internal auditors as not as interesting and too time-consuming. However, these evidence-gathering procedures often provide internal audit with opportunities to implement the most creative portion of the audit project. Assume, for example, that internal audit has performed detailed internal controls–oriented review of a large fixed-asset capital budgeting application where transactions are initiated from a variety of subsidiary systems and where the application eventually provides general ledger financial statement balances. Internal audit has tested system-to-system internal controls and concludes that they are adequate; they have also manually recalculated the depreciation expenses for several selected transactions and found them to be correct.

Can an internal auditor conclude that the fixed assets and accumulated depreciation numbers produced by this sample system are accurate? In a large organization, where fixed assets may represent a substantial portion of the balance sheet, an internal auditor may decide that there is far too great of a risk in relying solely on just this internal controls review. The several transactions selected for a recalculation compliance test may not be representative of the entire population, and there may be an error in certain classes of these transactions. Although application-to-application controls may have appeared proper, some types of transactions may be assigned to incorrect account groups. Without detailed CAAT based testing of this example fixed-assets system, it is possible that these errors could go undetected.

Auditors should have an understanding of when it is cost-effective and appropriate to develop CAATs to perform detailed tests of information systems applications in order to verify the correctness of transactions or account balances.

Some of the circumstances when internal audit should perform this more detailed application evidence gathering and testing include:

- There is a perception that the risk of relying just on documented internal controls is too high.

- Although internal audit may have performed limited walkthrough or compliance types of tests, the results of these tests may be somewhat inconclusive and will suggest a need for more detailed tests.

- In some instances, certain internal controls may be weak or difficult to identify, and internal audit may want to develop CAATs to perform detailed tests of the automated applications.

- Some complex or large automated applications are involved, such as the comprehensive ERP systems discussed in Chapter 21.

In many instances, the decision whether to rely just on internal controls reviews and limited compliance testing or to perform detailed tests of transactions will be a decision of audit management. However, the use of CAATs should be a key internal audit tool to employ in many situations. The nature of the audit tests to be performed, the extent of data, the complexity of the application, and the tools and skills available to internal audit should all be factors in this decision. Internal audit should become familiar with the various software products and techniques available for analyzing and testing computer system files. The implementation and processing of CAATs should be part of the skill set requirement for all internal auditors.

ENDNOTES

[1] *Computer-Assisted Audit Techniques*, American Institute of Certified Public Accountants, New York. Auditing guide now out of print.
[2] ACL Services Ltd., Vancouver, B.C., Canada.

PART SIX

Internal Auditor Tools and Trends

CHAPTER TWENTY-FOUR

HIPAA and Growing Concerns Regarding Privacy

24.1 BEYOND SARBANES-OXLEY: GROWING PRIVACY CONCERNS

As emphasized throughout this book, the Sarbanes-Oxley Act (SOA) is the most significant U.S. accounting and securities legislation since the early 1930s. While it certainly has launched a series of what we have called "new rules" for corporate governance and financial statement auditing, other recent legislation has also introduced other new rules that will have an impact on many internal auditors as well. This chapter will introduce two other newer federal acts that both have a privacy protection focus and will affect many modern organizations and their internal auditors. Federal legislation is often named after its main legislative sponsors. Senator Sarbanes and Representative Oxley have brought us SOA, as an example. Another newer law, named after its sponsors, is the Gramm-Leach-Bliley Act of 1999 (GLBA). GLBA requires financial institutions to further protect and audit their data and to take special care when sharing this data with others. While directed at financial institutions, GLBA affects many organizations, and this chapter will discuss its main components impacting internal auditors. Another act, the Health Insurance

Portability and Accountability Act (HIPAA) has introduced another set of privacy and security rules covering personal health-care records. While its focus is on health-care providers, HIPAA covers the kinds of personal privacy records that affect all U.S. organizations, and it has caused changes in such areas as information systems security and human resources functions. Internal auditors should have a general understanding of these still-evolving GLBA and HIPAA rules. Although focused on consumer finance and health-care issues that will not directly affect every internal auditor today, both have important privacy provisions that may soon become important in other, broader areas.

It is sometimes difficult to predict when new legislation will have a continuing and lasting impact or whether it will be just a law on the books with little ongoing compliance activity. The fifth edition of *Brink's Modern Internal Auditing*[1] for example, talked about the Foreign Corrupt Practices Act (FCPA) of the late 1970s. That legislation seemingly had some strong internal control documentation requirements that initially had many internal auditors thinking they would be kept very busy over the years keeping their organizations in compliance with these FCPA provisions. While the legislation remains on the books, there has been limited enforcement action since its enactment, and the FCPA's requirements covering internal control documentation have been all but forgotten by many today. We do not think that GLBA or HIPAA and certainly not SOA will go the same way as the FCPA, but such legislation and regulatory interests rise and fall. At the present time, internal auditors need to be aware of this privacy-related legislation and plan their review and internal control activities accordingly.

24.2 GRAMM-LEACH-BLILEY ACT

Officially known as the Financial Modernization Act of 1999, the Gramm-Leach-Bliley Act is a privacy related set of requirements with an objective of protecting consumers' personal financial information held by financial institutions. This privacy-related legislation has three principal parts: (1) the Financial Privacy Rule, (2) the Safeguards Rule, and (3) what are called "pretexting provisions." Each of these will be discussed in the following sections. GLBA gives authority to eight different federal agencies and the states to administer and enforce a new set of privacy-release rules that apply to what are generally called "financial institutions." These institutions include not only traditional banks, securities firms, and insurance companies, but also organizations providing many other types of financial products and services to consumers. Among these services are lending, brokering, or servicing any type of consumer loans; transferring or safeguarding money; preparing individual tax returns; providing financial advice or credit counseling; providing residential real estate settlement services; collecting consumer debts; and an array of other activities. With GLBA, these nontraditional "financial institutions" are now regulated by the Federal Trade Commission (FTC) either directly or through other federal and state agencies.

While an internal auditor working for a bank or insurance company today probably has been involved with the 1999 GLBA and its privacy-related provisions, the act is a newer rule that may affect many other organizations due to its expanded definition of what are called "financial institutions." GLBA rules are also being applied to many state-regulated financial institutions. As an example, insurance companies in the United States are regulated on a state-by-state basis with the National Association of Insurance Commissioners (NAIC) acting as a central coordinating and standards-setting group for these state chartered insurance commissions. The NAIC has imposed the federally mandated GLBA rules on its individual state regulated insurance companies. This is another example of how U.S. federal regulations move in some instances from a U.S. authority like the SEC, for SOA matters, to rules covering state laws as well as the similar international rules discussed in Chapter 29, "ISO and Internal Audit Worldwide Standards." We often forget that in the United States some corporate regulations and many other legislative rules are effective on a state-by-state basis. For example, motor vehicle driver licenses are issued by each of the states. Similarly, although the CPA examination is administered by the AICPA, CPAs are licensed on an individual state basis through individual boards of accountancy. Through the authority of the NAIC, a state-rule-coordinating body, GLBA rules are being adopted by most to the states in the United States.

(a) GLBA Financial Privacy Rules

U.S. consumers frequently encounter the GLBA and its Financial Privacy Rule today when they receive an often innocuous note from a credit card provider talking about their privacy rules for that credit card. The GLBA Financial Privacy Rule requires financial institutions to give their customers these privacy notices that explain the financial institution's information collection and sharing practices. This privacy notice must be a clear, conspicuous, and accurate statement of the company's privacy practices; it should include what information the company collects about its consumers and customers, with whom it shares this consumer credit information, and how it protects or safeguards the information. The notice applies to the "nonpublic personal information" the company gathers and discloses about its consumers and customers; in practice, that may be most—or all—of the information a company has about its customers. For example, nonpublic personal information could include the information that a consumer or customer puts on a credit or sales contract application; information about the individual from another source, such as a credit bureau; or information about transactions between the individual and the company, such as an account balance. Indeed, even the fact that an individual is listed as a consumer or customer of a particular financial institution is classified under GLBA as nonpublic personal information. Matters that an organization has reason to believe are lawfully public—such as mortgage loan information in a jurisdiction where that information is publicly recorded—are not restricted by GLBA.

GLBA-mandated privacy notices must contain the following information elements:

- The types of nonpublic personal information that an organization collects regarding its customer
- The types of nonpublic personal information the organization will disclose to others about the customer
- The parties to whom the organization discloses this information, other than under an exception to the prohibition on nondisclosure

- The customer or client's right to "opt out" of the disclosure along with simple rules for opting out

- Organization policies with respect to sharing information on a person who is no longer a customer or client

- Organization practices for protecting the confidentiality and security of the customer or clients' nonpublic personal information

Many consumers today pay little attention to these privacy notices even though they may state that the company that has their account data may share the consumer's name with others. Rather than the all-too-common consumer practice of crumpling and tossing this note, GLBA gives the customer the right to opt out of—or say no to—having this consumer private information shared with certain third parties. The privacy notice must explain how—and offer a reasonable way—they can opt out. For example, providing a toll-free telephone number or a detachable form with a preprinted address is a reasonable way for consumers or customers to opt out; but requiring someone to write a letter as the only way to opt out is not. The privacy notice also must explain that consumers have a right to say no to the sharing of certain information, such as credit report or application information, with the financial institution's separate divisions or affiliates.

GLBA puts some limits on how anyone that receives nonpublic personal information from a financial institution can use or redisclose the information. If a lender discloses customer information to a service provider responsible for mailing account statements, where the consumer has no right to opt out, that service provider may use the information only for limited purposes—such as, for mailing account statements—and may not sell the information or use it for marketing.

This GLBA Federal Privacy Rule gets more complex as we get into its details. Our intention here is not to give such a detailed explanation of this portion of GLBA, but to explain these privacy rules in general. An internal auditor should recognize that all personal financial information is very private and cannot just be arbitrarily sold or otherwise distributed. Consumers have rights to opt out, or say no, and the organization must keep appropriate records of these actions and respect consumer privacy rights. Internal auditors working with any financial institutions or applications should be aware of how GLBA privacy applies to the internal auditor's organization. The same is true for any organization that has a consumer-related credit granting and billing facility. A risk to an organization is that they may take the GLBA Privacy rules as an almost trivial matter, perhaps fail to honor an opt-out request or improperly sell a mailing list and then find them facing some type of class action litigation for damages due to the failure to comply.

(b) GLBA Safeguards Rule

The act's Safeguards Rule requires financial institutions to have a security plan in place to protect the confidentiality and integrity of personal consumer information. When consumers open an account or purchase some product, they will often disclose some element of personal information—such as an address, telephone number or credit card number—as part of that application transaction process. An organization must have a security plan in place to protect the confidentiality and integrity of that personal data. It should cover more that just the business continuity risks discussed in Chapter 18, "Business Continuity Planning and Disaster Recovery," and should include controls to prevent hackers from accessing data files, disgruntled employees from accessing customer information, or just simple carelessness. The GLBA Safeguards Rule requires that every financial institution, regardless of size, must create and implement a written information security plan for the protection of customer data. The scope and complexity of this security plan may be scaled to the size of the institution and the sensitivity of the information it maintains. The plan should be based on a risk analysis that identifies all foreseeable threats to the security, confidentiality, and integrity of customer information. Based on that risk analysis, financial institutions must document and implement security measures that include administrative measures such as employee training, technical protections including passwords, encryption controls and firewalls, and physical safeguards such as locks on doors and computers. Financial institutions must designate one or more of their employees to coordinate these safeguards, and must conduct periodic reviews to determine whether their security programs require updating in light of changed circumstances.

Internal auditors should be aware of how an organization can start becoming compliant with the GLBA safeguard rule through the following steps:

1. **Environmental Risk Analysis.** The organization should formally identify the internal and external risks to the security, confidentiality and integrity of all customer personal information. Risk analysis approaches were discussed in Chapter 5, "Understanding and Assessing Risks: Enterprise Risk Management." This process should cover all sources of personal information, whether on automated systems or manual records.

2. **Designing and Implementing Safeguards.** These safeguards are essentially the internal control procedures discussed in Chapter 4, "Internal Controls Fundamentals: COSO Framework," as part of the COSO framework and elsewhere throughout this book.

3. **Monitoring and Auditing.** Continuous monitoring processes, such as those discussed in Chapter 25, "Continuous Assurance Auditing, XBRL, and OLAP," should be in place. Internal audit can play an important monitoring and auditing role here by regularly scheduling reviews of the adequacy of the security plan, coupled with appropriate compliance tests.

4. **Constant Improvements Program.** As a result of any weaknesses found in audits or other tests, the organization should have a program in place to constantly improve its security plan. That program should be well documented to describe the plan's progress.

5. **Overseeing Security Providers and Partners.** Many partners and other organizations may have access to this same personal information or may just have access to systems network connections where that personal privacy can potentially be violated. Adequate policies, controls, and audit procedures need to be in place here as well.

The GLBA Safeguards Rule applies to a wide range of providers of financial products and services, including mortgage brokers, nonbank lenders, appraisers, credit reporting agencies, and professional tax preparers, as well as retailers that issue their own credit cards. Banks are not subject to the Safeguards Rule, but must comply with similar counterpart regulations that have been issued by federal banking agencies. Failure to comply with the Safeguards Rule may result in fines or other enforcement action by the FTC.

(c) GLBA Pretexting Provisions

Using an expression that will set off spell-checkers in most word-processing programs, GLBA prohibits "pretexting," the use of false pretenses, including fraudulent statements and impersonation, to obtain consumers' personal financial information, such as bank balances, under false pretenses. Pretexters use a variety of tactics to get personal information. For example, a Pretexter may call, claim she's from a survey firm, ask a few questions to perhaps get the name of one's bank, and then use the information gathered to call the target person's financial institution, pretending to be that targeted person or someone with authorized access to that account. She might claim that she's forgotten her checkbook and needs information about the account. In this way, the pretexter may be able to obtain personal information about the target victim such as a Social Security number, bank and credit card account numbers, information in someone's credit report, and the existence and size of personal savings and investment portfolios.

Under GLBA's pretexting provisions, it is illegal for anyone to:

- Use false, fictitious or fraudulent statements or documents to get customer information from a financial institution or directly from a customer of a financial institution

- Use forged, counterfeit, lost, or stolen documents to get customer information from a financial institution or directly from a customer of a financial institution

- Ask another person to get someone else's customer information using false, fictitious, or fraudulent statements or using false, fictitious or fraudulent documents or forged, counterfeit, lost, or stolen documents

Pretexting leads to a new security and privacy risk or exposure, "identity theft." This occurs when someone hijacks your personal identifying information to open new charge accounts, order merchandise, or borrow money. Consumers targeted by identity thieves usually don't know they've been victimized until the hijackers fail to pay the bills or repay the loans, and collection agencies begin dunning the consumers for payment of accounts they didn't even know they had. According to the FTC, the most common forms of identity theft are:

- *Credit Card Fraud.*   A credit card account is opened in a consumer's name or an existing credit card account is "taken over."

- *Communications Services Fraud.*   The identity thief opens telephone, cellular, or other utility service in the consumer's name.

- *Bank Fraud.*   A checking or savings account is opened in the consumer's name, and/or fraudulent checks are written.

- *Fraudulent Loans.* The identity thief gets a loan, such as a car loan, in the consumer's name.

A separate federal law, related to GLBA, The Identity Theft and Assumption Deterrence Act, makes it a federal crime when someone: "knowingly transfers or uses, without lawful authority, a means of identification of another person with the intent to commit, or to aid or abet, any unlawful activity that constitutes a violation of federal law, or that constitutes a felony under any applicable state or local law." Here, a name or Social Security number is considered a "means of identification," as is a credit card number, cellular telephone electronic serial number, or any other piece of information that may be used alone or in conjunction with other information to identify a specific individual.

GLBA is one of the new rules that will impact many internal auditors, particularly those working in any type of financial institution. While many aspects of GLBA are designed to protect consumer financial information, that definition has become so broad that GLBA affects a wide range of organizations and many internal auditors in the United States.

24.3 AUDITING FOR GLBA COMPLIANCE

Internal auditors working with financial and credit-granting organizations should become more aware of these GLBA rules as well as their general privacy rules that are applicable for many other organizations. The Web is the most appropriate source to obtain additional more detailed and current information on the act and its provisions. Two good sources are:

1. **Federal Trade Commission (FTC).** This government source provides an overview view of GLBA as well as its most current rules at: http://www.ftc.gov/privacy/glbact/.

2. **National Association of Insurance Commissioners (NAIC).** This is a state-by-state regulatory organization that has good GLBA information at: http://www.naic.org/GLBA/.

Exhibit 24.1 provides some general rules and steps for auditing compliance with GLBA controls and procedures. While these audit procedures must be expanded for some organizations, the objective of this exhibit is to provide some general audit steps to consider for an operational review of financial institutions to demonstrate GLBA compliance.

EXHIBIT 24.1

Audit Procedures for Gramm-Leach-Bliley Compliance

Internal audit should meet with financial management and counsel to assess whether the organization can be defined as a "financial institution" under the terms of the Gramm-Leach-Bliley Act (GLBA). If affected, internal audit procedures should include:

1. Determine the organization regularly sends out financial privacy notices, and assess follow-up procedures in place to correct returned letters or to provide answers to customers regarding these notices.

2. Assess record keeping and other controls regarding the privacy notice opt-out rules. Select a sample of customers who have requested to opt out and determine these privacy procedures are operating.

EXHIBIT 24.1 *(CONTINUED)*

Audit Procedures for Gramm-Leach-Bliley Compliance

3. Review general record privacy and security procedures over all GLBA-affected materials. Good practices here will include strong information systems password controls and office procedures covering paper-oriented records.

4. Determine that the organization has a formal security plan in place to protect the security and confidentiality of personal consumer information.

5. Determine that an environmental risk analysis is in place to formally identify all internal and external risks to the security, confidentiality, and integrity of all customer personal information.

6. Review continuous monitoring processes in place surrounding controls over customer personal information and assess their adequacy.

7. Review the adequacy of constant improvement programs surrounding GLBA security controls and comment on their adequacy.

8. Assess the adequacy of information programs within the organization to inform all employees of the requirements of GLBA and their need to protect customers' personal information.

9. Determine that adequate controls are in place to prevent violations of GLBA pretexting provisions.

10. Determine that the organization has taken adequate steps to inform other related organizations of GLBA provisions.

24.4 HIPAA: HEALTH-CARE AND MUCH MORE

A U.S.-based internal auditor today who is visiting a doctor for an annual physical or some other procedure will be asked to sign what looks like an innocuous disclosure permission agreement when checking in at the front desk. These permission documents ask the patient to agree to allow his or her medical records to potentially be shared or disclosed as part of that visit. If the auditor-patient asks why, the response will usually be that this is a "legal requirement of HIPAA." The medical patient's typical reaction is to sign the document and move on, not fully understanding this signature request. Although a health-care-related set of rules, HIPAA contains a set of privacy-related legislative rules that go beyond health care and will have an impact on many organizations and their internal auditors.

An internal auditor for a manufacturing company or a financial services organization might ask, "Why should I care about HIPAA?" Enacted in 1999 with some final rules still not released at the publication date of this book, the Health Insurance Portability and Accountability Act (HIPAA) has a major impact on the privacy and security of personal medical records as well as on many other personal records going forward. Individuals encounter HIPAA when visiting a doctor's office or for many other medical related matters. Human resources functions in organizations also are seeing the impact of HIPAA requirements today in their administration of employee health-care plans and medical treatment records. Of course, HIPAA has caused a large and ever-growing impact on the entire health-care industry and all affiliated delivery providers. Even more significantly, it will improve standards for a wide range of electronic-commerce-based business processes.

The original HIPAA legislation has four primary objectives:

1. Ensure health portability by eliminating preexisting condition job locks. This was the original motivation for the passage of HIPAA. People were diagnosed with some condition and then unable to acquire new health coverage when changing employers because information about that individual health condition was often cavalierly shared with others.

2. Reduce health-care fraud and abuse. The congressional hearings leading to this legislation were filled with comments and examples of alleged health-care fraud and abuse.

3. Enforce standards for health information. This is covered by the HIPAA privacy and security rules outlined below.

4. Guarantee security and privacy of health information.

This section will provide a brief overview of HIPAA objectives and the resultant rules covering privacy and security. While not an exhaustive introduction to all aspects of HIPAA, the paragraphs that follow will introduce it as another of the legislatively driven "new rules" that will affect many internal auditors. The progress of the HIPAA legislation illustrates how the government sponsored rule-making process often works and, perhaps, shows that we can expect the new PCAOB auditing standards rules will take some time to completely develop and be issued. HIPAA rules were initially issued in draft form following an early published schedule, the drafts resulted in lots of comments, revised rules drafts were issued with still more comments, and the final rules were issued much later that originally planned. The PCAOB auditing standards rules to come, discussed in Chapter 3, "Internal Audit in the Twenty-First Century: Sarbanes-Oxley and Beyond," will probably proceed in a similar manner.

(a) HIPAA Patient Record Privacy Rules

Ongoing concerns regarding medical patient privacy were the motivating reasons for the U.S. Congress originally passing HIPAA. We visit a medical care provider, discuss some concern or problem, and then expect treatment in a manner that is confidential or private. We do not want the results of that medical office or physician visit to be communicated back to our employer's human resource department, to some other insurance company that has no need to know, or to be left on a desk in the medical care provider's office for anyone to pick up. Even worse, we do not want any personal, confidential matters to be shared in a manner that may limit our future employment options. This personal information privacy concern is the basis for much of HIPAA. However, many parties need to have some information about our health-care condition to provide adequate coverage or reimbursement, and virtually all health-care operations require detailed and complex supporting systems. HIPAA privacy rules cover five general areas as are briefly outlined in the paragraphs following.

These comments do not provide an exhaustive coverage of and are not intended to be a reference source for HIPAA rules; they are intended to provide the non-medical professional with an overview of these HIPAA new rules:

- *Medical Records Uses and Disclosures.* An organization that is subject to HIPAA rules must take steps to limit the use and disclosure of personal medical information to "the minimum necessary to accomplish the intended purpose of the use, disclosure, or request" for nontreatment-related matters. We start this overview of HIPAA rules by directly quoting some of the words contained in the HIPAA rules. Using words such as "the minimum necessary" the act contains many such guidelines that will be subject to specific organization-by-organization practices that are to be validated through other rulings or litigation over time.

  This section of HIPAA rules goes on to specify that individual health information loses its HIPAA protection if the individual covered is "de-identified" in a manner such that this health information will not contain any of 18 specific identifiers of the individual and his or her relatives, employers, or household members. This requirement says a lot about HIPAA. In order to make a health-related information system HIPAA compliant, the legislation identifies these 18 specific factors that a specialist in database retrieval might use to identify an individual. That is, an individual's medical information that is placed in some type of file or information system is generally protected from general disclosure to others, but that information can be shared if it meets certain specific conditions.

- *Authorization Requirements.* This is the section of HIPAA that many users of health-care services first encounter. Health-care providers must obtain written approval to disclose health-care information on everything with the exception of emergency situations. An individual has the right to refuse such a disclosure and health-care providers must have a strong record retention requirement to keep track of all of these disclosures. These are the documents, as previously discussed, that an individual is asked to sign when visiting a physician's office.

- *Privacy Practice Communications.* Health-care providers must have published Privacy Practices that they should provide to health-care users. Individuals then have the right to formally request restrictions in this policy, and providers must accommodate reasonable requests.

- *Medical Record Access and Amendment Rights.* Individuals have the right to inspect and copy all or a portion of their personal health information. In addition, individuals have the right to request amendments to those health-care records. Finally, the health-care provider must keep a record of all other parties that requested access to these personal health-care records in the six-month period prior to any request.

- *HIPAA Privacy Administration.* Going beyond the records access and disclosure rules, HIPAA has an extensive set of privacy administrative requirements. These rules apply to what are called "covered entities"—medical offices, laboratories, hospitals, and all others involved with personal health care. These privacy administration rules include:

○ The provider must designate a "privacy official" who is responsible for the development and implementation of HIPAA policies and procedures.

○ The provider must train members of its workforce on these HIPAA privacy-related policies and procedures and must maintain documentation to demonstrate that the training has been provided.

○ A health-care provider must have in place administrative, technical, and physical safeguards to protect the privacy of personal health information.

○ The health-care provider must apply "appropriate sanctions" against employees who fail to comply with these privacy polices and procedures.

○ The provider must develop and implement policies and procedures that are designed to comply with the elements of the HIPAA regulations, and this documentation must be maintained in written or electronic form for six years.

While these HIPAA rules cover access to personal health-care information, they outline other areas that really define good operating practices that should be implemented elsewhere in the organization. An example would be the requirement that health-care providers maintain documentation covering their training programs. These types of rules have existed for FDA medical or drug programs, are now part of HIPAA, and are a good idea for most corporate training programs. Organizations sometimes spend resources in training their employees but do not bother to document that activity very well.

These rules and others in this chapter are important to an internal auditor working in a health-care-related organization, such as a hospital or medical claims insurance company. However, the rules extend to other areas as well such as medical insurance claims processing in an organization's human resources department or factory floor safety and accident reporting. Health-care-related organizations should have strong HIPAA compliance rules and procedures, but it is beyond the scope of this book to provide a detailed description of these rules. However, internal auditors will encounter areas where HIPAA compliance is required in many other environments. Exhibit 24.2 describes some HIPAA health-care procedures that should be in place in any organization

EXHIBIT 24.2

Internal Audit HIPAA Requirements Procedures

1. Is the organization defined as a health-care-related organization and subject to HIPAA rules? If not, there is no need to complete the steps.

2. Has an enterprise-wide information security officer been appointed for HIPAA compliance and has a general implementation plan been developed?

3. Have policies and procedures to protect patient health information been developed and implemented?

EXHIBIT 24.2 *(CONTINUED)*

Internal Audit HIPAA Requirements Procedures

4. Is there a process for the ongoing support and monitoring of HIPAA rules and regulations?

5. Are processes in place to develop comprehensive privacy and security policies, procedures, controls, and technologies?

6. Does the organization have a formal contingency plan in place that includes:
  - Application and data criticality analysis
  - Data backup planning
  - Disaster recovery plans
  - Emergency mode operations plan
  - Periodic testing and revisions to the plan

7. Are there formal information access control processes, including access authorization, access establishment rules, and access modification procedures?

8. Controls over access to information systems media should include processes for:
  - Accountability
  - Data backup
  - Data storage
  - Disposal of data

9. Personnel security policy/procedures should:
  - Ensure the supervision of maintenance personnel by an authorized, knowledgeable person
  - Maintain a complete record of access authorizations
  - Ensure that operating and maintenance personnel have proper access authorization
  - Include a personnel clearance procedure

10. Formal termination procedures should be in place, including the changing of appropriate combination locks and the removal from access lists.

11. Physical access controls throughout the facility should include:
  - Emergency mode operation plans
  - Equipment control into and out of facility
  - Facility security plans
  - Procedures for verifying access authorizations prior to physical access
  - Maintenance records
  - Need-to-know procedures for personnel access
  - Sign-in for visitors and escorts, if appropriate
  - Testing and revisions to the physical access plan

12. All networks and communications should be protected through:
  - Automatic logoff
  - Unique user identification
  - Passwords and PINs
  - Telephone callbacks

(b) Cryptography, PKI, and HIPAA Security Requirements

In addition to its medical records authorization and release privacy rules, HIPAA contains some very specific and, in many respects, difficult-to-implement information systems security requirements. It pushes to the edges of common computer security practices today and requires such things as secure electronic signatures even though, at the time of this publication, there are no technically mature techniques to provide such security on open networks such as the Internet. We are still at a point where a skilled computer hacker can intercept a cell phone call and such a call covering health-care-related matters could create a violation of HIPAA security requirements. Technology will change, control procedures will improve, the hackers will get ever smarter, and violations will be settled in the courts.

The basic reason behind these security rules was that the pre-HIPAA security of health-care administrative systems was often inadequate. Organizations often cannot improve this system security just by purchasing and installing new software but must first improve human-driven policies. The HIPAA security standards rules were not finalized and put into effect until April 2003. Full compliance with these rules is not required until April 21, 2005, a date that may be pushed out again into the future but that will continue to be a challenge for many organizations to implement. These rules apply to what HIPAA calls "covered entities" and include:

- Doctors and other health-care providers who process health-care claims electronically

- Health plans, including organizations that "self-insure"

- Health-care clearinghouses—billing services and others who provide data-formatting services for electronic claims submission

This means that these HIPAA security rules apply to all organizations, whether they are a single doctor's office, a major hospital, or a small professional office that handles its own health-care claims processing through self-insurance.

Security is a key HIPAA element for keeping personal health information private, and many first steps are mainly a matter of improving the design and function of organizational security-related systems. HIPAA security rules cover good security practices for much more than just medical records, such as requirements for strong disaster recovery standards. These published rules consist of both "required" and what HIPAA calls "addressable" rules. The latter are rules that an organization may not be required to implement due its small size and limited resources. The "required" HIPAA rules represent many good information security practices that are appropriate for any organization. Other HIPAA security areas are beyond the scope of this book, such as requirements for PKI, or a Public Key Infrastructure, environment that includes digital signatures.

(c) HIPAA Security Administrative Procedures

HIPAA requires administrative procedures to be in place to guard data integrity, confidentiality, and availability. These procedures must be carefully documented per HIPAA rules, and Exhibit 24.3 lists some of these "required" administrative procedures. We have only listed the implementation rules here in a very general manner, but published HIPAA rules tend to be very detailed. Many of these requirements, such as having a documented and tested contingency plan or formal policies for information access controls, are similar to the control procedures internal auditors have been recommending over the years. Some of these represent good practices that will already be in place in many organizations. Rule number 3 refers to the need for what is called a sanctions policy—a formal set of rules for people who violate the security policy. This is a good idea for most organizations! Now, as an administrative rule, an HIPAA-affected health-care provider will face a penalty if its established rules and procedures are found to be inadequate.

<hr>

EXHIBIT 24.3

HIPAA Required Implementation Specifications

The following provisions apply to what are called "covered" entities or organizations under HIPAA rules and must be part of an organization's HIPAA security and compliance plan.

1. **Risk Analysis.** Organizations must conduct a thorough assessment of the potential risks of information confidentiality, integrity, and availability.

2. **Risk Management.** Covered organizations must implement reasonable and appropriate security measures to reduce overall risks to an acceptable level.

3. **Sanctions Policy.** Sanctions or related penalties must be applied to workforce members who violate the organization's security policy. This might translate in to some type of a "three strikes and you're out" type of policy.

4. **Information Systems Security Activity Reporting.** Security logs, incident reports, and related security activity reports should be reported and reviewed on a regular basis.

5. **Incident Response.** Processes should be in place to identify, investigate, mitigate, and document security incidents.

6. **Backup Procedures.** Appropriate procedures must be in place to recover any loss of data.

7. **Disaster Recovery.** Every covered organization must establish procedures to cover any loss of data.

8. **Emergency Mode of Operations.** Processes must be in place to ensure the security of patient information when operating in an emergency mode.

9. **Related Business Contracts.** An organization must include language in contracts with suppliers of related services that require the supplier adopt adequate security measures to report security incidents to the organization, to ensure these subcontractors implement appropriate security measures, and to provide for the termination of the contract in case of a security breach.

10. **Disposal of Patient Information.** Policies and procedures should be in place to address the final disposition of such patient information as recycled disk devices.

11. **Media Reuse.** Processes must be in place to ensure the removal of sensitive information from electronic media, such as disk drives, before reuse.

12. **Unique User Identification.** Unique identifiers must be assigned to all systems users in order to prevent shared accounts and to track system behavior.

13. **Emergency Access Procedures.** Procedures must be established to all allow for the accessing of electronic information during an emergency.

14. **Documentation.** Procedures must be established to guarantee information security, maintain the documentation for a period of six years, and review it periodically.

HIPAA security requirements also include some physical safeguard rules that are similar to the physical access controls that have existed over data centers going back to the early days of mainframe computers. Here, however, HIPAA goes beyond the classic computer operations center and calls for strong guidelines and documentation over workstation use and location. While internal auditors typically have not expressed many internal control concerns regarding such matters as the physical controls surrounding the many networked terminals in a business environment, a nurse's or other workstation requires such strong controls in a medical environment.

(d) Technical Security Services and Mechanisms

HIPAA rules require that processes should be put in place to guard the integrity, confidentiality, and availability of data and to prevent unauthorized access to data that is transmitted over communications networks. The rules here, which will not be effective until at least 2005, will require information systems security controls that are often stronger than those found in many large corporations today and include:

- *Access Control.* Strong control mechanisms based on the context of the data or the role/position of authorized users must be established. In addition, control processes must always be in place to allow emergency access from data center operations if required.

- *Audit Controls.* Here and throughout all of the HIPAA rules are requirements for strong audit controls, including such things as documentation revision and traditional audit trails.

- *Data Authentication.* Strong systems controls over data integrity are required here. These are the same types of application controls discussed in Chapter 21, "Reviewing and Assessing Application Controls."

- *Entity Authentication.* Controls must be in place so that when one workstation attempts to access another, it is authenticated. This process may include passwords, telephone callbacks, or even biometric controls. This requirement goes beyond many organizational practices in place today.

- *Communications and Network Controls.* A wide range of controls is suggested here, including alarms, encryption, event reporting, message authentication, and others. The HIPAA-affected organization must implement a very secure network.

HIPAA requires that electronic signature controls be established that will provide the same legal weight to electronic data signatures as are associated with a traditional signature on a paper document. HIPAA rules require message integrity, no repudiation, and user authentication for any message with an electronic signature. However, it is well recognized that no "technically mature techniques" exist here today in an open network environment to comply with these HIPAA rules. Digital signature processes are in place today, but they are often somewhat cumbersome. Nevertheless, these digital signatures will be required until other techniques are developed. This is a classic case of the U.S. government establishing ideal or desired ideal or desired rules even when no practical solution exists today. Legislators sometime think that if they set a high standard, industry and other groups will charge ahead to make things happen. This sometimes does work, but if not, rules will be revised.

(e) Going Forward: HIPAA and E-Commerce

Although designed to protect and authenticate medical information, HIPAA rules outline some strong guidelines for all electronic-commerce processes. A major requirement here will be improved standards and processes for electronic signatures. There is still much to be accomplished before processes become common and commercially available, and the National Institute of Standards and Technology (NIST) is taking a leadership role in the development of a federal Public Key Infrastructure that supports digital signatures and other public-key-enabled security services. NIST is coordinating with industry and technical groups developing PKI technology to foster interoperability of PKI products and projects.

Ongoing HIPAA rules, many still to be released, will almost certainly push progress in many areas of security and integrity. Although developed for health-care organizations, these rules will have an impact on many organizations. Internal auditors should try to stay aware of these ongoing rules and required standards even though not working directly for a health-care organization. The chapter has provided a very limited introduction to these complex and important rules. An internal auditor can find more HIPAA information on the Web at two important sources:

- *U.S. Department of Health and Human Services.*   Copies of HIPAA rules and other materials are available from http://hhs.gov/ocr/hipaa/.

- *HIPAA Advisory.*   A site maintained by Phoenix Health Systems as a public service is a good source for HIPAA information at http://www.hipaadvisory.com.

24.5   OTHER LEGISLATIVE INITIATIVES: GROWING CONCERNS FOR PRIVACY

GLBA and HIPAA represent two important legislative initiatives that introduce new privacy and security rules. There are other recent and privacy-related U.S. federal initiatives, such as the Children's Online Privacy Protection Act (COPPA), which regulates the collection of children's personal information. Other new rules are international in nature such as the large set of privacy and security international standards, including International Organization for Standarization (ISO) Standard 15408, a framework to evaluate IT security. ISO standards are introduced in Chapter 29, although a combination of space limitations and their level of relevance to the practice of internal auditing have limited coverage of these other areas. A common thread for many of these new initiatives is personal privacy protections for much of the information about individuals that is kept in automated system records.

The HIPAA and GLBA legislation discussed in this chapter may very well point to other legislative initiatives in areas beyond health care and personal financial privacy protections. In addition, although it may take some time to fully develop, the COSO ERM risk model discussed in Chapter 5 may soon cause some major changes in the thinking of how we understand, organize, and protect business and other areas of risks. There will be many opportunities for internal auditors in current and future organizations.

ENDNOTE

[1] Moeller Robert, *Brink's Modern Internal Auditing*, 5th Edition, New York: John Wiley & Sons, 1999.

CHAPTER TWENTY-FIVE

Continuous Assurance Auditing, XBRL, and OLAP

25.1 WHAT IS CONTINUOUS ASSURANCE AUDITING?

Continuous assurance auditing (CAA) is the process of installing control-related monitors in automated systems such that these monitors will send signals or messages to auditors—usually internal auditors—if the automated system's processing deviates from one or another audit limit or parameter. This concept has been around for some years. In the earlier days of information systems auditing, the literature referred to similar monitoring concepts as Integrated Test Facilities (ITFs) or System Continuous Audit Review File (SCARF) facilities[1] although these concepts were seldom if ever implemented. These real-time audit monitors sounded very interesting but really could not be implemented in that earlier era of batch-processing and magnetic tape storage applications. The concepts behind ITFs and SCARFs later began to be described as continuous assurance monitoring techniques, or CAA. The concept continued to be a frequent topic at internal audit future-technology-related conferences through the 1990s. Finally, technology and, to some extent, the Sarbanes-Oxley Act (SOA), now are making CAA a very practicable alternative for auditing automated systems.

AICPA chair James Castellano's testimony to congress in its hearings regarding the fall of Enron emphasizes the importance of this approach. His February 2002 comments included:

> The transition to new reporting and auditing models is going to demand not only new audit approaches but personnel of the highest caliber. With this in mind, the profession has been working actively in the following areas: continuous auditing or continuous assurance involves reporting on short time frames and can pertain to either reporting on the effectiveness of a system producing data or more frequent reporting on the data itself.

This chapter will discuss CAA as an improved alternative approach for reviewing today's automated systems. Technology makes continuous auditing approaches much easier to implement, and SOA's requirements for almost real-time financial reporting makes these concepts very attractive. The concept leads to installed audit monitors and the ability to "close" an organization's financial reports on almost a real-time basis. Some larger organizations today have implemented various types of continuous auditing approaches, with this chapter considering some example implementations. CAA represents a dramatic change in the audit model and may change both auditor practices and skill requirements as it becomes more widely accepted.

Organizations today have multiple needs to retain all forms of operating and historical information, stored on information systems databases. When this stored data is organized on a series of large, complex, and interrelated databases, the concept has come to be known as a data warehouse. A data warehouse environment is an almost necessary component for implementing CAA as are the related data warehouse tools of data mining and Online Analytical Processing (OLAP). This chapter will briefly discuss these concepts and their applicability to internal audit processes. Internet concepts and the use of an Extensible Marking Language (XML) is another key component to CAA. Finally, the chapter will introduce XBRL, the AICPA initiated, Extensible Business Reporting Language. XBRL is an evolving tool that internal auditors should understand and will almost certainly be using in future years.

25.2 IMPLEMENTING CONTINUOUS ASSURANCE AUDITING

Auditing has gone through a series of conceptual changes over time. In its earliest days, auditing was a process of vouching and testing, a concept that goes back to the dictionary definitions of these terms. To "vouch" means to attest, guarantee, or certify something as being true or reliable, and an auditor performs tests to support that vouching process. This has been the detailed type of audit process that has been used for years. However, as systems became more highly automated, auditors began to primarily rely on reviews of internal controls to support their audit conclusions rather than "old-fashioned" vouching. If the controls were adequate and found to be working through tests of these controls, there was less need to perform the detailed transaction testing. In this second phase of auditing and through the early 1990s auditors placed a major emphasis on reviews of internal controls as the major component of their attestation work.

With too many systems and too many diverse controls to consider coupled with an ongoing emphasis on increased audit efficiency, auditors—particularly external auditors—began performing a formal risk analysis over their control environments with their audit emphasis placed only on higher-risk internal control areas. This audit risk analysis process was discussed in Chapter 5 "Understanding and Assessing Risks: Enterprise Risk Management," and could be considered a third phase of auditing after first, vouch and test, and second, internal control reviews. Many analyses of what happened after Enron as well as WorldCom, Tyco, HealthSouth, and a host of others raised many questions about the audit procedures used. How could these failures have happened? Why didn't the external auditors see these internal control weaknesses and other problems? One of the concerns often cited here was that financial reports were frequently unreliable. A second concern and criticism was that the supporting final audited reports were often delivered well after the official statement closing dates and contained many pro forma numbers. SOA now requires that financial reports be closed and issued on an increasingly tighter schedule, closer to the organization's period ending dates. That requirement points to the need for continuous close audits and auditor assurances—what may become the next phase or generation of audit techniques.

(a) What Is a Continuous Assurance Auditing System?

CAA is an audit technique that produces audit results simultaneously with, or within, a short period of time after the occurrence of actual events. Auditor-supervised controls are installed in major, enterprise-wide resource systems that include alarm monitors and continuous analytical analysis routines to either attest results or highlight items for immediate audit analysis. A CAA is generally independent of the underlying business application with processes that test transactional data against defined control parameters or rules. CAA processes today run automatically on a daily or weekly basis and generate exception reports or alerts for internal auditor follow-up. Similar to the traditional audit process, a CAA process is more detective than preventative.

In its most basic design, a CAA is an independent application that monitors another critical application. Exhibit 25.1 shows a CAA monitoring application for an automated payments system. This is a separate parallel set of software that monitors all payment activity through periodic reviews of activity through a payments transaction file. Activity summaries are reported through periodic reports, and any unusual items are highlighted in an exception report, probably through an e-mail notice. This type of system is very similar to the kinds of password security monitors that are in place in many organizations. Exception activity is reported on a regular basis, but any "red flag" violations are highlighted.

CAA applications imply more than just monitors that run against application transaction files and highlight exceptions. For many organizations, applications are much more complex. Enterprise resource planning (ERP) systems are an example. These are the all-inclusive application packages, by vendors such as SAP, PeopleSoft, or Lawson, that provide total systems solutions including accounting, the general ledger, human resources, and purchasing covering virtually all application areas in the enterprise. These are complex information systems

EXHIBIT 25.1

Payment System Continuous Assurance Audit Monitor

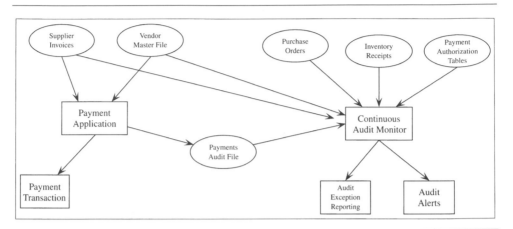

Source: Robert R. Moeller, *Sarbanes-Oxley and the New Internal Auditing Rules,* © copyright 2004, John Wiley & Sons. Used with permission.

where an average ERP implementation costs some $12 million and takes almost two years to implement. These implementations are built around a single or a closely federated set of databases. Any CAA set of monitors here must be much more complex because multiple transactions may update or depend on multiple tables. The CAA process is very useful here because it allows monitoring to be installed over a complex set of processes. This is also the ideal environment in which to install CAA because the monitoring activity can be built around the common database structure of an ERP implementation.

Exhibit 25.2 provides a conceptual view of the multiple audit review processes that are elements of CAA. At the base of the exhibit is a stream of measurable, information systems application processes such as might occur in a complex ERP. The audit team would then establish some metrics it wishes to monitor as well as supporting standards for those metrics. As a simple example, the United States has established money-laundering banking rules stating that all cash transactions over $10,000 are to be reported to regulators. An organization has a legal requirement to monitor and report those transactions. Metrics tools could be built into the ERP processes to monitor all cash transfer transactions with a standard that any amount over this $10,000 limit should be flagged. The process could have multiple levels of metrics and standards with exceptions fed up to a first level assurance process that would monitor the difference and, in some instances, send back a correcting feedback transaction to the ongoing process. The first level of monitoring here might be similar to the warning notes that are sent to a corporate systems user when his or her mailbox is over 90% full.

Other discrepancies would flow up to what the Exhibit shows as a second level monitoring or auditing process. This level would produce the reports to management or emergency exception notices. Beyond reports, this level could produce more significant audit or assurance actions. In the mailbox full example, CAA would initiate a transaction to prevent further accesses to the offending user.

There is also a third level to CAA to monitor the auditing process. Control procedures also would be built into the process to monitor ongoing CAA activity. This is the level that the organization could use to report CAA activities to external auditors or regulators.

The monitoring processes just described can be performed on multiple levels. The first CAA level might be to flag and extract all transactions that pass resources between the organization and some entity of interest, extracting all transactions that match auditor-defined criteria for further analysis, vouching, or reporting. An example might be monitors to screen for all financial transactions with some group of countries or companies of interest. A second level would be a bit more sophisticated and would include some limits or logical templates in the evaluation process, such as maximums and minimums in the monitors. On a third and more analytical level, CAA could examine the formal rules relative to the process monitored. An example here might be the use of system-generated values such as interest rates or asset returns and a comparison with auditor-initiated reasonableness tests of those assumptions compared with historical values.

EXHIBIT 25.2

Continuous Assurance Audit Process

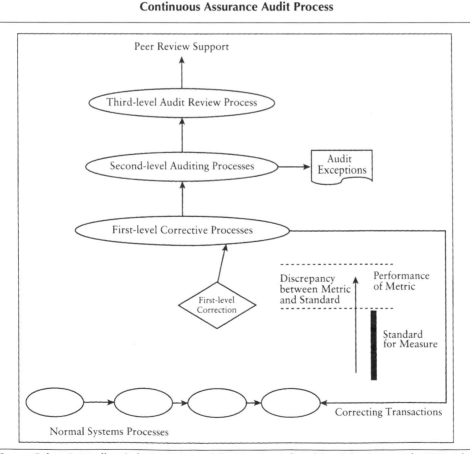

Source: Robert R. Moeller, *Sarbanes-Oxley and the New Internal Auditing Rules*, © copyright 2004, John Wiley & Sons. Used with permission.

At its most basic level, CAA introduces a heightened level of monitoring to application systems. Classic auditor points of control will "disappear" into the processing system, changing recording and measurement tools. The cycle time for making audit-based decisions or actions will very much decrease because it is based on systems measures. CAA creates an environment for 24 hours a day, 7 days a week (24/7) continuous auditing.

CAA processes already have been implemented at a variety of larger organizations. AT&T, for example, was an early leader, and CAA has become quite common in the insurance, stock brokerage, and medical-claims-processing industries. Built around an organization's ERP system, CAA is particularly useful for monitoring purchase and payment cycle applications with an emphasis on controls over potential vendor-related fraud. CAA is a valuable tool for any application area where cash is going "out the door," including employee travel accounting, insurance claims, and money-laundering controls.

(b) Resources for Implementing CAA

While the basic concept of implementing some form of audit monitor in an ERP or other business application seem relatively straightforward, the actual execution of CAA in an organization presents challenges. In order to be independent of other information systems applications, the CAA process must be installed with some level of independence from other outside parties. That is, if CAA has an objective to monitor all transactions over X dollars and some certain other conditions, those monitoring controls must be installed independently such that they cannot be bypassed. However, installing CAA in an ERP or any other business applications require some complex technical skills that may be beyond the capabilities of many internal auditors. Conversely, even if the internal audit group has the technical skills to install CAA in an organization's applications, IT management will look at any such proposal with a high degree of skepticism. IT management will not trust its auditors to install their own CAA monitoring software in a production system environment, but if IT agrees to take the CAA software module and test and modify it for production installation, the CAA's independence may be compromised.

The market is always changing, but this section introduces several vendor-supplied software solutions for installing CAA. The products or approaches discussed are not the only solutions to installing CAA, but represent some good starting points for an organization that is considering the use of CAA. While the concepts of CAA have been described for some time by "voices in the wilderness" at academic conferences, CAA is just beginning to be more widely recognized. Good sources for more information on CAA can be found at the Texas A&M University Mays Business School Center for Continuous Auditing at http://business.tamu.edu/cca/ as well as the Rutgers University accounting Web site, http://raw.rutgers.edu/. Both are involved with conferences on CAA, and papers from their past conferences can be found there. Partially based on presentations from past continuous auditing presentations, we have selected several CAA implementation examples.

(i) The KPMG CAA Approach.
The external audit firm KPMG in the United Kingdom has been working with a CAA approach called KOLA, KPMG On Line

Auditing.[2] KPMG installs their own desktop computer at the audit client site for CAA reviews, with read-only access to relevant databases running behind the organization's firewall. No software is loaded on the company's system, data does not routinely leave the client, avoiding security issues, and the organization's e-mail system is used to carry program instructions and report audit test outcomes. Databases are monitored using automated routines to notify the auditor for various levels of audit events, including pre-programmed responses for automatic escalation or prompts calling for manual responses for certain events conducted either remotely or in person. KOLA also allows data to be sent as file attachments for further analysis. Exhibit 25.3 shows this KOLA process as was presented at the previously referenced continuous auditing conference.

While the KOLA system has evidently never been implanted by KPMG on a worldwide basis, it appears to be an excellent approach to implementing CAA. It is described as platform independent, working with any database but with no software loaded onto the client organization's system. The KOLA computer, shown in the lower-right side of the exhibit, provides the capability to audit controls online for early, proactive audit problem identification.

(ii) ACL Continuous Assurance Systems. Many auditors over recent years have used software products developed by ACL,[3] a popular software product for computer-assisted audit analysis and retrievals and discussed in Chapter 23, "Computer-Assisted Audit Techniques." That same vendor provides an effective tool for CAA. The ACL approach here might be described as "first generation" CAA. ACL takes the approach that few organizations today have fully embedded

EXHIBIT 25.3

KPMG KOLA Continuous Assurance Audit Process

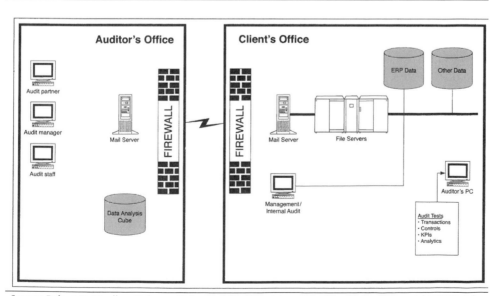

Source: Robert R. Moeller, *Sarbanes-Oxley and the New Internal Auditing Rules*, © copyright 2004, John Wiley & Sons. Used with permission.

and automated continuous auditing or monitoring applications and those most audit-related testing applications today are simply a series of automated data analysis tests that are manually initiated and run on a regular basis. The ACL approach goes a step further so that the auditor does not need to formally start and run the monitoring program. The ACL software is linked to organizational files and applications so that it can run in the background. The software is useful for such areas as detecting unusual transaction indicators of fraud or identifying duplicate and other overpayments. While not truly continuous, ACL suggests the auditors install and run this software based on completion of process steps and at periodic time intervals. The software then takes a slice of the data, capturing all transactions since the last test process. ACL continuous assurance software is used today by all of the "final 4" public accounting firms as well as a large number of major corporations in the United States. An organization today that is interested in implementing some beginning level of CAA might well consider starting with ACL's assurance product.

(iii) Dashboard Approach to Monitoring: Business Objects and Others. Complex information systems can be built with a wide variety of monitoring programs and displays to allow an operator to review performance and highlight any potential problems. This is similar to an automobile with a dashboard full of gauges that allow a driver to monitor performance because they show speed, progress by indicating miles traveled, status because they show the fuel remaining, and problems by displaying warnings for such items as low oil pressure. This dashboard approach allows the driver to monitor overall progress while the vehicle is in operation and to take action as required. That same dashboard approach can be used with business information systems.

The typical online application of today has a continuous display for that application. In a sales order application, designated users can access the progress of sales recorded, perhaps by product line or region, through an online terminal. However, that monitoring typically just covers that one sales application, and another screen must be called up to review related activities handled by other applications such as ongoing cash collections or returns. Today's ERP applications provide a better environment for such cross-application monitoring because all of the components of the ERP, from receiving to general ledger processes, are under a common database structure. In addition, several good software products are in place to allow an organization to install dashboard monitors to review overall progress of business transactions and other activities to allow for prompt remedial action when necessary. Perhaps two of the better software tools are the offerings of BusinessObjects[4] and Cognos.[5] Each of these firm's products allows an organization to tie a wide variety of diverse applications to a dashboard monitor, allowing users to monitor overall activity.

The console monitors on the classic mainframe computers acted as a dashboard and monitored all system activity with a constant stream of messages to the operator. The same concept can be applied to today's ERP applications. This will allow an organization and internal audit to move from an environment of monitored controls to the real-time monitoring of system operations with adjustments for continuous improvement.

25.3 INTERNET-BASED EXTENSIBLE MARKING LANGUAGES: XBRL

Business today is very much based on Internet-supported applications. The paper-based information reports and the batch systems that supported them have largely gone away. Virtually all organizations today are operating in an environment of Internet-supported systems and processes. While this is a very flexible approach, using the Internet can raise questions about document integrity from management and auditors. When reports were being produced in the classic closed-shop data center, whether on paper or by an online system, there was little question about the reported data provided that internal controls were adequate. As long as there were appropriate general and application controls in place, auditors had few questions about general data integrity and only had to perform traditional audit tests to acquire a level of assurance regarding the data. However, the "free and open" nature of the Internet can raise doubts or questions about the integrity of transmitted data. The question here is how does the user know that the file is actually what it is represented to be?

Coding or marking languages solve some of those concerns, and XBRL, a proposed industry standard for the publishing, exchange, and analysis of financial and business reports and data, offers an excellent solution. XBRL (*Extensible Business Reporting Language*) is an open standard marking language developed by a consortium of over 200 companies and agencies, and strongly supported by the AICPA. Delivering benefits to investors, accountants, regulators, executives, business and financial analysts, and information providers, XBRL provides for the publication, exchange, and analysis of complex financial information in corporate business reports in the dynamic and interactive realm of the Internet. XBRL provides a common format for critical business reporting processes, simplifying the flow of financial statements, performance reports, accounting records, and other financial information between software programs. XBRL defines a consistent format for identifying data and for business reporting to streamline the preparation and dissemination of financial data, and to allow analysts, regulators, and investors to review and interpret it. As a result, XBRL should save time and money when information consumers within and outside of a company analyze complex operations and financial data. In the post-Enron era of SOA, XBRL is an important tool for providing consistent business and financial reporting.

(a) XBRL Defined

XBRL is a new Internet standard similar to the use of HTML (Hypertext Markup Language) for browsing, MP3 for digital music, or XML (*Extensible Markup Language*) standard for electronic commerce. XBRL uses standard Internet XML data tags to describe financial information for public and private companies and other organizations. XBRL International is a professional affiliation of some 200 organizations as well as separate local jurisdictions that collaboratively produce standard specifications and taxonomies that anyone can license royalty free for use in their applications. Just as we have established formats for Internet e-mail addresses or Web access links, XBRL provides both a standard description and classification system for the contents of accounting reports. Data can be taken from an accounting information system and XRBL coded to produce an electronic annual report, including all financial statements, the auditors' report, and 10K notes. The document can then be read directly by computer programs or end users or, more likely, coupled with a stylesheet to produce a printed annual report, user-friendly Web pages, or Adobe Acrobat™ file. Similarly, internal business reports and regulatory filings can be output in a variety of forms.

"XBRL is . . . perhaps the most revolutionary change in financial reporting since the first general ledger."[6] XBRL provides a method for organizations to report their financial information in a format that can be easily read and understood by others. It allows for efficient data collection and publishing as well as serving as a tool for improved data validation and analysis. Exhibit 25.4 illustrates how XBRL can improve the transfer of data and information across systems and entities. As the exhibit shows, financial data from an organization's ERP, general ledger, and other financial systems can be all coded in XRBL. That coded information then can be used, either at the present time or in the future, for reporting to banks, the annual reports, SEC EDGAR[7] filings, and other applications. XBRL is a consistent approach for reporting to investors, credit agencies, governmental agencies, and other entities.

(b) Implementing XBRL

XBRL is an evolving standard where visionaries have praised the concept, where tools and standards have been established, and where there have been some but

EXHIBIT 25.4

XBRL Interoperability Uses

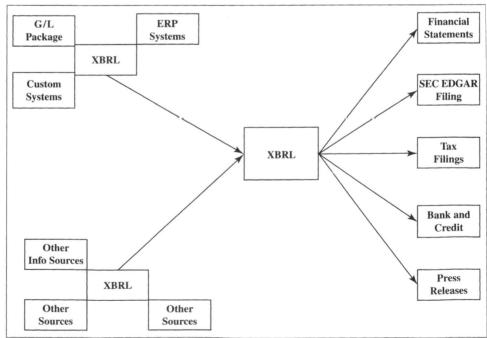

Source: Robert R. Moeller, *Sarbanes-Oxley and the New Internal Auditing Rules*, © copyright 2004, John Wiley & Sons. Used with permission.

not many early adopters to date. As examples of early adopters, Microsoft Corporation first filed its SEC 10K report in XBRL format for the year 2002, and General Electric is using it for its internal company reporting. Governmental regulators have seen the value of financial reports issued in a consistent and traceable format, and the U.S. Federal Deposit Insurance Corporation (FDIC) now requires that federal bank status Call Reports be submitted in XBRL format. Using the standard can save on costs and provide reporting flexibility by eliminating proprietary accounting system dump formats and doing away with manual copy-and-paste consolidation and reporting. We will probably see SEC requirements for the use of XBRL in the upcoming years.

As an Internet markup language for financial data, XBRL is similar to HTML for browsers, where the Internet user clicks on some tagged reference and is pointed to another site. Under XBRL, Internet financial data is tagged in a manner that is recognized and properly interpreted by other applications, based on a standardized XBRL vocabulary of terms, called a taxonomy, to map results into agreed-on categories. An example of this XBRL taxonomy is the markups or coding for well-defined concepts within the United States' generally accepted accounting principles (GAAP), including such areas as Accounts Receivable Trade or Allowance for Doubtful Accounts. No matter where it is located in the report format, a value can be recognized as the Allowance for Doubtful Accounts, whether it is found within one organization's reports or across multiple organizations'. However, GAAP may vary somewhat depending on if the organization is a retailer, a mineral extraction mining company, or any of many other variations, and XBRL qualifiers set these categories. A major savings with XBRL is the reduction of the data manipulation required when the organization needs to reposition the output from its financial systems to meet the needs of diverse users. A quarterly IRS tax form is very different in format and content from the format in a quarterly SEC filing, although the information needed to file both documents typically comes from the same financial database. With XBRL, information will be entered once and the same information can be "rendered" as either a printed financial statement, an HTML document for a Web site, an EDGAR SEC file, a raw XML file, or a specialized reporting format such as periodic banking and other regulatory reports.

Paperless reporting is facilitated here as well. Prior to XBRL, it has been necessary to extract financial information for reports from databases such as a general ledger, and that extracted information would then need to be processed multiple times depending on the needs of the user. For example, a typical balance sheet would need to be individually processed for SEC filings, for placement in the annual report, for examination by external auditors and for analysis by management. Each process could require an extra handling of the information to create the desired report. With XBRL, the information is coded once and ready for extraction electronically into reports for all information users. With the proper tools in place, the desired output for all uses of the balance sheet information can be transmitted electronically, without the need for paper-based reports, and there is only one authorized version of that balance sheet with its data appearing in other reports or sources where needed.

Although its use is limited to the early adopters today, XBRL is coming! Whether mandated by a regulatory reporting agency, launched by visionaries in the organization, or just because "everyone else" will soon be using XBRL to code their financial reports, most organizations will soon be using it as part of their financial reporting procedures. An internal auditor should now start having conversations with appropriate persons in the information systems as well as financial management to determine plans for XBRL implementations. As a first step, however, the interested internal auditor should gain some knowledge about it. Since it is an XML-based, royalty-free, and open standard, much information is available through the official Web site (www.xbrl.org). That site will point interested persons to a wide variety of papers, presentation sets, and descriptions of its use.

Because it is a new, evolving technology, there are some risks of error here. The organization needs to select an appropriate taxonomy and to appropriately tag their data. Going back to our earlier example, there will be one taxonomy for a manufacturing and distribution organization and quite another for a petroleum refinery. While this would be a fairly broad error, starting with the wrong one will cause multiple control problems. Once that taxonomy is selected, procedures need to be in place to ensure that the tagging of data is complete and accurate. This is the same type of control concern that Internet browser users occasionally encounter when one clicks on a link and gets pointed to the wrong or a nonexistent site. It is frustrating when surfing through the Web, but critical when retrieving or reporting financial data. Internal audit should review procedures to ensure that controls are in place for that XBRL data tagging. Even though these kinds of endeavors often start as a pet project by some member of the information systems group, that tagging should be documented in a controlled environment.

XBRL is rapidly becoming a "new rule" standard for Web-based financial reporting and supporting systems in the United States, in the European Union, and throughout the world. Some have predicted that it will become a standard to SEC reporting by as early as 2006, not that far away. As John Connors, CFO of Microsoft, stated in 2002 on releasing his company's financials in XRBL, "We see XRBL as not only the future standard for publishing, delivery and use of financial information over the Web, but also as a logical business choice."[8]

25.4 DATA WAREHOUSES, DATA MINING, AND OLAP

For many years, data storage was considered a rather mundane component of the information systems infrastructure. Data that was needed for immediate short-term access was stored on mass storage disk drives with other less essential data being copied to magnetic tape drives. However, those old rules have not worked that well as applications have grown larger and more complex and as users have become ever-more hungry to analyze and understand that protected data. Data storage has now become a major component of the information systems organization with many new tools and technologies.

While space limitations in this book as well as the breadth of the topic today restrict our discussion of storage management, internal auditors should develop an understanding of this increasingly important component of information systems. This section will briefly introduce several important storage management practices and concepts. Storage management control procedures are an important part of information systems general controls that are still too often ignored in older discussions on information systems controls.

(a) Importance of Storage Tools

Although we have mentioned the past use of tape drives and disk devices, computer equipment manufacturers have been experimenting with and introducing new storage devices over the years. In the mainframe, legacy systems world, the emphasis was always on trying to pack more data storage capacity on a reliable disk drive. During the 1970s, storage techniques ranged from the use of large rotating drum devices on some old mainframes to experiments with holographic light-based storage. Rotating disk devices and magnetic tape prevailed, and computer operations centers in the 1980s had large amounts of floor space devoted to these storage management devices. During that same period, an increasing amount of storage resided on desktop computers with their own very reliable and increasingly high-capacity "C drive" hard disks. Systems and databases were getting larger, and there was a need for some reliable tool to handle these ever-larger storage needs. Although there were other new product attempts as well, the storage world really changed when EMC Corporation[9] launched a kitchen-refrigerator-sized product called a Symmetrix that was really a massive array of hundreds of very-high-speed hard disks controlled and attached to each other and connecting computers through extremely fast and reliable Fibre Channel connections. Soon, other competitors launched similar storage management, capabilities increased, and storage costs dropped dramatically. Storage management as a separate technical profession was launched.

Many organizations experimented with these new storage device offerings, trying one or another unit due to user demands for more and more storage capacity. This led to storage management configurations in data centers called "just bunches of disks" (JBOD) with these storage devices all connected as best as possible to servers or central computer systems. A concept called network-attached storage (NAS) soon evolved whereby the storage devices were connected to a network to provide file-level access to the stored data. Specialized NAS servers were added to allow applications to determine the locations of stored data such that anyone on the NAS could access stored data, and additional capacity could be added easily. From NAS, we have moved to storage area networks (SANs) whereby all storage devices are installed in a configuration similar to the local area network of office desktop computer systems. With SANs, stored data can be spread across multiple devices with easy switching from one to another.

Technology moves forward, and today we have content addressed storage (CAS), which tends to move storage from being just an archive to an environment that can more easily respond to direct user and application requests in formats ranging from classic database formats to digital photos. Our point here is not to attempt to explain these technologies but to highlight that storage management is an increasingly important and evolving component of an organization's information technology environment. Internal auditors can provide a major service to management through reviews of storage management capabilities, including device utilization, performance, and traffic patterns. Storage management problems can limit system availability and present difficulties in meeting service level agreements.

(b) Data Warehouses and Data Mining

Over recent years, the concept of data warehousing has evolved into a unique and separate business application class. But, the internal auditor may ask the question, "What is a data warehouse?" A simple answer is that a data warehouse is managed data situated after and outside the operational information systems. Data warehousing's primary concept is that the data stored for business analysis can most effectively be accessed by separating it from the data in the operational systems. Many of the reasons for this separation have evolved over the years. In the past, legacy systems archived data onto tapes as it became inactive, and many analysis reports ran from these tapes to minimize the performance impact on the operational systems. Advances in technology and changes in the nature of business have made many of these business analysis processes much more complex and today data warehousing systems support the OLAP systems discussed later in this chapter.

Data warehousing systems are most successful when data can be combined, in the true concept of a central warehouse, from multiples operational systems at a place independent of the source applications. The data warehouse can effectively combine data from multiple applications such as sales, marketing, and production systems. Many large data warehouse architectures allow for the source applications to be integrated into the data warehouse incrementally. This allows for cross-referencing and time dimension data filtering, allowing an analyst to generate queries for a given week, month, quarter, or a year or to analyze data from the old and new applications.

Building a data warehouse can be a complex task for an organization. Data must be gathered from multiple sources, scrubbed to clean up problems, and then converted or transformed to a form suitable for the data warehouse databases. Exhibit 25.5 shows this general concept at a very high level. Assume that an organization has separate systems for order processing, product management, and marketing. The key information elements here will be transformed to a consistent data warehouse format, existing backups will be converted, and going forward, these systems will feed the data warehouse on a regular basis. The idea is not necessarily to move all application operations to the data warehouse repository but to convert them from their separate applications for future analysis. A way of thinking about the data warehouse concept is to considerer a department of accounting department analysts where each employee downloads some data to his or her desktop system and produces separate analysis reports. In a warehouse type of environment, all of the separate data might be combined on one server so that all analysts could combine and share data.

An objective of a data warehouse is to make information retrieval and analysis as flexible and as open as possible. Low-end tools such as simple query capabilities may be adequate for users that only need to quickly reference the data warehouse, while other users may require the use of powerful multidimensional analysis tools. Data warehouse administrators should be established to identify and assign access to these query tools. There is often a progression path to the higher-level tools for the data warehouse users. After becoming familiar with a low-level data warehouse tool, the user may be able to justify the cost and effort involved with using a more complex tool. Internal auditors should be aware of

EXHIBIT 25.5

Data Warehouse Transformation Example

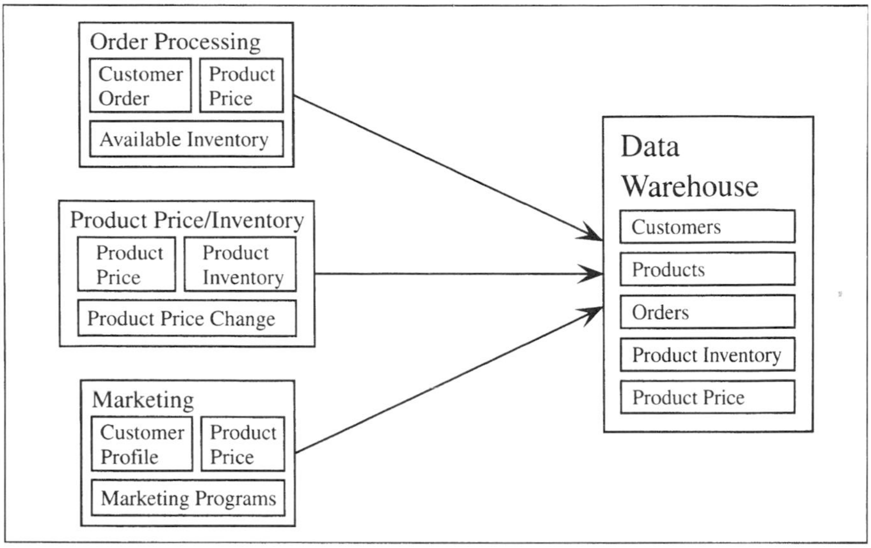

Source: Robert R. Moeller, *Sarbanes-Oxley and the New Internal Auditing Rules,* © copyright 2004, John Wiley & Sons. Used with permission.

the processes in place and the controls to limit access to authorized users. Because of the massive amount of historical data contained in a data warehouse, there is a need for a high level of security and privacy tools.

Many reports that are generated from a data warehouse facility will be just "canned" reports against warehouse summary data. They may be produced regularly or on request. In other instances, users may perform specific queries against the data warehouse accumulated summary data. The real strength of the data warehouse is its ability to allow analysts to perform what is called data mining. This is an evolving science where data-mining users start with summary data and drill down into the detail data looking for arguments to prove or disprove a hypothesis. The tools for data mining are evolving rapidly to satisfy the need to understand the behavior of business units such as customers and products. Even though this data mining may account for a very small percentage of the data warehouse activity, this is the key strength of the data warehouse for most organizations with such a facility. While the reports and queries off the data warehouse summary tables are adequate to answer many "what" questions, the mining-like drill down into the detail data provides answers to "why" and "how" questions.

A data warehouse can be a better single and consistent source for many kinds of data than the operational systems. However, because most information will not be carried over to the data warehouse, it cannot be a source of all system interfaces. Data warehousing is certainly a newer concept for internal auditors, and are only introducing the concept in a very general manner. The internal auditor seeking more information should do a Web search for some of the many sites discussing the topic or advertising data warehousing software products.

(c) Online Analytical Processing

As another new concept to many internal auditors, OLAP is the foundation for a range of essential business applications, including sales and marketing analysis, planning, budgeting, statutory consolidation, profitability analysis, balanced scorecard, performance measurement, and data warehouse reporting. Although OLAP is neither a new nor an obscure concept, it is not widely understood by management, internal auditors, and even many information systems professionals. OLAP is a category of software that enables analysts, managers, and others to gain insight into data through fast, consistent, interactive access to a wide variety of possible views of information that has been transformed from raw data to reflect the real dimensionality of the enterprise as understood by its users. The problem for many organizations is the mass of data and the need to better understand any related trends. Consider a large organization selling multiple product lines from various facilities. Which product lines are the most profitable? In which area or markets are sales increasing or declining? Do customer return patterns represent any overall trends? Answering these and other questions is the function of OLAP.

OLAP is the dynamic multidimensional analysis of consolidated enterprise data supporting the end-user analytical and navigational data. One way of thinking about OLAP concepts is to consider the model of a very complex, very large spreadsheet. We normally think of spreadsheets primarily as two-dimensional arrays of rows and columns where we can do searches, calculations, and types of analysis across these rows and columns as well as over multiple two-dimensional pages or spreadsheet tabs. However, sometimes data is too complex or there is just too much of it to place everything in an Excel-type spreadsheet. OLAP software comes in here with the following features:

- *Multidimensional Conceptual Views.* Calculations and modeling are applied across multiple dimensions, through hierarchies, and/or across members. Software tools can allow analysis across 8 to 10 dimensions.

- *Trend Analysis Over Sequential Time Periods.* Beyond the multidimensional process of looking at data, OLAP tools can consider any data item in terms of sequential time period trends.

- *Drill-Down Capabilities to Deeper Levels of Consolidation.* Using OLAP, the user can highlight a data element and then easily "drill down" to examine the basic data the created that item of interest.

- *Intuitive Data Manipulation.* OLAP tools have the ability to allow "if A, does this imply B?" levels of data manipulation.

- *Rotation to New Dimensional Comparisons in the Viewing Area.* OLAP allows a user to flip a complex database on its side and examine all of the data from that different perspective.

- *Reach-Through to Underlying Detail Data.* This really says that the OLAP user can better see the data trends that supported some conclusion.

These features are some of the major attributes of an OLAP application. Organizations typically implement OLAP in a multiuser client/server mode with an objective of offering users rapid responses to queries, regardless of database size and complexity. OLAP helps users synthesize enterprise information through comparative, personalized viewing, as well as through analysis of historical and projected data in various "what-if" data model scenarios.

There are a variety of software products in the marketplace that perform OLAP functions, but all of them today comply with a basic set of features that were first defined by the computer scientist, E. F. Codd. For background, Codd (1923–2003) was the original designer of the relational database model that is now used in many if not most information systems databases. Two examples of his relational database design are the Oracle and IBM's DB2 products built around his specifications. The general characteristics of an OLAP application, described previously, are part of Codd's general model and should be part of any installed OLAP application installed in the organization.

OLAP is not necessary for every organization. In some instances, an organization does not have the large amount of diverse data where OLAP procedures will be cost beneficial. Many other organizations know that they need OLAP-based solutions, but professionals tasked with selecting and implementing them may be new to the area, or may have lost track of its rapid developments. Selecting the right OLAP product is hard, but very important, if projects are not to fail. If an organization is considering the purchase of an OLAP product, internal audit should offer support to review the control procedures for the new software. If the organization is using OLAP software, internal audit should attempt to become familiar with the software product. Although we have talked about OLAP as a useful analytical tool for general business purposes, it may also be very useful for extensive audit queries over data.

25.5 NEWER TECHNOLOGIES, THE CONTINUOUS CLOSE, AND SOA

This chapter has tried to introduce some important new and evolving technologies that are important for internal auditors. Storage management represents a field of growing importance to the organization and its information systems resources. While there have always been data storage concerns going back to the days of unit record punched cards, the need for accurate and efficient storage processes is increasing. Internal auditors whose reviews of information systems controls in the past have been limited to computer hardware and network general control issues should begin to devote more attention to storage management.

Continuous assurance auditing is an approach that is growing in its acceptance and may soon affect all internal auditors. SOA Section 409, as discussed in Chapter 3, "Internal Audit in the Twenty-First Century: Sarbanes-Oxley and Beyond," requires all registered organizations to close their books for periodic financial reporting following tighter and tighter schedules. The external auditors performing those reviews as well as management are now requesting timely internal control assessments of those supporting systems. This really points to the growing importance of the continuous assurance auditing techniques discussed in this chapter. As these time requirements get tighter, management will demand tools to help close their books and produce financial reports on an even more prompt basis. The ultimate result will be the continuous close where the summarized results at the end of a business day represent the overall results for the organization up through the end of that business day. Many organizations today are already experimenting with these approaches, and the increasing SOA regulatory requirements as well as capabilities offered by technology today will continue to point organizations in that direction. This continuous close trend will point to new opportunities and internal controls concerns for internal auditors.

ENDNOTES

[1] The first edition of Robert Moeller's *Computer Audit, Control, and Security*, New York: John Wiley, 1989, discussed how internal auditors can build ITF and SCARF facilities. This edition is now out of print but a new edition is in preparation.

[2] Kevin Handscombe, KOLA, KPMG On Line Auditing. Paper presented at the Fourth World Continuous Auditing and Reporting Symposium, April 2002, Salford University, England.

[3] ACL Services, Ltd., 1550 Alberni Street, Vancouver, British Columbia V6G 1A5, Canada

[4] BusinessObjects Corporation, San Jose, CA and Paris, France.

[5] Cognos Corporation, Ottawa, Ontario, Canada.

[6] *Accounting Today*, September 2000.

[7] A long acronym whose meaning really does not matter today, EDGAR is the SEC's forms and filing database; it can be found at www.sec.gov.edgar.

[8] "Microsoft Become First Technology Company to Report Financials in XBRL." March 5, 2002, Microsoft PressPass, Microsoft.com.

[9] EMC Corporation, Hopkinton, MA. The author of this book worked with EMC in the past and helped to launch their Operations Management Consulting group.

Internal Audit Quality-Assurance and ASQ Quality Audits

26.1 ASQ AUDIT STANDARDS: A DIFFERENT APPROACH

While many think of only the CPA-type external or the Institute of Internal Auditors (IIA) internal auditors as *auditors*, other professionals also call themselves auditors. Examples here might be federal government contract auditors or others who audit health care or hospital standards. These auditors typically do not work in the corporations that are the domain of the CPA-type external or IIA-associated internal auditors. While the internal audit professional, who is highlighted in the title of this book, typically has little contact with them, quality auditors are another group of auditors who play an important role in many organizations. Administered through the American Society for Quality, they are an internal audit–like professional group that has its own standards and professional certification designations. Quality auditors have responsibilities to review a wide range of standards-compliance, work-simplification, and quality-related processes in the organization. These quality auditors have historically primarily operated "on the shop floor" of manufacturing or service organizations and often have had little contact with the IIA-type internal auditors in the same organization.

Although they have historically been separate from the IIA type of internal auditors that are the overall theme of this book, the classic quality auditor is becoming ever closer today to the IIA internal auditor than in the past. More accurately, both of these types of auditors are changing in terms of their objectives and approaches, bringing them closer together. This chapter will discuss the activities and functions of the quality auditor in today's organization. The classic IIA internal audit professional should have an understanding of the activities of quality auditors and how their work fits in the overall environment of corporate governance.

This chapter will also consider another aspect of internal audit quality assurance—QA reviews of an internal audit function performed by members of the internal audit team themselves or by contracted outside reviewers. The terminology can be confusing. A quality auditor is a separate professional who is a member of the ASQ. Quality assurance, or QA, refers to a process practiced by many internal audit functions. Large internal audit functions, in particular, can often gain some real value for themselves and for their overall organization by having an independent quality review of their internal audit practices and operations.

26.2 QUALITY AUDITOR STANDARDS AND PRACTICES

Although the expression quality auditor usually describes this professional, many in this ASQ-sponsored professional group call themselves internal auditors. While some of these quality auditors may belong to the IIA as well, they have their own professional organization, the Quality Audit Division (QAD) of the American Society for Quality (ASQ). That organization is the leading proponent of the quality movement in the United States with a wide range of publications, professional certifications, and separate divisions covering industries such as aerospace or pharmaceuticals as well as professional practices, such as the QAD. ASQ is very involved with the ISO worldwide quality standards, and its QAD is responsible for compliance audits against those ISO standards. ASQ quality audit professional certifications will be discussed in Chapter 28, "Professional Certifications: CIA, CISA, and More," and ISO in Chapter 29, "ISO and Internal Audit Worldwide Standards."

The QADs stated mission is "To support auditors and other stakeholders by defining and promoting auditing as a management tool to achieve continuous improvement, effective communication, and increased customer satisfaction." The use of the plain word "auditor" often causes some confusion. Although historically called quality auditors, this professional group often call themselves "auditors" today. In addition, there are both internal and external quality auditors. While a quality auditor may be a member of the IIA in addition to the ASQ, the external quality auditor has no regular relationship with the AICPA and its CPA designation. Exhibit 26.1 shows these different classifications or functions of quality auditors.

EXHIBIT 26.1

Classifications of Quality Auditors

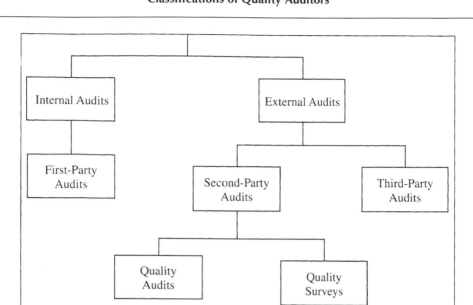

As shown in the exhibit, what are called first-party audits are performed by an internal quality auditor, within the organization, to measure its strengths and weaknesses against its own procedures or standards as well as any external standards adopted by the audited organization. We have mentioned the ISO standards, but there are numerous industry or specialty standards here as well. As an example, the automotive industry has its own quality-related standards. There may be a separate quality audit function within the organization, or the audits may be performed by regular employees who have appropriate training and certification.

A second-party audit is performed by an outside team. Frequently, in the quality audit world, a second-party audit takes place when an organization sends its quality auditors out to a supplier or vendor to perform a quality audit. These types of reviews are often structured as quality surveys or quality audits/assessments. In general, a quality survey is typically performed prior to the award of a contract to a prospective supplier to ensure that the proper capabilities and quality systems are in place. The quality audit/assessment is a comprehensive evaluation that analyzes such things as facilities, resources, technical capabilities, and other factors at some outside party. Second-party external audits are not at all like the well-recognized financial statement external audits. They are used here when an organization, the customer, wants to review the quality or other capabilities at a supplier or service provider. That supplier or provider may have little chance to say yes or no to the audit if they want repeated business with the organization sending the auditors. Second-party quality audits may be performed by the customer requesting the audit or through contracted consulting services.

Finally, third-party external quality audits are performed on the supplier by external participants other than the customer. Third party audits are performed by auditors certified by a recognized or registered authority to allow the supplier to attest that it meets the audited and attested standard. In another example, a government unit may perform mandatory audits on regulated industries such as for nuclear power facilities. The supplier being audited, in such a mandated audit situation, has no real opportunity to select the auditors or auditing organization. Although a totally different situation, this is similar to when a U.S. Internal Revenue Services (IRS) auditor informs an individual or organization that they will be visited by an IRS auditor to look at their tax records.

The ASQ currently has 11 separate certification programs covering various industry or specialty areas. One of these is the Certified Quality Auditor (CQA). Within the CQA are specialty designations for hazard analysis or biomedical auditing. These certifications require designated levels of work experience and successfully passing an examination. The author of this book is a Certified Quality Systems Engineer (CQSE). This is a challenging professional examination, and the CQA is equally challenging. ASQ quality auditors are involved in similar professional activities and have standards similar to IIA internal auditors, particularly those with the Certified Internal Auditor (CIA) certification. In addition to specialized professional publications, the ASQ has a series of specialized national meetings and conferences for ASQ quality auditors.

26.3   ROLE OF THE QUALITY AUDITOR

The various standards and guidance materials covering quality auditing are similar to the standards and approaches used by the IIA internal auditor. Quality auditors follow the same general procedures as "regular" internal auditors in their procedures for developing audit programs, reporting findings, and the like. Quality auditors usually are not involved with financial issues that come with reviews of financial internal controls or financial statement integrity. Quality audit procedures often follow published standards such as ISO 9000 as discussed in Chapter 28, and their audits often tend to be more quantitative and mathematical than the work of the typical internal auditor. The work of quality auditors is often closely aligned with the classic tools used by quality-assurance specialists.

An example might help explain a typical quality auditor tool, technique, and quality audit approach. Exhibit 26.2 shows a Pareto chart, a common diagram in quality-related groups. The idea here is to rank the types of errors or problems found by the auditor on the vertical axis with the most severe problems listed first. In this example, there were 62 cases of defect 1 during the period reviewed. Similarly, there were 58 cases of defect 2 with increasingly fewer cases for the other defects. The numbers of cumulative defects are plotted on the vertical axis. The line goes from 62 to (62 + 58 = 120) for the second point and continues. The idea behind a Parento chart is to see which defects require the most attention. The less than 10 instances of defect 6 shown here should require less management attention than other defects.

EXHIBIT 26.2

Pareto Chart Example

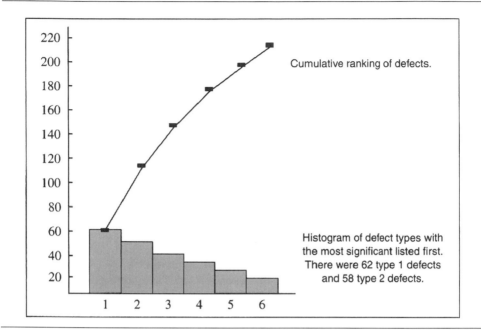

Cumulative ranking of defects.

Histogram of defect types with the most significant listed first. There were 62 type 1 defects and 58 type 2 defects.

While quality auditors have traditionally used tools such as Parento charts to review defects and make recommendations, in recent years the worldwide movement to ISO 9000 quality standards have very much changed their role. The ISO 9000 family of quality management standards was adopted in 1987, and sector-specific derivatives followed for the automotive, aviation, and telecommunications industries. Thousands of organizations have become registered or certified to these standards. Chapter 29 discusses ISO standards and their impact on all internal auditors. Organizations normally apply ISO quality standards in areas such a manufacturing, research, or distribution logistics. Over time, quality auditors became the owners of the ISO 9000 assessments.

ISO 9000 standards require more than just effective control. They call for examples of continual improvement, with the quality auditor given the responsibility to assess whether such improvement programs are in place. This can be a challenge. A system or process must be changed to improve it. This is just not a matter of working harder or being more careful. If there is no change in some aspect of a system or process, the outcomes will always be the same.

Quality auditors are often involved with tests for improvement based on their findings from an earlier review. To accomplish this continuous improvement, the data in a new review must be analyzed for trends and identification of weaknesses. The quality auditor then compares results to goals and objectives, and analyzes process data to identify risks, inefficiencies, and opportunities for improvement as well as negative trends. The results may be recommendations for changes in procedures, or in other elements of the process, such as improvements in acceptance criteria or methods of monitoring. Recommended changes in equipment or technology may also be among the quality auditor's recommendations for continual improvement. In many respects, quality auditors recommend more significant changes to the improvement cycle than have been the case for internal auditors.

26.4 QUALITY AUDITORS AND THE IIA INTERNAL AUDITOR

Although the two professional groups may have had few contacts and little in common in the past, there is an evolving level of integration today between IIA internal auditing and ASQ quality auditing. The term "quality auditing" is going away and is being replaced by just "auditing" in ASQ publications and in some ISO standards. The terminology used in both IIA and ISO standards is becoming increasingly consistent with standards revisions for each over recent years. ISO has defined an audit as a "systematic, independent and documented process for obtaining audit evidence and evaluating it objectively to determine the extent to which audit criteria are fulfilled."[1] The IIA's definition of internal auditing, discussed in Chapter 12, "Internal Audit Professional Standards," contains some quality-related words such as "assurance, adding value, risk management, systematic, disciplined, control, and process orientation." There appears to be some integration of quality auditing and internal auditing terminology into a generic assessment and business process improvement model.

There will probably be a growing convergence of internal auditing and quality auditing over the upcoming next years. An increasing number of organizations, worldwide, are seeking ISO registrations, and ISO 9000 standards are becoming more process oriented, customer focused, and business driven. With an emphasis on "effectiveness," an ISO 9000 registered company must demonstrate quality system effectiveness.

In some organizations today, the chief audit executive (CAE) also has been involved with the organization's quality audit function on at least a courtesy level. In the future, internal audit functions will almost certainly become more acquainted with their quality audit functions and should give consideration to sharing resources. Although their historical roots are different, both audit functions should become involved with value-added audit functions for the organization.

26.5 QUALITY-ASSURANCE REVIEWS OF AN INTERNAL AUDIT FUNCTION

Internal auditors have a special role in their service to the management in the modern organization. As has been described in many chapters of this book, internal auditors will visit a unit or component of an organization, review its controls, and make recommendations for improvements. The IIA-oriented modern internal auditor uses the *Standards for the Professional Practice of Internal Auditing*, described in Chapter 12, as well as the supporting practices and procedures discussed throughout this book. The CAE should have communicated these standards and practices to all members of the internal audit staff. Other members of the organization, that is, the auditees, should have a basic understanding that internal audit is following a set of good practices when it performs its reviews. However, beyond a high-level review by the external auditors, no one regularly "audits the internal auditors" to see if they are following both good practices and their own professional standards.

The effective modern internal audit function should look at itself from time to time to determine if all of its own components are following good internal audit practices and procedures. This is best accomplished if internal audit goes through an "audit the auditors" type of review over its own functions. The *Standards for the Professional Practice of Internal Auditing* refers to what are called *quality-assurance reviews.* IIA Standard 560 calls for the CAE "to establish and maintain a quality-assurance program" to appraise the quality of the audit work performed through ongoing supervisory reviews, reviews by internal audit of its own work, and reviews by external parties.

Internal audit quality-assurance reviews are a special type of audit—more than a normal management assessment of operations or an external auditor SAS No. 70 review, as was discussed in Chapter 10, "Working with External Auditors." While Standard 560 calls for three levels of review, this chapter will primarily focus on reviews of internal audit performed by normal internal audit operations, including members of other organizations or even a specialized department within internal audit. These reviews allow an internal audit function to assess the quality of its own procedures and its compliance with internal audit standards. This section describes the elements that should be included in an internal audit quality-assurance program and describes how internal audit can establish a program to perform these reviews.

(a) Benefits of an Internal Audit Quality-Assurance Review

Internal audit departments are sometimes viewed as operating outside of other mainstream organization functions. Internal audit reports to the audit committee with close ties with very senior levels of management, and has contact with all other functions in the organization through its operational and financial reviews. However, as a very specialized function, internal audit is not always considered when other organization performance measurement policies and procedures are established. This is not to suggest that internal audit is ignored. However, those implementing a new program of employee incentive pay, a major quality-assurance initiative, or some other employee benefit do not always consider the unique aspects of the internal audit function when designing the program. These programs are often focused on the organization's main functions, whether they are manufacturing, distribution, or financial.

As a very key function in the organization, however, internal audit needs a way to measure itself and to establish incentives to do a better job. This is one of the real benefits of an internal audit quality-assurance review. While internal audit itself is the prime beneficiary of these reviews, other stakeholders in an organization also benefit from a strong program of internal audit quality-assurance reviews. These reviews allow internal audit to demonstrate to management that it is doing a good job or taking corrective action to improve if necessary. Other parties, such as regulatory agencies, also may benefit from these reviews. They will provide them with a basis to better utilize the work of the internal audit department.

(i) Benefits to Internal Audit. The main beneficiary of any internal audit quality-assurance review program will be internal audit itself. As discussed beginning with Chapter 1, "Foundations of Internal Auditing," internal audit operates somewhat differently from many other functions in a typical organization and often cannot measure itself by such common measures of success such as sales, production, or administrative efficiencies. An external reviewer who understands the internal audit process and who has had exposure to other organizations can review internal audit operations from the perspective of both internal audit's compliance with professional standards and how its operations compare with other similar internal audit organizations. A review of compliance with internal audit standards also is valuable. As outlined in Chapter 12, IIA standards are comprehensive, covering all aspects of internal audit operations. While an internal audit function should have a program in place to follow these standards in all of its auditing activities, compliance with one or another specific standard may slip through inattention or just the pressure of completing audit projects. A quality-assurance review will allow a reviewer outside of day-to-day internal audit activities to assess how good a given audit function is doing in complying with internal audit standards. This can be a valuable benefit to the modern internal audit function.

The other area where internal audit can benefit from an internal quality-assurance review is the reviewer's comparison of the internal audit function with other internal audit organizations. Internal audit management does not always know how well it compares to other internal audit functions in terms of such things as its use of audit automation, efficiency in performing audit tests, or travel policies. CAEs can gather some of this information through their professional contacts at IIA meetings or other personal or professional contacts. However, these contacts do not always provide the same level of objectivity that would be found through the work of an independent reviewer who looked at several internal audit organizations. Even though one-on-one professional contacts are valuable, there can be a tendency for professional peers in different organizations to gloss over some faults or weaknesses when comparing their relative activities.

Internal audit quality-assurance reviews, performed by either outside parties or by a specialized function in the larger internal audit department, can add significant value to the internal audit organization. The review may point to areas where some internal audits were performed in a manner not fully in compliance with standards or where efficiencies could have been achieved by using different audit procedures. For example, the sample selection approach used in a given audit may have been too large. Although the audit's results were correct, a smaller sample might have produced the same audit conclusions but with greater efficiency. As a result of such quality-assurance reviews, internal audit management may be able to use the recommendations to improve its own overall operations.

(ii) Benefits to Management. Several levels of management, ranging from the managers directly responsible for internal audit areas reviewed to the audit committee, are all beneficiaries of internal audit quality-assurance reviews.

Although an internal audit team should certainly not show its latest quality-assurance review report to the auditee management of its next audit assignment, the findings of a good program of quality-assurance reviews should result in better and more efficient audits. All members of management—and managers directly responsible for units audited, in particular—will benefit from an efficient and effective internal audit organization. A program of quality-assurance reviews should help to ensure ongoing audit efficiency and effectiveness.

The audit committee and senior management will realize even greater benefits from a strong program of internal audit quality-assurance reviews. As has been discussed throughout this book, internal audit is a strong component in the system of internal controls. Senior management and the audit committee should understand the overall principles of internal control, but may not always fully understand the workings of their internal audit function. As a result of sharing the summarized results of an internal audit quality-assurance review with various levels of senior management, they will have a greater confidence in the quality of the reviews performed. This is a major benefit to the overall organization.

(b) Elements of an Internal Audit Quality-Assurance Review

An internal audit quality-assurance review is a formal process similar to many of the audit procedures outlined in other chapters. The review should be properly planned, follow a formal audit program, and be performed by qualified reviewers who can exhibit an appropriate level of independence. Whether performed by a special unit of internal audit charged with performing such reviews or by an outside consultant, the review should follow the same standards of independence and objectivity found in any internal audit. The only significant difference here is that the quality-assurance review will focus its efforts on internal audit procedures. The establishment of these requirements is an important first step necessary to launch an internal audit quality review function. Although management may want to vary the content of any review to reflect local concerns within an organization and its internal audit function, the review should concentrate on internal audit's compliance with the *Standards for the Professional Practice of Internal Auditing*, and any quality-assurance review should assess compliance with the principles outlined in these standards.

The specific details behind how the quality of internal audit operations will be measured depends on many factors, including the size of the internal audit department, directions by senior management specifying more emphasis on one area over another, and other factors. Nevertheless, all internal audit activities should be measured against compliance with these IIA standards.

A quality-assurance review is usually initiated through a detailed review of compliance with internal audit procedures. This would include such matters as an evaluation of the risk-assessment planning process, reviews of other planning documents, staff assignment procedures, a review of selected workpapers and reports used in actual audits, and all other planning and administrative materials used by internal audit in the course of performing its audit assignments. The purpose of this review approach is to measure the overall quality of internal audit's own procedures. While the specific procedures to be performed will vary with the size and activities of the internal audit department and its various activities, Exhibit 26.3 outlines the general procedures to be performed in an internal audit quality-assurance review. In addition to reviewing workpapers and administrative procedures, the quality-assurance review should focus on the auditees who either request reviews or have had reviews performed in their areas. An internal audit function contributes little to the quality of procedures in the overall organization if auditee management has serious concerns about the nature of the work performed, including the appropriateness of the audit conclusions reached and how those conclusions were communicated to management. The idea is not to determine that a representative group of auditees necessarily *like* the internal auditors who performed one or another review in their area but to assess whether the reviews were performed in an appropriately professional manner.

As a result of these review procedures and auditee surveys, the quality-assurance reviewer should summarize its results and prepare a report for the CAE. Based on report recommendations, a plan for improvement or corrective

EXHIBIT 26.3

General Procedures for a Quality-Assurance Review of Internal Audit

1. Define the areas to be included in the internal audit QA review—whether the entire function or just a separate component of internal audit, such as a separate division or geographic area.

2. Define the time period for the audits to be included in the QA review—whether from the conclusion of the last QA review or for the 12-month period prior to the announcement of the audit.

3. Determine who will be performing the QA internal audit review and ascertain that the reviewer understands both the IIA standards and supporting internal audit department procedures.

4. If internal audit has not had such a quality-assurance review within the last 24 months, take steps to ensure that both members of the internal audit staff and management understand the purpose and nature of the QA review.

5. If the QA review team plans to survey or interview auditees outside the internal audit department, make some preliminary plans to inform all affected persons.

6. Based on internal audits completed and in process, develop a general strategy for the number and types of audits to be selected for review. If special knowledge areas are to be included, such as computer security or automated design, determine that appropriate resources have been allocated.

7. Decide if the QA review will be on a top-level basis, checking for compliance to general standards or planned to include detailed reviews of selected audits, including workpaper reference checks or the reperformance of tests.

8. If problems are encountered in the course of the planned QA review, such as audits requiring a more detailed review, procedures should be prepared to evaluate the QA review's scope or schedule.

9. Develop a general procedure for the format and nature of the QA final audit report.

10. Develop a strategy for reporting the results of the QA review to other members of the internal audit department and to selected members of senior management.

action should be established. In some cases, if the reviewers found that certain completed audits did not follow good internal audit procedures, a program of ongoing review or corrective action should be established. If the quality-assurance review points out the need for such improvements as increased continuing education, a plan for corrective action should be established.

(i) Who Performs the Quality-Assurance Review? Although a CAE should see the value of a quality-assurance review, an independent party is often needed to perform the review. This is often fairly easy in a large, multiunit internal audit department where a team of centralized "corporate" internal auditors as well as others from differing divisional units can perform quality-assurance reviews of other divisional units. Although there is always the possibility for certain jealousies and unobjective appraisals, an in-house quality review, if properly managed, can be performed inexpensively as well as effectively and efficiently. For larger internal audit departments, in-house resources can even be devoted to performing periodic quality-assurance reviews.

Most internal audit departments are either not large enough to perform a separate quality-assurance review or may face other challenges that prevent them from having members of their organization perform quality-assurance reviews. A five-person internal audit group, for example, cannot realistically conduct a quality-assurance review with one member of the staff reviewing the other four. Internal audit management has two options here. They can both develop a self-assessment type of review and have all members of the smaller staff evaluate themselves, or they can contract with an outside party to perform the review.

The options available for outside parties who can perform a quality-assurance review include public accounting firms, consultants who specialize in such reviews, or internal auditors from other organizations. As another option, the IIA has a review program where it will schedule a team of professionals to perform the review. In addition to very small internal audit groups, some larger internal audit functions may find these outside source review approaches to be attractive. An internal audit self-assessment of its quality procedures can take the form of the control self-assessment (CSA) reviews discussed in Chapter 27, "Control Self-Assessments."

A larger internal audit organization can perform quality-assurance reviews using designated members of the department. In many respects, an internal auditor who is familiar with the organization, its procedures, and industry—but also understands general internal audit procedures—is often the best, most qualified person to review internal audit operations. Just as internal audit performs a review of another function, such as the purchasing department, the purchasing department could review itself by assigning certain people from its organization to perform this task. However, unless the purchasing department has had experience performing such self-assessments, the results of their review could be viewed as self-serving. Internal audit has an advantage over a function such as purchasing, as internal audit regularly exhibits its independence through its standards and other review activities. A larger internal audit function can perform its own effective quality-assurance reviews if it can demonstrate to others, both inside and outside of internal audit, that it is acting as an independent party.

Larger internal audit functions can also establish effective quality review programs internally by designating certain members of the organization the responsibility to perform quality-assurance reviews throughout the department. The internal audit function must be large enough to allow one auditor, or a small specialized group of auditors, to perform the quality-assurance reviews separate from normal audit activities. In a large internal audit department, there may be enough activity to justify a full-time quality-assurance function. In addition to the reviews, it could perform other activities such as developing audit procedures. This internal review arrangement will not work if members of the regular audit staff are regularly pulled from the normal schedule and asked to review their peers.

Although internal auditors have standards that require them to act independently, quality reviews of themselves can be viewed by some persons as either self-serving exercises or as programs to "get" one or another persons in the audit department. As mentioned, the reviews are best performed by an independent function within the internal audit organization and should otherwise follow normal internal audit procedures. That is, the internal audit quality-assurance function would schedule each of its reviews in the same manner that internal audit plans and schedules any normal audit. If it were doing a quality review of a separate organizational unit's internal audit function, it would schedule and announce the review like any normal audit. Once the review was completed, the manager responsible for the unit reviewed would respond to the audit report as would any other auditee. Copies of the final report would go to the CAE, who could take further action as necessary.

This is a particularly effective way to organize internal audit QA reviews when the audit functions are distributed throughout the organization. An outside quality-assurance reviewer would probably not get to all of the geographically remote units in the course of a single review. An in-house set of quality-assurance reviewers could.

Self-assessment reviews are often the most realistic way for a very small internal audit staff, perhaps with less than 10 members, to review its own operations. The staff might postpone normal scheduled audits and block out time to perform the self-assessment review. Time could be allocated for this type of review when the staff was not otherwise busy with scheduled audits.

A self-assessment review by the same internal audit staff responsible for normal audit procedures almost appears as if the auditees are auditing themselves! However, this is often the only way to review the quality of internal audit procedures in a small organization. Budget limitations usually prevent hiring outsiders to perform the review, and a small audit department could not justify the people resources. Members of the staff would be asked to step back and review all of the procedures performed in the course of a series of audits, including planning, workpaper documentation, audit report content, and a variety of other matters.

Rather than writing a report about itself, as is often done when persons outside of normal internal audit operations perform this type of quality-assurance review, findings from the self-assessment review are often shared through a series of introspective review meetings. Here, internal audit management and all parties involved would take steps to improve operations based upon the self-assessment review findings. For a smaller internal audit organization, self-assessment is usually a cost-effective way to measure quality assurance. People are often their own best critics!

26.6 LAUNCHING THE INTERNAL AUDIT QUALITY-ASSURANCE REVIEW

The CAE should take the lead in launching a quality-review program in the internal audit organization if a formal QA function is not already in place. While it does not matter who starts the review, the internal audit staff will recognize the importance of the CAE initiating the process. If the external auditors, for example, suggest such a review to members of the audit committee, all parties will have the underlying question, "What's wrong with our internal audit?" But, if internal audit itself initiates the process, they will have much greater flexibility to suggest the most appropriate parties to perform the review. When an organization's external auditors propose an internal audit quality-assurance review, the implication is that they will probably be contracted to do the work.

Internal audit may initiate a quality-review process by proposing the activity as part of the annual budgeting and planning process. A basic program can be outlined and resources allocated for either creating a separate quality-assurance review function in the organization or contracting the review process to an outside provider. If such a process is not already in place, the CAE should not think of this as a one-time process but a continuing mechanism to assess the quality of overall internal audit performance.

While any outside contractors should clearly be made to understand that they do not have an annuity for these reviews once they receive the first assignment, internal audit should think of this quality-assurance review process as an ongoing program rather than a one-time review. When a CAE proposes a program of internal audit quality-assurance reviews to the audit committee and senior management, there may be mixed messages received in return.

If the work is planned to be performed by a specialized in-house group, the question may be asked why existing internal audit staff can not be pulled off of other audit work to perform the reviews. The CAE needs to emphasize the importance of performing these reviews independently and in a manner that will not limit other planned audit activities. If the review is planned to be performed by a consulting firm specializing in such reviews, internal audit may have to explain why they would be preferable to the outside auditors. In either case, the CAE may find that convincing management of the need for the reviews and the approach to be used will require some "selling."

An internal audit quality-assurance review process will be readily accepted by management if internal audit presents a good plan to perform these reviews on an ongoing basis, if the reviews will allow auditees to provide some inputs regarding their impressions of the overall internal audit process, and if the quality-assurance review process points to an improved internal audit function in the organization. In addition to selling management on the need for such a quality-assurance function, internal audit management should inform all of the internal audit staff of the plans to form the function. Care should be taken to emphasize that the reviews are not intended to be a "witch hunt" but are designed to improve the overall quality of all audits performed. Properly explained, the process should be enthusiastically accepted by members of the internal audit staff.

Although an overall plan of performing QA reviews over a period of time is needed, established procedures necessary to perform a single, comprehensive review of an internal audit function. The necessary steps are to define objectives of a given review, to understand internal audit staff procedures, to survey or interview a selected group of auditees, and to report the results of the review to management and other interested parties. The quality-assurance review process often will be performed by a specialized, independent group within the internal audit. A section following discusses self-assessment reviews directly performed by members of internal audit on their own audit activities. These self-assessment reviews are particularly appropriate for a smaller organization.

(a) Quality-Assurance Review Approaches

An internal audit function launching a quality-assurance review program needs to make some basic planning and organizational decisions. In addition to deciding who will be performing the reviews, internal audit management must decide on the scope, depth, and breadth of the reviews to be performed. *Scope* here implies the amount of detail to be included in any review. Should the review include primarily internal audit administrative procedures or should it extend to detailed reviews of such areas as information systems audit practices or audit sampling approaches? *Depth* here refers to the amount of detail to be included in the quality-assurance review of any area. With an extended scope, the quality-assurance reviews might go down into the detailed audit procedures performed in each audit reviewed. It is one matter to determine that a selected audit project to be reviewed has a planning memo, a set of workpapers, and an audit report on file. In an extended scope review, the quality-assurance reviewers might examine the detailed audit procedures performed for each audit selected for the review. This might include a detailed review of workpapers and even the reperformance of some tests. *Breadth,* as used here, refers to the number of units to be included in any quality-assurance review. Should the quality-assurance review be just restricted to the larger centralized audit function at headquarters or should it extend to remote units? In other organizations, the geographically remote units may be subject to quality-assurance reviews but headquarters will not. In other instances, internal audit management will just review domestic units and not go overseas, or they will review one operating division but not others. Auditees may or may not be surveyed depending on the review approach selected.

Decisions should be made as to the frequency of planned quality-assurance reviews. In a large, geographically disbursed organization, a quality-assurance function will probably not be able to review every internal audit unit every year. The selection of who to review—and how often—should depend on the criticality of the internal audit function reviewed. The same risk-assessment techniques introduced in Chapter 4, "Internal Controls Fundamentals: COSO Framework," can be useful in helping internal audit management decide which areas are to be included as part of annual quality-assurance review plans. If a given area was subjected to an earlier quality-assurance review and areas in need of corrective action were identified, the quality-assurance review function may want to schedule an additional follow-up review in that area. Even if an outside consultant is used to perform its quality-assurance reviews, internal audit management should take a major role in deciding on the scope, depth, and breadth of the quality-assurance reviews to be performed by the quality-assurance reviewers over a specified, often one-year time period. Internal audit management should take the lead in specifying the types of reviews to be performed as well as the expected outputs from those reviews. Sometimes outside reviewers will have a tendency to do the work according to their own agenda. Management should make it known that the CAE is responsible for getting the quality-assurance review approach subject to risk-analysis studies and various other inputs from organization management.

While these comments have assumed that the CAE will have a strong input into the quality-assurance review process, the role of that same CAE in administering and reviewing internal audits should also be considered to be within the scope of any review of overall quality-assurance procedures. For example, if internal audit standards call for the CAE to sign the engagement memo and if the CAE ignores this duty, the quality-assurance review should highlight this discrepancy. This scope allows the review to assess the overall quality of performance by the entire internal audit function.

The CAE should assure the quality team performing the work that it has an obligation to effectively assess the overall quality of the internal audit function. Once the reviews have been selected, an approach established, and a plan developed, senior internal audit management should inform all members of the organization of the quality-assurance review plans. For a large internal audit organization with multiple units, that communication could take the form of a formal memo announcing the review plans and the need for cooperation. A sample memo is shown as Exhibit 26.4. A similar note should be directed to auditee groups that may be asked to participate in interviews or surveys. All parties need to be informed of the objectives of the quality-assurance review program. Even if internal audit has an ongoing review program, a notice similar to Exhibit 26.4 will remind organization members that the review program is starting another new, often annual cycle.

(b) Example of a QA Review of an Internal Audit Function

As an example, this section describes how a quality-assurance review might be performed by members of internal audit's overall organization who are scheduled to review an internal audit department at a separate, semi-independent division of the organization. The unit to be reviewed is called Axylotl Specialties, an independent unit that is 75% owned by the headquarters company, with the remaining 25% held by outside investors. Assume Axylotl Specialties' internal audit function ultimately reports to the CAE at headquarters but does not have day-to-day audit project–related contact with the headquarters audit staff. As with many decentralized organizations, the Axylotl Specialties internal audit function has been asked to follow general guidance from headquarters but has

EXHIBIT 26.4

Quality Review Engagement Letter Memo

MEMO

TO: XYZ Division Internal Audit Staff
From: Tom Goodguy, Quality Assurance Manager
Date: May ■,■■
Subject: Quality-Assurance Review

As part of our established internal audit procedures, the internal audit quality-assurance department periodically selects areas for review to assess compliance with department and general internal audit standards. Since we have not performed a review in your area for over two years, the XYZ Division internal audit function has been selected for a quality-assurance review starting May XX, XXXX. I will be directly managing this review and will be assisted by two staff members.

Please send me a current schedule of internal audits completed over the past year, as well as a copy of your current audit plan. We will select two audits completed over this period and will request a set of the workpapers in advance.

We plan to arrive at the XYZ Division internal audit offices on the morning of May XX and would like to meet with the internal audit management team at that time, and we will then advise you of the areas selected for detailed review. We expect that our fieldwork will require no more than two weeks. At the end of our fieldwork, we will meet with XYZ internal audit management to discuss our initial findings and recommendations.

Thank you for your cooperation and please contact me if you have questions.

Tom Goodguy

---

the freedom to establish some of its own local procedures based on the unique audit risks found in their business. In addition, Axylotl Specialties has its own audit committee.

This quality-assurance example review will follow the general procedures outlined in Exhibit 26.3 and assumes that the headquarters review team has had little contact with Axylotl Specialties. While this example assumes that the group to be reviewed is an independent unit of the parent corporation, these same basic procedures can be used by a variety of different reviewers and for varying internal audit units.

(i) Quality-Assurance Review Preliminary Planning.   The internal audit quality-assurance review team should follow some of the same procedures here that it might use if it were performing a normal internal audit, as has been described in previous chapters of this book. These might include:

- *Announce the Planned Quality-Assurance Review.*   The review should be announced to all members of the internal audit staff that might be affected by the review. Members of the internal audit staff might be offended if they do not know about the planned review and its objectives. The review announcement should contain a strong message that the purpose of the review is not to "get" anyone on the internal audit staff but to help the overall internal audit organization to become more efficient and effective.
- *Assign Resources to Perform the Review.*   Concurrent with or even prior to announcing the review, decisions need to be made regarding who is to perform the review. If an outside provider is used, objectives and review

schedules should be well defined. An internal audit quality-assurance review should have designated persons who will be performing the work and who will not be distracted by other projects.

- *Meet with Internal Audit Management.* In a large internal audit organization, the CAE is often responsible for initiating the review by scheduling it with the specialized function within internal audit that will perform the work or by contracting with an outside provider. Other members of the internal audit management team may not have that much knowledge about the planned review. Before starting the actual work, the review team should meet with appropriate members of audit management to advise them of its review approach and to discuss any special considerations that might affect the review approach. For example, the quality-assurance team may schedule a review at a separate, divisional internal audit function. Local internal audit management may explain some special considerations that might suggest that the reviewers avoid looking at one or another area. If the request is reasonable, the quality-assurance team should honor it, documenting that decision.

- *Meet with Other Members of Management.* Organizational management is normally quite aware of their internal auditors' work products through their presence in various operational areas or through audit reports. They may not be aware of the objectives of an internal quality-assurance review. This is the time for the review team leaders to meet with appropriate members of local management to explain their review objectives. The review team should also request some input from management regarding any of their concerns about the performance of internal audit. For example, management may feel that certain audit reports took far too long to be issued or that some members of the audit organization have not been acting in a professional manner. This type of input may point the review team to an examination of completion times for those audits mentioned or a review of training records for the audit staff.

After completing these first steps, the quality-assurance team should be ready to perform the actual review. Assuming that it has established a starting audit program, it may want to modify the scope and extent of its planned review based on these inputs. If a branch unit audit manager has indicated that a very critical audit is in process during the time of the review, the review team may want to avoid that review area so as to not disrupt other internal audit operations.

(ii) Quality-Assurance Internal Audit Review Procedures. An internal audit quality-assurance review is an independent assessment of the audit department's performance in compliance with internal audit professional and departmental standards. There is no single approach that applies to all internal audit departments and all reviews. Generally, a review will investigate internal audit office procedures and organizational standards and then will focus on individual completed audits to determine if the standards have been followed. Exhibit 26.5 describes some of the major review steps for a quality-assurance review of internal audit operations. The reviewers need to understand specific internal audit

EXHIBIT 26.5

Review Steps for a Quality-Assurance Review of Internal Audit

Audit _____ Location _____ Date _____

AUDIT STEP	Initials	W/P
1. Review I/A department procedures to determine if adequate emphasis is devoted to accuracy and quality issues. Highlight areas for potential improvement.	_____	_____
2. For current and past years, review the risk analysis and planning process. Assess whether appropriate attention was given to broad range of risks in organization.	_____	_____
3. Review the most current year of the completed audit plan:		
• Assess reasons for audits either never launched or still in process.	_____	_____
• Review the hours recorded for completed audits and compare to original plans. Document and determine reasons for major variances.	_____	_____
• Review the extent of special, nonplanned audits performed over past year and assess reasonableness.	_____	_____
4. Select a sample of audits completed of the past years and pull their complete workpaper files to ascertain:		
• Workpapers are in good order and follow I/A department standards.	_____	_____
• Audit programs support the risks identified, audit scope, and the work performed.	_____	_____
• All potential findings have been carried to the final audit report or otherwise received appropriate disposition.	_____	_____
• Appropriate audit reports or other communications were prepared following good internal audit standards.	_____	_____
5. Based on workpapers reviewed and other materials, assess I/A's use of audit automation, audit sampling, and other advanced techniques.	_____	_____
6. Interview key auditees from several audits completed to assess their impression of the professionalism of the I/A department.	_____	_____
7. Review I/A budgeting, travel expense, and time reporting procedures to determine the reasonableness and thoroughness of accounting procedures.	_____	_____
8. Review the continuing education activities within the I/A department to determine that appropriate attention is given professional training.	_____	_____
9. Review staff turnover within the department. If this seems high, investigate potential causes. If little turnover, discuss with the director plans for auditor career growth.	_____	_____

departmental procedures. This requires an initial study of documentation and other materials as a first step, just as internal auditors would review available documentation as a first step in their operational audits. Even if members of the same overall audit organization are performing the quality-assurance review, the review team should still review this internal audit documentation. It will reacquaint them again with operations and will allow them to better define their audit tests. This documentation standards review may also point to additional areas to emphasize in their detailed testing procedures. For example, the review may find that internal audit's standards for auditor project timekeeping are extremely complex. Because of this complexity, they may see a red flag that might suggest that auditors may have trouble completing the time reporting and therefore may not keep accurate time records. This might be an area for more detailed review.

Items reviewed within the internal audit department should be selected on a test basis. While this might not be an appropriate area to perform detailed statistical sampling test selection approaches, the review team should use judgmental sampling in the various areas reviewed. That is, internal audit might not care to reach an attribute sampling–type of conclusion, as was discussed in Chapter 16, "Gathering Evidence through Audit Sampling," the review teams should take care to make representative selections of all areas sampled. For example, if the quality-assurance reviewers are interested in whether internal audit has been performing an adequate risk analysis in various areas of the organization, the review team might judgmentally select several areas of overall organization operations and determine if an adequate risk analysis had been performed in those areas selected as part of the annual planning process.

The actual quality-assurance review procedures to be performed are essentially the same as for all other audits described throughout this book. The reviewers should identify an area from their established review program, select a representative sample of actual items, review or test the items selected, evaluate the tests, and document the results. The quality-assurance review team should take the same care in selecting and documenting its work as it would expect internal audit to follow in its regular audits. As with normal internal audits, when the review team finds what appear to be significant exceptions, it should discuss these potential findings with the internal auditors being reviewed to determine that there are no extenuating circumstances behind the potential findings. This is the same process normally followed in any internal audit, except that here the reviewers are auditing the auditors.

(iii) Reviews of Individual Completed Audits. In addition to reviewing overall audit group procedures, a quality-assurance review should always include a detailed review of a sample of completed audits. This review should not be made to second-guess the findings of the auditors who originally performed the work but to determine that the review followed good internal audit standards throughout all of the work, including planning, test procedures performed, workpaper documentation, and the completed audit report. While the steps described previously reviewed internal audit department standards, this phase of a quality-assurance review will assess compliance with these standards in the completion of actual audits.

Normally, a quality-assurance review team should select a representative sample of materials from completed audits over perhaps the past one-year period. This sample should include all types of audits, including operational, financial, information systems, and other types of special reviews. A good starting point is to look at an audit project report listing completed audits. From this, the review team should select the sample and pull the workpaper files and any other related data to describe the audit procedures performed, the conclusions reached, and the method of communicating those audit conclusions. This should not be a process to second-guess the auditors who performed the review. The reviewers should read enough of the workpapers to understand the audit objectives, the approaches used, and the conclusions reached. If the section reviewed has what appears to be a good process, where audit supervisors or others review all workpapers and appear to ask appropriate questions prior to the completion of normal audits, the quality-assurance review team can look at this sample review and satisfy itself it is working for all of the audits selected.

Once a review selection has been made, the quality-assurance reviewers should examine a sample of completed audit workpapers. This exercise will very much depend on the reviewers' understanding of departmental procedures. Here, in a review of individual workpapers, quality assurance should determine if those standards are being followed and if good auditing practices are used. The number and extent of areas that might be included in such a review will vary with the overall type and scope of the audit. They might include the following:

- *Audit Sampling Procedures Used.* Chapter 16 discussed procedures for the use of both statistical and nonstatistical sampling procedures. The internal auditors who did the actual work may have made a decision to only pull a limited judgmental sample when a better audit result might have resulted from the use of some type of statistical sampling approach. An appropriate quality-assurance comment is that the auditor in charge of the review did not appear to have considered the better results that might have been gained from statistical sampling techniques.

- *Compliance with GAAP or Other Accounting Standards.* While internal auditors will generally not be performing financial audits, many audits have some financial accounting ramifications. In many cases, these reviews may have been performed for the external auditors who would be responsible for reviewing the work and signing off on the conclusions developed. However, if the financial accounting procedures performed were strictly part of internal audit's review, the quality-assurance reviewer might want to consider the appropriateness of the financial accounting procedures as documented in the workpapers.

- *Appropriate Consideration of Information Systems Risks.* Operational audits sometimes do not consider the information systems risks associated with the area reviewed. For example, an operational or financial review might rely on the outputs of an information system, with no attention given to the controls surrounding that system. An appropriate quality-assurance review point is to comment on the assessment of information systems risks.

- *Use of Computer-Assisted Audit Techniques.* Chapter 23, "Computer-Assisted Audit Techniques," discussed the use of computer-assisted audit techniques to introduce efficiencies into the process of gathering audit evidence. If the audit workpapers reviewed do not show evidence of any considerations on the use of these techniques when the data reviewed might suggest this use, this may be an area for a review comment.

- *Use of Other Audit Automation Techniques.* Chapter 15, "Workpapers: Documenting Internal Audit Activities," discussed the preparation of workpapers to document audit activities. While many of the areas discussed there are appropriate for a quality-assurance review, the chapter emphasized some of the automated techniques that could be used to make the audit and workpaper-preparation process more efficient. Again, this is an area for potential quality-assurance review and comment.

These items are just limited examples of the many specific areas that might be included in a quality-assurance review of completed workpapers. The quality-assurance reviewers need to go through the selected workpapers in some detail and determine if internal audit best practices were followed during the review. In some instances, the quality-assurance reviewers may want to discuss the work with the internal auditors who completed the review and prepared the workpapers. While the audit workpapers should speak for themselves, the internal auditors who did the work can often provide additional background information on their reviews. While a need to ask specific questions about the audit procedures not described in the workpapers may point to lack of documentation, these questions are sometimes necessary for clarification purposes. Also, the quality-assurance reviewers will often want to interview or survey the actual auditees.

The actual audit report and its findings are also part of the quality-assurance review of the completed audit workpapers. The reviewers should determine that all points covered in the workpapers and identified as potential report findings have been included in the final audit report or otherwise given proper disposition. While the purpose of quality-assurance review is not to act as an after-the-fact "English teacher" who looks for style and small grammatical errors and the like, the reviews should assess whether the audit report has been clearly written and is in accordance with internal audit department standards. The reviewers may want to consider the elapsed time between fieldwork completion and report issuance. Too long of a delay in this report production may indicate some overall internal audit quality problems. The review of workpapers should include all of the steps documented in the internal audit process, from risk assessment and initial audit planning to the release of the final report, including auditee responses.

(iv) Auditee Interviews and Surveys. A quality-assurance review should include interviews or surveys with a sample of users of internal audit services. This process can take two different forms. The reviewers may want to interview both the auditees and users of audit reports as part of a quality-assurance review of selected internal audit projects. As an alternative, quality assurance may want to survey organizational management to better understand their impression of internal audit's services. Each of these surveys of persons outside of the internal audit department can have different dimensions and each may point to different potential conclusions.

Benchmarking is a different type of internal audit survey. This is where reviewers interview persons from audit departments in other organizations. The idea here is not to just review the quality of one or another individual audit but to assess how the entire internal audit department stacks up with similar internal audit functions in other organizations. This type of exercise is most meaningful when data is gathered from internal audit organizations of a similar size and in a similar industry. While some internal audit benchmarking is often done on a CAE level through informal professional contacts, quality assurance–sponsored internal audit benchmarking often formalizes this process and provides a better understanding of what internal audit departments in other organizations are doing.

Although the material discussed here is presented in the context of internal audit quality-assurance review work, internal audit management should consider the use of these survey and interview techniques for all audit work. An internal audit process often works outside of normal business processes, and internal audit should be able to gain considerable value from assessing what auditees thought of an audit just completed. Although the following sections are addressed to an internal audit quality-assurance function, some of these same concepts are applicable also to general internal audit management.

(A) QUALITY-ASSURANCE AUDITEE INTERVIEWS

After reviewing workpapers and other materials from a completed audit, the quality-assurance team will often find it valuable to interview some of the auditees. These are the persons whose functions were reviewed as part of the completed audit selected in the quality-assurance review. The idea here is to assess the level of internal audit professionalism as seen through the eyes of the auditees. Even though the quality-assurance team may have found the selected workpapers to be well organized and the audit report well written, internal audit has a potential quality problem if the auditees—the subjects of the audit—did not regard the internal auditors who performed the review as high-quality professionals.

Many factors can cause this type of feeling. For example, the field audit team may have worked late into the evening one day, but arrived at the audit site late in the morning the following day. Because the auditees did not know the team was working late, the auditees might have resented the auditor's work habits. Quality-assurance interviews with selected auditees might reveal this type of information.

Auditee interviews are usually initiated following a quality-assurance workpaper review. While not every auditee identified in the workpapers should be contacted, the review team might consider taking a small set of these persons to participate in an interview. Even though quality assurance may want to talk to several auditees identified in a single set of workpapers, all quality-assurance interviews should involve only one single auditee at a time. This one-on-one approach allows an auditee to be more open in expressing concerns regarding an audit.

Quality-assurance auditee interviews can provide much information about the quality of the internal auditors performing a review, but they can present difficulties. First, an auditee may not give totally honest responses to the interviewer's questions. The auditee being interviewed may not want to hurt the members of the audit team and will be reluctant to express honest opinions. Even worse, if a group of auditees is interviewed together as a focus group, there is a danger the session will transform itself into some form of a "feeding frenzy" where a large amount of negative, but unsupported bad news is communicated.

Exhibit 26.6 outlines the types of questions that a team of quality-assurance reviewers might ask a series of selected auditees. The interviewer should clearly state that the purpose of the review is to measure the overall quality of the audit procedures performed and not to "get" anyone. The auditee being interviewed should be assured that all responses will be kept confidential—similarly to the procedures followed in a normal audit. If appropriate, the interview responses should be summarized to capture total auditee impressions regarding the review.

EXHIBIT 26.6

Quality-Assurance Auditee Review Question

As part of our effort to maintain the highest level of professionalism, we are asking you to help review our performance in a recent audit performed in your department. We are interested in the_____ audit that took place between mm/dd/yy and mm/dd/yy and was led by_____.

Please take a few minutes to answer the following questions. If necessary use additional sheets and send your response in the enclosed envelope.

1. Did you understand the purpose and objective of the audit? Did you receive a formal letter announcing the audit?

2. Did the audit start when it was planned and finish as you expected?

3. Did the internal audit team maintain a professional attitude consistent with your department, in terms of such matters as their work hours, dress, and attention to work during the day?

4. Did the audit team appear to understand the area they were reviewing? Did they ask questions when appropriate? Did those questions appear excessive?

5. Was the audit performed so as not to hinder your normal work activities?

6. Were matters of audit concern, particularly those that were included in the final audit report, discussed with you in the course of the review?

7. Did the audit conclude with a formal exit meeting? Were the auditors' matters of concern discussed with you and did you have an opportunity to respond as appropriate and to provide additional data when necessary?

8. Was the audit report for the review delivered in a timely manner and did it reflect the final closing meeting and any additional clarifications that you may have added?

9. Were the audit recommendations in the final report appropriate and helpful?

10. In general, what was your overall opinion of the audit?

(B) Internal Audit Quality-Assurance Surveys

Interviews, as discussed previously, are generally limited to a small group of auditees involved with only a limited number of audits included in a quality-assurance review. In some instances, quality assurance may find some value in surveying all auditees in a given division, department, or larger organizational unit that has had contact with internal audit. This approach usually works best when quality assurance is reviewing the internal audit department in some geographically remote unit where the quality-assurance team has little knowledge of local internal audit operations. The survey might be mailed out prior to the arrival of the quality-assurance review team, with instructions to mail back the responses.

If this is done in advance, the internal audit quality-assurance team may be able to identify some potential concerns before the initiation of the actual quality-assurance review. The overall survey would have the same types of questions as in Exhibit 26.6. If this is to be sent to a separate unit of the organization, which may have its own separate internal audit function, the survey might be directed to all members of management who might have come in contact with internal audit rather than just to those who have been subjected to audits. This way, the quality-assurance team will be able to determine if some members of the organization who have never been included in an internal audit feel they should be included. The quality-assurance team conducting the survey should carefully classify the survey data to identify trends or issues.

(C) Internal Audit Benchmarking

Sometimes an internal audit quality-assurance team may want to determine how the practices in the internal audit function reviewed compare with those in other functions outside of their organizations. While a standard tenet of the IIA has been "progress through sharing," benchmarking is an expanded version of that sharing. In a traditional sharing exercise, the CAE or some other member of audit management may call directors of internal audit in other organizations to ask how they do something or to inquire as to their policy regarding some audit task. Benchmarking is a much more formal task where the best practices from a series of internal audit organizations are surveyed.

Benchmarking is used to measure nonaudit practices across different companies, and it is also a very effective tool for an internal audit quality-assurance review team. Although the quality-assurance team may have its own impression as to the best way to perform some audit procedure, it will often have no supportive evidence to show that its suggested approach is the best and is even used by other leading organizations. Quality-assurance benchmarking provides a way to assess how other internal audit departments are dealing with similar situations. For example, the quality-assurance team may find that the internal auditors reviewed are seldom using statistical sampling techniques in their reviews even though departmental standards call for their use as a suggested procedure. A good way to convince the audit managers and supervisors involved to use statistical sampling is to point out that a benchmarking survey has found that such sampling is used successfully by the internal audit departments in a series of leading and generally respected internal audit department organizations.

Benchmarking is a useful technique that can be used by internal audit in a variety of areas. Today, it is most frequently used by overall organization quality-assurance functions to compare cross-organizational practices. It is a useful technique for internal audit quality-assurance reviews.

(c) Reporting the Results of an Internal Audit Quality-Assurance Review

An internal audit quality-assurance review is an internal audit review of internal audit. Thus, the quality-assurance review should follow many of the same procedures as a normal internal audit, including planning, fieldwork, documentation of results, and then the audit report. A quality-assurance review is of little value unless its results are reported to internal audit management and others in some type of audit report. Depending upon the size of the internal audit department and the scope of the quality-assurance review, the completed review might follow a normal internal audit report, as was discussed in Chapter 15. That is, the quality-assurance reviewers should prepare a draft report with their quality-assurance review findings; the audit group reviewed would have an opportunity to respond to those findings, outlining the corrective action steps they plan to take; and the final product would be a quality-assurance report similar to regular internal audit reports.

A key difference between an internal audit quality-assurance report and a normal internal audit report is the report distribution. This report will normally be addressed to the CAE with copies to the audit committee but few if any other persons outside of internal audit on its distribution list. Since the report may cover some very specific and technical details of problem areas identified by the quality-assurance team, it may go into far greater detail than should be included in a well-drafted internal audit report. The quality-assurance review team is responsible for discussing areas where the internal audit area reviewed can improve its procedures; internal audit itself is responsible for making certain that appropriate corrective actions are taken. The CAE is normally responsible for deciding if persons outside of internal audit should receive a copy of the internal audit quality-assurance report. The CAE, for example, should give a copy to the audit committee as well as a selected number of senior managers and often to the external auditors. Quality assurance, however, should not assume that it can distribute the compiled report as desired. The CAE is responsible for determining that all aspects of the internal audit department follow good practices and that any appropriate corrective actions are taken.

A smaller internal audit department or an organization that has not devoted formal resources to performing formal, quality-assurance reviews should still take steps to monitor the quality of its internal audit activities. The quality of the internal audits performed can be measured through self-assessment surveys, which can take many forms, ranging from an open discussion in response to a "How are we doing?" type of question raised at a departmental session, through the completion of a formal self-assessment review or questionnaire. While the open discussion will give the CAE some information on how well the small audit department is doing, a self-assessment survey is most useful.

The idea is to ask each member of the internal audit department to complete a survey where they will respond to questions regarding their audit practices and how well they think that they, the individual auditors, as well as the department in total, think they are doing. Despite the size of the internal audit organization, all members of the team can evaluate how they feel they are performing as individuals, how they are performing as a team on their audit assignments, and how the overall audit department is performing in the eyes of each individual auditor. Each member of the audit department would be asked to complete a survey, tailored to the individual internal audit department, which emphasizes compliance with internal audit standards and the overall perceived quality of the work performed. A limited number of users of internal audit services might also be polled through this type of survey.

A small internal audit organization may be faced with the question of who should complete the survey. If the internal audit department consists of the CAE and perhaps only a staff of six, that director would know which of the internal audit staff completed the surveys based upon the nature of some criticisms or even the handwriting. These types of surveys are best run independently. The CAE might ask the human resources department to mail out the surveys and to compile the mailed-in results. This way, the survey responses would not be easily connected with the persons completing them and staff members would feel freer to express their opinions regarding the quality of internal audit department operations.

Once the survey results have been tabulated by the responsible nonaudit party, the CAE should share them with the audit staff. Although this type of assessment will not result in a formal findings and response type of audit report, members of the audit staff can collectively decide on various areas for internal audit improvement and should take steps to change internal audit operations as appropriate. Although not as comprehensive as the formal internal audit quality-assurance review described earlier in this chapter, an independent self-assessment review is a good exercise for the smaller internal audit department to evaluate the quality of its performance.

26.7 FUTURE DIRECTION FOR QUALITY-ASSURANCE AUDITING

Quality-assurance reviews are powerful tools that allow an internal audit department to measure how well it is performing. Internal auditors often review many other areas and freely make constructive suggestions, but they often do not take the opportunity to review themselves. A formal program of quality-assurance reviews will allow internal audit to better assess its own performance with reviews performed by a specialized function within internal audit, by various qualified outsiders, or by means of a self-assessment survey. Who performs the review will depend on the size and organization of the internal audit department, as well as on management's commitment to this type of review program.

In addition to reviewing how an individual internal audit department is doing and how well it is operating in compliance with internal audit standards, an internal audit department often needs to assess how it is performing when compared to internal audit functions in other organizations. This is where the concept of benchmarking is useful. An internal audit quality-assurance function can meet with other internal audit groups and determine how those groups are performing. Similarly, the well-run internal audit function should hold itself open to share its ideas and practices with other internal audit functions that are doing their own benchmarking.

No matter what specific approaches are used, the effective internal audit function needs to have an effective quality-assurance program in place. This will allow internal audit to comply with the *Professional Standards for the Practice of Internal Auditing*, as described in Chapter 12, and will otherwise allow internal audit to act as a strong, effective function in the organization.

ENDNOTE

[1] ISO CD2/ISO 19011 Milwaukee: ASQ Quality Press, 2000.

CHAPTER TWENTY-SEVEN

Control Self-Assessments

27.1 IMPORTANCE OF CONTROL SELF-ASSESSMENTS

One of COSO's recommendations, mentioned briefly in Chapter 4, "Internal Controls Fundamentals: COSO Framework," is that organizations "should report on the effectiveness and efficiency of [their] system of internal control." That internal control reporting can either be at a total organization level or be limited to individual organizations departments or functions. Chapter 6, "Evaluating Internal Controls: Section 404 Assessments," discussed the review of internal accounting controls from the perspective of the Sarbanes-Oxley Act (SOA) Section 404 requirements, and other chapters have covered various other aspects of internal controls reviews. The Institute of Internal Auditors (IIA) has introduced a different approach, called the control self-assessment (CSA) methodology, to help an internal audit function to look at its own controls or for helping others to review their internal controls. Based on the Total Quality Management (TQM) approaches of the early 1990s as well as the COSO framework discussed in Chapter 4, the CSA methodology has become a powerful new tool for internal auditors and others to better help to understand an organization's internal control environment. The approach requires the internal auditors to formally assemble a special team to assess those internal controls.

CSA was first initiated at Gulf Canada internal audit in 1987 as a tool to assess its internal control effectiveness as well as business processes. Facing both a legal consent decree requiring Gulf Canada to report on its internal controls and the difficulty resolving oil and gas measurement issues through the traditional audit process, its internal audit group launched a *facilitated meeting* self-assessment approach that involved gathering management and staff for interviews relating to, and discussions of, specific internal controls issues or processes. The process became a successful mechanism to assess informal, or soft, controls as well as the more traditional hard controls such as accounting balances.

CSA has been adopted by a number of major corporations as well as becoming part of IIA Standards of Professional Practice that were discussed in Chapter 12, "Internal Audit Professional Standards." This chapter briefly describes the CSA process and discusses the potential value to an organization in using CSA, how internal audit can launch CSA, and how to evaluate the data and results from a CSA project. CSA can be an important and useful tool for many internal audit organizations.

27.2 CSA MODEL

CSA is a process designed to help departments within an organization to assess and then evaluate their internal controls. In many respects, the CSA approach uses some of the same concepts found in the COSO framework internal controls model as discussed in Chapter 4. The CSA model says that an organization must implement strong control objectives and control activities in order to have a strong internal control environment. These two elements are surrounded by a good system of information and communication as well as processes for risk assessments and to monitor performance. This model is shown in Exhibit 27.1.

In some respects, CSA is an internal controls assessment process that has been viewed to be easily approachable for many. While some business professionals often look at a COSO internal controls risk assessment process as too "high level" and difficult to understand, CSA is an approach where individual departments in

EXHIBIT 27.1

The CSA Process

an organization can formally meet, in a facilitated group format, and assess the risks and internal controls within their individual departments or functions. Many internal audit departments have used CSA as a method to encourage departments or groups to better think about how to improve internal controls.

27.3 LAUNCHING THE CSA PROCESS

CSA is a process through which internal control effectiveness is examined and assessed not by a team of outsiders, but by people from within the function being assessed. Internal audit often takes a leadership role here. The objective is to provide reasonable assurance that good internal control business objectives will be met. The CSA concept requires the gathering of management and staff for interviews to assess their internal controls environment—a controls self-assessment. Because CSA requires all people in a function to participate in these sessions, from senior managers to staff, it often works best when someone outside of the department acts as a facilitator. While many people can take this CSA facilitator role, the two key groups that are ideal for this role might be internal audit with its internal controls review background or the quality function with its understanding of CSA-type processes.

Regardless of who acts as leader or facilitator, a CSA project should improve an organization's control environment by making all involved stakeholders more aware of organizational objectives and the role of internal control in achieving goals and objectives. Going forward, the CSA process should motivate employees to design and implement improved control processes and continually improve control processes. A CSA review is particularly effective when the internal control system reviewed is a large enterprise resource planning (ERP) system that covers all or most aspects of operations. This is a case where one basic automated system covers accounting, human resources, production, marketing, and more. Vendors such as SAP, PeopleSoft, and Oracle supply these all-encompassing applications. This type of application covers many aspects across an organization, and many participants often do not fully understand the internal control implications of their various actions.

The first step in launching CSA is for the chief audit executive (CAE) or some other person leading the initiative to "sell" the concept to senior management. In a smaller organization, the message may be that CSA should help the organization to improve internal control procedures and some aspects of SOA Section 404 compliance, while not embarking on a time-consuming, expensive exercise. Other potential benefits from such CSA process are:

- To increase the scope of internal control reporting during a given period
- To target internal control-related work by focusing on high-risk and unusual items discovered in the course of these CSA reviews
- To increase the effectiveness of corrective actions by transferring internal controls ownership and responsibility to operating employees

The CSA team leader then needs to decide what portion of the entity will use CSA, what functions or objectives to consider, and what level of stakeholders should be included in the assessments. The number and level of stakeholders will depend on the CSA approach selected. The three primary CSA approaches are *facilitated team meetings or workshops, questionnaires,* or *management-produced analysis*. Organizations often combine a mixture of more than one approach to accommodate their self-assessment.

Facilitated team meetings gather internal control information from work teams that may represent multiple levels within an organization. A facilitator, trained in internal control system design, should lead the sessions. A questionnaire-based approach uses surveys that are usually based on simple yes/no or have/have not responses. Process owners use the survey results to assess their control structure. The third approach, a management produced analysis' is really an internal audit type of analysis. Based on a management- or staff-produced study of the business process, a CSA specialist—probably an internal auditor—combines the results of the study with information gathered from sources such as interviews with other managers and key personnel. By synthesizing this material, the CSA specialist develops an analysis that process owners can use in better understanding and improving internal controls for the given process area.

The CSA approach and format used here will depend on the overall organizational culture as well as senior management decisions. In the event that a corporate culture does not support a participative CSA approach, questionnaire responses and internal control analysis can enhance the overall control environment. Ideally, the facilitated session is the best, where all employees meet on peer basis and discuss and evaluate their internal control issues and concerns on a discussion basis, led by a facilitator.

Just as there is some discussion on the role of internal audit in SOA Section 404 reviews, the same is true for CSA processes. There must be a decision as to whether internal audit or operating management will drive the CSA process. Some CSA practitioners believe that internal audit, as the arm of senior management responsible for internal control oversight, may be the appropriate driver for CSA. The presence of internal auditors in CSA-facilitated meetings is, in and of itself, an oversight control. Others believe that a self-assessment can only be effectively performed by operating management and/or work units. The involvement of internal audit, in this view, means that management will be less accountable for internal controls.

(a) Performing the Facilitated CSA Review

The basic concept behind a CSA review of an internal control system or process is to gather a group of people, across multiple levels of the organization and from multiple units, and then to gather extensive information about internal controls for that selected system or process. The idea is to select representative samples of stakeholders throughout the organization to meet and discuss the selected system's operations and controls. An internal auditor or some other communications specialist is then designated to head these workshops, lead discussions, and help draw conclusions.

Facilitated team workshops gather information from work teams representing different levels in the business unit or function. The format of the workshop may be based on objectives, risks, controls, or processes. Each has distinct advantages, depending on the internal controls area reviewed. Assume as an example, that an organization has installed a large, comprehensive ERP system that encompasses many major operations areas. Management has requested an internal control risk assessment of this major application. Because the ERP system covers many aspects of business operations, a decision is made to review systems controls through a series of "focus group" users gathering to discuss and review systems operations. Planning steps for organizing these CSA reviews should be developed into a CSA organization plan. Based on the extensive set of CSA materials published by the IIA,[1] this plan and a facilitated CSA session can follow any of four meeting formats:

- *Objective-Based CSA Facilitated Sessions.*   These sessions focus on the best way to accomplish a business objective, such as accurate financial reporting. The workshop begins by the team identifying the controls presently in place to support the system objectives and, then, determining any residual risks remaining if controls are not working. The aim of this format of workshop is to decide whether the control procedures are working effectively and that any remaining risks are at an acceptable level. This type of a facilitated session could begin by the facilitator asking participants to identify their group's control environment, emphasizing such areas in the control environment as:

  - The control consciousness of the organization.

  - The extent to which employees are committed to doing what's right and doing it the right way.

  - A wide variety of factors that encompasses technical competence and ethical commitment.

  - Intangible factors that are often essential to effective internal control.

- *Risk-Based CSA Facilitated Sessions.*   These sessions focus on the CSA teams listing risks to achieve internal control objectives. The workshop begins by listing all possible barriers, obstacles, threats, and exposures that might prevent achieving an objective and, then, examining the control procedures to determine if they are sufficient to manage any identified key risks. The aim of the workshop is to determine significant residual risks. This format takes the work team through the entire set of objective-risks-controls surrounding the entity reviewed. This would be followed by risk-based discussions. Teams would be asked to identify their risks by asking the questions:

  - What could go wrong?

  - What assets do we need to protect?

  - How could someone steal from us?

  - What is our greatest legal exposure?

  Sessions would then attempt to identify significant risks at their department, activity, or process level. For each identified risk, the groups should discuss the potential likelihood of occurrence and the potential impact. Those risks with a reasonable likelihood of occurrence and a large potential impact would be identified as significant.

- *Control-Based CSA Facilitated Sessions.* These sessions focus on how well the controls in place are working. This format is different than the two sessions previously described because the facilitator identifies the key risks and controls before the beginning of the workshop. During the CSA session, the work team assesses how well established the controls mitigate risks and promote the achievement of objectives. The aim of the workshop is to produce an analysis of the gap between how controls are working and how well management expects those controls to work.

- *Process-Based CSA Facilitated Sessions.* These sessions focus on selected activities that are elements of a chain of processes. Processes are a series of related activities that go from some beginning point to an end, such as, the various steps in purchasing, product development, or revenue generation. This type of workshop usually covers the identification of the objectives of the whole process and the various intermediate steps. The aim of the workshop is to evaluate, update, validate, improve, and even streamline the whole process and its component activities. This session format may have a greater breadth of analysis than a control-based approach by covering multiple objectives within the process and by supporting concurrent management efforts, such as reengineering, quality assurance, and continuous improvement initiatives.

Each of these formats can be effective for developing and understanding both the hard and soft controls in a function as well as the risks surrounding any significant internal control processes. The keys to success here are to have knowledgeable and well-prepared meeting facilitators to ask appropriate questions and to get all of the selected team members to participate. The other major key is to take detailed transcriptions of the meeting sessions. While not every word spoken has to be recorded, strong meeting highlights are needed. Recording major discussion points through the facilitator's large notes pad in front of the room often works well.

While the facilitator is a major driver here, CSA sessions can easily turn into disasters with the wrong people mix. Lower-level stakeholders may feel reluctant to discuss controls weaknesses if people that are more senior are in the session. Comments about risks or control weaknesses can get very personal if some of the team has major responsibilities for the systems or process discussed. Despite all of this, the CSA process can be a very worthwhile, but expensive, tool to look at a comprehensive system or process from multiple perspectives and to understand any internal control weaknesses.

(b) Performing the Questionnaire-Based CSA Review

A CSA facilitated review can be difficult and time-consuming, no matter whether relative risk, internal control, or process based. In many cases, a questionnaire format can be an effective way to gather control information. A questionnaire is prepared covering the process or system of interest and then distributed to a selected group of stakeholders to gain an understanding of the risks and controls in the area of interest. Exhibit 27.2 is an example CSA questionnaire for Planning and Budgeting processes. It was developed by the IIA, who also has an extensive set of other sample CSA questionnaires on its Web site: www.theiia.org.

The CSA team would circulate these questionnaires, with the respondent's name attached, to a selected group of stakeholders, monitor results to ensure that an appropriate number have been returned, and then compile the results. Questionnaires will not yield the discovery type of comments that would come out of focus groups but will give an overall assessment of the soundness of processes and internal controls. This is an effective way to gather basic CSA background data.

EXHIBIT 27.2

CSA Specific Function Questionnaire: Planning and Budgeting

The following questions might be used for a Planning and Budgeting CSA review.

1. Do you ensure that completed budgets are consistent with the strategic plan of the company?

2. Are policies and procedures in place to avoid understatement of expenditures?

3. Do you investigate all variances between actual expenditures and budgeted amounts, and, for all variances, are explanations required?

4. Do you ensure that the finalized budget and all revisions are properly documented and approved?

5. Have you assigned a person to receive all information regarding changes to the company that may affect the budget?

6. Is the budget preparation procedure (including approval level requirements) fully documented, and is it distributed to all management involved in the budget process?

7. Are procedures in place to provide adequate information to departmental management for their use in developing a budget?

8. Do you monitor trends in expenses?

9. Are calculations methods for expenses (including new categories) adequately explained?

10. Do you ensure that departments are given adequate time to complete and submit their budgets?

11. Have you identified one individual within each department who has the responsibility for completing the budget, and is assistance provided as needed?

12. Do you advise departments on what and how expenses are to be charged for acquisitions or disposed operations?

EXHIBIT 27.2 *(CONTINUED)*

CSA Specific Function Questionnaire: Planning and Budgeting

13. Are procedures in place to ensure that a limited number of authorized individuals have access to the budgets and that any additions, changes, and deletions are approved and traceable? If the budget is online, are all transactions identified by user ID, date, and transaction type?

14. Do you review the initial budgets and identify areas of possible cost reductions?

15. Are procedures in place to identify departments that consistently incur large expenditures at year-end to bring actual costs up to budget?

16. Are procedures in place to handle cash forecasts?

17. Do you monitor and require approvals for all capital expenditures?

18. Have you identified all of the documentation required of departments when submitting numbers for budgets, return on investments calculation, etc.?

19. Do you monitor project breakdown to ensure that large projects are not broken down into smaller projects to avoid approval requirements?

Source: Robert R. Moeller, *Sarbanes-Oxley and the New Internal Auditing Rules,* © copyright 2004, John Wiley & Sons. Used with permission.

(c) Performing the Management-Produced Analysis CSA Review

As an alternative to a survey or a facilitated workshop, a management-produced analysis is very similar to the type of operational review that an internal auditor would perform. This is one of the three CSA analysis approaches suggested by the IIA. Using this approach, management produces a staff study of the business process—almost a research study. The CSA specialist, who may be an internal auditor, combines the results of the study with information gathered from sources such as other managers and key personnel. By synthesizing this material, the CSA specialist develops an analysis that process owners can use in their CSA efforts.

The management-produced analysis approach, although endorsed by the IIA as one of three suggested CSA approaches, is difficult for the typical organization. It suggests an almost "academic" review by someone in the organization followed by some comparative research for subsequent analysis. We generally do not suggest this approach!

The IIA believes all the above formats strengthen the entity's control structure. Each entity should perform an analysis of external opportunities or threats as well as internal strengths and weaknesses to determine which format is most appropriate in the organization. Many CSA users combine one or more formats within a given facilitated meeting to best meet their needs.

27.4 EVALUATING CSA RESULTS

A CSA analysis, particularly if it covered multiple processes or systems, will result in a large amount of accumulated data. Some may support existing process strengths, others will point to internal control weaknesses in need of correction, and still others may point to areas in need of further research. In many cases, the work will validate the integrity and controls of the systems and processes reviewed.

The results of this CSA review will be similar to those of a COSO review of internal accounting controls—a disciplined and thorough method to evaluate significant internal controls. This might be a good first step to launch a SOA Section 404 analysis, as was described in Chapter 6. CSA provides a manner for reviewers to gain a better understanding of the multitude of soft controls that surround many processes or systems. Published documentation or focused controls review interviews may indicate that some controls exist. However, the back and forth from a facilitated session may reveal that "yes, there are control processes described in our systems documentation, but we always push the escape key to ignore the control warning messages." This can be an effective way to expose internal control vulnerabilities.

CSAs were introduced to the internal audit community in the late 1980s and subsequently were embraced by the IIA. Many private-sector organizations worldwide initiated successful CSA programs, and several state governments within the United States began requiring CSA-oriented internal control assessments. The auditing and accounting departments within those states complied with the regulations via questionnaires or management-produced analysis processes. The Federal Deposit Insurance Corporation (FDIC) and the Canadian Deposit Insurance Corporation (CDIC) now require financial institutions throughout the United States and Canada, respectively, to assess internal controls with specific CSA guidance compliance.

In recent years, the IIA has launched its first specialty certification, the Certification in Control Self-Assessment (CCSA). This examination-based certificate is designed to enhance senior management's confidence of a reviewer's understanding and knowledge of, and training in, the CSA process. The CCSA certificate and its requirements are discussed in Chapter 28, "Professional Certifications: CIA, CISA, and More."

The IIA believes that CSA effectively augments internal auditing. One of the primary responsibilities of the board and officers of any organization is providing stakeholders with assurance through oversight of the organization's activities. Internal auditing, by definition, assists members of the organization in the effective discharge of their responsibilities. Through CSA, internal auditing and operating staff can collaborate to produce an assessment of internal controls in an operation. This synergy helps internal auditing assist in management's oversight function by improving the quantity and quality of available information. The quantity is increased as internal auditing relies on operating employees to actively participate in CSA, thus reducing time spent in information gathering and validation procedures performed during an audit. The quality is increased since participating employees have a more thorough understanding of the process than an auditor can develop over a relatively short period of time.

ENDNOTE

1. *Control Self-Assessment: Experience, Current Thinking, and Best Practices*, The Institute of Internal Auditors Research Foundation, Altamonte Springs, FL, 1996.

PART SEVEN

The Professional Internal Auditor

CHAPTER TWENTY-EIGHT

Professional Certifications: CIA, CISA, and More

28.1 WHY SEEK PROFESSIONAL CERTIFICATION?

We live in a world today increasingly filled with various professional certification designations. Information systems professionals who work with Microsoft Windows, for example, can take an examination and become certified as Microsoft Certified Systems Engineers (MSCE). To obtain this certification, an individual must take and pass a comprehensive examination and also demonstrate some level of experience in having worked with appropriate types of software products. This certification may be viewed very positively by an employer looking for a candidate to fill a position requiring those job skills. A MSCE may give a candidate some additional points in the job selection process.

Other professional certifications may not be that valuable to some. For example, but not to pick on an industry, the insurance industry is filled with many types and levels of certifications. A purchaser of life insurance may encounter a salesperson who has a stream of different certification initials after the name on his or her business card. Among many others, this may include a

Certified Life Underwriter (CLU) certification. Does such a CLU certification have an influence on whether a consumer will buy life insurance from a CLU-designated salesperson over another? For many, the answer is probably NO. Those initials may help tell the consumer to recognize that the life insurance salesperson is experienced, but the sales pitch and price will often be deciding factors on the insurance purchase. Of course, the consumer will expect a greater knowledge of insurance processes from the salesperson with the CLU.

Internal auditors often face a similar decision. Many internal auditors join the profession with no specific certification requirements beyond their undergraduate college degrees. However, some hiring managers once assumed that potential internal auditor candidates must have a Certified Public Accountant (CPA) certificate to become qualified as an internal auditor. However, over time many realized the internal audit profession required people with different skills and qualifications than just a CPA. Things changed at the urging of Institute of Internal Auditors (IIA), and the result was the Certified Internal Auditor (CIA) certification. Today, beyond the CIA, an internal auditor can become a Certified Information Systems Auditor (CISA), a Certified Fraud Examiner (CFE), or acquire any of a series of other certifications. Some of these may be very valuable for a typical internal auditor, while others may receive little more than a "ho hum" from potential employers. This chapter will discuss some of the professional designations that are important to the modern internal auditor. In particular, we will look at the CIA and CISA certifications, including their qualification and examination requirements. In addition, the chapter will consider some of the other certification options important for internal auditors.

The chapter will not discuss the CPA examination. While certainly more oriented toward external auditors, the CPA is still the best recognized accounting, auditing, and internal control examination for all financial professionals, including internal auditors. It should be an objective for any internal auditor with a financial background who has not already attained CPA certification. The other professional examinations discussed in this chapter, such as the CIA, also should be considered strong objectives for many modern internal auditors.

28.2 CERTIFIED INTERNAL AUDITOR EXAMINATION

The Certified Internal Auditor (CIA) certification is the major professional certification for internal auditors, and is sponsored by the IIA. The CIA examination was first offered in August 1974 to 654 candidates, and the IIA has awarded more than 45,000 CIA designations to date. Administered by the IIA Board of Regents, the CIA is a seven-hour total examination that is offered worldwide twice a year and consists of the following sections:

Part I: The Internal Audit Activity's Role in Governance, Risk, and Control

Part II: Conducting the Internal Audit Engagement

Part III: Business Analysis and Information Technology

Part IV: Business Management Skills

By applying to become a CIA candidate, an individual agrees to accept the conditions of the program including its eligibility requirements, exam confidentiality, acceptance of the CIA's Code of Ethics, continuing professional education (CPE) requirements, and any other conditions enacted by the Board of Regents or the Certification Department.

To apply to take the CIA examination, candidates must hold a bachelor's degree or its equivalent, such as Chartered Accountant, from an accredited college-level institution; a copy of the candidate's diploma, transcripts, or other written proof of completion of a degree program must accompany the candidate's application. With the exception of full-time undergraduate degree students in their senior year, candidates will not be allowed to sit for the exam until the educational requirement is met.

Applicants who do not possess a bachelor's degree and who are unsure whether their educational achievements or professional designation qualify as equivalents can apply for a waiver from these educational requirements through a formal request to the Board of Regents, the final judge of the acceptability of professional or educational attainment offered in lieu of a bachelor's degree and of equivalents. Information submitted should be sufficiently detailed to enable the Board of Regents to determine equivalency.

CIA candidates must exhibit high moral and professional character and must submit a character reference form completed by another CIA, or the candidate's supervisor, manager, or educator. In addition, CIA candidates are required to have completed 24 months of internal auditing experience or its equivalent. Equivalent experience means experience in the audit/assessment disciplines, including external auditing, quality assurance, compliance, and internal control. Either a master's degree or work experience in related business professions (such as accounting, law, or finance) can be substituted for one year of experience. Work experience must be verified by a CIA or the candidate's supervisor. Candidates may sit for the CIA exam prior to satisfying their experience requirement, but they will not be certified until the experience requirement has been met.

In addition, the CIA exam is a nondisclosed examination. That is, candidates must agree to keep the contents of the exam confidential and therefore may not discuss the specific exam content with anyone except the IIA's Certification Department. Unauthorized disclosure of exam material will be considered a breach of the code of ethics and could result in disqualification of the candidate or other appropriate censure.

(a) The CIA Examination

Exhibit 28.1 shows an overview of the potential contents of the four parts of the CIA examination. As shown on the exhibit, candidates may be tested for the *Proficiency* or *Awareness* of a given subject area. Awareness means that the candidate must be aware of general issues in a topic area while proficiency says the candidate should have a strong understanding and knowledge of how to apply that subject area. Two subject points in Part IV might better explain this difference:

- *Part II Fraud Knowledge Elements.* Understanding "red flags" and types of fraud has been assigned a P for a proficiency level of knowledge. The CIA-qualified internal auditor should be proficient in these important areas.

- *Part II Fraud Knowledge Elements.* Interrogation techniques and forensic auditing only requires an A or an awareness level of understanding. Both of these areas are complex topics requiring an advanced level of knowledge.

The CIA examination covers a wide range of current topics that are significant to the modern internal auditor. Each of the four sections will have 75 to 125 multiple choice questions. The examination is periodically updated and reflects current topics of interest to internal auditors.

Exhibit 28.1

CIA Examination Summary

Part I: The Internal Audit Activity's Role in Governance, Risk, and Control

A. COMPLY WITH THE IIA'S ATTRIBUTE STANDARDS (15-25%)	Level P

1. Define the purpose, authority, and responsibility of the internal audit activity.
    a. Determine if the purpose, authority, and responsibility of internal audit activity are clearly documented and approved.
    b. Determine if the purpose, authority, and responsibility of internal audit activity are communicated to the engagement clients.
    c. Demonstrate an understanding of the purpose, authority, and responsibility of the internal audit activity.
2. Maintain independence and objectivity.
    a. Foster independence.
        1) Understand organizational independence.
        2) Recognize the importance of organizational independence.
        3) Determine if the internal audit activity is properly aligned to achieve organizational independence.
    b. Foster objectivity.
        1) Establish policies to promote objectivity.
        2) Assess individual objectivity.
        3) Maintain individual objectivity.
        4) Recognize and mitigate impairments to independence and objectivity.
3. Determine if the required knowledge, skills, and competencies are available.
    a. Understand the knowledge, skills, and competencies that an internal auditor needs to possess.
    b. Identify the knowledge, skills, and competencies required to fulfill the responsibilities of the internal audit activity.
4. Develop and/or procure necessary knowledge, skills, and competencies collectively required by internal audit activity.
5. Exercise due professional care.
6. Promote continuing professional development.
    a. Develop and implement a plan for continuing professional development for internal audit staff.
    b. Enhance individual competency through continuing professional development.
7. Promote quality assurance and improvement of the internal audit activity.
    a. Establish and maintain a quality assurance and improvement program.
    b. Monitor the effectiveness of the quality assurance and improvement program.	

EXHIBIT 28.1 *(CONTINUED)*

CIA Examination Summary

c. Report the results of the quality assurance and improvement program to the board or other governing body.
    d. Conduct quality assurance procedures and recommend improvements to the performance of the internal audit activity.
  8. Abide by and promote compliance with the IIA Code of Ethics.	

B. ESTABLISH A RISK-BASED PLAN TO DETERMINE THE PRIORITIES OF THE INTERNAL AUDIT ACTIVITY (15-5%)	**Level P**

1. Establish a framework for assessing risk.
  2. Use the framework to:
    a. Identify sources of potential engagements (e.g., audit universe, management request, regulatory mandate)
    b. Assess organization-wide risk.
    c. Solicit potential engagement topics from various sources.
    d. Collect and analyze data on proposed engagements.
    e. Rank and validate risk priorities.
  3. Identify internal audit resource requirements.
  4. Coordinate the internal audit activity's efforts with:
    a. External auditor
    b. Regulatory oversight bodies
    c. Other internal assurance functions (e.g., health and safety department)
  5. Select engagements.
    a. Participate in the engagement selection process.
    b. Select engagements.
    c. Communicate and obtain approval of the engagement plan from board.	

C. UNDERSTAND THE INTERNAL AUDIT ACTIVITY'S ROLE IN ORGANIZATIONAL GOVERNANCE (10-20%)	**Level P**

1. Obtain board's approval of audit charter
  2. Communicate plan of engagements
  3. Report significant audit issues
  4. Communicate key performance indicators to board on a regular basis
  5. Discuss areas of significant risk
  6. Support board in enterprise-wide risk assessment
  7. Review positioning of the internal audit function within the risk management framework within the organization.
  8. Monitor compliance with the corporate code of conduct/business practices
  9. Report on the effectiveness of the control framework
 10. Assist board in assessing the independence of the external auditor
 11. Assess ethical climate of the board
 12. Assess ethical climate of the organization
 13. Assess compliance with policies in specific areas (e.g., derivatives)
 14. Assess organization's reporting mechanism to the board
 15. Conduct follow-up and report on management response to regulatory body reviews
 16. Conduct follow-up and report on management response to external audit	

EXHIBIT 28.1 *(CONTINUED)*

CIA Examination Summary

17. Assess the adequacy of the performance measurement system, achievement of corporate objective **18.** Support a culture of fraud awareness and encourage the reporting of improprieties	
D. PERFORM OTHER INTERNAL AUDIT ROLES AND RESPONSIBILITIES (0-10%)	**Level P**

1. Ethics/Compliance
    a. Investigate and recommend resolution for ethics/compliance complaints
    b. Determine disposition of ethics violations
    c. Foster healthy ethical climate
    d. Maintain and administer business conduct policy (e.g., conflict of interest)
    e. Report on compliance
2. Risk Management
    a. Develop and implement an organization-wide risk and control framework
    b. Coordinate enterprise-wide risk assessment
    c. Report corporate risk assessment to board
    d. Review business continuity planning process
3. Privacy
    a. Determine privacy vulnerabilities
    b. Report on compliance
4. Information or physical security
    a. Determine security vulnerabilities
    b. Determine disposition of security violations
    c. Report on compliance	

E. GOVERNANCE, RISK, AND CONTROL KNOWLEDGE ELEMENTS (15-25%)	**Levels**
1. Corporate governance principles	A
2. Alternative control frameworks	A
3. Risk vocabulary and concepts	P
4. Risk management techniques	P
5. Risk/control implications of different organizational structures	P
6. Risk/control implications of different leadership styles	A
7. Change management	A
8. Conflict management	A
9. Management control techniques	P
10. Types of control (preventive, detective, input, output)	P
F. PLAN ENGAGEMENTS (15-25%)	**Level P**

1. Initiate preliminary communication with engagement client.
2. Conduct a preliminary survey of the area of engagement.
    a. Obtain input from engagement client.
    b. Perform analytical reviews.
    c. Perform benchmarking.
    d. Conduct interviews.
    e. Review prior audit reports and other relevant documentation.
    f. Map processes.
    g. Develop checklists.	

EXHIBIT 28.1   *(CONTINUED)*

CIA Examination Summary

3. Complete a detailed risk assessment of the area (prioritize or evaluate risk/control factors).

4. Coordinate audit engagement efforts with.

   a. External auditor
   b. Regulatory oversight bodies

5. Establish/refine engagement objectives and identify/finalize the scope of engagement.

6. Identify or develop criteria for assurance engagements (criteria against which to audit).

7. Consider the potential for fraud when planning an engagement.

   a. Be knowledgeable about the risk factors and red flags of fraud.
   b. Identify common types of fraud associated with the engagement area.
   c. Determine if risk of fraud requires special consideration when conducting an engagement.

8. Determine engagement procedures.

9. Determine the level of staff and resources needed for the engagement.

10. Establish adequate planning and supervision of the engagement.

11. Prepare engagement work program.

Format: 125 multiple-choice questions

Part II: Conducting the Internal Audit Engagement

A. CONDUCT ENGAGEMENTS (25-35%)	Level P

1. Research and apply appropriate standards:
   a. IIA Professional Practices Framework (code of ethics, standards, practice advisories).
   b. Other professional, legal, and regulatory standards.

2. Maintain an awareness of the potential for fraud when conducting an engagement.
   a. Notice indicators or symptoms of fraud.
   b. Design appropriate engagement steps to address significant risk of fraud.
   c. Employ audit tests to detect fraud.
   d. Determine if any suspected fraud merits investigation.

3. Collect data.

4. Evaluate the relevance, sufficiency, and competence of evidence.

5. Analyze and interpret data.

6. Develop work papers.

7. Review work papers.

8. Communicate interim progress.

9. Draw conclusions.

10. Develop recommendations when appropriate.

EXHIBIT 28.1 *(CONTINUED)*

CIA Examination Summary

11. Report engagement results.	
a. Conduct exit conference.	
b. Prepare report or other communication.	
c. Approve engagement report.	
d. Determine distribution of report.	
e. Obtain management response to report.	
12. Conduct client satisfaction survey.	
13. Complete performance appraisals of engagement staff.	
B. CONDUCT SPECIFIC ENGAGEMENTS (25-35%)	Level P
1. Conduct assurance engagements.	
a. Fraud investigation	
1) Determine appropriate parties to be involved with investigation.	
2) Establish facts and extent of fraud (e.g., interviews, interrogations and data analysis).	
3) Report outcomes to appropriate parties.	
4) Complete a process review to improve controls to prevent fraud and recommend changes.	
b. Risk and control self-assessment	
1) Facilitated approach	
(a) Client-facilitated	
(b) Audit-facilitated	
2) Questionnaire approach	
3) Self-certification approach	
c. Audits of third parties and contract auditing	
d. Quality audit engagements	
e. Due diligence audit engagements	
f. Security audit engagements	
g. Privacy audit engagements	
h. Performance (key performance indicators) audit engagements	
i. Operational (efficiency and effectiveness) audit engagements	
j. Financial audit engagements	
k. Information technology (IT) audit engagements	
1) Operating systems	
(a) Mainframe	
(b) Workstations	
(c) Server	
2) Application development	
(a) Application authentication	
(b) Systems development methodology	
(c) Change control	
(d) End-user computing	
3) Data and network communications/connections (e.g., LAN, VAN, and WAN)	
4) Voice communications	
5) System security (e.g., firewalls, access control)	
6) Contingency planning	
7) Databases	
8) Functional areas of IT operations (e.g., data center operations)	

EXHIBIT 28.1 *(CONTINUED)*

CIA Examination Summary

9) Web infrastructure	
10) Software licensing	
11) Electronic funds transfer (EFT) and Electronic data interchange (EDI)	
12) e-commerce	
13) Information protection (e.g., viruses, privacy)	
14) Encryption	
15) Enterprise-wide resource planning (ERP) software (e.g., SAP R/3)	
i. Compliance audit engagements	
2. Conduct consulting engagements	
a. Internal control training	
b. Business process review	
c. Benchmarking	
d. Information technology (IT) and systems development	
e. Design of performance measurement systems	
C. MONITOR ENGAGEMENT OUTCOMES (5-15%)	**Level P**
1. Determine appropriate follow-up activity by the internal audit activity.	
2. Identify appropriate method to monitor engagement outcomes.	
3. Conduct follow-up activity.	
4. Communicate monitoring plan and results.	
D. FRAUD KNOWLEDGE ELEMENTS (5-15%)	**Levels**
1. Discovery sampling	A
2. Interrogation techniques	A
3. Forensic auditing	A
4. Use of computers in analyzing data	P
5. Red flag	P
6. Types of fraud	P
E. ENGAGEMENT TOOLS (15-25%)	**Levels**
1. Sampling	A
a. Nonstatistical (judgmental)	
b. Statistical	
2. Statistical analyses (process control techniques)	A
3. Data gathering tools	P
a. Interviewing	
b. Questionnaires	
c. Checklists	
4. Analytical review techniques	P
a. Ratio estimation	
b. Variance analysis (e.g., budget vs. actual)	
c. Other reasonableness tests	
5. Observation	P
6. Problem solving	P
7. Risk and control self-assessment (CSA)	A

EXHIBIT 28.1 *(CONTINUED)*

CIA Examination Summary

8. Computerized audit tools and techniques	P
a. Embedded audit modules	
b. Data extraction techniques	
c. Generalized audit software (e.g., ACL, IDEA)	
d. Spreadsheet analysis	
e. Automated work papers (e.g., Lotus Notes, Auditor Assistant)	
9. Process mapping including flowcharting	P
Format: 125 multiple-choice questions	

Part III: Business Analysis and Information Technology

A. BUSINESS PROCESSES (15–25%)	Levels
1. Quality management (e.g., TQM)	A
2. The International Organization for Standardization (ISO) framework	A
3. Forecasting	A
4. Project management techniques	P
5. Business process analysis (e.g., workflow analysis and bottleneck management, theory of constraints)	P
6. Inventory management techniques and concepts	P
7. Marketing - pricing objectives and policies	A
8. Marketing - supply chain management	A
9. Human resources (Individual performance management and measurement; supervision; environmental factors that affect performance; facilitation techniques; personnel sourcing/staffing; training and development; safety)	P
10. Balanced scorecard	A

B. FINANCIAL ACCOUNTING AND FINANCE (15–25%)	Levels
1. Basic concepts and underlying principles of financial accounting (e.g., statements, terminology, relationships)	P
2. Intermediate concepts of financial accounting (e.g., bonds, leases, pensions, intangible assets, R&D)	A
3. Advanced concepts of financial accounting (e.g., consolidation, partnerships, foreign currency transactions)	A
4. Financial statement analysis	P
5. Cost of capital evaluation	A
6. Types of debt and equity	A
7. Financial instruments (e.g., derivatives)	A
8. Cash management (treasury functions)	A
9. Valuation models	A
a. Inventory valuation	
b. Business valuation	
10. Business development life cycles	A

EXHIBIT 28.1 *(CONTINUED)*

CIA Examination Summary

C. MANAGERIAL ACCOUNTING (10-20%)	
1. Cost concepts (e.g., absorption, variable, fixed)	P
2. Capital budgeting	A
3. Operating budget	P
4. Transfer pricing	A
5. Cost-volume-profit analysis	A
6. Relevant cost	A
7. Costing systems (e.g., activity-based, standard)	A
8. Responsibility accounting	A
D. REGULATORY, LEGAL, AND ECONOMICS (5-15%)	Level A
1. Impact of government legislation and regulation on business	
2. Trade legislation and regulations	
3. Taxation schemes	
4. Contracts	
5. Nature and rules of legal evidence	
6. Key economic indicators	
E. INFORMATION TECHNOLOGY - IT (30-40%)	Level A
1. Control frameworks (e.g., eSAC, COBIT)	
2. Data and network communications/connections (e.g., LAN, VAN, and WAN)	
3. Electronic funds transfer (EFT)	
4. E-commerce	
5. Electronic data interchange (EDI)	
6. Functional areas of IT operations (e.g., data center operations)	
7. Encryption	
8. Information protection (e.g., viruses, privacy)	
9. Evaluate investment in IT (cost of ownership)	
10. Enterprise-wide resource planning (ERP) software (e.g., SAP R/3)	
11. Operating systems	
12. Application development	
13. Voice communications	
14. Contingency planning	
15. Systems security (e.g., firewalls, access control)	
16. Databases	
17. Software licensing	
18. Web infrastructure	
Format: 125 multiple-choice questions	

EXHIBIT 28.1 *(CONTINUED)*

CIA Examination Summary

Part IV: Business Management Skills

A. STRATEGIC MANAGEMENT (20-30%)	*Level A*

  1. Global analytical techniques
   a. Structural analysis of industries
   b. Competitive strategies (e.g., Porter's model)
   c. Competitive analysis
   d. Market signals
   e. Industry evolution

  2. Industry environments
   a. Competitive strategies related to:
    1) Fragmented industries
    2) Emerging industries
    3) Declining industries
   b. Competition in global industries
    1) Sources/impediments
    2) Evolution of global markets
    3) Strategic alternatives
    4) Trends affecting competition

  3. Strategic decisions
   a. Analysis of integration strategies
   b. Capacity expansion
   c. Entry into new businesses

  4. Portfolio techniques of competitive analysis

  5. Product life cycles

B. GLOBAL BUSINESS ENVIRONMENTS (15-25%)	*Level A*

  1. Cultural/legal/political environments
   a. Balancing global requirements and local imperatives
   b. Global mindsets (personal characteristics/competencies)
   c. Sources & methods for managing complexities and contradictions
   d. Managing multicultural teams

  2. Economic/financial environments
   a. Global, multinational, international, and multilocal compared and contrasted
   b. Requirements for entering the global marketplace
   c. Creating organizational adaptability
   d. Managing training and development.

C. ORGANIZATIONAL BEHAVIOR (20-30%)	*Level A*

  1. Motivation
   a. Relevance and implication of various theories
   b. Impact of job design, rewards, work schedules, etc.

  2. Communication
   a. The process
   b. Organizational dynamics
   c. Impact of computerization

EXHIBIT 28.1 *(CONTINUED)*

CIA Examination Summary

3. Performance
  a. Productivity
  b. Effectiveness
 	
4. Structure
  a. Centralized/decentralized
  b. Departmentalization
  c. New configurations (e.g., hourglass, cluster, network)	

D. MANAGEMENT SKILLS (20–30%)	*Level A*

1. Group dynamics
  a. Traits (e.g., cohesiveness, roles, norms, groupthink)
  b. Stages of group development
  c. Organizational politics
  d. Criteria and determinants of effectiveness
 	
2. Team building
  a. Methods used in team building
  b. Assessing team performance
 	
3. Leadership skills
  a. Theories compared and contrasted
  b. Leadership grid (topology of leadership styles)
  c. Mentoring
 	
4. Personal time management	

E. NEGOTIATING (5-15%)	*Level A*

1. Conflict resolution
  a. Competitive/cooperative
  b. Compromise, forcing, smoothing, etc.
 	
2. Added-value negotiating
  a. Description
  b. Specific steps
 	
Format: 125 multiple-choice questions	

Source: Printed with permission of The Institute of Internal Auditors - 247 Maitland Avenue - Altamonte Springs, Florida 32701-4201 U.S.A.

(b) Maintaining CIA Certification

An internal auditor does not have to be a member of the IIA to take the CIA examination or to hold the certificate, although the IIA highly encourages membership. All CIA's, whether IIA members or nonmembers, must be familiar with the IIA's *International Standards for the Professional Practice of Internal Auditing* and agree to abide by The IIA's Code of Ethics, which sets forth a standard of conduct for all internal auditors.

Upon certification, CIA's are required to maintain their knowledge and skills and to stay abreast of improvements and current developments in internal auditing standards, procedures, and techniques. Practicing CIA's must complete and report 80 hours of Continuing Professional Education (CPE) every two years.

The CIA is really a worldwide certification as opposed to the CPA certification, which is a U.S. certification issued by individual states, or various national versions of Chartered Accountant certifications. The CIA is the only internationally recognized designation for internal auditors. The exam is offered in English, French, Spanish, and Portuguese at more than 200 exam sites throughout the world. It is also offered in Chinese, Czech, German, Hebrew, Italian, Japanese, and Thai at select international locations.

28.3 OTHER IIA-SPONSORED CERTIFICATIONS

In addition to the CIA, the IIA's Board of Regents offers several other professional certification examinations and certificates, the Certification in Control Self-Assessment (CCSA), the Certified Government Auditing Professional (CGAP), and the Certified Financial Services Auditor (CFSA). Each of these is separate, three-hour examinations that also can be taken as a substitute for Part IV of the regular CIA examination.

(a) CCSA Requirements

Chapter 27, "Control Self-Assessments," described the IIA's Control Self-Assessment (CSA) process. As a means to promote and encourage CSA-related activities, the CCSA professional certification has been established. In contrast to the experience requirements of the CIA examination and the rigor of the two-day examination, the CCSA is a single three-hour, 125-question examination that tests candidates for their knowledge of CSA processes in the following broad areas:

Domain 1. CSA Fundamentals (5–10 percent)

Domain 2. CSA Program Integration (15–25 percent)

Domain 3. Elements of the CSA Process (15–25 percent)

Domain 4. Business Objectives/Organizational Performance (10–15 percent)

Domain 5. Risk Identification and Assessment (15–20 percent)

Domain 6. Control Theory and Application (20–25 percent)

Each of these domain areas covers the CSA process in much more detail than was presented in Chapter 27. The examination is based on the same topic proficiency and awareness approaches as found in the CIA examination. Based on information published in the IIA Web site (www.theiia.org), Exhibit 28.2 shows the examination knowledge requirements for Domain 3 as an example. That Web site also contains some sample examination questions. After completion of the CCSA examination, the candidate should be an experienced CSA session facilitator, as was discussed in Chapter 27.

Candidates for the CCSA are not required to have CIA credentials or even to be internal auditors. The experience requirements for the CCSA are that the candidate has had some level of experience in the control self-assessment field. Other requirements, such as accepting the code of ethics and continuing education are similar to the CIA. The CCSA will give the practitioner a level of expertise in this area, but it almost needs to be combined with another certification such as the CIA. Completion of this examination will serve as a substitute for Part IV of the regular CIA examination.

EXHIBIT 28.2

CCSA Examination Domain 3 Topics

Note: The topics tested on the CCSA exam are framed in the context of a variety of industry situations. Candidates are not expected to be familiar with industry-specific controls, but should be able to relate to risks and controls that generally apply to business processes in various industries.

Domain 3 - Elements of the CSA Process: 15–25%

A. Management's priorities and concerns (P)

B. Project and logistics management (P)

C. Business objectives, processes, challenges, and threats for the area under review (P)

D. Resource identification and allocation (A)

 1. Participants
 2. CSA team

E. Culture of area under review (P)

F. Question development techniques (P)

G. Technology supporting the CSA process (P)

H. Facilitation techniques and tools (P)

I. Group dynamics (P)

J. Fraud awareness (A)

 1. Red flags/symptoms of fraud
 2. Communication and investigation channels
 3. Responding to evidence

K. Evaluation/analytical tools and techniques (trend analysis, data synthesis, scenarios) (A)

L. Formulating recommendations or actions plans (practical, feasible, cost-effective) (P)

M. Nature of evidence (sufficiency, relevance, adequacy) (A)

N. Reporting techniques and considerations (types, audience, sensitive issues, access to information) (P)

O. Motivational techniques (creating support and commitment for recommendations) (A)

P. Monitoring, tracking, and follow-up techniques (A)

Q. Awareness of legal, regulatory, and ethical considerations (A)

R. Measuring CSA program effectiveness (A)

P = Candidates must exhibit proficiency (thorough understanding; ability to apply concepts) in these topic areas.
A = Candidates must exhibit awareness (knowledge of terminology and fundamentals) in these topic areas.

(b) CGAP® Requirements

There have been references throughout this book to government auditors but no explanation of their tasks and skills. Whether working for one of the many branches of the U.S. government or at a state or local level, an internal auditor working in a government environment is faced with a different set of knowledge and skill requirements than the typical internal auditor working in the private sector. Attainment of the Certified Government Auditing Professional® (CGAP) certification allows a candidate to demonstrate these governmental auditing skills.

The CGAP is a specialty certification designed specifically for and by government auditing practitioners. This examination is available in the United States only at this time. It tests a candidate's comprehension of government auditing practices, methodologies, and environment, as well as related standards and control/risk models.

The requirements for the CGAP are similar to those of the CIA and CCSA just described. Candidates for this three-hour examination must have had two years of auditing experience in a government environment (federal, state/provincial, local, quasi-governmental areas, authority/crown corporation). Work experience must be verified by a CGAP, a CIA, a CCSA, a CFSA, or the candidate's supervisor. The CGAP covers the following areas or domains:

Domain 1. Standards and Control/Risk Models (5–10 percent)

Domain 2. Government Auditing Practice (35–45 percent)

Domain 3. Government Auditing Methodologies and Skills (20–25 percent)

Domain 4. Government Auditing Environment (25–35 percent)

Although this book does not at all cover the often very specialized field of governmental internal auditing, Exhibit 28.3 shows five sample questions, taken from the IIA Web site, for this examination. These certainly are topics that have not been discussed throughout this book, and they show the specialized knowledge requirements of government auditors. The IIA lists a series of reference sources to help a candidate prepare for the CGAP examination.

EXHIBIT 28.3

CGAP Examination Sample Questions

1. In a financial statement audit, Government Auditing Standards (Yellow Book) require that the scope of the review of compliance and internal control over financial reporting be specifically communicated to all of the following EXCEPT the:

(A) audit client.

(B) audit committee.

(C) requestor of audit services.

(D) funding agency.

2. It is important that an internal audit department's statement of purpose, authority, and responsibility detail:

(A) the delineation of responsibilities between the internal and external auditors.

(B) the organizational status of the internal audit function.

(C) whether the agency head will present audit findings to the oversight committee.

(D) under what circumstances the internal audit director may have confidential access to the oversight committee.

EXHIBIT 28.3   *(CONTINUED)*

CGAP Examination Sample Questions

---

3. A meter-reading audit for a municipal utility includes the following audit program steps:
   - Determine whether meter readings used in customer billings are free of significant error.
   - Analyze the average read time per day for each meter reader.
   - Review controls over the accurate transmission of meter-reading data from handheld devices to the organization's computer.

Which of the following types of audit services are included in these audit program steps?
   I. efficiency audits
   II. information technology audits
   III. financial statement audits
   IV. quality audits

(A) I only

(B) I and IV only

(C) II and III only

(D) I, II, and IV only

4. An internal auditing department plans to begin an audit of a city's highway maintenance department. One of the audit objectives is to determine whether fixed assets employed in highway maintenance are properly reflected in the accounting records. In meeting this objective, which of the following audit approaches is likely to be most effective?

   (A) inspecting fixed assets used in the highway maintenance process and tracing to the asset subsidiary ledger

   (B) scanning the asset subsidiary ledger for credit entries

   (C) selecting items from the asset subsidiary ledger and recalculating depreciation

   (D) examining documentation concerning the cost of fixed assets used in the highway maintenance process

5. Which would be part of the compliance segment of a performance audit?

   (A) Performance reports comply with reporting guidelines.

   (B) Laws and regulations significant to the entity are being followed.

   (C) Activities required by law or policy are being carried out.

   (D) Laws and regulations significant to the audit objective are being followed.

(c) CFSA Requirements

The Certified Financial Services Auditor® (CFSA) is another of the IIA's specialty certifications, demonstrating an individual's competence and professionalism in the financial services internal auditing (banking, insurance, and securities). This exam is available in the United States and Canada only at this time. The examination covers the following domain areas:

Domain 1. Financial Services Auditing

Domain 2. Banking

Domain 3. Insurance

Domain 4. Securities

Each if these financial domains can be very different as the specialized knowledge requirements for banking are often very different from the field of insurance. Exhibit 28.4 shows the application topic outline for insurance—a broad range of topics.

EXHIBIT 28.4

CFSA Examination Topic Outline for Domain 3 Insurance

INSURANCE INDUSTRY CFSA TOPICS

A. Applications/processes

  1. Marketing, Sales, and Distribution

  2. Underwriting

  3. Reinsurance

  4. Actuarial

  5. Claims

  6. Financial Reporting

  7. Compliance

  8. Investment Operations

  9. Risk Management

 10. Premium Audit

 11. Administration

B. Laws and Regulations

  1. The McCarran Ferguson Act

  2. State Insurance Commissions

  3. The NAIC

  4. The Securities and Exchange Commission

  5. ERISA

  6. State Model Laws

C. Products

  1. Life, Pension, and Annuity

    a. Individual Insurance

      i) Whole Life

      ii) Term Life

      iii) Universal Life

      iv) Endowments

    b. Group Insurance

      i) Life

      ii) Accident and Health

      iii) Accidental Death and Dismemberment

      iv) Disability

      v) Dental

      vi) HMOs

      vii) Managed Care

      viii) Utilization Management

      ix) Preferred Provider Organizations

      x) Administrative Service Only

    c. Pensions

      i) Qualified Plans

      ii) Tax Favored Individual Retirement Plans

      iii) Qualification Rules

      iv) Plan Discrimination

EXHIBIT 28.4 *(CONTINUED)*

CFSA Examination Topic Outline for Domain 3 Insurance

v) Savings Plans
vi) Vesting
vii) Fiduciaries
viii) Prohibited Transactions
ix) Annuity
x) Fixed Annuities
xi) Variable Annuities

   d. Reinsurance

2. Property and Casualty Products
   a. Workers' Compensation
   b. General Liability
   c. Automobile
   d. Homeowners'
   e. Umbrella Coverage
   f. Financial Guarantees
   g. Other

28.4 CERTIFIED INFORMATION SYSTEMS AUDITOR EXAMINATION

Previous chapters have mentioned the hopefully friendly rivalry between the IIA and what was once the EDP Auditors Association (now the Information Systems Audit and Control Association [ISACA]). What is now ISACA was founded by internal auditors who felt the IIA was not giving enough attention to technology and information systems issues. The two professional groups have been operating in a somewhat parallel manner, and ISACA has an IT related certification examination similar to the IIA's CIA. This is the Certified Information Systems Auditor (CISA) examination and professional designation. The CISA examination is open to all individuals who have an interest in information systems audit, control, and security. The examination is offered once per year worldwide. In addition to successfully passing the CISA examination, a minimum of five years of professional information systems auditing, control, or security work experience is required for certification. Substitutions and waivers of such experience may be obtained as follows:

- A maximum of one year of information systems experience *or* one year of financial or operational auditing experience can be substituted for one year of information systems auditing, control, or security experience.

- 60 to 120 completed college semester credit hours (the equivalent of an associate or bachelor degree) can be substituted for one or two years, respectively, of information systems auditing, control, or security experience.

- Two years as a full-time university instructor in a related field (e.g., computer science, accounting, information systems auditing) can be substituted for one year of information systems auditing, control, or security experience.

Experience must have been gained within the 10-year period preceding the application date for certification or within five years from the date of initially passing the examination. Retaking and passing the examination will be required if the application for certification is not submitted within five years from the passing date of the examination. All experience is verified independently with employers.

Per ISACA guidelines, the tasks and knowledge required of today and tomorrow's information systems audit professional serve as the blueprint for the CISA examination. Exhibit 28.5 shows the subject areas that are included in the CISA examination. Each of these is supported by a far greater list of knowledge requirements as defined in the ISACA Web site (www.isaca.org) or in a variety of reference materials listed there as well. Each of these seven points is supported by much more detailed requirements outlining the specific knowledge area in each. These detailed lists of knowledge requirements may seem rather formidable to the typical non-information-systems-oriented internal auditor!

EXHIBIT 28.5

CISA Examination Content Areas

1. *Management, Planning, and Organization of IS (11%)*
   Evaluate the strategy, policies, standards, procedures and related practices for the management, planning, and organization of IS.

2. *Technical Infrastructure and Operational Practices (13%)*
   Evaluate the effectiveness and efficiency of the organization's implementation and ongoing management of technical and operational infrastructure to ensure that they adequately support the organization's business objectives.

3. *Protection of Information Assets (25%)*
   Evaluate the logical, environmental, and IT infrastructure security to ensure that it satisfies the organization's business requirements for safeguarding information assets against unauthorized use, disclosure, modification, damage, or loss.

4. *Disaster Recovery and Business Continuity (10%)*
   Evaluate the process for developing and maintaining documented, communicated, and tested plans for continuity of business operations and IS processing in the event of a disruption.

5. *Business Application System Development, Acquisition, Implementation, and Maintenance (16%)*
   Evaluate the methodology and processes by which the business application system development, acquisition, implementation, and maintenance are undertaken to ensure that they meet the organization's business objectives.

6. *Business Process Evaluation and Risk Management (15%)*
   Evaluate business systems and processes to ensure that risks are managed in accordance with the organization's business objectives.

7. *The IS Audit Process (10%)*
   Conduct IS audits in accordance with generally accepted IS audit standards and guidelines to ensure that the organization's information technology and business systems are adequately controlled, monitored, and assessed.

A set of CISA test questions is posted in the ISACA Web site to give an internal auditor a feel for the complexity of this examination. A sample of 12 of these test questions is posted in Exhibit 28.6. An internal auditor can quickly determine that the CISA is a fairly technical test given questions even in this sample asking about TCP/IP of denial-of-service considerations. The CISA examination has similar education, experience, and continuing education requirements as were found with the CIA examination discussed previously.

EXHIBIT 28.6

CISA Sample Test Questions

1. **In a risk-based audit approach, an IS auditor, in addition to risk, would be influenced by:**
   - A. the availability of CAATs.
   - B. management's representation.
   - C. organizational structure and job responsibilities.
   - D. the existence of internal and operational controls.

2. **The extent to which data will be collected during an IS audit should be determined, based on the:**
   - A. availability of critical and required information.
   - B. auditor's familiarity with the circumstances.
   - C. auditee's ability to find relevant evidence.
   - D. purpose and scope of the audit being done.

3. **The PRIMARY advantage of a continuous audit approach is that it:**
   - A. does not require an IS auditor to collect evidence on system reliability while processing is taking place.
   - B. requires the IS auditor to review and follow up immediately on all information collected.
   - C. can improve system security when used in time-sharing environments that process a large number of transactions.
   - D. does not depend on the complexity of an organization's computer systems.

4. **Which of the following data entry controls provides the GREATEST assurance that the data is entered correctly?**
   - A. Using key verification
   - B. Segregating the data entry function from data entry verification
   - C. Maintaining a log/record detailing the time, date, employee's initials/user id, and progress of various data preparation and verification tasks
   - D. Adding check digits

5. **Capacity monitoring software is used to ensure:**
   - A. maximum use of available capacity.
   - B. that future acquisitions meet user needs.
   - C. concurrent use by a large number of users.
   - D. continuity of efficient operations.

6. **Which of the following exposures associated with the spooling of sensitive reports for offline printing would an IS auditor consider to be the MOST serious?**
   - A. Sensitive data can be read by operators.
   - B. Data can be amended without authorization.

EXHIBIT 28.6   *(CONTINUED)*

CISA Sample Test Questions

    ○ C. Unauthorized report copies can be printed.

    ○ D. Output can be lost in the event of system failure.

7. **Which of the following types of firewalls would BEST protect a network from an Internet attack?**

    ○ A. Screened subnet firewall

    ○ B. Application filtering gateway

    ○ C. Packet filtering router

    ○ D. Circuit-level gateway

8. **Applying a retention date on a file will ensure that:**

    ○ A. data cannot be read until the date is set.

    ○ B. data will not be deleted before that date.

    ○ C. backup copies are not retained after that date.

    ○ D. datasets having the same name are differentiated.

9. **A digital signature contains a message digest to:**

    ○ A. show if the message has been altered after transmission.

    ○ B. define the encryption algorithm.

    ○ C. confirm the identity of the originator.

    ○ D. enable message transmission in a digital format.

10. **Which of the following would be the BEST method for ensuring that critical fields in a master record have been updated properly?**

    ○ A. Field checks

    ○ B. Control totals

    ○ C. Reasonableness checks

    ○ D. A before-and-after maintenance report

11. **A TCP/IP-based environment is exposed to the Internet. Which of the following BEST ensures that complete encryption and authentication protocols exist for protecting information while transmitted?**

    ○ A. Work is completed in tunnel mode with IP security using the nested services of authentication header (AH) and encapsulating security payload (ESP).

    ○ B. A digital signature with RSA has been implemented.

    ○ C. Digital certificates with RSA are being used.

    ○ D. Work is being completed in TCP services.

12. **To prevent an organization's computer systems from becoming part of a distributed denial-of-service attack, IP packets containing addresses that are listed as unroutable can be isolated by:**

    ○ A. establishing outbound traffic filtering.

    ○ B. enabling broadcast blocking.

    ○ C. limiting allowable services.

    ○ D. network performance monitoring.

28.5 ANOTHER ISACA CERTIFICATION

ISACA has recently launched a new certification and examination, the Certified Information Security Manager (CISM). This program was launched in 2004 and a base of certified CISMs was established by grandfathering professionals who already had strong levels of information systems security experience. The CISM program appears to be very similar to the CISSP examination and certification discussed below.

The CISM is a new test and certification with little track record today. Because it is supported by the very strong and credible ISACA organization, we can expect to see it grow in terms of statues and recognition. However, these examinations and certifications often take time to become highly recognized among managers and professionals. While preparing and sitting for any professional examination is an excellent learning exercise for any professional, an internal auditor may want to wait to see how the CISM develops and is recognized before preparing to receive certification here.

28.6 CERTIFIED FRAUD EXAMINER CERTIFICATION

Concerns regarding fraud and fraud investigations are becoming increasingly important to all auditors. Chapter 11, "Fraud Detection and Prevention," discussed fraud and fraud detection as well as the new fraud-related auditing standard, SAS No. 99. That chapter also discussed how professional audit organizations in the past had stated that it was not the auditor's responsibility to investigate and detect fraud. However, in our present post-Sarbanes-Oxley Act (SOA) era, internal and external auditors now have a strong responsibility to investigate for fraud and to take appropriate actions when it is identified.

There is a professional organization that is very involved with fraud-related issues for the internal auditor, the Association of Certified Fraud Examiners (ACFE). The organization has its own professional examination and certification, the Certified Fraud Examiner (CFE). Obtaining a CFE designation is regarded as an indicator of excellence in the antifraud profession. Members experience growth, both professionally and personally, and can position themselves as leaders in the antifraud community.

The CFE examination covers four fraud-related broad areas:

1. Criminology and Ethics
2. Financial Transactions
3. Legal Elements of Fraud
4. Fraud Examination and Investigation

To many internal auditors, these are topic areas that are beyond their experience and training. The ACFE, of course, has its own publications, conferences, and local chapters provide an internal auditor with a greater level of information about fraud and fraud investigations.

Although a relatively new professional organization, the ACFE has quickly gained prominence in this post-SOA era. While the ACFE has its own Web site, much of the fraud materials published in newer AICPA Web pages on fraud and discussed in Chapter 11 are strongly based on ACFE materials. In addition, the ACFE Web site contains a sample examination to allow an internal auditor to determine if he or she is ready to take the CFE test. The CFE test is an entirely online exercise where the candidate registers and takes the examination over a machine-timed interval.

28.7 CISSP AND INFORMATION SYSTEMS SECURITY CERTIFICATION

A professional organization known as the International Information Systems Security Certification Consortium or (ISC)^2 is responsible for one of the more challenging professional certifications and examinations, the Certified Information System Security Professional (CISSP). This professional examination and its CISSP designation are well recognized but difficult to achieve for many. This is really a certification for information systems security professionals and not the ordinary internal auditor.

The CISSP program is on a much higher, much more technical level than other training programs that an internal auditor frequently encounters. The examinations are tightly proctored, training materials are reviewed and approved by (ISC)^2, and the overall quality of the examination is high. If an internal auditor encounters someone in an auditee organization with CISSP certification, that person will almost certainly be someone with a high-level knowledge of information systems security.

28.8 ASQ INTERNAL AUDIT CERTIFICATIONS

Chapter 26, "Internal Audit Quality Assurance and ASQ Quality Audits," talked about the American Society for Quality (ASQ) and its quality auditor certifications. The ASQ sponsors a wide range of examinations and certifications for all aspects of its operations. One that may be of interest is their Certified Quality Auditor (CQA) certification. A Certified Quality Auditor is a professional who understands the standards and principles of auditing and the techniques of examining, questioning, evaluating, and reporting to determine a quality system's adequacy and deficiencies. The CQA analyzes all elements of a quality system and judges its degree of adherence to the criteria of industrial management and quality evaluation and control systems. The difference here between a regular internal auditor and a CQA is that the latter often works in a quality-assurance group and spends more time on process-oriented reviews as opposed to the IIA internal auditor's financial and operational reviews.

To achieve the CQA designation, the candidate is required to pass a five-hour, multiple-choice written examination that measures comprehension of the quality audit profession. As the minimum professional requirements, a quality auditor:

- Must possess the knowledge to effectively conduct different types of objective, ethically based audits, using and interpreting applicable standards/requirements.

- Must be able to develop and communicate an audit plan within a defined scope that identifies applicable standards, necessary personnel, required documents and tools, and an audit agenda.

- Must be able to effectively execute an audit plan, including opening the meeting, performing the audit, and the closing meeting using generally accepted auditing techniques and verifying, documenting, and communicating findings as appropriate for the audit.

- Must be able to objectively present verified nonconformance to the audited standard and evaluate the effectiveness of the resultant follow-up/corrective action activities in an ethical and timely manner.

- Must know and be able to apply basic auditing tools and techniques, such as flowcharting, the concept of variation, observation techniques, and physical examination techniques. A CQA must also demonstrate a general knowledge of quality-control tools, descriptive statistics, and applicable sampling theories.

The requirements listed here are similar to those of the IIA-oriented internal auditor but the CQA uses different approaches and terminologies. For example, the previous list references such things as "verified nonconformance to the audited standard" or "the concept of variation." These are specialized ASQ terms, but many concepts go back to standard internal audit processes. The CQA examination is highly based on the ASQ's Body of Knowledge, a comprehensive set of key knowledge areas and practices for the CQA. This is a document that is reviewed by the ASQ professional organization and then updated after republication.

The ASQ has two other quality auditor certifications, one for biomedical quality audits and the other for HACCP-based (or process-safety) systems. The ASQ is very responsive to build a separate certification when there appears to be a special demand. These are just different areas of quality auditing.

28.9 OTHER CERTIFICATIONS FOR INTERNAL AUDITORS

As discussed at the beginning of this chapter, some professions have a large number of professional certifications available to them, depending upon an auditor's job requirements and skills. There is no one list here, but the certification depends upon the auditor's needs and interests. The requirements for all of them are similar, usually consisting of specified requirements to take the examination, passing it and receiving the "Certified . . ." designation, followed by continuing education requirements to keep the certification current.

The basic value of these certification examinations is to focus an internal auditor on the details of one or another professional area and then to receive that certification to demonstrate skills to others. As an example of how this works, this author has worked extensively with the Capability Maturity Model (CMM) as was described in Chapter 20, "Software Engineering, the Capability Maturity Model, and Project Management." For some time, there was no formal certification that demonstrated a professional's knowledge of CMM. In response to this gap, the ASQ has launched a Certified Quality Systems Engineer (CQSE) examination and certification that is heavily oriented to CMM. Although the author felt he had good CMM skills, taking and passing the CSQE was a way to demonstrate to others one's knowledge about CMM.

28.10 WHY GET CERTIFIED FOR ANYTHING?

As discussed throughout this chapter, there is a wide range of certifications available and often appropriate to internal auditors. A professional certification is a way for an internal auditor to demonstrate to peers and others that the audit professional has some unique and important professional skills. Professional certifications are important and more importantly, the knowledge gained through obtaining a certificate allows an internal auditor to work more efficiently and effectively in service to management. Certification, and in particular the CIA, is important for internal auditors. The CAE should encourage all members of the internal audit group to become certified as CIAs and/or as CISAs. This is a measure of internal audit professionalism and becomes an important attribute when the CAE can talk about the professionalism of the internal staff when talking to the audit committee and senior management.

Individual internal auditors should use these certification examinations as a measure of their own professionalism. These are important indicators of one's knowledge, interests, and abilities. For both those within an organization's internal audit function and those moving beyond it, certifications are measures of one's knowledge and interests in the profession.

ISO and Internal Audit Worldwide Standards

29.1 IT IS NOT JUST A UNITED STATES ISSUE

The Sarbanes-Oxley Act (SOA) is a U.S. law that was enacted in response to financial frauds in U.S. corporations such as Enron and WorldCom. The only non-U.S. corporation often cited at the time was Tyco, with headquarters in Bermuda. Tyco, who's CEO was involved with flagrant financial excesses, was really a U.S. corporation that had transferred its corporate registration to Bermuda for tax purposes. At that time, journalists and politicians elsewhere in the world and particularly in European Union (EU) countries initially tut-tutted that this financial fraud was just a U.S. problem. They particularly resented the SEC's plans to impose SOA rules on international corporations whose securities are registered in U.S. exchanges.

It did not take long to realize that the United States was not the one and only with regard to financial fraud. In February 2003, the major Dutch food distributor Royal Ahold admitted an "accounting irregularity" of some $500 million. Ahold had operations throughout the world and was found to have misstated its accounting and financial records to show better results. Early 2004 brought in another multibillion fraud at Parmalot, a worldwide producer and distributor of dairy and bakery products, based in Parma, Italy. Among other matters, the external auditors there bought off on fraudulent bank balance confirmations of fictitious bank balances, with seemingly not much due diligence.

While the investigations of Ahold and Parmalot were continuing, a corruption trail was initiated in France against some 37 people from the major oil company, Elf, who were accused of siphoning off over $400 million of corporate funds through the 1990s. The CEO was the main miscreant there. When asked at the trial to justify his use of Elf corporate funds for the purchase of a $9.3 million Paris mansion, a country chateau, and $4.5 million for a personal divorce settlement, after 18 months of marriage, the ex-CEO stated, "I allowed myself to get carried away." The United States is not alone in corporate accounting scandals!

This chapter will look at SOA from an international perspective. Although some rules have yet to be released, we will look at the SOA rules from the focus of a non-U.S. corporation with an emphasis on internal auditors. The chapter will also provide an overview of International Auditing Standards (IAS), a set of guidelines with U.S. roots that are now evolving into their own worldwide set of guidance standards.

Many professional have seen the words "ISO Registered" included in customer brochures and other advertising materials. While the United States often pushes its standards on the rest of the world, ISO[1] (the English designation for the International Organization for Standardization) an international set of guidelines that many U.S. organizations have adopted. (As an aside, the acronym ISO does not match the name. The abbreviation is different in various languages such as OIN in French, but the abbreviation ISO is used as a worldwide standard name.) ISO is really important for today's global economy, and internal audit can help to assure effective ISO compliance. This chapter also introduces ISO quality standards, the ISO registration process, and ISO quality audits. Another U.S.-imported international standard, the Information Technology Infrastructure Library (ITIL) of service delivery and support processes was discussed in Chapter 22, "Infrastructure Service- and Support-Delivery Controls."

29.2 SOA INTERNATIONAL REQUIREMENTS

When SOA was enacted in 2002, the initial legislation covered all companies with SEC registration, whether United States or international. Many foreign-registered companies initially assumed that they would be exempt from all or at least some final not yet published rules. A large number of foreign companies come under SOA rules, however. As of early 2004, for example, the New York Stock Exchange listed 474 non-U.S. companies from 51 countries with a combined global market capitalization of approximately $4.3 trillion. Among other differences, these SOA-compliant organizations historically did not always follow U.S. GAAP, their audit committee rules are different, and they sometimes only reported annually. To appease its foreign companies, the SEC has offered a number of limited exemptions or special accommodations, including modifications to the attorney conduct rule and the use of non-GAAP financial measures, among others. They were also allowed more time to become compliant. Nevertheless, SOA applies to any foreign company with its securities registered on a U.S. exchange.

Like their U.S. counterparts, foreign companies are required to provide certification of their financial statements by their chief executives and chief financial officers. Thus, the non-U.S. CFOs and CEOs are subjecting themselves to possible U.S. legal actions. For violators, the prosecution process may be challenging, but a foreign national who has even been indicted under a United States law will have trouble even visiting the United States in future years until the matter is resolved. In addition, at the time of this publication, only a few foreign companies have openly opted out of the U.S. markets because of this changing regulatory environment. With some exemptions, SOA rules apply worldwide to all SEC-registered organizations.

SOA has really raised the bar for foreign corporations to seek listings on U.S. exchanges, but the United Kingdom and European Union (EU) are currently studying the same issues. There will be a move over the upcoming years toward tighter governance standards in all of the major foreign countries, making SOA and related regulations more palatable for all.

29.3 INTERNATIONAL ACCOUNTING AND AUDITING STANDARDS

Internal and external auditors based in the United States had thought of the AICPA and its Auditing Standards Board (ASB) as the body that, for many years, had established auditing standards for U.S. organizations. At least, that was prior to SOA and the Public Corporation Auditing Oversight Board (PCAOB) that now has the authority to establish auditing standards in the United States. Of course, a major objective of any audit is to review compliance against some recognized standard or principle. One of the major tenets of internal control, under COSO and any other internal audit for that the entity audited, is compliance with laws and regulations. That legal compliance becomes a standard for audits of internal accounting controls. Financial audits also assess the fairness of accounting procedures per established accounting standards. Those standards in the United States are based on Generally Accepted Accounting Principles (GAAP), as well as very specific accounting rules proscribed by the Financial Accounting Standards Board (FASB). These U.S. auditing and accounting standards are not the same throughout the world.

Standards such as double entry bookkeeping are accepted and recognized throughout the world. Others may have the same intent but are different in various national entities. The practice of driving on the right- or left-hand side of the road is such an example of a national practice. No matter which standard is followed, automobile drivers can still easily get from point A to B as long as all drivers follow the same rule. The same is true for auditing and accounting standards and practices. It only becomes a bit more complex because we are an increasingly global economy, and accounting and auditing practices in Belgium, for example, need to be comparable to those in its nearby neighbor France. In addition, there is a need for some consistency with standards between many countries such as both Germany and the United States. As our individual organizations become increasingly global, internal auditors should at least have a general understanding of the differences and consistencies across international borders.

Accounting and auditing standards had been established over the years on a country-by-country basis by professional or governmental boards as well as by some international standards-setting bodies. Individual countries may sometimes fully or only otherwise only generally accept these international standards. The United States is an example of the latter. With strong established practices in many areas, the United States often takes the lead for some standards and goes its own way regarding others. All internal auditors, whether in the United States or worldwide, should gain a general understanding of these "rules" and how they might apply to an auditor's organization and what body establishes the standards. The latter can be confusing.

As we move into the world of international organizations, we run into a gaggle of initials used to describe these various organizations. One can just think of the United Nations (UN) with UNESCO, FAO, UNICEF, UNCTAD, and many more. International auditing accounting and standards use the same or similar often confusing sets of initials. There are International Standards of Auditing (ISAs), as well as International Accounting Standards (IASs). The ISA auditing standards are established by the International Federation of Accountants (IFAC) through its International Auditing and Assurance Standards Board (IAASB) who issues these (ISAs) as well as International Auditing Practice Statements (IAPSs). To complicate the picture, there is also the International Organization of Supreme Audit Institutions (INTOSAI) whose Auditing Standards Committee contributes to the work of IAASB.

The ISA auditing standards are fairly consistent with the pre-PCAOB + United States. SAS documents or probably with the yet to be issued auditing standards under PCAOB. Exhibit 29.1 lists the current ISA auditing standards. They are not totally consistent with the U.S. SAS documents. ISAs are released after publication of an exposure draft and are published in over 20 languages including French, German, Russian, and Spanish. More than 70 countries have indicated that they either have adopted IASs or feel that there are no significant differences between their standards and the ISA international standards. The United States is one of the "no significant differences" countries here. In many cases, the ISAs followed the issuance of U.S. SAS documents. For example, the recently revised ISA 240 closely follows SAS No. 99 on auditing for fraud as was discussed in Chapter 11, "Fraud Detection and Prevention." To provide a flavor of these standards, Exhibit 29.2 shows ISA No. 610 on considering the work of internal auditors. The typical auditor, particularly internal auditor, does not need to have a detailed understanding of these international standards of auditing at present. However, as we work in a more global environment, they will become increasingly important.

Acronyms again, the International Accounting Standards Board (IASB) publishes accounting standards in a series of pronouncements called International Financial Reporting Standards (IFRS). Those pronouncements also are sometimes designated as "International Accounting Standards" (IAS). They somewhat provide a basis or foundation for all counties worldwide and, in particular, provide accounting standards for a developing country that does not have established accounting standards. Most developed countries have established accounting standards that generally follow United States, British, German, Swiss,

EXHIBIT 29.1

International Standards on Auditing

Introductory Matters

ISA 100   Framework of International Standards on Auditing

ISA 120   Assurance Engagements

Responsibilities

ISA 200   Objectives and General Principles Governing an Audit of
                 Financial Statements

ISA 210   Terms of Audit Engagements

ISA 220   Quality Controls for Audit Work

ISA 230   Documentation

ISA 240   The Auditor's Responsibility to Consider Fraud and Error
                 in an Audit of Financial Statements

ISA 250   Consideration of Laws and Regulations in an Audit of a
                 Financial Statement

ISA 260   Communication of Audit Matters with Those Charged with
                 Governance

Planning

ISA 300   Planning

ISA 310   Knowledge of Business

ISA 320   Audit Materiality

Internal Control

ISA 400   Risk Assessments and Internal Control

ISA 410   Auditing in a Computer Information Systems Environment

ISA 420   Audit Considerations Relating to Entities Using Service
                 Organizations

Audit Evidence

ISA 500   Audit Evidence

ISA 510   Initial Engagements—Opening Balances

ISA 520   Analytical Procedures

ISA 530   Audit Sampling and Selective Testing Procedures

ISA 540   Audit of Accounting Estimates

ISA 550   Related Parties

ISA 560   Subsequent Events

ISA 570   Going Concern

ISA 580   Management Representations

EXHIBIT 29.1 *(CONTINUED)*

International Standards on Auditing

Using Work of Others

ISA 600   Using the Work of Another Auditor
ISA 610   Considering the Work of Internal Auditing
ISA 620   Using the Work of an Expert

Audit Conclusions and Reporting

ISA 700   The Auditor's Report on Financial Statements
ISA 710   Comparatives
ISA 720   Other Information in Documents Containing Audited Financial
                Statements

Specialized Areas

ISA 800   The Auditor's Report on Special Purpose Audit Engagements
ISA 810   The Examination of Prospective Financial Information

Related Services

ISA 910   Engagements to Review Financial Statements
ISA 920   Engagements to Perform Agreed-Upon Procedures Regarding
                Financial Statements
ISA 930   Engagements to Compile Financial Information

Source: Robert R. Moeller, *Sarbanes-Oxley and the New Internal Auditing Rules,* © copyright 2004, John Wiley & Sons. Used with permission.

or French rules. The IAS standards historically were not inconsistent with those country-by-country standards. An auditor doing work in the developing country that does not have any strong accounting standards should look to the IAS materials to form a basis for appropriate accounting standards. Going forward, all countries that are members of the EU are now required to adopt the IASB international accounting standards by 2005. This will eliminate country-by-country standards within EU countries.

In a step toward eliminating the existing differences between U.S. GAAP and international standards, FASB and IASB are presently examining and selecting the better of these standards in each of the 15 areas, including how companies make restatements when accounting standards change and in the classification of short- and long-term liabilities. This effort toward harmonization comes as all publicly listed European companies prepare to meet international accounting standards by 2005. Companies that are also publicly listed in the U.S. will have to meet the U.S. standards under SOA, as well. The goal is to reach a consensus on standards by at least 2005. This push for a convergence of standards is really a result of the U.S. corporate scandals that led to SOA. The more recent Dutch accounting scandal at Ahold will have the same effect. We should soon see the two sets of standards—international standards and U.S. GAAP—converge.

EXHIBIT 29.2

ISA 610—Considering the Work of Internal Auditing

Introduction

1. The purpose of this International Standard on Auditing (ISA) is to establish standards and provide guidance to external auditors in considering the work of internal auditing. This ISA does not deal with instances when personnel from internal auditing assist the external auditor in carrying out external audit procedures. The procedures noted in this ISA need only be applied to internal auditing activities which are relevant to the audit of the financial statements.

2. The external auditor should consider the activities of internal auditing and their effect, if any, on external audit procedures.

3. "Internal auditing" means an appraisal activity established within an entity as a service to the entity. Its functions include, amongst other things, examining, evaluating and monitoring the adequacy and effectiveness of the accounting and internal control systems.

4. While the external auditor has sole responsibility for the audit opinion expressed and for determining the nature, timing and extent of external audit procedures, certain parts of internal auditing work may be useful to the external auditor.

Scope and Objectives of Internal Auditing

5. The scope and objectives of internal auditing vary widely and depend on the size and structure of the entity and the requirements of its management. Ordinarily, internal auditing activities include one or more of the following:

- Review of the accounting and internal control systems. The establishment of adequate accounting and internal control systems is a responsibility of management which demands proper attention on a continuous basis. Internal auditing is ordinarily assigned specific responsibility by management for reviewing these systems, monitoring their operation and recommending improvements thereto.

- Examination of financial and operating information. This may include review of the means used to identify, measure, classify and report such information and specific inquiry into individual items including detailed testing of transactions, balances and procedures.

- Review of the economy, efficiency and effectiveness of operations including non-financial controls of an entity.

- Review of compliance with laws, regulations and other external requirements and with management policies and directives and other internal requirements.

EXHIBIT 29.2 *(CONTINUED)*

ISA 610—Considering the Work of Internal Auditing

Relationship between Internal Auditing and the External Auditor

6. The role of internal auditing is determined by management, and its objectives differ from those of the external auditor who is appointed to report independently on the financial statements. The internal audit function's objectives vary according to management's requirements. The external auditor's primary concern is whether the financial statements are free of material misstatements.

7. Nevertheless some of the means of achieving their respective objectives are often similar and thus certain aspects of internal auditing may be useful in determining the nature, timing and extent of external audit procedures.

8. Internal auditing is part of the entity. Irrespective of the degree of autonomy and objectivity of internal auditing it cannot achieve the same degree of independence as required of the external auditor when expressing an opinion on the financial statements. The external auditor has sole responsibility for the audit opinion expressed, and that responsibility is not reduced by any use made of internal auditing. All judgments relating to the audit of the financial statements are those of the external auditor.

Understanding and Preliminary Assessment of Internal Auditing

9. The external auditor should obtain a sufficient understanding of internal audit activities to assist in planning the audit and developing an effective audit approach.

10. Effective internal auditing will often allow a modification in the nature and timing, and a reduction in the extent of procedures performed by the external auditor but cannot eliminate them entirely. In some cases however, having considered the activities of internal auditing, the external auditor may decide that internal auditing will have no effect on external audit procedures.

11. During the course of planning the audit the external auditor should perform a preliminary assessment of the internal audit function when it appears that internal auditing is relevant to the external audit of the financial statements in specific audit areas.

12. The external auditor's preliminary assessment of the internal audit function will influence the external auditor's judgment about the use which may be made of internal auditing in modifying the nature, timing and extent of external audit procedures.

13. When obtaining an understanding and performing a preliminary assessment of the internal audit function, the important criteria are:

   a. *Organizational Status:* Specific status of internal auditing in the entity and the effect this has on its ability to be objective. In the ideal situation, internal auditing will report to the highest level of management

EXHIBIT 29.2 *(CONTINUED)*

ISA 610—Considering the Work of Internal Auditing

and be free of any other operating responsibility. Any constraints or restrictions placed on internal auditing by management would need to be carefully considered. In particular, the internal auditors will need to be free to communicate fully with the external auditor.

b. *Scope of Function:* The nature and extent of internal auditing assignments performed. The external auditor would also need to consider whether management acts on internal audit recommendations and how this is evidenced.

c. *Technical Competence:* Whether internal auditing is performed by persons having adequate technical training and proficiency as internal auditors. The external auditor may, for example, review the policies for hiring and training the internal auditing staff and their experience and professional qualifications.

d. *Due Professional Care:* Whether internal auditing is properly planned, supervised, reviewed and documented. The existence of adequate audit manuals work programs and working papers would be considered.

Timing of Liaison and Coordination

14. When planning to use the work of internal auditing, the external auditor will need to consider internal auditing's tentative plan for the period and discuss it at as early a stage as possible. Where the work of internal auditing is to be a factor in determining the nature, timing and extent of the external auditor's procedures, it is desirable to agree in advance the timing of such work, the extent of audit coverage, test levels and proposed methods of sample selection, documentation of the work performed and review and reporting procedures.

15. Liaison with internal auditing is more effective when meetings are held at appropriate intervals during the period. The external auditor would need to be advised of and have access to relevant internal auditing reports and be kept informed of any significant matter that comes to the internal auditor's attention which may affect the work of the external auditor. Similarly, the external auditor would ordinarily inform the internal auditor of any significant matters which may affect internal auditing.

Evaluating and Testing the Work of Internal Auditing

16. When the external auditor intends to use specific work of internal auditing, the external auditor should evaluate and test that work to confirm its adequacy for the external auditor's purposes.

17. The evaluation of specific work of internal auditing involves consideration of the adequacy of the scope of work and related programs and whether

EXHIBIT 29.2 *(CONTINUED)*

ISA 610—Considering the Work of Internal Auditing

the preliminary assessment of the internal auditing remain appropriate. This evaluation may include consideration of whether:

a. the work is performed by persons having adequate technical training and proficiency as internal auditors and the work of assistants is properly supervised, reviewed and documented;

b. sufficient appropriate audit evidence is obtained to afford a reasonable basis for the conclusions reached;

c. conclusions reached are appropriate in the circumstances and any reports prepared are consistent with the results of the work performed; and

d. any exceptions or unusual matters disclosed by internal auditing are properly resolved.

18. The nature, timing and extent of the testing of the specific work of internal auditing will depend on the external auditor's judgment as to the risk and materiality of the area concerned, the preliminary assessment of the internal auditing and the evaluation of the specific work by internal auditing. Such tests may include examination of items already examined by internal auditing, examination of other similar items and observation of internal auditing procedures.

19. The external auditor would record conclusions regarding the specific internal auditing work that has been evaluated and tested.

Note: This document is one of the ISA International Auditing Standards as used in the European Union and other countries outside of the United States.

Source: Robert R. Moeller, *Sarbanes-Oxley and the New Internal Auditing Rules,* © copyright 2004, John Wiley & Sons. Used with permission.

For internal auditors, the IIA's Standards, as discussed in Chapter 12, "Internal Audit Professional Standards" are international standards and apply to all internal audits no matter the country. Internal auditors may encounter different accounting standards or even different local financial statement auditing standards, but the overall IIA professional standards should always be followed. Regarding these accounting and auditing standards, we can almost certainly expect that the ISA and IAS standards will take the place of country-by-country standards, with the exception of those in the United States with its international leadership role.

29.4 COSO WORLDWIDE: INTERNATIONAL INTERNAL CONTROL FRAMEWORKS

Chapter 4, "Internal Controls Fundamentals: COSO Framework," discussed the COSO internal control framework that has been part of U.S. auditing standards and is now a component of the SOA internal control requirements under PCAOB. While COSO was launched in the United States, other countries have implemented their own internal control frameworks. This section will introduce two of them, the

CoCo framework from Canada, and the U.K. Turnbull report framework. These frameworks were released after COSO and have some very attractive features.

As internal auditors increasingly work on a global basis, there is much value in at least having an understanding of these slightly varying internal control standards. Just as we are seeing some convergence in auditing standards, as discussed in the previous section, we should soon see the same with international internal control frameworks. The EU is in the process of developing such a control framework. At present, the several internal control structures are different, but all have similar overall control objectives.

(a) CoCo: Canada's Equivalent of COSO

The Canadian Institute of Chartered Accountants (CICA) is the professional financial auditing and accounting organization in Canada. Similar to AICPA's awarding of the CPA certificate, the CICA awards Chartered Accountant certifications. After the release of the COSO framework and the AICPA's incorporation of it in U.S. audit standards, the CICA established a study group in 1995 to issue guidance on designing, assessing, and reporting on the control systems of organizations. The result is the Criteria *of Co*ntrol (CoCo) framework.

This CoCo framework was introduced in Chapter 7. According to CoCo, control comprises those elements of an organization—including its resources, systems, processes, culture, structure, and tasks—that, taken together, support people in the achievement of the organizations' objectives. CoCo was defined in Chapter 7 and described in Exhibit 7.9. Some of the wording here differs slightly from the U.S.-oriented COSO. While CoCo defines control objectives similar but not identical to COSO, it emphasizes that the essence of control is purpose, commitment, capability, monitoring, and learning within that framework represented. Each of these represents a set of internal control criteria summarized on the exhibit. The criterion for commitment, for example, consists of the following:

- Shared ethical values, including integrity, should be established, communicated, and practiced throughout the organization.

- Human resource policies and practices should be consistent with an organization's ethical values and with the achievement of its objectives.

- Authority, responsibility, and accountability should be clearly defined and consistent with an organization's objectives so that decisions and actions are taken by the appropriate people.

- An atmosphere of mutual trust should be fostered to support the flow of information between people and their effective performance toward achieving the organization's objectives.

The CoCo model has similar detailed criteria for the other three major elements. Based on these elements, CICA has been shaping these internal control concepts and developing a new terminology that might ultimately become codified in future standards. CICA guidance goes on to state that management's overriding objective is to ensure, as far as practical, the orderly and efficient conduct of the entity's business. Management discharges its internal control responsibilities through actions directed to:

- *Optimizing the Use of Resources.* Internal control assists management in optimizing the use of resources by ensuring as far as practical that reliable information is provided to management for the determination of business policies, and by monitoring the implementation of those policies and the degree of compliance with them.

- *Prevention or Detection of Error and Fraud.* A management internal controls objective is the prevention and detection of unintentional mistakes or errors and fraud—the intentional misrepresentation of financial information or misappropriation of assets. The guidance goes on to state that any controls here should be *cost-effective.* The cost of a possible control should be weighed against the relative likelihood of error and fraud occurring and the consequences if any were to occur, including the effect on the financial statements.

- *Safeguarding of Assets.* An organization's assets should be safeguarded partly through internal controls and partly through business policies. Internal control protects against loss arising from *unintentional* exposure to risk in processing transactions or handling related assets. The degree of *intentional* exposure to risk is determined by business policies.

- *Maintaining Reliable Control Systems.* These are the policies and procedures established and maintained by management either to collect record and process data and report the resulting information or to enhance the reliability of such data and information. Management requires reliable control systems to provide information necessary to operate the entity and produce such accounting and other records necessary for the preparation of financial statements.

The preceding paragraphs have briefly outlined the CoCo framework. While it is very consistent the U.S. framework, CoCo represents a tighter, easier-to-grasp model of internal control than COSO. The CoCo control framework represents a different way of thinking about internal control and provides a good way for management to think about how their organizations are performing. We would recommend that all auditors take a more detailed look at the CoCo model. A good starting point is www.cica.ca.

(b) Internal Control Standards in the United Kingdom

Organizations seem a bit more complex as we move over to what typically, those in the United States, call England or the United Kingdom. Similarly to Canada, the professional designation is Chartered Accountant, a certificate that is obtained through auditing experience and passing a comprehensive examination. Their professional organization is The Institute of Chartered Accountants in England and Wales as well as separate organizations for Ireland and for Scotland. There are separate Chartered Accountant designations and organizations for management accounting and public finance. Affiliated with the Charted Accountants institutes, the Auditing Practices Board (APB) establishes and publishes statements of the principles called APBs, similar to what were U.S. SAS documents.

The United Kingdom was faced with some of the same concerns as the United States regarding improper financial reporting during the 1990s. Their focus was more on inappropriate statements made by directors but included failures of internal control as well. The result was the 1999 study *Internal Control: Guidance for Directors on the Combined Code.*[2] The report is known as the 1999 Turnbull report on internal control, named after the chair of the committee that launched it, and Combined Code is the name of the United Kingdom's corporate governance legislation. The report is oriented toward directors of public companies and places a strong emphasis on objective setting, risk identification, and risk assessment when evaluating internal controls. The report calls on directors to regularly consider the following factors:

- The nature and extent of the risks facing the company
- The extent and categories of risk that it regards as acceptable for the company to bear
- The likelihood of the risks concerned materializing
- The company's ability to reduce the incidence and impact on the business risks that do materialize
- The costs of operating particular controls relative to the benefit thereby obtained in managing the related risks

This set of considerations is very similar to some of the risk assessment approaches discussed in Chapter 5, "Understanding and Assessing Risks: Enterprise Risk Management." What is significant about the U.K. Turnbull approach to developing an effective system of internal controls is the emphasis on understanding business objectives and then analyzing risks as first steps to designing effective internal controls. Turnbull then suggests a framework for evaluating the effectiveness of internal controls. The idea is to understand the risks, to design controls based on those risks, and to perform tests to evaluate the controls.

Although there are some differences in the text, Turnbull provides the same three basic objectives for internal controls as was discussed for COSO and CoCo: effectiveness and efficiency of operations, reliability of internal and external financial reporting, and compliance with applicable laws and regulations. The really important concept of the Turnbull approach is its emphasis on risk assessment and developing controls for high-impact and higher-likelihood risks. COSO provides the same general guidance, but the U.K. Turnbull approach perhaps does a better job of establishing a risk-based internal control environment. There is nothing to conflict with COSO, and an internal auditor might find value in reviewing the Turnbull report in greater detail.

(c) Internal Control Frameworks Worldwide

With a wide range of independent national accounting authorities and some differences in business practices worldwide, there are other variations of internal control frameworks or models worldwide. Most follow the COSO framework today with its CoCo or Turnbull variations. For example, in Australia there are the Australian Conditions for Control (ACC). It is not the objective of this book to summarize internal control practices on a country-by-country basis.

Although not discussed that specifically in the COSO framework, internal audit has a more prominent role in other models. Perhaps because internal auditors in the past in the United Kingdom sometimes were regarded as little more than corporate "policemen," the Turnbull materials very much stress the importance of internal audit in improving the internal control framework. Turnbull states that an internal audit function should be able to:

- Provide objective assurance to the board and management as to the adequacy and effectiveness of the company's risk management and internal control framework

- Assist management to improve the processes by which risks are identified and managed

- Assist the board with its responsibilities to strengthen and improve the risk management and internal control framework

Developed before SOA, this is excellent guidance for internal audit to understand risks and to help improve the internal control structure in any organization worldwide.

29.5 ISO AND THE STANDARDS REGISTRATION PROCESS

Standards at all levels are essential in our global economy. They are documented agreements containing technical specifications or other precise criteria to be used consistently as guidelines, or definitions, to ensure that products, processes, and services are fit for their purpose. For example, the physical structure of a credit card is based on a standard that defines such features as an optimal thickness so that the cards can be used worldwide. Standards contribute to making life simpler, and to increasing the reliability and effectiveness of the goods and services we use.

Most international standards are based on guidelines from the International Organization for Standardization (ISO) in Geneva, Switzerland. Founded in 1946, ISO has some 200 technical committees covering a wide range of areas. Virtually all countries in the world are ISO members. ISO standards are frequently detailed documents that follow recognized numbering schemes. ISO 9000 covers quality standards and describes the documentation requirement to support such quality assertions. For an organization to claim that it follows a certain level of quality under the ISO 9000 series, it must first document these processes in very precise detail. It will then invite in an outside auditor or registrar to review this documentation and concur that the documentation is appropriate, in a process similar to a financial external audit. The organization can then claim that they are ISO compliant with the standard of interest.

ISO standards and registrations represent a different dimension and area of interest for many internal auditors primarily interested in operational and financial controls. The quality auditors, discussed in Chapter 26, "Internal Audit Quality Assurance and ASQ Quality Audits," have been responsible for auditing according to the ISO standards. However, with the ever-increasing globalization of businesses, all internal auditors should have an understanding of these ISO 9000 quality standards as well as the process for achieving ISO certification.

(a) ISO9000 Quality Standards Overview

Prior sections of the chapter discussed the letters and acronyms associated with international auditing and internal control international standards. The same is true—and perhaps even more so—for the ISO series of standards and guidelines. We will not attempt to cover all of them here but only provide an overview of some of these standards. Much more information can be found at www.iso.ch. The primary ISO quality standards here are:

- *ISO 9000:2000, Quality Management Systems: Fundamentals and Vocabulary.* This standard is a starting point and defines the fundamental terms and definitions used in the ISO 9000 family to avoid misunderstandings in their use.

- *ISO 9001:2000, Quality Management Systems: Requirements.* The requirement standard used to assess the ability to meet customer and applicable regulatory requirements and to thereby address customer satisfaction. This is the only standard in the ISO 9000 family against which third-party certification is covered.

- *ISO 9004:2000, Quality Management Systems: Guidelines for Performance Improvements.* A standard to provide guidance for continual improvement of quality management systems to benefit all parties through sustained customer satisfaction

These are the three prime ISO quality standards; the 2000 on these numbers means that this set was updated in the year 2000. In addition, these are numerous supporting guidelines with numbers such as ISO10005:1995, ISO10006:1997, and ISO10012-2:1997 covering such areas as standards for preparing the QA plan, project planning standards, and statistical process controls. The whole idea is that there are general standards or guidelines for virtually all areas of the quality process. For example, there is a guideline for training the staff in quality processes, ISO10012:1999. If the question is asked whether an organization or one of its functions has adequately trained the staff in certain quality processes, the response might be to point to this guideline and detailed documentation to support compliance.

As discussed, detailed descriptions regarding all ISO standards, and the Quality Management standards, can be found in the public access ISO Web site (www.iso.ch). ISO charges for the complete copies of many of these documents, but the Web site is a good starting point to learn more about ISO and its quality standards. The ISO review process here is similar to a normal internal audit in that the organization establishes goals, applies the appropriate standards, implements those standards, and then reviews them. The ISO standards referenced are quite detailed. For example, ISO 19011 for auditing covers over 30 printed pages and really details the entire quality audit process. Other ISO standards are equally as detailed.

The overall ISO process is really a process of establishing effective documentation of existing processes. If an organization claims that they have "world-class" production standards, under ISO they need to develop detailed documentation that supports that contention. This may include the results of detailed testing or a statistical process analysis. A strong system of documentation is really a key to establishing a level of ISO quality standards compliance.

(b) Quality Audits and Registration

Although neither IIA internal auditors nor external auditors give much attention to quality auditors in their professional literature, there are some strong analogies between these groups of auditors. In a financial audit, the internal and external auditors perform periodic reviews of internal accounting controls installed by management prior to the period end date. Their work is based on auditing standards, and management procedures will have been based on strong, supporting internal control processes. As a final step, the external auditor reviews the financial reports for the period as well as other supporting materials and attests to the fairness of these financial reports through the CPA's signature. The audited financial statements are filed with the SEC and become part of the annual report to shareholders.

Quality audits are based on the ISO standards just discussed. Management should have established quality processes as part of normal operations and will review compliance to those standards through internal self-checks or reviews by the organization's quality audit function. In order to publicly state that the organization is ISO compliant, its quality systems are reviewed and registered through an external quality auditor function, a quality audit registrar. Although not all are tied to the same SEC reporting cycle, the results of quality audits allow organizations to tell outsiders that they are ISO compliant. Similar to investors requiring a set of audited financial reports; customers often will require that same ISO certification, particularly in international transactions.

A major difference between an audited financial statement and ISO quality standards is that when an organization adopts quality standards, they must strive for the continual improvement of their quality management system along with ongoing customer satisfaction. Continual improvement is a process of increasing the effectiveness of the organization to fulfill its quality objectives, and ISO 9001 requires that an organization plan and manage the processes necessary for the continual improvement of its quality management system. Data should be obtained from various sources, both internal and external, to assess the appropriateness of quality system goals. This information can also be used to improve the performance of your processes. These benefits must be strengthened through effective internal auditing and management review of system performance. Like all systems, it either improves or becomes less effective. It does not remain static for long.

ISO standards provide guidance to establish and maintain an ongoing set of quality audits for an organization. The standard utilizes the Plan-Do-Check-Act cycle to define the audit program. Some of the key actions addressed are:

- Establishing the objectives and extent of the audit program
- Establishing the responsibilities, resources, and procedures
- Ensuring the implementation of the audit program
- Monitoring and reviewing the audit program to improve its efficiency and effectiveness
- Ensuring that appropriate program records are maintained

Documentation is a key element in any quality system. Exhibit 29.3 illustrates the tiered level of ISO quality documentation. At Tier 1, or at the very top, there is a need for a very high level ISO quality document for the organization.

EXHIBIT 29.3

ISO Quality System Documentation Tiers

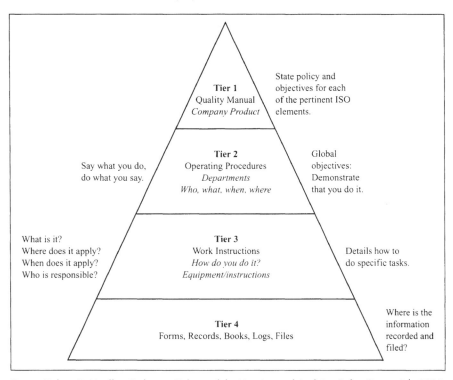

Source: Robert R. Moeller, *Sarbanes-Oxley and the New Internal Auditing Rules*, © copyright 2004, John Wiley & Sons. Used with permission.

There is a hierarchy of more detailed documentation as we step down tiers here to the detailed forms, files, and records at the Tier 4 foundations. This is the same level of documentation that internal auditors have been commenting on for years. The difference with ISO quality audits is that an organization *must have* an adequate set of documentation as well as an ongoing process to improve it.

A key component of the ISO process for internal auditors is the ISO continuous improvement and quality audit process. As discussed in Chapter 26 as well as here, the typical IIA-trained and -oriented operation or financial internal auditor today is often isolated from quality auditors—even within the same organization. This situation should change. Quality auditors are moving out of the production floor and are now more frequently just calling themselves internal auditors. However, the name and title is not as important as the overall function. The quality auditor is perhaps much more concerned about the importance of continuous improvement and the documentation necessary to support it. This should be an important aspect of the work of all internal auditors.

All internal auditors should gain at least a general understanding of the ISO 9000 quality management standards and process. Acceptance of ISO 9000 standards allows essentially any organization to improve its standards of quality and service to customers as well as internal members of the organization.

EXHIBIT 29.4

ISO Quality Management Principles

Principle 1. Customer Focus

Organizations depend on their customers and therefore should understand current and future customer needs, should meet customer requirements, and strive to exceed customer expectations.

Principle 2. Leadership

Leaders establish unity of purpose and direction of the organization. They should create and maintain the internal environment in which people can become fully involved in achieving the organization's objectives.

Principle 3. Involvement of People

People at all levels are the essence of an organization, and their full involvement enables their abilities to be used for the organization's benefit.

Principle 4. Process Approach

A desired result is achieved more efficiently when activities and related resources are managed as a process.

Principle 5. System Approach to Management

Identifying, understanding, and managing interrelated processes as a system contributes to the organization's effectiveness and efficiency in achieving its objectives.

Principle 6. Continual Improvement

Continual improvement of the organization's overall performance should be a permanent objective of the organization.

Principle 7. Factual Approach to Decision Making

Effective decisions are based on the analysis of data and information

Principle 8. Mutually Beneficial Supplier Relationships

An organization and its suppliers are interdependent, and a mutually beneficial relationship enhances the ability of both to create value.

Source: Robert R. Moeller, *Sarbanes-Oxley and the New Internal Auditing Rules*, © copyright 2004, John Wiley & Sons. Used with permission.

Exhibit 29.4 summarizes the major principles behind ISO 9000. If an internal auditor's organization is already involved in an ISO registration effort, internal audit should get involved with the processes, helping where it can and otherwise embracing ISO's concepts. If the organization has done nothing with ISO, the CAE should review the costs and benefits of ISO registration and consider recommending it to other members of the management team.

29.6 ISO 9001:2000 INTERNAL AUDITS

The ISO materials are a comprehensive set of detailed standards guidelines. An organization must first go through the detailed documentation and procedural changes to become compliant with an ISO standard, such as the ISO 9001:2000 quality standards, and then arrange to have an independent registrar come in an audit those standards to certify compliance. This process is both similar and quite different from the audits of financial statements for public corporations. Internal audit can take a similar but not required role in each of these cases.

In a financial audit environment, the external audit firm will follow established PCAOB and SAS audit standards and test and evaluate the fairness of financial records according to GAAP. In an ISO audit, an authorized registrar will evaluate both an organization's conformance to applicable ISO standards and then their actual conformance with these documented procedures. This is really a different approach from the financial statement audit process that has been very familiar to many internal auditors. Quality auditors, as were discussed in Chapter 26, can also play a very important role here in reviewing an organization's compliance with ISO standards in advance of any formal ISO registrar reviews and as part of reviews to ensure a program of continuous improvement in an organization.

Chapter 26 discussed how the American Society for Quality (ASQ) quality auditor is increasingly becoming similar to Institute of Internal Auditors (IIA) auditors. With ISO standards becoming increasingly important to all organizations worldwide, all internal auditors should develop an understanding of the concepts and philosophy of the ISO process and participate in ISO internal audits when they have the opportunity. The primary objectives of these audits should be:

- *To verify conformance with applicable ISO standards.*   As discussed, these standards are very detailed. To claim compliance with them, an organization is expected to operate in conformance with those standards.

- *To verify conformance with documented procedures.*   ISO very much calls both for applicable processes to be well documented and for organizations to follow their own documented procedures.

- *To verify the effectiveness of processes in the system.*   This is a somewhat different dimension from most traditional operational audits. Rather than just determining that whether some process is or not documented, the ISO auditor will perform tests to determine if the process is effective.

- *To identify opportunities to improve the system.*   This objective is very much what internal auditors have been doing in their service to the management mission discussed throughout this book. With ISO audits, these suggestions are expected in most audits.

Many organizations today are taking steps to become ISO compliant. Internal auditors who have not been involved with the ISO certification process in the past, should establish strong communication with their quality-assurance function. Some organizations have quality-assurance functions that are more closely aligned with manufacturing engineering than with operational auditing. If so, internal audit can offer its normal audit review skills to that quality function to help launch an ongoing program of ISO audits. At the same time, internal audit can use these contacts to gain knowledge about ISO standards and the quality audit process.

ISO quality standards are a worldwide set of processes that will become increasingly important to all organizations and business functions in the future. This is an international set of standards that should become part of every internal auditor's knowledge base.

29.7 ANOTHER STANDARD: ISO 14000 ENVIRONMENTAL MANAGEMENT

Environmental control issues are becoming increasingly important on a worldwide basis. There is a worldwide recognition that organizations cannot just drain industrial or human waste into a nearby river, burn it while watching the smoke drift away, or bury it with no concern that it might seep back into the water supply. Strong environmental rules have been established throughout the world to encourage people and organizations to create a cleaner and safer environment. Those violating the rules or standards may be subject to penalties including large fines and public approbation. Depending on the organization, its industry, and even its geographic location, the management of these environmental risks can be very complex. Rules are difficult to follow and subject to interpretation, but regulations require a high level of documentation to attest that the environmental procedures are working. Although there are many rules and regulations, it is not in society's interests to have large cadres of "environmental police" to monitor these rules. Rather, organizations are encouraged to "self-police" their environmental compliance standards.

As a result, organizations have established what are called environment management systems (EMS), which have some close analogies to the systems of internal control discussed throughout this book. An EMS is a series of control procedures designed to provide the organization as well as outsiders with assurances that the company's environmental control system is working. Standards have been established, similar to the ISO 9000 quality standards, to monitor the success of an organization's EMS. These standards come under the designation of ISO 14000 and define the procedures that an organization must have in place to attest that they have an effective EMS. ISO 14000 procedures were first released in 1996 and are supported by a set of guidance materials similar to those of ISO 9000. Exhibit 29.5 summarizes some of the principle requirements of ISO 14000. The emphasis is very much on documentation standards.

Audits of EMS procedures under ISO 14000 may become increasingly important to internal auditors as concerns regarding EMS procedures increase. While many organizations have industrial engineers and others on their staffs who have a good understanding of the manufacturing and other processes covered by ISO 9000 quality standards, there is presently a wide need for knowledge about EMS procedures, because an important aspect of an EMS audit under ISO 14000 involves a review of supporting documentation and the control systems in place to manage their environmental management systems. While a typical internal audit may not be an "expert" in this often specialized area, many internal auditors have the skills and understanding to communicate these requirements and procedures to others in the organization.

Whether it be ISO or many of the other standards discussed in this chapter, the overall rules covering many areas are going worldwide. In many respects, this is an element of our increasingly global economy where countries throughout the world communicate with one another. Internal auditors should consider the implications of these current and increasingly important worldwide standards as elements of their internal audit work.

EXHIBIT 29.5

ISO 1400 Major Requirements

1. Senior management should be responsible for defining an environmental policy that is:
   a. Appropriate to the company's environmental impacts
   b. Committed to continual improvement
   c. Committed to prevention of pollution
   d. Committed to regulatory compliance
   e. Committed to other related requirements to which company subscribes
   f. Documented, implemented, and maintained

2. Procedures should be in place to identify the environmental aspects that the company can control or influence. Aspects with significant impacts should be considered when setting objectives and targets, and the information should be kept current.

3. Procedures should be in place to identify environmental legal requirements.

4. All employees whose work may have a significant environmental impact should be competent and receive appropriate training.

5. Procedures should be in place to make employees aware of:
   a. Importance of conformance with environmental policy and procedures
   b. Requirements of the EMS
   c. Actual and potential significant environmental aspects of work activities
   d. Environment benefits of improved person performance
   e. Potential consequences of departing from specified operating procedures

6. Procedures should be in place for communication with internal and external parties regarding environmental aspects and the EMS.

7. Procedures should be in place to document all environmental documents in a current manner.

8. Procedures should be in place to identify potential, accidental, and emergency situations.

9. Procedures are needed to respond to accidents and emergency situations, including periodic testing where practicable.

10. Documented procedures should be in place to monitor and measure activities that can have a severe environmental impact.

11. Procedures should be in place to define the responsibility and authority to:
    a. Handle and investigate nonconformance
    b. Take action to mitigate impacts
    c. Initiate complete corrective and preventive action, appropriate to the magnitude of the problem

12. Detailed records shall be maintained of all environmental activities.

13. Programs and procedures should be in place to audit the EMS on a regular basis.

14. Management should perform a regular and periodic review of the EMS.

Source: Robert R. Moeller, *Sarbanes-Oxley and the New Internal Auditing Rules*, © copyright 2004, John Wiley & Sons. Used with permission.

ENDNOTES

[1] International Organization for Standardization, www.iso.ch
[2] Published by The Institute of Character Accountants in England & Wales. A PDF version is available through www.icaew.couk/internalcontrol.

CHAPTER THIRTY

Future of the Modern
Internal Auditor

30.1 INTERNAL AUDITING PROFESSION TODAY

An ongoing objective of this book has been to present an overview of major professional issues surrounding internal auditors. Some of these are technology driven, some based on evolving professional standards, and others are impacted by technology. These issues continually change and evolve—an important concept for an active profession! As examples, the fourth edition of this book, released in 1982, included a lengthy discussion of the significance of the then new Foreign Corrupt Practices Act (FCPA) and its requirements calling for organizations to document their internal controls. The FCPA was mentioned again in the 1999 fifth edition but because there never were any major enforcement actions regarding it, this edition has given the FCPA only a limited reference. Similarly, the fifth edition talked about some internal audit computer technology approaches that seemed interesting then, but have since never received much further recognition. Things change, and no one has a full-functioning crystal ball to envision the future.

This edition has also introduced some newer rules or trends that are important to internal auditors today and some of which probably will continue to be in the future. A good example here is the Sarbanes-Oxley Act (SOA) and the requirements of its Section 404 reviews. These were discussed in Chapter 3, "Internal

Audit in the Twenty-First Century: Sarbanes-Oxley and Beyond," and Chapter 6, "Evaluating Internal Controls: Section 404 Assessments," as well as referenced throughout this edition. SOA and the new regulator of the of the external auditing profession, the Public Corporations Accounting Oversight Board (PCAOB), will almost certainly continue to have an ongoing impact on auditing, and internal auditing as well, in the years going forward. Of course, SOA and the PCAOB have been with us for less than two years at this time of publication. Its emphasis may change over time, and a future seventh edition of this book may view matters differently.

Other matters discussed in this edition may change as well, with resultant impacts on internal auditors. Nevertheless, the topics discussed in this sixth edition represent perhaps a "best guess" at the internal auditing profession today and some of the directions it may be headed. However, to avoid the very long time lags between editions, this author and the publisher, John Wiley & Sons, will issue periodic updates to this book. These will be limited-scope documents that will cover such areas as PCAOB new rules that will have an impact on internal auditors. These are planned to be offered by the publisher to purchasers of this sixth edition in the future.

Going forward, the modern internal auditor should always try to stay informed on ongoing professional, procedural, and technical issues impacting the practices and profession of internal auditing. This sixth edition has tried to address some of these issues, and this last chapter will conclude with some evolving issues and trends that may have an impact on all internal auditors in the future. The message for all internal auditors is to keep informed on issues and developments, including those reported by the Institute of Internal Auditors (IIA), the Information Systems Audit Control Association (ISACA), or other professional groups.

30.2 EVOLVING ISSUES AND TRENDS

Issues surrounding SOA and the ongoing emphasis on corporate governance through the United States, as well as much of the world, show that ongoing interest and importance in the profession of internal auditing is both growing and changing. As an example, the IIA had some 60,000 members at the time of the 1999 fifth edition. In only five years, professional membership has grown by some 50% to over 90,000! This growth trend follows a seemingly reduced level of interest in the profession through the mid-1990s where the major public accounting firms seemed to be taking responsibility for much of the internal audit profession through their outsourcing agreements with major corporations worldwide. A renewed appreciation of strong internal control processes and the passage of SOA has changed things. IIA membership and the need for increased internal audit services will only increase as the years go forward.

The sections following highlight some evolving issues that may become important to internal auditors in the near future. While no one can accurately predict the future, the previous fifth edition highlighted some areas that were not all that common then but have become important for internal auditors today. A major topic was the fifth edition discussion on the importance of ethics and codes of conduct as part of organization corporate governance. Some other areas that may be important for the modern internal auditor in the years going forward are discussed in the following sections.

(a) Importance and Significance of SOA 404 Reviews

Although SOA has multiple requirements, many managers and internal auditors think of it today just in terms of the requirements of its Section 404 requirements, as were discussed in Chapter 6. These rules call for management to arrange for a review and assessment of its internal controls such that the external auditors can subsequently examine and attest to those internal controls reviews as part of their independent audits of an organization's financial statements. As often happens with U.S. legislation, it takes some time for the formal rules to be finalized, and the final rules here were not issued until March 9, 2004.[1]

Compliance with these new SOA requirements has and continues to be a major effort by many major corporations worldwide. The completed internal controls documentation as well as the results of supporting testing has to be very thorough and complete, and a problem with this work in its early days is the question of how much is enough? That is, external auditors can review and attest the internal controls documentation for all areas in an organization. However, time and logistics constraints predict that the external audit firms will not look at every process or every organization entity. Some may be just too small or insignificant, but there have been few guidelines to date. Almost certainly, as the years go forward, there will be accepted practices here helping all parties to determine what is really material or what should be carefully documented and tested.

Internal audit's role in these Section 404 reviews is still up in the air. As discussed in Chapter 10, "Working with External Auditors," internal auditors may do these internal controls reviews and testing as independent units in support of organization management, they may act as contractors to their external auditors in their assessment reviews, or they may just step aside and continue their normal internal audit reviews with essentially no participation in this Section 404 process. Although things certainly may change, this author predicts that internal auditors will increasingly take the role of documenting and testing an organization's internal controls for a subsequent external auditor attestation. This type of role would very much raise the stature on internal audit and its role in corporate governance in future years.

(b) Other SOA Issues: Whistleblower Programs and Internal Audit

Although many professionals today think of SOA just in terms of its Section 404 internal controls documentation and testing requirements, the act covers a wide variety of other topics and issues, as were discussed in Chapter 3. Some of these cover such areas as audit committee membership or other corporate governance issues and have little direct impact on internal auditors today. As discussed in Chapter 9, "Whistleblower Programs and Codes of Conduct," SOA's whistleblower provisions may have a growing significant impact on internal auditors in the years going forward.

Under these rules, any stakeholder who sees some perceived accounting or internal controls irregularity can "blow the whistle" and call the matter to the attention of management, regulators, or even litigators. These rules can present a massive minefield for organizational management, who will take extreme steps to avoid creating a whistleblower situation. Because they are often among the first to see these problems, internal auditors can take a strong rule in supporting management as well as helping to protect them from potential whistleblower situations. In the years going forward, internal auditors should take a much more active role in strengthening codes of conduct and other ethics programs in the organization and in providing strong support for compliance in these areas.

(c) PCAOB, External Audit Firms, and Internal Audit

As discussed throughout this book, the role of PCAOB as the new regulator of the public accounting industry is just getting started. When first launched, PCAOB adopted the existing Statements on Auditing Standards (SAS) that were issued by the AICPA's Auditing Standards Board. PCAOB is just beginning to issue its own standards or rules, but there has been little to date beyond the previously referenced final rules on Section 404 reviews. Perhaps as is common with many governmental regulators, there almost certainly will be an increasing number of new rules and standards in the years ahead. These may cover improvements on existing SAS documents or may expand to other areas where regulators feel there is a need for auditing standards. In the opinion of this author, new rules may very well move in a direction similar to the U.S. Food and Drug Administration (FDA) rules for approving new drugs. That is, there may be detailed new rules requiring extensive documentation and evidence retention. The future will perhaps see a much more regulated external audit process!

What does the newly evolving PCAOB and its rules mean for internal auditors? Internal audit received essentially no specific mention in the SOA legislation, but regulators certainly recognize the importance of internal audit and of a strong internal audit function as an important factor in an organization's internal control structure. Internal auditors should keep aware of new or proposed PCAOB rules going forward. Some will have an impact on the external audit process and not directly on internal audit. Others, however, may affect internal auditors and their organizations. All internal auditors and, in particular Chief Audit Executives (CAEs), should monitor the PCAOB's activities and understand its new and proposed rules. In addition, internal audit should convey these rules to senior management and the audit committee to communicate the impact of any new changes on the organization. Most new rules are initially issued in draft form with a period for public comment. Individual internal auditors and CAEs representing their organizations should take an active role in this public comment process. This is the manner in which new rules are established.

The role of the major public accounting firms is changing! What was once the "Big 8" set of major firms has currently dwindled to what some call the "Final 4." These firms are under massive pressure to comply with new rules under changed roles. In addition to SEC investigations and regulatory pressures, these firms face the potential for massive financial damages through civil litigation. If a firm has been the external auditor in what has been found to be a many-year, multibillion dollar fraud, these auditors will face litigation from the harmed investors. Damage suits can be in the billions of dollars, and this trend can only go so far. As this book goes to press, several of the Final 4 firms are in this situation with the potential of more to come. What will be the outcome? Our prediction will be less dependence on the Final 4 firms for auditing, with the PCAOB contracting out some of this work for other qualified consulting firms. A series of smaller auditing firms may perform pieces of an overall audit with the PCAOB taking a central project management role. Of course, these comments are very speculative, and the impact of the changes they suggest on internal auditors, if any, is yet to be determined.

(d) Continuous Close and Information Systems Changes

As another evolving trend, SOA section 409 and the PCAOB are calling for almost real-time close the books financial reporting. It is no longer acceptable for an organization to come to a calendar quarter close and not report its results for that quarter until well into the end of a subsequent quarter. Pressures for the continuous close and related continuous assurance auditing, as discussed in Chapter 25, "Continuous Assurance Auditing, XBRL, and OLAP," will become important requirements for organizations going forward. This requires new software systems and procedural tools as well as increasingly tight internal controls. Reviews of these new systems require different approaches by internal and external auditors as well as management. Internal auditors should attempt to gain an understanding of these evolving trends and develop appropriate internal audit review techniques. If not already in place, an internal audit function should adopt better information systems auditing tools and procedures.

(e) Evolving Worldwide Standards

Many internal auditors operating outside of the United States today look at SOA and the evolving PCAOB rules as a set of U.S.-based rules that are being imposed on them, no matter where they are domiciled. While there is certainly a truth to that statement today, we are rapidly moving to a set of worldwide standards. While some of these are discussed in Chapter 29, "ISO and Internal Audit Worldwide Standards," on international accounting and auditing rules, there may be many more changes yet to come. In addition to auditing and accounting rules, we shall see an increased emphasis on the quality-assurance rules issued by the Internal Organization for Standardization (ISO) and briefly discussed in Chapter 26, "Internal Audit Quality Assurance and ASQ Quality Audits," on quality audits. ISO represent a series of rules that have started in Europe and have moved to worldwide acceptance. While there will always be local differences, all organizations will be increasingly affected by these evolving worldwide standards. Internal auditors in multinational organizations increasingly run in to these new worldwide rules and standards. The modern professional internal auditor should continue to be aware of the worldwide rules and adapt internal audit procedures to recognize them when appropriate.

(f) Ongoing Security and Privacy Concerns

Chapter 24, "HIPAA and Growing Concerns Regarding Privacy," discussed growing concerns about security and privacy. This will become an increasingly important issue for society and all internal auditors. The Internet and wireless communications allow individuals and organizations worldwide to be connected with one another. While some of this is very important, privacy and security are today and in the future an ever more important concern. The modern internal auditor should keep informed about legislation as well as potential abuses in these areas and develop skills to understand and evaluate them. Some of this requires increased technical skills, but much of this requires an ongoing appreciation for these trends and their associated risks.

30.3 MODERN INTERNAL AUDITING

This book has tried to present an overview of the profession of internal auditing today, the tools and techniques that an internal auditor can use, and some speculation on where the profession is headed. Internal auditing represents an important function in the organization today and an increasingly important professional direction for individuals. It is also a fascinating field where the effective internal auditor must have some financial and operational, as well as information systems, skills. These are tools that an internal auditor can develop and build upon as work progresses from one audit area to another. Legislation such as SOA has changed many things, but internal audit continues to be a group that provides important and valuable service to management in today's organizations.

Victor Brink could hardly be aware of many of these changes when he drafted his first edition in 1942. However, he was suggesting professional changes then to a profession that often did little more than balance checking accounts and reconcile similar accounts in support of external auditors. That evolving profession he suggested, modern internal auditing, has become much more important and vital to management. Internal auditing has and continues to change. The modern internal auditor today is much different in some respects from Vic Brink's internal auditor and will continue to change as the years and demands of internal audit services evolve.

ENDNOTE

[1]PCAOB Release No. 2004-001, March 9, 2004. www.pcaobus.org

Index